Conducting Research in Psychology

Measuring the Weight of Smoke

Second Edition

Brett W. Pelham
State University of New York, University at Buffalo

Hart Blanton
University of North Carolina, Chapel Hill

THOMSON

™

WADSWORTH

Australia • Canada • Mexico • Singapore • Spain
United Kingdom • United States

This book is dedicated to our mothers, Tina Blanton
and the late Dottie Pelham.

THOMSON

WADSWORTH

Sponsoring Editor: *Marianne Taflinger*
Assistant Editor: *Jennifer Wilkinson*
Editorial Assistant: *Nicole Root*
Technology Project Manager: *Darin Derstine*
Marketing Manager: *Lori Grebe*
Marketing Assistant: *Laurel Anderson*
Advertising Project Manager: *Brian Chaffee*
Signing Representative: *Diana Rothberg*
Project Manager, Editorial Production: *Mary Noel*

Print/Media Buyer: *Vena Dyer*
Permissions Editor: *Charles Hodgkins*
Production Service: *Greg Hubit Bookworks*
Copy Editor: *Jamie Fuller*
Text Designer: *Sharon L. Kinghan*
Cover Designer: *Denise Davidson*
Cover and Interior Cartoons: *Brett Pelham*
Compositor: *Shepherd, Inc.*
Printer: *Webcom, Ltd.*

Printed in Canada
3 4 5 6 7 0   6 05 04 03

Library of Congress Control Number: 2002102410

ISBN 0-534-52093-6

Wadsworth/Thomson Learning
10 Davis Drive
Belmont, CA 94002-3098
USA

Asia
Thomson Learning
5 Shenton Way #01-01
UIC Building
Singapore 068808

Australia
Nelson Thomson Learning
102 Dodds Street
South Melbourne, Victoria 3205
Australia

Canada
Nelson Thomson Learning
1120 Birchmount Road
Toronto, Ontario M1K 5G4
Canada

Europe/Middle East/Africa
Thomson Learning
High Holborn House
50/51 Bedford Row
London WC1R 4LR
United Kingdom

Latin America
Thomson Learning
Seneca, 53
Colonia Polanco
11560 Mexico D.F.
Mexico

Spain
Paraninfo Thomson Learning
Calle/Magallanes, 25
28015 Madrid, Spain

Brett Pelham

Hart Blanton

About the First Author

Brett Pelham grew up as the second of six children outside the small town of Rossville, Georgia. Brett received his B.A. from Berry College in 1983 and received his Ph.D. from the University of Texas at Austin in 1989. He wrote the first edition of this book while working as an associate professor at UCLA, and he is currently an associate professor at SUNY, Buffalo. He studies person perception, stereotyping, social inference, and the self-concept. He teaches courses in social psychology, research methods, statistics, social cognition, and the self-concept. In his spare time, he enjoys juggling, painting, sculpting, listening to alternative rock music, cooking, and traveling. He doesn't enjoy weightlifting or running, but he occasionally does these things to compensate for a diet rich in Coca-Cola. In June of 2001, he won a Gold Medal in the triple jump and placed fifth in the 1500 meters in the prestigious Southwestern U.S. Regional Master's Track and Field Championships in San Diego, CA. To the best of his memory, there was exactly one person in his age group who placed worse than him in each of these events. He is thankful for that one person in each event.

About the Second Author

Hart Blanton grew up as the second of three children in a small town in Appalachian Virginia. Hart received his B.A. from Virginia Tech in 1990 and received his Ph.D. from Princeton University in 1994. He worked on the second edition of this book while at SUNY Albany. In 2002, he moved to the psychology department at the University of North Carolina, Chapel Hill. He studies group processes, self and identity, health psychology, social cognition, social influence, and social comparison. He has taught courses in research methods, social psychology, statistics, the self, social comparison, and social influence. In the summer, he enjoys motorcycle trips and gardening. In the winter, he vows to take up skiing or snowboarding or something like that. He enjoys weightlifting because he finds value in setting aside a chunk of time each day for a completely mindless goal pursuit. His diet consists of a wide variety of carbohydrates, but he cannot tell the difference between Coke and Pepsi (see the Blind Taste Test in this text). He is physically stronger than exactly one other author of this textbook.

Brief Contents

Contents

Chapter 7
Experience Carefully Exploited:
Quasi-Experimental Research Designs   184

Chapter 8
Research Design   218

Chapter 13
Putting Your Knowledge to Work:
20 Methodology Problems   348

Coda   360

Appendix
An Experimental Replication of the Depressed
Entitlement Effect Among Women   361

Preface to the First Edition

Several years ago, I came to a very painful conclusion: Most undergraduate students dread courses in research methods. In one of my pre-course evaluations, one frank and articulate student summarized this sentiment by writing that "few things could be more boring, useless, intimidating, or impenetrable than research methods." I was disturbed by this sentiment because I had agreed to teach a course in experimental research methods. I was also shocked because I firmly believed that few things could be more interesting, useful, inviting, or intuitive than research methods. If this belief strikes you as strange, it will be my goal in this book to convince you that most people's distaste for research methods has a lot more to do with the way research methods are typically written about than it does with the nature of research methods *per se*.

To make this point in a different way: I suspect that, with a little effort, I could write a boring, useless, intimidating, and impenetrable book about skydiving, juggling, or romantic trysts. The key to doing so, I think, would involve a heavy focus on the *rules and technical details* of skydiving, juggling, or trysting without much focus on the *experience* of these inherently interesting activities. In my opinion, this common approach to writing about research methods is one of the major reasons that this topic has such a bad reputation. The approach adopted in this book is a hands-on, practical approach that should give you a feel for what it is like to actually conduct research in psychology. Perhaps more important, it should also allow you to apply some of your familiar intuitions to the topic of research methods. In other words, if you can choose an outfit for yourself, play a board game, or recommend a good restaurant, you probably have the capacity to become an expert in research methods. In fact, if you are one of those rare people who does *not* have these mundane skills, I suspect that it is because you have been reading too many books on research methods! Perhaps this book can help you translate your technical expertise into some simple skills you can use in your daily life. For the rest of you, the crux of the approach adopted in this book will be to help you translate your familiar but sophisticated life skills into the skills that can make you a proficient experimenter.

Because I happen to study social psychology, another important thing that I have tried to do in this text is to emphasize what is *social* about psychological research methods. Being a good experimental psychologist requires the use of the same methodological rules that apply to all other scientific disciplines. However, the fact that people are social beings generates some practical dilemmas that are not likely to plague researchers in astrophysics, metaphysics, or psychophysics (a branch of perceptual psychology). The most ubiquitous of these problems is that when people know that their behavior is being studied, they often behave unnaturally. The challenge of experimental psychology is to study "natural" behavior in unnatural (laboratory) situations. It is the clever solutions psychologists have developed to deal with this problem that make experimental research methods in psychology a little different, and perhaps a little more interesting, than experimental research methods in general. My point is that good experimental psychology is not just good science; it is a combination of good science and good art. It takes a good scientist to generate tests of psychological theories, but it takes a good artist (and occasionally a good con artist) to translate these tests into laboratory experiences that are psychologically real to research participants. I hope that what you enjoy most about this book is learning how psychologists go about the difficult business of studying realistic behavior in unrealistic situations.

Acknowledgments

Marianne Taflinger, senior acquisitions editor, not only convinced me to write this book but also gave me excellent advice about how to do so—at all stages of the book's development. I am also indebted to the outside reviewers of the manuscript on which this book is based, who all made insightful and constructive suggestions that allowed me to improve the content and presentation of this book: Bernard C. Beins, Ithaca College; Brian C. Cronk, Missouri Western State College; Joel S. Freund, University of Arkansas–Fayetteville; Thomas E. Nygren, Ohio State University; and Carl Scott, University of Saint Thomas.

Brett Pelham

Preface to the Second Edition

In an intensive marathon session in Albany, New York, we worked to convert (1) the first edition of this text and (2) many pages of notes, revisions, and new material into (3) the revised textbook you see here. We also spent a great deal of time engaged in mostly friendly methodological debates that led to numerous improvements to the first edition of this text. The most concrete product of all of our work was the expansion of the text to include two new chapters, one devoted exclusively to quasi-experiments and one devoted exclusively to design. We also expanded the text in numerous other ways. For instance, we expanded discussions of the role of theory and theory testing in research, we elaborated on questionnaires and sampling techniques, and we expanded the original discussions of both confounds and validity. The first author is a little embarrassed to admit that we also corrected some of his originally idiosyncratic ideas to make the coverage of this text more consistent with standard use of a few key methodological terms.

Our methodological debates occasionally led to more profound debates about things such as (1) whether the two main clauses in a compound sentence must be separated by a comma (yes, they must), (2) whether a supersaturated solution of sugar and water will crystallize when it cools (no, it won't), (3) whether the beta weights in a simultaneous multiple regression equation share any of their "unique" variance (in an important sense, yes, they do), and (4) whether the comic-book character Spider-Man would have been more credible if he had produced his webs naturally rather than artificially (scientifically, yes; literarily, no). We think that the way we resolved many of our debates is informative. We resolved first debate by asking an *authority* (an English professor). We resolved the second by making an *observation* (we heated water, added more sugar than we would have ever thought possible, and waited to see if the resulting syrupy liquid crystallized when it cooled). We resolved the third debate (about statistics) by relying on *logic,* and we will spare you the details. Finally, we could resolve the fourth debate only by using *intuition.* It would make more sense scientifically if Spider-Man produced his webs naturally, just like a real spider. However, real spiders also spin their webs from, well, their butts. Intuitively, we agreed that this would create a whole host of image problems for any self-respecting superhero.

In addition to giving you a quick preview of how people know things (the topic of Chapter 1), this account also reveals something about why we wrote this book. Whether discussing profound questions involving the philosophy of science or debating ridiculous questions involving comic-book characters, each of us lives and breathes psychology more than we would like to admit. That is, we have to admit that there is nothing we enjoy thinking about more than research and the scientific method. Although this fact sometimes drives our friends and loved ones crazy, we hope that our friends and loved ones have not suffered in vain. That is, we sincerely hope that this text will help you appreciate the wonder and precision of the scientific method. If you have always been fascinated by most people's favorite topic (human nature), we hope to add to your fascination by helping you understand exactly how psychologists know what they know about this intriguing topic.

About the Supporting Materials

InfoTrac® College Edition is an extensive online database of 3,800 periodicals that is accessible over the Internet 24 hours a day, 7 days a week available free to students whose instructors choose to order the book with this service. Included in InfoTrac College Edition are such journals as *Science, American Psychologist, Journal of Social Psychology, Journal of Cross-Cultural Psychology,* and a variety of other periodicals that can be used to see how research is reported in the media.

CogLab is an online set of 32 experiments in which students can experience phenomena, such as the Stroop effect, directly. Go to http://coglab. wadsworth.com.

The Instructor's Manual/Test Bank, authored by Brett Pelham and Mauricio Caravallo, has pleased us for its enthusiastic reaction by its users. We've provided a course syllabus, suggestions as to how to use the test items in class, advice about how to use the Hands-On Activities presented in the book, and answers to the Methodology Exercises. There are also detailed summaries for each of the chapters that expand upon material that appears in the book. In the Exam Questions section, we took great pains to avoid the letter "C" bias on the 25 multiple-choice questions provided for each chapter, two sets of matching items, four examples of essay questions and model answers, and three examples of short-answer questions. Further, since students have remarked that our exams are difficult, we suggest ways to provide "easier" items. New to this edition are features for each chapter such as InfoTrac College Edition search terms, 2–3 Web sites, and material to integrate CogLab into your course. There are correlations, suggestions, and CogLab test questions as well.

A Brief Note to Students

For both aesthetic and pedagogic reasons, we have not included any definitions in the margins of this text. However, to help you identify crucially important theoretical and technical terms, we have printed these terms in boldface (like **this**) throughout the text. In addition, you will notice that when introducing the crucial terms, we always provide an explicit definition, description, or summary of the term. These explicit definitions of key terms are summarized more formally in the glossary that appears at the end of the book. Theoretical and technical terms that are important but secondary to the crucial terms are typically printed in italics (like *this*), and they, too, are almost always accompanied by an explicit definition. Finally, to help you organize your knowledge of research methods, we have organized the material in each chapter of the text by using major and minor headings. Paying attention to these headings should help you to organize your knowledge around the major themes we have suggested in each chapter.

Acknowledgments

The first author thanks his dad, who first taught him to be a critical thinker, and his mom, who first taught him to be patient with his dad. The first author also thanks Dennis Selvidge, Julian Shand, Robert McCrae, David McKenzie, Daniel McBrayer, and Edward Vatza, who taught him to love science. Bill Swann and Dan Gilbert taught the first author almost everything important that he learned in graduate school, and Janet Spence taught him to be patient with Bill Swann and Dan Gilbert.

During the ten years that the first author was at UCLA, he benefited enormously from the wit, warmth, and wisdom of Paul Abramson, David Boninger, Marilynn Brewer, John Hetts, Anne Peplau, Jim Sidanius, Shelley Taylor, Heidi Wayment, and Bernie Weiner. Bernie Weiner was the wittiest. The rest of you, as you all know, were all the warmest and wisest. The first author also thanks those who helped him learn to teach research methods: Khanh Bui, Tom DeHardt, Pam Feldman, Marie Helweg-Larsen, Paul Mallery, and Eve Rose. During the past few years (while at SUNY, Buffalo), the first author was also lucky enough to have Sandra Murray and Derek Taylor as dear friends and devoted colleagues. You have both taught him more than you will ever know. Finally, it should go without saying that the person to whom the first author can only tip his cap, the person from whom he has learned more about science than anyone else, is the ever thoughtful Curtis Hardin.

The second author wishes to thank many people, too. However, as you can plainly see, the first author used up so much space that the second author only had room to thank his generous and brilliant colleague, Jim Jaccard (selected at random from the numerous wonderful people who will all be thanked personally).

Both authors wish to thank Susan Polan for her nurturance and tolerance during the preparation of the second edition. Finally, both authors are grateful for the helpful suggestions of the following reviewers: Janet Andrews, Vassar College; Wendy Francis, The University of Texas at El Paso; Matthew Johnson, Binghamton University, State University of New York; Doug Matheson, University of the Pacific; Dawn McBride, Illinois State University; Celia Reaves, Monroe Community College. Tracy DeHart carefully reviewed both the first and second editions of the book. Her wise, open advice and wide-open eyes were invaluable.

Brett Pelham

Hart Blanton

Chapter 1

How Do We Know?

For if we show that what follows from the thing in
question is not the case, we shall have demolished the
thing in question. . . .
  —Aristotle
    (in Barnes, 1984)

Thus I arrived, by the end of 1919, at the conclusion
that the scientific attitude was the critical attitude,
which did not look for verifications but for crucial
tests; tests which could *refute* the theory being tested,
though they could never establish it.
  —Karl Popper
    (1974/1990)

Introduction: What This Text Is About

It is said that in the late 16th century, Sir Walter Raleigh made
a very audacious bet. In an effort to impress Queen Elizabeth I,
he bet a young courtier that he could *measure the weight of
smoke*. The courtier considered Sir Walter's claim ridiculous
and eagerly accepted the bet. After establishing the details of
the wager, Sir Walter produced two identical cigars and
weighed them on a very precise scale. He then lit one of the
two cigars and placed it back on the scale. After the cigar
burned away, Sir Walter weighed the remaining ashes and
announced that the weight of the smoke was to be found in
the ashes. Specifically, it was the *difference* between the
weight of the intact cigar and the weight of the ashes. The
courtier had to agree and reluctantly paid the bet.

It is highly unlikely that this story is true. For one thing,
cigars that aren't continually puffed on typically do not

remain lit. For another, it wasn't until the late 18th century that Antoine Lavoisier demonstrated (by means of some very careful experiments) that the part of a burning object that seems to disappear when burned continues to exist but goes elsewhere (Harré, 1981). Although this story may not be very accurate, it is very scientific. For one thing, this story illustrates that things that appear to be immeasurable can sometimes be measured very well. For another, this story illustrates that it often takes a good deal of creativity, and a small leap of faith, to figure out *how* to measure the seemingly immeasurable. If Sir Walter Raleigh had actually made a bet about measuring the weight of smoke, he could have won the bet only if the young courtier possessed an intuitive appreciation of the law of conservation of matter. That is, Sir Walter's argument about the cigars is valid only if one takes it on faith that matter can neither be created nor destroyed.

In psychology, we are in the business of measuring things even more fleeting and ephemeral than smoke. The objects of our research attention are elusive concepts like passion, perception, prejudice, and persuasion. We cannot directly observe any of these psychological concepts, but we can often make reasonable inferences about them by making *indirect* observations. This is why, when asked what he does for a living, one of the authors sometimes tells people that he is in the business of measuring the weight of smoke. When asked what this book is about, we are tempted to give the same answer. It is about how to answer some elusive questions about people by making use of careful, albeit typically indirect, observations.

Preamble for Chapter 1

In this first chapter we have tried to set the stage for the chapters that follow by familiarizing you, in both formal and informal ways, with the nature of the scientific method. We consider this a very important goal. By specifying the basic underpinnings of science, we hope to prepare you to think about psychology as an enterprise that is just as scientific as physics or chemistry. By specifying how reasonable and intuitive the basic underpinnings of science are, we also hope to introduce you to the idea that you can translate your common sense—things that you know tacitly or implicitly—into formal knowledge of scientific research methods.

Imagine we told you that what you now have in your hands is the world's first custom-designed textbook. We wrote this particular version of the book with you and you alone in mind, tailoring the content and presentation of the book to your own unique personality. As ridiculous as this sounds, try to keep an open mind about it while you read our professional evaluation of your personality:

> You feel good when other people like and admire you. However, you
> sometimes have a tendency to be self-critical. You have some personality
> weaknesses, but you are generally able to compensate for them. Though you
> try not to appear this way to others, you tend to be worrisome and insecure
> on the inside. You have a great deal of unused energy that you have not
> turned to your advantage. At times you have serious doubts about whether

you have made the right decision or done the right thing. You prefer a certain amount of change and variety and become dissatisfied when hemmed in by restrictions and limitations. You pride yourself on being an independent thinker and do not accept other opinions without satisfactory proof. You have found it unwise to be too frank in revealing yourself to others. At times you are introverted, wary, and reserved; at other times you are extroverted, affable, and highly sociable. Though you have weaknesses that sometimes bother you, you have many talents and are above average at a surprising number of things. Where character is concerned, two of your biggest strengths are your ability to get along with others and your self-insight. You have a clear and balanced sense of your strengths and weaknesses. Most of all, you rarely deceive yourself; you are in touch with the real you.

You should now be having at least two reactions to this description. First, you should find it surprisingly accurate. Second, you should be curious to know *how* it could be so accurate. To address the second reaction first, what you have just read is a *Barnum description,* aptly named after the famous circus promoter P. T. Barnum. Like many psychics and astrologers, Barnum knew that most people readily confuse statements that are true of *people in general* with statements that are true of *them in particular* (see Forer, 1949; McKelvie, 1990). When Bui (1997) gave a description very much like this one to undergraduates at UCLA, she found that the typical student reported that it was highly accurate. When asked how well this personality profile described them on a 9-point scale whose upper endpoint was labeled *extremely well,* the large majority of students responded with 7s, 8s, or 9s (the mean was 7.5, and the most common response was 8).

To appreciate how truly *un*informative a Barnum description really is, consider how you would have felt about the description if it had been a little more transparent that it describes virtually everybody: "You dislike being publicly humiliated, and you enjoy it when important people tell you that you are wonderful. You prefer working with your hands over working with your feet. You hate waiting in long lines, having root canals, contracting serious illnesses, and getting into motor vehicle accidents. . ."

"I was hoping you could tell me something mildly favorable—yet vague enough to be believable."

But what do Barnum descriptions have to do with psychological research methods? For starters, your curiosity about the apparent accuracy of our original Barnum description is an example of your general curiosity about human affairs. Nothing, absolutely nothing, is more interesting to people than people, and this has probably been true of people for as long as people have existed. For finishers, Barnum descriptions are also a good reminder of the difference between intuitive and scientific ways of understanding behavior. More specifically, Barnum descriptions are not very scientific. Instead, they bear a close resemblance to some of the earliest ways that human beings explained human behavior. To fully appreciate the kinds of explanations for human behavior that are currently offered by psychologists, one should place these explanations in some kind of historical context. From this perspective, the story of how people's explanations for human behavior have changed over time is a story of great progress. It is also a testament to the power of systematic research methods to uncover truths that would be difficult if not impossible to uncover through intuition or casual observation. We hope that we will not sound overly enamored of scientific research methods if we say that the hundred or so years in which people have conducted systematic research on human behavior have taught us more than we learned in the hundreds of centuries that preceded the last hundred years.

A Brief History of Human Knowledge
Metaphysical Systems

The earliest explanations for human behavior (and for the physical world as well) appear to have been **metaphysical** or supernatural explanations. Metaphysical explanations are explanations that violate what scientists now consider established physical laws, primarily by attributing behavior or experiences to nonphysical forces such as spirits or deities. The earliest category of metaphysical explanations for human behavior was probably **animism,** the belief that natural phenomena are alive and influence behavior. The common members of many prehistoric bands of hunter-gatherers, along with the distinguished members of many ancient civilizations, appear to have endorsed a wide variety of animistic beliefs. For example, a common belief among many ancient people was that possessing parts of certain animals (e.g., a buffalo's hide, an eagle's feathers) would endow the owner with some of the psychological properties of the animal in question. Similarly, among ancient people almost everywhere, natural phenomena such as the wind, sun, and rain were often assumed to have wills or temperaments. Even early scientists and philosophers sometimes explained natural phenomena in animistic terms. For example, Plato apparently believed that the universe was literally alive and had a soul at its center. According to at least some interpretations, Aristotle argued that gravity reflects the desire of physical objects to return to "mother earth" (Rensberger, 1986).

More subtle versions of animistic thinking appeared in Aristotle's analysis of human personality. In his *Physiognomics,* Aristotle heartily endorses the idea that people who possess the *physical* attributes of certain animals possess the habits and dispositions of those same animals. According to Aristotle, just as people with thick necks were strong in character and fierce tempered (like bulls), people with long, thin necks were backward and cowardly, like deer. Similarly, it seemed self-evident to Aristotle that "men with small *ears* have the disposition of monkeys" and that "those with large ears [have] the disposition of asses." And speaking of asses, Aristotle did not limit his analysis to facial features. He also argued that "*Buttocks* pointed and bony are a mark of strong character" and that curved toes and nails "on the evidence of birds with curved claws" are a sign of disrespect or rudeness (Aristotle, in Barnes, 1984). (Though we hate to quibble with Aristotle, we should note that we have never met an insolent sparrow.)

Animistic explanations such as these seem naive by today's standards, but the natural appeal of animistic and anthropomorphic explanations has not completely disappeared from modern thought. Any car lover who has ever assumed that his reliable old Dodge Dart will not be as good to its new owner as it was to him, any cat lover who has ever assumed that his tabby genuinely loves and admires him, and any PC lover who has ever commented that her aging laptop "is still thinking" about a command (or that her out-of-date software program "is temperamental") has engaged in highly animistic ways of thinking.

A second very old category of metaphysical explanations shares many of the features of animism but is still a potent force in the lives of millions of people everywhere. This second category of metaphysical explanations includes **mythology and religion.** Mythological and religious systems make the assumption that deities (who exist in some kind of spiritual rather than physical plane) play an important role in human behavior. Religious explanations for behavior are typically much more sophisticated and comprehensive than animistic explanations, but they share the basic assumption that non-physical forces determine much of what people do. The point of placing religious systems in this historical sequence is not that they are right or wrong relative to more scientific explanations. It is merely that they are different. They are built on a different set of assumptions than those upon which scientific systems are built (though scientists, too, make plenty of assumptions). As you will see later, religious and scientific systems of thought are also built upon very different sources of evidence. For now it may be instructive to remember that, in addition to being an important part of the lives of people everywhere, religions are also systems of understanding and explaining human behavior.

A third very old category of metaphysical systems is **astrology.** Astrology appears to have been first practiced by the ancient Egyptians, who, like Dionne Warwick and her psychic friends, made the assumption that human behavior is determined by the activity of celestial bodies. An interesting aspect of astrology is that, despite its demotion to a form of entertainment in the last hundred years or so, it does make some very scientific assumptions about human behavior. For example, serious astrologers are very focused on accuracy and precision in measurement. They believe that if one is to give a person the most accurate astrological reading possible, it is necessary to know the exact year, month, day, and time of day of that person's birth, along with the exact latitude and longitude of the person's birth location (Candlish, 1990). Thus, according to *some* of the criteria of good science, astrologers are almost as scientific as astrophysicists. Of course, according to many other criteria, they are the perfect model of decidedly *un*scientific ways of thinking. We will return to this topic later. For now, suffice it to say that metaphysical systems such as animism, mythology, and astrology were eventually abandoned by *scientists* in favor of explanations based on (1) a different set of assumptions about how the world works and (2) a different way of deciding what to believe.

Philosophy

One of the earliest systems of thought to compete with metaphysical systems was **philosophy.** As it is practiced today, philosophy refers to the study of knowledge, behavior, and the nature of reality by making use of logic, intuition, and empirical observations. However, early philosophers often borrowed concepts from less scientific ways of thinking. Many early European philosophers worked hard to make sure that their ideas were consistent with the Bible or with the works of Aristotle or Plato—who, as you may recall, both endorsed some highly animistic beliefs. As late as the 17th century, the brilliant philosopher Descartes, who almost single-handedly transformed thinking about human behavior into a scientific enterprise, accepted the argument that nerves were hollow tubes through which "animal spirits" flowed to the brain. As philosophy matured, however, its practitioners came to rely increasingly on logic and empirical observation. Among contemporary philosophers, arguing for an idea or opinion solely on the basis of authority is considered a sign of weakness.

The focus on logic among philosophers had its roots in early Greek philosophers such as Plato and Aristotle, and it has never really fallen out of favor. In contrast, the focus on empirical observation, though championed by Aristotle himself, never really seemed to catch on until the concept got a big jump start from Descartes in the 1600s. After Descartes, the value of making empirical observations grew in popularity during the days of British empiricists such as Locke, Hume, and Hartley. This principle reached its philosophical heyday after August Comte convinced most 19th-century philosophers that a comprehensive theory of knowledge and human behavior should follow the principle of *positivism* (Schultz, 1981). That is, it should be based only on observations that can be made with absolute certainty. By the middle of the 19th century, the concept of empiricism—the idea that the best way to learn about the world is to make observations—not only took firm hold in philosophy but also became one of the core assumptions of the scientific method. Because psychology emerged as an independent field of study in the mid- to late 19th century, and because it emerged partly in the wake of philosophy, it should come as no surprise that psychologists, especially experimental psychologists, place a great deal of stock in systematic observation. Before we discuss psychology, however, it would be useful to remind ourselves that psychology owes only about half of its genealogy to philosophy. Psychology also grew out of physiology and the physical sciences.

Physiology and the Physical Sciences

Although philosophers believe in empirical observation, very few philosophers gather data to test their theories and hypotheses. Psychology probably owes its current emphasis on systematic observation to its roots in the physical sciences, especially **physiology.** Physiology is the study of the functions of and interrelations between different parts of the brain and body. Physiologists study topics as diverse as how voluntary and involuntary muscle tissues differ and whether different areas of the brain can perform the same basic cognitive or emotional functions. Virtually everything we know about physiology has been discovered using the experimental method. Before William Harvey's landmark experiments on the circulation of blood in 1628, scientists had little or no idea that blood is pumped throughout the body by the heart. Similarly, the tenacious belief that nerves were Lilliputian pipelines for animal spirits was put to rest once and for all by means of the experimental method. A few simple experiments conducted by biologists like Luigi Galvani and Alessandro Volta demonstrated that it is an electrical rather than a spiritual charge that must be applied to a frog's nerves to produce muscle movements. Finally, it wasn't until researchers began to experimentally destroy certain parts of the brains of animals that they were able to determine that different areas of the brain were charged with different physical and psychological tasks. For example, Marshall Hall's experiments with decapitated animals in the early 1800s provided some of the first convincing evidence that reflex movements are determined by the spinal cord and not the brain. (We said that experimental physiology was enlightening, not that it was always beautiful to behold.) What a supergenius like Descartes could never quite resolve in a lifetime of careful speculation, a regular genius like Volta all but proved with a battery and a single, freshly severed frog leg (see Asimov, 1964). And what Volta left unfinished, subsequent generations of smart folks with a little training in experimental physiology proved beyond the slightest doubt (Schultz, 1981).

We are trying to make two distinct points. The first point is that the experimental method is an incredibly powerful way to answer research questions—whether they are physical questions about quantum mechanics or social psychological questions about Chrysler mechanics. The second point is that experimental psychologists owe a great deal of what is good about their discipline to the traditions and methods developed and refined by physiologists and other physical scientists. Now that we have paid some tribute to the metaphysicians, philosophers, and physiologists who preceded scientific psychology, let's take a brief look at the development of scientific psychology. Although it would be a mistake to equate science with experimentation (many scientific studies are not experiments), most historians of psychology would probably agree that psychology first became a science when psychologists first began to conduct experiments. Thus, we begin with an account of when psychologists first seized upon the experimental method.

Experimental Psychology

Most historians of psychology agree that experimental psychology was invented in Germany sometime around the mid- to late 1800s. The only point of disagreement is whether the German guy who invented it was named Fechner, von Helmholtz, Weber, or Wundt.[1] Although most people have bestowed this honor on Wundt, one could easily make an argument for almost any of these gifted researchers. To a greater or lesser extent, they all studied perceptual and sensory processes in the mid- to late 1800s, and they all made use of experimental methods. However, Wundt was the most psychologically minded one in the bunch. Both his desire to break consciousness down into its component parts and his heavy emphasis on experimental methods probably reflected his extensive training in physiology. However, Wundt was also quite interested in higher-order mental processes. In fact, in one of his earliest and most important works (the *Beitrage,* published in 1862), he expressed a keen interest in creating a field he called *social psychology,* and he eventually published a ten-volume book entitled *Folk Psychology* between 1900 and 1920. Surprisingly, however, Wundt felt that the experimental method that was so crucial to understanding basic psychological experience was ill suited to the study of complex cognitive and social processes. Of course, it is a major theme of this text that nothing could be further from the truth.

In the past 120 years or so, **psychology** has become both decidedly experimental, and decidedly scientific. In fact, like many other researchers, we define psychology as the scientific study of human behavior. That brief definition warrants an entire textbook on research methods because of the single word "scientific." In a nutshell, this book is about how to go about the business of psychology scientifically. Your brief foray into the history of how people have understood their physical and social worlds should have given you some appreciation for how scientific approaches to understanding human behavior differ from other approaches. However, to gain a fuller appreciation of what it means to study human behavior scientifically, it would probably be useful to give some additional thought to exactly how scientists go about their business. The first thing to know about scientists is that, like pastors, politicians, and pastry chefs, scientists make some very important assumptions. Knowing what scientists take for granted can help make us better methodologists because many of the specific principles that are dear to the hearts of methodologists can be derived from the general principles that almost all scientists take for granted. Fundamental principles that are more or less accepted on faith are often referred to as **canons.** There appear to be at least four such fundamental principles that are accepted by almost all scientists.

The Four Canons of Science
Determinism

One hallmark of scientific thinking is the assumption of **determinism.** This is the doctrine that the universe is orderly: the idea that all events have meaningful, systematic causes. Even animistic and astrological systems of thought are partly deterministic. Astrologers appear to believe that something about the motions and positions of celestial bodies *causes* people to behave in certain predictable ways. They can't (or won't) tell us exactly what it is about Neptune's rising or Venus's falling that causes Serena to have had bad luck last Wednesday, but it is presumably *something* systematic. Otherwise, why not assign people to astrological signs at random? Whereas there may be some deterministic slippage in astrological systems, there is little room for such slippage in science.[2] Some psychologists have even argued that people (and perhaps many other animals) are predisposed to think in causal terms. Whether we are predisposed to do so, there is plenty of evidence that we are wont to do so. As an example of the power and utility of causal thinking, consider the following problem (adapted from Tversky & Kahneman, 1982):

A cab was involved in a hit-and-run accident at night. Two cab companies, the Green and the Blue, operate in the city. You are given the following data:

1. 85% of the cabs in the city are Green and 15% are Blue.
2. A witness identified the cab as Blue.

The court tested the reliability of the witness under the same circumstances that existed on the night of the accident and concluded that the witness correctly identified each one of the two colors 80% of the time and failed 20% of the time. What is the probability that the cab involved in the accident was Blue? If you are like most people, your intuitions are telling you that it is about .80, which corresponds very well to the reliability of the witness. In numerous studies, this is exactly what Tversky and Kahneman (1982) found. The median ("middle") and modal ("most common") answer for a large group of participants was .80.

Now, if you can somehow cleanse your cognitive palate, consider a slightly different version of the same problem. In this version, you learn exactly what you learned above except that the information about the cab companies is a little different. Specifically, replace statement (1) in the original problem with the following statement:

1'. Although the two companies are roughly equal in size, 85% of cab accidents in the city involve Green cabs and 15% involve Blue cabs.

Now think again about the accident, the reliability of the witness, and the probability that the cab involved in the accident was Blue. What is this probability?

Although the correct answer hasn't changed, your intuitions about the answer may have. When Tversky and Kahneman gave this logically equivalent version of the problem to a different group of participants, the median answer changed to .60, which indicates that participants in this second group were making at least partial use of information about *base rates*. Base-rate information is information about the proportion of things in a target population—in this case, either the proportion of Green and Blue cabs in the city, or the proportion of Green and Blue cabs involved in accidents. The main point of the cab problem, by the way, is that when people are provided with both base-rate information and some kind of subjectively useful competing information (in this case, a witness's report), they don't make very good use of the base-rate information. However, if you revised your answer downward once you realized that most accidents in this city are *caused* by Green cabs, you were improving the accuracy of your judgment by being more sensitive than usual to base-rate information when it was expressed in causal terms (see Ajzen, 1977, for additional evidence along these lines). The correct answer to the cab problem, by the way, is .41. In light of the facts that (1) Green cabs are 5.67 times as likely to be involved in accidents as are Blue cabs and (2) the witness's judgment was pretty poor (only 30% better than the chance performance level of 50%), you should have adjusted your answer *quite a bit* in the direction of Green cabs (see Tversky & Kahneman, 1982, for a more detailed explanation). The fact that most people come a lot closer to the correct answer when the base-rate information is framed in causal terms attests to the tendency of people to prefer to think, and possibly to be predisposed to think, in causal terms.

Further evidence that people may be predisposed to think in causal terms comes from research that deals more directly with how people perceive covariation. Consider the information about glorks and zarks presented in Table 1.1. Based on the information in this table, decide which of the two groups, zarks or glorks, you find more likable. Please make this judgment before you read any further! If you are like most people, you probably found the glorks at least a little more likable than the zarks. If you did in fact conclude that you'd prefer to invite a glork rather than a zark to your next dinner party, you probably fell prey to a common judgmental bias known as the *illusory correlation* (Hamilton & Gifford, 1976). In a number of judgment situations very much like this one, Hamilton and his colleagues found that people falsely infer a connection or correlation between group membership and the likelihood of engaging in nice versus nasty behavior. More specifically, they typically judge small groups like the zarks to be less likable than large groups like the glorks.

This perceived correlation is referred to as illusory because in the preceding example (and in many others like it) there is no connection between group membership and behavior. In the particular example given here, both glorks and zarks are exactly twice as likely to help the nems as they are to harm them. There just happen to be twice as many glorks as zarks. If we consulted Tversky and Kahneman to help us describe this situation, they would probably remind us (1) that base rates for helping are twice as high as they are for harming, (2) that base rates for glorks are twice as high as they are for

TABLE 1.1 *Prosocial and antisocial behavior of zarks and glorks*

Group:	Who Harmed the Nems?	Who Helped the Nems?
Zarks:	T, a zark, harmed the nems.	E, a zark, helped the nems. N, a zark, helped the nems.
Glorks:	R, a glork, harmed the nems. O, a glork, harmed the nems.	A, a glork, helped the nems. S, a glork, helped the nems. L, a glork, helped the nems. P, a glork, helped the nems.

zarks, and (3) that in this case, there is no need to adjust anything for base rates—except perhaps in the sense that, in light of base rates, there is no reason to be impressed by the fact that four different glorks helped the nems. Helping is simply popular; glorks are simply populous.

Presumably, the fact that people often perceive connections where none truly exist plays an important role in the development and maintenance of stereotypes (see Hamilton & Rose, 1980). Did you notice, for example, that in most people's eyes, the statistical minority group (the much maligned zarks) was judged more harshly than the statistical majority? The well-established finding that people often perceive connections between things that aren't really connected also suggests that people may be a little too ready to see the world in terms of causes. If this is true, people do not appear to be alone in this tendency. Behaviorists who condition animals such as rats and pigeons have identified an animal analogue of this judgmental bias. More specifically, Skinner demonstrated that if you place an animal in a box and drop reinforcements in a food tray at random intervals (irrespective of what the animal is doing), the animal will often behave as if there is a contingency (i.e., a connection) between some behavior it may have spontaneously emitted during the "training" session and the delivery of the reinforcement. For example, if a pigeon happened to be standing on one foot prior to the (random) delivery of a food pellet, the pigeon might engage in this behavior several times again. Of course, if the pigeon does this long enough, another pellet will eventually be dropped into the food tray. The exact behavior that is "falsely conditioned" in this way will differ from one pigeon to the next, but conditioning will often occur nonetheless. Skinner (1948) referred to this false conditioning process as *superstitious conditioning*. At the risk of anthropomorphizing, the pigeon appears to have formed an illusory correlation between the arbitrarily produced behavior and the arbitrarily delivered food pellet. If pigeons could invite people to dinner parties, they too might prefer the company of glorks.[3]

The principle of determinism has a close corollary. This is the idea that science is about **theories.** A theory is simply a statement about the causal relation between two or more variables. It is typically stated in abstract terms, and it usually has some degree of empirical support (though many people would quibble with this final part of the definition). Theories wouldn't be very useful in the absence of determinism, because in the absence of determinism, orderly, systematic causes wouldn't exist. Although many people think of psychology as a "soft" science that may not be as theoretical as "hard" sciences like physics or biology, theories play exactly the same role in psychology that they play in physics or biology. They identify abstract, hypothetical constructs that presumably tell us something about how the world operates. From this perspective, psychological constructs such as relative deprivation or selective attention are just as scientific as physical and biological constructs such as relativity or natural selection (see Hedges, 1987).

Just as laypeople tend to think deterministically, laypeople also tend to think theoretically. Most people have well-elaborated "theories" about things as diverse as police officers, baseball games, and golden retrievers. Moreover, much like scientists, people often inherit these theories from their ancestors, and they are often reluctant to part with them. Social psychologists have a host of terms for these naive (untrained) causal theories; they include terms such as causal schema, script, stereotype, self-concept, and working model. In fact, when Fritz Heider (1958) wanted to summarize the way in which common people understand their social worlds, he referred to people as "naive scientists." By this he meant that people have little or no formal training in explaining the social world but go about doing so in much the same way that scientists typically go about explaining the physical world.

Regardless of what the cab problem, the illusory correlation, superstitious conditioning, and the construal of people as naive scientists have to do with laypeople's assumptions that the universe is chock-full of orderly causes, scientists have long made this assumption. They accept this canon largely on faith in much the same way that a rabbi accepts the Torah largely on faith. To be anti-Torah in any serious way would probably mean being something other than a rabbi. Similarly, to be devoutly antideterministic would probably mean being something other than a scientist. However, being enamored of determinism isn't the only thing that makes a person a scientist. There are at least three other things you probably need to believe in if you want to be a card-carrying scientist.

Empiricism

Scientists not only assume that the universe obeys orderly principles; they also assume that there are good and bad ways of *figuring out* these orderly principles. The best method, according to scientists, is to follow the canon of **empiricism,** that is, to make *observations.* Of course, you are already familiar with the concept of empiricism because, as we noted earlier, it is one of the favorite tools of modern philosophers. It is an even more favorite tool of scientists, and psychologists are no exception. Like astrophysicists and psychophysicists, psychologists assume that the best way to find out how the world works is to make observations. It may seem patently obvious to you that making observations is a great way to find things out, but this is a relatively modern assumption—even among philosophers and scientists.

This point should be brought home for you anytime you hear someone use the phrase "I got it straight from the horse's mouth." What people typically appear to mean by this is "I got it straight from the source" (often an expert source)—meaning that they are reporting firsthand rather than secondhand information. Like many other common phrases, this one has been around for so long that it has come to take on a subtly different meaning from the one originally intended. Apparently, the phrase originated when a group of philosophers were debating the number of teeth that a horse should have (see Rensberger, 1986). We don't know exactly how many teeth a horse should have, and apparently the philosophers didn't either. If we may take a little creative license to reenact this discussion, a biologically inclined philosopher may have argued that as a member of the family *Equidae,* a horse should, like a quagga or a zebra, have exactly 34 teeth. A more theologically inclined philosopher may have retorted that, as a scripturally unclean, noncloven-hoofed grazer, the horse should have fewer teeth than a cow and should therefore have somewhere in the neighborhood of 28 teeth. Of course, we have no idea *exactly* what logical or intuitive arguments were used by the philosophers, but the point is that the debate was extremely long and extremely speculative. Eventually, however, one of the philosophers put an abrupt end to the debate by posing a simple but profound solution. He suggested that if everyone really wanted to know how many teeth a horse has, they should just go out, find a horse, look it in the mouth, and count its teeth (unless, perhaps, it proved to be a gift horse, but that's a different story). In other words, he suggested that *making an observation* is a good way to find things out about the world.

This second canon of science is probably the least controversial of the four. After all, throughout human history, there have been plenty of empiricists. As we noted earlier, one of the things that distinguished Aristotle from many of his contemporaries was his emphasis on systematic observation. Similarly, Galileo's biggest claim to fame is a legendary experiment in which he simultaneously dropped a heavy and a light cannonball from the Leaning Tower of Pisa. As the famous story goes, the two balls obligingly fell at precisely the same rate, invalidating the Aristotelian theory that the rate at which objects fall is directly proportional to their weight. This is an excellent example of Galileo's extreme faith in empiricism. However, there is a serious problem with this example. The problem is that Galileo *never performed* this celebrated experiment (see Asimov, 1964; Glenn, 1996; Rensberger, 1986). Moreover, the reason he never did so is quite interesting. Galileo *did* place a great deal of faith in empiricism. However, he apparently placed an even greater deal of faith in himself (or, to be more precise, in his powers of reasoning). Galileo solved this gravitational puzzle logically, and then *challenged his detractors* to perform the crucial experiment.

Galileo's logic took the form of a thought experiment that went something like this: Imagine that we held a heavy object directly underneath a light object and simultaneously dropped the two objects. According to Aristotle, the heavy object should outpace the light object in its descent toward the earth, leaving it behind. Fair enough. Now imagine that we reversed the situation by holding the light object directly *underneath* the heavy object before releasing them. According to Aristotle, the light object should actually slow the heavy object down! To Galileo this seemed ridiculous. By combining arguments such as these with some additional arguments about wind resistance, Galileo convinced himself that if one could eliminate the problem of wind resistance, all objects would fall at the same rate. Apparently, Galileo convinced his detractors as well. When he challenged them to prove him wrong by performing the much acclaimed experiment with cannonballs, they declined the invitation. The point is that Galileo was so confident of his prediction that he challenged *others* to test it empirically.

Because empiricism has become one of the guiding assumptions of modern science, you shouldn't be too surprised to learn that a lot of other famous scientists have placed a great deal of faith in it. However, you might be at least a little surprised to learn that a lot of laypeople, and at least a few famous religious thinkers, have also placed a great deal of stock in empiricism. When someone says that "the proof of the pudding is in the eating" or tells someone else to "put up or shut up," this person is expressing an intuitive appreciation of empiricism. Similarly, when the much maligned "doubting Thomas" said that he could not truly believe that Jesus had risen from the dead unless he could be allowed, among other things, to place his finger in the holes in Jesus' hands, he was identifying himself as an empiricist. Of course, this hasn't done much for Thomas's popularity with followers of Christianity. However, for at least one famous Christian, preaching the merits of empiricism never caused much of a ruckus. When the apostle Paul wrote that "faith without works is dead," part of what he appears to have been saying is that works count for something special because works, unlike faith, are readily observable. If Paul had been addressing a group of cooks rather than a group of disciples, he might have said that the proof of the pudding is in the eating. If he had been addressing a group of athletes or gamblers, he might have reminded them that talk is cheap and asked them to put up or shut up.

Parsimony

A third basic assumption of most scientific schools of thought is a sort of scientific tie-breaker. It is a pragmatic recommendation about the kind of theory or explanation that a good scientist should prefer. Virtually all scientists agree that if we are faced with two competing theories that do an equally good job of handling a set of empirical observations, we should prefer the simpler, or more **parsimonious,** of the two. As the word "parsimony" is commonly used by nonscientists, it refers to extreme stinginess or frugality. This is good to remember because the canon of **parsimony** says that we should be extremely frugal in developing (or choosing between) theories—by steering away from unnecessary concepts. Mechanics and engineers would probably appreciate parsimony because parsimony is a sort of theoretical analogue of the mechanical idea that it is preferable to make machines that have the smallest possible number of moving parts (because this leaves fewer parts to break down).

Because people often confuse science with closely related fields like technology and higher mathematics, parsimony is probably the canon that is least consistent with most laypeople's intuitions about science. When people see a "scientific" figure or diagram that resembles the wiring schematic for a telephone dispatch system—full of circles, boxes, arrows, and cryptic labels—they tend to think "How scientific! I wish I could understand it!" The point of parsimony is that if something is good science you *should* be able to understand it. If forced to choose between two pretty good theories that both explain the results of your experiment, choose the one that your great-aunt Josephine will understand better. Unless your great-aunt Josephine is a retired electrical engineer, it will almost never be the one that looks like a wiring diagram. Arnold Buss (1988) has appropriately labeled the tendency for psychologists to be intrigued by models with lots of boxes and arrows "boxology." And he has noted that boxology is very *un*scientific—because it is very unparsimonious.

One of the first people to make a potent argument for parsimony was the medieval English philosopher William of Occam, and for this reason the principle of parsimony is sometimes referred to as "Occam's razor." To paraphrase Occam, the principle of parsimony states that it is intellectually inappropriate to make more assumptions than you absolutely have to (Duffy, 1993). In the late 1800s, another famous Englishman, the animal psychologist C. Lloyd Morgan, made a very similar point. Morgan argued that we should avoid making too many assumptions when we try to understand the behavior of animals. The version of this point he emphasized in his debates with the famous animal psychologist George Romanes is the one for which he is best known. Morgan was very frustrated with Romanes's elaborate (and typically anthropomorphic) explanations for animal behavior. For example, Romanes (1882) frequently assumed that animals possess complex ideas, engage in reasoning by analogy, and make use of the "logic of feelings" in pretty much the same way that human beings do (see Figure 1.1). Morgan's recommendation to animal psychologists was that whenever one can explain animal behavior in terms of simple mental activities such as conditioned associations, it is inappropriate to explain these behaviors in terms of higher mental functioning. In the early days of scientific psychology, behaviorists such as John B. Watson and B. F. Skinner took "Lloyd Morgan's Canon" a step further by assuming that we should strive to explain human as well as animal behavior using a small set of relatively simple principles. From this perspective, Watson and Skinner were even bigger fans of parsimony than the two men whose names have become virtually synonymous with this basic tenet of science.[4]

At the risk of undermining our basic argument about the canon of parsimony, it is worth noting that it may not *always* be parsimonious to explain human and animal behavior using different theories. In the case of explaining how a housecat opens a door, for example, we agree that it is inappropriate to assume that a cat's thoughts and feelings about doors are as complex as a carpenter's. However, what if you were trying to explain why chimpanzees do some of the amazing things they do? For example, like people, chimpanzees easily learn to recognize themselves in mirrors. Chimpanzees also make and use tools, and they appear to engage in strategic deception as well as strategic cooperation. For instance, the Dutch primatologist DeWaal (1996) once observed an amorous but low-ranking male chimpanzee display his erect penis to a desirable female (to protect the chimp's identity we'll call him C. H.). C. H. expressed his affection for this beautiful female chimp by simply facing her, sitting upright, and spreading his legs. However, when the alpha male in this troop wandered by, C. H. quickly and strategically placed his hand over his penis—and casually looked away. Is it more parsimonious to explain this behavioral sequence using the principles of operant conditioning or to describe it using words such as fear, jealousy, and deception? Considering the fact that chimpanzees share about 98% of their genetic information with human beings (Diamond, 1992), DeWaal suggests that it would sometimes be more parsimonious to explain similar behaviors in human beings and chimpanzees using a single theory rather than two completely different theories. This controversial example should illustrate that whereas there is a great deal of consensus concerning the basic canons of science, there is somewhat less consensus regarding exactly how and when to apply these canons.

A final perspective on parsimony is to consider it an extension of the idea that science is a very theoretical enterprise. One of the most important things a good scientific theory does in the first place is to simplify and organize a great number of otherwise disparate observations—by tying them together into some kind of coherent causal story. A good theory about why people fall in love, for example, can simplify and organize a great number of otherwise

FIGURE 1.1   At the time this photo was taken, Devon was a 2-year-old housecat. In this series of photos, Devon is opening a door to get to some tuna the first author placed on the other side (and his housemate, Tasha, is capitalizing on his efforts). The animal psychologist George Romanes (1882, pp. 421–422) observed a cat very much like Devon and described the cat's behavior as follows: "Cats . . . have a very definite idea as to the mechanical properties of a door. . . . First the animal must have observed that the door is opened by the hand grasping the handle and moving the latch. Next, she must reason. . . . If a hand can do it, why not a paw? . . . the pushing with the hind feet after depressing the latch must be due to adaptive reasoning." How parsimonious is this explanation?

unrelated observations about romantic attraction. The idea behind parsimony is that as long as we are at the business of simplifying and organizing, we might as well *keep* at it until we have made things as simple as possible. When it comes to scientific journeys, most scientists believe in traveling light.

Testability

The final, and perhaps the most important, canon of science is the assumption that scientific theories should be **testable** (confirmable or disconfirmable) using currently available research techniques. The canon of testability is closely related to the canon of empiricism because the techniques that scientists typically use to test their theories are *empirical* techniques. It is hard to be a believer in empiricism without also being a believer in testability (and even harder to be a believer in testability without also being a believer in empiricism). After all, empirical tests of an idea often reveal that the idea is not as correct as its proponents had originally assumed. In addition to being closely related to the canon of empiricism, the concept of testability is even more closely associated with the more specific philosophy of **falsifiability.** The idea behind falsifiability is that scientists should go a step beyond putting their theories to some kind of test by actively seeking out tests that could prove their theories *wrong* (see Abramson, 1992). During the period of tremendous scientific advancement that occurred in the early to middle part of the 20th century, Karl Popper became very famous for espousing this idea.

During his youth, Popper had been an ardent devotee of Marxism, but as he began to think about how Marxism compared with some alternate schools of thought, he began to realize that most Marxists accepted Marxist doctrines uncritically—going about their lives as if all the predictions of Marxism were self-evident truths. His feeling was that if he was to devote himself to a school of thought, it would have to be one that could survive some kind of critical test.

Popper (1974/1990) spends the early portion of his book *Unended Quest* describing his conversion to a philosophical and scientific school of thought known as *logical positivism.* Logical positivists believe that science and philosophy should be based solely on things that can be observed with absolute certainty. Many of them also believe that the way to go about testing scientific theories and hypotheses is to actively try to disconfirm them. Popper (1974/1990) described a crucial step in his conversion to this critical school of thought by describing his delight at the way Einstein wrote about his general theory of relativity:

> But what impressed me most was Einstein's own clear statement that he would regard his theory as untenable if it should fail in certain tests. Thus he wrote, for example: "If the redshift of spectral lines due to the gravitational potential should not exist, then the general theory of relativity will be untenable.". . . This, I felt, was the true scientific attitude.

Among psychologists, concepts such as testability and falsifiability are extremely important because many early psychological theories (e.g., the work of Freud and other psychoanalysts) were difficult to put to any kind of objective test. Prominent behaviorists such as E. C. Tolman and Clark Hull improved this state of affairs when they followed the example of many physicists and popularized the idea of operationism, or **operational definitions.** Operational definitions are definitions of theoretical constructs that are stated in terms of concrete, observable procedures. It is a thorn in the flesh of psychologists that much of what we wish to understand (e.g., hunger, fear, attention, prejudice, etc.) is not directly observable. Operational definitions solve this problem by connecting unobservable traits or experiences to things that *can* be observed. For example, researchers such as Tolman and Hull operationally defined hunger in terms of hours of food deprivation or proportion of normal body weight after extended food deprivation (Schultz, 1981). Unlike the nebulous experience of hunger, things like time and weight can be readily observed or measured. Of course, there is no way to know with absolute certainty that a rat (or a person) that hasn't eaten in two days is experiencing hunger, but it is an extremely reasonable assumption. More important, it is an assumption that makes theories involving internal states such as hunger the objects of empirical investigation.

Operational definitions also lend themselves well to precise quantification. An elephant that hasn't eaten in 48 hours should be somewhat hungrier than one who hasn't eaten for 36, and should be much, much hungrier than an elephant who has just eaten. It would be highly presumptuous to assume that an elephant that hasn't eaten for 48 hours is *twice* as hungry as an elephant that hasn't eaten for 24, but if we plot hours of food deprivation against a quantitative, operationally defined measure of learning (e.g., the number of wrong turns taken prior to reaching a goal box in an enormous maze) we can begin to say something precise about how hunger relates to learning in elephants. And if we are in the business of theory testing, we might be able to say that a particular theory of hunger and learning is in need of revision.

Operational definitions are so much a part of scientific ways of thinking that most modern scientists probably take them for granted. However, if we define both science and operational definitions pretty loosely, it could be argued that operational definitions have been around as long as science has. A case in point has to do with an operational definition of intelligence that was (somewhat begrudgingly) adopted by the Greek philosopher-scientist Thales. Thales was arguably the first true scientist. That is, he was apparently the first person in recorded history to address questions about the basic nature of the universe without falling back on magical or metaphysical explanations. Although Thales cared little for money, he apparently cared a great deal about being smart. After becoming legendary for his intellect, Thales was apparently insulted by jealous critics who asked him (if we may translate loosely from the Greek), "If you're so smart, why ain't you rich?" Thales happened to have an excellent understanding of weather, and according to Asimov (1964), Thales responded to this obnoxious question by buying up olive presses in a year in which his meteorological observations told him it would be an excellent year for olives. During that year's bountiful olive harvest, Thales charged bountiful rates for the use of his olive presses. Thales thus became an instant olive baron, and having proven his point, went back to work as a real scientist.

Like most of the other scientific concepts we have discussed so far, operational definitions are not unique to science. Long before Tolman and Hull were imploring their fellow psychologists to convert the unobservable into the observable, rabbis and referees were doing much the same thing—and for much the same reason. They wanted observable answers to important but elusive questions having to do with things like the will of God or the relative skill of two soccer teams. In the case of religious figures, ancient Jewish prophets, when faced with difficult decisions about the will of God, used to place "prayer cloths" on the ground around dusk and consult these cloths the next morning to ascertain what they assumed were God's wishes. Most frequently, the presence or absence of dew on the cloth would be taken to indicate which of two potential courses of action was to be taken. Of course, prophets who made use of such prayer cloths were making some pretty big assumptions about the connection between dew and their chosen deity, but the issue is not that they did or didn't make good decisions this way. It is that even people with no training in scientific methods can appreciate the logic of operational definitions.

Most sports and games provide more familiar examples of operational definitions. In fact, to our knowledge, there is no such thing as a competitive sport or game that does not make use of operational definitions. In basketball, for example, the operational definition of scoring a basket is propelling the ball from a legal position on the court so that it falls downward through a metal hoop that is suspended 10 feet in the air on some kind of backboard. Nothing else players do, no matter how spectacularly athletic, will score a basket for their team. Of course, the ability to do this while following all the other rules of the game is one good, solid indicator of the abstract, hypothetical construct most people call basketball-playing ability. To appreciate the utility of operational definitions, imagine trying to play a complex game like basketball, football, or chess *without* operational definitions. It is hard to know how winners and losers would be decided, and it is quite possible that there would never *be* any losers. If we asked the members of opposing baseball teams to introspect on their skills and decide who should be declared victorious, we strongly suspect that both teams would typically decide that they were superior. Operational definitions play a similar role in science. If we simply asked proponents of a theory what they think of their theory's chances of being correct, we would find that very few theories ever got disconfirmed.

Because operational definitions are so important, it might be useful for you to consider some concrete examples of operational definitions. Table 1.2 summarizes at least two distinct ways in which psychologists might operationally define constructs as varied as cognitive load and interpersonal attraction. Whereas no one way of operationalizing any of these constructs is perfect, they all share the positive trait of making abstract hypothetical concepts measurable (and thus testable). To flesh one of these examples out in more detail, consider the two operational definitions of "memory." The first definition, the number of words from a list a participant can recall after a delay, is very intuitive. If we want to know how well you learned the words in a list, we can simply ask you to recall the words and count up the number of words you listed correctly.

TABLE 1.2. Some abstract psychological concepts and some potential operational definitions for them.

Concept	Operational Definition
Depression	1. Total number of symptoms a person reports having experienced (e.g., sadness, loss of appetite, sleep disturbance) in a structured interview
	2. A person's true-false responses to an anonymous, 20-item pencil-and-paper survey (e.g., "During the past four weeks, I have had serious thoughts of harming myself.")
Cognitive load	1. Whether participants are given 5 seconds or 50 seconds to estimate the answer to a problem
	2. Whether participants are instructed to keep a running total of a series of 1-digit numbers that appear in the center of a computer screen (while they are listening to a story)
Attraction	1. How close participants sit next to a confederate who is always seated at the end of a row of chairs
	2. Whether a person is married to someone
Memory	1. The number of words from a list a participant can recall after a delay
	2. The specific word a participant makes when presented with a word fragment such as "ele_____."

However, unless you happen to know a lot about memory, the second definition, the specific word a participant makes when presented with a word fragment such as "ele_____," may not make much sense. How could you test people's memory by asking them to complete a word fragment?

Let's begin by considering how *you* completed this word fragment. What was the very first word that came to mind for you? If you made the word "elephant," we suspect it is because you were exposed to this word a few minutes ago—when you were reading about operational definitions of hunger. If we hadn't mentioned elephants in this example (or if you had just taken the elevator from your elementary calculus class on the eleventh floor), we suspect that you'd be way more likely to have made a different word.

As it turns out, word fragment tasks are excellent measures of certain kinds of memory. When a person cannot recall a specific word, but this word nonetheless influences how the person completes a word fragment task (or some other cognitive task), memory researchers would say that the person has an implicit (i.e., unconscious) memory for the word (Schacter, 1996). To frame this a little differently, everyone knows that people can sometimes *recognize* words that they cannot *recall*. Measures of recognition memory (e.g., "Did you see the word 'apple'?") are often more sensitive than measures of recall memory (e.g., "List all the words you can remember."). Memory researchers happen to know that word fragment measures are sometimes even more sensitive than measures of recognition. Having a cool operational definition can sometimes allow researchers to learn things they never could have learned without it. Judging from research using measures of implicit memory, we have learned that people sometimes "know" things that they themselves do not realize.

Speaking of memory, you may recall that we said operational definitions are important because they make theories testable or disconfirmable. What, exactly, makes a theory disconfirmable? In addition to operational definitions, it's also things like clear and parsimonious statements of what the theory predicts. However, one additional thing to keep in mind is that testability and disconfirmability refer as much to the attitude of a theory's proponents as they do to the nature of a theory itself. For example, very few voters would consider conducting an experiment to decide whether to become a Republican or a Democrat. Similarly, if Zeke tells you that there is no kind of empirical evidence that could persuade him to change his opinion of shellfish or Zen Buddhism, you can be pretty sure that he did not arrive at his opinions scientifically. The cornerstone of the scientific perspective is thus openness to criticism and revision. In fact, Popper has argued that it is openness to criticism and revision, rather than the use of any specific methods or procedures, that makes a field of study scientific.

The degree to which a belief system is open to revision is an important determinant of the kinds of evidence or support that advocates of the belief system will typically be most interested in scrutinizing. For example, scientists place very little stock in authority, but popes and presidents typically consider authority the bottom line. To gain a final bit of perspective on how scientific belief systems differ from other common belief systems, it might be useful to consider four different kinds of support for beliefs and see how each kind of support is typically viewed by advocates of different belief systems.

Four Ways of Knowing About the World

One of the best ways to learn about a person's thinking style is to ask that person a difficult question and then ask the person to explain how he or she arrived at the answer. For example, consider the proposal that there is a gravitational attraction between the tip of your left thumbnail and the planet Pluto. Is there? Use any reasonable method that is currently at your disposal, but do not read any further until you have come up with an answer.

If you guessed that there is no such attraction, you might have come to this conclusion in several different ways. First of all, your **intuitions** may have simply told you that such an idea seems far-fetched. Second, you may have tried to make use of **logic,** reasoning that if the tip of your left thumbnail is attracted to things as bizarre and distant as the planet Pluto, then you'd have some noticeable difficulties keeping it in your possession. Though it is less likely, you may have also consulted some sort of **authority** figure. If your roommate, the physics major, was handy when you were reading this question, you may have simply asked him or her the answer to the question. Finally, although it would have been desirable to do so, it is extremely unlikely that you made any kind of empirical **observation** to test this idea because doing so would be virtually impossible. The correct answer, by the way, is that there is indeed a gravitational attraction between the tip of your left thumbnail and the planet Pluto. The universal law of gravitation states (and empirical research has thus far confirmed) that there is a gravitational attraction between all the matter in the universe. One reason you are at little risk of having a tiny piece of your thumbnail wrenched from your thumb in a meteoric descent toward Pluto is that gravitational attraction falls off as a squared function of the distance between the objects in question. As long as you stay close to Earth and far away from other celestial bodies, you will save a lot of money on manicures.

As far as we can tell, the four methods of "knowing" you may have consulted when trying to answer this question—namely, authority, intuition, logic, and observation—come pretty close to exhausting all the basic ways in which people decide what they believe. Each of these ways of knowing plays a role in almost all kinds of belief systems. However, the relative emphasis placed on each varies dramatically from one belief system to the next. Consider authority. Authority refers to status or prestige, typically based on things like expertise or legitimately acquired power. Laypeople appear to place a great deal of emphasis on authority or expertise when making day-to-day decisions. In fact, the tendency to do so is prevalent enough that it has been labeled the *expertise heuristic* by researchers who study attitudes and persuasion (e.g., see Chaiken, Liberman, & Eagly, 1989; Hovland & Weiss, 1951; Petty & Cacioppo, 1986; Smith & Mackie, 1995). Whereas scientists and philosophers claim to place little stock in authority, believers in virtually all governments or religions consider authority (e.g., the president, the Buddha, the Torah, the Constitution) the final word on many important beliefs and decisions.

Governments and religions are also similar in that both systems appear to consider intuition an important way of understanding the world. The U.S. Declaration of Independence makes the bold, intuitively appealing statement, "We hold these truths to be self-evident. . . ." As another example, most religions and governments take the intuitively appealing position that people are free to make all their own choices in life. Many philosophical and scientific views call this intuitive claim into question because it is potentially at odds with the canon of determinism (see Skinner, 1971). Debates about topics like freedom versus determinism, which have taken on great importance among philosophers and scientists, are not nearly so important to ministers and prime ministers. One reason this is true is that religious and political thinkers place great faith in intuition. In contrast, scientists and philosophers place greater faith in logic, and may become deeply troubled by logical paradoxes. Politicians are more likely to put paradoxes to a vote. Ministers are more likely to leave them in the hands of a higher power.

Although the typical scientist and the typical philosopher might both prefer logical rather than intuitive solutions to a debate, scientists and philosophers differ somewhat in the relative emphasis they place on logic. To the typical philosopher, logic is likely to take preeminence even over observation as the touchstone against which all other things are judged. Philosophers as a group devote an enormous amount of their intellectual efforts to discerning

TABLE 1.3 Relative importance of different ways of knowing to different belief systems

Religion	Government	Philosophy	Science
1. authority	1. authority	1. logic	1. observation
2. intuition	2. intuition	2. observation	2. logic
3. logic	3. logic	3. intuition	3. intuition
4. observation	4. observation	4. authority	4. authority

Note: Rank-orderings are from (1) most to (4) least important.

the correct and incorrect rules of reasoning (Copi, 1978). Philosophers seem to have learned that they cannot always believe their eyes. To the typical scientist, logic can be incontrovertible, but it can also be impenetrable, and it takes a backseat to observation as the primary mode of figuring out the world. Whereas the philosopher finds comfort in the use of contrapositives, the scientist finds more comfort in the use of counterbalancing. Scientists prefer experimentation over argumentation.

The relative importance of authority, intuition, logic, and observation for religion, government, philosophy, and science are listed in Table 1.3. Although it is possible to quibble with the exact rankings, a gross analysis of the table should clarify an important distinction between scientific and nonscientific belief systems. Scientists and nonscientists make use of very different techniques for figuring out the world.

Two final notes are in order about the four ways of knowing. The first note is that there is no guarantee that one way of knowing will be superior to others across all possible situations. Observation compels scientists to create particle accelerators; intuition compels people to create families, sculptures, and governments. If the Declaration of Independence had been written by political scientists rather than politicians (e.g., "Recent research in public policy suggests a number of useful generalizations about self-governance . . ."), we suspect that it would have generated a bit less enthusiasm among colonists struggling with their allegiances to the British Crown.

The second note is that these distinctions between different ways of knowing are convenient simplifications. Furthermore, true genius often consists of finding the balance between different ways of understanding the world. For instance, Thomas Jefferson was a scientist as well as a politician, and his scientific side often influenced his political arguments. Unlike many of his contemporaries, for example, Jefferson argued that systems of government, like scientific theories, should change with the times on the basis of new evidence. When asked, in 1816, whether the Virginia constitution should be revised, Jefferson remarked:

> I am certainly not an advocate for frequent and untried changes in laws and constitutions. . . . But I know also, that laws and institutions must go hand in hand with the progress of the human mind. As that becomes more developed, more enlightened, as new discoveries are made, new truths disclosed, and manners and opinions change with the change of

circumstances, institutions must advance also, and keep pace with the times. We might as well require a man to wear still the coat which fitted him when a boy, as civilized society to remain ever under the regimen of their barbarous ancestors.

(Letter to Samuel Kerchreview, July 12, 1816)

Good thinkers rarely limit themselves to a single way of understanding the world. As a very different example, when Galileo finally got around to doing some empirical studies of gravity, he was plagued by the inaccuracies of the current technology of measurement. Instead of waiting a couple of hundred years for the invention of a good stopwatch, he slowed things down by studying the behavior of bodies *rolling down inclined planes* (Asimov, 1964; Harré, 1981). By doing so, Galileo was able to demonstrate quite convincingly that heavy and light objects "fell" at the same rate. In addition, he was able to show something more subtle, and perhaps more important. Things don't simply fall at a constant rate: they constantly accelerate. Of course, accepting Galileo's conclusions requires us to make some logical inferences about the compatibility of rolling and falling, but this is exactly the point. Galileo was not simply a good logician or a good observer. One of his unique talents was his ability to blend logic and observation into a seamless set of arguments that could knock someone's socks off (and predict how quickly they would fall to the floor).

HANDS-ON ACTIVITY 1

Galileo's Dice

One of the points emphasized in Chapter 1 is that scientists and nonscientists typically rely on different "ways of knowing." Although Chapter 1 emphasized the idea that the different ways of knowing may lead to different conclusions, this is not a hard-and-fast rule. In fact, we suspect that more often than not, the four different ways of knowing lead people to the same conclusion. To give you some direct experience with different ways of knowing, and to demonstrate that they may sometimes diverge and sometimes converge, your instructor will divide you up into three or four groups. Each group will adopt a different approach to answering the question that a group of gamblers once posed to Galileo. Readers who want a little more detail about this problem should consult Freedman, Pisani, Purves, and Adhikari (1991), whose discussion of this problem provides most of the factual basis for this activity.

About 400 years ago, some gamblers were playing a popular game involving three standard, six-sided dice. The game involved betting on how many spots would appear when the three dice were rolled, and most of the gamblers believed that the probability of rolling a 9 (a total of nine spots) was the same as the probability of rolling a 10. However, some gamblers had the gut impression that a 10 was slightly more likely than a 9, and their casual observations seemed to confirm this intuition. The gamblers who believed that a 9 and a 10 were equally likely made a simple, logical argument in favor of their position. They noted that when rolling three six-sided dice, there are *exactly six* different combinations of numbers that add up to 9:

1, 2, 6   1, 3, 5   1, 4, 4   2, 2, 5   2, 3, 4   3, 3, 3

There are also *exactly six* different combinations that add up to 10:

1, 3, 6   1, 4, 5   2, 2, 6   2, 3, 5   2, 4, 4   3, 3, 4

Thus it seemed logical to these gamblers that the chances of rolling a 9 and the chances of rolling a 10 are equal. Because the gamblers could not reconcile their intuitions, their observations, and their logical analysis, they did what any reasonable person would do: They consulted an authority. In particular, they took their puzzle to Galileo, and he was able to solve it to everyone's satisfaction. Before you learn about Galileo's solution, we would like you to directly experience some of the different ways of approaching this problem to see what kinds of conclusions you would generate if you were using only one particular way of knowing to answer the question. Before you learn which group you are in, take a look at the different approaches to the problem that will be adopted by the different groups.

Group 1 (the Logical Counters of Ways)

If you are assigned to this group, you will be asked to adopt a specific *logical* approach to the problem. It will be your job to work through the logical problem, come to a conclusion about the problem, report your degree of confidence in your conclusion, and defend your answer to the members of the other groups.

Group 2 (the Logical Expected Evaluators)

There is more than one logical approach to solving this problem. If you are assigned to this group, you will be given some clues about a different *logical* approach to the problem. This particular approach will involve applying the logic of *expected values* to the problem to see whether a 9 or a 10 comes closer to the expected value (the long-run average) of all possible rolls of three dice. Like the members of the other two groups, you will draw a conclusion, report your confidence in the conclusion, and defend your answer to the other groups.

Groups 3 and/or 4 (the Empiricists)

If you are assigned to this group or groups, you will have the painstaking but important task of making a series of *observations* to try to answer the question. Specifically, you will be given a set of three dice and asked to roll them as many times as possible (e.g., 200 times) while the other groups work on their approach to the problem. By recording (1) the total number of rolls you make, along with (2) the number of 9s you roll and (3) the number of 10s you roll, you should begin to get some sense of how likely these two rolls are in general, along with some sense of which—if either—of the two is *more* likely.

Be ready to draw a conclusion, state your confidence in the conclusion, and defend it to the other groups. If you are a member of one of two different groups of empiricists, you should probably take note of how well the other group of empiricists "replicates" your own group's findings.

What about Intuition and Authority?

Finally, notice that you were not asked to create a group of people who approach the problem by consulting either their intuitions or their local authority. We suspect that you'd have a very hard time solving the problem intuitively. Even if you did, we suspect that you wouldn't be all that confident in your answer. The reason we didn't ask anyone to consult an authority is that this would take only a few seconds. You'd simply ask your instructor for the correct answer and record it without necessarily knowing why this answer is correct.

When all three or four groups are done, we hope you will have solved this problem.

More Detailed Instructions for Groups 1 and 2

There are no special instructions for groups 3 and 4 other than those given above. Here are the detailed instructions and clues for groups 1 and 2. For now, you should read *only* the instructions for your own specific group. After the activity is done, everyone should read the instructions that were provided to every group so that you can gain a fuller appreciation of the different ways of knowing that are a part of this activity. Alternatively, some instructors may wish to allow everyone to try *all* the approaches, to allow people to appreciate more fully each way of knowing.

Group 1 (the Logical Counters of Ways): Galileo's insight into this problem was quite simple—at least in retrospect. Whereas it is true that there are exactly six *general* ways to roll a 9 or a 10 with three dice, Galileo realized that there could be different numbers of *exact* ways to roll each of these values. To illustrate what he meant by exact ways, Galileo recommended that people keep track of the three separate dice by making each die a different color. Galileo made a careful list of (1) all the specific ways of rolling a 9 and (2) all the specific ways of rolling a 10. For example, one specific way to roll a 9 is to roll a 1, 2, 6 (a 1 on the die arbitrarily designated as the first, a 2 on the die arbitrarily designated as the second, and a 6 on the die arbitrarily designated as the third). But of course, there are other ways to roll a 9, including other specific orders for the combination 1, 2, and 6. Your job is to make an exhaustive list of all the specific possible ways to roll both 9s and 10s. One good way to do this is to copy down the six combinations that yield a 9 and then list all the specific ways that you could possibly observe each combination (e.g., exactly how many ways [orders] are there to roll a 1, a 2, and a 6?). Finally, note that if you want to state your conclusions in terms of probabilities (the number of unique ways to observe the outcome you care about divided by the total number of possible outcomes), you will need to divide your values by the total number of unique ways to roll three dice. This is $6 \times 6 \times 6$. Do you see why it is $6 \times 6 \times 6$?

1st die   2nd die   3rd die

Group 2 (the Logical Expected Evaluators): If you have had much experience rolling a pair of six-sided dice, you know that some rolls are much easier to get than others. As it turns out, the most common roll for a pair of standard dice is a seven (a total of seven spots). This should make a lot of sense. If you think about the *expected value* of a *single* die (the value you'd expect to see if you rolled the die an infinite number of times under ideal conditions) you should realize that it's the *average* of all the six possible *equally likely* rolls [(1 + 2 + 3 + 4 + 5 + 6)/6 = 3.5]. If the expected value (the long-run average) of one die is 3.5, it should not be surprising that the expected value of two dice is 2 × 3.5, or 7.0. If you remember that the probability of different dice rolls forms a very loose approximation of the normal distribution, you should see another reason why 7 is the most common roll. It's the mean, and the mean in a nearly normal distribution like the one describing dice rolls is the single most likely outcome. An illustration of the distribution of all possible rolls of two dice appears below. This figure shows how the *mean* outcome is also the *most likely* outcome, and how the probability of each roll tapers off as it departs further and further from 7 (e.g., a 6 is more likely than a 5, which is more likely than a 4, etc.). In this frequency distribution, each square represents a single specific outcome among the 36 possible outcomes. For example, the figure shows that there are exactly 6 ways out of 36 to roll a 7 and only 1 way to roll a 12 (rolling a 6 on each of the two dice).

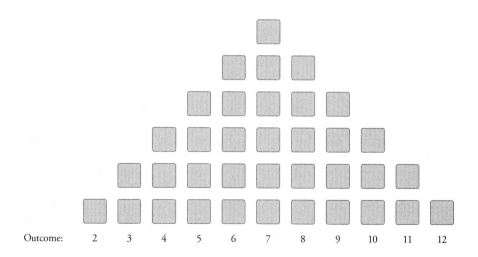

Outcome: 2   3   4   5   6   7   8   9   10   11   12

If you are wondering what this two-dice example has to do with the problem with three dice, ask yourself (1) whether a 9 or a 10 (rolled with three dice) should be closer to the *expected value* of three dice and (2) what approximate shape you would expect the distribution of three dice to take. This should lead you to the answer to this question.

Questions

Here are some questions for all three groups (to be answered at the conclusion of your own group activity, before learning anything about the details of what the other groups concluded):

1. Which roll do you think is most likely, a 9, a 10, or neither?

2. How confident are you of this answer? Answer using a single number from the following scale:

1	2	3	4	5	6	7	8	9

NOT AT ALL CONFIDENT   EXTREMELY CONFIDENT

3. What is your best guess as to the *exact* probability of rolling a 9 with a fair set of three dice? What about a 10? How confident are you of this precise set of guesses? Answer using the same scale:

1	2	3	4	5	6	7	8	9

NOT AT ALL CONFIDENT   EXTREMELY CONFIDENT

Class discussion should focus on the advantages and disadvantages of each approach, along with the advantages of treating one technique as a check on the others. If there are two groups of empiricists, it is usually interesting to compare the scores. How these two groups of scores compare should tell you something about issues such as sampling error, effect size, and sample size in research.

Notes

1. For a more detailed discussion of this issue, see Schultz (1981, pp. 56–57). Schultz notes, for example, that Wundt was the only one in this distinguished group to set himself the explicit task of founding a new discipline.

2. Actually, proponents of chaos theory might argue that the universe isn't completely deterministic. For an interesting discussion of this topic, see Stewart (1989).

3. The best evidence that people may be predisposed to think in ways that reflect some kind of belief in systematic causes comes from developmental studies of infants (for example, see Spelke, 1991). Even evidence that very young infants possess certain kinds of causal knowledge, however, is open to multiple interpretations (see Baillargeon, 1994). For our purposes, suffice it to

say that scientists are not alone in their assumption that the world operates on the basis of systematic, predictable causes.

4. Of course, an even more important reason why Watson and Skinner didn't like to speculate about higher-order mental processes is that they felt that these processes are impossible to observe (they did not, however, argue that they don't exist). In other words, behaviorists like Watson and Skinner were big fans of empiricism. Although we are big fans of behaviorism, we feel that the devotion of many behaviorists to empiricism may have been a little too extreme. Physicists cannot *directly* observe black holes, subatomic particles, or radio waves, but they can test theories about them empirically by making indirect observations—that is, by examining the consequences of these hypothetical entities for things, such as the refraction of light, that we *can* observe, so long as we have the right instruments.

2

How Do We Find Out?
The Logic of Scientific
Discovery

[L]aws haven't the slightest interest for me—except in
the world of science, in which they are always changing; or in the world of art, in which they are unchang-
ing; or in the world of Being in which they are, for
the most part, unknown.
   —Margaret Anderson

In this chapter, we build on the foundation laid in Chapter 1
by discussing the basic goals and procedures of science, with
an emphasis on the science of psychology. We begin by arguing that the primary goal of any science is to establish laws of
nature, and we distinguish laws from theories and hypotheses. We then examine the role of observation and reasoning
in science, and in so doing we distinguish between inductive
and deductive approaches to scientific thinking. Next, we
identify three distinct approaches to scientific hypothesis testing and discuss some of the ways in which each approach is
compatible or incompatible with the basic goals of science.
Finally, we describe how the basic principles of science translate into a general set of procedures that virtually all psychologists (and most other scientists) follow when they conduct
research. This chapter thus complements Chapter 1 by further
elaborating the basic foundations of the scientific method. It
then sets the stage for the remainder of the book by briefly
outlining the basic procedures of psychological research.

Laws, Theories, and Hypotheses

If you are a psychology major, you probably take it as a given that psychology is a science. However, you probably won't be surprised to learn that many *non*-psychologists (including some scientists) assume that it is impossible to study human behavior scientifically. Some people even react with annoyance or indignation when they learn about psychologists' latest efforts to understand important phenomena such as love, morality, or altruism. To some people, it is disturbing to imagine that wonderful things like love are subject to orderly laws. As the poet e. e. cummings put it, "he who pays any attention to the syntax of things will never wholly kiss you." By this, he seemed to mean that it is easy to ruin a good experience by overanalyzing it. We couldn't agree more with this opinion. In fact, we agree with it because scientific research has confirmed it! For example, taste testers who think too much about the basis of their preferences while sampling jellies have a lot of trouble telling the difference between really succulent and really sucky jellies (Wilson & Schooler, 1991). However, this does *not* mean that we shouldn't seek scientific explanations for important experiences such as love, altruism, and the taste of strawberry jelly. It just means that we shouldn't allow what we learn about the nature and causes of these important experiences to get in the way of the personal fulfillment these experiences can bring us. We don't have to be afraid of knowledge.

Of course, critics come in many shapes and sizes, and some critics argue that although it would be highly *desirable* to understand things like infatuation or gustation, it simply is not possible. Such critics correctly point out that no one can ever predict *exactly* what another person will do. However, this criticism doesn't hold up to close scrutiny. The fact that psychologists cannot predict the behavior of one specific person is no more troubling than the fact that meteorologists often cannot predict the behavior of one specific cloud. Meteorologists *can,* however, predict the weather (loosely speaking, the behavior of large groups of clouds), just as psychologists can predict the behavior of large groups of people. Researchers who study interpersonal attraction couldn't tell you *for sure* whether Rupert is going to fall in love with Rita tomorrow, but they could identify a long list of conditions that would make this more likely than usual. The fact that prediction is imperfect doesn't mean that rules don't govern human behavior. On the basis of scientific studies of interpersonal attraction, for example, we know that people gravitate toward other people who (1) are physically attractive, (2) are familiar rather than unfamiliar, and (3) are highly competent (but not *too* competent). The same kind of research also shows that we are strongly attracted to others whose earlobe shapes closely resemble our own! If you throw a large group of Ruperts and Ritas together at a dance, researchers who know about things like this can predict reasonably well who ends up dancing together.

In short, like vulcanologists and virologists, psychologists are in the business of seeking out laws that allow them to make precise predictions of human behavior. The fact that such predictions are rarely perfect is no reason to give up hope. From this vantage point, the goal of every branch of science, from anthropology to zoology, is to discover **laws.** Although the search for scientific laws is as old as science itself, the scientist who did the most to draw attention to the importance of laws was Sir Isaac Newton (1642–1727). Newton was probably the most important scientist to have ever lived. When Newton wasn't busy inventing integral calculus or the reflecting telescope, he was busy developing his three famous "laws of motion." In his second law of motion, Newton asserted that the "acceleration of an object is directly proportional to the net force acting upon it and inversely proportional to its mass." Roughly speaking, this means it's a lot easier to throw a rock at a barn than to throw a barn at a rock (unless the rock happens to be the Rock of Gibraltar). However, this rough translation does little justice to the beauty, precision, and utility of this law. Knowledge of this law, for example, has allowed scientists to put telecommunication satellites into orbit around the earth, and thus you wouldn't be able to use your cell phone if scientists didn't understand this law. It's important to realize that Newton proposed this law without *any qualification* because he was confident that it would predict the acceleration of *any object in any circumstance.* This law applies whether the accelerating object in question is a soccer ball, a human cannonball, or a giant ball of gas better known as a star. That is the beauty of a law. *A law is a universal statement of the nature of things that allows reliable predictions of future events.*

As we have already noted, psychologists are often unable to predict the future, and so we can only feel humbled by Newton's laws. Does this mean psychology is not a science? Nope, not at all. Like the goal of any science, the goal of psychology is to try to develop laws. It is not the fault of psychology that it has not yet mastered the practice. If this sounds like a cop-out, it shouldn't. Even if we could identify laws of human behavior, this would not necessarily allow us to predict every detail of a person's behavior. In fact, even Newton's laws of motion would fail if held to this high standard. To illustrate, imagine that you go to a baseball game and discover that the person seated next to you is none other than Sir Isaac Newton. You compliment him on looking so young for a man of more than 360 years, and he compliments you on your mastery of the complex rules of baseball. He deftly answers a couple of difficult questions about your upcoming calculus exam, and you deftly explain the difference between a fastball and a slider. In short, you are both having a wonderful time. Just as you are about to explain the concept of a change-up, the batter makes contact with a blazing fastball. Do you suppose Newton will be any better than you are at predicting whether this hit will be a home run? Probably not. You probably feel just as capable as old Isaac when it comes to everyday prediction. Of course, Newton would be excellent at this sort of prediction if he were given all the relevant "data" (e.g., the speed and mass of the ball, the speed and mass of the bat, the angle of contact of the bat and ball, etc.). Newton is not to be blamed for developing laws that are hard to apply in complex situations.

The same is true for psychologists. A psychologist will not always be able to predict the specific actions of your roommate, Jennifer. Nevertheless, a well-trained psychologist should be able to make some predictions that untrained people would be unable to make. Furthermore, the psychologist's ability to make correct predictions about Jennifer should increase (1) to the degree that the behavior in question was well studied (e.g., psychologists know more about human memory than they do about human taste in music) and (2) to the degree that the psychologist was given a great deal of relevant data about Jennifer (e.g., her nickname is J-Lo, she has a lesion in the ventromedial portion of her hippocampus). It might be unrealistic to think that we will ever succeed in developing psychological laws or that we will ever get our hands on all the data we'd need to do so, but these are just two of the many challenges that make psychology exciting.

To say that the goal of psychology is the establishment of laws is not to overlook the fact that a great deal of psychology focuses on less grandiose pursuits. We can't all be Sir Isaac Newton. Most contemporary psychologists are content to try to develop and test **theories.** As mentioned in Chapter 1, *a theory is a general statement about the relation between two or more variables.* Good theories share all the features of good science emphasized in Chapter 1. First, they should be deterministic. Thus, they should be logical and orderly, emphasizing the systematic *causal* relations between variables. Next, they should be empirically grounded. This means that they should generate predictions about readily observable events. Next, they should be parsimonious. A good theory is a simple and concise statement that allows you to predict a wide variety of conceptually similar behaviors (e.g., feelings of closeness among siblings, the strength of commitment among marriage partners, cohesion among the members of a junior high school debate team). Finally, a good theory should be testable. As we will explain later in more detail, theories do much more to advance scientific understanding when they prove to be wrong than when they prove to be untestable.

Taking all this into account, how do theories differ from laws? The main difference between laws and theories is their breadth or universality. Laws are comprehensive, fundamental statements about reality. In contrast, theories have *boundary conditions;* there are plenty of times when they do not apply. Even the best of theories offer accurate prediction only in certain circumstances. A psychologist who develops a theory of aggression, for instance, usually knows that this theory will not predict all forms of aggression in all situations. If the theory is a good one, however, it will offer reliable prediction of aggression under a reasonable, and specifiable, set of circumstances. For instance, a theory may apply well to most forms of physical aggression, but it may explain very little when it comes to verbal aggression.

Because theories have boundary conditions, it is possible for more than one theory to be true. This occurs, for instance, when one theory predicts behavior in one set of circumstances (or for one group of people) and another theory predicts the same kind of behavior in a different set of circumstances (or for a different group of people). To illustrate, each of the following theories enjoys a good deal of support under at least some circumstances: "Alcohol produces aggression," "frustration produces aggression," and "exposure to violent media images produces aggression." Each of these theories is correct a good deal of the time, but none is valid for everyone under every possible circumstance. As a result, a good theory not only states specific relations between specific variables, but it also states the conditions under which these relations do and do not apply. Furthermore, two or more correct theories will sometimes cancel one another out. For example, if a person grew up watching a lot of violent TV but the person never drinks alcohol and is not currently frustrated, this person's nonviolence would not invalidate the theory that exposure to violent TV causes aggression.

This analysis of theories helps to address a response we sometimes encounter when we tell friends (or unfortunate strangers) about some new and exciting psychological theory. Sometimes, the friend or stranger will criticize the theory by noting that they know someone who does not usually behave in the manner suggested by the theory (e.g., "You say frustration leads to aggression, but whenever my friend Leonard is frustrated, he just goes shopping."). Although exceptions such as this are interesting, they do little to invalidate a theory. Instead, they simply remind us that the theory falls short of being a law. Incidentally, this explains why very few people refuse to believe in basic laws of nature ("You say gravitational forces exist everywhere, but whenever my friend Leonard is dropped from a high place, he floats magically in the air."). Another way to say this is that human behavior usually has multiple determinants. This is known as the principle of **equifinality:** the notion that the same behavior is often produced by many different causes (McKearney, 1987–1988). Because of equifinality, psychologists sometimes disagree about the conditions favoring one theory over another, and so good theory testing will often take the form of determining each theory's proper domain of application (Greenwald et al., 1986). This sort of theory testing is especially important when different theories lead to contradictory predictions. For instance, some have argued that "alcohol consumption causes aggression" (Taylor & Gammon, 1975), whereas others have argued that "alcohol consumption causes helping" (Steele, Critchow & Liu, 1985). Clearly, both theories are sometimes true. However, to determine whether your inebriated friend Leonard is going to help or hurt you in a specific situation, you will need to know which theory applies. For example, if Leonard is inebriated enough to think he can fly, he might hurt you while trying to help you.

As it turns out, laws and theories do not account for every kind of statement scientists can make about the relation between two or more variables. A third category of research statements is **hypotheses.** To test a theory, a person should use the theory to derive specific predictions that can be readily tested. *Hypotheses are predictions about specific events that are derived from one or more theories.*[1] For hypotheses to serve as tests of specific theories, the hypotheses must follow in a clear and logical fashion from the theories in question, preferably under conditions clearly specified by the theory. Many times, a theory clearly and obviously leads to a specific hypothesis in a given circumstance. In these instances, hypothesis testing boils down to theory testing. A lack of support for the hypothesis translates into a lack of support for the theory that produced it. More often, researchers may be uncertain about the conditions under which the theory applies. Thus, they will test hypotheses in specific circumstances to see whether these circumstances fall within the boundary conditions of the theory. At other times, two different theories might make opposing predictions in the same conditions, and researchers might then outline two rival hypotheses. If the results support one theory to the detriment of the other, the theory that lost out *may* prove to be false. However, it is quite possible that this particular set of circumstances simply favored the theory that seemed to win out. A creative researcher (i.e., a fan of the losing theory) might be able to identify a different set of circumstances in which there would be much stronger support for the second theory.

Through the benefit of extensive hypothesis testing, researchers can determine exactly when (if ever) specific theories are true. If a wealth of research on relevant theories accumulates, researchers might be able to integrate this knowledge and propose a law. In truth, because psychology is a young science, psychological research does not yet seem to have produced any hard-and-fast laws. For the time being, however, it appears that what psychology lacks in laws it has more than made up for in theories. In fact, psychological theories are almost as plentiful as psychologists. Most of these theories (especially the good ones) can be used to generate dozens of specific hypotheses about human behavior.

The Science of Observation

As we pointed out in Chapter 1, one of the most important concepts distinguishing science and nonscience is **empiricism**—basing knowledge on observations. The notion that we should base what we know on what we observe now seems pretty obvious, but this was a major advance in the history of science. But how did some ancient philosopher's advice about counting horses' teeth evolve into one of the cornerstones of the scientific method? How, exactly, did scientitsts come to appreciate the value of observation? Furthermore, how do scientists make the difficult trip from scientific observation to scientific conclusions? Although there are many answers to these two closely related questions, it is clear that Francis Bacon deserves a great deal of the credit. In the early part of the 17th century, Bacon boldly proclaimed that scientists can uncover hidden truths from everyday observation. However, Bacon appreciated just how hard it is to do this, and so he made some very specific recommendations about how to make and interpret scientific observations.

To benefit from careful scientific observations, Bacon argued, you must apply the **method of induction.** Making use of induction means making many observations under controlled conditions and arriving at a general statement about how things are. Induction, then, is *reasoning from specific instances to general principles.* We engage in induction all the time. After observing dozens of incidents in which specific cats and dogs always fight like, well, cats and dogs, we might come to the general conclusion that cats and dogs always hate each other. Similarly, after observing hundreds of individual birds that can all fly, we might boldly assert that all birds can fly. In scientific circles general conclusions drawn in this way (e.g., "dropped objects always fall toward the earth") usually come to be known as theories, and these theories can often be tested against new observations that are made in a variety of new situations. If the new observations are consistent with the statement, then the statement survives. If not, the statement is either discarded or revised. If the statement is revised, it is then tested against new observations, and the whole process starts over again. With the benefit of continuous revisions, the general statement should become more and more accurate. Eventually, it may become so precise and well supported that it evolves into a law. To put this in a nutshell, the inductive technique Bacon supported requires careful, systematic observation, and in scientific circles it usually leads to a more or less continuous cycle of revisions based on precisely these observations. Careful induction is much more of a pain in the butt than casual observation, but the idea is that it eventually pays off (no pain, no gain, you might say).

Bacon was one of the first people to appreciate the merits of learning from systematic observation. Like a bold explorer, he pushed scientific frontiers to new limits. Like a bold explorer, Bacon was also one of the first people to be attacked when other people realized where he was headed (fortunately for Bacon, he was dead and gone by the time the attack reached its climax). In the 18th century, the method of induction came under vigorous attack by the British philosopher David Hume. Hume felt that Bacon was dead wrong. He argued that observation is *not* the appropriate dividing line between science and nonscience. Hume identified what is now called **the problem of induction.** The problem of induction is simple. Careful induction requires scientists to make a great number of observations. Scientific progress is a long journey that contains many steps. This seems reasonable enough. After all, it shouldn't be child's play to develop laws of nature. But how do you know when you've made *enough* observations to be sure that your law is true? According to Hume, you *never do*. Even if you have made *hundreds* of observations, *all* of which are consistent with your general conclusion (i.e., your law or theory), it is always possible that the very *next* observation you make will prove you wrong by violating your conclusion.

The history of science is full of examples of seemingly well-established theories that were later proven to be wrong. For instance, we now know that earth is not at the center of the universe, that the heart is not the seat of human emotions, that you cannot determine a person's character by reading the bumps on his or her head, and that people are not the only animals to create and use tools. To pick a slightly more controversial example, social psychologists who study person perception once believed that there is a fundamental human tendency to attribute a person's actions to that person's enduring personality (rather than attributing the actions to situational factors). This is, in fact, a pretty potent and pervasive tendency. Consider the last time another driver cut you off on the freeway or drifted erratically into your lane. We suspect that you may have leapt to the conclusion that your fellow commuter was *not* the world's most competent driver. Perhaps you were right. However, why not leap to the conclusion that this person must have been sick with worry over an ailing parent, must have spilled a drink in his or her lap, or must have been rushing a sick orphan to the hospital? People *do* seem to be predisposed to explaining other people's behavior in terms of these other people's enduring character traits.

Lee Ross (1977) was so impressed with this tendency for people to favor dispositional ("He's a lousy driver.") over situational ("He's distracted.") explanations that he labeled this tendency the "fundamental attribution error." Many researchers subsequently embraced this label. Ross's use of the word "fundamental" suggested that this attributional tendency was a basic feature of human social judgment. Moreover, at the time, this was a very reasonable conclusion. But here's the rub. Not long after this label took hold, Miller (1984) collected cross-cultural data suggesting that people from India do not make the fundamental attribution error.[2] Social psychologists thought that they had uncovered something basic to human judgment because they had run numerous carefully designed studies showing this effect. Miller's findings changed the whole picture.

This example illustrates the problem of induction. Like politicians whose personal lives have not been closely scrutinized, scientific assertions that are strongly supported today might be strongly rejected tomorrow. But let's imagine that Miller had observed a very robust fundamental attribution error in India. Would this have settled things once and for all? We hope you can see that it wouldn't have. As Hume correctly noted, the fact that all our observations to date have been consistent with a law or theory does not mean that this will always be the case in the future. Someone might run a study tomorrow showing that one of psychology's most cherished theories is incorrect. Because we can never know if this will happen, induction does not allow us to uncover unwavering laws of human nature. Induction is always probabilistic.

So how can we resolve this dilemma? The most popular answer is probably that we can complement our use of induction by making use of **deduction** as well. Deduction refers to *reasoning from the general to the specific. In science, deduction thus occurs when a general statement (a theory) is used to develop predictions (hypotheses) that are then tested against observations.* Karl Popper (the same guy who promoted logical positivism; see Chapter 1) was particularly fond of the deductive method. Recall that Popper argued that good theories have to be falsifiable, which means being open to empirical tests. Popper also noted that empirical tests can never prove that a theory is correct. Thus, Popper was a big fan of subjecting theories and laws to empirical tests even though he strongly believed that no theory or law can ever be *proven*. Why is it impossible to prove a theory or law? For precisely the reason that Hume mentioned: You can never be sure that you have subjected the idea to every possible test. In this sense, a scientific law strongly resembles a governmental law. Obeying a law hundreds of times does not prove that Tracy will never break it. In contrast, breaking the law only once permanently establishes Tracy's guilt.

As this example shows, *it is possible to prove that a theory is false, but it is not possible to prove that it is true.* But if scientists can never, ever prove their theories correct, why should they bother to test them in the first place? Why continue to court rejection when acceptance is unattainable? One answer to this question is that folks like Popper and Hume may have overstated their cases. Of course, we can never prove anything with absolute certainty, but we can sometimes show that something is true under a wide variety of circumstances. As philosophers interested in absolute truths, Hume and Popper may have set the bar a bit too high. If we're willing to live with a little bit of uncertainty, we don't need to worry about our ultimate shortcomings. A second way of responding to the uncertainty of the scientific method is to realize that there is a great deal to be learned from failure (from falsifying a theory). Popper himself made this very point. It is sometimes more useful to know what is *not* true than it is to know what is true. From this viewpoint, scientists do not travel toward truth so much as they walk away from falsehood. In other words, the debate over what is scientifically knowable is partly a matter of how you choose to frame things.

Consider an analogy from the world of art. Word has it that Michelangelo was once asked by what method he was able to carve masterpieces such as his statue of David. He replied that it was easy. All he did, he said, was get a big block of marble and then remove everything that was not David. In this same way, psychology starts with a big block of possible truths and then it slowly, methodically, removes the ones that are not true. Does this ever leave anything good behind? Ever seen Michelangelo's *David?*

So what's the bottom line on induction and deduction? Our position is that even scientists who make careful use of both induction and deduction live in a tenuous world where their most beloved theories may be discarded when they prove to be wrong. Nonetheless, most scientists also realize that their erroneous theories, if they receive attention from other scientists, will serve as the inspiration for the superior theories that someday replace them. The goal of science is not to get things right so much as it is to be a part of making things righter. Finally, it is worth noting that scientists do not let go of their theories quite as quickly as you might expect. Clever experiments that fly in the face of existing theories *sometimes* inspire people to abandon old theories, but at other times, they merely inspire people to fly off the handle and attack the researchers who collected the new data! This is not entirely unhealthy, and if it is done well, it does not involve personal attacks (physical or otherwise). Instead, the healthy skepticism that is a natural part of scientific thinking often translates into a healthy sense of skepticism regarding novel and provocative findings. Old theories do not usually die easily.

Three Approaches to Hypothesis Testing

The processes of induction and deduction provide a partial answer to the question of how scientists go about the business of deciding what is true. However, a different way to address this same question is to ask how scientists test hypotheses. From our perspective, there are three basic ways that scientists seem to test hypotheses. However, before we discuss the details of scientific hypothesis testing, we would like to ask you to test a couple of hypotheses yourself. Let's begin with a very simple hypothesis about a set of cards containing letters and numbers. Imagine that you were presented with the set of cards depicted in Figure 2.1 and told that *every card has a letter on one side and a number on the other.* You may take this as a given (e.g., there are no cards containing letters on both sides). Having established this much, you would like to test a proposed hypothesis about the cards. That is, you

FIGURE 2.1   The cards used in Wason's (1971) hypothesis-testing task

would like to determine for certain whether the hypothesis is correct or incorrect. The hypothesis is that *every card containing a vowel must have an even number on the other side*. If this is not true, then the hypothesis is wrong. Of course, one approach to testing the hypothesis would be to turn over all four of the cards, but this isn't very efficient. Not all cards need to be turned over to test the hypothesis. Your goal is to carry out a complete and accurate test of the hypothesis while turning over *only the cards necessary* to do so. Given this constraint, which cards would you turn over?

Most people report that they would turn over two cards: the card showing the E and the card showing the 4. Let's do this. In this case, the E has a 2 on the other side, and the 4 has an A on the other side. The obvious conclusion would appear to be that the hypothesis is correct. After turning over the E and the 4, this was certainly the first author's conclusion when Bill Swann (the professor who would eventually become his dissertation advisor) asked him to test this hypothesis many years ago. It was also the conclusion of the large majority of participants who were given this same problem by Wason (1971) in his studies of hypothesis testing. The problem with this common approach to hypothesis testing is that it is wrong. First of all, there was no need to turn over the 4 at all. The stated hypothesis was that every vowel *had to have an even number on the other side*. This could still be completely true if some or even all of the consonants *also* had an even number on the other side. The rule simply didn't say anything about consonants. If you are at all like the first author, you probably looked at the other side of the card with the 4 because you were somehow hoping or expecting to see a vowel. Strike one. If you are even more like the first author, you are now saying to yourself, "So big deal, I turned over a card I could have left unturned. I still drew the right conclusion. After all, every vowel *does* have an even number on the other side." Does it? Let's turn over the 7 to make sure. As it turns out, the 7 has a U on the other side. U is definitely a vowel, and unless you are very, very liberal in rounding numbers upward, 7 is definitely *not* an even number. Strike two. As it turns out, the hypothesis is false. If you are even *more* like the first author, you are now struggling to find a way to feel rational about your choice of the E and the 4. Perhaps you are complaining that the question was vaguely worded or misleading. Strike three. Don't be so defensive!

Unless Bill Swann is standing in front of you right now and smiling because you were so predictably wrong, you still have one up on the first author.

Wason and his colleagues referred to the systematic bias they observed in this and several other studies as the **positive test bias.** This refers to the tendency for people who are evaluating hypotheses to attempt to *confirm* rather than to *disconfirm* these hypotheses. Of course, this intuitive approach is highly inconsistent with the logic of good science. However, it probably does not surprise you to learn that laypeople do not usually concern themselves with behaving scientifically. More often than not, people who are asked to test a hypothesis look long and hard for evidence that would support the hypothesis while looking past equally important evidence that could disconfirm it. Although Popper would certainly disapprove of this bias toward confirmation, the tendency for people to adopt a confirmatory approach to hypothesis testing is pretty pervasive. For instance, research in social psychology also suggests that when people are testing social hypotheses (e.g., "Is Zoe an extrovert?"), they are inclined to seek out evidence that is consistent rather than inconsistent with their preexisting expectations. For example, when people are asked to find out whether someone like Zoe is an extrovert, most people ask a preponderance of questions that are designed to elicit extroverted responses. For example, people are more likely to ask Zoe what she would do to liven things up at a dull party than they are to ask her when she is most likely to be interested in spending time alone. Almost anything Zoe says about livening up a dull party is likely to make her sound pretty extroverted— regardless of whether she really is the life of the party.

One well-documented social psychological analogue of the positive test bias is **behavioral confirmation,** the tendency for social perceivers to elicit behaviors from a person that are consistent with their initial expectancies of the person (Snyder & Swann, 1978). One of the best-known examples of research on behavioral confirmation is a study by Snyder, Tanke, and Berscheid (1977). These researchers gave some men the hunch that women they were getting to know over a laboratory "telephone" were either sociable or shy (by giving the men fake photos depicting either extremely attractive or unattractive women). The men who *thought* they were talking to highly attractive women later reported that they had expected the women to be highly sociable and entertaining. Moreover, in the course of their conversations with the presumably attractive woman, the men made these expectations come true. The men were more animated and entertaining themselves when they thought they were talking with an attractive woman. The most interesting aspect of this study, however, is that the women on the other end of the phone (who knew nothing about the misleading photographs) *confirmed* the men's originally false expectations by behaving in a highly sociable fashion themselves (as confirmed by raters who did not see the photos and only listened to what the women were saying).

Large bodies of research on self-fulfilling prophecies, experimenter bias, and stereotyping tell a very similar story (see Allport, 1954; Darley & Gross, 1983; Hamilton & Sherman, 1994; Rosenthal & Jacobson, 1966). Once we get an idea in our heads, most of us tend to engage in hypothesis-confirming

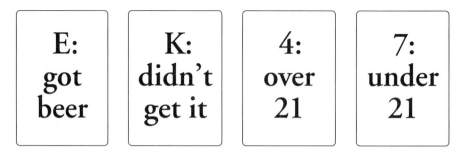

FIGURE 2.2   A set of cards involving a concrete, familiar version of Wason's problem (adapted from Cox & Griggs, 1982)

behaviors that may falsely convince us that the idea is correct. Of course, an important consequence of confirmatory judgment biases is that people often believe that they have confirmed hypotheses that are not true. Moreover, once we have been exposed to some tentative evidence in support of our theories or ideas, we also become very reluctant to give them up—even in the face of strong disconfirming evidence that comes along later (e.g., see Ross, Lepper, & Hubbard, 1975; Swann, 1987, 1992). In fact, Dan Gilbert and his colleagues have gathered evidence suggesting that it may be impossible for human beings to *comprehend* a statement without initially encoding the statement as true (see Gilbert, 1991).

If you are one of those people who fell prey to the positive test bias, and if you are still feeling a little foolish, why not try a different version of the E, K, 4, 7 problem? We strongly suspect that if we had originally given you this alternate version of the problem, you would have performed brilliantly. Here is the problem: Imagine that you are working as the manager of a local bar. Your job is to test the following hypothesis: *If a person has been served an alcoholic beverage, then that person must be at least 21 years of age.* Now look at the four cards (representing four different people) depicted in Figure 2.2. On one side, each card tells you whether a person is at least 21 years of age. On the other, each card tells you whether that person was served an alcoholic beverage. As you can see, Person E was served an alcoholic beverage, and Person K was not. Further, Person 4 is over 21 years of age, and Person 7 is not. Which cards would you need to turn over to evaluate this hypothesis?

As you can see, this situation is logically identical to the E, K, 4, 7 situation. Being a vowel has the same logical status as drinking a beer, being an even number has the same logical status as being over 21, and so forth. When Cox and Griggs (1982) gave this kind of familiar, concrete problem to a large group of participants, they found that very few people fell prey to the positive test bias. Most people correctly went right for the equivalent of the E (the person who was drinking a beer) and the 7 (the 17-year-old who got caught trying to use his older brother's expired Arizona driver's license). And most people, exactly like you, were quite correct.

What does all of this have to do with the ways in which scientists typically evaluate hypotheses? The main connection is that psychologists (and other scientists) sometimes show the same bias as laypeople who are evaluating unfamiliar hypotheses. They spend a great deal of time and energy trying to validate their hypotheses and spend little or no time and energy trying to prove these same hypotheses wrong. On the other hand, like laypeople, scientists do not *always* engage in confirmatory approaches to hypothesis testing. Instead, they usually fall into one of three different camps. The three general approaches that scientists seem to adopt when testing hypothesis include *validation, falsification,* and *qualification.* We now review each of these three basic approaches to hypothesis testing.

Validation

The most common approach to hypothesis testing among scientists is probably validation, and psychologists are no exception to this rule. **Validation** is an approach to hypothesis testing in which researchers attempt to gather evidence that supports or confirms a theory or hypothesis. It is the rough scientific equivalent of the positive test bias. When researchers adopt this approach toward research, they make implicit choices about what kind of data to examine, and they may even engineer laboratory situations that are highly conducive to supporting their theory or hypothesis. Is this fair? Popper would certainly be critical of this approach, and it'd be hard to blame him. On the other hand, this problem is serious only if scientists pretend that their tests of their hypotheses are free of any bias. For example, researchers who are testing a novel theory sometimes want to know if the theory is true under *any* circumstances. In such a case, any conscious or unconscious biases toward selecting just the right sample or just the right situation might be forgivable. After all, if a phenomenon proves to be interesting, future researchers will almost always try to identify the limitations (i.e., the boundary conditions) of the theory.

To illustrate, consider Festinger's (1957) theory of *cognitive dissonance.* Cognitive dissonance theory states that when a person simultaneously holds two beliefs that are dissonant (i.e., logically inconsistent), the person will experience an aversive state of arousal. The theory further states that the person will be highly motivated to *reduce* this aversive arousal (i.e., this dissonance) by making the two beliefs more compatible. Many hypotheses can be derived from this theory, and some of them are probably wrong. However, in the early days of dissonance theory, researchers wanted to know if the theory had any merit whatsoever. Thus, they began by creating contrived laboratory situations in which they expected people to do some pretty interesting things to reduce their cognitive dissonance. In so doing they were actively trying to confirm the new theory. In one famous study (Festinger & Carlsmith, 1959) participants spent an hour engaging in an extremely boring peg-turning task. The experimenter then convinced participants that they would be doing him a big favor if they could tell an unsuspecting person (who was waiting to begin the same task) that the wearisome task was extremely interesting. Although the experimenter made people feel he really needed their help, he did not absolutely insist on the favor. Instead, he made people feel personally responsible for their behavior by letting them know that, as much as he

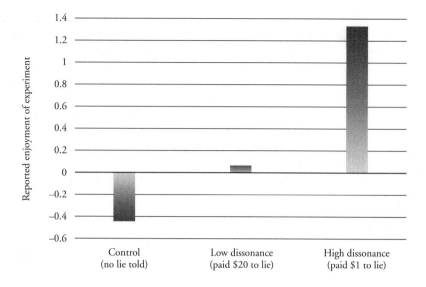

FIGURE 2.3 Dissonance reduction: participants' ratings of how much they enjoyed a boring task as a function of whether they were induced to lie about the task and how much money they were offered to do so (from Festinger & Carlsmith, 1959)

needed their help, participants had the choice not to help him. In a sense, participants didn't *really* have a choice about helping the experimenter. Virtually every one of the thousands of participants who have been placed in situations like this one have agreed to help the experimenter—and harm the person waiting to begin the study—by agreeing to tell the lie. In other words, the experimental situation is carefully engineered to give participants the illusion that they freely chose to lie about the task when the experimenter was actually in full control of participants' behavior.

The experimenter was also in control of whether people had an *excuse* for the glaring contradiction between their direct experiences of boredom and their direct reports of fascination because the experimenter offered people different amounts of reward for "helping him out." In one condition, the experimenter offered people the paltry reward of $1 to lie to the potential peg-turner. In a second condition, he offered people a $20 reward to tell the same lie. Presumably, $20 was enough to prevent people from experiencing a great deal of dissonance about telling the lie. However, $1 was not. How could the $1 participants reduce this dissonance? One way would be to decide that the task was quite a bit more enjoyable than they had originally thought. This is exactly what the poorly paid participants did. They justified their deceptive behavior by *changing their attitudes* to be more consistent with their behavior. In comparison with the well-paid participants (or an additional group of participants who were not induced to lie at all), the $1 participants reported that they felt the experimental task was quite interesting. The results of this study are summarized in Figure 2.3.

Notice that Festinger and Carlsmith didn't try to dream up a situation in which people's dissonance would have no psychological consequences, nor did they try to dream up a situation that *should* lead to dissonance according to Festinger's theory but *wouldn't* do so in practice. Instead of looking for evidence that could invalidate dissonance theory, they looked for evidence that could confirm it. As you will soon see, this didn't prove to be a serious problem because many generations of future researchers worked hard to identify the precise boundary conditions of this interesting theory. Nonetheless, in light of what you learned about the positive test bias and about the inductive problem, you may be a little concerned that researchers often adopt the approach of validation. If you are of this opinion, you might be happy to learn that psychologists sometimes adopt a very different approach to hypothesis testing. Sometimes, psychologists take Popper's advice to heart and engage in the strategy of *falsification* rather than validation.

Falsification

Falsification is an approach to hypothesis testing in which researchers attempt to gather evidence that *invalidates* or *disconfirms* a theory or hypothesis. If you are still wondering why anyone would actively strive to disprove something, remember Popper's philosophy of logical positivism and the lesson of the positive test bias. Theories or hypotheses that survive careful attempts at falsification are all the better for it. And theories that do not, according to Popper, should be discarded (hopefully, in favor of *better* theories).

In truth, it is hard to find examples of theorists who have tried hard to falsify their *own* theories. Trying hard to falsify your own theory is a little like trying hard to find out if your 14-year-old daughter has taken up smoking. Researchers know they *should* actively look for evidence that their theories are wrong, just as concerned parents know they should actively look for evidence that their children have taken up smoking. Instead of asking Jennie an innocuous question such as "You're not a smoker, are you?" it might be better to ask Jennie to take a saliva test that would reveal if she has smoked lately. But just as most parents really want to believe that their kids are truthful, most psychologists really want to believe that their theories are truthful.

Fortunately, science is different from parenting in at least two important ways. First, some aspects of falsification are simply an inherent part of scientific investigation. Because scientists have to justify and carefully describe their methods to other scientists, they can't usually get away with biased approaches to hypothesis testing. Along similar lines, any study that involves careful, objective data collection can yield results that are the opposite of what a researcher might have hoped or predicted. Some aspects of the scientific method promote falsification whether a researcher likes it or not. To put it a little differently, you must be trained to follow a minimal set of rules if you wish to be a scientist. Unfortunately, no training of any kind is required if you wish to be a parent. A second way in which being a scientist is different from being a parent is that whereas children are rarely interrogated by anyone other than their parents, theories are often scrutinized by a great number of scientists, including those whose biases run contrary to those of a theory's proponents. Whereas Dr. Jordan is unlikely to try to falsify his own theory of memory, Dr. Ericson (who proposed a competing theory of memory) may be quite happy to falsify Jordan's theory. Like most other sciences, psychology has a healthy tradition of adversarial theory development. Accordingly, researchers from different "camps" often try to validate their own theories while trying to falsify the theories from opposing camps.

Research on cognitive dissonance theory provides some good examples of exactly this kind of process. Researchers often tried to disconfirm or falsify cognitive dissonance theory as a way of advancing compelling alternative theories. One researcher who became extremely well known for trying to falsify dissonance theory was Daryl Bem (1967, 1972). Bem was skeptical of some of the underlying assumptions of cognitive dissonance theory, and he conducted a series of very clever studies designed to cast doubt on this famous, heavily studied theory. Bem's criticism of dissonance theory was based on the fact that he wasn't a big fan of motivational processes. He developed a theory that accounted for the results of previous studies of cognitive dissonance without making any assumptions about the aversive motivational state that Festinger called cognitive dissonance.

In one classic study Bem asked participants to judge the attitudes of *another person* (a college sophomore named Bob Downing) who had ostensibly taken part in a study identical to the Festinger and Carlsmith $1 and $20 study. In other words, Bem repeated all the crucial manipulations and procedures of the Festinger and Carlsmith study but had people judge the attitudes of *someone else* who was turning tedious pegs and spinning dubious tales at the request of an experimenter. Bem's participants judged Bob Downing exactly the same way the real Bob Downings had judged themselves in the original study. When Bob told the white lie for $20, or wasn't asked to tell a lie at all, Bem's participants inferred that Bob probably thought the peg-turning task was quite boring. However, when they learned (as Bob presumably had in the actual study) that Bob had described the apparently boring task as interesting for only $1, they concluded that Bob must have felt that the task was pretty interesting.

Because these findings bear such a striking resemblance to the findings of Festinger and Carlsmith, you may be wondering why such findings would cast doubt upon dissonance theory. The reason is that one of the core assumptions of dissonance theory is the assumption that *aversive arousal* is a crucial component of cognitive dissonance. Presumably, it is this aversive arousal that fuels dissonance reduction (including dissonance-based attitude change). But Bem demonstrated attitude change (differences in the attitudes people attributed to another person) in a situation in which his participants should have been extremely unlikely to experience any kind of aversive arousal. Telling people *yourself* that a boring task was interesting might make you experience some discomfort, but watching a stranger do so shouldn't cause you any personal discomfort at all.

So why did Bem's participants conclude that Bob Downing was a big fan of peg-turning when he said so for only $1? Because people are pretty good at drawing reasonable inferences about a person by observing that person's behavior in context. Even if Bob hated the task, he would probably say it was interesting for $20. But if Bob said that the task was interesting for only $1, he

TABLE 2.1 A tale of two theories: Cognitive dissonance or self-perception?

I. How **cognitive dissonance theory** explains Festinger and Carlsmith's findings:
  A. In the $1 condition:
    1. "I just told someone that this peg-turning task is interesting."
    2. "That *really* bothers me! Why would I have said that when I don't believe it?"
    3. "I certainly wouldn't have done it for a dollar. I still feel bad."
    4. "But wait, maybe it's not so boring after all. Yeah, that's it. I actually *liked* it."
  B. In the $20 condition:
    1. "I just told someone that this peg-turning task is interesting."
    2. "That *really* bothers me! Why would I have said that when I don't believe it?"
    3. "For $20, that's why! I'd say just about anything for $20!"
    4. "Yep, the task is pretty boring. I just said it was interesting to get the money."
II. How **self-perception theory** explains the same findings:
  A. In the $1 condition:
    1. "I just told someone that this peg-turning task is interesting."
    2. "Hmm . . . that's interesting. I wonder why I said that?"
    3. "Let's see; I don't think I would have done it for a mere dollar."
    4. "The only logical conclusion is that I must have liked it more than I thought."
  B. In the $20 condition:
    1. "I just told someone that this peg-turning task is interesting."
    2. "Hmm . . . that's interesting. I wonder why I said that?"
    3. "Well, the experimenter did pay me $20 to say it. That's certainly a good reason"
    4. "Yep, the task is pretty boring. I said it was interesting to get the money."

must have actually thought it was pretty interesting. In social psychological terms, Bem adopted an *attributional* perspective on how people understand the behavior of other people. He referred to his particular attributional perspective as *self-perception theory,* and he argued that attribution theories such as self-perception theory could account not only for his findings but also for the large body of findings that researchers had previously explained in terms of cognitive dissonance theory. In the case of the original dissonance studies, Bem argued that people made use of exactly the same attributional principles they use to understand *others* to understand *themselves.* Just as an outside observer might calmly conclude that Bob must like the task if he said it is interesting for only $1, Bob, too, might calmly conclude that he must like the task if he said it is interesting for only $1. Bem's insight was that when we are trying to figure out our own attitudes, we might use the same rules we use to figure out other people. To get a better feel for the difference between cognitive dissonance theory and self-perception theory, and the way each theory explains Festinger and Carlsmith's findings, you might want to refer to Table 2.1.

At the risk of sounding a little repetitious, the main difference between these two accounts is that only dissonance theory assumes that the experience of *discomfort* (i.e., "aversive arousal") is the driving force behind attitude change. Self-perception is not a highly motivational theory; it just assumes that people want to figure out the world (themselves included). Notice that if you make Bob the actor in the top half of Table 2.1, the description no longer makes sense. Why should it make *you* feel guilty, uncomfortable, or nervous to see that some stranger (Bob) told a white lie? Cognitive dissonance theory cannot readily explain our judgments about other people's attitudes. In contrast, the self-perception account (in the lower half of Table 2.1) still makes perfect sense if you make Bob the actor. You wonder why Bob did it (without feeling guilty or uncomfortable) and you draw a logical conclusion based on whether Bob was paid a lot of money to do so. Self-perception theory explains the original Festinger and Carlsmith study, and it also explains Bem's replication involving people's judgments of Bob Downing.

Although Bem's findings did not guarantee that there is no such thing as cognitive dissonance, they cast doubt on the idea that dissonance reduction processes are the driving force behind the kinds of attitude change observed in experimental tests of dissonance theory. Although dissonance reduction processes *could* be the reason Festinger and Carlsmith's $1 participants decided they liked peg-turning, self-perception theory has a leg up on dissonance theory because it is more parsimonious. First, unlike dissonance theory, self-perception theory does not require any elaborate assumptions about aversive states of arousal. Second, if we extend the principle of parsimony to the understanding of research traditions (rather than single studies), it seems more parsimonious to endorse a single theory that can explain two different research traditions than it does to endorse both of the theories. Now that you realize that Bem was only trying to falsify cognitive dissonance theory because he was trying to validate a theory of his own, you may wonder if Popper would have approved of Bem's approach to hypothesis testing. We suspect that Popper would have been pretty pleased. After all, Popper didn't have anything against theories. He simply wanted people to put theories, anyone's theories, to the kinds of critical tests that could lead to at least one theory's rejection.

Qualification

If you are the open-minded person you have always prided yourself on being, you may still be wondering if there isn't enough room in a big field like psychology for *both* cognitive dissonance theory and self-perception theory. As it turns out, there is. Moreover, one of the main reasons that we know this has to do with a third basic approach to hypothesis testing. This third approach, which we will refer to as **qualification,** has become increasingly popular with psychologists over the past couple of decades. Qualification is an approach to hypothesis testing in which researchers try to identify the boundary conditions under which a theory or hypothesis is and is not true. In many cases, this strategy can lead to the integration of two apparently contradictory theories by specifying the conditions under which *each* of the theories is correct. During the numerous debates between advocates of dissonance and self-perception theory, some researchers began to speculate that each of the two theories was correct under different conditions.

One of the best-known efforts to integrate or qualify each of the two theories was a paper by Fazio, Zanna, and Cooper (1977). These researchers argued that a crucial determinant of when people engage in dissonance reduction versus self-perception has to do with the precise degree to which people's behavior is inconsistent with their attitudes. According to Fazio et al., when people engage in behaviors that are only *slightly to moderately* inconsistent with their own attitudes (inconsistent behaviors that still fall within people's "latitudes of acceptance"), people will experience little or no aversive arousal and will engage in self-perception processes. In contrast, when people engage in behaviors that are *highly* inconsistent with their own attitudes (inconsistent behaviors that fall in people's "latitudes of rejection"), people will be likely to experience a great deal of aversive arousal and will engage in dissonance reduction.

Fazio et al. tested their ideas by using a variation of an established technique for inducing dissonance-based attitude change. In particular, they induced people to write attitude-inconsistent essays and were careful to make some participants feel that they had freely chosen to write the essays. Importantly, for some of these high-choice participants, the attitude-discrepant essays they were asked to write differed greatly from their original attitudes (and should have aroused dissonance). In contrast, for other participants, the essays fell within a range that participants had identified as discrepant but still acceptable (meaning that writing the essays should have aroused little dissonance). If Fazio et al. expected to see attitude change in both conditions, how could they know that the two kinds of attitude change were the results of different psychological processes? They found out by making use of an experimental manipulation that they expected to influence dissonance reduction but *not* self-perception. Specifically, they gave some participants the impression that the small booths in which they were taking part in the laboratory study would make most people feel nervous and uncomfortable. For people who were experiencing aversive arousal (a.k.a. cognitive dissonance), this would give them the opportunity to mistakenly attribute their arousal to the unnerving booths rather than to their decision to write the unnerving essays. Thus, Fazio et al. expected that this unusual manipulation would eliminate dissonance-related attitude change (in the high discrepancy condition) but would have no influence on self-perception processes (in the low to moderate discrepancy condition).

This is exactly what they found. The suggestion that the booth could make people uncomfortable completely eliminated attitude change for the participants who had written the extremely discrepant essays. However, this dissonance-erasing manipulation had no effect whatsoever on attitude change for people who had written the discrepant but not completely disagreeable essays. These participants showed plenty of behavior-consistent attitude change regardless of whether they were given an excuse to ignore any potential feelings of dissonance. (For further evidence of the limiting conditions of dissonance-based attitude change, see Collins & Hoyt, 1972.)

If you noticed that Fazio et al.'s experiment is a bit more complex than some of the experiments mentioned earlier, you are correct. One drawback to qualification as an approach to hypothesis testing is that it is inherently complicated. It requires researchers to have some sophisticated ideas about the world, and it requires more complicated experiments and more complicated statistical analyses than do simpler approaches to hypothesis testing. A theory will usually have to reach a pretty advanced state of development before researchers can begin to offer reasonable speculations about the boundary conditions under which the theory is most and least likely to be correct. Despite this fact, however, a huge advantage of qualification is that it combines the desirable features of both validation and falsification. Moreover, because of the inherent complexity of human social behavior, research based on qualification will typically represent a closer approximation to reality than simpler approaches based solely on either validation or falsification. Qualification is probably the best road to uncovering laws.

Although qualification has become an increasingly popular approach to hypothesis testing in psychology, it could be argued that some of the confirmatory biases that are an inherent part of validation can easily become an inherent part of qualification. For example, researchers who are interested in falsification or qualification are typically just as interested in producing a specific pattern of research findings as are researchers interested in validation. It is simply the case that the specific pattern of results they are interested in confirming is a little bit more complex than the pattern of results that might be expected by a researcher who is interested in validating a simpler, less-well-developed hypothesis. In other words, it could be argued that the distinctions made here have a lot more to do with the stage of development of a particular research question than they do with the basic approach that psychologists adopt to test their hypotheses. From this perspective, researchers are almost always trying to validate some theoretical perspective. It is the nature and complexity of the theoretical perspective that changes, and not necessarily the nature of how researchers test their theories. Regardless of which particular perspective you personally come to adopt on hypothesis testing, it is important to keep in mind that scientists are probably prone to some of the same hypothesis-confirming biases that characterize human judgment in general.

To add a limitation to this limitation, our discussion of hypothesis testing may give you the false impression that it is extremely easy to gather support for a scientific theory or hypothesis. After all, if most researchers spend a disproportionate amount of time trying to validate their theories, then most researchers must generate misleadingly large amounts of evidence in favor of their theories. As we noted earlier, however, there are at least two important checks on this problem. The first is that there are so many different theories (and scientists) out there. As illustrated by our abbreviated history of cognitive dissonance theory, this means that many common theories of human social behavior are opposed by *competing* theories that are advocated by opposing camps. While some dedicated researchers are busy trying to show that "birds of a feather flock together," other equally dedicated researchers are just as busy trying to show that "opposites attract." If both camps are advocating theories that are true in some circumstances, then both camps will benefit from having worthy adversaries. The opposing camp that does not kill your own theory will only make your theory stronger. To relate all this more directly to qualification, researchers who appreciate the merits of more than one theory (i.e., qualificationists) sometimes bridge the gap between validation and falsification by trying to figure out exactly *when* each of a given set of competing theories is correct. You might think of these researchers as the scientific equivalent of U.N. peacekeepers. They go around and ask "Can't we all get along?" With any luck, these peacekeepers will be able to identify research boundaries that both sides can agree upon.

As we noted earlier, a second reason that validation does not get completely out of hand has to do with the difference between scientific approaches to discovery and the scientific method. Even when researchers carefully, actively, even shamelessly, seek out evidence in support of their ideas (including their ideas about how to integrate two opposing theories), they are held to certain scientific standards of "proof." Another way of putting this is that scientists cannot expect to convince others to accept any evidence in support of their theories unless this evidence passes some very strict standards. But what are these standards? What are the basic rules of the game of psychology? In a sense, the rest of this book is designed to answer this question. However, because the primary goal of this chapter is to acquaint you with the logic of scientific discovery, this chapter would be incomplete without a brief summary of the basic research paradigm that has become the gold standard of psychological research: an ideal set of research procedures that serve as the model for almost all psychological research. We refer to this paradigm as the *experimental* paradigm because it is grounded in the assumption that experimentation is the most useful tool for figuring out the true causes of human behavior. However, this paradigm is much broader than experimentation per se. As you will see, it provides some basic rules and guidelines for almost any kind of systematic research.

The Experimental Paradigm

The backbone of almost all psychological research methods is the **experimental paradigm** developed and refined by R. A. Fisher beginning in the 1920s. Before we get into the details of the experimental paradigm, it would probably be useful to give you a working definition of words like "experiment" and "paradigm." **Experimentation** refers to an approach to scientific investigation in which researchers manipulate one or more variables to examine their effect on some other variable or variables. The more specific term **experiment,** on the other hand, refers to a particular study in which the researcher has made use of experimentation. Thus, what makes a study an experiment is the fact that the researcher **manipulated** an independent variable or variables. That is, the researcher isolated and systematically varied the state (e.g., presence versus absence) or level (e.g., physical or psychological intensity) of the variable. As we are using the term here, a **paradigm** refers to a widely shared set of guiding assumptions and research methods that make up a scientific research tradition. Although paradigms also have something to do with scientific theories or worldviews (Kuhn, 1970), the experimental paradigm has more to do with ways of going about research than it does with the specific laws, theories, or hypotheses that the research is designed to examine. Paradigms are a bit like laws (or canons) in that it takes a great deal of evidence, some extremely convincing arguments, or both to get scientists to abandon them in favor of alternate paradigms. Consistent with this idea, Kuhn (1970) has argued that most major scientific advancements come about in fits and starts. According to Kuhn, scientific change or progress is a lot like major changes in government. It typically takes a "scientific revolution" or "paradigm shift" to bring about meaningful advances.

What is the experimental paradigm? As we will refer to it here, the experimental paradigm is the general approach toward research that has become the accepted standard in psychology over the past 75 years or so. It refers to how participants are selected for a study, how they are assigned to conditions once they become involved in a study, how studies are carried out, and how the findings of a study are interpreted. Like any major paradigm, the experimental paradigm owes its existence to the creativity and persistence of many people, but the person who is most responsible for the development of the experimental paradigm in biology and the social sciences is R. A. Fisher. In the 1920s and 1930s Fisher wrote two landmark books that dramatically shaped the way psychologists (and many other scientists) think about research. Collectively, these two books, *Statistical Methods for Research Workers* (1925) and *The Design of Experiments* (1935), probably represent the biggest analytical breakthrough in the history of psychology.

Fisher was a scientific genius who spent much of his time obsessing about issues such as buttercups and horse manure. That is, as an agricultural biologist, Fisher wanted to answer practical questions having to do with things like the amounts or compositions of manures that would maximize crop yields. Fortunately for psychologists, plants are a lot like people. Every plant is different, and this makes it difficult to know with any certainty whether a given plant grew large because it grew in just the right kind of manure or whether some other uncontrolled factor (e.g., spacing, degree of exposure to sunlight, genetic predisposition) was the real reason for the plant's unusual size. This meant that Fisher had to figure out ways of making *general inferences about causes* from a limited number of observations of particular plants. He was just as interested in figuring out exactly what makes sugar beets grow big as psychologists are in figuring out exactly what makes people gamble, experience hallucinations, get divorced, or become devoted beet growers. We said that it is fortunate for experimental psychologists that plants are like people because Fisher's solutions to his inferential problems turned out to be just as applicable to people as they are to sugar beets and buttercups.

To summarize Fisher's contributions, he developed and refined three important techniques that constitute the experimental paradigm. Two of these techniques are ways of getting control over observations, and the remaining technique is a way of drawing inferences from those observations. These three techniques include manipulation, randomization, and calculation (statistical testing).

Manipulation

Fisher emphasized and formalized the long-standing scientific tradition of *manipulating* variables to examine their effects on other variables. The variables an experimenter manipulates have come to be known as **independent variables,** and the variables that these independent variables are expected to influence have come to be known as **dependent variables.** A good way to remember this is that the dependent variable is referred to as dependent because it is expected to *depend upon* (i.e., to be caused by) the independent variable.

At a bare minimum, this means that any true experiment must have at least two groups of participants, an *experimental group* (the group that receives the experimental treatment or manipulation) and a *control group* (the group that does not). This convenient simplification sometimes breaks down a bit because treatments aren't always all or nothing. For example, Fisher might have conducted an extremely simple experiment in which he tested the effectiveness of a standard, well-understood 1% solution of some fertilizer to a 2% solution of the same fertilizer. Both groups received a treatment, but the treatment was different for the two groups. Similarly, a social psychologist interested in stereotypes might warn people not to be sexist and then examine their potentially sexist completions of sentence fragments under conditions of *relatively high* versus *relatively low* time pressure (e.g., people might be placed under high or low amounts of time pressure as they try to complete a sentence such as "A woman who dates a lot of men is _____.")[3] In studies such as these, it is somewhat arbitrary which of the two groups we call the experimental group (though researchers typically reserve this label for the group that gets the more interesting or unusual of the two treatments). Regardless of whether an experiment has a group that receives no treatment at all, the crucial idea behind the manipulation of variables is that there are two groups that are treated differently in *one and only one way.* When this happens (and when certain other experimental precautions are taken), we can be reasonably certain that any differences in the behavior of the two groups are attributable to the manipulation alone. That is, we can be reasonably sure that we have identified one of the *causes* of the behavior in question.

Although most researchers are trained to think that careful laboratory studies always need an experimental group and a control group, there are some exceptions to this rule. Occasionally, a finding can be so unusual or so inherently interesting that there is no real need for a control group. Can you think of any famous studies in psychology that did not have a control group? One example is Milgram's (1963) classic study of obedience to authority. In this study, 65% of a group of normal, healthy men from all walks of life delivered what they thought were extremely painful and potentially life-threatening shocks to a "learner" who was presumably having difficulty learning a set of word pairs. Why wasn't it all that important for Milgram to have a control group? Because you already have one stored inside your head! It's the 99–100% of normal, healthy people that most of us assume would *never* jeopardize another person's well-being just because a guy in a white lab coat told them to shock the beans out of him. Milgram gathered some tentative evidence for this assumption by describing his study very carefully to a group of psychiatrists and asking them to estimate the proportion of people who would deliver the most extreme levels of shock to the victim. The psychiatrists guessed that almost no one would behave like the typical participant in Milgram's study.

Of course, if Fisher were around today, he might insist that Milgram should nonetheless have included a control group. After all, doing so would allow for a direct comparison of the obedience of people under different conditions (rather than a comparison of the observed findings with our intuitions). As it turns out, Milgram did this in some follow-up experiments, and in so doing he identified some of the important predictors of when people are most obedient. For example, Milgram's original participants did not have to look at or touch their victim. They delivered their shocks from a room adjacent to the learner's room by flipping a series of switches on a machine. In subsequent experiments, when participants had to touch the learner by forcing his hand onto a "shock plate," rates of obedience dropped dramatically (see Miller, Collins, & Brief, 1995, for a further discussion).

This analysis should clarify the important idea behind the manipulation of variables and the closely associated idea of having an experimental group and a control group. It is being able to make precise comparisons of *the ways things are* (in the presence of the variable you care about) with *the way they would have been* (in the absence of the variable you care about). Notice, however, that even when we do have an experimental group and one or more control groups, we still have to make an inference. When we conclude that our manipulation had its expected effect, we are assuming that the participants in our experimental group *would have* behaved exactly like the participants in our control group if they hadn't gotten the experimental treatment. Is this a reasonable assumption? After all, people are different. Maybe the people in our experimental group behaved the way they did because they were just that sort of people. Ignoring this potential problem for a moment, there is another equally serious potential problem. Even if we correctly assume that the people in our experimental group would have behaved exactly like the people in the control group had they never received our treatment, how can we generalize from this small group of observations to people (or sugar beets) *in general?* Recall that Fisher, like most psychologists, wanted to draw general conclusions from his studies.

Randomization

Fisher was keenly aware of each of these problems. In fact, he realized that the two problems have very similar solutions. The solution he popularized for each of these problems is *randomization*—an additional control technique that is a crucial component of the experimental paradigm. To deal with the second problem first, it is solved by making use of **random sampling** (also known as **random selection**). Random sampling is a technique for deciding which participants (or seedlings) make it into your study in the first place. Psychologists who make use of random sampling first identify the group of people about whom they wish to draw inferences (e.g., Asian American women, 5-year-olds, professional artists, or simply people in general). They then choose their participants from that population such that everyone, absolutely everyone, has an equal chance of being selected into the study. The random part of random sampling might involve putting names or phone numbers in a hat and literally mixing them up and pulling some of them out. More commonly, however, it will involve a reliance on something like a computer program with a random number generator or a set of tables of random numbers. Random sampling is a pretty simple concept, but doing it right can present some very serious difficulties. For example, if you are interested in studying voters, you can't literally place the names of all the registered voters in the United States in a 3-acre hat and then pull out a couple of hundred names. For this reason survey researchers have developed some very detailed and sophisticated techniques for randomly sampling people in accurate and efficient ways (we'll say more about this later). For the present purposes, however, it is sufficient to be familiar with the way random sampling works in an ideal world (or when the sample of people about whom you wish to draw inferences is pretty limited—that is, when you *can* use simple random sampling).

The main point behind random sampling is that when you make use of it, you maximize the chances that the people in your study are exactly like the people in the population about which you wish to generalize. In fact, the *more* you make use of random sampling (e.g., the more people you randomly sample, or the more closely your imperfect sampling technique resembles simple random sampling), the more likely it is that your sample will be *exactly* like the population of people about whom you wish to generalize. If you wonder why random sampling works better when there are more people in your sample, think about the extreme case of randomly sampling every single person in a population. Once you had sampled the entire population, your sample would *be* the population. Now think about the other extreme: What if you randomly sampled a *single person* from a population? What are the chances that this person would be exactly 67.21 inches tall and 51% female, with an IQ of exactly 100 and exactly 13.17 years of education (and so forth)? Having said this, one of the surprising things about random sampling is how well it works when the number of people sampled is relatively small. Major polling services such as the Gallup group can predict the behavior of millions of voters in U.S. presidential elections, typically within a couple of percentage points, from samples of only a few thousand people. Moreover, only a fraction of the typical error rate in carefully conducted surveys has to do with actual sampling error (or "bad luck" with random sampling). Most of it has to do with other problems, such as getting people to honestly report their true opinions or knowing who will actually vote (so that nonvoters aren't counted in the sample—see Freedman, Pisani, Purves, & Adhikari, 1991).

So if we make use of random sampling, we can be pretty sure that our sample tells us something about the population from which we sampled. But once we have selected a group of participants for our experiment, how can we ensure that our experimental group is as similar as possible to our control group? It may have occurred to you by now, as it did to Fisher long ago, that you could take advantage of randomization again. Fisher's solution to the problem of equating experimental and control groups was **random assignment.** This is a technique for assigning participants to conditions in an experiment such that every participant has an equal chance of being assigned to any of the conditions of the experiment. Because most experiments make use of a manageable number of participants, a few researchers engage in random assignment by literally pulling numbers (or codes for experimental conditions) out of a hat. As another example, in an extremely simple experiment made up of only an experimental and a control group, an experimenter might repeatedly flip a fair coin, numbering the tosses and recording all the outcomes. The first toss would determine the condition to which the first participant is assigned, the second toss would determine the condition to which the second participant is assigned, and so forth until the list of assignments is completed. The insight of Fisher and other groundbreaking statisticians was that this "arbitrary" way of assigning people to experimental conditions is superior to a host of other highly systematic ways of trying to equate experimental and control groups. The concept of random assignment is important enough that we have designed a special activity (a methodology exercise; see Chapter 6) to give you some direct insight into how random assignment works.

Because random sampling and random assignment are closely related, a final note about the precise relation between the two is probably in order. Text-books on research methods typically emphasize the fact that random sampling and random assignment are very different things. Yet beginning students often tend to confuse the two. In this case we tend to empathize with the students. Although it is obviously important to keep these two methodological terms straight, it makes sense that students would confuse the two terms because these two distinct forms of randomization do *exactly the same thing*—only at very different stages of the research process. *Both of these forms of randomization maximize the likelihood that two separate groups of people will be as similar as possible.* The only difference has to do with which groups of people you are most worried about. If you want to make sure that the people in your study are exactly like the people in the real world, choose people at random from the real world to decide who makes it into your study (make use of random sampling). On the other hand, if you want to make sure that the people in your experimental group are exactly like the people in your control group, choose people at random once you already have your sample of participants, to decide who makes it into each group (make use of random assignment).

We will return to the topics of random sampling and random assignment at many other points in this text. For now the most important point about randomization is that it constitutes the second of the crucial techniques that characterize modern psychological research methods. Thus randomization makes it possible for researchers to make general inferences from specific observations. However, moving from the specific to the general is still an inference, and it is important to make this inference carefully. The third component of the experimental paradigm, inferential calculation, or **statistical testing,** provides a specific set of rules and procedures for making this inference as carefully as possible.

Inferential Calculation (Statistical Testing)

The basic idea behind statistical testing is that decisions about what to infer from a set of research findings need to be made in a logical, unbiased fashion. One of the most highly developed forms of logic is mathematics, and statistical testing involves the use of objective, mathematical decision rules to determine whether an observed set of research findings is "real." The logic of statistical testing is largely a reflection of the skepticism and empiricism that are crucial to the scientific method. When conducting a statistical test to aid in the interpretation of a set of experimental findings, researchers begin by assuming that the **null hypothesis** is true. That is, they begin by assuming that their own predictions are wrong. Typically this means assuming that the experimental group and the control group are not really different and that any apparent difference between the two groups is simply due to luck or sampling error. After all, random assignment is good, but it is rarely perfect. It is always *possible* that any difference an experimenter observes between the behavior of participants in the experimental and control groups is simply due to chance. The main thing statistical hypothesis testing tells us about an experiment is exactly *how* possible it is (i.e., how likely it is) that someone would get results as impressive as, or more impressive than, those actually observed in an experiment if chance alone (and not an effective manipulation) were at work in the experiment.

The same logic applies, by the way, to the findings of *all* kinds of research (e.g., survey or interview research). If a researcher correlates a person's height with that person's level of education and observes a modest positive correlation (such that taller people tend to be better educated), it is always possible—out of dumb luck—that the tall people in this specific sample just happen to have been more educated than the short people. Statistical testing tells researchers exactly how likely it is that a given research finding would occur on the basis of luck alone (if nothing interesting is really going on). Researchers conclude that there is a true association between the variables they have manipulated or measured only if the observed association would rarely have occurred on the basis of chance.

Because people are not in the habit of conducting tests of statistical significance to decide whether they should believe what a salesperson is telling them about a new line of athletic shoes, whether there is intelligent life on other planets, or whether their friend's taste in movies is "significantly different" from their own, the concept of statistical testing is pretty foreign to many budding methodologists. However, anyone who has ever given much thought to how American courtrooms work should be extremely familiar with the logic of statistical testing. This is because the logic of statistical testing is almost identical to the logic of what happens in an ideal courtroom. With this in mind, our discussion of statistical testing will be focused around the metaphor of what happens in the courtroom. If you understand courtrooms, you should have little difficulty understanding statistical testing.

As mentioned above, researchers performing statistical tests begin by assuming that the *null hypothesis* is correct—that is, that the researcher's findings reflect chance variation and are not real. The opposite of the null hypothesis is the **alternative hypothesis.** This is the hypothesis that any observed differences between the experimental and the control group *are* real. The null hypothesis is very much like the *presumption of innocence* in the courtroom. Jurors in a courtroom are instructed to assume that they are in court because an innocent person had the bad luck of being falsely accused of a crime. That is, they are instructed to be extremely skeptical of the prosecuting attorney's claim that the defendant is guilty. Just as defendants are considered "innocent until proven guilty," researchers' claims about the relation between the variables they have examined are considered incorrect unless the results of the study strongly suggest otherwise ("null until proven alternative," you might say). After beginning with the presumption of innocence, jurors are instructed to examine all the evidence presented in a completely rational, unbiased fashion. The methodological equivalent of this is to examine all the evidence collected in a study on a purely objective, *mathematical* basis. After examining the evidence against the defendant in a careful, unbiased fashion, jurors are further instructed to reject the presumption of innocence (to vote guilty) only if the evidence suggests *beyond a reasonable doubt* that the defendant committed the crime in question. The statistical equivalent of the reasonable doubt principle is the **alpha level** agreed upon by most statisticians as the reasonable standard for rejecting the null hypothesis. In most cases, the accepted probability value at which alpha is set is .05. That is, researchers may reject the null hypothesis and conclude that their hypothesis is correct only when findings as extreme as those observed in the study (or more extreme) would have occurred by chance alone less than 5% of the time.

　　If prosecuting attorneys were statisticians, we could imagine them asking the statistical equivalent of the same kinds of questions they often ask in the courtroom: "Now, I'll ask you, the jury, to assume, as the defense claims, that temperature has no effect on aggression. If this is so, doesn't it seem like an *incredible coincidence* that in a random sample of 40 college students, the 20 students who just happened to be randomly assigned to the experimental group—that is, the 20 people who just happened to be placed in the uncomfortably hot room instead of the nice, comfortable, cool room—would give the stooge almost *three times* the amount of shock that was given by the people in the control group? Remember, Mr. Heat would have you believe that in comparison with the 20 participants in the control group, participants number 1, 4, 7, 9, 10, 11, 15, 17, 18, 21, 22, 24, 25, 26, 29, 33, 35, 36, 38, and 40, as a group, just *happened* to be the kind of people who are inherently predisposed to deliver extremely high levels of shock. Well, in case you're tempted to *believe* this load of bullsh—." "I object, your Honor! The question is highly inflammatory," the defense attorney interrupts. "Objection overruled," the judge retorts. "As I was saying, in case any one of you on the jury is tempted to take this claim seriously, I will remind you that we asked Dr. R. A. Fisher, an eminent mathematician and manurist, to calculate the *exact probability* that something this unusual could happen due to a simple failure of random assignment. His careful calculations show that if we ran this experiment a *thousand times* without varying the way the experimental and control groups were treated, we would expect to observe results as unusual as these less than *one time in a thousand!* Don't you think the defense is asking you to accept a pretty incredible coincidence?"

A final parallel between the courtroom and the psychological laboratory is particularly appropriate in a theoretical field like psychology. In most court cases, especially serious cases such as murder trials, successful prosecuting attorneys will usually need to do one more thing in addition to presenting a body of physical evidence pointing to the defendant. They will need to identify a plausible *motive,* a good reason why the defendant might have wanted to commit the crime. It is difficult to convict people solely on the basis of circumstantial evidence. A similar state of affairs exists in psychology. No matter how "statistically significant" a set of research findings is, most psychologists will place very little stock in it unless the researcher can come up with a plausible reason why one might expect to observe those findings. In psychology, these plausible reasons are called *theories.* It is quite difficult to publish a set of significant empirical findings unless you can generate a plausible theoretical explanation for them.

We will discuss the nuts and bolts of statistical testing in more detail in Chapter 10, which deals exclusively with the topic of statistics. However, if you can develop a keen grasp of the basic Fisherian logic that lies at the heart of almost all statistical tests, you will be in a very good position to understand the logic and procedures underlying any particular statistical test you may come across in almost any research setting. Furthermore, if you can develop an appreciation of the logic of Fisher's experimental paradigm, you will be in a good position to appreciate all kinds of experimental and nonexperimental research methods.

Notes

1. Occasionally, hypotheses may also be generated on the basis of a researcher's intuitions (in the absence of any formal theory). However, we suspect that very few hypotheses are generated in a true theoretical vacuum. In most cases, researchers who generate hypotheses intuitively base them either on tacit or implicit (i.e., unconscious) theories or on folk wisdom. Folk wisdom has roughly the same logical status as a theory. For example, the opposing ideas that "opposites attract" or that "birds of a feather flock together" can each be converted into formal theories.

2. There is actually some controversy regarding whether people in Eastern cultures commit the fundamental attribution error. Regardless of one's position on this specific controversy, our basic point remains. Scientists often draw reasonable conclusions based on the scientific method only to later learn that these conclusions were wrong.

3. If your level of sexist conditioning is as high as ours, "popular" (a nonsexist completion) was *not* the first completion to come to mind. In their work on ironic processes of mental control, Wegner, Erber, and Bowman (1993; cited in Wegner, 1994) conducted exactly such a study. They found that people who were trying their best not to be sexist were much more likely to generate sexist completions when they had very little time to formulate their responses. This is consistent with a large literature in social cognition and stereotyping that suggests that many aspects of stereotypes are overlearned and thus infect the belief systems of even highly egalitarian or open-minded people (see Devine, 1989; Banaji & Hardin, 1996).

3

Moving from Fact to Truth: Validity, Reliability, and Measurement

People who say "lightning never strikes twice" oughtta go out and get a better lightning rod.
　—William Stacy Pelham

Fact is stranger than truth.
　—Junior Samples (from the TV show *Hee Haw*)

In this chapter, we discuss validity, reliability, and measurement scales as they apply to psychological research. There are many ways to think about and assess both validity and reliability, and maximizing both validity and reliability is crucial to all forms of psychological research. As we will explain, however, it is not possible to maximize all types of validity and reliability simultaneously. This is true, for instance, because specific research methods that increase one kind of validity often have the drawback of decreasing some other kind of validity. For this reason, we suggest ways of trying to capitalize on the advantages of a given method while minimizing its disadvantages. Finally, we conclude the chapter by discussing the important question of scaling and measurement in psychological research, with an emphasis on how scaling and measurement relate to validity and reliability.

Three Strange Stories

One of us has a friend who says that everyone he has ever met is interested in at least two of the five most boring things on earth: weather, politics, train trips, golf, and aerobic exercise. We're sure that this person is wrong. We say this because we happen to know of some interesting stories or events that have to do with at least three of these five topics.

Let's start with weather. Did you know that on January 9, 1934, in Boulder, Colorado, the high temperature reached 77°? Exactly two years earlier, on January 9, 1932, the high temperature in Paris Water Works, Illinois, reached a balmy 80°.

Now in case you don't get too excited about weather, here's a story about a train trip (adapted from Plous, 1993). Not too long ago, one George D. Bryson took the train from St. Louis to New York City. Along the way, Mr. Bryson decided to stop over for a couple of days in Louisville, Kentucky, a city he had never before visited. Mr. Bryson got off in Louisville and asked a clerk at the station to recommend a local hotel. Mr. Bryson took the advice of the clerk and proceeded to the Brown Hotel, where he was given room 307. After checking in—just for fun—Mr. Bryson asked if he had any mail. The desk clerk obligingly handed him a letter addressed to "Mr. George D. Bryson, Room 307." Of course, if Rod Serling (from the *Twilight Zone*) had been telling this story, the man would have learned that there was an identical George Bryson who was living his life in another time dimension, exactly two days ahead of him. The real story is a little less bizarre. The last person to have occupied room 307 just happened to have been a *different* Mr. George D. Bryson, and the first Mr. Bryson had failed to pick up his last piece of mail.

Of course, this story could have been even stranger. For example, if the same thing had happened to either Jerry Derryberry, Jr. (who is a cousin of the first author) or Bubba Skaggs (who is an old friend of the first author), it'd be a little more impressive. For every guy in the world named Jerry Derryberry, Jr. or Bubba Skaggs, there must be at least 20 or 30 guys named George D. Bryson. Speaking of Bubba Skaggs, that takes us to our third strange story. During the late 1970s, Bubba was a student at a small, private liberal arts college near Rome, Georgia. Bubba swears that, prior to taking a college course in beginning golf, he had never touched a golf club in his life. (On the basis of both his name and his reputation for honesty, we are strongly inclined to believe him.) On the first day of Bubba's beginning golf class, the instructor pointed across an open field to a large tree that stood about 100 yards away. An old tire was hanging from the tree and swaying gently in the warm Georgia breeze. The instructor announced that if anyone in the class could drive a golf ball through the tire on his or her first attempt, this person would receive an A in the course and be excused from attendance. Like all the students this instructor had taught over the years, the other students in Bubba's class failed miserably in their shots at the tire. Then came Bubba. Although Bubba probably provided a textbook example of horrible form, he dropped the first golf shot of his life right in front of his target and watched gleefully as it bounced right through the middle of the tire. (The instructor made him take the rest of the course anyway.)

By now you may be wondering what hot winter days, George D. Brysons, and lucky golf shots have to do with research methods. The main answer has to do with your likely reaction to each of these stories. In particular, your reaction should reflect something important about your intuitive appreciation of reliability and validity. For example, we suspect that you're not planning to pack up your swimsuit this coming January and head off to Paris Water Works,

Illinois, for a balmy vacation. Furthermore, despite Bubba's impressive debut as a golfer, we suspect that you're not wondering why you never saw him on the leader board at the Masters Golf Tournament. This is because you have a clear intuitive appreciation of the fact that almost all measurements include components of error or noise (i.e., good or bad luck). In simpler terms, the main thing you probably appreciate is the fact that Junior Samples was right. In a very important sense, fact *is* stranger than truth. The *fact* is, it was quite warm in Paris Water Works on January 9, 1932. The *truth* is, winters in Paris Water Works are typically colder than a pair of brass underwear. The *fact* is, Bubba hit a great golf shot his first time up to the tee. The *truth* is Bubba was a raw beginner who never became a highly skilled golfer. Because our only glimpses at psychological truths are based on particular facts (particular manipulations and measurements), we need to know as much as we can about the validity and reliability of our psychological manipulations and measurements. This is because the validity and reliability of our manipulations and measurements in any investigation are important determinants of the degree to which our research findings (our facts) are likely to be good approximations of the truth.

Validity

Let's begin with a discussion of **validity.** The validity of a psychological statement refers to the relative accuracy or correctness of the statement. Sometimes the term is used narrowly—to describe individual propositions or research claims. At other times it is used much more broadly—to describe a particular investigation, or even an entire research program. Like many other broad concepts, validity takes a variety of forms and has a range of different meanings. These include statistical conclusion validity, divergent and convergent validity, discriminant validity, predictive validity and so forth (see Campbell & Fiske, 1959; Cook & Campbell, 1979; Shadish, Cook, & Campbell, 2002). In this chapter, however, we will focus on the four forms of validity that will provide you with the basic foundation you will need to understand the key challenges facing empirical psychologists. These four types are internal, external, construct, and conceptual validity.

Internal Validity

Internal validity refers to the extent to which a set of research findings provides compelling information about *causality*. When a study is high in internal validity, we can confidently conclude that variations in the independent variable caused any observed changes in the dependent variable. Of course, we can never conclude anything with absolute confidence, and so issues of validity are always relative rather than absolute. Given this caveat, however, laboratory experiments tend to be very high in internal validity. This is true because laboratory experiments do two very important things. First, they control for individual differences. Second, they allow researchers to isolate their independent variables from potential sources of contamination.

As an example, suppose you were a methodologically sophisticated but biologically naive researcher who wanted to know if water causes plants to grow. You might purchase 20 healthy bean plants and randomly assign each plant to an experimental or a control group. You might then place all the plants in a hothouse for a month and water the experimental plants twice a day, leaving the poor control plants to wither away from thirst. Finally, at the end of the month, you might measure the heights or weights of the plants. Because the first author has unintentionally placed dozens of innocent house-plants in the control condition of this hypothetical experiment throughout his adult life, he knows that your control plants would be much smaller and much less healthy than your experimental plants. We hope you realize that if you performed this simple experiment carefully and sensibly, your findings would be likely to reveal an important truth about the causal role of a regular water supply in plant growth. In other words, your study would be very high in internal validity.

Internal validity is crucial to testing theories because theories are all about causality. As we noted in Chapters 1 and 2, a theory is "a general statement about the *causal* relation between two or more variables." If a study does not say much about causality, then it makes a limited theoretical contribution. This point is simple enough. However, the problem is that it is surprisingly diffi-cult to demonstrate that one variable is the cause of another. Most researchers who wish to understand causality rely heavily on the framework proposed by the 19th-century philosopher John Stuart Mill. Mill argued that three require-ments must be met to establish firmly that one thing causes another. The first condition is probably the easiest. It's **covariation.** For one variable to cause another, Mill argued, changes in one variable must correspond with changes in the other. As an example, high levels of frustration often go hand in hand with high levels of aggression. This suggests that frustration *might* cause aggression, but it does not guarantee it. We need to know more. For one thing, we'd want to see if aggression is causing frustration rather than the reverse. Simple covariation is consistent with both possibilities.

This leads us to Mill's second requirement, **temporal sequence.** To argue that changes in one variable cause changes in a second, the changes in the first variable must *precede* the changes in the second. This is not always easy to tell. For instance, researchers commonly measure a wide range of variables at the same time, to see if different variables covary with one another in ways that are consistent with a particular theory. With this kind of research design, it is impossible to establish temporal sequence, and thus it is impossible to know what caused what. In light of this problem, researchers sometimes mea-sure variables over time (in prospective or longitudinal studies) to see if changes in one variable do, in fact, precede changes in a second. Although this is a big improvement over a cross-sectional design, a researcher can never be certain that the potential cause that he or she selected was the *only* poten-tial cause whose changes preceded changes in the other variable. For instance, if our longitudinal study of adolescent development showed that increases in kids' heights predicted their increased interest in sex, it would be unwise to conclude that height causes interest in sex. Other variables that are likely to have covaried with an increase in height (e.g., puberty) seem like much better causal candidates than height per se.

This leads us to the third and final requirement for establishing causality, **eliminating confounds.** Unfortunately, unless a researcher can conduct a true experiment on his or her topic of interest, eliminating confounds can be *extremely* difficult. In addition to the example of height and puberty, let's consider a slightly trickier confound. Specifically, consider the finding that, as the national levels of ice cream sales increase, national homicide rates also increase. Do ice cream sales cause murders?! Should we outlaw the production and distribution of ice cream as a means of lowering homicide rates? Probably not. In this case, it seems extremely likely that both ice cream sales and homicide rates are influenced by a third variable, namely seasonal variation in the weather. When it's hot out, people buy more ice cream. In addition, when it's hot out, people become more easily frustrated, and so they become more prone toward violence. This relation is a clear example of a confound, also known as the **third-variable problem.** Because heat is causing changes in both variables, the two variables will covary with one another and give the false appearance of a causal relation. So far, so good. We figured out—and logically eliminated—the confound involving heat and ice cream. Now we know that frustration, specifically the frustration of being overheated, is the true cause of homicide. Or do we? Unfortunately, it is possible that frustration, heat, and ice cream sales are all confounded with something *else* that it is the true cause of homicide. Worse yet, this true cause may be a lot less interesting than frustration. Perhaps people simply (1) drink more alcohol, (2) socialize more, (3) get out of doors more, or (4) travel more when it is hot out. All these variables are probably confounded with the weather. Furthermore, any or all of these variables could conceivably contribute to homicides. For instance, if homicides are more likely to occur when people are drinking, or when people are socializing, this is a serious problem for our explanation based on frustration.

As we will explain in more detail in Chapter 6, the research design that is best suited to establishing causality (i.e., internal validity) is the laboratory experiment. The fact that laboratory experiments allow researchers to assess covariation, to establish the temporal sequence of events, and to eliminate a great number of confounds (by means of random assignment and the manipulation of variables) means that they are the ideal research tool for establishing internal validity. Nonetheless, laboratory experiments have drawbacks as well as advantages, and one of these drawbacks is that they are not always very high in a second very important kind of validity—namely, external validity.

External Validity

External validity refers to the extent to which a set of research findings provides an accurate description of what typically happens in the real world. When a study is high in external validity, or *generalizability,* we can confidently conclude that the findings of the study will apply to other people, other physical or social environments, and perhaps even other cultures. As it turns out, life is complex enough that even the most basic research findings fail to generalize to every imaginable sample or situation in which we might hope to apply them. For instance, even in the case of our simple experiment on water and plant growth, there are some clear limits to the truth behind our finding. If a group of researchers tried to repeat our study using cacti rather than bean plants, it is unlikely that they would observe the same results (daily watering kills most cacti). Even if we stick with bean plants, our experiment certainly does not tell us everything there is to know about plant growth. If we had kept all our plants in a dark closet rather than a hothouse, or restricted their access to soil or carbon dioxide, we might have failed to realize that water plays a role in plant growth only when certain other preconditions are met. Another way to put this is that external validity is closely associated with the important concept of boundary conditions. When the boundary conditions of a specific research finding are very narrow, this finding is low in external validity.

It should go without saying that people are at least as complex as plants. For example, suppose we were interested in empathy and helping. If we manipulated empathy in the laboratory and found that it makes male college students more likely than usual to help a female student who appears to be in distress, we could be pretty certain that it was our manipulation of empathy and not something else that caused our participants to behave this way in the lab. However, we couldn't be quite so certain that a different manipulation of empathy would have the same effect on the members of a Gaelic knitting group who are asked to donate money to charity.

If you are wondering how anyone could ever keep track of all the hundreds of ways in which a research finding should be generalizable, you might be happy to learn that most of the concerns researchers have about external validity can be mapped onto only two forms of generalizability. First, researchers are often concerned about *generalizability with respect to people*. In these instances, researchers want to know that the results they observed in a given sample would occur in other samples (i.e., for other kinds of people). Researchers become particularly concerned about this issue when their samples are composed exclusively of people who are all members of the same social group (e.g., people over the age of 65, White men, firefighters, new mothers). For instance, in social and cognitive psychology, studies are often conducted on large groups of mostly White college students. This has led many to question whether the results of such studies generalize to more diverse groups of people (Sears, 1986.). Similarly, some have criticized the entire field of psychology because the bulk of psychological research has been conducted in the United States and Western Europe (Markus & Kitayama, 1991). If we truly wish to understand human nature, we should study a broad range of human beings.

A second concern regarding generalizability (and thus a second form of external validity) is *generalizability with respect to situations*. This second form of external validity has to do with the degree to which a set of research findings applies to different real-world settings or contexts. Researchers may become particularly worried about this issue when a research setting bears little resemblance to any real-life situations. Suppose, for instance, that a laboratory researcher frustrates some of her participants by having them work on a fascinating intellectual task that they are never allowed to complete. She finds that her frustrated participants (as compared with nonfrustrated participants) are later more likely to insult a mildly annoying confederate who bumps into them in the hallway. Is it safe to assume that these findings would generalize to predict real-world incidents of "road rage"? It is not at all clear. Findings in the hallway do not always travel well to the highway.

Are there any studies that tend to be high in external validity? Yes. *Passive observational studies,* especially when they are conducted on diverse groups of people in real-world situations, tend to be high in external validity. If you showed that incidents of road rage in a large and ethnically diverse city such as Los Angeles are more likely to occur on days when traffic (a.k.a. frustration) is heavier than usual, you would have some pretty good evidence for the external validity of your finding. On the other hand, a drawback of this approach would be that you couldn't be sure that it was frustration per se (rather than variations in the time of day or the day of the week) that was the true cause of road rage. This is the dilemma that almost all researchers face in psychology. Laboratory studies tend to be high in internal validity but low in external validity. Passive observational studies tend to be high in external validity but low in internal validity. This concept of trade-offs between internal and external validity is sufficiently important that we will expand on it in great detail in Chapter 6. For now, remember that few studies can be extremely high in both internal and external validity. As a culinary metaphor, being really high in both internal and external validity is like being really nutritious and really delicious. Both of these things are highly desirable properties of food, but they do not usually go hand in hand.

Construct Validity

A third important form of validity is **construct validity.** Construct validity refers to the extent to which the independent and dependent variables in a study truly represent the abstract, hypothetical variables of interest to the researcher. That is, it has to do with whether the manipulated and/or measured variables in a specific study accurately reflect the variables the researcher hoped to manipulate or measure. Yet another way of putting this is that construct validity is a direct reflection of the quality of a researcher's *operational definitions.* To the degree that a researcher's operational definitions do a good job of converting the abstract to the observable, construct validity is high.

Fortunately, some important hypothetical constructs are easy to convert to measurable events. For instance, hours of food deprivation is probably a very good proxy for the theoretical construct "hunger." Conversely, operationalizations that are less than ideal will sometimes stick out like a sore thumb. The amount of time participants in an experimental waiting room spend reading a *Zagat Restaurant Guide* is a questionable proxy for hunger because it is likely to reflect many things other than hunger (e.g., socioeconomic status, interest in fine dining). Whether a person wears eyeglasses is an even poorer index of hunger because it is difficult to dream up any possible connection between this event and hunger. We don't want to offend any hunger researchers by trivializing the richness and complexity of hunger, but one nice thing about hunger is that it's pretty easy to come up with good operational definitions of it.

On the other hand, many important hypothetical constructs are more difficult to convert to measurable events. One of the biggest challenges facing researchers who study highly unobservable cognitive or emotional constructs is maximizing the construct validity of their independent and dependent variables. Sometimes it is hard to know how to measure a variable because the theoretical construct itself is poorly understood, complex, or multifaceted. As an example, imagine you wanted to know if self-esteem is associated with satisfaction in close, long-term romantic relationships. Are people who are usually happy with themselves usually happier than usual with their romantic partners? To figure this out, we'd need to decide what we mean by constructs such as self-esteem and romantic satisfaction. One popular view of self-esteem is that it is merely the sum of people's positive and negative attitudes about themselves (Marsh, 1993). A second view emphasizes the idea that self-esteem contains components of both competence ("Am I good at stuff?") and likability ("Do people like me?"; see Tafarodi & Swann, 1995). A third view is that self-esteem consists of both what you *think* about yourself (your cognitions) and how you *feel* about yourself (your affect; Pelham & Swann, 1989). Furthermore, whereas some people view self-esteem as a stable personality trait, others might argue that it is better understood as a state than as a trait (Heatherton & Polivy, 1991). And if you think self-esteem is hard to get a handle on, remember that we still haven't decided how to assess romantic satisfaction. We don't want to overstate this problem. There is actually pretty good consensus regarding the best ways to measure constructs such as self-esteem and romantic satisfaction. Nonetheless, part of the challenge, and fun, of research is coming up with good measures of what you wish to study. When researchers begin to disagree with one another about the best way to measure something, this is often when things get interesting. It then becomes the challenge of researchers in a field to determine whether different operationalizations of the same underlying construct have different consequences for different aspects of human thought, feeling, and behavior.

Conceptual Validity

The final form of validity we wish to emphasize is **conceptual validity.** Conceptual validity refers to how well a specific research hypothesis maps onto the broader theory that it was designed to test. Recall from Chapter 2 that the deductive method asks you to develop hypotheses from general theories, which are then tested against observations. For these tests to be informative, however, the hypotheses must first be appropriate to the theory. As a specific example, recall from Chapter 2 that Festinger and Carlsmith (1959) hypothesized that people would be more likely to change their attitudes to be consistent with a lie if they were paid $1 as opposed to $20 for telling the lie. This specific hypothesis was derived from a much more general theory. The theory, cognitive dissonance theory, states that people have a need to resolve inconsistencies in their thoughts and/or actions. Most people can readily see that this specific hypothesis followed logically from cognitive dissonance theory. For the sake of comparison, let's imagine that Festinger and Carlsmith (1959) had decided to test cognitive dissonance theory by testing the specific hypothesis that people prefer $100 to being poked in the eye with a sharp stick. After all, with a little creative stretching, an interesting theory like cognitive dissonance theory *could* conceivably be used to generate this incredibly uninteresting prediction. If most people possess the belief that they love being paid and hate being poked, then shouldn't it arouse cognitive dissonance to choose a poke in the eye over $100? So shouldn't people minimize their dissonance by gravitating toward the money?

It seems like a safe bet that if Festinger and Carlsmith had run this alternative study, they would have observed very strong support for their predictions. In fact, unless their participants were downright crazy, it seems likely that *no one* would have chosen a stick in the eye over $100. After dozens of successful replications of this finding, perhaps dissonance theory would have been elevated to the exalted status of a psychological law! Perhaps not. The problem here is twofold. First of all, this kind of prediction is not really one of the first things to come to mind when one gives some serious thought to cognitive dissonance theory. In other words, the prediction does not follow all that logically from cognitive dissonance theory. Second, it is very easy to generate this prediction in the *complete absence* of cognitive dissonance theory. Worse yet, most of the theories that do readily suggest this specific prediction are extremely obvious, extremely well established, or both.

Most psychologists would probably agree that the basic hypothesis in Festinger and Carlsmith's $1 and $20 study did follow quite logically from cognitive dissonance theory. Furthermore, at the time, there were very few other theories around that would generate the same predictions (remember that self-perception theory didn't come around until much later). When there is clear consensus regarding the kind of hypotheses that follow logically from a theory, it is easy for researchers from different theoretical camps to agree about the best way to test the theory. At times, however, researchers will disagree, and these disagreements often reveal differences in people's preexisting assumptions about human nature.

As a more contemporary example of a research finding that is high in conceptual validity, consider a provocative study of close relationships conducted by Murray, Holmes, and Griffin (1996). Murray et al. developed a theory regarding *positive illusions* in close relationships. Positive illusions are *unrealistically favorable views of one's relationship partner.* As an example, if Sondra is in love with Jason, she might believe that Jason is as handsome as Brad Pitt and as funny as Woody Allen. In reality, Jason might be about as smart as Brad Pitt and about as handsome as Woody Allen. Some theories of clinical and social psychology suggest that these unrealistic beliefs would wreak havoc in Sondra and Jason's relationship. After all, there's a word for people who are out of touch with reality, and this word is "crazy." However, Murray et al. assumed that for a relationship to survive the day-to-day threats and crises that always come along (e.g., a minor argument, a slightly flirtatious phone call from Brad Pitt), most people need to believe that they have latched onto someone who is truly special, someone who approaches their ideal partner. In a sense, then, illusions about one's partner are a healthy defense against the sometimes harsh realities of close relationships.

But how could you ever *measure* illusions? How could you know whether Sondra's view of Jason is unrealistically favorable? A simple way that Murray et al. developed was to compare what people thought about their partners with what *these partners* thought about themselves. If Sondra's general evaluations of Jason are much more favorable than Jason's own self-evaluations, it seems pretty likely that she has developed an overly generous view of Jason. Of course, without subjecting Jason to dozens of objective tests of his true level of wonderfulness, we can never know with absolute certainty whether Sondra has overestimated Jason's wonderfulness (e.g., the degree to which he is kind, patient, understanding, hardworking, etc.). But if we make some reasonable assumptions, we can be pretty darn sure—just as we can be pretty darn sure that people who are paid $20 to tell a white lie won't sit around wondering why they told the lie.

So far, so good. Murray et al. found a simple way to assess something that, at first blush, would seem very difficult to measure. But where to go next? Recall that their theory suggested that optimistic illusions in close relationships are *good* for people. The next step, then, was to decide what "good" is and to measure it. This turned out to be a lot easier than measuring illusions. One very good outcome in a relationship is how *satisfied* people are with their relationships. Murray et al. assessed relationship satisfaction using a simple, reliable, and valid measure, and they then tested to see whether people whose partners viewed them in unrealistically favorable ways were, in fact, more satisfied with their relationships. They were. That is, the more people's partners idealized them (relative to how they viewed themselves), the more satisfied people reported being with their relationships. People who were idealized by their partners also reported experiencing less conflict in their relationships, suggesting that the benefits of being idealized were pretty general. Finally, Murray et al. observed this same pattern of results in both dating and married couples—suggesting that their model applies to at least two different kinds of important relationships.

To appreciate why Murray et al.'s study was high in conceptual validity, you should also know that there are a few other theories in social psychology that make predictions opposite to those made by Murray et al.'s theory. For example, an interpersonal variation on cognitive dissonance theory would suggest that it would make people feel uncomfortable to know that someone they loved held views of them that were radically inconsistent with (i.e., dissonant with) their own self-views (see also Swann, 1987). It is largely because the theory of positive illusions makes unique predictions that this study was high in conceptual validity. Finally, notice that Murray et al. did *not* ask participants who were idealized by their partners if they preferred being idealized to receiving a sharp stick in the eye. Murray et al.'s theory of positive illusions *could* be used to generate this prediction, but a study testing this prediction wouldn't be very high in conceptual validity.

If you think that conceptual validity sounds a lot like construct validity, you are correct. In addition to the fact that both forms of validity start with the same three letters, both construct and conceptual validity have to do with how well what a researcher *did* maps onto what the researcher *meant, said, or should have done*. However, there is an important difference between these two forms of validity. Whereas construct validity has to do with how well a specific manipulation or measure maps onto the specific hypothetical construct in which a researcher was interested (i.e., is spitting on someone a good measure of aggression?), conceptual validity is much broader. It has more to do with whether the researcher should have been interested in that specific hypothetical construct in the first place (e.g., does dissonance theory *really* lead to this novel hypothesis about aggression, or does the prediction come out of left field?). In short, whereas construct validity has more to do with specific manipulations and measures in specific studies, conceptual validity has more to do with research hypotheses and, in some cases, entire research programs.

Reliability

In addition to validity, another crucial aspect of almost all research is reliability. **Reliability** refers to the consistency or repeatability of a measure or observation. Reliability can be broken down into three basic forms. Before we discuss these three distinct forms of reliability, however, we would like you to take part in a thought exercise that should reveal that you already possess a pretty sophisticated understanding of reliability. Imagine that you had the simple but important task of developing a highly reliable measure of the overall quality of food at a particular restaurant. That is, assuming that you had plenty of time and money at your disposal, imagine that you wanted to find out everything the average restaurant patron would want to know about the caliber of the food at the restaurant. What steps would you take to develop a reliable measure of the quality of the food? To make the question more specific, focus on three issues in your answer. First, how many *tasters* or raters would you send to the restaurant? Second, which *foods* would you have your rater or raters try? Third, how many *times* (on how many occasions) would you send your rater or raters to the restaurant? Please answer each of these questions before you read any further.

Hopefully, you provided the same kind of answer to each question. The best answer to each question is "as many as possible." You would maximize the reliability of your measure by asking many *observers* to make many *observations* on many *occasions*. The selection of multiple observers, for instance, would decrease the likelihood that one or two raters with bad taste in food would unduly bias the ratings. Although researchers are rarely able to do this, the best way to select your multiple raters would be to randomly sample them from the pool of people about whom you wish to make inferences (the likely patrons of the restaurant). The selection of multiple dishes or observations (perhaps a random sample of foods actually ordered by patrons of the restaurant) would guarantee that you didn't give the restaurant good ratings because you happened to try the bul gogi or the penne al vodka, the two main courses at which the restaurant happens to excel. Finally, by returning to the restaurant on multiple occasions, you would guarantee that your sampling procedure accurately reflected any daily or hourly variations in the quality of the food (based on things like which chefs were working or how long the fish for the sushi had been sitting in the kitchen). These three important variables—observers, observations, and occasions—correspond to the three basic forms of reliability: interobserver agreement, internal consistency, and temporal consistency.

Interobserver Agreement

Interobserver agreement, also known as **interrater reliability,** refers to the degree to which different judges independently agree upon an observation or judgment. When you ask your roommate or romantic partner whether your maroon sweatshirt clashes with your green pants, you are demonstrating an implicit understanding of one of the important forms of reliability. If you are the only one who thinks your maroon sweatshirt looks good with the green pants but the two of you agree that it goes well with the black pants, you would be wise to go with the black ones, for which your informal measure of interobserver agreement is relatively high. Many important real-world judgments involve interobserver agreement. For example, performances in figure skating, gymnastics, and diving typically are evaluated by a group of several highly trained judges. Each judge carefully and independently observes each performance and provides a single numerical rating of the performance. These ratings are then averaged together to yield a summary judgment of the quality of a performance. Moreover, the judges of many of these athletic competitions appear to have some appreciation of the fact that the individual ratings should be consistent with one another. In an effort to make their ratings more consistent, judges sometimes discard the highest and lowest ratings given to each competitor for a given performance (e.g., the score for a floor routine that received ratings of 9.5, 9.8, 9.8, 9.8, 9.8, 9.9, and 10.0 would be the average of the four 9.8s and the 9.9).

It is important to note that the ratings of multiple judges are useful only if these ratings are made by *trained* and *independent* judges. Depending on the complexity of what is being coded, raters may need to spend several minutes, several hours, or even several months learning a coding scheme before they are ready to serve as judges. For example, if you wanted to be able to determine whether the participants in your research project were clinically depressed, your raters would all need to undergo extensive training in some kind of structured clinical interview technique. Most such techniques require a minimum of a couple of weeks of training, even for a person who is already trained in many facets of clinical psychology. On the other hand, if you merely needed to decide how frequently your participants smiled during a 4-minute videotaped interaction with a confederate, you might be able to develop your own coding scheme and train yourself and your two research assistants to make reliable ratings of these smiles in an hour or two. Regardless of the complexity of a coding task, judges are free to discuss their ratings with one another in detail during the training phases of this aspect of research. However, once they actually begin making their ratings for a given research project, they should *not* discuss their ratings with other judges. The main reason for this rule is that violating the principle of independence of ratings can falsely increase the reliability of a set of ratings without necessarily increasing their validity. If you ask your sister what she thinks of your maroon sweatshirt, and she checks with your mom before answering, you didn't really have the opinions of two separate raters. And if your mom happens to be a big fan of green pants, you might not make a valid decision about your wardrobe.

Although the use of multiple judges is important to the establishment of interobserver agreement, it is also important to note that the ultimate goal of measurement in research is a high level of reliability rather than a high number of judges. When interobserver agreement is extremely high, researchers will often have two or three raters judge a subset of all their observations, measure the level of interrater reliability, and then fall back on the ratings of one or two raters once it has been shown that the behavior in question can be judged with a high degree of reliability by the raters in question. In other cases, when it is harder to get a reliable set of ratings about a behavior, researchers may make use of a team of multiple raters for all their observations.

When are the ratings of a group of judges most likely to serve as a key variable of interest to a researcher? Whenever the researcher is studying a behavior and whenever this behavior cannot be assessed in a simple physical way (such as the number of times that a participant presses a shock button or whether a participant gives money to someone who asks for it). Behavioral ratings from multiple raters are particularly likely to be useful when participants themselves do not have the ability or the motivation to introspect on their experiences and report what is happening. For example, if we wanted to determine how nervous people appeared during an interaction with an attractive confederate, it would probably be unwise to ask people questions about their own nonverbal behavior. However, it should be no problem to train a group of research assistants to make these kinds of ratings objectively and reliably.

Internal Consistency

Another form of reliability that applies to a great deal of psychological research is internal consistency. Measures of **internal consistency** provide information about the degree to which all the specific items or *observations* in a multiple-item measure behave the same way. This form of reliability is probably the broadest of the three discussed here—in the sense that it is applicable to many different kinds of measurements (e.g., the specific items in a multi-item behavioral measure, the specific questions in a self-esteem survey). The only key is that the construct the researcher cares about (e.g., aggression, helping, extroversion, self-esteem) must be represented by more than one particular question or indicator. That is, the variable of interest must be assessed by asking people more than one specific question or making more than one specific behavioral observation.

For instance, if we wanted to develop a simple four-item survey measure of extroversion, we might ask people to make self-ratings on four different traits. Specifically, people could be asked to report the degree to which they were (1) outgoing, (2) friendly, (3) talkative, and (4) gregarious. If the same

TABLE 3.1 Hypothetical responses of an extrovert and an introvert on a four-item measure of extroversion

Haruki's Responses:							Michiko's Responses:						

Haruki's Responses:

1. I am outgoing.

  1   2   3   4   5   6   ⑦
not at   very
all true   true

2. I am friendly.

  1   2   3   4   5   6   ⑦
not at   very
all true   true

3. I am talkative.

  1   2   3   4   5   ⑥   7
not at   very
all true   true

4. I am gregarious.

  1   2   3   ④   5   6   7
not at   very
all true   true

Michiko's Responses:

1. I am outgoing.

  ①   2   3   4   5   6   7
not at   very
all true   true

2. I am friendly.

  1   ②   3   4   5   6   7
not at   very
all true   true

3. I am talkative.

  ①   2   3   4   5   6   7
not at   very
all true   true

4. I am gregarious.

  1   2   3   ④   5   6   7
not at   very
all true   true

people who reported that they were outgoing also reported being highly friendly, talkative, and gregarious, and if most of the other possible comparisons that could be made between items also revealed that people's responses were consistent (e.g., if people who said they were very friendly also said they were very talkative), then our measure of extroversion would be internally consistent.

On the other hand, suppose that a lot of people didn't know the meaning of the word "gregarious." What would happen to people's responses on this item? They probably wouldn't be consistent with people's ratings on the other items. Like most introverts, most extroverts might just circle the middle of our 7-point scale, indicating their uncertainty about this item. Table 3.1 illustrates the hypothetical survey responses of a very introverted and a very extroverted participant who filled out this measure. Notice that Haruki, our bubbling extrovert, made highly consistent responses on three of the four items. Now notice that Michiko, our placid introvert, also made highly consistent responses on three of the four items. If the responses of most of our other participants were like those of Haruki and Michiko, we would have an otherwise highly reliable measure with one bad item. What should we do with this item? We should throw it out—exactly the way you'd throw out the ratings of an Olympic ice-skating judge whose ratings disagreed with those of the other judges, and exactly the way you'd throw out the sweet-and-sour soup item from your restaurant survey if judges' ratings of this dish disagreed with their ratings of the other dishes on your survey. If judges' ratings of the sweet-and-sour soup didn't behave in the same way as their ratings of the bul gogi, the polenta, the hot dogs, and the moo goo gai pan, you wouldn't want to use the sweet-and-sour soup item in your survey of the quality of food at different restaurants.

The distinction between observations and observers is pretty subtle. The best way to keep them straight might be to stick with our restaurant example and to realize that each of these two distinct forms of reliability can be applied to this situation. To assess interobserver agreement, we would probably examine the *total food ratings* (the summary scores) of all our individual judges for each restaurant to be sure that the judges agreed with one another about the quality of food at each of the individual restaurants. The object of this analysis would be *judges,* and we would want to ignore the role of different items in the scale and focus on whether the *summary* food ratings made by each judge agreed, restaurant by restaurant, with the summary judgments of the other judges. On the other hand, to assess the internal consistency of our 30-item measure of food quality, we would want to ignore the role of individual judges by collapsing across all the judges. That is, we would average the ratings of all the judges for each specific food item at each specific restaurant and determine whether 30 *items* behaved the same way across the total pool of many specific *restaurants*. Alternately, we could calculate an index of interobserver agreement separately within each restaurant (and then, perhaps, average this value across all the restaurants).

Although internal consistency is most often an issue for the reliability of survey measures (such as measures of attitudes or self-esteem), internal consistency can also apply to behavioral measures. As an example, if we wanted to develop a reliable observational measure of the nonverbal indicators of people's level of discomfort during an interaction, we might get a team of judges to observe (1) the degree of gaze aversion, (2) the amount of fidgeting, and (3) the level of physical distance participants maintained between themselves and an interaction partner. The internal consistency of our summary measure of nonverbal discomfort would be assessed by determining whether the people who scored high or low on any one of these specific measures also tended to score in a similar fashion on the other remaining measures. To the degree that this was true, the nonverbal measure of apparent discomfort would be high in internal consistency. To the degree that it was not, it would be very hard to argue that we were truly measuring a reliable construct.

Temporal Consistency

A third important form of reliability is **temporal consistency, or test-retest reliability.** This refers to the degree to which an item or a scale correlates positively with itself over time. Like internal consistency, temporal consistency or test-retest reliability is most applicable to survey measures of attitudes, moods, self-conceptions, or personality traits. In the case of temporal consistency, however, researchers are interested in knowing the degree to which the scores of individual participants are stable versus unstable *over time.* It is possible, in principle, for a measure to be high in internal consistency but low in temporal consistency. For example, if you developed a ten-item mood measure, you would probably expect the measure to be internally consistent. People who reported that they were currently feeling *pleasant* should also report feeling *happy, elated,* and so forth. On the other hand, you probably *wouldn't* expect people who reported being in a good mood today to report being in exactly the same kind of mood two weeks later. People may differ somewhat in their chronic or general mood level, but almost by definition, mood is highly variable.

Coming back to our restaurant example, suppose that someone instituted the bizarre policy that all restaurants had to employ trainee chefs during at least 50% of their business hours. If this were true, it would be quite possible for the restaurants in a sample to produce consistently better food on some days (when the master chef was working) than on others (when the trainee was working). If this were true, a measure of the internal consistency of food at the various restaurants would probably remain very high (the master chefs would produce a wide array of delicious foods and the trainees would produce a wide array of less delicious foods). But a measure of the temporal consistency of restaurant ratings would be much lower because of more or less random fluctuations over time in who happened to be working at a given restaurant on a given day.

It is also possible for a measure to be low in internal consistency but high in temporal consistency. For instance, suppose you developed a three-item measure of overall athletic ability consisting of separate measures of strength, speed, and endurance (e.g., a weightlifting score, a score in a 100-meter dash, and a score in a 10,000-meter run). The internal consistency of this measure would probably be pretty low because it is unlikely that these three scores would be highly correlated with one another. Most people who can lift a great deal of weight usually suffer by comparison in 10,000-meter runs. Nonetheless, it seems very reasonable to assume that most people's performance scores in these individual events would remain relatively stable over time. People who are strong, speedy, or tireless today would probably be similar kinds of people next week or next month. If each individual performance score proved to be temporally stable, but the three different scores didn't correlate well with one another, we might decide to keep these scores separate, but we wouldn't have to worry much about their reliability. We'd conclude that athletic performance isn't a single, unidimensional thing like height (if it were, the three measures *would* correlate very well with one another). However, we would be happy to know that our three individual measures of each of these three separate things was pretty reliable (i.e., temporally stable).

The "More Is Better Rule" of Reliability

Although reliability can be broken down into at least three different categories, one idea that is common to all three forms of reliability is the idea that the reliability of most measures is likely to increase as we increase the number of observers, observations, or occasions that go into the measure. All else being equal, ten raters will usually produce more reliable ratings than five, 20-item self-esteem scales will usually be more reliable than 10-item scales, and an assessment of people's attitudes that was based on observations made at four different times will typically be more reliable than an assessment collected at a single session. If it is not intuitively obvious to you why this is the case, consider the following thought question. Imagine that you are told that you will be paid $1,000,000 if you can beat Michael Jordan in a game of one-on-one basketball. Mike has generously offered to let you start with the ball, and he has told you that he will allow you to decide how many points will constitute a game. Taking it as a given that your chances of winning would be extremely slim, would you prefer to play a game to 20 baskets or a game to 1 basket? If you have good intuitions about reliability, you should greatly prefer the 1-basket game. In a 1-point game, there is always a slim chance that you could get off a quick shot before Mike decided to take you seriously. And of course, if your shot happened to fall, you would win the game. In a game to 20, however, the likelihood that you could string together 20 such lucky shots would be much, much lower. The principle behind this is that a small number of observations is more likely than a large number of observations to reflect the operation of chance or error.

This thought exercise should also make it clear that reliability and validity are not completely separate concepts. After all, if a 20-point game gives Michael Jordan a better chance of beating you, then the 20-point game must be higher in validity than the 1-point game. This is generally true; more reliable measures are usually more valid measures. One good way to think about this is that reliability is a *necessary* but not a *sufficient* condition for validity. As a physical example of this, imagine that you were given an oversized ruler that had been mislabeled with 1-inch marks made at 4-inch intervals. The ruler would probably yield highly reliable or consistent measurements, but the measurements obviously would not be valid. Now imagine that you were asked to make some extremely precise measurements and were given a metal yardstick whose length was perfectly accurate only at a temperature of 70°. At lower temperatures the yardstick would shrink a little, and at higher temperatures it would expand a little. Although this yardstick would yield measurements that weren't perfectly reliable, the validity of these measurements would still be very high. And the *more* measurements we took of something using this yardstick (under a variety of different temperatures), the more closely we would approximate the object's true length—because the underestimates and the overestimates would begin to average out.

The ancient measuring unit known as a cubit illustrates this point in a slightly different way. The ancient definition of a cubit is that it is the length of a man's arm from the elbow to the fingertips. For most men today, this is somewhere around 18 inches. If we modernize this male-centered measure to include the 51% of the human population that happens to be female, the value would change a little, but the concept is obviously the same. A "true" cubit, by definition, is the average value of a cubit for everyone on the planet. However, if we asked people to report the length of a specific object in cubits, we would get different answers from different people. Whereas a typical NBA center might correctly report that a DVD is only a fifth of a cubit wide (because his arms are so long), a typical jockey might correctly report that a DVD is about a third of a cubit wide. There would still be some agreement (some reliability) in a large set of such measures as long as we had people measure objects of greatly differing sizes (the measurements of both the center and the jockey would clearly show, for example, that SUVs are much wider than DVDs). When averaged across a reasonable number of judges, the reliability of this method for assessing length would be high, but it certainly wouldn't be perfect. However, if we averaged the length estimates (in cubits) for a variety of standard objects provided by *every person on earth,* the average length estimate for each object—by definition—would be *perfectly* valid. For example, if a cubit proved to be 16.81 inches (because that's exactly how long the average human arm is from elbow to fingertip), then we could rest assured that the average length estimate we'd receive for an object that was exactly 16.81 inches long would be exactly 1 cubit (assuming, of course, that people were properly trained to measure things in cubits). In other words, adding a large number of measures together not only increases reliability, but it usually increases validity as well.

One final point to consider where reliability is concerned is that all three common forms of reliability can be readily quantified using some relatively simple statistics. For example, a common statistical indicator of internal consistency is *Cronbach's alpha (α).* Alpha values strongly resemble correlations, and they are closely tied to the average correlation that exists between multiple indicators of a single construct. Similarly, to assess temporal stability, researchers can simply take a measurement on two different occasions and correlate people's scores at time 1 with the their scores at time 2. In this case, the statistical indicator of reliability in question doesn't resemble a correlation; it *is* a correlation. Appropriately enough, it is referred to as a *test-retest correlation.* In contrast, there are no statistics we can easily compute to determine the degree of internal, external, construct, or conceptual validity possessed by a given study. Most forms of reliability can be assessed statistically; most forms of validity can only be assessed logically or intuitively.

Measurement Scales

In our discussions of validity and reliability, we have thus far ignored an important set of distinctions among different kinds of measures. As it turns out, both reliability and validity are influenced by the kinds of measurement scales researchers use to assess their dependent variables. Similarly, one of the important determinants of the statistics a researcher may use to analyze his or her research findings is the nature of the measurement scales used to assess the dependent variables. Most psychologists and statisticians identify four distinct kinds of variables or measurement scales, and these distinctions correspond roughly to the mathematical complexity or sensitivity of the different scales. As you might guess, more sensitive scales usually allow more reliable, and thus more valid, measurement.

Nominal Scales

The simplest kind of measurement scale a researcher can use is a **nominal,** or **categorical, scale.** As the word "nominal" implies, nominal scales are scales that involve meaningful but potentially arbitrary and nonnumerical *names* or categories. Gender is a good example of a nominal variable. For most practical purposes, it takes on only two mutually exclusive and exhaustive values, and these values have nothing to do with counting or quantity. If we wanted to keep track of gender in a survey study, we could code men as 1 and women as 2. However, we could just as meaningfully code women as 1 and men as 2 (or code men as 1492 and code women as 1776). This is because numbers in nominal scales work simply as tags or labels (names) for different categories. Product identification numbers, license plate numbers, social security numbers, months or days of birth, and telephone numbers are good examples of variables that are nominally scaled. Many clinical diagnostic categories and health outcomes also constitute nominal variables. A bone is either broken or intact. A woman is either pregnant or not. A patient might or might not qualify as schizophrenic, autistic, or clinically depressed. A golf shot either falls through the center of a tire (or into a cup) or it doesn't. There is no in-between, and there are no numerical properties that are inherently a part of these arbitrarily assigned numerical categories.

Ordinal Scales

The first step toward scales that do have clear numerical properties is **ordinal scales.** As the name implies, ordinal scales are scales that involve *order* or ranking. A person's birth-order or ranking in a dessert contest is an example of an ordinal variable. Like categorical scales, ordinal scales involve a set of mutually exclusive and exhaustive labels. In the case of ordinal scales, however, there is a clear ordering or hierarchy to the labels. Just as a ranking of 1st always precedes a ranking of 2nd, a ranking of 145th always precedes a ranking of 146th. Although ordinal scales provide some information about the relative value or position of different people or things (e.g., the *L. A. Times* is the largest newspaper in the city; Shira finished third in the state bench-press championships), they are not at all sensitive to the absolute differences between these things. Knowing that someone finished second in a three-person footrace against both Michael Johnson and the comedian Drew Carey wouldn't tell us much about a person's precise running speed.

Of course, unscrupulous researchers, advertisers, and reporters may sometimes take advantage of the imperfect or relative properties of ordinal scales by selectively reporting rankings that portray an observation in the best possible light. For example, there is a story that back in the early days of the Cold War, President John F. Kennedy ran a two-person long-distance footrace against Soviet Premier Nikita Khrushchev. It is said that *Pravda* gave a technically correct but misleading report of the outcome of this race. Specifically, *Pravda* reported that both men ran in a grueling long-distance footrace (without revealing that they were the only ones in the race). *Pravda* further reported that whereas Khrushchev finished in second place, Kennedy finished next to last.

Interval Scales

Whereas ordinal scales do not provide any information about absolute differences between stimuli, **interval scales** do. Interval scales are measurement scales that make use of real numbers designating "amounts" to reflect relative differences in magnitude. Unlike ordinal scales, interval scales can sometimes take on negative values (–12° F is a value on an interval scale of temperature). Although there are some differences of opinion on this point, most definitions of interval scales also specify that interval scores are separated by equal values. This is true in theory, but it typically is not quite the case in practice. Although the difference between 10 and 15 is numerically the same as the difference between 40 and 45, the difference between these scores on some psychological scales will not necessarily be identical. Interval scales are important because most psychological scales are interval scales. For example, SAT, GRE, and IQ scores are reported on interval scales. In the case of SAT and GRE scores, the scales start at 200, have a theoretical mean of 500, and have an upper limit of 800. Unlike ordinal scales or rankings, interval scales easily accommodate ties. Hundreds of people in a large sample can and do receive Quantitative SAT scores of exactly 560. Other common examples of interval (or nearly interval) scales include self-esteem scores, measures of attitudes made on 5-, 9-, or 32-point Likert scales, and measures of marital satisfaction or liking for a confederate.

Ratio Scales

Ratio scales are very much like interval scales except that they have two important additional properties. The first property is that single unit differences on ratio scales *always* have exactly the same value or meaning (the same magnitude) along all possible points of the scale. For instance, the difference between 100 and 101 kilograms is *exactly* the same as the difference between 7 and 8 kilograms. However, it is a second property that most clearly distinguishes ratio scales from interval scales. This is the fact that ratio scales always have a true zero point, a point at which none of the quantity under consideration is present. Of course, this means that ratio scales can never take on values less than zero. One practical consequence of the nature of ratio scales is that they allow us to speak meaningfully about *ratios of values*. For example, it is correct to say that a 90-year-old is twice as old as a 45-year-old, that a 50-pound bag of potatoes is five times as heavy as a 10-pound bag, or that participants in an experimental condition were given ten times the monetary reward given to participants in a control condition. However, it would not be correct to say that a person with an IQ of 140 is twice as smart as a person with an IQ of 70 (which is why the first author didn't feel much like he was being flattered when his older brother used to tell him that he had the IQ of two morons). Similarly, it would also be incorrect to say that the participants who received ten times as much as their peers in the control condition were ten times as *happy* as those who received the smaller rewards.

As suggested above, almost all psychological scales are interval scales rather than ratio scales. This doesn't mean that psychological scales are inherently imprecise. In fact, psychologists usually design their interval scales in the hopes that these scales will *approximate* true ratio scales. Some early methodologists such as Guttman and Thurstone even designed empirical techniques for devising scales whose intervals very closely approximate equal psychological intervals (e.g., see Edwards & Thurstone, 1952). However, because of the extreme convenience and relative usefulness of simple Likert scales, many social, clinical, and personality psychologists make heavy use of Likert scales (or adaptations thereof) in their research.

Conversions and Perversions in Scaling and Measurement

It is often possible to convert a higher-level measurement scale to a lower-level scale, but the reverse is not the case. For example, if we asked 100 golfers to make a drive at a hole and measured exactly how far in feet each shot fell from the hole, this would constitute a ratio measure. A shot that landed 25 feet short of the hole would be twice as close to the hole as a shot that landed 50 feet short, and three times as close as a shot that landed 75 feet short. These ratio scores could easily be converted to interval scores that no longer preserved ratio information. They could also be converted to rankings—from best to worst, for example. Finally, these ratio scores could be simplified even further by simply categorizing them as on or off the green or in or out of the rough.

As mentioned earlier, some kinds of measurement scales appear to be somewhat more reliable than others. In addition to the fact that it was based on a single observation, one of the reasons that Bubba's solitary golf shot was not a highly valid or reliable indicator of his golfing skill is that this single observation was made on a nominal scale. A dichotomous, nominal scale such as this (particularly one with such a low probability of "success") would constitute a reliable and valid indicator of people's golfing skills only if we asked people to take a very large number of golf shots and counted up the total number of successful shots. Tiger Woods should be more successful than Bubba on this kind of measure, but it would literally take thousands of observations to figure this out (to make this particular measure reliable). On the other hand, if we simply marked an X on the ground beneath the tire, asked people to take a swing at the tire, and measured how far each shot landed from the tire, we would have a much more sensitive (ratio) measure of how good each shot was. A couple of dozen shots should now yield an extremely reliable and valid measure of people's golfing skill. This analysis suggests an important principle of measurement. Whenever we have a choice in measurement, we will usually be better off making use of interval or ratio scales rather than nominal or ordinal scales.

The idea that researchers should try to develop measurement scales that are as sensitive as possible applies within as well as between different kinds of scales. As it turns out, some kinds of Likert scales appear to be more reliable (and thus potentially more valid) than others. For instance, Nunnally (1970) has suggested that researchers will typically increase the reliability of single-item scales as they increase the number of response options. Thus 5-point Likert scales will typically be more reliable than simple true/false scales, and 9-point Likert scales will also be more reliable than 5-point Likert scales. As it turns out, increasing the number of response options beyond about nine doesn't appear to add very much to the reliability of single-item scales. On the other hand, it doesn't diminish reliability either. The decision about exactly what kind of scale to use is constrained not only by issues of reliability but also by practical issues

TABLE 3.2   *The Self-Attribute Questionnaire*
(adapted from Pelham & Swann, 1989)

This measure assesses different aspects of self-concept. For the eight items below, *rate yourself relative to other college students of your own age and sex* by using the following percentile scale (where 5 means better than only 5% of other people, 50 means exactly average, and 95 means better than 95% of other people):

05 10 15 20 25 30 35 40 45   50   55 60 65 70 75 80 85 90 95

well below   average   well above
    average   average

(For example, if one of the traits that followed were height, a woman who was slightly below average in height would probably enter 40 or 45 in the blank next to that question.)

Enter a value between 5 and 95 in each blank:

_____ 1. intellectual or academic ability

_____ 2. social competence or social skills

_____ 3. artistic ability

_____ 4. musical ability

_____ 5. athletic ability

_____ 6. common sense

_____ 7. leadership ability

_____ 8. sense of humor

such as familiarity or clarity to research participants. As a concrete example, the first author revised the Self-Attributes Questionnaire (SAQ) a few years ago to make use of the 19-point scale that appears in Table 3.2. The old version of this measure made use of a 10-point scale that was more sensitive near the endpoints than it was in the middle. Although we do not consider the new scale disproportionately better than the original, the new scale is probably a closer approximation of a ratio scale. Unlike the units in the original scale, the measurement units in the new scale are all equal in size. Furthermore, if participants reported their self-views in a perfectly accurate fashion, it would be the case that people who reported that they were at the 50th percentile on a specific SAQ dimension could outperform twice as many people as those who reported that they were at the 25th percentile. This would mean, of course, that the scale was a rough-and-ready approximation of a ratio scale (though not a true ratio scale). Of course, it is a huge assumption that people evaluate themselves in an unbiased fashion on the SAQ (people don't). However, if we assume that any biases in self-evaluation are a constant that does not depend heavily on how many scale points we include in the SAQ, the new version of the SAQ should be a closer approximation of a ratio scale.

A final note about scaling is that psychological measurement scales do not merely extract information *from* participants. At times measurement scales also communicate information *to* participants. This means that the precise wording of psychological scales can sometimes have a large impact on what people tell us. A clever demonstration of this fact was performed by Schwarz, Hippler, Deutsch, and Strack (1985), who asked people how long they spent watching television every day. Some participants reported their TV watching habits on a 6-point scale that ranged, in equal half-hour increments, from a low value of *up to 0.5 hour* to a high value of *more than 2.5 hours* per day. Other participants filled out a 6-point scale that also contained equal half-hour increments, but began at *up to 2.5 hours* and ended at *more than 4.5 hours*. Only about 16% of the people who filled out the first scale reported that they watched TV more than 2.5 hours per day. In contrast, more than 37% of the people who filled out the second scale reported watching more than 2.5 hours per day. *The range of options that we choose to present to our participants can greatly influence what they choose to tell us.*

Even asking people two logically equivalent versions of the same question can sometimes lead to very different answers. Consider the question that Tversky and Kahneman (1981) posed to their research participants:

> Imagine that the U.S. is preparing for the outbreak of an unusual Asian disease, which is expected to kill 600 people. Two alternative programs to combat the disease have been proposed. Assume that the exact scientific estimate of the consequences of the program are as follows:
>
> > If Program A is adopted, 200 people will be saved.
> > If Program B is adopted, there is 1/3 probability that 600 people will be saved, and 2/3 probability that no people will be saved.

Which of the two programs would you favor? If you are like most people, you would favor program A. In Tversky and Kahneman's study, 72% of their participants chose this cautious, or "risk-aversive," option. People's responses to this question clearly showed that most people don't like to take risks. Or do they? In a second version of this same question, Tversky and Kahneman described the unusual disease in precisely the same way but framed the two programs differently. Now the two programs were described as follows:

> > If Program C is adopted, 400 people will die.
> > If Program D is adopted, there is 1/3 probability that nobody will die, and 2/3 probability that 600 people will die.

Try to start with a clean slate and make your selection again. Which program would you prefer? When the question was framed in this way, only 22% of the people surveyed chose the risk-aversive option (option C). Notice, however, that options A and C are *logically identical*. The consequences of both programs are that 400 people will die and 200 people will be saved. Are people risk aversive, or are they risk takers? The answer depends dramatically on how the same question is put to people.

Does this mean that we can never know anything about whether people are cautious? Not at all. Tversky and Kahneman's research suggests that a more balanced way to frame questions such as this one would be to describe the outcomes of each program in terms of both gains and losses. Moreover, even if we chose to ask a question one and only one way, this doesn't mean that we couldn't study people's judgments about risk. For example, imagine that you were going to play a gambling game in which you were offered a choice between (1) a guarantee of $10,000 and (2) a 50% chance of winning $30,000. Would you opt for the sure thing or the gamble? In situations like this, most people are risk aversive (i.e., most people choose the sure thing). On the other hand, if we asked you the same question but gave you a choice between (1) a guarantee of $1 and (2) a 50% chance of winning $3, our suspicion is that you'd be much more likely to go for the risky option. Finally, assume that we conducted a true experiment in which we posed the two different versions of this question to two different groups of 50 people. If we observed that people were much more likely to choose the risky option in the case of the low-stakes version of the question, we could reasonably conclude that people are *less* risk aversive than usual when the stakes are low. Any biases in the way we had worded our question would be constant across the two conditions, and we could still draw some reasonable inferences about our manipulation (i.e., about what makes people more or less risk aversive).

In case we haven't quite driven home the point that validity and reliability are extremely important aspects of psychological research, we'd like to close this chapter by repeating this familiar theme. As a matter of fact, you could think of this entire textbook as a detailed recipe for maximizing the validity and reliability of psychological research. If you'd like your methodological world simplified even further, we can do so by adding that *everything* really boils down to validity. As important as reliability is, it is only important insofar as it contributes to validity. As you learn about the various research techniques we scrutinize and celebrate in this text, you should probably keep it in mind that you are almost always learning about some specific way of maximizing validity. In other words, the major goal of this book is to outline things researchers can do to maximize the validity of their research. Before you learn about the specific tools needed to achieve this goal, however, it might be useful to learn about the most common pitfalls that can get in the way of the goal. Chapter 4 is designed with this idea in mind: to prepare you for what is to come by exploring the most common threats to the validity of psychological research.

4

How Do We Misinterpret? Common Threats to Validity

This was a creature, more troublesom to be drawn, then any of the rest, for I could not, for a good while, think of a way to make it suffer its body to ly quietly, in a natural posture; but whil'st it was alive, if its feet were fetter'd in Wax or Glew, it would so twist and wind its body, that I could not any wayes get a good view of it; and if I killed it, its body was so little, that I did often spoile the shape of it, before I could thoroughly view it: for this is the nature of these minute Bodies, that as soon, almost, as ever their life is destroy'd, their parts immediately shrivel, and lose their beauty. So it is . . . with. . . . Animal substances; the dead body of an Ant, or such little creature, does almost instantly shrivel and dry, and your object shall become quite another thing, before you can half delieneate it. . . .

 —Robert Hooke
  (Micrographia, 1665) on the difficulty of rendering drawings
  of ants from microscopic observations

For if we wish to form a picture of the nature of these elementary particles, we can no longer ignore the physical processes through which we obtain our knowledge of them. . . . In the case of the smallest building particles of matter, every process of observation produces a large disturbance. We can no longer speak of the behaviour of the particle independently of the process of observation.

 —Werner Heisenberg
  (1955) on the impossibility of precisely assessing certain
  properties of subatomic particles

One Strange and Lucrative Story

When Brett Pelham (the first author of this text) was in the third grade, he did a very unscrupulous thing. He had gotten into the habit of selling and swapping candy, toys, and magnets with the other kids in his third-grade class, and on this particular day he really needed a quarter. Unfortunately, all he had to work with was a lead fishing weight. The lead weight couldn't be made into any kind of toy, and it didn't do anything fun or exciting. In fact, being made of lead, it wouldn't even stick to a magnet. In a moment of inspiration (or perhaps desperation) Brett decided that the fishing weight was actually a lucky charm, and he further decided to try to pawn it off on his good friend David Hare. David had traded with Brett before, and when Brett claimed to possess a lucky charm that he was willing to sell for only a quarter, David was justifiably skeptical. Brett proposed a simple test of the efficacy of the charm. He told David to put the charm in his pocket and ask Jill Long to give him a dime so that he could buy an ice cream. (At Happy Valley Elementary School, ice cream was always available right after recess, and the price was only a dime.) Brett wasn't sure if he really expected the scam to work, but he figured that if it didn't, he would be none the worse for it. Of course, if it *did* somehow work, Brett would have his desperately needed 25 cents (or 2½ ice creams, to put it in perspective). After putting the charm to the test, David came back to Brett beaming with joy and announced (1) that Jill Long had given him the dime and (2) that he would be delighted to purchase the charm.

One of us would like to believe that Brett was smart enough to pull the wool over David's eyes, but in all honesty, Brett was almost as persuaded about the efficacy of the "charm" as David was. Brett vividly remembers being *extremely* reluctant to sell the charm once he learned how well it had worked. His ultimate decision to sell probably says a lot more about his inability to delay gratification than it does about his intellectual precocity. Of course, we all know now that the test Brett proposed to David had some very serious flaws. In retrospect it's pretty clear that David's profitable exchange with Jill Long had a lot more to do with David's ability to be charming (and Jill's profound generosity) than it did with the charming powers of a lead fishing weight.

This story is a fitting introduction to the topic of threats to validity because the crucial test described in the story has some intuitive appeal but suffers from many of the problems that characterize research studies that are low in validity. In the case of the test of the fishing weight, Brett had asked David to do several problematic things: to make a single observation, to gather data from a biased sample of "participants" (himself and Jill), and to fail to include the equivalent of a control group (i.e., some observations in which he asked people like Jill for money *without* the charm). These are the kinds of issues that are the topic of this chapter: issues that determine the validity of a set of research findings. Many of the specific threats discussed here have been discussed in detail by Cook and Campbell (1979). Thus, much of this chapter (and much of what we know about psychological research methods) is a tribute to their insights.

This chapter focuses on four general categories of threat to the validity of a set of research findings. We divide each of these four general categories of threat into two or three more specific categories of threat, and in the case of each specific threat, we discuss exactly what kind of validity it threatens (e.g., internal or external validity). Finally, we also make some suggestions for how to reduce or eliminate each threat to validity. To begin with the broad categories first, we will argue that almost any threat to the validity of a research finding can be placed under one of four broad headings. These include the ideas that (1) people are different, (2) people change, (3) the process of studying people changes people, and (4) variables that systematically accompany a treatment variable (i.e., confounds) change people. Let's begin with the idea that people are different.

People Are Different
Individual Differences

Your mother loves stir-fried vegetables and classical music. Your father cares little for either. *You* are wondering intensely how we knew about your parents' taste in food and music. Another reader whose parents have precisely the same taste is far less curious. These are simple examples of the fact that people are different. Although everyone seems to know that people are different, not everyone appreciates the implications of this simple fact for research methodology. As it turns out, one of the most common categories of threats to validity is based on this obvious fact about people.

The type of research claim that is most susceptible to this threat is probably best thought of as a pseudo-experiment or false experiment. However, because people often treat pseudo-experiments as if they were true experiments, it is worth beginning our list of threats to validity with a discussion of how individual differences could cloud the interpretation of this intuitively appealing but analytically appalling approach to research. As the term is used here, a **pseudo-experiment** is a research design in which someone tests a claim about a variable (e.g., a product, a charm, a clinical treatment) by exposing people to the variable of interest and noting that these people feel, think, or behave as expected. Examples of claims based on pseudo-experiments include things like "Melanie wore her lucky bowling shoes and bowled a 247," "Rhonda took the Ivy Review SAT Course and aced her SATs," and "David carried a fishing weight in his pocket and got a dime from Jill Long." Although there are other problems with claims such as these, the most serious problem is that some particular people happen to be good at bowling, taking exams, and getting dimes. In the absence of some kind of comparison with a *control group,* we have no idea what would have happened if the same person had engaged in the same behavior *without* being exposed to the variable of interest. Individual differences are a very good alternate explanation for the findings observed in pseudo-experiments, especially those involving a small number of research participants.

To be more specific about individual differences as they are being discussed right now, individual differences are a threat to the *internal* validity of a researcher's claim. The researcher maintains that some variable of interest causes changes in another variable, but simple individual differences provide an equally plausible account of the observed findings. With this in mind, you might recall that R. A. Fisher came up with a research design that is relatively immune to threats to internal validity—including threats based on individual differences. Fisher refined the *experimental method,* which involves making use of random assignment, the manipulation of variables, and inferential statistics to draw conclusions about a treatment variable of interest. Suppose we identified a group of 50 prospective SAT takers, none of whom planned to take an SAT review course. If we randomly placed half of these students in a review course, and we found that they scored higher on the SAT than their untutored peers, we could greatly increase our confidence that the review course contributes to superior performance. As we will see in Chapter 8, a second solution to the problem of individual differences is to make use of *within-subjects,* or *repeated-measures,* designs. If we chose a group of 20 people who were in the market for a lucky charm and had each person (unknowingly) engage in the same behavior *with and without* carrying a charm, we would be in a good position to determine the efficacy of the charm.

Selection Bias and Nonresponse Bias

The fact that people are different can be a threat to external as well as internal validity. If people are different, and a sampling technique somehow favors one particular kind of person, we might draw general conclusions about people (in either experimental or nonexperimental studies) that apply only to the particular people, or kinds of people, that we have sampled. Sampling people from an unrepresentative sample (by using imperfect sampling techniques) is referred to as **selection bias.** A famous example of selection bias that led to a failed prediction about a U.S. presidential election occurred back in 1936, when researchers were still struggling to develop valid sampling techniques. A group of researchers from the prestigious *Literary Digest* mailed postcards to *10 million* Americans and asked them who they planned to vote for in the upcoming election. Well over 2 million people returned the postcards, and the results of the poll suggested strongly that the Republican candidate, Alf Landon, was the people's choice. Of course, the results of this gigantic poll were wrong. Otherwise, you'd probably see a tiny profile of Alf Landon every time you looked at a dime (and there might also be a famous muppet from outer space named Franklin). The Democratic candidate, Franklin D. Roosevelt, won the election in a landslide.

Why were the *Literary Digest* pollsters wrong? Because they made use of biased sampling techniques. In particular, they sampled their pool of potential voters by selecting names from places like telephone directories and automobile registration records. Not surprisingly, the kinds of people who owned cars and telephones back in the depression-riddled 1930s were pretty rich. As it turns out, the 1930s represent a turning point in American voting patterns. This just happens to have been the time in American history when people began voting with their purses. Thus, in 1936, wealthy people were much more likely to vote Republican. Although this is not always mentioned in discussions of the *Literary Digest* error, not everyone expected Alf Landon to win. In particular, researchers from the recently formed Gallup organization conducted a much smaller poll of about 50,000 people (that's a sample about 1/48th the size of the *Literary Digest* sample!). In their poll, the Gallup group used methods that much more closely approximated true random sampling. These procedures appear to have been much less biased than those of the *Digest.* In contrast to the predictions of the *Digest,* the Gallup group predicted that Roosevelt would get about 56% of the vote. In actuality, he got 62%. The Gallup pollsters were less than perfect, but they correctly predicted that Roosevelt would win.

Another important form of bias that played a role in the *Literary Digest* error is **nonresponse bias.** Nonresponse bias is closely related to selection bias except that in the case of nonresponse bias it is the respondents themselves who are the source of the bias. Because people who choose to answer surveys are systematically different from people who choose not to do so, surveys that have low response rates may yield information that is highly misleading. In the case of the *Literary Digest* error, only about 24% of those who were mailed postcards asking them about the election bothered to return the cards. Although this still yielded a very large sample, the size of this sample was meaningless. More than 2 million badly sampled voters are still badly sampled. Modern survey researchers have developed a wide range of solutions to the problem of nonresponse bias. For example, Gallup pollsters now conduct most of their interviews over the phone rather than by means of mail-in surveys. This increases response rates from about 25% to about 65% (see Freedman, Pisani, Purves, & Adhikari, 1991). A less-than-perfect 65% response rate can still be a huge problem sometimes. Thus, modern survey researchers have also developed sophisticated ways of adjusting for nonresponse bias.

One might assume that modern pollsters and survey researchers would have learned their lesson from the *Literary Digest* error, but the results of poorly conducted polls can still garner a great deal of public attention. Back in the early 1990s, *TV Guide* reported the results of a poll of people's attitudes about television. In particular, they asked people if they would be willing to forgo *ever* watching television again for an absurdly huge amount of money (something like a million dollars). A ridiculously high proportion of those polled reported that the rough psychological equivalent of being given a dump truck full of money would not be enough to convince them to abandon TV forever! As much as Americans (the current authors included) rely on TV for daily doses of enlightenment, we were shocked to learn about the results of this poll. When we later learned that *TV Guide* had sampled people who (1) just happened to subscribe to their weekly TV magazine and (2) had bothered to return their questionnaire, we were less shocked.

To bring the issue of selection bias a little closer to home, Sears (1986) argued that the common practice of relying heavily on samples of convenience (i.e., on college students) in research may represent a serious shortcoming of much psychological research. In fact, Sears argued that some of our most important conclusions about human nature may be somewhat wide of the mark. For example, he argued that research on attitudes may underestimate the stability and potency of people's attitudes. Because college students are still forming many of their important attitudes, their attitudes may be less likely to predict behavior than the attitudes of a typical sample of older adults. Similarly, Sears argued that college students may be more obedient to authority than are older adults. Although it is possible to take issue with some of his assertions (e.g., that college students are highly deferent to authorities), it is hard to argue with his general point.

Although selection bias clearly threatens the external validity of descriptive findings, it does not necessarily threaten the internal validity of an experimental finding. The degree to which it does so depends heavily on the precise manner in which people are sampled, the precise topic of investigation, and the still more precise question of how the researcher operationalized his or her independent and dependent variables. For example, if a researcher demonstrated that college students perform more poorly on a written problem-solving task when it is phrased abstractly rather than concretely, it seems unlikely that a group of truck drivers or dairy farmers would perform better on the abstract problem. On the other hand, if a researcher manipulated the degree to which solving a problem required either traditionally measured IQ or "practical intelligence" (i.e., common sense), we might want to be more cautious in generalizing our findings to a more pragmatically inclined sample (see Sternberg, 1996).

Finally, it is important to realize that the efficacy or utility of a sampling technique depends as much on the group of people about whom we would like to generalize as it does on the group of people we have sampled. If we are interested in the attitudes of truck drivers, college students, or fashion models, it would obviously be highly inappropriate to collect data from a random sample of American voters. Less obviously, if we wanted to draw general conclusions about "people" or "adults," and we had selected a truly random sample of Americans, we would still need to consider the fact that we had sampled people from one particular culture. Some cross-cultural researchers have suggested that many of the psychological principles that Westerners take for granted may not apply very well to the typical inhabitants of Eastern or collectivistic cultures (see Markus & Kitayama, 1991; Triandis, 1989; but cf. Hetts, Sakuma, & Pelham, 1999).

People Change

Another category of threats to validity is based on the idea that people differ not only from one another but also from *themselves*. That is, people sometimes change. You are not exactly the same person you were four years ago. You also are not the same person when you are with your best friend that you are when you are with your mom (unless your mom happens to be your best friend). Just as differences between people can sometimes masquerade as meaningful research findings, differences in the *same person* across time and situations can sometimes do the same. This can be true even when researchers make use of both a pretest and a posttest to assess changes in people's behavior. If people change for reasons that have nothing to do with a researcher's treatment, then these changes can lead to some very inappropriate conclusions about the treatment. We break these changes down into two categories. One is history and maturation. The other is regression toward the mean.

History and Maturation

History and maturation each represent common threats to internal validity. These threats are most likely to be a problem when a researcher conducts a pretest-posttest study in which all participants receive the treatment of interest (i.e., in a repeated measures study in which there is no control group). As the name implies, **history** refers to changes that are occurring more or less across the board in a very large group of people such as a nation or culture. In contrast, **maturation** refers to the specific developmental or experiential changes that are occurring in a particular person, or a particular age cohort, over time. During times of famine in a particular culture or region, most people lose weight. During adolescence, most people grow and gain weight. Like individual differences, history and maturation represent a serious threat to validity only when a researcher does not conduct a true experiment. However, history and maturation still pose serious problems even when a researcher attempts to control for individual differences by assessing the responses of the same person before and after a treatment.

For example, imagine that a researcher was interested in improving people's dancing ability by using mental imagery. Assume that the researcher convinced a group of 20 adolescent ballet dancers to take part in a 12-week mental imagery study in which the dancers spent 5 minutes per day vividly imagining graceful dance moves. Suppose further that the researcher measured people's performance during a dance recital both before and after the 12-week treatment and found that the average participant increased the quality of his or her dances by about a point on a well-validated 14-point scale of dance performance. Although the researcher might wish to conclude that mental imagery can improve people's dancing ability, it would probably be much more reasonable to conclude that 12 weeks of dance classes, or perhaps 12 weeks of simple physical maturation, led to the average increase.

How could the researcher correct this problem? By conducting a true experiment in which he or she randomly assigned dancers to either a mental imagery condition or a control condition (a condition that did *not* include any mental imagery training). If the study were conducted with an appropriate level of care, and if the gains posted by the experimental group were significantly larger than those posted by the control group, it would be reasonable to attribute the difference in improvement between the two groups to the experimental imagery treatment. Learning and maturation would almost certainly happen, but they should happen equally to dancers randomly assigned to each of the two conditions.

Where threats to validity are concerned, the problems of history and maturation can also refer to relatively short-term changes in a person's physical or psychological state, changes that may occur over a couple of weeks, or even a few minutes, rather than a few months. One of our favorite examples of relatively short-term "maturation" comes from an episode of the 1960s TV show *The Beverly Hillbillies*. In this episode, Granny claims to have developed a home cure for the common cold. When queried about her remedy, Granny dictates that people afflicted with severe cold or flu symptoms should (1) drink her special, home-brewed elixir once a day, (2) consume plenty of other fluids, and (3) rest in bed for about two weeks. Less entertaining examples of this logic appear frequently in TV commercials for pain relievers. Such commercials often include testimonials from people who, for example, had a throbbing headache, took a dose of a pain reliever, and felt better a little while later. Anyone who has ever had to endure a headache when no pain reliever was handy knows that throbbing headaches eventually stop throbbing. Sound evidence of the relative superiority of a particular pain reliever would require evidence from a true experiment in which a control group received a brand of pain reliever other than the one being advertised.

Regression Toward the Mean

A phenomenon that is closely related to maturation also represents a threat to internal validity, and it is important enough to deserve a discussion of its own. This threat to validity is **regression toward the mean:** the tendency for people who receive high or low scores on a particular measure to score *closer to the mean* on a subsequent testing. Changes in human performance due to regression toward the mean are most frequently attributed to a treatment when researchers conduct the kind of pretest-posttest designs that are also susceptible to threats like history and maturation. However, in the pure case of regression toward the mean, changes that are mistaken for experimental treatments occur when research participants do not experience any true changes (such as maturation) but score differently than they did originally when they take a retest of a particular measure of personality or performance.

If this sounds a little puzzling, consider a concrete example as an illustration. Suppose you are shooting a few baskets with your friend Elizabeth, who used to play high school basketball and is rumored to be a very good free-throw shooter. When you press her to tell you *exactly* how good she is, she replies that she hasn't played much in the past six months but adds that her free-throw shooting percentage in high school was 80%. Being the skeptical type, suppose you hand her the ball and ask her to shoot 20 free throws to document her prowess. Now suppose she makes an impressive 19 of 20 shots. That's 95%, which is quite a bit better than what she claimed. Would you call your friend a liar and insist that her free-throw percentage in high school must have been 95%? We're guessing you wouldn't. And you shouldn't. Simple things like luck (a couple of good rolls on shots that normally don't fall) or having a "good day" (e.g., having gotten a good night's sleep) are likely to have made a contribution to her stellar performance at the stripe. Finally, suppose you were asked to predict how many free throws (out of 20) Elizabeth would make *tomorrow*. You probably shouldn't predict 19. If Elizabeth was truly an 80% free-throw shooter in high school, and if she hasn't changed much lately,

TABLE 4.1 *Regression toward the mean in professional sports*

1. Randy Johnson, 1995 American League Cy Young Winner:
   - 1995 ERA = 2.48   1996 ERA = 3.67
2. Greg Maddux, 1995 National League Cy Young Winner:
   - 1995 ERA = 1.63   1996 ERA = 2.72
3. Emmitt Smith, 1995–1996 NFL Rushing Leader:

1995–1996 Season:	1996–1997 Season:
average yards per carry: 4.7	average yards per carry: 3.5
total rushing yards: 1,773	total rushing yards: 1,204
rushing touchdowns: 25	rushing touchdowns: 12

4. Rankings by Total Tournament Winnings, 1994 Men's PGA Tour:
Nick Price, #1   Greg Norman, #2   Mark McCumber, # 3
Rankings of the same three players as of October 7, 1996:
Nick Price, #46   Greg Norman, #10   Mark McCumber, #33

Note: ERA = earned run average (average number of earned runs a pitcher allows per nine innings pitched). Lower ERAs indicate superior pitching performance.

you would probably predict better if you guessed that her performance would match her "true score," which appears to be about 80% (or 16 out of 20).

The only problem with this analysis is that people often fail to appreciate just how pervasive and predictable regression toward the mean really is. For example, many parents, coaches, and trainers of fighter pilots appear to believe that punishment is a more effective training tool than is reinforcement. Kahneman and Tversky (1973) noted that experienced trainers of fighter pilots expressed a great deal of confidence in this belief about the effects of rewards and punishments on performance in the cockpit. They defended the belief by noting that reinforcing pilots for excellent performance was typically followed by a drop in performance. In contrast, they noted, punishing pilots for poor performance was typically followed by an improvement in performance. In both cases, of course, the changes in the pilot's behavior can be readily explained by regression toward the mean. Some additional observations that are consistent with regression toward the mean appear in Table 4.1.

People who believe that award-winning rookie athletes experience a "sophomore slump" (because they get lazy or arrogant), or that physically punishing kids for aggressive behavior leads to a reduction in the offensive behavior may also be failing to appreciate the potency and ubiquity of regression toward the mean. In fact, in a wide range of areas in which people must use less-than-perfect indicators to make inferences about a person's traits or abilities, human judges often fail to appreciate regression toward the mean. For instance, when a top-selling CD wins a major award or breaks a sales record, people often express disappointment that the subsequent CD didn't do as well as the one that preceded it. Moreover, fans and critics alike often struggle to understand what caused the artist to lose his or her touch in the subsequent album. A good example of this kind of analysis came after Hootie and the Blowfish's *Cracked Rear View* CD sold millions of copies in 1994 and 1995.

Their next album, *Fairweather Johnson,* was reasonably successful but it sold considerably less well than the blockbuster CD that preceded it. In his unofficial Web page, one of the otherwise admiring fans of this group lamented the mistake that he felt could cost Hootie and the Blowfish their careers:[1]

> Can you recall an 80s band named "Men at Work?" Well they too had great success with their first album like Hootie. Here's where the similarities get ugly; Men at Work's second album did OK but not as good as the first album. . . . same with Hootie. Then Men at Work took a year off, again just like Hootie is planning to do. Finally when Men at Work came back and put out their 3rd album (Two Hearts) it BOMBED big-time! Sooo, let's hope this time off is good for Hootie and that they don't end up . . . like Men at Work. . . .

How can things like free throws, album sales, or IQ scores reflect regression toward the mean even when there is no real change in a person's talents or traits in a given area? The key to answering this question centers around the distinction between a *performance* or *observed score* (e.g., scoring 132 on an IQ test, making 19 of 20 free throws, producing a CD that sells over 10 million copies) and a *true score:* an underlying ability or trait that the observed score presumably reflects (being smart, being a good free-throw shooter, being musically gifted). Almost by definition, true scores are much more stable than observed scores. They reflect the stable characteristics of the person in an idealized setting in which things like good or bad luck are held constant. In contrast, performances or observed scores are influenced not only by true scores (real attributes of the person in question) but also by *error* (chance factors that influence performance). These sources of error are things that are unsystematic and difficult or impossible to predict. They include both fluctuating personal variables like physical health, fatigue level, or brief lapses in attention, and fluctuating environmental variables like room temperature, wind conditions, or whims in the public's musical taste.

Regression toward the mean is such an important concept that we have included a special activity on regression toward the mean at the end of this chapter. Until you have completed that exercise, the best way to think of regression toward the mean is that it exists because performance is always a joint product of skill and luck. Unusually good or bad performances are typically composed of a combination of relatively low or high ability, *plus* unusually bad or good luck. The ability factor doesn't usually change at a second testing, but luck typically does. Our best guess about luck is that it is likely to be average anytime we assess it, and this means, for example, that really good luck is usually followed by luck that isn't quite so good. This, of course, leads to scores or performances that aren't quite so good.

As mentioned earlier, the kinds of studies that are most likely to be influenced by regression toward the mean are pretest-posttest studies that do not involve a control group. For instance, imagine that you identified a group of people in a physical education course who all scored below the mean on a measure of free-throw shooting. After recording each person's score, you might give all these people some coaching in free-throw shooting. If you tested them again and found that the average person showed large gains in free-throw shooting percentage, there would be two good explanations for the observed changes. One possibility is that the coaching was successful. The other is that the group showed regression toward the mean. This should be the case because, *as a group,* your free-throw shooters are likely to have had below-average luck at the free-throw line during the pretest. On the whole, their luck during the posttest should be neither bad nor good, and thus the average score for the group as a whole should increase.

How can you separate regression toward the mean from an experimental treatment? The easiest way would be to divide your group of poor shooters in half (at random) and to give half of the group no coaching. If the group that received coaching showed a larger increase than did the control group, it would be reasonable to conclude that your coaching techniques had been effective. The same situation would apply if you identified a group of people who scored high on a self-report measure of depression and gave half of them two weeks of intensive psychotherapy. Unless you had a control group that did *not* receive therapy, you wouldn't know if the observed improvements in the well-being of your treatment group reflected (1) the effectiveness of your therapy or (2) regression toward the mean. In fact, in the extreme case, you could give people therapy that actually made them worse and still see improvements in your treatment group! If your control group showed significantly *more* improvement than your treatment group, this would be very bad news indeed for the usefulness of your treatment. In other words, if people who were left to their own devices improved more than people who got the treatment, it would be better to leave people to their own devices.

The Process of Studying People Changes People
Hooke, Heisenberg, and (Perhaps) Hawthorne

As suggested by the quotation that begins this chapter, Robert Hooke (1665) experienced great difficulty performing early microscopic studies of ants and other small insects. The primary difficulty that plagued Hooke is the fact that ants, like people, do not always welcome being studied. Hooke's eventual solution was to put his uncooperative subjects to sleep by placing them "into a drop of very well rectified spirit of Wine." When the spirits evaporated, the ants were preserved intact, ready for careful microscopic examination. Two hundred and ninety years later, Werner Heisenberg (1955) wrote of a similar but even greater problem, the impossibility of observing certain properties of subatomic particles without changing the nature of the particles. Heisenberg's uncertainty principle dictates, among other things, that there is no way to know simultaneously both the position and the momentum of subatomic particles such as protons or electrons. Translating loosely, one aspect of the Heisenberg uncertainty principle is that subatomic particles do not like to be observed. Although the amount of error or unpredictability introduced by the uncertainty principle is very small, its theoretical implications have been large enough to turn modern physics on its head.

At about the same time that physics was being reinvented by people like Heisenberg and Einstein, researchers at the Hawthorne Plant of the Western Electric Company (in Chicago, Illinois) were presumably learning that studying people can be just as tricky as studying ants or electrons. Researchers at the Hawthorne Plant were interested in the effects of environmental factors such as lighting on worker productivity. According to traditional interpretations of the Hawthorne studies, the workers at the Hawthorne plant responded to almost *any* changes in working conditions by working harder than usual. For example, both increases and decreases in lighting levels appeared to make people work harder. Over the past 70 years or so, researchers have dubbed this effect—the increases in productivity that occur when workers know they are being studied—the **Hawthorne effect.** According to some contemporary researchers (see Dooley, 1995), however, the Hawthorne effect actually has a somewhat shaky empirical foundation. At least some of the quasi-experimental manipulations performed in the Hawthorne studies may have been confounded with other factors such as personnel changes. On the other hand, even if the Hawthorne effect is a bit of a misnomer, a large body of research in psychology suggests that the act of studying people can dramatically change the way that people behave. Researchers who have documented the numerous ways in which studying people can change people would probably argue that the study of ants or subatomic particles doesn't sound so tricky after all.

Testing Effects

One of the specific ways in which studying people changes people is similar to the threats to internal validity discussed in the last section. This threat to internal validity is testing effects, and like the threats discussed in the last section, this threat is also a problem in pretest-posttest designs that have no control group. However, testing effects belong in the category of study-induced threats because such effects are a direct consequence of studying people. **Testing effects** refer to the tendency for most participants to perform better on a test or personality measure the second time they take it. This improvement typically occurs even on clinical and IQ tests, and it often occurs even when people are given an alternate form of the test at the second testing.

There are many potential explanations for testing effects. To a great extent, testing effects probably reflect learning on the part of the test taker. In the case of an IQ test, for example, test takers may belatedly come up with a good strategy for approaching a certain kind of test question. Similarly, highly motivated takers of IQ tests might even go to the trouble to look up the answers to some of the questions that they were unable to answer. In the case of tests of physical skills, the simple act of taking the test provides practice at the task. In the case of attitude, personality, or self-concept measures, on the other hand, what people may learn is what the test measures or what kinds of responses are socially desirable. In the case of many psychological tests, yet another way of thinking about testing effects is that they may represent a form of *attitude polarization*. Research on attitude polarization has shown that

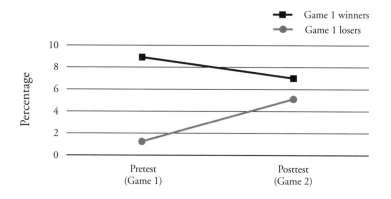

FIGURE 4.1   Simultaneous regression toward the mean and testing effects for novice bocci ball players

simply allowing people to give a little thought to their attitudes often leads them to become more extreme in these attitudes. Because most people's scores on most socially desirable psychological measures tend to be positive, we might expect that the simple opportunity to think about or express these attitudes—by filling out a psychological measure—will lead to a strengthening or polarization of these attitudes (Tesser & Valenti, 1981).

Regardless of exactly why testing effects occur, they may masquerade as treatment effects anytime a researcher tests a group of participants twice without including a pretested control group. Testing effects can even occur for people who score at or above the mean on a psychological measure. Because testing effects are in opposition to regression toward the mean for people who initially obtain high scores on a particular measure, you may be wondering how testing effects and regression toward the mean can both be true. They both are true, and in fact they can both occur even in the same study or performance situation. Figure 4.1 illustrates a hypothetical data set in which regression toward the mean and testing effects occur simultaneously. For this hypothetical group of beginning bocci ball players, the score of the average participant increased by exactly a point (from 5.0 to 6.0) from the first to the second game. At the same time, the group of low scorers (those who had lost their first game) scored better in game 2, and the group of high scorers (those who had won their first game) scored worse in game 2. The reason there could still be a testing (or practice) effect is that the 4-point gains of the initial losers more than made up for the 2-point losses of the initial winners.

There are several ways to correct the problem of testing effects. As suggested above, one simple way is to conduct a true experiment with a pretested control group. This will not eliminate testing effects, but it will allow you to separate them from your experimental treatment. On the other hand, if you are strongly interested in obtaining a posttreatment score that is not in any way influenced by a pretest, you can conduct a true experiment in which you simply eliminate the pretest. Although this approach may not be quite as sensitive or statistically powerful as the approach that makes use of a pretest, notice that this simplified design still allows you to draw firm conclusions about your treatment. For example, if you identified a large group of children who were at risk for developing low self-esteem, you could randomly determine that half of them would receive an experimental intervention—without ever measuring anyone's self-esteem prior to the intervention. As long as you randomly assigned the children to the two groups, you could safely assume that the initial self-esteem levels of the two groups were identical. Barring a failure of random assignment, any meaningful differences that existed between the two groups *after* the intervention would thus have to be a consequence of the experimental intervention. Finally, if you had no other choice (e.g., if ethical or practical concerns made it impossible to have a control group), you could minimize the possibility of testing effects by waiting as long as possible to administer your posttest (and perhaps using an alternate version of the test). Presumably, if you waited long enough, your participants might forget most of what they learned by taking the initial test.

Experimental Mortality (Attrition)

It would be nice if the worst thing that ever happened to people when they took part in psychological research was to learn the lowdown on a particular psychological test. Unfortunately for researchers as well as for participants, another thing that some participants learn about some investigations is that they wish to withdraw from them. The failure of some of the participants in an experiment to complete the study is known as **experimental mortality,** or **attrition.** Depending on exactly what form it takes, this problem can represent a threat to internal validity, a threat to external validity, or a threat to both.

One troublesome form of experimental mortality happens in experiments or longitudinal studies that take a very long time to complete. In the case of lengthy experiments, people may get tired or bored and fail to respond at certain crucial points in the study. In the case of longitudinal survey studies, people may move away to Chicago or Kamchatka. As a more detailed example, consider a lengthy experiment on implicit learning (learning without awareness). Implicit learning is a very interesting topic. It has to do with how people can be taught to behave as if they know things (such as rules for categorizing stimuli) without being able to consciously report the basis of their knowledge (see Reber & Kotovsky, 1997, for an example). However, from the perspective of research participants, studies of implicit learning can be extremely boring because they require people to process seemingly meaningless stimuli for very long periods (for hours or occasionally even days at a time).

Suppose a researcher wanted to see if people could implicitly learn some of the important grammatical rules of an artificial language. To find out, imagine that she exposed her participants to an experimentally generated language for a total of 12 hours (over a period of four days). Suppose further that the researcher manipulated limitations on people's working memory to test her prediction that people will show implicit learning only when they are able to devote their full attention to the experimental task. Finally, suppose that a lot of people got sick of reading a meaningless artificial language for 12 precious hours of their lives. That is, assume that the researcher's study was plagued by a high rate of experimental mortality. To be more specific, imagine that she started out with 40 participants divided evenly between her two conditions but lost exactly 6 people in each of the two conditions of her study. Finally, assume that the remaining 28 participants confirmed her predictions perfectly. Only the participants in the low-load (high-attention) condition showed evidence of implicit learning.

Can the researcher confidently conclude that her manipulation had its intended effect? In other words, is her study high in internal validity? Probably so. Although the 12 people who dropped out of her study are almost certainly different from the 28 who stayed in, it is noteworthy that the proportion of people who dropped out of the study (the attrition rate) is *exactly the same* in the two different conditions. Studies in which there is an equal level of attrition across all of the experimental conditions suffer from simple or **homogeneous attrition.** Any individual differences associated with attrition should thus be constant in the two different conditions. This does not mean that the study is perfect. Instead it means that the high attrition rate observed in the study is predominantly a threat to *external* rather than internal validity. There is a good chance that these findings apply only to the kind of highly motivated, tolerant, or easygoing person who can endure 12 hours of exposure to artificial language. Whether the results would generalize to the kinds of people who dropped out of the study is open to debate.

There is a second form of mortality that does represent a serious threat to internal validity. This more troublesome form of mortality is referred to here as differential or **heterogeneous attrition.** Heterogeneous attrition occurs when the attrition rates in two or more conditions of an experiment are noticeably different. Suppose, for example, that in an even more tedious version of the hypothetical study described above, the cognitive load manipulation turned out to be just enough to make the study interesting for participants. If this were true, we might expect participants in the boring control condition to drop out of the study at a much higher rate than participants in the cognitive load condition. For the sake of simplicity, imagine that no one dropped out of the mildly captivating load condition while fully half of the participants in the wearisome control (i.e., no load) condition dropped out. Now suppose that the 10 abnormally persistent people who endured the tedious control condition learned their grammar better than did the 20 normal people who had an additional task to keep them occupied. This would be a highly ambiguous finding. We wouldn't know if it was the experimentally manipulated surplus of mental capacity or the naturally occurring surplus of mental tenacity that led to the superior performance of the 10 unique people in the control condition. Another way of putting this is that differential mortality rates erase all the normal benefits of random assignment. After heterogeneous attrition, the people in one condition of the study are systematically different from the people in some other condition of the study.

What can be done to reduce or eliminate the problems associated with mortality or attrition? The first thing is to do anything within reason to keep people from dropping out of your study. Communicating the personal or scientific importance of the study to participants and presenting the study to people with authority and enthusiasm are good starting points. When done carefully, warning people that the study may not be all that exciting may also be helpful. Whenever it is possible to do so, scheduling breaks or rest periods for participants is yet another helpful strategy. Finally, offering people significant academic or financial rewards for completing the study is sometimes an additional option.

When all this is not enough, there is one additional thing that researchers might consider if they are concerned about differential attrition, especially in studies that are not very time-consuming. If there is some particular aspect of the study that is aversive, and if the participants in one condition of the study aren't supposed to be exposed to this aspect of the study, put them in this condition *after* they've completed the part of the study they were originally expected to complete. Presumably, some of them will drop out of the study. This is good because it will allow you to delete these participants from the condition that normally would have had very few experimental casualties. That is, it will allow you to *equalize* attrition in the two conditions of your experiment. Moreover, it will also allow you to compare those who eventually dropped out with those who didn't to determine how serious a threat attrition really was in the first place. Of course, like the other solutions to attrition, this solution also raises serious pragmatic and ethical issues. For example, is it ethical to offer people large amounts of money to endure painful electric shocks so that very few people will drop out of your study? Is it ethical to expose so many people to painful shocks? In principle, solutions to the problem of attrition can mean the difference between a methodologically sound study and a study that is very low in both internal and external validity. In practice, researchers must consider the ethical implications of any strategies designed to equalize attrition across experimental conditions.

Participant Reaction Bias

In addition to testing effects and experimental mortality, a third way in which the process of studying people can threaten validity occurs almost anytime people realize that they are being studied. The broad term for this specific category of threats is **participant reaction bias:** the bias that occurs when people realize they are being studied and behave in ways that they normally wouldn't. Because people are complicated, they may respond to the realization that they are being studied in a wide variety of ways. However, most forms of participant reaction bias can be boiled down to about three basic varieties. First, people may try to do what they think the researcher expects. Second, people may try to do the opposite of what they think the researcher expects. Third, people may try to do whatever will make them look good. More briefly put, people may be too cooperative, people may be too stubborn, or people may be too egotistical. These incidental motivations all represent a threat to internal validity because any of them may mask or mimic the potential effects of the independent variables under investigation.

The first, and probably the most problematic, form of participant reaction bias is **participant expectancies.** Participant expectancies occur when participants consciously or unconsciously try to behave in ways they believe to be consistent with the experimenter's hypothesis. Participants might do this for several different reasons: in an effort to please the experimenter, in an effort to feel normal, or as part of a desire to fill an implicit social contract with the experimenter (see Grice, 1975). Of course, participants can try to do as expected only when the expectations are somehow revealed to them (when experimenters tip their hands, so to speak). Characteristics of an experiment itself that subtly suggest how people are expected to behave are referred to as **demand characteristics,** and demand characteristics often play a role in the operation of participant expectancies.

A great deal of research on human aggression has been criticized on account of participant expectancies or demand characteristics. In numerous laboratory and field studies of the *weapons effect,* Berkowitz and his colleagues (e.g., Berkowitz & Lepage, 1967) have shown that the mere presence of a gun can act as a cue that triggers aggressive responses. More specifically, Berkowitz and Lepage (1967) gave male participants the opportunity to shock a confederate who the participants believed had previously chosen to shock them. The participants delivered more shock than usual in retaliation when a rifle and a revolver (as opposed to a couple of badminton racquets) happened to be sitting near the shock key. On the basis of studies such as these, Berkowitz has argued that cues that are associated with aggression can eventually come to elicit aggressive responses on their own.

Critics have argued that demonstrations of the weapons effect are likely to reflect the operation of participant expectancies or demand characteristics. From this perspective, instead of stimulating aggressive thoughts because of classical conditioning, the guns that happen to be lying around in experiments on the "weapons effect" are stimulating participants' thoughts about how the experimenter expects them to behave. Although there is still some debate over this issue, Berkowitz and colleagues have presented at least some evidence suggesting that demand characteristics or participant expectancies are unlikely to account for the weapons effect. For instance, Turner, Simons, Berkowitz, and Frodi (1977) reported that either making participants more suspicious than usual or increasing participants' awareness of the experimental hypothesis tended to *decrease* participants' levels of aggressiveness in the presence of weapons.

In the case of the weapons effect, the tendency of well-informed participants to be experimentally uncooperative was pretty good news for Berkowitz. In many other cases, however, the tendency of research participants to rebel against an experimental manipulation isn't so reassuring. In fact, the tendency of participants to try to disconfirm an experimenter's hypothesis represents a second form of participant reaction bias, namely **participant reactance.** Although there could be other reasons, the main reason that participants might work hard to *disconfirm* an experimental hypothesis is probably grounded in people's basic desire for autonomy or independence (see Brehm, 1966). No one likes to feel like a puppet, and if people get the feeling that the experimenter is pulling their strings, they may pull back by doing the opposite of what they think the experimenter expects. To see how this could be a problem, imagine that Berkowitz had incorrectly hypothesized that guns serve to make people fearful and thus *reduce* aggressive behavior. Assume further that he cranked up the volume on his manipulations by making people highly aware of the presence of the guns. If people responded with reactance to their natural inclinations and failed to shock other people in the presence of the guns (even though they otherwise would have wanted to do so), it might appear that the guns had made people fearful when they had actually made people uncooperative! This would clearly represent a threat to internal validity. On the other hand, assuming that participant reactance normally works in opposition to an experimenter's predictions, it can still be a problem. In particular, reactance could easily mask the operation of a true effect, leading researchers to falsely reject a valid hypothesis.

A third form of participant reaction bias could also threaten internal validity by working either for or against an experimental prediction. This third form of bias is referred to as **evaluation apprehension.** Evaluation apprehension refers to people's concerns about being judged favorably or unfavorably by another person (Rosenberg, 1965a). It can easily threaten the validity of a research study by causing people to do whatever they expect will portray them in a favorable light (i.e., by trying to look good in front of the experimenter). To stick with studies of aggressiveness, people who might privately wish to shock the beans out of an annoying confederate might refrain from doing so during an experiment because they realize that their shocks are being counted up as an index of aggression. If the presence of a weapon somehow clued people in to this possibility, the weapon might decrease aggressive behavior in the laboratory when the most common effect of weapons in the real world is to make people more aggressive. Alternately, if an experimenter somehow communicated to participants that aggressiveness was a highly desirable trait, the presence of guns could artificially promote aggressive behavior in the laboratory even if guns truly had no such effect under normal circumstances. Similarly, as suggested by traditional interpretations of the Hawthorne effect, either increases or decreases in illumination levels could falsely appear to increase worker productivity. One way in which they could do so would be by making workers behave as if someone important was constantly looking over their shoulders.

Fortunately, there are several things that researchers can do to reduce or eliminate most forms of participant reaction bias. First of all, researchers can take steps to guarantee the *anonymity* or privacy of their research participants. In the case of survey research on attitudes or the self-concept, this safeguard is especially important. Self-concept researchers who are concerned about evaluation apprehension almost always instruct participants not to put any identifying information on their surveys. Researchers may also ask participants to seal their surveys up in plain, unmarked envelopes before they turn them in. If participants are taking the surveys in a relatively public setting such as a classroom, researchers may even give them brightly colored cover pages so that they can cover up their responses as they fill out the surveys.

In purely experimental research in which there is some chance that people will guess the experimental hypothesis, it is sometimes possible to gain control over participants' expectancies by giving participants in the experimental and the control group exactly the same expectancy—typically one that has little or nothing to do with the real predictions of the experiment. This false expectancy is often part of a **cover story,** a false and often elaborate story about the nature and purpose of the study. In Milgram's classic study of obedience, the cover story was that participants were playing the role of teacher to teach word pairs to a learner. In Asch's study of conformity, the cover story was that participants were helping the experimenter learn about visual perception and judgment. In studies such as these, the researchers go to great lengths to convince their participants that they are studying something that has little or nothing to do with the real purpose of the study. Although the use of deception to reduce participant reaction bias can be extremely effective, its utility must be weighed against the ethical implications of telling people elaborate lies.

A less actively deceptive approach to some forms of participant reaction bias involves keeping participants in the dark in various ways. For instance, in some studies researchers can simply keep people blind to the experimental conditions to which they have been assigned. In more naturalistic studies with behavioral-dependent measures, researchers can also make use of surreptitious (secret) or **unobtrusive observations.** In the case of studies making use of unobtrusive measurements, research participants do not realize that they are being studied at all. Even in laboratory experiments in which people do know that they are being studied, the use of unobtrusive measures may prevent people from realizing which aspect of their behavior is being studied. For example, if we wanted a direct measure of how much someone liked a similar versus a dissimilar experimental confederate, we could simply ask participants how much they liked the confederate on a typical Likert scale. However, if we were concerned that participants might not be willing to report their true feelings about the confederate, we might unobtrusively measure how much physical distance participants maintained between themselves and the confederate during a staged interaction (e.g., by seeing how far participants sat from the confederate when they were working with the confederate at a large table).

Yet another approach to reducing the effects of evaluation apprehension requires researchers to convince their participants that researchers can read people's minds. This may sound a bit far-fetched, but Jones and Sigall (1971) developed a technique based on exactly this idea. More specifically, Jones and Sigall brought people to their laboratory and hooked them up to a phony lie detector. Because Jones and Sigall had previously gone to the trouble to measure their participants' attitudes in a pretest, they were able to convince their participants that the machine could read people's minds (by detecting minute changes in the way participants held onto an "attitude wheel"). Jones and Sigall found that when people were hooked up to this *bogus pipeline,* they were more willing to admit having negative feelings about stigmatized group members such as Blacks and the physically handicapped. In their review of research using the bogus pipeline, Roese and Jamieson (1993) reported that the bogus pipeline has turned out to be an extremely useful technique for getting people to report how they really feel about things.

Another approach to minimizing almost any kind of participant reaction bias (especially evaluation apprehension) is to make use of *indirect* measures of people's attitudes and opinions. As an example of indirect measures, consider a clever study of attitudes and behavior conducted by Vargas, von Hippel, and Petty (1998). These researchers were interested in people's attitudes about cheating. Among other things, they wanted to know if people who have relatively favorable attitudes about cheating might be more likely to cheat than people who have more traditional (i.e., unfavorable) attitudes. The problem with trying to study this important question is that very few people are willing to admit being thumbs-up on cheating. Vargas et al. solved this problem by developing an *indirect measure* of attitudes about cheating. Along these lines, they asked participants to make some judgments about the appropriateness of *another person's* decision to obtain a copy of a highly desirable and presumably expensive library book—by claiming to have lost the book and paying the library a modest replacement fee. Not surprisingly, some of Vargas et al.'s participants reported that they considered this morally questionable act morally bankrupt. In contrast, other participants (like the CEOs of some large energy companies) reported that they considered the act to be little more than a matter of creative bookkeeping. Vargas et al. assumed that their participants' true attitudes about cheating would play an important role in how they evaluated the morally ambiguous book buyer. Specifically, they assumed that people who had relatively lax attitudes about cheating would be less likely to view the book buyer as dishonest. In other words, these researchers used people's judgments of the morally ambiguous target as an indirect measure of their attitudes about cheating. This indirect measure proved to be directly related to cheating behavior. Specifically, the indirect measure was a good predictor of their participants' actual tendencies to cheat on a test involving extremely difficult anagrams.

The key to the success of indirect measures is that they constitute a pencil-and-paper version of *unobtrusive* measures. That is, when participants fill out indirect measures of attitudes, they don't realize what is actually being measured. Another way in which researchers can measure attitudes without having to worry about participants catching on to what is being measured is to measure attitudes that participants do not realize they possess. After all, if participants do not realize that they possess a specific attitude, it will be pretty hard for them to hide this attitude from an experimenter. Of course, if participants are unaware of their own attitudes, you may be wondering how an experimenter could ever measure these attitudes. Researchers have recently addressed this problem by developing *implicit* (i.e., nonconscious) measures of people's attitudes. For example, Greenwald, McGhee, and Schwartz (1998) used the Implicit Association Test (IAT) to assess people's unconscious associations about objects as varied as insects, flowers, and ethnic groups. There are now many versions of this test, but the basic idea behind the test is always the same. It is to see how easily (i.e., how quickly) people can associate different things. For example, if a person found it easy to pair photos of Black faces with negative words such a "death" but found it easy to pair photos of White faces with positive words such as "peace," Greenwald and colleagues would consider this an indicator that the person possessed negative implicit (i.e., unconscious) attitudes about Blacks.

Researchers have also developed a wide variety of measures to assess people's unconscious attitudes about *themselves*. Hetts and colleagues refer to people's unconscious attitudes about themselves as *implicit self-regard* or *implicit self-esteem*. To measure implicit self-esteem, Hetts, Sakuma, and Pelham (1998) activated people's thoughts about themselves and then examined how these activated thoughts influenced the ways in which people subsequently processed information. One measure that Hetts et al. used was an adaptation of a very useful priming technique pioneered by Fazio and colleagues (Fazio, Jackson, Dunton, & Williams, 1995; Fazio, Sanbonmatsu, Powell, & Kardes, 1986). This procedure required people to make some rapid judgments about words that appeared on a computer screen. Participants might be quickly exposed to a priming word such as "me" or "I." Shortly after a priming word disappeared, participants were asked to identify a favorable or unfavorable word (e.g., "good" or "bad") that was flashed in the same spot on the computer screen. If the presentation of self-relevant primes (e.g., "me") makes it easier than usual for a person to identify favorable words (and has the opposite effect for unfavorable words), researchers using this technique assume that this person is *high* in implicit self-regard. That is, this person appears to possess mostly positive associations about the self. On the other hand, if getting a person to think about the self makes it easier than usual for him or her to process negative words (and harder to process positive words), researchers assume that the person is relatively *low* in implicit self-regard. Hetts et al. have found that implicit self-regard is not correlated with traditional (explicit) measures of self-esteem. Nonetheless, implicit self-regard is correlated with a number of important behaviors and judgments (e.g., the kind of culture in which a person was reared, people's tendencies to make self-serving performance judgments; see Hetts, Sakuma, & Pelham, 1998; Hetts & Pelham, 2001; and see Greenwald & Banaji, 1995; Wilson, Lindsey, & Schooler, 2000, for extensive discussions of unconscious aspects of social attitudes).

To summarize work on indirect and implicit attitudes: This work appears to provide some promising solutions to the problem of participant reaction bias. In the past few years, research using implicit measures has mushroomed, and it appears that this interest in implicit social judgments will only increase in the years to come (for a description of an additional measure of implicit self-esteem, see Kitayama & Karasawa, 1997; Koole, Smeets, van Knippenberg, & Dijksterhuis, 1999). Given the popularity and utility of unobtrusive *behavioral* measures in the past, along with the theoretical and practical importance of finding ways to reduce participant reaction bias, we are optimistic about the potential of these recently developed measures. If you are interested in seeing exactly how an implicit measure works, you might wish to check out a popular and informative Web page that will allow you to take the Implicit Association Test developed and refined by Tony Greenwald,

Mahzarin Banaji, Shelley Farnham, Laurie Rudman, and Brian Nosek. At the time of this writing the Web address was http://buster.cs.yale.edu/implicit/. If you have trouble with this Web address, you can always try a Web search using "IAT" or "Implicit Association Test" as search terms.

Variables That Accompany a Treatment Change People

A final category of threats to the validity of research consists of things that researchers unintentionally allow to vary along with their independent variables. Each of these two distinct threats can be quite difficult to detect, and each represents a threat to internal validity. The first threat applies almost exclusively to experiments, and the second threat can apply to any kind of design but is least likely to apply to experiments.

Experimenter Bias

One of the most subtle, and interesting, threats to validity can happen when experimenters' expectations about their studies bias their experimental observations. Appropriately enough, this unintentional bias on the part of experimenters is referred to as **experimenter bias,** and it may take either of two distinct forms. The first form of experimenter bias occurs when researchers make biased observations in an experiment. Because experimenters are only human, they sometimes see what they expect to see and observe support for their hypothesis when an unbiased observer might not see any. A second form of experimenter bias occurs when experimenters actually treat their participants differently according to their expectations about how their participants should perform. In the case of this second bias, even a perfectly objective observer might observe differences in the behavior of people in different experimental conditions. However, these differences would have more to do with subtle differences in the way the experimenter treated the participants than they would with the true manipulations of interest.

"'Maze-dull', 'a little slow', 'maze-impaired.'
It all starts to get to a guy after a while."

In one of the first studies to call attention to experimenter bias, Rosenthal and Fode (1963) observed each of these two forms of experimenter bias. They trained a group of highly motivated experimenters and asked them to test the performance of groups of carefully bred "maze-bright" and "maze-dull" rats in a laboratory maze. As Rosenthal and Fode expected, the maze-bright rats learned their way around the mazes more quickly than did the maze-dull rats. This seemingly trivial finding may seem a little less trivial when you consider the fact that the two groups of rats were actually identical. Rosenthal and Fode simply got a bunch of run-of-the-mill, maze-mediocre rats and randomly split them into the two different groups. The important thing is that Rosenthal and Fode's bright and highly motivated experimenters *thought* that some of the rats were brighter (and perhaps more highly motivated) than the others. Why did the rats that were labeled more favorably perform more favorably? Because the experimenters unwittingly *treated* them more favorably. The experimenters not only petted the presumably bright rats more and handled them with greater care, but also encouraged the rats more when the rats were running in the mazes. Rosenthal and Fode also observed evidence of experimenter bias when they looked carefully for coding errors committed by the experimenters. The coding errors favored the presumably maze-bright rats quite a bit more frequently than they favored the less highly regarded maze-dull rats.

It is important to realize that Rosenthal and Fode's experimenters were not consciously engaging in any form of scientific dishonesty. They were simply letting their expectations get the better of them—in much the same way that hypothesis testers who are asked to solve the E, K, 4, 7 problem often let their hypotheses about vowels and even numbers get the better of them. It is very hard to look for what you do not expect to see. As an anonymous social critic once put it, "I'll see it when I believe it." Rosenthal and colleagues might add that if we believe something strongly enough, we may do more than simply see it; we may also unknowingly work to make it happen (see Snyder, Tanke, & Berscheid, 1977).

You may have noticed that there is a very fine line between experimenter bias (also known as experimenter expectancies) and the participant expectancies discussed in the last section. At some point, experimenter expectancies can get translated into participant expectancies, and the research participants can thus become unwitting participants in the experimenter's self-fulfilling prophecies. However, there are some differences between these two forms of bias. In addition to the obvious difference about who does the expecting, there is another difference, and this difference is the reason we have categorized experimenter bias as something that occurs when experimenters unwittingly allow something else to accompany their experimental manipulations. In its prototypical form, experimenter bias refers to things that have nothing to do with an experimental manipulation (unintentionally giving some rats a few extra pets, unknowingly smiling more at the teacher's pet, offering subtle encouragement to the participants who are expected to persist longer at unscrambling anagrams). To put it differently, experimenters who fall prey to experimenter bias have unknowingly allowed one or more *confounds* to spoil their manipulations. In contrast, participant expectancies can occur even when a study is perfectly executed by the experimenter. The only trouble with participant expectancies is that participants are sometimes smarter than experimenters give them credit for being. Nothing extraneous that the experimenter is doing is covarying with the experimental manipulation. The participants simply figure the manipulation out.

As subtle and potentially injurious as experimenter bias is, it is relatively easy to fix. Researchers who wish to avoid experimenter bias simply need to keep themselves *blind* to (i.e., unaware of) their participants' treatment conditions. This can be done, for example, by having one researcher interact with participants while a separate researcher keeps track of participants' experimental conditions using arbitrary code numbers. When this is not possible, it is often possible to standardize most aspects of the instructions that participants receive (e.g., by recording and presenting the instructions in audiotaped form). The only portion of the instructions that is changed is the portion that is essential to the experimental manipulation. Finally, whenever possible, researchers concerned about the biasing influences of any kind of expectancies often make use of a **double-blind procedure** in which both the experimenter and the research participants are kept unaware of the participants' treatment conditions.

When approaches such as these cannot easily be adopted, researchers have occasionally resorted to deceiving their experimenters! In a study of the "door-in-the-face" technique for increasing compliance, Cialdini and Ascani (1976) did exactly this. In particular, Cialdini and Ascani trained experimenters to ask college students to perform a painful but socially desirable favor: giving blood. In a control condition, the experimenters simply asked participants to give blood (tomorrow). In the door-in-the-face condition, the experimenters preceded this same request (to give blood tomorrow) with a gigantic and unreasonable request that everyone refused: agreeing to give blood every six weeks for the next two years. Because the experimenters in this study approached students on a college campus and hit them up with their requests, it was impossible to keep the experimenters blind to participants' conditions. Cialdini and Ascani informed their experimenters that they should expect to see lower rates of compliance with the target request among those in the door-in-the-face (ridiculous request first) condition. Moreover, they did this knowing full well that they could be setting the stage for experimenter bias. However, because they actually expected their door-in-the-face condition to elicit *higher* than usual levels of compliance, they were stacking the deck *against* their hypothesis. As everyone but the experimenters expected, Cialdini and Ascani found that participants who received the door-in-the-face manipulation were much more likely to agree to give blood the next day. Moreover, after the door-in-the-face participants had actually given blood, they were also about twice as likely as participants in the control condition to agree to give blood again in the future. The results of Cialdini and Ascani's experiment are summarized in Figure 4.2. Experimenter bias cannot provide a very good explanation for these findings.

FIGURE 4.2   Giving blood and agreeing to give blood again as a function of compliance technique used during recruitment (from Cialdini & Ascani, 1976)

Confounds

As suggested above, experimenter bias represents a potent but subtle way in which researchers unintentionally allow a secondary variable to accompany the independent variable in which they are interested. There is a second, very broad, category of such accompanying variables that also represents a serious threat to internal validity. This second category of threats is confounds. A **confound** is a broad term for any design problem in which some additional variable (sometimes referred to as a nuisance variable) varies systematically along with the independent variable. Because the simplest version of a true experiment involves only two variables (a single independent variable and a single dependent variable), confounds are sometimes referred to as "the third variable problem." They are best thought of as design mistakes because they occur when something a researcher hadn't thought about (or couldn't help) could be responsible for the researcher's observed findings. Although confounds are much more likely to plague nonexperimental than experimental research, even the best-laid plans of the best experimenters sometimes prove to be susceptible to confounds.

Before analyzing confounds in experimental research, let's consider a relatively simple confound in correlational research. Imagine we told you that we had obtained strong evidence that tattoos are a leading cause of death. We did so by conducting a 10-year longitudinal study of 12,000 middle-aged men. In this hypothetical study, we simply documented the number of tattoos that each man had and examined death rates over the 10-year period for men with different numbers of tattoos. Figure 4.3 illustrates the findings from this hypothetical study. The findings clearly show that the more tattoos men had, the more likely they were to die during the 10-year period. In a sample this large, these findings would undoubtedly be highly significant. Does this mean that tattoos are a public health menace? Obviously not. There are quite a few variables that are confounded with the number of tattoos people have that provide a much more reasonable account of these findings. Because we are both Southerners,

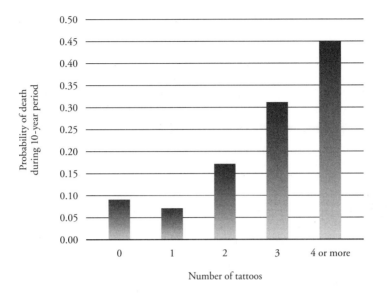

FIGURE 4.3 Probability of death from all causes as a function of number of tattoos possessed (data are hypothetical).

and because one of us is a Southerner who has quite a few tattooed relatives, we hesitate to contribute to stereotypes of the tattooed. Nonetheless, restricting our analysis to what the first author has directly observed in his own tattooed relatives, we are willing to suggest that, among other things, men who have a lot of tattoos might be more likely than their untattooed peers to (1) use tobacco products, (2) drive motorcycles, (3) eat high-fat, low-fiber diets, (4) consume large quantities of alcohol, (5) fail to wear their seat belts when driving, (6) get into bar fights, (7) fail to get adequate medical treatment for their high blood pressure or diabetes, and (8) insult people who routinely carry handguns. Because any of these "third variables" might be enough to explain the observed findings regarding tattoos and death rates, few people would be tempted to conclude that tattoos play a direct role in causing death.

Because confounds are typically much harder to identify than our tattoo example might suggest, many correlational studies suffer from confounds. In fact, many carefully designed laboratory experiments suffer from potential confounds. As an example, consider some carefully designed experimental studies of mood and helping. Theory and common sense suggest that under at least some circumstances, people who are in a good mood might be especially likely to offer help to those who need it. Early experiments designed to test this hypothesis involved giving some people positive feedback about their personalities to see if the increase in positive mood would lead to increases in helping. Although studies such as this supported the idea that happiness leads to helpfulness, it is possible that giving people positive feedback might do more than simply elevate their mood. Positive feedback also increases people's beliefs about their competence, and people who think they are competent appear to be more likely to help others, even when their feelings of competence do not necessarily put them in a good mood. For example, people who are told that they have a knack for handling rats are more likely to help people threatened by rats than are people who are told that they shouldn't quit their day jobs to become rat handlers.

Because Isen and Levin (1972) were aware of this potential confound, they developed a manipulation of mood that was not confounded with people's beliefs about their competence. Specifically, they gave cookies to some men who were sitting in a library to see if those who had been given the cookies would be more likely to help a fellow student. The men who had just been given cookies were indeed more likely to help. However, this alternate manipulation of mood appears to be confounded with a different variable. Specifically, people who receive something nice (like a cookie) from a stranger have just been exposed to a *prosocial model,* and exposure to prosocial models is known to increase helping behavior (Bandura, 1977). To correct for this and other problems, Isen and colleagues eventually developed the "found dime" paradigm for manipulating mood. Researchers who make use of this mood manipulation simply arrange for some participants to "find" a dime (or some other amount of money) in a place such as a public telephone booth. It presumably takes very little skill to pick up a found dime. In addition, the only thing modeled by the unknown person who presumably left a dime behind is forgetfulness. Nonetheless, Isen and her colleagues have found that this uncontaminated manipulation of mood reliably increases a wide variety of helping behaviors (Isen, 1987). Because the concept of confounds is so important, we will discuss this concept (and Isen and Levin's experiments) in much more detail in Chapters 5 and 6.

What can researchers do to eliminate confounds from their research? Although there are no guarantees when it comes to avoiding confounds, one simple thing that researchers can do is to conduct true experiments. Relative to other research designs, true experiments are less likely to contain confounds. This is because the combination of random assignment and the ability to isolate and manipulate specific independent variables provides a great deal of insurance against confounds. In addition to running true experiments, researchers who wish to avoid design mistakes can do what laypeople do when they are trying to avoid making mistakes. They can be careful. Reading as much as possible about what has already been done on your topic and giving a great deal of thought to the design of your experiment can greatly reduce the likelihood that you will either (1) repeat the mistakes of previous researchers or (2) generate novel mistakes of your own. Finally, a third potential solution to the problem of confounds is to measure any variables that are likely to be confounded with the variable or variables in which you are interested. Doing so will allow you to assess whether a potential confound is really something to worry about (by seeing if it is correlated with either your independent or your dependent variable). In addition, it will allow you to make certain kinds of statistical corrections for the potential confound about which you are worried. Statistical techniques such as the analysis of covariance (ANCOVA), partial correlation, and multiple regression are specifically designed to allow researchers to see if their independent variables are still associated with a dependent variable once the effects of a potential confound have been statistically removed. Although some of these techniques are beyond the scope of this book, the methodology exercise on partial correlation should give you some basic insights into how it is possible, at least in principle, to remove the effects of confounds before looking for any effects of the independent variable or variables in which you are most interested.

Instead of providing a laundry list of threats to validity, in this chapter we have tried to organize some common threats to validity around four broad themes. We hope that this organizational scheme provides a good way of thinking about threats to validity. In the case of internal validity, however, there is an even simpler organizing scheme that can be used to appreciate the threats discussed here. If we had to come up with a single category for threats to internal validity, this threat would have to be *confounds,* broadly defined. If you think about any of the specific threats discussed in this chapter (e.g., individual differences, history, testing effects, etc.) you should be able to see that in the case of each specific threat the core of the problem is that *something else* that the researcher hadn't taken into account was accompanying the researcher's independent variable. Whereas the researcher had tried to isolate the cause of some outcome of interest, this cause turned out not to have been isolated after all. Things like preexisting differences between people, differences in how much an experimenter smiled at someone, or differences in people's familiarity with a test from pretest to posttest were always confounded with whatever variable the researcher really cared about. Because there are a great number of ways in which confounding variables can accompany other variables of interest, there are a great number of threats to internal validity. Fortunately, there are also a great number of things we can do to correct these threats.

HANDS-ON ACTIVITY 2

Regression Toward the Mean

As you just learned, one common threat to the validity of many research claims (and a source of many naive theories about human behavior) is regression toward the mean. As you probably recall, regression toward the mean refers to the tendency for people who obtain high or low scores on a particular measure to score *closer to the mean* when they are retested on the same measure. Many people who understand the definition of regression toward the mean have a great deal of trouble seeing exactly *why* this should be the case. What is it, exactly, that causes extreme scores to become less extreme the second time around? The simple answer is chance. To the degree that people's scores on a particular measure are partly determined by chance as well as by stable properties of people, we would expect high scorers on a measure (as a group) to have been somewhat luckier than low scorers (as a group). Because luck isn't something that people carry around with them, it is reasonable to expect that people who have recently had good or bad luck will have average luck the next time we test them. So long as luck or chance plays a substantial role in determining people's performance on a measure, people's high or low scores on that measure will typically regress toward the mean on a subsequent testing.

To give you a concrete example of how this works, we would like you to engage in a simple group activity that will allow you to see how chance factors combine with stable properties of people to produce regression toward the mean. After randomly assigning you to one of two groups (a group of "high rollers" and a group of "low rollers"), your instructor will give you either two or three standard six-sided dice. In particular, the high rollers will receive three dice, but the low rollers will receive only two. Notice that in this activity the number of dice you are allowed to roll is a stand-in for some *stable property of people* such as skill or ability at a task (in this case, the task of rolling a lot of spots with two or more dice). Thus, we know that if we asked each of the high rollers and each of the low rollers to roll the dice a thousand times, the average score (i.e., the "true score") of each of the high rollers would be about 10.5 and the average score of each of the low rollers would be about 7.0. You can think of the number of dice you get to roll as a stand-in for your true *ability* at this game. But suppose we asked each of you to roll your dice only once. In this case, each person's score (i.e., the total number of spots each person rolled) would be influenced not only by the number of dice he or she was rolling but also by the luck of the particular roll (that is, by chance or measurement error). To see how chance events can produce regression toward the mean, let's play two rounds of a very simple dice game. Round 1 will be a stand-in for a pretest, and round 2 will be a stand in for a posttest.

After you have been randomly assigned to be either a high or a low roller, your instructor will ask you to roll the dice, and she or he will publicly record your score. After each person in the class has rolled his or her dice on the first round of the game, each person will be assigned to a *new* group according to the value of his or her roll. Unlike the ability grouping based on people's true scores (i.e., the number of dice people are allowed to roll), this new grouping will be based on *performance* (i.e., the total number of spots people actually rolled during round 1). In particular, your instructor will perform a *median split* (i.e., a "split down the middle") on your round-1 scores and place each person in either the upper or the lower half of the class according to this measure of performance. The easiest way to do this is to tally up all the scores at the end of round 1 and to physically place people on opposite halves of the room based on their performance during round 1. Finally, after sorting people into the two groups, you and your instructor should compute and publicly record an average *pretest score* for each of the two groups. Of course, by necessity the score for the high performers will be quite a bit higher than the score for the low performers.

Once the pretest scores have been computed, each person will roll the dice again during round 2. The score people receive during round 2 can be thought of as a posttest score, and it is important that each person generate a posttest score by rolling the *same number of dice* that he or she rolled during round 1 (because truly being a high or low roller is a stable property of each person). As each person rolls the dice again, your instructor will publicly record the scores for round 2. When everyone has rolled the dice a second time, it will be time to compute the average posttest score for the two performance groups. Unless something very unusual happened, you should observe regression toward the mean. That is, the average score for the high performers should have decreased, and the average score for the low performers should have increased.

Questions for Group Discussion

1. First, assuming that you observed at least some evidence of regression toward the mean, why exactly did this happen?

2. Notice that one difference between this demonstration and real life is that in the demonstration it is possible to observe directly the stable properties of people (in this case people's "dice-rolling ability"). When we can't look inside people and see their "true scores" we are forced to rely solely on measures of performance as proxies for ability. However, suppose we developed a measure so valid and reliable that it allowed us to categorize people perfectly on the basis of their true scores (e.g., their true ability at a task). Would we expect to see any more or any less evidence of regression toward the mean in a case such as this? If you are uncertain, notice that the observations you generated in this demonstration could be used to answer this. That is, if you assigned people to groups on the basis of their *true* status as a high or low roller and then computed pretest and posttest scores for the true high and low rollers, what would you be likely to observe?

3. Finally, notice that the degree to which chance plays a role in people's scores on a measure can be thought of as a proxy for the *reliability* of that particular measure. What is the general relation between the reliability of a measure and the amount of regression toward the mean that you'd expect to observe on this measure? For example, if a measure involved an even larger component of chance than the measure we used today (e.g., suppose everyone rolled only a single die but some people rolled a six-sided die and some people rolled a seven-sided die), would you expect to see more or less evidence of regression toward the mean?

Special Notes to the Instructor

This demonstration works best with a group of exactly 20 students. Using 20 students will create two groups of exactly 10 participants, making it very easy to compute the means that serve as the basis of the demonstration. There are likely to be some ties when you are trying to perform your median split. To increase the chances that you will observe regression toward the mean, you might want to break any ties by sending people to performance groups that are at odds with their "true scores." Alternately, of course, you could allow tied participants to take part in a "roll off" to determine their assignment to one of the two performance groups. Finally, if you would like to try a simpler and more dramatic demonstration of regression toward the mean, you might consider having students play two rounds of some kind of psychic guessing game. Because performance on this test will consist *solely* of error or luck, you will typically see a tremendous amount of regression toward the mean on the second round of this game. The authors thank Dr. Tara MacDonald for suggesting this last demonstration.

Notes

1. The Web site was http://www.thecore.com/~webuser/hootie_html/news.html. Except for the potential error involving regression toward the mean, we give the site a pretty enthusiastic thumbs-up.

Chapter 5

Nonexperimental Research Designs

You can observe a lot just by watching.
—Yogi Berra

This chapter provides our first detailed look at the nuts and bolts of psychological research methods. Specifically, it provides descriptions of some of the most commonly used nonexperimental research designs. We begin with a description of case studies or single-participant designs. We follow this with a description of single-variable studies whose purpose is to describe the state of the world. After discussing single-variable research (e.g., epidemiological research, public opinion surveys), we discuss four kinds of multiple-variable or *correlational* research (e.g., archival research, survey and interview research). In the case of each design, we show how measurement in naturalistic settings provides opportunities to maximize external validity. However, this opportunity often comes at the cost of increased concerns about internal validity. It is addressing these concerns about internal validity that represents much of the challenge, and the excitement, of correlational research.

Describing the World of a Single Participant: Case Studies

One of the most interesting ways in which researchers study human behavior is by conducting **case studies,** that is, by making careful analyses of the experiences of a particular person or group. Case studies are most likely to capture our attention when they focus on people whose extraordinary experiences would be difficult or impossible to re-create in the laboratory. Moreover, case studies often involve remarkable people with conditions so rare that it would be very difficult to identify and study them in large numbers (either in the laboratory or in the real world). When people develop amnesia, survive massive head injuries, compose symphonies as children, or remain children forever (by failing to mature and age), inquiring minds want to know about it. Inquiring scientific minds also want to know about it. However, unlike casual analyses of people's behavior, scientific case studies are usually aimed at uncovering general psychological principles. Like any other approach to research, that is, case studies are usually designed to generate, delineate, corroborate, or invalidate theories. Pretty often, case studies are carried out when little if any systematic research has been conducted on a topic. In such cases, the careful, detailed observations that make up good case studies can provide researchers with the insights they need to develop new theories, theories that are eventually tested out on large groups of people.

The psychologists who make the most frequent use of case studies are clinical psychologists and behavioral neuroscientists. That much being said, we suspect that theory development in other areas of psychology could be greatly enriched by the use of case studies. In fact, most researchers who would never consider conducting case studies themselves would probably have to agree that we have learned a great deal from case studies. In fact, one of the most famous and influential studies in the history of psychology was a case study that was documented more than 150 years ago. For both historical and theoretical reasons, the story behind this particular case study still fascinates many researchers. The story in question is the story of Phineas Gage.

Please Don't Try This at Home: The Case of Phineas Gage

Phineas Gage was a likable, energetic, and industrious foreman who had an excellent but hazardous job. In the summer of 1848, he was supervising a large group of workers who were laying down railroad tracks near the town of Cavendish, Vermont. Gage was a hands-on supervisor who personally performed some of the most dangerous tasks required to construct a railway. On the day that Gage became famous, he was blasting away some rocks when a freak accident cost him a substantial portion of his brain. During the accident, Gage was holding onto a tamping iron, a 43-inch-long, 13¼-pound iron rod about as thick as a broomstick. When Gage unwittingly tapped the tool into a large charge of explosives, the rod was suddenly transformed into a high-speed projectile. It blasted through Gage's face in a split second, entering below his left eye and exiting the top of his head. The bar landed over 100 feet away, and took with it a large chunk of Gage's brain. Phineas Gage's life wasn't over, but it was forever changed.

In addition to a lot of luck, Gage's youth and strength somehow allowed him to survive both this incredible accident and the infections that followed in its wake. Within two months, Gage was considered cured and was back on his feet again. He was now blind in his left eye, and he must have had a very nasty scar on the left side of his face. Otherwise, however, he seemed to have experienced very few physical repercussions from the accident. Gage could speak normally and had lost none of his senses or physical abilities. Even his higher-order mental capacities, such as his memory and attention, seemed to have been spared any meaningful damage. However, there was one pretty dramatic consequence of Gage's accident. As Damasio et. al. (1994) put it, "Gage was no longer Gage." Despite his normal-to-superior cognitive capacities, this previously likable and disciplined man had been turned into nothing short of a social and emotional disaster. Both his language and his behavior became abusive and socially irresponsible. He made such an art of cursing that people often tried to keep women and children away from him. He could no longer hold down a regular job, and he had little or no ability to manage his money or his emotional life. Gage appears to have been robbed completely of the ability to make important decisions, and he alienated almost everyone who had ever cared about him.

Gage's case is interesting for many reasons. For instance, after some of the scientific dust settled over the case, it eventually convinced most scientists that damage to specific brain areas is in fact associated with specific kinds of psychological deficits. Almost 150 years after Gage's life-altering accident, researchers were still analyzing his injury and publishing scientific papers on its apparent consequences. For example, Damasio et al. (1994) used state-of-the-art neuroimaging techniques (magnetic resonance imaging) to analyze Gage's skull and make inferences about the precise brain regions that were likely to have been damaged during his accident. These sophisticated studies suggested that it was primarily damage to the *prefrontal cortex* that was responsible for the social and emotional deficits that plagued Gage after his accident. Studies with modern-day Phineas Gages, people who have sustained other forms of injury to the prefrontal cortex, have confirmed the same predictable constellation of social and emotional problems. A sketch of Gage's skull, suggesting the approximate location of the damage to his brain, appears in Figure 5.1.

FIGURE 5.1   A sketch of Phineas Gage's skull

My Life as a Dog: The Case of Stephen D.

Sometimes case studies give us a glimpse into how different the world would be if our normal experiences were cranked up or down a couple of notches. By providing information about the extremes of human experience, such studies often provide some clues to the adaptive significance of ordinary experiences that most people take for granted. When such extremely unusual experiences can be attributed to some physical or chemical change in a person's brain or body, they may also yield important insights about the biological underpinnings of many ordinary human experiences (as was the case with studies of Phineas Gage). A great number of case studies of this variety have been documented by the neurologist Oliver Sacks. In Sacks's clinical experience, he has come across an enormous number of patients whose unusual experiences cast ordinary experience in a whole new light. One such patient was Stephen D.

Stephen D. was an otherwise ordinary medical student with an unfortunate addiction to amphetamines. One night he had an intensely vivid dream that he was a dog. When he awoke the next day, he found that pieces of his dream had become reality. The main sense in which this was true was olfactory. Stephen awoke with an appreciation of smells that practically hijacked his entire way of being. Quoting liberally from Stephen D. himself, Sacks (1985) provides a colorful description of Stephen's transformation:

> 'I had never had much of a nose for smells before, but now I distinguished each one instantly—and I found each one unique, evocative, a whole world.' He found he could distinguish all his friends—and patients—by smell: 'I went into the clinic, I sniffed like a dog, and in that sniff recognised, before seeing them, the twenty patients who were there. Each had his own olfactory physiognomy, a smell-face, far more vivid and evocative, more redolent, than any sight face.' He could smell their emotions—fear, contentment, sexuality—like a dog. He could recognise every street, every shop, by smell—he could find his way around New York, infallibly, by smell.

"Hey, isn't that ole' Rex Conley over there? Why I haven't smelled him in years!"

Stephen's incredible world of smell evaporated after about three weeks and never returned. Ultimately, Stephen's loss of his extreme sensitivity to smell was probably a blessing. While possessed of his incredible sense of smell, Stephen reported having great difficulty thinking and reasoning. The richness and potency of his immediate sensory experiences simply did not allow him the luxury of sitting back and analyzing the world in an intellectual fashion. Dogs would apparently make poor philosophers or rocket scientists. Sacks concludes that Stephen's experience was probably an amphetamine-induced dopaminergic excitation. In other words, a neurotransmitter that plays an important role in smell was artificially kicked into overdrive and briefly gave Stephen a dog's perspective on the world.

Really, Really Late Night with Peter Tripp

Whereas Phineas Gage and Stephen D. never asked to become objects of intense psychological scrutiny, a few people have become the objects of intensive scrutiny by choice. About 30 years ago Peter Tripp was a successful New York disc jockey who decided to stage a 200-hour "wakeathon." What would happen to a person who went without sleep for eight consecutive days? The first thing, as you might guess, is that the person would get very, very sleepy. If your study habits are as poor as the first author's were when he was in college, you may have some idea of what it was like for Tripp to stay awake for 40–50 hours. He not only experienced an enormous desire to sleep but also started to have difficulty thinking and performing routine activities. However, these problems paled by comparison with what followed after 100 hours of sleep deprivation. At this point, Tripp began to have active and intense hallucinations. Shoes grew cobwebs, clocks grew human faces, clothing turned into worms, and many things burst into flames in his presence. Three days later, after about 170 hours of wakefulness, Tripp was barely able to maintain contact with reality and often questioned who he was. By the end of the horrific experience, Tripp had become nothing short of a raging lunatic, and he had to be restrained by the scientists who were monitoring his excruciating personal experiment (see Suter & Lindgren, 1989, for a more detailed summary).

As Suter and Lindgren (1989) noted, Tripp's experiences seem to suggest that extreme levels of sleep deprivation are virtually intolerable. However, Suter and Lindgren also noted that at least one other high-profile case of prolonged sleeplessness yielded findings that were much less dramatic. In 1965, a student named Randy Gardner apparently stayed awake for a full 11 days as part of a high school science project. Gardner appeared on national television at the end of his 11-day ordeal, and he exhibited very few of the problems that had plagued Tripp. Anyone who observed a weary but essentially normal Gardner would have wondered if Tripp might have had a couple of loose screws well before his wakeathon. The consequences of extreme sleep deprivation are apparently less predictable than those of having an iron bar blasted through one's prefrontal cortex.

The Life and Very Hard Times of Sarah

Although Peter Tripp's self-inflicted nightmare seems bad, it pales by comparison with the extended nightmare that many abusive parents chronically inflict on their children. Understanding the consequences of exposure to physical and sexual abuse is an important social problem. The way victims respond to such abuse also provides psychologists with some important raw material for forming or evaluating theories of stress, coping, and the self-concept. For example, many self-concept researchers would like to know exactly how victims of chronic abuse deal with the trauma. If such victims are able to do so at all, how do they manage to develop a positive sense of self? In the book *Sarah: A Sexual Biography,* Abramson (1984) provides some clues to questions such as this by analyzing the life of a young woman he calls Sarah.

Sarah was the product of a broken home: an irresponsible-to-abusive biological father, an abusive-to-reprehensible stepfather, and a passive mother who did little or nothing to protect Sarah from the sexual assaults, physical abuse, and insults that she received at the hands of her stepfather. As a result of this abuse, Sarah became sexually active at a very early age, entered numerous abusive and neglectful relationships (sexual and otherwise), worked for a few months as a high-paid prostitute, and wandered all over the United States and Europe trying to figure out who she was and what she wanted out of life. (She could afford to travel, by the way, because some members of her family happened to be extremely wealthy.)

Although Sarah's candid reports of her life and times revealed dozens of seemingly self-destructive decisions, she ultimately appeared to resolve many of her conflicts. By the end of Sarah's story, she had adopted a very traditional, and seemingly healthy, lifestyle. She had a loving husband and had become a devoted mother and homemaker. According to Abramson, Sarah's transformation from victim to victor provides evidence of the presumably universal motives to feel good about ourselves and to make sense of our worlds. Of course, just as people differ enormously in their responses to sleep deprivation, they differ enormously in their responses to a childhood full of assault and battery. Many people (including Sarah's sister) respond to the kind of abuse that Sarah experienced by becoming severely depressed or even psychotic. Although Sarah's story provides us with a successful example of how a particular person was able to fulfill her basic needs for coherence and self-worth, it can provide us with only preliminary clues about how something as complex as the self-concept takes shape in adulthood.

The Man Who Forgot His Wife and His Hat

Although no case study can definitively answer basic research questions, case studies *can* sometimes be used to test specific research hypotheses. As an example of just this kind of case study, consider a study of memory and the self-concept presented by Tulving (1993). During the mid- to late 1980s, researchers interested in memory and the self-concept began to collect evidence suggesting that *trait information* (e.g., "I'm introverted," "I'm a great cook") and *autobiographical information* ("I went to the library instead of the party on Friday," "The curried chicken I cooked up last week was delicious") are represented separately in memory. This means, for instance, that once people have developed an abstract representation of their level of introversion or culinary prowess, they should be able to tell you exactly how introverted they are, or exactly what caliber of chef, without having to retrieve any specific memories of difficult conversations or delectable collations (see Klein, Sherman, & Loftus, 1996).

Klein et al. tested this hypothesis experimentally, and they came up with some good evidence for it. For instance, in some studies Klein et al. manipulated whether people had or had not recently retrieved biographical memories that were relevant to a specific trait. They then asked people to make a trait judgment about themselves on the same dimension that had just been activated during the autobiographical memory task. To the degree that people's trait judgments (i.e., people's self-views) are intimately connected to their autobiographical memories, doing the autobiographical memory task first should make it easier for people to judge the self-descriptiveness of the traits. However, to the degree that autobiographical information and trait information are functionally independent in memory, remembering a specific behavior first shouldn't really have any effect on the second judgment. Klein et al. found that unless people knew very little about themselves in a specific area (i.e., unless people hadn't yet formed a coherent self-view), autobiographical retrieval did little or nothing to facilitate trait judgments in a given area.

The strong form of Klein et al.'s hypothesis is pretty radical. It suggests that people who can't recall a single introverted or extroverted thing they have ever done might still be able to tell you precisely how introverted or extroverted they are. This should sound at least a little outlandish. How can people know that they are good cooks if they can't recall a single time when they ever did any cooking? And even if they do decide that they're great cooks, would anyone else be able to validate such claims by independently agreeing with the judgments? Tulving was intrigued enough with this version of Klein et al.'s hypothesis that he decided to put it to a direct test. Enter K. C.

K. C. was born to an upper-middle-class Canadian family in 1951. He was a good son and a pretty successful student. His life was relatively uneventful until at age 30 he was nearly killed in a high-speed motorcycle accident. Like Phineas Gage, K. C. experienced a severe head injury. Like Phineas Gage, K. C. was also a survivor. Nonetheless, after more than seven months of hospitalization and rehabilitation, it was clear that K. C. would no longer be able to care for himself. Despite having a normal to above-average IQ, K. C. was forced to live under the direct care of his parents. The reason for K. C.'s dependence on others is the fact that he developed one of the most profound cases of amnesia ever known. His amnesia was particularly pronounced when it came to *episodic* memory, that is, memory for autobiographical events. As Tulving (1993) put it, K. C. became "incapable of recollecting any events or happenings from any period of his life once they receded beyond the reach of short term memory . . . a time span measured in a few minutes." K. C. lives forever in the present.

Although K. C. couldn't tell you what he had for breakfast this morning or what he was doing ten minutes ago, he isn't completely devoid of abstract knowledge about his physical and social world. For instance, he has no difficulty using language, he can somehow remember the difference between stalagmites and stalactites, and he can identify the location of his family's summer cottage on a map. However, the most amazing thing about K. C. is that, despite having no memory of anything he has ever done, he can tell you exactly what kind of person he is. In other words, K. C. still has a self-concept. In fact, like most people without any kind of memory problem, K. C. appears to possess a self-concept that is (1) relatively stable over time and (2) highly consistent with what his mom thinks about him. To examine this second idea, Tulving asked both K. C. and K. C.'s mother to rate K. C.'s personality using the kind of standard trait terms that self-concept and personality researchers use all of the time. K. C. and his mother agreed very well about what traits K. C. did and did not possess. In fact, even when forced to make "either-or" judgments about trait terms that K. C. had originally found impossible to distinguish (e.g., when asked to report whether K. C. is more "artistic" or more "musical," or to report whether he is more "quarrelsome" or "selfish"), K. C. and his mother agreed on 73% of the traits. Finally, because K. C. underwent some dramatic personality changes after his accident, it was possible to see how much of K. C.'s self-concept reflected the "new" versus the "old" K. C. When K. C.'s mom was asked to make separate ratings of the old and the new K. C., only her ratings of the *new* K. C. agreed closely with K. C.'s self-ratings. In combination with the experimental findings of Klein et al., K. C.'s case study strongly suggests that people's abstract self-views are quite distinct from their episodic or autobiographical memories.

By the way, the fact that case studies often focus on highly unusual people does *not* mean that it's impossible to study such people using other research designs. It's simply that really unusual people are hard to gather up in large numbers (imagine trying to run an entire experiment using only participants named Jerry Derryberry, Jr.). Nonetheless, researchers who put their minds to it can sometimes overcome this practical barrier. As a case in point, Lieberman, Ochsner, Gilbert, and Schacter (2001) wanted to know whether amnesiacs (people like K. C.) would reduce their cognitive dissonance surrounding events that they had completely forgotten. (Recall that dissonance occurs when people become aware that they possess two contradictory beliefs.) Lieberman et al.'s research strongly suggests that amnesiacs reduce their cognitive dissonance in much the same way that people with intact memories do. This is interesting because it suggests that at least some aspects of the dissonance reduction process are probably unconscious. Even if amnesiacs consciously reduce their dissonance while they still remember what caused it, for example, it looks like dissonance reduction persists even when people can no longer remember the *source* of their dissonance. Ever known that you *really* liked something without having any idea why? That kind of thing must happen to K. C. all the time.

What Makes a Case Study Scientific?

As illustrated by the diversity of the case studies summarized here, case studies are almost always a rich source of ideas for theory building, and they can also be used to test the plausibility of existing theories. This raises the question of what makes a case study scientific. Laypeople describe the quirks and eccentricities of their friends all the time. Supermarket tabloids provide extensive accounts of the deeds and misdeeds of the rich and famous. Do such analyses qualify as case studies? Scientifically speaking, the answer is no. Unless the goal of these accounts is the development or refinement of *theories* of human behavior, they should not be considered case studies. An important difference between scientific and informal analyses is that scientific analyses of extraordinary events often demystify them by explaining them in terms of established scientific principles—principles that presumably apply to everyone, given the right circumstances. As a brief example of the difference between case studies and less reputable news stories, consider the fictional case of Mr. Zelick, a modern-day "Elephant Man." Instead of speculating, as a tabloid author might, that Mr. Zelick was bitten by a radioactive elephant and may have fathered the love-child of an aging soap opera vixen, a scientific analysis would be more likely to provide a deterministic, empirically grounded, parsimonious, and testable explanation for Mr. Zelick's strange behavior:

> Yes, it's fascinating that Mr. Z. thought he was an elephant, ate only peanuts and acacia bark, and (according to his medical records) gained over 80 pounds during the three weeks that he suffered from this delusion. Given Mr. Z.'s chronic problems with nasal congestion, it is even more impressive that he developed the ability to hold nearly a pint of water in his nose and showered naked in public by spraying the water on his back. Although his condition is highly unusual, careful radioimaging of Mr. Z.'s brain suggests a straightforward account for this transformation. . . . It now seems likely that *anyone* who suffers a lesion in this specific area of the ventromedial hypothalamus will develop the same syndrome of physical and behavioral symptoms.

Needless to say, only this second hypothetical account would qualify as a scientific case study. By providing detailed records of rare events, case studies try to explain unusual events by relying on established scientific principles.

To provide a complementary perspective on what makes a case study scientific, it is necessary to consider the attitude of the authors of case studies toward how audiences should respond to them. Abramson (1992) argued that the crucial determinant of whether a case study is scientific is the same standard Popper set for what makes *anything* scientific. We use case studies to develop and sometimes test theories that are open to *falsification*. As discussed in Chapters 1 and 2, scientific statements and analyses are those that are open to disconfirmation. Science is all about openness to criticism and revision. According to this definition, *any* approach to increasing knowledge, be it history, particle physics, or musicology, qualifies as scientific as long as its proponents are willing to change their minds in the face of information that raises doubts about their original positions. Although the specific facts behind case studies are rarely refuted, the *conclusions* drawn from these facts are often the subject of serious scientific debate. For instance, no one seriously questions whether Phineas Gage was the victim of an unusual and unfortunate accident. However, early interpretations of Gage's behavior raised some interesting, and testable, questions about the degree to which different mental and emotional functions were tied to specific brain areas (e.g., see Damasio, 1994). The story of Phineas Gage didn't teach behavioral neuroscientists everything there is to know about the prefrontal cortex, but it did inspire them to begin asking the right questions.

Of course, case studies, like all other approaches to research, have their drawbacks. For example, case studies do not always lend themselves well to the use of operational definitions or statistical analyses. In addition to these rational critiques, we suspect that the lack of respect for case studies sometimes observed in some scientific circles has at least a little to do with the legacy of Sigmund Freud. Because Freud was an ardent fan of case studies, and because he is much better known for his creativity and imagination than for the scientific rigor of his analyses, case studies may have gotten something of a bad rap among many researchers. This is unfortunate because, like more contemporary research designs, case studies can yield some extremely important information about the nature of human experience. (It is also unfortunate because Freud, though wrong about a lot of details, was pretty darned insightful.)

Describing the State of the World at Large: Single-Variable Research

Although case studies typically focus on a single person or group, they can be a rich source of information about people in general. Nonetheless, one of the biggest drawbacks of case studies is the fact that we do not usually know how well the results of a case study apply to people in general. The fact that most case studies focus on highly unusual people sometimes adds to this concern. This is a theoretical as well as a practical problem. Sometimes nothing could be more important than knowing exactly how well a specific observation describes people in general. Single-variable studies are designed with precisely this goal in mind: to describe some specific property of a large group of people. As examples, single-variable studies might address questions about the popularity of gun control below the Mason-Dixon Line, the prevalence of clinical depression in Canadian high schools, or the proportion of eligible voters in Barcelona who plan to vote for an incumbent in a mayoral election. If these questions seem largely descriptive rather than theoretical, it is because they are. Because single-variable research focuses on a single question or type of question, it cannot usually be used to answer questions about causes.

Although there are a couple of exceptions to this general rule, the exceptions exist only when there is a strong reason to expect a large group of people to do something other than what they turn out to do. For instance, if a representative survey of American women revealed that 89% of women were dissatisfied with their bodies, this would lend some support to the claims of many clinical and social psychologists that women are socialized to adopt unrealistic, and potentially unhealthy, body images. A search for the causes of this phenomenon would be the next logical step. For now, however, let's stick with the first step. What kind of single-variable studies are performed by researchers who simply want to provide accurate descriptions of the world?

Describing Populations

Two of the most important types of single-variable research are the census and the population survey. The goal of each of these techniques is to produce a clear picture of a specific group of people, that is, a population. Of course, there is one important goal behind a census that doesn't really apply to population surveys. This is the goal of simply counting the number of people in a population. To illustrate each of these two techniques, imagine that a researcher wanted to determine how satisfied students enrolled in Canadian colleges and universities are with their educations. How could this be done? One obvious way would be to identify *all* the students enrolled in Canadian institutes of higher learning in a given year. Every single student could then be given an inventory assessing educational satisfaction. Needless to say, this would not be very easy to do. First, it would be extremely difficult for anyone to obtain such an exhaustive list of students in the first place. Second, even if they could, it would be even more difficult, expensive, and time consuming to contact everyone on such a huge list. This example reveals the difficulty of conducting a census. A **census** is a body of data collected from every (or virtually every) member of a population of interest. In the Unites States, for example, government officials conduct a census every ten years. This is an enormous and expensive undertaking, and this is part of the reason that the U.S. government does it only every ten years.

Because it is incredibly difficult to conduct a true census, researchers more typically estimate the characteristics of populations by using **population surveys.** Ideally, a population survey uses *random selection* (also known as *random sampling*) to identify a subset of all the people in a population. Data from this subset are then used to make inferences about the attributes of the total population from which these people were sampled. Because there is good reason to expect a randomly selected sample to be similar to the people in the larger population, we can usually rest assured that the sample provides an accurate picture of the population. The main advantage of a population survey over a census, then, is that it is *much* easier to conduct a population survey than a census.

At first blush, it might not seem that much easier to conduct a population survey than a census. For example, to get a random sample of Canadian college students, we might need to begin with a very long list of students (all of them!). As we mentioned before, this is not really feasible. Survey researchers get around this problem by using **cluster sampling.** Researchers who use cluster sampling create a manageable list of all the possible *locations* in which they can find members of the population in which they are interested. In the present example, this would mean creating a list of every college and university in Canada. That'd be a pretty long list, but it'd seem like nothing compared with the original list of individual student names. The next step would be to select a reasonable number of schools from the larger list. Suppose we randomly sampled 20. Working from this list, we could contact the registrars of the 20 schools and ask each registrar for a list of each official student body. Then we might randomly sample 50 students from each school to produce a total sample of 1,000 students. Assuming we could persuade most of these students to respond to our population survey, this limited number of students would provide the information we used to make an estimate of the attitudes of the total population.

With the benefit of cluster sampling, we can make some very good guesses about the attitudes of extremely large groups of people. However, it should go without saying that the characteristics of our sample will rarely be *exactly* like the characteristics of our population. Let's say, for instance, that exactly 80% of the college students in our survey said they were satisfied with their educational experience. We know that a little bit of good or bad luck with sampling may have influenced this careful, scientific estimate. It's unlikely that *precisely* 80% of all Canadian college students are satisfied with their educations. But just how far off could our estimate be? Could the correct answer be 20%? Fortunately, there is an easy way to answer this kind of question. By performing a couple of simple calculations, we can estimate how much error is likely to exist in any specific set of population survey findings. The error that may have gone into our estimate is called **sampling error.** Sampling error reflects the likely discrepancy between the results one obtains in a specific sample and the results one would have been likely to have obtained from the entire population. This value is also called the *margin of error.* Using conventional probability values, a 3% margin of error in our study would mean that we could be 95% sure that the actual proportion of students in the population who are stisfied with their educations is 80%, *plus or minus* this 3% error value. To put it a little more simply, this would mean that the actual proportion of Canadian college students who are satisfied with their educations is very likely (95% likely) to be somewhere between 77% and 83%. That's not a perfect estimate, but most people would probably be pretty satisified with it.

One of the interesting things about carefully conducted surveys is that very precise estimates of population characteristics can usually be obtained using samples that are much, much smaller than the population of interest. As an example, assume there are roughly a million students enrolled in colleges and universities in Canada. If we used a careful sampling technique such as cluster sampling to estimate the percentage of students who are satisfied with their educations, we'd obtain a sampling error of about 3% in a sample of only 1,000 students. Granted, 1,000 people is a lot, but it's certainly a lot less than a million. We'd cut down our work (i.e., our data collection) by a factor of a *thousand* and get nearly the same gain in information. If we had some way of using true random sampling, by the way, our estimate would become even more accurate. And if we used cluster sampling to estimate the attitudes of an extremely large group of people (e.g., the residents of China, whose population is well over a *billion* people), we'd be about as accurate as in this estimate involving only a million people. (Incidentally, you may have heard that the residents of China are more modest than most people in the rest of the world, and we recently heard a good explanation for why this might be the case. In a country of over a billion people, even if you *truly are* one in a million, you must face the painful mathematical conclusion that there are at least a thousand other people exactly like you.) Because the population survey is such a powerful research tool, it has been used in a wide variety of applied domains in which researchers need to know about the characteristics of a particular population. Two of the more important applications of population surveys are in the areas of *epidemiological research* and research on *public opinion.*

Epidemiological Research

As it is defined by scientists in general, **epidemiology** refers to the scientific study of the causes of disease. But when *clinical psychologists* speak of **epidemiological research,** they are typically referring to descriptive studies that focus primarily on the prevalence of different psychological disorders within meaningful, well-defined populations. Clinical epidemiologists who wish to estimate the proportion of people in a population who suffer from specific disorders such as depression, schizophrenia, obsessive compulsive disorder, or substance abuse face a particularly daunting task. To attain the ideals of population surveys, they would like to randomly sample a population of interest and conduct clinical diagnostic interviews with each person in their sample to determine the precise percentage of people who meet strict clinical criteria for a disorder. An example of research that approximated this ideal state of affairs is the Epidemiological Catchment Area (ECA) project conducted in the United States in the early 1980s (see Regier & Burke, 1987). In the ECA studies, interviewers sampled large groups of people using a variation on the cluster sampling procedure just described. One variation from a strict cluster sampling procedure was that, to avoid undersampling mentally ill people who weren't living at home, the researchers supplemented their large community samples at each of five sampling sites with smaller samples of people who were institutionalized in or near each site (in places like hospitals, prisons, and nursing homes).[1]

Needless to say, this enormous study posed some enormous practical and technical problems. For example, how could the researchers minimize nonresponse bias (the bias that occurs when some people refuse to take part in a study)? This is particularly problematic in research of this sort because people who suffer from mental illness are precisely the kind of people who might be most unwilling or unable to respond to a request to be interviewed. When all was said and done, the researchers found creative ways around this and other practical problems, and thus they were able to come up with some good estimates of the frequency and distribution of different mental illnesses. For example, in comparison with previous estimates of illness rates that were estimated indirectly from the use of mental health services, the results of the ECA studies suggested that anxiety disorders, especially phobias, are much more common than researchers had previously believed. Although the ECA studies were largely descriptive, many of the findings that have emerged from these studies appear to have important practical and theoretical implications for the understanding and treatment of mental illness.

Although the ECA studies should primarily be considered single-variable studies, it is important to note that studies that focus exclusively on a single variable are extremely rare. After all, the only thing researchers need to do to turn a single-variable study into a multiple-variable study is to measure a second or third variable. Most of the theoretically interesting findings from the ECA studies involved two or more variables rather than one. As an example, the ECA studies revealed some interesting things about gender and the prevalence of different mental disorders. First of all, in contrast to the findings of many existing studies, the results of the ECA studies suggested that there is little or no *overall* difference between women and men in rates of mental illness. However, on an illness-by-illness basis, there were some notable differences. For instance, relative to men, women were about twice as likely to be diagnosed as clinically depressed but more than five times *less* likely to be diagnosed with either antisocial personality disorder or disorders involving the abuse of alcohol (Regier & Burke, 1987). Both clinical psychologists interested in the causes of mental illness and social psychologists interested in gender and socialization are likely to be intrigued by these differences.

Research on Public Opinion

Another important form of single-variable research that typically requires the use of population surveys is research on **public opinion**—research designed to determine the attitudes and preferences of specific populations, such as voters or consumers. As we are using the phrase here, public opinion research also includes **marketing research,** that is, research designed to assess consumers' attitudes about and preferences for different products and services. You may wonder why political groups, government agencies, and manufacturers are willing to go to so much effort to find out people's attitudes about everyday things like guns and butter. One simple answer is purely pragmatic. It makes good economic and political sense to know the attitudes of one's consumers and constituents before trying to sell them either a new brand of soft drink or a new brand of foreign policy.

For the sake of argument, however, assume that someone interested in public opinion decided to save some research money by estimating public opinion intuitively instead of using a population survey. Although the intuitive approach does have some obvious advantages when it comes to time and money, it also comes with certain serious risks. To get a feel for how the intuitive estimation of public opinion works, try your hand at estimating the results of a survey study conducted on a group of UCLA students (Pelham, 1998). Six of the 28 questions these students answered can be found in Table 5.1. For the purposes of this activity, let's generously assume that the sample was fairly representative of UCLA students.

To make this exercise work, take out a sheet of paper and record your best guess for each of the six questions. Please do so before you read any further! If your judgments follow some of the basic principles of cognitive and social psychology), we're betting that these judgments, while generally pretty accurate, reflect a couple of interesting biases. First of all, we're guessing that your judgments probably reflect some degree of conservatism, or what we might call *regression toward the midpoint*. As a potential example, compare your estimate for question 2 with the 87% of UCLA students who actually

TABLE 5.1 Estimating public opinion (from Pelham, 1998)

In a recent survey, what percentage of UCLA students reported that:

1. they typically carry $1.50 or more in coins in their pocket or purse? _____%
2. they have ever been camping? _____%
3. they had worn blue jeans at least once in the week prior to the survey? _____%
4. they preferred ice cream over apple pie as a dessert? _____%
5. they had ever visited Disneyland? _____%
6. they would choose a $40,000 Mercedes Benz over $30,000 in cash? _____%

Note: The proportions of students answering each question in the affirmative are as follows: (1) 47%, (2) 87%, (3) 94%, (4) 51%, (5) 99%, (6) 16%.

reported that they had been camping. We're guessing that your estimate was at least a little lower than this pretty high value.

Before we discuss your estimates for any of the other questions, let's take a slightly different approach to these questions. Imagine that you had been a participant in the original study. Stop to consider how *you* would have answered question 1. That is, do you typically carry more than $1.50 in coins in your pocket or purse? If you do, we're guessing that your estimate on this question was higher than the correct answer of about 47%. On the other hand, if you do *not* typically carry around large quantities of change, we're guessing that your estimate was lower than the correct answer of 47%. Why should your own coin-carrying habits have anything to do with your guess about how other people would answer this question? From a purely rational standpoint, they *shouldn't*. But the point is that they probably do. Research on the *false consensus effect* (Ross, Greene, & House, 1977) has shown that most people overestimate the proportion of other people whose attitudes and behaviors are similar to their own. Among the UCLA students who answered the questions sampled in Table 5.1, false consensus effects occurred on 25 of 28 questions. For example, people who reported carrying around a lot of change estimated that 75% of the students in their class also carried around a lot of change. Those who did *not* report being heavy change carriers disagreed. As a group, they estimated that only 25% of their fellow students typically carried around a lot of change.

The finding that human judges frequently fall prey to biases such as regression and false consensus suggests that people who need to make decisions based on public opinion could run into trouble if they rely too heavily on their intuitions. Because social judgments are both statistically regressive and egocentric, people who are members of small minorities may be especially prone to overestimate the proportion of people who share their opinions. In the UCLA study, for example, the 13% of the students who reported that they had never been camping estimated that 50% of their UCLA peers had never been camping. To translate this into practical terms, if you are a marketing researcher who wants to know about the size of the market for camping equipment, the last person you should ask (if you're only going to ask one person, that is) is someone who has never been camping. Similarly, if you want to know what most people think about a radical change in public education policies, you would probably do well to ignore the opinions of the three specific people who personally formulated the radical new policy.

Incidentally, problems such as egocentric biases and regression toward the midpoint in judgment are made worse by the fact that people who make erroneous judgments often place undue confidence in these judgments (see Fischhoff, 1982). Because of this tendency toward overconfidence, novice marketers and politicians might often place undue confidence in their intuitions regarding other people's attitudes and opinions and thus forgo conducting systematic surveys to gather important descriptive data about the people they wish to influence or understand. If you really want to know what a particular population thinks about something, you should locate a random sample that is drawn from this population and ask them what they think. You could then use the responses you get from this small sample to obtain fairly accurate estimates of the views of the larger population.

Limitations and Drawbacks of Population Surveys

Population surveys are a highly cost-effective way to learn a lot about a population of interest. For this reason, they are usually much better than surveying everyone (taking a census of people's attitudes) or sampling no one (performing an intuitive assessment of people's attitudes). This being said, there are some serious limitations to the use of population surveys. First and foremost, population survey research requires a very careful consideration of a wide variety of potentially complex sampling issues. Although we do not wish to overstate this problem, most people who wish to conduct population surveys will want to consult a trained expert in survey research. As the popular commercial warning says, "Please don't try this at home." Consider, for instance, the numerous sampling issues researchers must have had to address in the Epidemiological Catchment Area studies. In addition to developing an effective sampling scheme and dealing with nonresponse bias, the directors of this nationwide project had to train a great number of interviewers to conduct valid and reliable clinical interviews. Furthermore, when a potential respondent did not speak English, this raised a whole host of issues regarding translations and minority representation. Although population surveys are much easier and cheaper than censuses, the complex problems that must be solved in population surveys sometimes makes these surveys more expensive and labor intensive than one might think.

Over the past decade or so, a growing problem for researchers who conduct almost all kinds of population surveys is that the American public has become increasingly skeptical of unsolicited surveys, regardless of their content. Ironically, then, the growing popularity of survey research, especially the popularity of telephone and mail surveys, has made it increasingly difficult to conduct this kind of research (because many people have grown weary of responding to surveys). Telemarketers and salespeople who disguise their pitches as research surveys further compound this important problem. In a world where people are bombarded with offers to purchase time-shares in Puerto Vallarta or change their long distance telephone company, well-intentioned researchers who wish to assess people's political attitudes or find out how Americans would most like to see health care reformed are facing an uphill battle that seems to grow a little steeper every year.

Finally, the fact that population surveys so effectively achieve their goal of being highly representative creates an additional problem for population survey researchers. Unlike experimenters who study college students, epidemiologists, market researchers, and public opinion pollsters have to be prepared to deal with a very wide range of research participants. This means that survey and interview questions have to be written so that people of varying ages, educational levels, language skills, and cultural backgrounds can readily understand all the questions. Given this constraint, researchers usually keep their population surveys short and to the point. Doing so necessarily limits the total amount of information researchers can gather from each individual participant. A closely related problem has to do with the diversity of the population survey *research setting* (most often, participants' homes). Unlike participants who have settled into the quiet confines of the laboratory, participants who pick up the phone and agree to respond to a public opinion poll may continue to watch *Wheel of Fortune,* pedal on an exercise bike, or both, while responding to the survey. This loss of control relative to the laboratory is not always this extreme, but it is an inherent part of many population surveys. The diversity of survey respondents and the noisy nature of many survey settings create problems for survey researchers that laboratory researchers rarely have to face.

Single-Variable Convenience Samples

Before we move on from single-variable to multiple-variable research, we should point out that there are a couple of forms of single-variable research in which researchers justifiably show very little concern for whether the people they sample are representative of some larger group of people. Sometimes, it is possible for a clever researcher to create a demonstration of human judgment or behavior that is so interesting, or disturbing, that it is surprising to see it occur in *any* sample. If the responses of normal, healthy people from any walk of life challenge researchers' well-established assumptions about human nature, these findings are likely to generate quite a bit of scientific interest. For instance, as you may recall, Milgram's (1963) original obedience study caused quite a stir even though he did not make use of random sampling (and did not include any kind of explicit control group). By showing that 65% of normal adults were willing to deliver potentially life-threatening shocks to a stranger merely because an authority figure told them to do so, Milgram documented a behavior so disturbing and surprising that he did not need a randomly sampled experimental and control group.

More recently, a great deal of research on **judgment and decision making** has challenged a different but equally cherished assumption about human nature. One spin on the Milgram obedience studies is that Milgram showed that human beings are not quite as *principled* as we might hope. There is also a great deal of single-variable research in judgment and decision making showing that human beings are not quite as good at *using principles* as we might hope. Moreover, much of this research is also based on convenience samples (usually college students). Because it is usually possible to specify exactly how a rational, logical decision maker would make certain kinds of judgments, and because systematic errors in people's judgments often reveal something about the decision rules people use to arrive at these judgments, it is often useful simply to know how good people are at making basic cognitive or social judgments. In other words, it is often highly informative to know the proportion of people who make a specific judgment or decision correctly. As an example, consider the following story about Linda.

> Linda is 31 years old, single, outspoken, and very bright. As a college student, she majored in philosophy and was deeply concerned with issues of discrimination and social justice. She also participated actively in antinuclear demonstrations. Please choose the most likely alternative:
>
> 1. Linda is a bank teller.
> 2. Linda is a bank teller and is active in the feminist movement.

When Tversky and Kahneman (1983) gave this problem to a large group of college students, they found that 85% of their participants indicated that the second option was more likely than the first. Presumably, almost everyone who reads the brief vignette about Linda develops an image of her that is much more consistent with the second description. Linda doesn't sound much like a bank teller at all, but most people seem to conclude that she's more likely to be a *feminist* bank teller than she is to be a bank teller. This highly intuitive conclusion turns out to be highly illogical. One of the fundamental laws of probability theory is the idea that a conjunctive or compound event (both A and B) can never be more likely than one of its component parts (either A alone or B alone). In the case of Linda, it *cannot* be the case that Linda is more likely to be a feminist bank teller than she is to be a bank teller. The reason this cannot be true is that the category of bank teller includes *all* bank tellers, both feminist and nonfeminist alike. When a person violates this basic principle of probability theory by judging a compound event to be more likely than one of its component events, that person has committed what Tversky and Kahneman call the *conjunction fallacy*.

Many areas of research on judgment and decision making make whole or partial use of single-variable designs. Likewise, most of the same studies use convenience samples (college students) rather than random samples to make their points. Knowing that 85% of people will readily violate a basic principle of logic is inherently informative. This is true in much the same way that it is inherently informative to know that about 65% of people will sometimes violate a basic principle of social responsibility (e.g., by delivering intense shocks to a hapless victim). Of course, just as epidemiologists, pollsters, and marketing researchers often build on their single-variable population surveys by trying to identify the predictors of depression or preferences for Alf Landon, researchers interested in judgment and decision making often try to identify when people are more or less likely to make suboptimal judgments (see Fischhoff, 1982; Gilbert, 1989; Pelham & Neter, 1995; Tetlock, 1985). However, a common starting point for studies looking at when and why people stray from ideal standards of judgment is first to conduct single-variable studies that simply document that people often go astray.

Correlational Methods: Multiple-Variable Research

Once researchers have developed a descriptive account of the variables in which they are interested, they typically become interested in understanding the causes of these variables. That is, they become interested in identifying the variables that are responsible for their observations. Of course, this represents a quest for internal validity, and no method surpasses exerimental methods for their potential to identify causes. For reasons we will describe in detail later in this book, however, many important research topics do not lend themselves well to experimentation. When this is the case, researchers sometimes test their theories and hypotheses about people by making use of what we call **correlational methods.**

The basic idea behind correlational research is to generate a fixed set of observations about a group of people and to test hypotheses about the associations between different variables. Do men and women differ in their attitudes about capital punishment? Are the typical residents of China, Japan, or India really more modest than the typical residents of the United States? Do cities with warmer climates have higher crime rates? Although it is not usually all that difficult to answer these interesting questions, it is usually extremely difficult to know what theoretical conclusions we can draw from them. Recall that theories are causal satements about the relations between two or more variables. This means that correlational research can be used in theory testing only to the degree that this research allows us to draw some reasonable conclusions about causality.

For example, suppose one wanted to argue that depression influences people's specific self-views. That is, suppose a resarcher wanted to argue that when people become depressed, they start to see the world through the filter of their unhappiness and so they rate themselves more negatively than they ordinarily would (see Bargh & Tota, 1988; Pelham, 1991b). If a researcher measured depression by means of a careful clinical interview and then assessed the favorability of people's specific self-views using a pencil-and-paper survey (e.g., "I am attractive," "I am a good leader"), correlational analyses could be carried out to document that people who are more depressed do in fact possess more negative self-views. However, even if this connection between depression and self-evaluation could be established, a critic could make at least two good arguments against the idea that depression *causes* people to view themselves negatively. First, there could be a *third variable* that is actually responsible for the observed association between depression and self-evaluation. Second, the problem of *reverse causality* could be at work. Let's use this example as an opportunity to discuss each of these problems in detail.

First of all, the critic could argue that some third variable is actually responsible for the association between depression and people's specific self-views. For instance, it could be that *anxiety or low self-esteem* (which are both strongly correlated with depression; see, for example, Dobson, 1985) represents the real reason why depressed people tend to view themselves negatively. To be a little more specific, the critic might argue that anxiety causes people to feel depressed and also causes people to develop negative views of their attractiveness or leadership abilities. To the degree that this is true, a successful intervention designed to lower depression will *not* cause people to develop more favorable self-views (unless the intervention also happens to lead to decreases in anxiety).

The problem discussed here is the familiar problem of *confounds*. As suggested in Chapter 4, nonexperimental approaches to research are almost always susceptible to confounds, and so the careful researcher must take steps to consider the plausibility of confounds (i.e., third variable explanations) before making any claims about causality. There appear to be three distinct kinds of confounds that can cloud the interpretation of almost any kind of research finding. Two of these kinds of confounds represent threats to internal validity. They raise serious questions about causality. The third kind of confound is more of a threat to construct validity, and it can thus lead a researcher to draw faulty inferences about the precise nature of a causal relation, even if a true causal relation definitely exists in a set of data.

Person Confounds

The first confound is the classic case. It's what we will call a **person confound.** This occurs when a variable (such as depression) seems to cause something because people who are high or low on this variable also happen to be high or low on some *individual difference* variable (i.e., some personality variable or demographic characteristic) that is associated with the outcome variable of interest. This sort of confound was just illustrated. People who are depressed usually tend to suffer from a lot of anxiety as well. As a result, a finding that seems to show that depression influences people's self-views may actually reflect the influence of anxiety on people's self-views. The only way to address this ambiguity with correlational data is to measure the confounding variable of interest and make some kind of statistical adjustment. (In case you are wondering how this statistical adjustment works, you will have the opportunity to see it at work firsthand in the methodology exercise on partial correlation at the end of this chapter.) For example, in an effort to determine whether depression or anxiety is causing changes in self-views, one could pit these two competing predictors against one another in a regression analysis designed to predict self-views. If one found that depression was associated with people's self-views only because it *happened to be correlated* with anxiety, the original correlation would not provide any support for our original theory of depression.

Environmental Confounds

A second important kind of confound is the **environmental confound.** Environmental confounds are very much like person confounds except that they refer to environmental (i.e., situational) rather than personological nuisance variables. As an example, stressful life events might cause people to become more depressed while simultaneously lowering people's self-views. If this happens, it might appear that depression is influencing self-views when it is not. Life events are influencing depression, and the *same* life events are also influencing self-views. Environmental confounds and person confounds are obviously similar in that they both represent clear threats to the internal validity of a research finding. They are obviously different in that they refer to events that exist outside versus inside the person. In the case of both person confounds and environmental confounds, a third variable clouds the picture of whether one variable truly causes another. Does depression really cause people to adopt negative self-views, or is it the anxiety that so often goes hand in hand with depression? Or is it the negative life events that often cause depression in the first place? It is important to realize that in each of these instances, there was a meaningful association between depression and the person confound or environmental confound that was creating interpretational problems. Like height and weight, depression and anxiety really are correlated. The same is true for depression and negative life events.

Operational Confounds

In contrast to both person confounds and environmental confouds, there is a third kind of confound in which a researcher inadvertently and unknowingly *creates* a correlation between two measures that, in reality, are *not* correlated. This produces an **operational confound.** Operational confounds are closely tied to the notion of *operational definitions.* They occur when a measure designed to assess a specific construct such as depression, memory, or foot size inadvertently measures *something else* as well. Operational confounds are easiest to distinguish from person or environmental confounds when this something else that is inadvertently measured (1) *has nothing to do* with the predictor variable that the researcher really wished to measure but (2) has a lot to do with whatever outcome the researcher wished to predict.

As an example, suppose that Dr. Young decided to develop a pencil and paper measure of depression. Furthermore, for some very good reasons Dr. Young wanted to measure depression without really tipping participants off to what he was measuring. Thus, he might want to steer away from normally useful survey items such as "I feel so miserable that I can't stand it," or "I have recently contemplated suicide." Instead, he might decide to focus disproportionately on the physical or somatic symptoms of depression. The typical items in his survey might thus include "I've had trouble concentrating lately," "I have trouble getting out of bed in the morning," "I've lost some of my interest in food," and "I don't sleep as well as I used to." Nice job. This measure might allow Dr. Young to assess depression without really cluing people in to what he was measuring. Furthermore, imagine that Dr. Young randomly sampled 500 Americans and found that those with higher scores on his measure reported having more negative beliefs about themselves. This included people's assessments of their physical and cognitive skills as well as their assessments of their level of physical attractiveness. People scoring high on his new measure were even more likely to report, for example, that "My life feels like it is out of my control." Can Dr. Young conclude that depression causes people to view themselves and their social worlds more negatively than usual? Unfortunately not. Despite all the sophisticated advice that you offered Dr. Young when he hired you as a high-paid methodological consultant, Dr. Young unintentionally allowed a construct that has nothing to do with depression to sneak into his measure.

This construct is called age. If you look back over the questions in Dr. Young's measure, you can see that senior citizens, especially those whose bodies have begun to give out on them a little, would probably be more likely than their younger counterparts to endorse the questions in Dr. Young's depression inventory. Dr. Young had *hoped* that people who said they had trouble getting out of bed would always be reporting a common symptom of depression. Instead, however, the older people in his sample might simply be reporting that it was physically hard to get out of bed in the morning! To add insult to injury, it would come as no surprise to learn that most old people do not feel quite as able-bodied or attractive as they did back when Grover Cleveland was president. Furthermore, if the ravages of time have confined some older people to wheelchairs or extended-care facilities, you can see why they might feel that they no longer have complete control over their lives. In short, an operational confound might be at work. Age is not really correlated with depression, but age seeped into Dr. Young's *measure* of depression, and age is also correlated with Dr. Young's outcome measure (specific self-evaluations of ability, attractiveness, and control).

Notice that this criticism of Dr. Young's research is based on the assumption that *something* about his new measure really does *cause* people to report negative self-views. In this specific case, it just happens to be something that is a lot less interesting than depression. In this particular case, what he measured does cause negative self-views. He just didn't measure exactly what he thought he was measuring. There are several ways to fix an operational confound. First, you can discard or revise your measure to remove the confound that you unknowingly built into it. In other words, you can go back to the drawing board. A second approach is to do the same thing you would have done if you were worried about a person confound or an environmental confound. You could *measure* the construct that you think is really accounting for the action (in this case, age) and perform statistical tests that are designed to tell you which of two competing variables is really responsible for an outcome. Finally, a third approach is probably a little more intuitive. Run a replication study in which you focus exclusively on participants who are roughly the same age. For instance, if Dr. Young had conducted his study on students enrolled in an introductory psychology course, he would have little to worry about when it came to this specific operational confound (because there would probably be few, if any, senior citizens in this sample). As you can see, just as there are multiple ways to get into trouble in correlational research, there are usually multiple ways to try to get out of it.

A Reminder About Reverse Causality

The three confounds we reviewed here all have the unfortunate effect of causing the researcher to draw faulty inferences about the meaning of a connection between two or more variables. As serious as all these confounds are, they are only part of the story. As you may recall, researchers who rely on correlational methods must worry not only about confounds or third variables. In addition, they have to be concerned about *reverse causality*. In our running example involving depression and negative self-views, a researcher who has controlled for every conceivable person, environmental, and operational confound might be tempted to conclude that depression does indeed cause people to evaluate themselves negatively. However, it is always possible that negative self-evaluations lead to depression rather than the reverse. Believing that one is incompetent might cause a person to become depressed.

To address the problem of reverse causality, researchers often follow people over time and make repeated assessments of the variables in which they are interested. **Longitudinal,** or **prospective, designs** such as this can go a long way toward suggesting causal connections between variables. (Recall that one of John Stuart Mills's time-honored requirements for establishing causality is showing that changes in one variable precede changes in the other.) However, longitudinal analyses are not a foolproof guarantee against reverse causality. Imagine that we conducted a longitudinal study in which we measured children's school performance at ages 8, 9, and 10. Furthermore, imagine that increases in children's school performance during the first year of the study predicted increases in parents' income during the second year of the study. It would be pretty wacky to conclude that children's grades cause parents' incomes. A more likely interpretation of the findings is that as parents' incomes increase over the long haul (beginning when children are born, perhaps), children do better in school (e.g., because of improvements in children's health, diet, or access to computers in the home). To definitively establish that changes in one variable lead to changes in another, it is usually necessary to conduct an experiment.

As this review reveals, correlational research is always susceptible to the third variable problem (i.e., confounds) as well as the bidirectionality problem, both of which are summarized in Figure 5.2. This might make you wonder why researchers interested in testing theories would ever bother to conduct correlational research. There are many answers to this question, but for now we will focus on only two. First, for reasons that we will discuss in much more detail in Chapter 7, there are many things that simply cannot be studied ethically or efficiently in the laboratory. Second, precisely because researchers know about the threats imposed by confounds and reverse causality, they try to design correlational studies in ways that will help minimize these threats. Although correlations are rarely taken as proof for a specific causal argument, carefully conducted correlational studies that rule out a large number of confounds and deal honestly with questions regarding reverse causality can do a great deal to advance our knowledge. Another way to put this is that the gain in external validity that is often provided in correlational studies sometimes compensates for any losses in internal validity. Finally, as you are about to learn, there are a wide variety of correlational research methods, and some of these methods are relatively immune to some specific types of confounds. Others are sometimes immune to reverse causality. Thus, by learning to make use of multiple research methods, researchers can sometimes maximize both

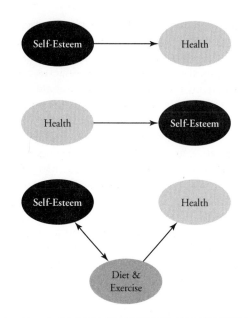

FIGURE 5.2 *The bidirectionality problem and the third variable problem: If self-esteem is positively correlated with physical health, (1) self-esteem may directly contribute to good health, (2) good health may directly contribute to self-esteem, or (3) a third variable (such as good health habits) may be the true cause of good health—and may happen to be correlated with self-esteem.*

the internal and external validity of their correlational research. With this idea in mind, let's take a look at three different examples of correlational research methods, each of which has something unique to offer us. We begin with a discussion of archival studies, move on to observational studies, and conclude with a discussion of field studies.

Archival Research

When a topic is ethically sensitive, when a variable is difficult or impossible to manipulate, or when a researcher is especially motivated to conduct a study that is high in external validity, researchers may make use of archival research designs. **Archival research** refers to research in which investigators examine naturally existing public records to test a theory or hypothesis. There is almost no limit to the kinds of data sources that can be used in archival studies. To provide only a few examples, police reports, records of jury decisions, hospital records, weather reports, outcomes of sporting events, marriage licenses, speeches made by politicians, divorce records, newspaper circulation rates, census data, and telephone directories have all provided the database for archival research designs.

An excellent example of an archival research design is provided by Peterson and Seligman (1987), who were interested in self-evaluation and physical well-being. These researchers collected old newspaper records of interviews conducted with famous baseball players who had all been inducted into the Baseball Hall of Fame. The researchers were particularly interested in how the players explained positive and negative things that happened to them on the baseball diamond. More specifically, the researchers wanted to know if there are any long-term consequences of making *self-serving* or *self-protective* attributions for one's successes and failures in life (e.g., "I won the big game today because nobody could hit my new curveball," "I lost the big game today because I got a lot of bad calls on my new curveball"). To see if egoistic attributions had positive consequences, they got a group of blind judges to rate all their interviews for the degree to which the players made self-serving and self-protective attributions for their athletic performances. They then correlated these ratings with a very simple and important health outcome: how long the players lived. For these men, making self-serving attributions appeared to have lifesaving consequences. The players who made more self-enhancing and self-protective attributions *lived* noticeably longer than players who were less self-serving!

Phillips's research on emulative suicide ("copycat suicide") also provides an excellent example of archival research. Phillips and colleagues made use of public records of suicides along with information about the media coverage received by different suicides. In several studies of this type, Phillips documented national or statewide increases in suicide rates following highly publicized suicides. He also found that when more television networks covered a particular suicide, subsequent increases in suicide rates were greater than when a suicide was less well publicized. These findings were especially prevalent for teenagers, who are known to be more suggestible than adults. More troubling still, Phillips found that media discussions of suicide in the form of public-service programs had much the same effect as the sometimes reckless suicide stories that appear in the news (e.g., see Phillips & Carstensen, 1986).

A third example of archival research is relevant to many different areas of psychology. To be more specific, researchers interested in attitudes, person perception, prejudice, stereotyping, and political psychology have conducted numerous archival studies of ethnicity and capital punishment. Quite a few large-scale studies, mostly conducted in the southeastern United States, have examined the rates at which prosecuting attorneys ask for the death penalty for Black versus White defendants who are being tried for murder. For example, Paternoster (1983) examined the decisions of prosecuting attorneys to request the death penalty in 1,805 South Carolina homicide cases. Because records of criminal proceedings provide quite a bit of information about the characteristics of alleged murderers and their victims, it is possible to relate different characteristics of defendants and victims to the harshness of various penalties meted out by the legal system. Paternoster's analysis suggested that when it comes to requests for the death penalty, justice is far from blind. When a Black defendant had allegedly murdered a White as opposed to a Black victim, prosecutors were *40 times* more likely to request the death penalty when presenting the case to the court. Moreover, research that has controlled for variables that could conceivably be confounded with ethnicity (e.g., socioeconomic differences between Black versus White defenders, severity of the crime

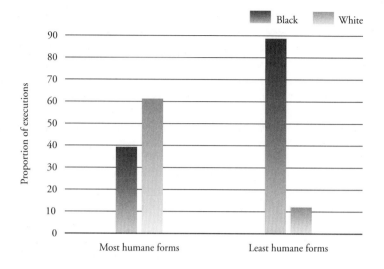

FIGURE 5.3 Ethnicity of person executed and brutality of capital punishment, 1608–1991 (from Sidanius & Pratto, 2000)

committed, number of victims) has found that ethnicity is still strongly associated with requests for capital punishment when these confounds are statistically controlled.

Other archival studies of this type have revealed that Black defendants are also more likely to *receive* the death penalty once convicted. In fact, archival studies that have adopted a historical perspective on capital punishment have revealed that there are even differences in the *kind* of capital punishment that has been meted out to White versus Black offenders. In particular, Sidanius and Pratto (2000) analyzed records of more than 7,000 executions performed in the United States over a 383-year period (between 1608 and 1991). They broke the executions down into three categories based on how gruesome or brutal the executions were. At one end of this category, they included relatively humane (i.e., less gruesome) forms of execution (namely, asphyxiation in the gas chamber, being shot, or receiving a lethal injection). At the other extreme, they included only the most brutal or gruesome forms ("pressing, breaking on the wheel, burning, hanging in chains, bludgeoning, and gibbeting"). Their findings were simple—and sobering. Among those executed using relatively humane methods, 61% were White and 39% were Black. In contrast, among those executed using the most heinous methods, only 11.6% were White and 88.4% were Black. A summary of these findings appears in Figure 5.3.

The great advantage of archival research is its potential for high levels of external validity. Although it is obviously possible to conduct a highly contrived archival study that has little to do with real-world behavior, studies such as those reviewed here generally get high marks for external validity. If you were interested in studying suicide, and you wanted to find a dependent measure that translated well into real suicides, you would be hard-pressed to find a better measure than records of real suicides. Archival research can also maximize both external and construct validity by eliminating any worries about whether a set of research findings occurred because the people being studied were trying to manage a positive impression with an experimenter (this is a pretty common concern in certain kinds of lab experiments). For instance, unlike laboratory participants who are asked to rate the aggressiveness of a Black or White target person, prosecutors who have to decide whether to request the death penalty for a particular Black or White defendant probably do not stop to consider whether their request will someday be analyzed by a social scientist.

Although external validity is often high in archival research, researchers usually have to work very hard to maximize the internal validity of such research. For instance, if you wanted to be absolutely positive that fluctuations in national suicide rates were caused by fluctuations in media coverage of suicides, you would want to consider a wide range of potential confounds, such as a slumping economy, disturbing historical events, or the possibility that grief over the death of a well-loved celebrity rather than copycat suicide was responsible for Phillips's findings. For these reasons, Phillips examined a very wide range of third variables that could have spuriously produced his findings. To provide only one example, he showed that media attention to the suicides of people who were almost universally disliked (e.g., a leader of the KKK) produced increases in suicide rates. In contrast, media attention to the nonsuicidal deaths of extremely beloved people (e.g., President Kennedy) did not yield increases in suicide rates. Grief apparently has little to do with Phillips's findings.

Of course, ruling out confounds does little or nothing to address the important issue of reverse causality, and Phillips was aware of this problem. In the case of his findings regarding suicide, it is conceivable that increases in suicide rates increase the amount of ink that newspapers decide to devote to stories of suicides. To address this concern, Phillips carried out painstaking analyses using many data sets, and he showed time and again that the news stories regarding suicides always *preceded* increases in suicide rates. Fortunately, some archival researchers do not have to worry about reverse causality the way Phillips did. That is, in some archival research reverse causality simply is not a serious worry. Because some events simply cannot cause others, archival researchers can sometimes capitalize on this fact. It seems pretty unlikely, for instance, that being executed in a cruel versus a more humane way ever changes a person's ethnicity. Along similar lines, consider the finding that people are more likely to commit aggressive crimes on days when it is particularly hot (Anderson, 1987; 1989). As we noted in Chapter 3, heat may be confounded with other sources of aggressive behavior. However, it is extremely unlikely that aggressive behavior is a cause of warm temperatures. Although archival research must always be interpreted with some degree of caution, there comes a point at which the most parsimonious account for a carefully studied real-world phenomenon is the idea that one variable caused another.

Despite the enormous advantages that archival research can have when it comes to external validity, one potentially frustrating aspect of archival research is the fact that people who generate public records of real-world events often do so for reasons that have nothing to do with research. Psychologists might fantasize about a world in which people who create public records are always thinking first and foremost about research opportunities ("OK, Jimmy, I know you're new at this, but I don't want you writing any more stories about aggressive crimes that don't include official records of temperatures on the day of the crime!"). However, the reality is that people who create public records have their own goals and agendas. When observations can't be carefully planned in advance, researchers have little choice but to wait around (or look around) for observations that happen to be relevant to the research question in which they are interested. By doing this, they relinquish some control over the quality of their data. In the case of emulative suicide, for instance, it could be a problem if coroners are sometimes reluctant to *label* probable suicides as suicides. After all, coroners are people, and people might stretch the truth around the edges a little to avoid stigmatizing a deceased person and thus causing increased suffering for the person's family. If this happens sometimes, the differences in suicide rates following media exposure might have *nothing* to do with actual suicide rates! Instead, they might have more to do with what coroners are willing to label a suicide. This would happen, by the way, if high-profile stories about suicides cause coroners to feel more comfortable reporting the truth when they detect a suicide. Phillips examined this alternative hypothesis in a very simple and compelling way. In follow-up studies, he showed that high-profile suicides led to increases in "hidden suicides." For instance, there are significant increases in single-auto accidents, in which people seemed to lose control of their car for no reason and die, following suicide stories. Moreover, these automobile accidents happen more often to people who more strongly resemble the person who committed suicide. Thus, young people are disproportionately more likely to crash their cars when a young rather than an old person has committed suicide. Phillips suggested that these car accidents reflect the known tendency for people to commit suicide in private, by manufacturing auto accidents that will cause their untimely death.

In case you're still not convinced, Phillips also showed that the *kind* of motor vehicle accidents that increase following well-publicized suicides are the kind that are more likely to reflect suicides. When a person is trying to commit suicide by crashing his or her vehicle (e.g., by pressing the gas rather than the brake when heading toward an embankment), the person should be more likely to die quickly following the crash. Sure enough, Phillips showed that accidents involving rapid deaths increased at a higher rate following suicides than did accidents involving slow deaths. Still not convinced? Phillips also tackled the coroner coding problem directly rather than indirectly. If coroners change their coding tactics after front-page suicides, rates of all other kinds of deaths should go down to about the same degree that rates of suicides go up after front-page suicides. They don't. Suicide rates go up while deaths from all other causes remain constant. All this being said, Phillips's research shows just how far archival researchers often must go in order to address potential biases in their data sets. Another way around this problem is to avoid analyzing data that someone else has collected. In this spirit, some researchers tackle their questions head-on by collecting their own data.

Observational Research

Research in which investigators record the real behavior of people in their natural environments is often referred to as **observational research.** Notice that observational research is very similar to archival research. The behaviors that researchers examine in observational research are always real, and the researchers do not manipulate anything. The difference between observational and archival research is the fact that, in observational research, the people making the observations are the researchers themselves. This not only gives researchers some control over exactly *what* they observe but also gives them some control over *how* they observe it. From a methodological perspective, the best kind of observational research is usually **unobtrusive,** meaning (1) that researchers do not interfere in any way with people's natural behavior and (2) that people do not realize that they are being studied. An excellent example of unobtrusive observational research was conducted by Colett and Marsh (1974). Colett and Marsh were interested in gender differences in mundane social behavior. To examine the specific gender differences in which they were interested, they placed a video recorder on the seventh floor of a building overlooking a busy walkway. However, they were less interested in walking than they were in squeezing. Specifically, they focused their observations on instances in which people had to squeeze past one another to get where they were going. Under these conditions, they found that 75% of the men in their study faced their fellow pedestrians as they squeezed by them. In contrast, only 17% of the women faced others as they squeezed by them.[2]

Of course, Colett and Marsh couldn't say exactly *why* men and women use different techniques to slip past strangers. One possible theory is that men are inherently more sociable than women. As a case in point, the two of us would like to confess that we often get together over coffee or tea and do nothing but sit around and talk for hours with our closest male friends. In contrast, most of the women we know get together with other women only when they want to play some kind of competitive sport or watch TV. Our casual observations of women under such circumstances have also revealed that many women who get together under such conditions hardly talk to one another at all—at least not until they've had a few beers to help break the awkwardness. Colett and Marsh realized that there could be more than one way to explain their findings, and so they took a second look at their observations. They found that in the rare instances in which women *did* slip past other people in a facing direction, they often engaged in a very telling behavior: They covered their breasts by folding their arms across their chests. So much for our theory!

Another example of an unobtrusive observational study also involves getting from one place to another, and it also involves gender. However, this study has to do with zipping through instead of squeezing past. McKelvie and Schamer (1988) made unobtrusive observations of whether drivers obeyed

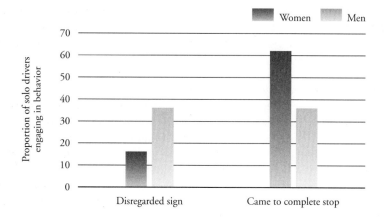

FIGURE 5.4 *Gender behavior at stop signs at night (from McElvie & Schamer, 1988)*

posted stop signs. Specifically, they made 600 unobtrusive observations at stop signs, coding for whether people (1) stopped completely, (2) performed a "slow stop," or (3) failed to stop at all. They also coded for driver gender and whether each driver was carrying any passengers. Finally, they made observations both during the day and at night to determine whether people's behavior might differ as a function of whether it was dark. It did. When a driver was alone in the car and there was no oncoming traffic, rates of both *complete* stops and *non*stops increased at night. That is, at night there were increases in both the number of people who obeyed the letter of the law and the number of people who disregarded the law completely. However, these transformations at night depended very much on gender. As summarized in Figure 5.4, solo male drivers who approached intersections at night were just as likely to disregard the stop sign (36%) as they were to stop completely (also 36%). On the other hand, solo female drivers who approached the same intersections at night were much more likely to do the right thing (62% stopped completely and only 16% disregarded the sign). McKelvie and Schamer couldn't check to see if the women who failed to stop were busy folding their arms across their chests, but these findings certainly suggest that women were exercising a certain kind of caution. The shroud of night seemed to make women more concerned about safety. It seemed to make men less concerned about getting caught for blowing a stop sign.

Unobtrusive measures are not limited to studies of locomotion. They can also be used to see how long people stay in one place. Because the "hatching chicks" exhibit was the most popular exhibit at Chicago's Museum of Science and Industry for many years, this meant that museum officials were required to replace the floor tiles around this exhibit about every six weeks. Floor tiles around the other exhibits typically lasted for years. This unobtrusive measure thus provided a nice index of popularity that museum officials could use to determine patrons' attitudes (see Webb, Campbell, Schwartz, &

Sechrest, 1966). In a similar way, mechanics who examine the rear shocks on a car to estimate the car's true mileage are also using wear and tear as an unobtrusive measure. By the same token, horse traders who examine a horse's teeth for signs of excessive wear (i.e., signs of excessive age) are also relying on unobtrusive measures. Incidentally, just to keep you up-to-date on all of your horse aphorisms, people are referring to exactly this kind of critical inspection when they say "Don't look a gift horse in the mouth." Unobtrusive measures may occasionally be misleading (e.g., a young horse may have had a bad dentist), but unlike people, they never lie on purpose.

Measures of wear and tear are not the only common form of unobtrusive measure. People's accents may tell you something about where they grew up. Their clothing may tell you something about their bank accounts. If you wanted to get a relative estimate of auto theft rates in different U.S. cities, you might sample a few grocery store parking lots and count the portion of cars that have Clubs™ or other lock-on devices attached to their steering wheels. Private detectives who want to know if someone smokes unfiltered Camels may resort to rummaging through the person's trash to determine his or her brand loyalties. Presumably, Sherlock Holmes would have performed the same assessment much less directly (e.g., by listening for subtle speech cues that reveal evidence of damage to the throat).

When it comes to external and internal validity, observational studies are in much the same boat as archival studies. Their tremendous potential for external validity is grounded in features of the research that sometimes get in the way of internal validity. Nonetheless, by being creative in their choice of measures and thorough in their efforts to control for confounds, researchers who conduct observational studies may reveal important facts about people that would be difficult to uncover any other way.

Questionnaire and Interview Research

To paraphrase Gordon Allport (1961), one of the most common ways to gather information about people's thoughts, feelings, and behaviors is to simply *ask* people about their thoughts, feelings, and behaviors. In questionnaires and interviews, this is exactly what researchers do. The number and variety of questionnaires (i.e., self-report ratings) and interviews (i.e., oral question-and-answer sessions) that have been used in psychological research are almost as large as the number and variety of *researchers* who perform this research. However, the logic of almost all forms of questionnaire and interview research is the same. The basic idea is to generate a fixed set of questions and pose them to a large group of people. People are expected to differ on all the variables measured, and a researcher ultimately expects people who are high or low on one variable (e.g., achievement motivation) to be high or low on some other variable (e.g., educational attainment). The questions in such research usually focus on two or more primary variables that the researcher expects to be related, but good survey studies will usually include measures of additional variables—you guessed it, variables that may be *confounded* with the variables in which the researcher is most interested.

Because questionnaires and interviews rely solely on the responses of individual research participants, research claims based on questionnaires and interviews are probably even more susceptible than other correlational designs to the specific category of confounds that we have labeled *person confounds*. This is because the specific characteristics that influence a person's response to one question will often influence the same person's responses to another question. For instance, Eileen, a person who is especially motivated to present herself in a desirable light to an interviewer might deny experiencing symptoms of depression and simultaneously exaggerate her feelings of competence in specific areas. In contrast, Matt, a person who tends to catastrophize (perhaps in order to receive sympathy) might actually exaggerate both his feelings of depression and his specific feelings of incompetence.

Thus, individual differences in the way people try to impress other people (including the researcher) might falsely inflate the true association between depression and people's specific self-views. As this example reveals, researchers who make use of questionnaires and interviews should work hard to ensure that their participants report what they truly believe. It is in part for this reason that researchers often go to great lengths to provide their participants with anonymity (i.e., privacy) in research. For similar reasons, researchers sometimes minimize their interactions with their participants, to minimize participants' concerns about looking good. If you have ever participated in a questionnaire study, you may have felt that the whole experience was a little impersonal. As long as you did not also feel unappreciated, this should have actually helped the researcher get more accurate data. At other times, of course, a study requires much closer interactions between experimenters and participants. In many clinical interviews, for example, the interviewer must walk a careful line between being polite, professional, and caring, and being so involved with a participant that the participant develops excessive concerns about doing or saying the right thing.

Assuming that researchers who conduct questionnaires have taken all the usual precautions to deal with confounds and reverse causality (with a little extra attention paid to person confounds), the actual business of carrying out questionnaires and interviews is pretty straightforward. Probably the most important thing researchers need to decide is how much room they will give participants to answer questions as they see fit. More specifically, questionnaires and interviews can be categorized in terms of whether they involve *open-ended* or *closed-ended* questions. Open-ended questions are those that give people free rein to respond however they wish. An example of an open-ended question is "What are your personal views on religion?" In contrast to this approach, closed-ended questions force people to choose their answers from a limited number of specific options. A closed-ended version of the same question might be:

Do you believe in God? (Circle one answer.)   no   yes

Notice that, in principle, the open-ended question allows the person to write or say almost *anything*. The person answering this question could produce an extemporaneous critique of existentialist philosophers, recite the Bhagavad Gita, or reply that religion is a private matter that people shouldn't discuss with others. The closed-ended question is much more restrictive (and not always as informative). However, it is also *much* easier to analyze. Whereas a researcher might spend hours developing a coding scheme for people's spontaneous replies to the first question, the second question would most likely be coded on a simple nominal scale (e.g., by using the numbers 0 and 1, for example).

Alternatively, once a researcher has decided to use a closed-ended question, the researcher might ask participants to answer the question using a continuous rather than a dichotomous scale. This is a common practice in psychology, and it is most typically done using variations on *Likert scales*. This method requires people to convert the subjective strength or intensity of their thoughts and feelings to some kind of linear scale. For instance, a variation on the question regarding whether people believe in God might read as follows:

To what degree to you believe in God? (Circle one answer.)

0	1	2	3	4	5	6	7	8	9	10
not at all					somewhat				completely	

As you can see, this second question provides much more sensitive information than the original question. In general, questions that provide a larger range of responses can be used to pick up smaller and smaller associations in correlational research. This is because these questions typically allow researchers to make finer distinctions between people. For instance, some people who would respond with a 1, 2, or 3 on this last question might have answered yes to the previous version of the question. If so, the original (dichotomous) question would lump together people whose belief in God hangs by a thread with those who believe in God with every fiber of their being. The second measure would usually be much more sensitive than the first.

Assuming that one has designed a closed-ended question that has a nice range of values, however, a researcher might still choose to use an open-ended response format to help see what information he or she could be missing by relying exclusively on closed-ended questions. To illustrate, consider research by Schuman and Scott (1987). They asked Americans to identify "the most important problem facing this country today." In one condition of their study, they listed four options—pollution, the energy shortage, legalized abortion, and the quality of public schools. To be as fair as possible, they also reminded people that they could choose *any other problem* that they wished. Thirty-two percent of those surveyed chose public education as the country's most important problem. However, when they asked people an open-ended version of the same question (that is, when they didn't list any answer options), only 1% of those surveyed spontaneously mentioned education! If you want to know what's on people's minds, it's probably best not to put anything there before you ask. The answers we get to research questions often depend on the questions we ask.

A variety of rules of thumb for constructing good self-report and interview questions will be discussed later in this text. For now, it is important to remember that many of the limitations on the degree to which researchers can draw reasonable inferences from questionnaire and interview research depend on exactly how well their studies are designed. Researchers who collect data using questionnaires and interviews can place greater confidence in the conclusions they draw from their research if they measure and control for potential confounds, take reasonable precautions to minimize self-presentational concerns among their participants, and give serious thought to the problem of reverse causality. In this way, they can capitalize on their opportunities to maximize external validity while minimizing the usual concerns regarding internal validity.

Summary

The nonexperimental designs discussed in this chapter all have an important place in the toolbox of the versatile methodologist. Moreover, like the tools in a real toolbox, each of these methodological tools has its own specialized purpose—and its own limitations. Case studies provide us with detailed portraits of the experiences of an individual person, but exactly what they reveal is sometimes in the eye of the beholder. Even when the findings of a case study are crystal clear, there is no guarantee that these findings are a reflection of general principles of human behavior. In some ways, single-variable studies such as epidemiological studies, descriptive studies of people's attitudes, or studies of judgment under uncertainty represent the polar opposite of case studies. They focus on a single variable rather than many variables, and they make use of many participants rather than a single participant. Such studies often do a great job of describing the state of the world at large, but they do not necessarily tell us very much about exactly why it is that way. Finally, multiple-variable, correlational research designs, such as archival studies, unobtrusive observational studies, and questionnaires share many of the strengths of case studies and descriptive studies. In particular, they usually involve observations or recollections of the experiences of people in their natural environment. These studies take us a step closer to understanding the causes of a phenomenon because they assess the relation between two or more variables. Despite this, such studies are typically open to more than one causal interpretation and concerns regarding this problem often inspire researchers to venture into the fascinating world of the experimental laboratory, a world we will explore in detail in the next chapter.

METHODOLOGY EXERCISE 1

Partial Correlation

After Galton's development of the correlation coefficient, the most dramatic and useful development in nonexperimental statistics has probably been the development of covariance techniques such as partial correlation. A partial correlation is a lot like a regular correlation. Like a regular correlation, for example, a partial correlation always ranges in value from –1 to +1, with higher absolute values indicating a stronger linear relation between two variables of interest. Instead of reflecting the simple (descriptive) relation between two variables, however, a partial correlation reflects the unique relation between two variables when the effect of a third variable is (mathematically) taken into account. Partial correlation is thus very useful because it takes you a step closer to seeing the causal relation between two variables. For example, suppose a researcher randomly sampled 1,000 Los Angeles–area residents, weighed them, gave them a test of verbal ability, and correlated the two scores. Would you be surprised to learn that the correlation between weight and verbal ability was +.60? (You should be. If weight and verbal ability truly went hand in hand, professional wrestlers would all have doctorates in astrophysics.) What if you learned that the researcher had sampled people of all ages? In this case, you would probably realize very quickly what was going on. Weight just happens to be associated with age, and age is, for obvious reasons, strongly related to "verbal ability." What the researcher would really like to know, then, is whether there is any relation between weight and verbal ability when age is held constant. To find out the answer, the researcher would need to conduct a partial correlation. If the partial correlation was positive and significant, you could put aside one possible third variable (age) as an alternative explanation for the researcher's findings.

Although hypothetical examples like this are useful, it is probably easiest to see how a partial correlation works by computing one in your head—using the reasoning skills you have been honing since you weighed only a few pounds. This is your assignment, and we are betting that it is much easier than you might think. The data you will evaluate come from an unobtrusive observational study we recently conducted. To test the suspicion that a colleague's daughter, Lisa, was stealing cookies from the psychology department cookie jar, we made observations on 12 different days. At the end of each day we recorded (1) whether Lisa had visited the psychology department and (2) whether any cookies were missing from the cookie jar. To convert the data to numerical form, we coded them as follows: For Lisa's presence in the department, a "0" meant that she *had not* and a "1" meant that she *had* visited the department on a given day. For cookie thefts, a "0" meant that cookies *had not* been stolen and a "1" meant that cookies *had* been stolen on a given day. A summary of the data appears below.

Hypothetical Data from Observational Study of Cookie Thefts

	Cookies Stolen?	Lisa Visited?
Day 1:	No (0)	No (0)
Day 2:	No (0)	No (0)
Day 3:	No (0)	No (0)
Day 4:	No (0)	No (0)
Day 5:	No (0)	No (0)
Day 6:	No (0)	Yes (1)
Day 7:	Yes (1)	No (0)
Day 8:	Yes (1)	Yes (1)
Day 9:	Yes (1)	Yes (1)
Day 10:	Yes (1)	Yes (1)
Day 11:	Yes (1)	Yes (1)
Day 12:	Yes (1)	Yes (1)

Questions

1. We conducted an analysis of these data and recorded the correlation. Which of the five answers below do you think it was? To check your intuitions about this answer, you can actually calculate the correlation coefficient by using the following formula:

$r = (\text{matches} - \text{mismatches})/n$

where "matches" refers to observations for which the two variables take on the same value and "mismatches" refers to observations for which the two variables take on different values. For example, if there were 10 matches and 4 mismatches in a set of 14 observations, the correlation would be $(10 - 4)/14$ or about .43. (Incidentally, this simple formula works only when you are correlating two dichotomous variables whose outcomes are equally likely—as they are here.)

(a) $r(10) = -.67, p = .018.$
(b) $r(10) = -.13,$ n.s.
(c) $r(10) = 0.00,$ n.s.
(d) $r(10) = +.13,$ n.s.
(e) $r(10) = +.67, p = .018.$

Assume that these are the only data you have at your disposal. What conclusion would you draw based on the magnitude and significance of this test? Based on the data you have so far, how likely is it that Lisa is guilty of at least some of the cookie thefts?

More data. Now suppose that we had conducted a more complete study—one in which we also observed the behavior of a second child, Bart, on the same 12 days. Because Lisa and Bart are both children of our colleague Homer, they tend to come as a package (i.e., their presence in the department is positively correlated). Because this is the case, you could think of Bart as a third variable or confound. It is obviously possible that Bart is the true culprit. Statistically, it is possible to conduct a partial correlation to get a better idea of who is responsible for the cookie thefts. In fact, not only could we compute a partial correlation between Lisa's presence and cookie thefts (controlling for Bart's presence), but we could also compute a partial correlation between Bart's presence and cookie thefts (controlling for Lisa's presence). In other words, we could try to see who is the true cause of the cookie thefts. The complete data for this study appear below.

Complete Data for Observational Study of Cookie Thefts

	Cookies Stolen?	Lisa Visited?	Bart Visited?
Day 1:	No (0)	No (0)	No (0)
Day 2:	No (0)	No (0)	No (0)
Day 3:	No (0)	No (0)	No (0)
Day 4:	No (0)	No (0)	No (0)
Day 5:	No (0)	No (0)	No (0)

Day 6:	No (0)	Yes (1)	No (0)
Day 7:	Yes (1)	No (0)	Yes (1)
Day 8:	Yes (1)	Yes (1)	Yes (1)
Day 9:	Yes (1)	Yes (1)	Yes (1)
Day 10:	Yes (1)	Yes (1)	Yes (1)
Day 11:	Yes (1)	Yes (1)	Yes (1)
Day 12:	Yes (1)	Yes (1)	Yes (1)

More Questions

2. If we gave these data to a computer, the computer would give us a very clear idea of who is responsible for the cookie thefts (in the form of a couple of partial correlations). Based on the additional data provided above, whom would you blame? In answering this question, be sure to report whether you feel you now have a better grip on who was responsible for the cookie thefts. In your answer include:

(a) Your estimate of the partial correlation between Bart's presence and cookie thefts. A good way to think about this is to ask yourself what portion of the blame for the cookie thefts should most reasonably be placed on Bart—given what you know about everything that is going on. If Bart seemed to deserve about half of the blame, for example, you might estimate his correlation at about .50 (or about .71, but this is a detail you don't need to worry about). (You do not necessarily have to hit the answer to the partial correlation right on the head, but you must logically defend your answer.)

(b) Your estimate of the partial correlation between Lisa's presence and cookie thefts. That is, how uniquely responsible is Lisa for the cookie thefts? (Be sure to defend your answer.) A hint: Some days are much more informative than others. Be sure to tell *which* days and why.

3. The power of partial correlation might lead some people to conclude that we no longer need laboratory experiments to assess causal relations between variables. Attack or defend this position. A hint: Recall the inductive problem from Chapter 1. What if Lisa had a great number of siblings and you could observe only one or two of them at once? Alternately, what if Homer occasionally trusted Lisa to come to the department by herself, but always accompanied Bart? A second hint: In the cookie example, it is obvious that causality can run in only one direction (i.e., it seems unlikely that disappearing cookies can cause Bart or Lisa to appear in the department), but what if you were trying to assess the relation between income and education, controlling for personality? Would partial correlation be any more or less informative than it was in the case of missing cookies? A final hint: Partial correlation controls for any confounding variable or variables that you were insightful enough to measure and add to your statistical analysis. For which variables does random assignment control?

Notes

1. When a sample size is chosen to yield the specific level of sampling error that researchers are willing to accept (e.g., 2% versus 5%), this sample size is based on the *population as a whole* rather than subgroups within the sample. Thus, a sample that will yield a 3% sampling error for estimates of disease prevalence for a specific population of 10 million people will always yield a somewhat larger sampling error for estimates of disease prevalence in small subsamples within the population (e.g., for African Americans). Researchers deal with this problem by oversampling subgroups they want to study so that these subgroups have sampling errors that are not excessively large.

2. The first author learned about the Colett and Marsh study many years ago in a graduate research methods course, and he took detailed notes about the study. However, when he tried to locate the original research report summarizing the study, he was unable to find it even after engaging in an extensive set of electronic searches.

6

Experience Carefully Planned: Experimental Research Designs

Regard no practice as immutable. Change and be ready to change again. Accept no eternal verity. Experiment.
—B. F. Skinner

This chapter focuses on experiments, including both laboratory and field experiments. We begin the chapter by briefly reviewing the history of experimentation, with an emphasis on how R. A. Fisher integrated the two crucial ingredients of experimentation as applied to human research participants. These two ingredients are the manipulation of variables and random assignment. We follow this with a discussion of the advantages and disadvantages of experiments, with an emphasis on how to maximize the advantages and minimize the disadvantages. Finally, we conclude the chapter with a discussion of the trade-offs between internal and external validity.

A Wonderful Method

In the classic Frank Capra film *It's a Wonderful Life,* the protagonist, George Bailey, gets the opportunity to see what the world would have been like if one and only one thing had been different—if he had never been born. As you well know if you are familiar with the movie, this experience profoundly changes George's view of his life. He sees exactly how important he proved to be to his friends, his family, and his community, and he thus comes to appreciate how wonderful his seemingly difficult life really is. This touching film often brings a tear to our eyes because it so beautifully illustrates the value of laboratory experiments. OK, we're kidding, but not entirely. This film really does illustrate what is wonderful about laboratory experiments. Lab experiments show us exactly how the world changes when you change *one and only one thing.* In so doing, they give us information about causality that is otherwise extremely difficult to obtain.

In the real world, after all, it is incredibly rare for one and only one thing to change in a person's life, and this is why, in the real world, it can be very difficult to pinpoint the exact causes of a person's behavior. If Renelle becomes a happier person after receiving a big promotion, is it because her level of occupational prestige increased, because she began making more money, because she was given more flexible work hours, or because she always looks forward to summer and just happened to receive her promotion in late May? It's very hard to know. Whoever coined the Latin phrase *ceteris paribus* ("all else being equal") must have appreciated this problem. If you want to know whether one thing alone affects something else, you must hold *everything else* but that one thing constant. Everything else is an awful lot, and the beauty of experiments is that they provide researchers with an elegant way of doing just this—*ceteris paribus,* manipulating one and only one thing.

By now, you know that another way of describing the wonderful thing about experiments is that experiments tend to be very high in internal validity. Recall that a study is high in internal validity only to the degree that the researcher can confidently assert a causal relation between the independent and dependent variables. Internal validity is crucial to theory testing because all theories are statements about the causal relations between variables. When a researcher can't be sure about causes (when internal validity is low), the researcher can't claim to have gathered good support for his or her theory. It is largely for this reason that researchers often conduct experiments. By now, you also have a pretty good idea of what an experiment is. But so far, we haven't really fleshed out the details of what experiments are, exactly how they are conducted, and what they can and cannot do for us. This is the primary goal of this chapter.

A Brief History of True Experiments

So let's begin at the beginning, starting with the simplest possible kind of experiment. To be considered an *experiment,* first and foremost, a study must make use of a **manipulation.** A manipulation occurs when an experimenter systematically alters the levels of a variable (i.e., the *independent variable*). The goal in so doing is to see if changes in the independent variable lead to corresponding changes in some outcome variable (i.e., the *dependent variable*). If a manipulation does, in fact, lead to changes in the dependent variable, an experimenter can feel fairly certain that the independent variable caused this change. If these effects are predicted from a known psychological theory, this theory moves up in the world of science. If these effects either contradict or fail to support a known psychological theory, this theory moves down in the world of science. Perhaps the theory is falsified and thus rejected. However, it is much more likely that researchers will modify the theory in light of this new information about the theory's limitations. We have referred to this process elsewhere as identifying the *boundary conditions* of a theory. Identifying the boundary conditions of a theory is a very important part of the scientific process, and a great deal of psychological research is all about this process. In science, as in life, it is sometimes just as important to know what someone or something cannot do as it is to know what that someone or something can do. In short, experiments can tell you exactly what a manipulation can and can't do.

It is difficult to say who invented manipulation, for much the same reason that it is difficult to say who invented cooking, the wheel, or agriculture. In other words, manipulation has been around for so long that it's impossible to say who invented it. When prehistoric people made crude tools and weapons by chipping away the edges of flint stones, they were manipulating natural objects to achieve certain desired results. In so doing, they were learning important lessons about the world (e.g., flint makes better blades than granite). Similarly, when prehistoric people learned that exposing meat to fire increases its shelf life, they were learning from direct manipulation. Nonetheless, it took ancient philosophers and scientists a long time to settle on manipulation as the preferred tool for figuring out the world. Aristotle made some very important contributions to science, but manipulation wasn't really one of them; he preferred argumentation to experimentation. In our opinion, the person who probably deserves the most credit for bringing manipulation to center stage in science was Galileo Galilei, who popularized the idea of manipulation by performing some of the first systematic experiments in science. Remember his experiments rolling balls down inclined planes? With a little help from people like Sir Isaac Newton (the famous physicist and mathematician) and John Locke (one of history's biggest fans of empiricism), the idea of manipulation eventually took hold in the social as well as the physical sciences.

But manipulation is only half the story. Once we enter the realm of social science, manipulation alone does not make true experiments. True experiments also require the use of *random assignment*. It is impossible to overstate the importance of random assignment to experimental research in psychology. Because random assignment is an essential ingredient to modern experimentation, you should probably know something about how this essential research technique was cooked up. There was a time long ago when researchers woke up at the crack of dawn, walked to their labs in the snow, and, if you can believe it, weren't lucky enough to live in a world with random assignment. In the early history of psychology, that is, random assignment simply hadn't been invented yet. In these early days, researchers were still uncertain of their methods. From their knowledge of the physical sciences, psychologists knew that manipulation was a crucial tool for learning about causes. However, psychologists faced a huge problem rarely faced by physical scientists. We might think of it as the problem of ceteris *non* paribus. When a physicist or chemist manipulates some aspect of the physical world, it is very easy to do so using objects or substances that are known to be *identical*. Take two identical objects, expose only one to radiation, heat, or dihydrogen oxide (i.e., water), and you can easily observe the consequences of your manipulation. It's not hard at all to create two or more identical physical objects (samples of pure sodium, 50-gram ball bearings) that become the objects of your scientific manipulations. Now, try doing this with *people*. (It's called cloning, it's potentially unethical, it takes a long time, and it didn't exist a hundred years ago.)

The history of the true experiment in the biological and social sciences is essentially the history of how researchers got around this thorny problem. It's the problem of *individual differences* we brought up in Chapters 2 and 4. So early experimenters realized that individual differences were a huge barrier to experimentation, but they didn't quite know how to overcome them. A common approach adopted in the old days was "matching." By matching each participant in an experimental condition with a very similar participant in a control condition, researchers hoped to guarantee that their experimental and control groups would be "equal" prior to their experimental manipulations. As it turned out, however, matching wasn't all that it was cracked up to be. The biggest two problems were (1) that it was really hard to do and (2) that it didn't really work. The researcher who managed to match experimental and control groups on one dimension (such as intelligence) often found that these groups differed on many other dimensions (such as age or sex, for example). Some researchers tried matching their participants on several dimensions at the same time, but this often proved to be very difficult. Where do you find an exact match for a 6' 3" tall, 308-pound, 25-year-old plumber with an IQ of 124, a low need for achievement, a moderately active sexual history, and seven siblings? And, even if you could find this guy's twin brother, Zeke, how would you get him here from Alabama to participate in your experiment?

Even more to the point, even if two or more groups of participants were matched on a large number of different dimensions, one would never know for sure that the groups were equivalent on *all* of the dimensions that might influence the results of an experiment. Imagine, for example, that you were a political and cognitive psychologist who was a little ahead of your time in 1896. You wanted to study the effects of classical conditioning on people's attitudes toward the current U.S. president, Grover Cleveland (see Staats & Staats, 1958, for some useful details about how you could do this). Specifically, you wanted to see if pairing pleasant versus unpleasant words (e.g., "happiness," "vomit") with President Cleveland's last name would eventually influence how much people said they *liked* President Cleveland. Let's further assume that you used matching to create two very similar groups of participants, one of whom always saw Cleveland's surname associated with pleasant words during a judgment task and one of whom always saw his surname associated with unpleasant words during the very same task. After working very, very hard at it, you matched the two experimental groups pretty well on five presumably important variables: age, income, gender, ethnicity, and political party affiliation. Hopefully, you can see that any of these variables could influence how much people would like President Cleveland. So far, so good.

Now suppose that the people who saw the name "Cleveland" paired with words like "love " and " chocolate" did, in fact, report liking this name more than the people who saw the same name paired with words like "disease" and "slime." Could you be sure that it was the conditioning manipulation, and nothing else, that led to this group difference? Maybe. After all, the two groups were very similar on five different variables that might predict how much people liked Cleveland. Or maybe not. What if you learned that four of the ten people in the positive word condition (and none of the people in the other condition) happened to be from Cleveland, Ohio? Or what if most of the people in the positive word condition happened to be highly optimistic people who view the world (including U.S. presidents) through rose-colored lenses? Or what if more members of the negative word group had recently been laid off from their jobs? Isn't a president usually one of the first people to get the blame for economic woes? The list could go on and on. Your imperfect experiment wouldn't be useless, but it certainly wouldn't be airtight. The impossibility of establishing a "perfect match" is similar to the inductive problem discussed in Chapter 2. A researcher simply cannot know with certainty that two matched groups have been equated on all the relevant dimensions that could influence the dependent variable. Even if two groups are matched on many, many variables, they may still differ from one another on some important variable that was not considered by the researcher.

The solution to this tricky problem proved to be **random assignment,** popularized by R. A. Fisher in the 1920s and 1930s. Random assignment is the closest thing to magic that researchers have ever discovered. It is a strange blend of precision and chaos—almost the opposite of matching. Whereas matching involves placing people in conditions on a very systematic basis, random assignment involves placing people in conditions on a totally arbitrary basis. Technically, this means that *every participant has an equal chance of being assigned to any particular condition of an experiment.* For example, an experimenter might assign people to conditions in a study either by flipping a fair coin or by drawing names from a hat to decide each participant's condition. Whenever laypeople "draw straws" or flip a coin to give two or more people an equal chance of experiencing something (the chance to receive a kickoff, the mission of crossing an enemy minefield) they are expressing an intuitive appreciation of the logic of random assignment. And random assignment, like coin flips, is very fair and logical. Besides being a lot easier and quicker than matching, random assignment does what matching cannot. It equalizes two or more groups on practically every dimension imaginable.

Notice that we said that randomization equalizes *groups.* The insight behind random assignment was that two groups can be virtually identical as groups even though each group is made up of very different specific people. To see that random assignment really does this, we encourage you to try your hand at the random assignment exercise at the end of this chapter. For now, just remember that random assignment assigns people in an arbitrary fashion to different groups. Thus, there is no reason to expect the groups to differ from one another before the experimental manipulation is performed. Of course, random assignment isn't perfect. Occasionally you will get a lot of particularly helpful, angry, or religious people in one group just the way you will occasionally get a lot of salt on one particular french fry, receive five cards of the same suit in one specific poker hand, or hit a bull's-eye twice in a row out of blind luck. On the whole, however, random assignment does a surprisingly effective job of equating two or more experimental groups. Better yet, random assignment doesn't just equate groups on the 2, 3, or 15 dimensions that one particular experimenter might care about. It essentially equates groups on *every* dimension imaginable (especially when you average across many different experiments or use a very large sample).

Finally, any worries a researcher might have that random assignment didn't work perfectly in his or her particular experiment can be addressed by conducting statistical tests. That is, the reason researchers conduct statistical tests on their data is to see if any differences that they observe between conditions are "real." In the context of experiments, statistical testing helps researchers determine whether any observed differences between experimental conditions are greater than those that one would expect on the basis of luck alone. That is, precisely because researchers know that random assignment isn't absolutely perfect, they have developed some simple statistical tests to help them determine when to believe a set of results. If a pattern of experimental findings could easily reflect minor imbalances in random assignment, the researchers have to conclude that their manipulations probably didn't have any effect. Conversely, researchers conclude that their manipulation had its predicted effects only when the two treatment groups in an experiment differ in predictable ways that greatly exceed the kind of differences you'd expect based on chance alone.

Needless to say, we wouldn't be devoting an entire chapter to true experiments if we didn't feel that they represent an extremely useful research technique. In the next section of this chapter we describe some of the most important advantages of true experiments relative to other research designs. As you will see, the two most important advantages are that experiments do what they were designed to do: they solve the problem of individual differences and they help to minimize confounds. These are the two main reasons why true experiments are usually very high in internal validity. However, experiments have several other important advantages, some of which have more to do with other forms of validity.

Strengths of True Experiments
True Experiments Eliminate Individual Differences

To illustrate how true experiments solve the problem of individual differences, let's take a close look at both (1) a classic study of mood and helping (Isen & Levin, 1972) and (2) a contemporary study of behavioral priming (Bargh, Chen, & Burrows, 1996). Isen and Levin wanted to see if positive mood contributes to helping. Specifically, they proposed that people who are feeling happy are more likely than usual to help those who need help, because helping allows people to maintain a good mood. To test this theory, they developed a simple and clever mood manipulation that involved (1) giving some people free cookies and (2) observing whether these people were more likely than usual to help a stranger. The participants were men who were sitting in a campus library, and the opportunity to help someone else came when an unfortunate fellow student (a trained research assistant who was in cahoots with the experimenters) dropped his books. Isen and Levin found that the men who received a cookie were more likely to help the student than were a comparable group of men who did not receive a cookie. They concluded that the cookie caused an increase in helping. If this conclusion was correct, then the results would support their theory of mood and helping. But was it correct? Was this study high in internal validity? Does being in a good mood really make people helpful?

Isn't it possible that the men who got cookies were simply different in some important ways from those who did not get cookies? Compared with the men in the control condition, maybe a lot of these cookie recipients were from Cleveland, Ohio (where people are reputed to be unusually helpful). Or maybe they simply had more time on their hands. The differences in helping behavior across conditions might have occurred for reasons that had little or nothing to do with the independent variable. That is, the real explanation for Isen and Levin's findings might be individual differences. Right? Wrong. Although anything is possible, it's highly unlikely that these two groups of men were highly different prior to receiving their level of the experimental manipulation. The reason is that Isen and Levin used *random assignment* to place the men in different conditions. Whenever Isen and Levin selected a man in the library as an unwitting participant, they consulted a random number table to determine the man's treatment condition. For the sake of simplicity, assume that the table simply contained a long string of 0s and 1s. If the first number consulted happened to be a 1, the first participant identified would be assigned to the experimental condition and would thus receive a cookie. If the next number consulted happened to be a 0, the next participant would be assigned to the control condition and would *not* receive a cookie. If the experimenter followed this procedure carefully (e.g., without peeking to see the first number before seeing the first participant), then it is highly unlikely that the men in the experimental and control conditions differed in any important ways. Random assignment solves the problem of individual differences.

Let's consider a more contemporary example. Bargh, Chen, and Burrows (1996) conducted a laboratory experiment in which they primed their participants to think about stereotypes of old people versus a control topic. Participants thought they were taking part in a study of language proficiency. The language proficiency task required participants to unscramble 30 sets of words to form 30 sentences. In reality, the scrambled sentences were a priming manipulation. For half of the participants, the scrambled sentences almost always referred to old people. They thus contained key stereotypic words such as "Florida," "gray," "wrinkle," "retired," "old," "forgetful," and "bingo." Other participants unscrambled 30 sentences that had nothing to do with old people. The key words were words such as "thirsty," "clean," and "private." Bargh et al. assumed that activating people's associations about old people might cause people to behave in ways that they stereotypically associate with the members of this social group. The idea is that if you have recently been thinking about grandmothers, you might actually *behave* in a slightly more grandmotherly fashion than usual. Short of inviting their participants to bake cookies and pinch the cheeks of small children, how could Bargh et al. test this idea in the lab? Like this: By telling participants that they were done with the study of language proficiency, thanking participants, giving them their research credit, and then *secretly timing them* to see how quickly they walked down the hall as they left the study! Their logic, of course, is that it is a stereotype of old people that they walk slowly.

They accomplished this last, crucial task with the aid of a research assistant who appeared to be casually hanging out in the hallway. This assistant (who had no idea which set of sentences participants had unscrambled) timed each participant as he or she walked down the hallway toward an elevator. Those who had been thinking about old people walked quite a bit more slowly than those in the control condition. By now, you probably realize that individual differences (e.g., differences in walking speed, differences in whether people were in a hurry) do *not* provide a plausible alternate explanation for this finding. In case you're still a little skeptical, we should add that, to remove any lingering doubts about whether their results were a fluke, Bargh et al. ran this walking study twice from start to finish, and they got exactly the same results in both studies. They also observed very similar findings in two other studies in which they used different specific priming manipulations. For example, by priming rudeness versus politeness in one study, they were able to get students to behave rudely versus politely to an experimenter who appeared to be ignoring them. We haven't done the math, but the likelihood that the results of all four of Bargh et al.'s priming studies are due to four separate failures of random assignment is roughly equal to the likelihood that Grover Cleveland will be elected the next U.S. president (by narrowly carrying Florida). Random assignment solves the problem of individual differences.

True Experiments Eliminate Other Kinds of Confounds

As you may recall from Chapter 5, the individual difference problem we just discussed may be thought of as a confound. A **confound** is a nuisance variable that (1) varies systematically with the independent variable and (2) influences the dependent variable in the same way you'd expect the independent variable to do. If Bargh et al. *had* somehow confounded walking speed with their experimental priming manipulation, this confound would completely undermine their claim about how priming affects behavior. Although random assignment solves the problem of individual differences, it does not guarantee that an experiment is completely free of confounds.

The reason for this is that random assignment, in and of itself, fixes only one specific kind of confound, **person confounds.** You first learned about person confounds in Chapter 5, when we discussed them in the context of correlational research. To translate person confounds into the language of true experiments rather than correlational studies, person confounds exist when individual differences covary with an experimental treatment condition and are related to the dependent variable. As we hope you just saw, person confounds are much less problematic in true experiments than they are in other kinds of research.

However, person confounds are not the only category of confounds. A second category of confounds is **procedural confounds.** Procedural confounds in experimental research are the exact equivalent of the *environmental confounds* we discussed in the context of nonexperimental research. We use the term "procedural" here to reflect the fact that experiments consist of planned procedures rather than naturally occurring events. Procedural confounds occur when an experimenter unwittingly manipulates two or more things at once. They happen when something the experimenter did not intend (a seemingly innocuous or tangential aspect of a procedure) is allowed to covary with the independent variable. For example, suppose that an experimenter interested in stereotyping wanted to manipulate the ethnicity of a person who asked strangers for a favor. He happened to have three excellent research assistants who were eager to work on the project: John (a White man), Stacey (a Black woman), and Mauricio (a Latino man). The researcher decided to do the study in a busy shopping mall. He began by carefully training the three confederates to make exactly the same polite request for help to many different male shoppers ("Excuse me, sir, could you possibly lend me 35 cents to make a phone call?"). The three confederates found a way to sample shoppers at random, and the dependent measure was the proportion of shoppers who gave a confederate money. As expected, shoppers were more likely to help the White as opposed to the Latino confederate. Surprisingly, however, the Black confederate received the most help of all. The results of the study seem to suggest that people's attitudes toward Blacks are more favorable than we might have assumed. However, there's a pretty serious procedural confound at work here, and we hope you spotted it. The confederate who got the most help happened to be the only confederate who was female. Under conditions such as these, people are more likely to help women than men.

Does this mean that true experiments don't provide much protection against procedural confounds? Absolutely not. They provide a great deal of protection in the sense that, unlike other research techniques, true experiments allow researchers to manipulate one and only one variable at time. Researchers simply have to make sure that they don't miss out on this wonderful opportunity by making procedural errors. Good experimenters take many steps to ensure that the *only* aspects of their procedures that vary across conditions are the ones that they intended. For instance, in their study of mood and helping, Isen and Levin used a male book dropper in both experimental conditions. They also made sure that the book dropper stood roughly the same distance from the participants in the two mood conditions, and they even trained him to drop the same number of books in both conditions. Furthermore, they made sure that the book dropper was always blind to whether a participant had been given a cookie. This assured that the confederate wouldn't change his behavior across conditions in subtle ways he himself might fail to realize. True experiments conducted carefully minimize the chances of procedural confounds.

Nonetheless, even when researchers take every conceivable step to eliminate person and procedure confounds, a third type of confound can still occur. We refer to this third category of confound as an **operational confound.** As we noted when discussing confounds in nonexperimental designs, our use of the word "operational" reflects the fact that this boils down to making a mistake in one's operational definition of a construct. When applied to laboratory experiments, operational confounds differ from the other two types of confounds in a very important way. Namely, they do not pose a threat to the internal validity of lab experiments. Instead, they pose a challenge to the construct validity of the manipulation and thereby influence the way researchers should interpret an experiment. We still know that the independent variable (and nothing but the independent variable) caused the observed changes in the dependent variable. However, we become worried that the independent variable maps onto a construct that the experimenter didn't originally have in mind.[1]

Recall from Chapter 3 that a manipulation has construct validity only to the extent that it truly reflects the underlying variable that is of focal interest in a theory. When an operational confound occurs, a manipulation influences more than one psychological construct, each of which may influence the dependent variable. As a result, what we had hoped was a very clean, simple manipulation proves to be dirtier and more complex than we had intended. As a result, we don't know for certain why our experimental and control groups behaved differently. To illustrate, let's return again to the study by Isen and Levin (1972). Isen and Levin gave their participants a cookie because they believed that it would put participants in a good mood. They were correct. Free cookies do, in fact, put most people in good moods. However, receiving a free cookie may have influenced helping in this study for reasons that had little or nothing to do with mood. An alternative reason that receiving a cookie may have led to helping behavior is that people who received the cookie from a stranger were exposed to a *prosocial model* (Bandura, 1977). Modeling refers to copying the behavior of other people, and modeling is an extremely well-documented phenomenon. It is thus possible that the participants in Isen and Levin's study who observed someone else being helpful (by passing out cookies to strangers, at no charge) decided to be helpful themselves (by picking up books for strangers, at no charge).

After all this, you may be a little disappointed to learn that being in a positive mood may not necessarily lead to helping after all. Cheer up, have a cookie; it looks like positive mood *does* contribute to helping. The reason we know this is that Isen and colleagues eventually developed a way of manipulating mood that eliminated the operational confound involving modeling. Specifically, as we noted briefly in Chapter 4, Isen and colleagues developed the "found dime" procedure—a procedure that does not appear to be contaminated by any other psychological constructs. Researchers who make use of this manipulation randomly put money in the pockets of some participants and not others. Specifically, they arrange for some participants to "find" a dime (or some other amount of money) in a place such as a public telephone booth. In this way, the only thing modeled by the unknown person who presumably left the money behind is forgetfulness. Nonetheless, this uncontaminated manipulation of mood reliably increases a wide variety of helping behaviors (Isen, 1987). This suggests that at least part of the reason cookies make people more helpful has to do with the fact that cookies (like found dimes) put people in good moods.

Finally, it is worth noting that whereas all true experiments fix the problem of individual differences, some specific kinds of true experiments help minimize confounds more readily than others. In particular, true experiments that are conducted in the *laboratory* make it a little easier to eliminate confounds than do true experiments conducted in the field (i.e., in the real world). The reason for this is that in the laboratory, researchers can play God by creating exactly the kind of psychological situation they want to create. For example, it is slightly easier to get people to eat cookies or find dimes in the laboratory than it is in the real world (where distractions sometimes interfere with such manipulations). More important, the freedom experimenters have to create highly unusual situations in the lab can help researchers separate variables that are typically confounded in the real world. For instance, in the real world people are typically exposed to things that they like more often than they are exposed to things that they dislike. So the *frequency* with which people are exposed to things is naturally confounded with the *favorability* of these same things. In the lab, however, it is very easy to expose people to some things more frequently than to others, independent of their favorability. The laboratory, then, is a place where natural confounds can often be eliminated. As an example from physics, consider Galileo's theory that bodies of differing weights fall at the same rate. This is a difficult theory to test outside the laboratory because an object's weight (and especially its density) is strongly confounded with the degree to which it is affected by wind resistance. Feathers and soap bubbles are easily carried away by the wind. When cannonballs and taxicabs are carried away by the wind, it's time to look for an underground shelter. In the laboratory we can minimize this potent natural confound. Under the highly artificial but scientifically informative context of a vacuum, a feather drops like a stone. In a very similar way, when psychologists bring participants into the psychological vacuum of the laboratory, they can easily conduct experiments that minimize confounds.

As we have suggested thus far, researchers can avoid virtually any kind of confound in their research if they follow three simple steps: (1) randomly assign participants to conditions, (2) eliminate procedural and operational confounds, and (3) move studies to the laboratory. Doing these things has two large advantages: Researchers don't have to worry too much about either individual differences or confounds. However, experiments, especially laboratory experiments, also have a few other important advantages, and our description of experiments would be incomplete if we did not make some mention of these additional advantages.

True Experiments Allow Researchers to Observe the Invisible

A third major advantage of experiments, especially laboratory experiments, is that they allow researchers to observe things that they could not observe any other way. Just as microscopes and telescopes allow biologist and astronomers to see what they could never see with the naked eye, sophisticated psychological measurement techniques allow psychologists to do the same. The list of experimental techniques that allow psychologists to observe things that would be unobservable outside the lab is growing on an almost daily basis. For example, researchers who study attitudes and persuasion can determine whether people like or dislike things by measuring very low levels of electrical activity in the specific facial muscles that play a role in smiling or frowning (see Tassinary & Cacioppo, 1992). Computerized response latency measures, magnetic resonance imaging (better known as MRI), and implicit memory measures (remember the "ele _____"?) are just a few of the hundreds of possible ways to measure the otherwise unmeasureable in the laboratory.

As a more elaborate example, consider Patricia Devine's (1989) influential study of the the cognitive bases of prejudice and stereotyping. Devine hypothesized that prejudiced beliefs might exist at two distinct levels of mental representation. Specifically, she suspected that people possess both automatic (overlearned, nonconscious) and controlled (carefully considered, consciously reportable) stereotypic beliefs. This general idea that belief systems have automatic, nonconscious components was pretty well accepted by cognitive and social psychologists by the time that Devine applied it to stereotyping. For example, it is well established that proficient readers such as yourself are not consciously aware of what they are doing when they convert letters on a page into meaningful words and ideas. After years of practice, much of your "knowledge" about reading has become so automatized that you are no longer consciously aware of it. The same thing is true of many other beliefs and behaviors (e.g., beliefs about how to drive a car). As a potential example of how automatic reading is for you, check out the first sentence of this paragraph. As you were reading it, did you notice the repetition "the the"? Most people wouldn't. The reason most people wouldn't is that part of being a proficient reader is learning to ignore certain kinds of redundant information when reading. To get back to the point: Devine wanted to extend established research on automatic and controlled information processing to the important topic of prejudice. She felt that even highly nonprejudiced people might possess overlearned, automatic associations about ethnic minority groups. Furthermore, she tested this idea, not by waiting to observe evidence of this in a naturalistic setting but by conducting a controlled laboratory experiment.

In her experiment, Devine subliminally exposed people to a long list of words and then examined their judgments about an ambiguously aggressive, race-unspecified target person named Donald.[2] For some people, the word list to which they were subliminally exposed before judging Donald consisted mostly of words that are stereotypically associated with African Americans (e.g., "ghetto," "basketball," "Negroes"). For others, the subliminal word list consisted mostly of words that were stereotype-irrelevant (e.g., "thought," "water," "people"). In other words, Devine manipulated the accessibility of people's automatic associations about African Americans. She expected that doing so would influence people's subsequent judgments of Donald's aggressiveness (because aggression is part of the stereotype of African Americans). It did. People who, without knowing it, had been exposed to the stereotype-relevant primes judged Donald to be more aggressive than did people exposed to the relatively neutral primes. Thus, Devine demonstrated that beliefs that occur outside a person's conscious awareness can influence that person's social judgments. More important, Devine also demonstrated that this automatic priming effect occurred even for participants who had extremely egalitarian attitudes about African Americans. Just as being less racist than average didn't provide people with any immunity from this priming effect, being more racist than average didn't make people especially susceptible to it. Needless to say, demonstrating that people's conscious and nonconscious belief systems operate differently would have been extremely difficult to do without the benefits of experimentation (and the precise experimental techniques, such as priming, that have been developed and refined as part of the experimental paradigm).

True Experiments Provide Information About Interactions

The first three advantages of experimentation are all connected to the idea that experimentation allows researchers to carefully isolate the independent and dependent variables that they wish to investigate. A fourth advantage of experimentation is that experiments are well suited not only to the isolation of variables but also to the careful, systematic blending of variables. To be more precise, experiments provide especially clear and useful information about how multiple variables work together to determine behavior. To put this more methodologically, experiments are typically better than are naturalistic designs at providing information about *interactions* between *two or more* independent variables. This is a statistical term indicating that the effect of one independent variable on a dependent variable is different at different levels of the *other* independent variable. By giving researchers complete control over their independent variables, experiments make it easier than usual to disentangle two or more variables for the purpose of detecting interactions. This is true in great part because lab experiments often allow researchers to separate two or more variables that may be highly correlated in the real world.

For instance, suppose a researcher wished to know how highly popular versus unpopular children respond to acceptance versus rejection from peers. This would be hard to study in a natural situation such as the classroom for two closely related reasons. First, almost by definition, highly popular students rarely experience rejection. Second, highly unpopular children rarely experience acceptance. In the laboratory, this would be very easy to fix: Identify the two groups of children you want to study, create two forms of false but convincing experimental feedback, and use random assignment to decide which kind of feedback (acceptance or rejection) each kid gets. In this way, plenty of popular kids would experience rejection, and plenty of unpopular kids would experience acceptance. You could then see, for example, whether popular versus unpopular kids respond differently to exactly the same experimental feedback. (You're correct. This study would be just as ethically sensitive as it would be informative. We promise to come back to the complex issue of ethics in Chapter 9.)[3]

In short, experiments help researchers figure out when the combined influence of two or more independent variables is different from the sum of their individual influences. When this happens, when two or more independent variables work together in unexpected ways, we have observed a statistical interaction. It may seem a little ironic that we need to *separate* two or more variables to appreciate how they work *together*. We will say more about inter-actions later on, but for now a couple of culinary analogies might help to clar-ify this point. Imagine that cocoa, sugar, and butter *always* came together as a package. That is, assume that neither chefs nor scientists had any way of ever separating these three ingredients. If this were the case, you would have no possible way of knowing that the combination of these three ingredients is much more delicious than any one ingredient in isolation. We know of no shops devoted exclusively to sugar, to butter, or to cocoa, but we can think of many devoted to that curious and addictive combination best known as choco-late. The same thing is true, by the way, for good ingredients that become worse rather than better when you put them together. If you were trying to invent a new dessert, and you suspected that two delicious ingredients tasted even more delicious together, you'd need to isolate the two ingredients. Then you'd want to blend them (and only them) together before adding them to your recipe. If the two individually delectable ingredients (say, for example, peppermint and orange) tasted horrible together (as they do when you have some orange juice after having just brushed your teeth), you would probably keep experimenting instead of throwing them both into your novel recipe for key lime pie.

Interactions are very important because they identify the limiting conditions of a specific theory. Recall that all theories have their boundaries: conditions under which they do and do not apply. No theory is correct under all possible circumstances. Many times, researchers thus conduct experiments with the spe-cific intention of determining when a specific theory is and is not true. As dis-cussed in Chapter 2, this approach to hypothesis testing is known as *qualifica-tion,* and qualification requires the analysis of interactions. To illustrate qualification as it might apply to a specific research finding, consider the bound-ary conditions of a typical *semantic priming* effect. **Semantic priming** refers to the finding that people recognize most words more quickly than usual when they have just been exposed to words that have a similar meaning (Neely, 1977). For instance, you should be able to identify the word "money" more quickly than usual if you have just been exposed to the word "bank." Interest-ingly enough, this priming effect occurs even when a prime (the word that comes first) is flashed up so briefly that people don't realize they were exposed to it. Is this priming effect really based on the semantic overlap (i.e., the over-lap in *meaning*) between different words? To find out, you might use the word "bank" as a prime for the word "money" under neutral control conditions, and hope to replicate the usual priming effect (people should recognize the word "money" more quickly than usual). However, to test the limiting conditions of this effect, you might use exactly the same prime for participants who had just read a story about the *banks* of the Mississippi River. Under this set of condi-tions (when the meaning of the word "bank" has been temporarily altered), the usual priming effect would probably disappear. This interaction between (1) the presence versus absence of a prime and (2) the temporary meaning of the prime would be easy to detect in an experiment. Furthermore, it could tell you some-thing important about the nature and limits of semantic priming.

True Experiments Minimize Noise

In addition to all the other strengths we have mentioned, there is one final strength of experimentation that applies to a much greater extent to *laboratory* experiments than to experiments in general. Nonetheless, this advantage is worth mentioning, not only because the large majority of experiments happen to be conducted in the laboratory, but also because this advantage is so important in its own right. In contrast to most other research settings, laboratory settings provide researchers with a unique ability to minimize **noise.** Students often confuse noise with confounds, but the two concepts are quite different. As you know very well by now, experimental confounds are nuisance variables that covary systematically across experimental conditions, raising the question of whether a large difference between an experimental and a control group really means anything after all. In contrast, noise refers to extraneous variables that influence the dependent variable but are evenly distributed across experimental conditions. Nonetheless, noise creates so much variability in the dependent variable that it makes it hard to see the true effects of any independent variables.

To appreciate the problem of noise, consider some of the many variables that are likely to influence how long it takes a person to recognize words that appear in the middle of a computer monitor (this is an extremely useful measure of information processing). To begin with some features of words themselves, both the frequency of a word in the English language (e.g., "good" vs. "goop") and word length (cat vs. catastrophe) have a big influence on how quickly people recognize words. A wide variety of contextual factors ranging from the size of the computer screen to the brightness of the testing room might also influence how quickly people respond in such a task. Finally, many individual differences (e.g., fluency in English, level of achievement motivation, visual acuity) influence people's responses. Suppose we decided to test the hypothesis that an experimenter's ethnicity (don't worry; this time we got rid of procedural confounds) influences participants' ability to recognize words related to ethnicity. If we allowed all these other factors to vary randomly, it would be *extremely* difficult to detect a real effect of the treatment in the midst of all this noise. However, if we took advantage of the control we have in the laboratory by holding all these sources of noise constant (e.g., by selecting only fluent speakers of English, controlling screen size and illumination levels, keeping word length more or less constant, etc.), we'd have a much better chance of detecting a true effect of the experimenter's ethnicity.

Concerns about reducing noise sometimes motivate psychologists to use highly homogenous samples of research participants, that is, participants who do not differ very much from one another (e.g., college students, children of the same age and/or gender). By studying groups who are similar in some important way, researchers often hope to eliminate much of the noise that occurs as a result of individual differences. As discussed below, however, the use of noise-free laboratories and homogenous samples has caused many people to ask whether the results of laboratory studies generalize to the "real world," where noise and individual differences abound. For the present purposes, suffice it to say that this is a reasonable question, but it is certainly no reason to abandon the precision and control over independent and dependent variables that is so readily afforded by the laboratory.

Summary

A simple way to summarize almost everything we have said about experimentation thus far is to say that experiments provide researchers with clear and compelling information about *causality*. An even simpler way to put it is to say that experiments are especially high in internal validity. This is especially important because the whole goal of science is to understand causes. True experiments that use random assignment, that take steps to eliminate procedural and operational confounds, and that police noise yield a lot of information about causes that would usually elude researchers using most any other method. Experiments thus allow researchers to determine whether the independent variable, the whole independent variable, and nothing but the independent variable has an impact on some outcome of interest. As R. A. Fisher (1935) put it, virtually every new thing human beings have come to know throughout history is based on "learning by experience." In this regard he added, "experimental observations are only experience carefully planned in advance." Experimentation is about making careful observations, under the best possible viewing conditions.

Are True Experiments Realistic?

Although experimentation may be the cat's meow, anyone who has been around a meowing cat for very long knows that meowing cats have some drawbacks. In this next section, we discuss the most serious potential disadvantage of experimentation, the fact that experiments may be unrealistic. We then devote a great deal of attention to the question of what can be done to address this potential problem. We will expand on the potential list of disadvantages of experiments in Chapter 7, by the way, when we discuss quasi-experiments, close cousins of true experiments that represent a different answer to the question of how to make the results of laboratory experiments more realistic.

The Problem: Artificiality

Perhaps the most common criticism of experiments is that they are "artificial" and thus may not reflect what happens in the real world. Consider the Isen and Levin (1972) study described near the beginning of this chapter. These authors showed that receiving a cookie made people more helpful than usual. But how often do people receive a cookie prior to witnessing someone else's need for help? This must rarely happen, and so it is worth asking whether more realistic mood manipulations (e.g., watching a happy movie, winning money at a casino) would have exactly the same effect on people's likelihood of helping a stranger whose car has broken down on the New Jersey Turn-pike. If realism is a mild problem for Isen and Levin's study of helping, it might appear to be a total disaster for Festinger and Carlsmith's (1959) study of cognitive dissonance. Have *you* ever been asked to perform a boring peg-turning task? Did the person who asked you to do so offer you $1 or $20 to tell a stranger that the boring task was actually quite interesting? If so, we sus-pect that this happened while you were a participant in a psychological exper-iment. Does this famous study tell us anything about how a hit man would reduce his dissonance when he realized that he had accidentally killed the wrong person? What about an 11-year-old girl who smokes a cigarette to impress a friend when she has always believed that smoking is bad?

The lack of realism in psychology experiments has received a great deal of critical attention. In the late 1960s and early 1970s, the field of social psy-chology experienced a sort of crisis in confidence regarding this issue. Because experimental laboratories are artificial situations and because they often use convenience samples of college students, a growing contingent of psycholo-gists became concerned about the ability of laboratory research to say anything meaningful about the real world. In its most extreme form, this criticism holds that laboratory research can tell us only how a particular group of people will respond to particular manipulations while they are in the laboratory—and nothing about how anyone else responds to anything else while they are any-place else. Can laboratory research tell us anything about broad principles of human nature? In Chapter 3, you learned that this concern has to do with the *external validity* of laboratory research. External validity refers to the extent to which a set of research findings provides an accurate description of what typ-ically happens in the real world. An externally valid laboratory finding applies to lots of different people in lots of different natural situations.

The Solution: Two Forms of Realism

In a climate where many people were questioning the value of laboratory experiments, some researchers decided to take a stand in favor of experimen-tation. One pair of influential researchers who took such a stand was Aronson and Carlsmith (1968). In the spirit of Fisher's original claim that experimenta-tion is merely experience carefully planned, Aronson and Carlsmith argued that there is no inherent reason that lab experiments have to be low in external validity. Furthermore, they made some concrete, practical suggestions about what researchers can do to maximize the external validity of psychological experiments. According to Aronson and Carlsmith, concerns about the artifi-ciality of laboratory experiments, though well-intended, missed the most important point behind these experiments. The point is not so much to emu-late reality as to reveal what lies beneath the surface of reality. Nonetheless, Aronson and Carlsmith noted that one simple way to make laboratory experi-ments more realistic would be to make them more physically similar to the real world. To use their terminology, studies that physically resemble the real world are high in **mundane realism.** To increase mundane realism, simply make a study as similar as possible to the real world setting you care about. If you are interested in studying gambling behavior, for example, you might consider setting up a real roulette wheel, hiring a research assistant to deliver free beers to your participants, and giving them a real stake of casino chips that they could gamble with under different experimental conditions (say, for example, after having had three regular or three alcohol-free beers). The setting of this study would strongly resemble the setting of a real casino, and thus it might reassure some people that the study's findings would travel well to real casinos. Although there is some merit to this approach, Aronson and Carlsmith argued that laboratory experimenters can best increase the external validity of their research findings by means of a radically different approach. They argued that rather than pursuing mundane realism, laboratory experimenters would usually be a better off pursuing **experimental realism.**

Experimental realism refers to the degree to which a research study is psychologically meaningful to research participants. We might also call it *psychological realism*. If a study is high in mundane realism when it *looks* just like the real world, a study is high in experimental realism when it *feels* just like the real world. The issue behind experimental realism is that research participants should truly experience the psychological states in which the experimenters are interested and thus behave naturally and spontaneously rather than artificially or self-consciously. A good example of a research program that appears to have been very high in experimental realism is Asch's (1955, 1956) research on conformity. Conformity was particularly interesting to psychologists in Asch's day because many psychologists had been personally affected by the events of World War II. Researchers hoped that gaining a better understanding of conformity could give them a better understanding of some of the horrible events of this war. At a much more mundane level, just about everyone knows what it is like to want to be like others. Asch knew this very well. If he had been strongly concerned about mundane realism, Asch could have asked teenagers to come into the laboratory to see how individual teenagers would respond to subtle group pressures to try a cigarette. Alternatively, Asch could have asked a group of upper-level managers to try to reach a difficult financial decision, to see if those who held a minority viewpoint would conform to the opinions of the majority. Instead of doing either of these things, Asch created a completely novel situation that bore very little physical resemblance to the schoolyard or the boardroom.

Asch did this by bringing participants to his laboratory for what appeared to be a boring study of visual perception. From the perspective of Asch's participants, their job was very simple: to make a series of judgments about the lengths of some lines. After taking a seat at a table with six other people who appeared to be co-participants, the real participants patiently waited their turns to announce which of three lines printed on a card was equal in length to a standard line. An example of one of the stimulus sets used by Asch appears in Figure 6.1. The first couple of trials of this experiment passed uneventfully as the real participants watched their peers announce the obvious answers to Asch's perceptual questions. However, in several crucial trials, most participants found themselves rubbing their eyes in disbelief. One by one, each of the first five participants calmly and confidently provided

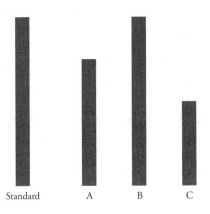

FIGURE 6.1   One of the stimulus sets used in the Asch (1955) study of conformity

patently *incorrect* answers to the questions. In some trials, for instance, these trained research assistants announced that line A was identical to the standard.

This placed the real research participants in a big dilemma. Would they shoot straight from the hip and deviate from the unanimous judgments of the other group members? Or would they ignore what their eyes were telling them and cave in to the subtle but potent pressure of the group? Most participants (75%) caved in and conformed on at least some of the crucial trials. If the facial expressions of Asch's participants were any indication of their state of mind during the experiment, this study was *very* high in experimental realism. In some of the surviving photos of participants in these studies, participants appeared to be dumbfounded by the misguided judgments of their peers, and yet they often parroted these incorrect judgments to the experimenter as if they were their own. This is exactly the sort of conformity process that researchers wanted to understand. Asch's methodology proved to be an excellent tool to study conformity not only because it maximized experimental realism but also because it readily permitted the use of experimental manipulations. In a careful set of studies using this line-judging procedure, Asch systematically manipulated a variety of variables that proved to have a potent effect on conformity rates. For instance, when Asch planted a single dissenter in the otherwise unanimous majority, conformity was reduced to about 20% of the original levels. This finding suggests that adolescents would be in a much better position to avoid smoking if they could locate a single "ally" who was willing to march to the beat of a healthier drummer. Although the unique and contrived setting that Asch created bore little resemblance to most real-world settings, the psychological experiences of Asch's participants appear to have been very genuine and meaningful. His participants truly were confused, they truly did not want to risk the rejection of others, and they truly reported judgments that flew in the face of reality.

Another classic example of an experiment that appears to have been high in experimental realism is Triplett's (1898) study of competition and performance. From his own experience as a bicyclist, Triplett noticed that trained athletes appeared to perform better when competing head to head with other athletes than when performing alone. For example, Triplett's careful observations of highly trained cyclists revealed that they produced better times when racing against one another than when racing against the clock (typically in an effort to break a record). If you think about how enormously important fast times are to highly trained cyclists, you might assume that these highly motivated and conditioned athletes would always push themselves to the limits of their abilities every time they raced—whether they were racing against the rapidly turning hands of a stopwatch or the rapidly churning legs of another rider. But Triplett noticed that the presence of a competitor seemed to improve people's performances. To put his observations to an experimental test, Triplett brought 40 children to his laboratory and had them play a game in which they tried to pull a small flag as quickly as possible around a 4-meter racecourse. They did so by reeling in a long silk string that was attached to a fishing reel. Triplett observed the same thing among kids trying to reel in flags that he had observed in the real world of athletes trying to reel in trophies. The presence of competitors facilitated performance.

Was Triplett's study high in experimental realism? Ironically, some of the best clues come from some of the rare participants in his experiment who did *not* confirm Triplett's predictions regarding social facilitation. Although Triplett found that competition *usually* facilitated performance, he also noted that competition sometimes caused people, especially young children, to become "overstimulated," leading to *decreases* in performance. In the interest of fairness, Triplett described the participants who disconfirmed his expectations just as carefully as he described those who confirmed them. He noted that whereas virtually everyone in his experiment *tried harder* to do well when competing against another person, some people's efforts did not pay off. After providing a statistical summary of the behavior of the ten participants who fell apart under the pressure of competition, Triplett provided a verbal description that suggests that his experiment was indeed high in experimental realism:

> This [reduction in performance] seems to be brought about in large measure
> by the mental attitude of the subject. An intense desire to win, for instance,
> often resulting in over-stimulation. Accompanying the phenomena were
> labored breathing, flushed faces and a stiffening or contraction of the muscles
> of the arm. A number of young children of from 5 to 9 years, not included in
> our group of 40, exhibited the phenomena most strikingly, the rigidity of the
> arm preventing free movement and in some cases resulting in an almost total
> inhibition of movement. The effort to continue turning in these cases was by
> a swaying of the whole body.

Triplett studied adults as well as children in his experiment, and his descriptions of the adults also make it clear that his participants cared deeply about his experimental task. Incidentally, we want to remind you that Triplett was forthright enough to describe the behavior of participants whose behavior was *disrupted* rather than facilitated by the presence of other people. Interestingly, Triplett's observations of the participants who fell apart under social pressure are consistent with contemporary research showing that the presence

It was just Lenny's luck to draw a first-round match
against last year's champion.

of other people can either *facilitate* or *disrupt* performance. Which effect the presence of other people has on performance depends on the degree to which the behavior being performed is easy or well learned. The presence of other people contributes positively to our performance only when the behavior in question is easy or well practiced (Zajonc, 1965).

A more contemporary example of a study high in experimental realism can be found in Judith Edney's (1979) research on the *commons dilemma*. In her research on this social trap, Edney introduces a group of real participants to an experimental game in which they are allowed to remove desirable resources (such as nuts, candies, or game tokens) from a common pool that is replenished after each round of play (after each time that all participants have individually had an opportunity to withdraw as many units as they wish from the pool). Edney's participants learn at the outset of the game that the experimenter will *double* all the remaining units of the resource at the end of each round (for a limited number of rounds or until the pool of resources is exhausted, whichever comes first). So if her participants played it smart, they would all withdraw nothing from the pool until the final round, at which time an equal split of the resources would give everyone more than any one participant could have possibly gained by taking everything on the first round. Experimental gaming studies such as these have consistently yielded an interesting and distressing finding: People rarely cooperate. Very few groups make it past the first round without exhausting the pool of resources. In fact, during the first round of the game, participants usually begin a mad dash to grab the resources. Some groups of participants have even knocked bowls of nuts to the floor as they scrambled to claim the lion's share of the initial pool of resources. As contrived as this situation might be, it appears to contain the essential psychological ingredients of many real-world commons dilemmas (e.g., the bulldozing of tropical rain forests or the overfishing of lakes and rivers). This artificial situation strongly piques people's interest in a limited resource, and it produces meaningful levels of greed based on mutual distrust.

To get a better feel for the lengths to which psychologists will sometimes go to create an ideal experimental environment, consider the following passage in which MacDonald, Zanna, and Fong (1995) describe the use of deception in a study of how alcohol influences judgment. To address concerns that some of their previous experimental findings might be attributable to placebo effects (i.e., to people's expectancies about how alcohol influences judgment), MacDonald et al. conducted a simple study in which they tried to convince all their participants (even those who were not intoxicated) that they had consumed quite a bit of alcohol:

> Nevertheless, to ensure that our results were not due to expectancy effects, we ran a placebo experiment, comparing the responses of people who received alcohol (n = 27) with those in a placebo condition (n = 23). Participants in the placebo condition were led to believe that they were consuming alcohol and Wink [a brand of soda] through smell, sight, and taste cues, but they were really receiving only a minute amount of alcohol. From our reading of alcohol studies that include a placebo condition . . . we took a number of steps to ensure that our manipulation was convincing to participants. While participants were completing a measure in another room, we sprayed the room where they would be consuming their drinks with a mixture of water and alcohol to provide smell cues. Participants also saw us pour their drinks: We had put flattened tonic water into an alcohol bottle so that participants in the placebo condition could see us pouring a clear liquid from an alcohol bottle into their drinks. Finally, we put a very small amount of alcohol (1 teaspoon) disguised as lime juice on top of their drinks so that the first taste of their drinks was mostly alcohol. Our manipulation did indeed convince placebo participants that they had consumed alcohol: Despite the fact that their actual breathalyzer readings were .000% or .001% in all cases, the average BAL [blood alcohol level] estimate for the placebo group was .072%, which was comparable to the actual BAL of participants in the intoxicated condition (M = .067%). None of our placebo participants expressed any suspicion during the debriefing—in fact, a number of them reacted with surprise and disbelief that they were not actually intoxicated.

MacDonald et al. follow this description with a footnote that adds a colorful and concrete picture of the effectiveness of their placebo strategy:

> One participant in the placebo condition actually refused to believe that he was not intoxicated. After the experimenter showed him the breathalyzer reading of .000, he argued that the breathalyzer must be "rigged," and he insisted on remaining in the laboratory until he felt sober enough to leave.

MacDonald et al. then demonstrated that there were important differences between the behavioral intentions of the participants in the placebo condition and the intentions of those in the intoxication condition. Relative to those who thought they were intoxicated but were actually sober, those who actually were intoxicated were less negatively disposed toward the idea of drinking and driving. MacDonald et al. appear to have captured a sobering psychological truth about drinking and driving. The fact that careful laboratory experiments often require the use of deception raises some difficult ethical issues. These issues are important enough that we will discuss them in detail in Chapter 9.

Is There a Recipe for Experimental Realism?

At this point, you may have noticed that we identified a serious criticism of experimentation and then quickly countered this criticism with a discussion of how experimental realism can save the day. Having said this much, we hasten to add that, just as nonexperimental researchers need to think long and hard about internal validity, laboratory experimenters need to think long and hard about external validity. Experimental realism only comes to the rescue when we know how to dial the right number. That is, experimental realism increases our confidence in the external validity of experimental research findings only when we can be certain that the participants in an experiment do, in fact, experience the psychological states the experimenter hoped to create. This can be difficult to establish. It essentially boils down to deciding whether a measure or manipulation is high in *construct validity.*

Construct validity provides us with a good way of thinking about experimental realism. For example, it highlights the fact that assessing any kind of validity often boils down to thinking carefully about whether a researcher did things the way he or she should have. Was Festinger and Carlsmith's famous experiment high in construct validity? As a big point in their favor, the whole reason that this study became so famous is that it struck most people that these experimenters had found an excellent way of creating dissonance in the laboratory. On the other hand, creative researchers who were not huge fans of cognitive dissonance theory were able to come up with a variety of alternate perspectives on what happens in the hearts and minds of participants who take part in studies of cognitive dissonance. Bem (1967), as you may recall, raised some excellent questions about whether Festinger and Carlsmith's participants were truly experiencing cognitive dissonance. (Remember the Bob Downing study?) In the end, however, critical analyses of cognitive dissonance theory only made the theory stronger by identifying its boundary conditions.

So how, exactly, do we know when a study is high in experimental realism? Unfortunately, it is hard to say. In fact, creating experimental realism is probably as much an art as it is a science. If there is a crucial ingredient, it is probably the same kind of thing that goes into activities like acting, stage direction, and puppeteering. It is the ability to identify the gist of a psychological experience and translate it into the precise but limited language of the lab without losing anything important. To paraphrase a famous definition of pornography, most psychologists would probably say that even though they cannot provide a simple formula for guaranteeing experimental realism, they can always recognize it when they see it. Fortunately, there are also empirical answers to questions about experimental realism. If you're not so sure that you've latched onto a manipulation that is high in experimental realism, you can always ask your research participants themselves what they think. Specifically, researchers can include *manipulation checks* in their experiments. We'll discuss manipulation checks in more detail in Chapter 9. However, the basic concept of a manipulation check is pretty simple. A manipulation check is a measure designed to see if a manipulation truly put people in the psychological state that the experimenter wished to create. For instance, if you were trying to manipulate the physical attractiveness of a confederate who asked participants for a favor, you could ask participants to report how physically attractive they found the confederate with whom they interacted. Alternately, if you were worried that questions about the confederate's attractiveness would make participants suspicious, you could show photos of the confederates to a group of people who didn't actually take part in the study and have them make some ratings. In either event, you could address the psychological realism of your manipulation empirically.

If one defines "ingredients" loosely, it may be possible to identify an additional ingredient of experimental realism. Unfortunately, high levels of experimental realism usually require the use of at least some minimal level of *deception*. Pretty frequently, the quest for experimental realism requires researchers to convince their participants that they are taking part in one kind of study when they are actually taking part in a study of something completely different. At a bare minimum, experimental realism almost always requires a more passive sort of lie in which experimenters fail to inform participants up front about the precise reasons the study is being conducted. In other words, experimental realism is about creating convincing illusions that cause people to experience the precise situations you care about as a researcher. Just as Festinger and Carlsmith weren't really studying peg-turning, Asch wasn't really interested in visual perception. Even Edney, whose study involved no elaborate lies or cover-ups, was interested in much more than a simple game involving nuts.

The use of deception appears to be on the wane in psychology, and we personally see this as a favorable development. Although there are times that it is very difficult to study phenomena at all without using deception, the routine use of deception can erode people's trust in the science of psychology. We will return to this issue in Chapter 9. For now, we simply note that a shift away from using deception in laboratory experiments reflects a changing sensibility among psychologists. To some degree, this change may reflect a tendency for researchers to forgo the experimental realism of the laboratory in pursuit of the mundane realism in the world around them. For better or worse, researchers who tell their participants that they are interested in visual perception or peg-turning are not studying topics such as conformity or cognitive dissonance. Increasingly, they are studying topics such as visual perception or peg-turning.

Trade-Offs Between Internal and External Validity

It has been suggested many times that there are strong trade-offs betweeen external and internal validity, as if researchers often need to choose one form of validity over the other. However, as suggested by our discussion of experimental realism, the methodological trade-off between internal and external validity isn't quite as hard-and-fast as one might think. After all, we just saw that cleverly designed laboratory studies that mimic the psychological states occurring in everyday life can sometimes prove to be very high in external validity. By the same token, carefully designed naturalistic studies that do not use experimental manipulations and that do not take place in the laboratory sometimes prove to be very high in internal validity. This is important to remember because experimental and nonexperimental results will sometimes contradict one another, and the conclusion that people most often jump to is that the laboratory study must be more internally valid than the field study. A potential case in point comes from social psychological research on depression. In the late 1970s, laboratory researchers carefully documented what became known as the "sadder but wiser" effect. In a highly influential laboratory study, Alloy and Abramson (1979) found that depressed and nondepressed students possessed very different opinions of their level of control over a series of lights in a laboratory contingency task. You might expect the pessimistically biased depressed students to underestimate their degree of control over the lights. After all, most of us tend to assume that depressed people view the world in negatively biased ways. However, this is not what Alloy and Abramson observed. Instead, the depressed students reported highly *accurate* views of their degree of control over the experimental task. The biased ones were the nondepressed students, who greatly overestimated their degree of control. This study, along with many subsequent laboratory studies, led most researchers to conclude that it is depressed rather than nondepressed people who see the world as it really is.

However, in the early 1990s, Dunning and Story (1991) pointed out that the laboratory judgment task used by Alloy and Abramson might not be telling the whole story about depression. They suggested that a more reasonable index of the accuracy of people's judgments could be obtained by asking people to make predictions about real, personally meaningful life events that could conceivably befall them in the future (e.g., getting placed on academic probation, getting dumped by a relationship partner, getting fired or demoted at work). When Dunning and Story compared people's *predictions* about the events (e.g., "I think that five of the ten bad things you asked me about will happen to me this semester") with the *actual occurrence* of the events over the course of the semester (e.g., "three of the ten bad things on your list actually happened to me this semester"), they observed results that were strikingly different from those of Alloy and Abramson. They found that it was actually the depressed people who were more optimistic! As Alloy and Abramson might have expected, the depressed people did make somewhat gloomy predictions about their futures. However, the *actual futures* of the depressed people were noticeably gloomier than what these depressed people had predicted. In contrast, the futures of the nondepressed students were typically about as rosy as they had predicted.

Despite the rigorous nature of Alloy and Abramson's laboratory task, they may have drawn an inaccurate conclusion about the true relation between depression and judgment. Depression may actually foster optimism rather than accuracy or pessimism (see Pelham, 1991b, for additional evidence that depression is occasionally associated with optimism). Of course, Dunning and Story do not argue that depression is good for you. Depression is a leading cause of suicide and has many other negative consequences. Their point was that laboratory studies may have yielded a misleading answer to the specific question of how depression biases judgments and predictions. On the other hand, even if we assume that Dunning and Story's story about depression and judgment is the bottom line, this does not mean that Alloy and Abramson's research was uninformative. First, there are probably some real-world judgments that bear a greater resemblance to Alloy and Abramson's contingency task than they do to Dunning and Story's prediction task. For these kinds of judgments, Alloy and Abramson may still be correct. Second, if we assume that one of the goals of research is to move toward greater and greater approximations of the truth, Alloy and Abramson's work played an extremely important role in revealing truths about depression by prompting a tremendous amount of research (including the research of Dunning and Story) on this important topic.

A similar example of an internally valid naturalistic study that convinced some people to rethink findings from the laboratory can be found in the research on temperature and aggression. The results of laboratory experiments involving direct manipulations of temperature have been surprisingly complex and somewhat inconsistent. For example, some experiments have revealed that increases in temperature lead to increases in aggression only when research participants have received *positive* rather than negative evaluations from the potential target of their aggressive behavior (Baron & Bell, 1976). Other experiments have revealed that increases in temperature increase aggression only to a point (they suggest that the relation between temperature and aggression is curvilinear).

In contrast to the mixed bag of findings that have been observed in the laboratory, field studies have consistently yielded much clearer and simpler findings. Specifically, most passive observational studies have revealed simple, linear relations between temperature and aggression. For example, among drivers in frequently sweltering Phoenix, Arizona, rates of aggressive horn honking at a stopped car increased as a direct function of temperature. Moreover, the increases were most pronounced among drivers who had their windows rolled down on hot days (and presumably didn't have the relief provided by air conditioning; Kenrick & MacFarlane, 1986). Similarly, in a large archival study of violent and nonviolent crime, Anderson (1987) observed that rates of hostile crimes such as murder, rape, and assault were higher in hotter cities than in cooler cities and were higher than usual during hotter quarters and hotter years within a given city. Moreover, rates of less violent crimes showed little or no increase as temperatures climbed. Similar findings have been observed in other natural settings. For example, in an archival analysis of over 800 major-league baseball games, Reifman, Larrick, and Fein (1991) found that pitchers were more likely to hit batters during games played on hot days. This tendency for hotter days to produce more beanballs appears to be linear: The hotter the day, the more likely pitchers are to throw at batters rather than at strike zones.

It is noteworthy that the participants who have been studied in naturalistic investigations such as these have never known that their aggressive behavior was the subject of psychological scrutiny. In lab experiments, however, it seems much more likely that some participants may have been able to guess that their aggressive behavior was the subject of psychological investigation (see Anderson, 1989). As we noted earlier, another reason that field experiments may yield better than usual information about causality in the case of research on temperature and aggression is that we can confidently assume that aggression does *not* cause heat. In many other areas of research, bidirectionality is possible. For example, do high levels of self-esteem cause people to seek out favorable social feedback, or does favorable social feedback lead people to develop high self-esteem? Either causal account is plausible. Moreover, because temperature is a simple, objectively measurable environmental variable, it is probably a little easier than usual to disentangle the effects of temperature from the effects of naturally occurring confounds (such as unemployment rates or seasonal variations in testosterone levels) that might also account for the observed connection between temperature and aggression. For reasons such as these, we suspect that in comparison with lab experiments, carefully conducted naturalistic studies of temperature and aggression may be just as high in internal validity. That is, they may provide equally accurate information about the causal role of heat in aggression, even though they disagree with the results in the laboratory. In short, inconsistencies between experimental and correlational results do not mean that one result or the other needs to be discarded. Often, these inconsistencies reveal a more interesting story than one would learn from a reliance on one method or the other.

When causal claims seem reasonable in field research, the boost in external validity that comes from field settings makes for some very compelling research statements. Nonetheless, we want to make it clear that laboratory experiments still hold certain clear advantages over correlational or passive observational studies. First, recall that despite some interesting exceptions, laboratory experiments *usually* yield superior information about causality. Second, even when it comes to sensitive topics such as aggression, laboratory experiments may yield important insights into the psychological mechanisms that are responsible for a research finding documented in the field. For example, Rule, Taylor, and Dobbs (1987) conducted an experiment in which they asked people to complete ambiguously aggressive story stems under cool or hot working conditions. They found that, relative to cool and comfortable participants, their overheated participants generated story completions containing significantly more negative emotions, more themes of frustration, and more themes of aggression. These findings suggest that one specific route through which temperature leads to aggression is by making aggressive thoughts more *cognitively accessible* than usual. Needless to say, it would be hard to document this kind of thing in a passive observational study. To paraphrase Fisher, observations such as these have to be carefully planned in advance. As this example should also suggest, the most compelling way to make a solid case for a theory (e.g., a theory of heat and aggression) would be to make use of a wide variety of different methods and hope that they all converge on the same conclusion. Laboratory findings such as those of Rule et al. have helped researchers figure out the precise *reasons* why so many other researchers have found correlational evidence that heat fosters aggressive behavior. Thus, field research told researchers what they should try to understand, and the laboratory research helped them do exactly that.

As a final comparison between laboratory and naturalistic studies, we want to emphasize the fact that good, careful naturalistic studies are not good and careful just because they happen to be conducted outside the laboratory. Simply going to "the field" is no guarantee of *any* kind of validity, external or otherwise. Although it is often assumed that conducting a study in the field guarantees that the study will be high in external validity, this is not always the case. In principle, field settings can be just as narrow and delimiting as lab settings. The real world, after all, isn't simply one gigantic, homogeneous field (see Banaji & Crowder, 1989). As a case in point, consider a very creative field experiment on self-awareness and socially undesirable behavior. A good deal of theory and research suggests that self-awareness (the awareness of our personal identities as well as our internal ideals and standards) reduces the likelihood that people will engage in socially undesirable behaviors such as lying or cheating. Beaman, Klentz, Diener, and Svanum (1979) decided to test this idea by conducting a field experiment focusing on trick-or-treaters who had the opportunity to steal pieces of candy. As the Halloweeners were entering a home, Beaman et al. manipulated the kids' levels of self-awareness in two distinct ways (by asking some of the kids their names and by sometimes placing a mirror in front of the bowl of candy). Regardless of the kids' level of manipulated self-awareness, the adult who interacted with the kids always directed them to the bowl of candy, asked them to take only a *single* piece, and walked away. As illustrated in Figure 6.2, the kids who were least likely to take extra candy were those who were most likely to have been made highly self-aware. Specifically, among the kids who had been asked their names and who were also exposed to the mirror, only about 9% took extra candy. In contrast, among those who had been asked their names but who were not exposed to the mirror, almost 38% took extra candy. Among those who had not been asked their names, the presence of the mirror made no difference.

Although this clever study involved the real behavior of real kids in the real world, this does not guarantee that these results would generalize to the hundreds of different real situations in which self-awareness might be expected to influence behavior. This study simply shows that self-awareness *can* influence behavior in some instances. If you think about it, you'll realize that this is exactly what a laboratory study always shows you. It shows that certain variables can influence certain outcomes in certain situations, but this only begs the question of how often these variables do influence these outcomes and in how many different situations. From this perspective, assessing the generalizability of a research finding should be done by seeing just how well the finding really does generalize across people and situations, and this question can never be answered by a single study, regardless of its methodology. No matter where a set of findings occurs, the question of external validity has to do with the degree to which the findings can be obtained in a wide variety of different settings using a wide variety of sensible manipulations and measures. In the case of self-awareness, by the way, there is good evidence that self-awareness plays an important role in reducing the likelihood that people will behave dishonestly. In a wide variety of settings, self-awareness

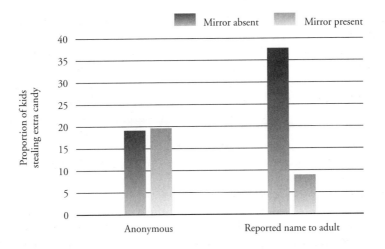

FIGURE 6.2 *Proportion of trick-or-treaters stealing candy as a function of anonymity and presence of mirror (from Beaman et al., 1979)*

manipulations have had a potent effect on people's tendencies to behave dishonestly (e.g., see Diener & Wallbom, 1976). This is just one example of how a little study can advance a big idea.

METHODOLOGY EXERCISE 2

Random Assignment

As you know, random assignment is one of the defining features of true experiments. To see how well random assignment works, why not try it yourself? Below there is a table describing 20 people who differ on all kinds of variables, from height to self-esteem. What would happen if you randomly assigned each person to an experimental or a control condition for a hypothetical experiment? Would your experimental and control groups be similar on all the dimensions listed? To find out, start at the top of your list and flip a fair coin to determine each person's condition. If the coin lands on heads, circle the **e** next to that person's participant number to indicate that you have assigned that particular person to your *experimental* group (and enter that person's scores in the appropriate set of blanks below the list). If the coin lands on tails, circle the **c** next to that person's participant number to indicate that you have assigned that person to your *control* group (and enter the person's scores in the other set of blanks). When you have worked your way through the entire list of 20 people, you should compute group means on each of the variables listed and enter them (rounded to the nearest hundredth of a point) in the spaces provided at the bottom of the table (or, if you're reluctant to mark up this book, use a photocopy of the table).

Pcond.	Age	IQ	Height	Surgency	Self-esteem
1 ce	16	145	73	10	42
2 ce	17	73	64	12	48
3 ce	21	86	70	9	30
4 ce	39	108	71	1	36
5 ce	18	58	72	5	38
6 ce	37	109	70	9	42
7 ce	31	91	68	7	28
8 ce	25	124	73	9	39
9 ce	23	64	66	6	40
10 ce	21	121	61	6	36
11 ce	28	93	71	5	45
12 ce	21	107	74	6	44
13 ce	26	94	64	4	43
14 ce	25	114	72	9	35
15 ce	31	78	68	7	40
16 ce	15	104	71	6	45
17 ce	25	128	68	7	42
18 ce	17	81	66	7	41
19 ce	21	136	65	9	38
20 ce	23	97	75	6	42

Experimental Group ($n = $ ____)   Control Group ($n = $ ____)

#	Age	IQ	Height	Surg.	Esteem	#	Age	IQ	Height	Surg.	Esteem
___	___	___	___	___	___	___	___	___	___	___	___
___	___	___	___	___	___	___	___	___	___	___	___
___	___	___	___	___	___	___	___	___	___	___	___
___	___	___	___	___	___	___	___	___	___	___	___
___	___	___	___	___	___	___	___	___	___	___	___
___	___	___	___	___	___	___	___	___	___	___	___
___	___	___	___	___	___	___	___	___	___	___	___
___	___	___	___	___	___	___	___	___	___	___	___
___	___	___	___	___	___	___	___	___	___	___	___
___	___	___	___	___	___	___	___	___	___	___	___
___	___	___	___	___	___	___	___	___	___	___	___
___	___	___	___	___	___	___	___	___	___	___	___
___	___	___	___	___	___	___	___	___	___	___	___
M_e	___	___	___	___	___	M_c	___	___	___	___	___

Questions

1. On the whole are the two groups as similar as you expected? (This question could be answered correctly with either a yes or a no. The important thing is to explain your answer.)
2. Do the two groups differ meaningfully on any of the variables measured? That is, did random assignment appear to work better for some variables than for others? (This question isn't as easy as it may seem. Be sure you give some thought to the fact that the different variables are scored in very different ways. For example, IQ scores of 101 and 107 are pretty similar. Is a 6-point difference in age equally small? A clue: standard deviation.)
3. Remembering (a) that any differences you observed must have been the result of chance and (b) that experimenters typically take it for granted that their experimental and control groups are identical prior to any manipulations, imagine that your participants differed noticeably on only one variable—self-esteem. Describe briefly an experiment or kind of experiment in which this preexisting difference between your groups might have disastrous consequences. Describe a different kind of experiment in which this particular difference would be unlikely to pose any problems. Be specific about why the failure of random assignment would be problematic in one study (and would not be problematic in the other).
4. Next, assume that you had a group of 40 people at your disposal rather than 20. What advantages and disadvantages would the extra 20 people pose? Make sure you frame at least one of your answers to this question in terms of the goal of random assignment.

Notes

1. If you defined internal validity in terms of underlying constructs rather than experimental manipulations, this argument would no longer be valid. Conceptual validity would reduce internal validity because a hypothetical variable other than the one the experimenter had in mind could be the real reason for the observed changes in the dependent variable. Because most methodologists define internal validity in terms of *manipulations and measures* (i.e., independent and dependent variables) rather than hypothetical constructs, this is the approach we adopt in this text.

2. By *subliminal* priming, we mean presenting words (or other stimuli) to people very, very briefly and following the briefly presented words immediately with some kind of *mask*. In Devine's case this meant presenting words for 80 milliseconds (a little less than 1/12th of a second) and following the words immediately with a series of random letters. The important thing about subliminal priming is that people are unaware of having seen the priming words (and cannot tell you what the words were). Nonetheless, the priming words often influence people's judgments in subsequent tasks.

3. You're also correct that, technically speaking, this is not a true experiment. This is the case because one of the independent variables was measured rather than manipulated. However, the basic point remains. It's much easier to combine multiple independent variables in experiments than in other research designs.

Experience Carefully Exploited: Quasi-Experimental Research Designs

But Daniel resolved not to defile himself with the royal food and wine, and he asked the chief official for permission not to defile himself in this way . . . but the official told Daniel, "I am afraid of my lord the king, who has assigned your food and drink. Why should he see you looking worse than the other young men your age? The king would then have my head because of you." Daniel then said . . . "Please test your servants for ten days: Give us nothing but vegetables to eat and water to drink. Then compare our appearance with that of the young men who eat the royal food and treat us in accordance with what you see." So he agreed to this and tested them for ten days.
—Daniel *1:8–14*

One Very Old Story

Unless you are well versed in both the ancient book of Daniel and the modern logic of quasi-experiments, you may not be in the best position to appreciate the important methodological lesson behind Daniel's proposal to this chief official of the Babylonian King, Nebuchadnezzar. In the interest of learning as much as possible from the Israelites he had conquered, King Nebuchadnezzar brought a group of scholarly young Jews into his palace for some intellectual discussions. The king rolled out the red carpet by providing these young men from the enemy camp with the same royal food and wine that he provided to his own royal servants. It seems safe to assume that Nebuchadnezzar would have been annoyed to learn that these young men refused to eat his royal food (they refused the food, by the way, because it wasn't kosher). This put the king's chief official in a difficult position. He really liked these young men, and he personally didn't mind it if they wanted to pass up on all these royal delicacies. However, if he allowed these young men to eat nothing but the rough equivalent of bread and water, he figured they would soon become unhealthy. At this point, the king would demand to know what was going on. Heads would roll, and the chief official's head would probably roll first. Daniel proposed a simple quasi-experiment designed to address the chief official's worries about their highly restricted diet, and you now know why.

So Daniel was apparently a pretty smart cookie (despite the fact that his diet never included any). But would Daniel's proposal have differed if he had known about the beauty and power of the experimental method? Could he have proposed a more sophisticated design? Perhaps he should have proposed the following test instead:

> Please test your servants for ten days: *Randomly assign half of them to receive vegetables to eat and water to drink, and assign half of them to receive royal food to eat and wine to drink.* Then have trained judges who know not of the experimental manipulation compare the appearances of the servants in the vegetable-and-water lot with those in the royal-food-and-wine lot. Let conventional statistical tests be used to determine if these two groups differ from each other, and treat us in accordance with the results of these analyses.

Although this design may *sound* more sophisticated than Daniel's design, it is actually what we sometimes like to call an ill-conceived, or *Dumas,* design (it's pronounced Dew-*moss,* but if you add the letters "b" and "s" in certain strategic locations, you'll see what we mean). This design would be useless as a test of Daniel's position because his position was tightly linked to his deeply held religious beliefs about diet. Daniel *wasn't* arguing that vegetables and water build better bodies than royal food and wine. Instead, he was proposing that God would keep him and his friends healthy *even if* they ate only vegetables and water. This story thus illustrates one of the most important reasons why people don't always conduct true experiments to test important ideas. They often don't because they often can't.

Before we discuss exactly why researchers can't always conduct true experiments, let's pause to appreciate the research design that Daniel actually proposed. The proposed design is a pretty good example of a **quasi-experiment.** Quasi-experiments are research designs in which researchers have only partial control over their independent variables. Strictly speaking, this means that participants are assigned to one or more conditions in a study by some means other than random assignment. This is what makes a study a quasi-experiment, and quasi-experiments are what this chapter is all about. After reviewing some of the considerations that lead researchers to conduct quasi-experiments, we will explain the logic of conducting and interpreting quasi-experiments. As we will show, the use of quasi-experimental designs can sometimes pose problems for a study's internal validity. However, these problems can often be addressed by identifying meaningful control groups that test for the influence of possible confounds. When threats to internal validity are carefully addressed, quasi-experiments become an extremely useful research tool because, relative to true experiments, quasi-experiments typically provoke fewer concerns about external validity.

Why Quasi-Experiments?

As Cook and Campbell (1979) put it, quasi-experiments are "experiments that have treatments, outcomes measures, and experimental units, but do not use random assignment to create the comparisons from which the treatment-caused change is inferred." As an example of one common kind of quasi-experiment, consider a hypothetical study of instructor teaching styles and student performance. Suppose that at the end of a ten-week statistics course, a researcher gave a standardized quiz to the students of two different statistics professors, Professor Simone and Professor Hardine. If Professor Simone's students outperformed the students of Professor Hardine, it might be because Professor Simone has developed an exceptional teaching style. However, it could also be because Professor Simone has developed a reputation for being exceptionally difficult. Only the brightest and most motivated students may have the gumption to sign up for his course in the first place. As this example illustrates, quasi-experiments often raise concerns about internal validity because *person confounds* might be causing the appearance of effects that would disappear if random assignment were used. Nevertheless, as we hope to demonstrate in this chapter, quasi-experiments can be quite effective at identifying causes and effects when researchers pay careful attention to potential confounds.

For now, we simply point out that quasi-experiments are often the method of choice among researchers who wish to maximize both internal and external validity. One of the primary reasons for this is that true experiments are often impossible to conduct. In other words, all else being equal, possible studies are to be preferred over impossible ones. To illustrate, it simply is not possible to randomly assign people to be male or female, but we know that sex and gender play tremendously important roles in human social behavior. Thus, we often study gender even though we cannot manipulate it. Similarly, it is not possible to experimentally manipulate natural disasters, the presence or absence of motorcycle helmet laws, or the attitudinal similarity of romantic partners. Nevertheless, these variables have some extremely important consequences, and so we don't allow our inability to study them using random assignment to stand in the way of studying them. On a closely related note, some topics than *can* be studied experimentally are still very difficult to study experimentally. Experimentation sometimes requires equipment and resources that many researchers cannot afford (such as computers, video cameras, royal food and wine, and particle accelerators). Sometimes we are forced to abandon "experience carefully planned" in favor of the observations that are provided by nature.

On top of all this, even when random assignment could be done, there are many instances in which it *shouldn't* be done. For ethical reasons, many potentially informative manipulations that could be performed in principle will be avoided in practice. For example, if we really wanted to know more about the causes of AIDS, lung cancer, or heart disease, we could probably make some pretty rapid progress by choosing a group of research participants and exposing a randomly assigned half of them to HIV, asbestos, or diets high in saturated fats. Clearly, there are limitations on what researchers can study using the experimental method. This is true for studies of psychological as well as physical outcomes. If researchers manipulated psychological variables that are thought to influence physical well-being (e.g., social support during bereavement, psychological stress during pregnancy), they could be randomly assigning some people to conditions that lead to serious health problems. Careful, longitudinal studies of pregnancy, for example, have shown that women who experience high levels of stress during pregnancy are more likely than usual to give birth to premature or low birth weight babies (e.g., see Lobel, Dunkel-Schetter, & Scrimshaw, 1992; and see Taylor, Repetti, & Seeman, 1994, for a general review). When it comes to important life outcomes involving physical health, Mother Nature's cruelest manipulations are best left to Mother Nature. Ethical concerns also come into play in the study of sensitive, socially relevant topics such as stereotyping, prejudice, intergroup relations, and aggression. Consider, for example, trying to manipulate the degree to which White people hold intolerant versus egalitarian attitudes about ethnic minorities. Even if such a thing were experimentally feasible, it certainly would be unethical. Few experimental psychologists would feel comfortable creating a group of racists.

Kinds of Quasi-Experiments

To summarize thus far, quasi-experiments are often the design of choice over true experiments for the simple reason that quasi-experiments can often be conducted when true experiments cannot. The fact that people often conduct quasi-experiments when it is impossible or unethical to conduct true experiments might tempt you to think of the quasi-experiment as the cubic zirconium of the methodological world, but nothing could be further from the truth.[1] Quasi-experiments are better thought of as hybrid designs that combine many of the desirable features of both experimental and nonexperimental research designs. Sometimes quasi-experiments do this by bringing measured rather than manipulated variables to the laboratory, and at other times they do so by allowing researchers to investigate a naturally occurring event that approximates an experimental manipulation. Another way to say this is that there are different kinds of quasi-experiments. In this chapter we focus predominantly on the two most commonly used quasi-experimental designs. We refer to these as person-by-treatment quasi-experiments and natural experiments.

Person-by-Treatment Quasi-Experiments

In social, personality, and clinical psychology, the most common kind of quasi-experiment is probably the **person-by-treatment quasi-experiment.** Person-by-treatment quasi-experiments are designs in which the researcher *measures* at least one independent variable and *manipulates* at least one other independent variable. Thus, person-by-treatment quasi-experiments almost always take place in the laboratory, and researchers who use this design always use random assignment to get experimental control over at least one of the independent variables. The only catch is that they also *measure* at least one other independent variable (e.g., self-esteem, extraversion, depression). To illustrate, a clinical researcher interested in depression might identify patients at a clinic who are interested in taking part in laboratory research. Participants would qualify for the study only if they clearly did or clearly did not meet the diagnostic criteria for a major depressive episode. Depression would thus be a measured independent variable. However, once depressed and nondepressed people arrived at the laboratory, they might be asked to perform an experimental task designed to put them in either a positive or a negative mood. Importantly, participants would be randomly assigned to this experimental condition, independent of their level of depression. The dependent measure might be the kind of explanation people offered for negative life events (e.g., being fired from a job, being rejected or ignored by a friend). If the results of this hypothetical study resembled the results of real quasi-experimental studies of depression, we might find that depressed and nondepressed participants explained negative events differently (i.e., depressed people blamed themselves more than nondepressed people) only when participants were in an experimentally induced negative mood.

In social and personality psychology, researchers often do a similar thing by using pencil-and-paper measures of attitudes or personality to create different experimental groups. Specifically, researchers often **prescreen** people on an individual-difference measure by giving the measure to a large group of people prior to the time that they run their laboratory study. The researchers then use these pretest scores to identify two or more **extreme groups.** Extreme groups are groups of people taken from the upper and lower ends of the distribution of an individual-difference measure. The idea behind creating extreme groups is to create categories of research participants who closely resemble the other members of their own groups on the dimension of interest but who differ greatly from the members of the other group. For instance, a researcher might use pretest data on a well-validated self-esteem measure to identify groups of people who score in the top or bottom 25% of a distribution of self-esteem scores. In this way, the researcher creates two groups that can be considered qualitatively different from each other. Notice that this would not be true if the researcher created groups by identifying people in the top or bottom half (i.e., top or bottom 50%) of the total distribution of scores. This second procedure is known as a **median split,** and it used to be a commonly used technique. However, the problem with this approach is that the people who fall near the cutoff score for the two groups (e.g., those who fall either barely below or barely above the median score) are much more similar to one another than they are to the extreme members of their own groups (e.g., those with esteem scores at the 10th and 90th percentiles). It is for this reason, among others, that contemporary researchers usually steer away from the use of median splits. As was the case in our clinical example, however, this selection procedure is only half the story. A study only becomes a quasi-experiment once participants are brought to the laboratory and exposed to an experimental manipulation.

Quasi-experiments that make use of extreme groups might seem to suffer from a serious problem. Specifically, it might seem worrisome that researchers who study extreme groups will not learn anything about people in the middle of the distribution. It is certainly true that you do not learn much about people that you do not study. However, *in most instances,* it is pretty safe to assume that people who possess a medium amount of an attitude or personality trait will respond to treatments in "medium amounts" when compared with people who score at the extremes. The advantage of using only extreme groups in quasi-experiments has to do with *test sensitivity* or the power to detect real effects when they exist. Most researchers feel that *if any effects are to be found,* they will usually find them using the extreme groups method. On the other hand, if researchers do not find any effects using extreme groups, it is usually unlikely that effects will be found at the center of the distribution. This rationale allows researchers to conduct quasi-experiments using a smaller number of people (pulled from the extremes) than they would need if they were to study people across the full range of their individual difference measure. This is particularly important if a laboratory manipulation is difficult, expensive, or time-consuming. Thus, there are some simple, pragmatic reasons to use extreme groups in quasi-experiments. Incidentally, choosing extreme groups is the rough equivalent of what true experimenters almost always do when they manipulate variables in the lab. For instance, if you were manipulating temperature to see if people behave more aggressively than usual when it is hot, it would *not* usually be wise to create 10 or 12 different temperature conditions. Instead, you'd probably just settle on a single comfortable and a single uncomfortable temperature. If a critic had good theoretical reason to believe that medium levels of a variable (like temperature or self-esteem) would yield effects that you had not originally anticipated, then nothing would be holding him or her back from replicating your quasi-experiment and adding a middle group to the mix.

To illustrate a person-by-treatment study that used extreme groups, consider a laboratory study of attitude change by Swann, Pelham, and Chidester (1988; Study 1). These researchers wanted to change the attitudes of people who are highly certain of their opinions. Previous research suggested that this would be a very tall order. Unlike people who aren't so sure of what they think, people who are highly certain of their opinions typically *resist* other people's efforts to change their opinions. These researchers suspected that it might be possible to turn this resistance to an advantage in some persuasion settings. This particular laboratory study focused on female students at the University of Texas who possessed relatively traditional sex-role preferences. *All* the women in the study possessed relatively traditional sex-role attitudes, but some of them were highly certain of their conservative attitudes, and some of them were much less certain. Notice that women were *not* randomly assigned to have different levels of self-certainty. Although it might be possible, in principle, to manipulate self-certainty, this study treated self-certainty as an individual-difference variable. Thus, self-certainty was measured in a pretest, and participants were categorized as high or low in self-certainty before being brought to the laboratory for an experimental manipulation.

In one experimental condition, these old-fashioned women were exposed to a common persuasion technique. Namely, they were asked a series of lead-ing questions that subtly encouraged them to make relatively *liberal* state-ments (e.g., "Why do you think women make better bosses than men?" "What do you like best about men who are sensitive to others?"). Because these women were asked to adopt a view that was different from their own, Swann et al. expected them to adopt more liberal attitudes—*but only when they orig-inally weren't very sure of their attitudes.* In the other experimental condition, participants were exposed to a paradoxical persuasion technique. Specifically, they were asked a series of *extremely conservative* leading questions (e.g., "Why do you think men always make better bosses than women?" "Why do you sympathize with the feelings of some men that women are better kept barefoot and pregnant?"). Because these questions implied an *extremely* con-servative position, Swann et al. felt that participants who knew exactly where they stood would actively resist the premises of the questions (e.g., "Well, I'm not exactly a radical feminist, but it makes me mad when men treat women like they were put here on earth to make babies!"). By working hard to make it clear that they disagreed with the radically conservative positions implied in these extreme questions, these highly self-certain participants would thus have to take a stand in a slightly liberal direction. Having done so, they should decide that they were a little more liberal than they had once thought (see Bem, 1967; Festinger & Carlsmith, 1959).

This study supported Swann et al.'s predictions, and Figure 7.1 summa-rizes the main findings. As you can see, the effects of the two different per-suasion techniques depended on who was being persuaded. Among the women who were uncertain of their opinions, those exposed to the conven-tional (leading liberal) persuasion technique became more liberal, and those exposed to the paradoxical (leading conservative) technique showed little change. On the other hand, among the women who were highly certain of their opinions, the opposite pattern was observed. Those who were asked leading liberal questions showed little attitude change, and those who were asked leading conservative questions became more liberal.

Many attitude and self-concept studies make use of designs very much like this one. Researchers who conduct these studies expect different *persons* (i.e., people with different attitudes, personalities, or self-conceptions) to respond differently to different *treatments* (i.e., different experimental manip-ulations)—thus the name "person-by-treatment" quasi-experiment. As another example of this kind of quasi-experiment, consider a hypothetical study of how people's self-concepts influence their choice of social interaction part-ners. Suppose you arranged for your participants to help you with some "mar-keting research" by playing a game of skill and hand-eye coordination with a stranger (actually a confederate). Furthermore, suppose that you made certain that your real participants always overheard a conversation between the con-federate and the experimenter during a break in the action. Specifically, sup-

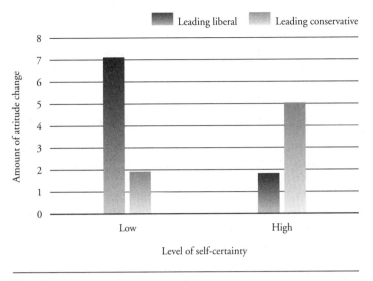

FIGURE 7.1   Effects of self-certainty and persuasion technique on attitude change (from Swann, Pelham, & Chidester, 1988)

pose you randomly assigned your participants either to hear the confederate evaluate them positively ("Wow, she seemed really athletic; I guess this study was right up her alley") or negatively ("I guess this study wasn't much fun for her; she doesn't seem very athletic"). Which type of feedback would your participants prefer? At first blush, it seems obvious. It seems that participants would prefer the positive feedback because we all like to hear people say nice things about us. Wouldn't you rather hang out with someone who thinks you're athletic than with someone who thinks you're athletically challenged?

According to *self-verification theory,* it depends. A person's preference for positive or negative feedback should depend not only on the favorability of the *feedback* but also upon the *self-concept* of the person receiving the feedback. In the case of this hypothetical quasi-experiment, it should depend on the favorability of the athletic self-views of the people who overhear the comment. Self-verification theory is a self-consistency theory (in the same family as cognitive dissonance theory). One of the interesting predictions of self-verification theory is that people should prefer to associate with other people who view them the same way they view themselves. This seems pretty straightforward, but self-verification theory takes an extreme view and argues that people with negative self-views will actually choose to hear negative rather than positive feedback when it is consistent with their own self-views. Thus, self-verification theory predicts that people who perceive themselves as unathletic will express more interest in interacting with the confederate when this person evaluates them negatively rather than positively. Of course, the opposite should be true for people who believe that they are highly athletic.

They should express more interest in interacting with the confederate when this person evaluates them positively rather than negatively. In studies very much like this one, this is what Swann and his colleagues have found (e.g., see Swann, Pelham, & Krull, 1989). People with negative self-views prefer to interact with people who hold negative impressions of them, but people with positive self-views prefer to interact with people who hold positive impressions of them.

Person-by-treatment quasi-experiments such as those discussed here offer an excellent way to examine the role of people's self-views in their interpersonal preferences. However, because researchers do not have experimental control over the variables that they have measured, they can never know for certain that their measured variables per se are truly responsible for their findings. In the study by Swann, Pelham, and Chidester (1988), for example, it is possible that some other individual-difference variable (such as reactance or stubbornness) rather than self-certainty was the true determinant of how people responded to the two different kinds of leading questions. This is the problem of *person confounds* discussed in Chapters 5 and 6. The experimenter is only measuring (and not manipulating) the individual-difference variable, and if that variable is important, it should be associated with many other variables. If you were to run a study that looked at people who were high versus low in self-esteem, just think of how many variables would probably correlate with that individual difference. Variables shown to correlate with self-esteem include gender, socioeconomic status (SES), depression, anxiety, professional success, physical health, and life satisfaction. Any one of these variables might offer a competing (third variable) account for any observed effects of self-esteem. As a result, researchers will need to consider these confounds and test to see if they are leading to the effects observed. In a similar way, researchers who conduct person-by-treatment quasi-experiments must consider *operational confounds*. As already mentioned, it is possible that a measure of self-esteem might accidentally measure another variable, such as age. If so, this too should be considered in analyses. We will discuss strategies a researcher might take to deal with confounds in the next section. For now, you should realize that the *inductive problem* simply won't go away! It is always possible that researchers will correct for a dozen important confounds but fail to consider a 13th confound that is the true cause of a commonly observed effect.

Natural Experiments

In person-by-treatment quasi-experiments, the researcher maintains partial control over the world by measuring individual differences and then manipulating other variables of interest. Thus, the researcher still has experimental control over at least one of his or her independent variables. In the second type of quasi-experiment, the experimenter does not use true random assignment at all and thus relinquishes experimental control completely. Control is "released to the wild," and all the variables of interest are measured. Quasi-experiments such as this one are often referred to as **natural experiments** because they involve naturally occurring "manipulations." It might seem odd to think that nature ever plays the role of experimenter, but there are plenty of times when this is true. Think of a time in your life when you were blind-sided by some random life event that was caused by factors that had nothing to do with you or with any other aspects of your life. In essence, you were chosen "at random" by fate to experience some event. Perhaps you happened to be standing near a tree at the very moment that a branch snapped and caused you some serious injury. Or perhaps fate brought you good luck rather than bad. Perhaps you just happened to win a raffle conducted at the local Home Depot™ store and won a lifetime supply of duct tape. Attorneys and insurance agents often refer to events such as snapping tree branches as "acts of God." They are random events that people themselves do not choose. Winning a lottery or a raffle is very similar in the sense that doing so happens as a result of a person's selection at random.

Of course, it would be hard to convert the extremely rare hypothetical events we described here into a quasi-experiment. That is, it's hard to imagine a quasi-experiment investigating "the stress-buffering effects of winning duct-tape lotteries after succumbing to tree-branch injuries." However, many random events occur frequently enough that they can be studied with large samples. Consider natural disasters. In any given year, many people who live in the midwestern United States will have their homes damaged or destroyed by tornadoes while their neighbors somehow escape the same fate. Tornadoes have been known to destroy one home completely and do practically no dam-age to a very similar home that is 50 feet away. Although people living in the Midwest probably differ from people living in other parts of the United States, it seems unlikely that tornadoes seek out one particular type of midwesterner more than another. Thus, within the Midwest, tornadoes reach out to touch a mostly random group of people. It would thus be reasonable for a researcher to see if midwesterners who have their homes struck by tornadoes experience higher rates of anxiety, depression, or post-traumatic stress disorder than midwesterners who have somehow been spared. In this way, a researcher could treat "tornado exposure" as a naturally occurring independent variable while treating outcomes such as anxiety or depression as dependent variables.

If natural manipulations always met the strict definition of absolute ran-domness, then it would be reasonable to think of natural experiments as true experiments. Most often, however, natural experiments focus on events that are more or less arbitrary but, strictly speaking, do not occur *completely* at random. In the case of tornadoes, for example, certain regions of a state or county (e.g., the kind of wide open spaces where people are likely to be farmers) might be more susceptible to tornadoes than others. A quasi-experimenter studying tor-nado victims and nonvictims who lived in the same very small geographic area wouldn't have to worry very much about this potential confound. In contrast, however, a researcher comparing victims in Dorothy County with nonvictims in Glinda County would have a little more to worry about.

As another example, consider a researcher who wants to determine if seat-belt laws influence traffic fatality rates. The researcher might compare states that have such laws with those that don't. Evidence that traffic deaths are lower in states that require the use of seat belts might show that seat-belt laws save lives. In truth, however, there might be third variables at work. For instance, seat-belt laws might be passed in states that also impose stricter than usual speed limits, or states that make greater efforts to crack down on drunk driving. In these cases, researchers will often treat these natural events *as if* they were experimental manipulations, but they will usually have to work hard to establish the comparability of their two different treatment groups. In the case of states with different seat-belt laws, for example, researchers might try to demonstrate that states that did and did not pass seat-belt laws had comparable traffic fatality rates just prior to the time that they adopted different laws regarding seat belts. This would help a lot, but the researchers would still need to make sure that nothing else changed at the same time that the seat-belt laws changed.

Another way of gaining control over an independent variable in a quasi-experiment is to measure any differences that do exist between people exposed to two different levels of a natural manipulation—that is, to measure any existing confounds. Researchers could then gain statistical control over such confounds by conducting special analyses that statistically equate two otherwise different groups. As a simplified example, suppose that a state that passed strict seat-belt laws in 1990 had a higher proportion of licensed female drivers than a similar state that did not pass such laws that same year. This is a problem because, on average, female drivers are safer than male drivers. If researchers knew this, however, they could simply compare fatality rates in the two states *controlling for gender*. One of the numerous ways one could do this would be to compare fatality rates (or better yet, changes in fatality rates) *within each gender* across the two states.

As examples such as this one suggest, the distinction between natural experiments and nonexperimental correlational designs is not always as clear as one might like. However, to the degree that the levels of a naturally occurring variable truly are determined arbitrarily, we are on safe ground labeling a naturalistic study a quasi-experiment. A potential point of debate in this regard might have to do with studies of naturally occurring events that can be defined categorically (so that we have the appearance of treatment conditions) but that do not happen all that arbitrarily. For example, it wouldn't make sense to most researchers to consider a person's status as a prisoner or a non-prisoner as a natural manipulation. However, what about convicted offenders who have committed exactly the same crime just before or just after their 18th birthdays? Unless one believes that something dramatic happens to people between the ages of 17.9 and 18.0 years, the important variable of whether offenders are tried as juveniles or adults would seem to be largely arbitrary in this specific case. Thus, it would seem appropriate to conceive of this situation as a natural experiment looking at the long-term consequences of being placed in the adult versus the juvenile justice system. The tricky part of deciding whether a study is a natural experiment centers around the question of exactly *how* arbitrary natural manipulations must be to count as arbitrary. This is further complicated by the fact that researchers can sometimes equate groups statistically that do not start off as equivalent.

Note: Same pattern held for last games other than game 7.

FIGURE 7.2   The home-field disadvantage in crucial World Series baseball games, 1924–1982 (from Baumeister & Steinhilber, 1984)

To muddy the waters a little further, many *archival studies* of real-world events also qualify as natural experiments. After all, records of tornadoes, traffic fatalities, and crimes can often be found in archival sources. As an example of an archival study that also qualifies as a quasi-experiment, consider a study of professional baseball players conducted by Baumeister and Steinhilber (1984). They tested the hypothesis that baseball teams sometimes choke under the pressure of trying to claim a "desired identity" (a World Series pennant) in front of a home audience. Baumeister and Steinhilber expected that the familiar "home-field advantage" observed in baseball games would be an advantage only during the *first few games* of a seven-game World Series. They argued that when a team played a decisive seventh game at home, playing in front of a home-field audience might actually become a disadvantage (because people feel more pressure to please those they care about than to please a bunch of strangers). Baumeister and Steinhilber also noted that the scheduling of World Series games is *not* based on the win-loss records of the two teams and it is *not* affected by the size of their fan base. As a result, inferior teams (e.g., the New York Yankees) are awarded the "home-team advantage" just as often as superior teams (e.g., the Atlanta Braves, the Arizona Diamondbacks). This is done, by the way, by simply treating the National League team as the home team one year and treating the American league team as the home team the next. This is about as close as one could possibly come to flipping a coin, and thus it is highly appropriate to consider the home-field advantage in the World Series a natural manipulation.

Baumeister and Steinhilber analyzed the outcomes of World Series games played from 1924 to 1982. They conducted many different analyses, but one of the simplest and most informative involved a comparison of the number of games won by home and visiting teams in games 1 and 2 versus game 7. The results of this analysis are summarized in Figure 7.2. As you can see, the home team won about 60% of the early games in a series (59 out of 98 games).

Note: Same pattern held for last games other than game 7.

FIGURE 7.3 Average number of fielding errors committed in World Series baseball games (from Baumeister & Steinhilber, 1984)

When it came to a decisive game 7, however, the home team won less than 40% of the games (10 out of 26). Is it reasonable to conclude that this finding reflected "choking" on the part of the home team? To find out, Baumeister and Steinhilber supplemented their analysis of wins and losses with an analysis of the number of fielding errors committed by the home and visiting teams (in the same games they analyzed for wins and losses). These results appear in Figure 7.3. As you can see, the average number of fielding errors committed by the home team was twice as high in game 7 as it was in games 1 and 2. Error rates for the visiting team actually dropped slightly from games 1 and 2 to game 7. However, a statistical test showed that this drop was not significant. This effect is consistent with Baumeister and Steinhilber's hypothesis, and it thus offers nice support for their theory of choking under pressure. When the stakes get as high as they can possibly get, it looks like the familiar home-field advantage in baseball becomes a home-field disadvantage.

Other Categories of Quasi-Experiments

The two kinds of quasi-experiments we have reviewed here do *not* cover the universe of all possible kinds of quasi-experiments. By jointly considering exactly how people come to be assigned to different groups, what kinds of treatments people receive, and where people receive their treatments, it is possible to generate many other kinds of quasi-experimental designs. As it turns out, none of these other designs is as popular as person-by-treatment quasi-experiments or natural experiments. Nonetheless, to give you a better feel for quasi-experimental designs, we provide you with a couple of brief examples of these alternative designs.

One kind of quasi-experimental design that is probably more useful in applied settings than in basic research settings is roughly the opposite of the person-by-treatment quasi-experiment. Specifically, there are times when researchers want to study people who have already sorted themselves into natural groups that cannot be pulled apart. Furthermore, sometimes these groups of people are highly similar rather than highly different. Finally, rather than exposing each group to both levels of an experimental manipulation, a researcher might expose each group to a *different* level of a single manipulation. We might refer to this design as a *natural groups with experimental treatment* design because it involves taking two naturally occurring groups of people and treating them differently in a very precise way. This design yields useful data only if we can safely assume that the two groups (1) were extremely similar in some important way(s) to begin with but (2) were subsequently exposed to different levels of an experimental treatment, without otherwise being treated differently. This design is the rough equivalent of a simple two-groups experimental design except that the two similar groups are not created using random assignment. The two groups already exist, and for legal, ethical, or pragmatic reasons, they cannot be reconfigured.

An excellent example of this design is the quasi-experiment that Daniel proposed to the king's chief official. Presumably, the two groups of men who ate very different diets were highly similar in physical size and strength prior to the manipulation. If they became different after the manipulation, it would seem pretty safe to attribute this emerging difference to the manipulation. When a company changes the health insurance plan for one group of employees without changing the plan for a very similar group, this might set the stage for a quasi-experimental study of the effects of the new plan on preventive medicine. If a city imposes stricter physical requirements for its firefighters' exam but does not make the same change for police officers, then the stage is set for a very different quasi-experiment. In cases such as these, we obviously could not reassign people to occupations to take advantage of random assignment. However, if we carefully assessed changes in people's health or physical prowess before and after the imposed changes, we could probably get a good feel for the consequences of the new policies.

It might also seem possible to generate novel quasi-experimental designs by combining natural manipulations with laboratory manipulations, or by assessing individual differences among people and then waiting for them to experience truly arbitrary natural events. These things are indeed possible, but in reality, these kinds of designs are extremely rare. For instance, it is very rare for researchers to be able to identify people who are likely candidates for a natural manipulation *prior to* the time that people actually experience the natural manipulation. If we knew that the residents of Ozburg, Kansas, were going to be hit by a tornado next month, we'd know the unknowable. Moreover, we'd also have a pretty big ethical obligation to warn people about the upcoming disaster. On the other hand, some natural manipulations are easier to predict and control than others, and creative researchers have occasionally created what might be termed *nature-by-treatment* studies. For instance, Pyszczynski, Greenberg, and Solomon (1996) conducted such a study to see how people psychologically defend themselves against thoughts of death. They did so by approaching research participants who did or did not happen to be standing within view of a funeral home (this was the natural manipulation). They then asked these participants to evaluate a person who either praised or criticized the American way of life (this was the experimental manipulation). As predicted, Pyszczynski et al. found that people were much more critical of a person who disagreed with the basic values of their culture when people were faced with a subtle reminder of their own mortality. When reminded of our own fragility, we rise to the defense of the core beliefs and values that we share with the other members of our social worlds.

As you can see, then, quasi-experiments come in many shapes and sizes. However, there are some theoretical and pragmatic constraints that limit our ability to conduct quasi-experiments. The biggest of these constraints is probably that good quasi-experiments must solve the tricky problem of comparability.

Comparability

To appreciate the role of comparability in quasi-experiments, let's return to the Baumeister and Steinhilber study of home-field status in baseball playoff games. We suggested that home-field status constitutes a good natural manipulation because teams are assigned to this condition independent of their win-loss records. It is just as important, however, that the home-team status variable can be studied by creating *comparable and non-overlapping groups*. These groups can easily be compared with one another to determine the effects of home versus visiting team status. In many instances, however, random events occur, but researchers who want to study them are left guessing about what kinds of comparisons they should make to do so. As an example, consider how a researcher might study a freak natural disaster. Suppose a meteor were to strike a rural farming community in the Midwest (those poor midwesterners!). Suppose further that the meteor happened to wipe out a large grain-collection facility at the outskirts of town, dealing a devastating blow to the local economy. You'd have to agree that this event was about as random as it possibly could be. The meteor could have hit anywhere on the earth's surface, and the people in this community did nothing to bring this event about. As honky-tonk singer Delbert McClinton would say, these folks were "victims of life's circumstances." Given this fact, it would be entirely appropriate to view the meteor strike as a natural manipulation. However, suppose a group of psychologists came along in the ensuing months to see if the meteor had caused increased levels of post-traumatic stress disorder (PTSD) in this community. The psychologists would run into a big problem: *They would need to find a reasonable comparison group.*

As you know from Chapter 6, experiments require comparison groups because raw numbers are rarely informative on their own. To know what a number means, a researcher must compare it with some other number to show that it is bigger or smaller than would be expected. To illustrate, imagine that researchers observed that 2.9% of the residents in this farming community were experiencing PTSD three months after the meteor strike. Should they conclude that the meteor lead to an *increase* in PTSD? Is a 2.9% rate of PTSD higher or lower than the national average? What about the national average for rural farming communities? What about the average for rural midwestern farming communities? Does it matter how big the communities are? Or what crops they grow? Clearly, to assess whether the meteor had any effect, one must identify some sort of group against which the group of interest can be compared.

The identification of a control group can be a very difficult task. Imagine, for instance, that researchers decide that they should compare PTSD levels in the meteor county with levels in the county just to the west. A consultant points out, however, that people in this county might be too close to the meteor strike because they also use the grain-collection facility that was destroyed by the meteor. Thus, there could be carryover effects, raising the PTSD levels in that county as well. When the researchers move another county to the west, they hit a community that has a large Amish population. The meteor struck a county that did *not* have a large Amish population, and so this new county would not make a useful comparison. When the researchers move one county further to the west, however, they cross the state line and thereby encounter numerous social, economic, and political changes (not to mention different state laws regarding health care, which could influence rates of PTSD). For this reason, the researchers decide to look two counties to the *east* of the county where the meteor fell (skipping over the county just to the east because of concerns about carryover effects). When they do this, they come to a large, mostly urban county that includes the state capital, and they thereby encounter a whole host of new problems. It may seem that these poor researchers are almost as unlucky as the poor people who happened to be the victims of the meteor, but we hope you see the point. It is often difficult to find an ideal control group when you are unable to make use of random assignment.

In short, even when events occur to some people more or less at random, it is not always clear where to find a group of people who are in all other ways exactly like these people. This problem is just as pronounced when a researcher identifies an unusual group of people that he or she wishes to study in the laboratory rather than in the field. Suppose, for instance, that a researcher wanted to study the laboratory responses of people with clinical levels of a specific phobia (e.g., extreme fear of heights). People who possess phobias probably differ from the majority of people in a population in a wide variety of ways, and thus a comparison with a group of adults who do not suffer from any form of clinical disorder whatsoever might not be ideal. A better control group, for example, might be people who have an equally serious but qualitatively different clinical disorder (e.g., a minor form of depression, a different kind of phobia). The fact that it is so difficult to identify the ideal comparison group in many quasi-experiments is one of the primary reasons researchers developed the notion of "patching."

Patched-Up Designs

Recall the extremely useful phrase *ceteris paribus* ("all else being equal"). This phrase reminds us of the core principle behind true experiments: If you want to show that an independent variable is influencing a dependent variable, you must hold *everything else* but the independent variable constant across experimental conditions. As you know, this requires both random assignment (to deal with person confounds) and procedural control (to deal with operational confounds). This very high level of control is not possible with quasi-experiments. By using nonrandom assignment to conditions and moving to the real world, researchers increase the risk of confounds. In the world of quasi-experiments, that is, all else is not *exactly* equal. Extraneous personality and environmental factors might cause the appearance of a treatment effect when no treatment effect actually exists.

Because it is not possible to hold all possible extraneous variables constant across quasi-experimental conditions, researchers must often decode the meaning of observed treatment effects by using a different method. This method is called **patching.** Patching occurs when a researcher adds new conditions to a study to help establish the size of a quasi-experimental effect, to test for the influence of conceivable confounds, or both. The end result is often what Campbell and Stanley (1966) referred to as a **patched-up design.** Patched-up designs thus occur when researchers continually add *control groups* to a quasi-experimental design. In the end, a carefully patched-up study will often resemble a patchwork quilt, with many different conditions sewn in to the original design, each to deal with different specific concerns. When using this approach, it is the researcher's responsibility to think of all the possible control groups that should be included to help clarify the exact meaning of any effects that are found. In a sense, then, quasi-experiments require researchers to focus their attention not only on the groups or conditions that are of interest but also on the groups or conditions that are not of interest.

This is a good idea. To illustrate its use, we ask you to consider a hypothetical example in which a researcher tests a simple, applied idea about teaching methods. With this example, we will attempt to demonstrate how careful attempts to establish the validity and magnitude of an effect will result in a systematic increase in control groups. After this detailed example, we will walk you more briefly through a series of real quasi-experiments that used archival methods to document the potency of a laboratory research finding in the real world.

Example 1: Evaluating a Teaching Tool

We hope it will come as no surprise to you that the two of us both teach research methods at our own universities. Relying on our individual experiences as instructors, we have occasionally debated the merits of posting study guides on our course Web pages. In this vein, imagine that one of us thinks that study guides help students make the most of a course because motivated students can study ahead and come to class a bit more prepared than they otherwise would. Imagine, however, that the other one of us thinks that study guides encourage an overreliance on the guides and underreliance on lectures. (This is a polite way of saying that he thinks study guides may encourage students to skip class). To resolve this debate, we could run a study to examine the impact of study guides on class grades. Let's imagine that the one of us who believes in the benefits of study guides—we'll call him Dr. Pelton—decided to run a study-guide efficacy study. As you will see, the simplest kind

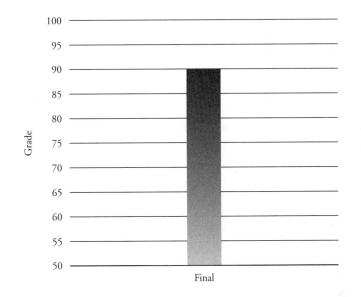

FIGURE 7.4   *One-group design*

of study one might be tempted to run will require a great deal of patching to become convincing.

Imagine that Pelton posts study guides for the course on his course Web page, so that students can easily download the guides well in advance of the midterm and the final exam. After doing this, Pelton determines that the class average on the final exam is 90 out of 100. This finding is illustrated in Figure 7.4. We've seen this sort of design before in the tornado study, and we now call it a **one-group design.** All our participants are in one group, the group that received the quasi-experimental treatment. As you may recall from Chapter 4, this design without a control group is also an example of a *pseudo-experiment* (it is a bit atypical, however, because pseudo-experiments usually focus on a single person whereas we looked at an entire group). As we hope you'll agree, the results of studies such as this are uninformative because they do not provide meaningful comparisons. We do not know if a 90 is typical for students in the class, if it is high for them, or if it is low.

To see whether the study guides influenced class grades, we need to have some sort of comparison to show that the grades are different than they would have been in the *absence* of the study guides. To get at this, we might patch in a new condition. For this purpose, Pelton could create a comparison by introducing the study guides for the final exam but not for the midterm. It would then become possible to compare grades on the midterm, taken before the study guides were provided, with grades on the final, taken after the posting. This design is referred to as a **one-group pretest-posttest design** (Campbell & Stanley, 1966). Using this design, Pelton could see if grades improved after the study guides were posted. Assume that when Pelton did this, he observed a significant increase in grades, from 82 to 90. The results of

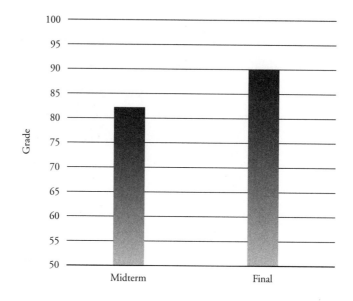

FIGURE 7.5   One-group pretest-posttest design

this patched-up study are shown in Figure 7.5. This design is an improvement over a one-group design, but it would still be open to many alternative explanations. It is possible, for instance, that grades increased over the semester as students adapted to Dr. Pelton's awkward lecture style, or learned to decipher his strangely worded tests (a form of testing effects). It is also conceivable that Dr. Pelton simply developed a final exam that was easier than the midterm. Finally, experimenter bias could be at work because Dr. Pelton was aware of when he administered the study guide manipulation. Thus, he might have unknowingly treated the students differently in other ways after the manipulation. If so, this 8-point increase from the midterm to the final might have been observed even if the study guides had not been posted. It is conceivable that the study guides actually made things worse! Without them, perhaps the class average would have increased even more.

Instead of trying to look for change in this specific class, Dr. Pelton could try a different kind of patch by comparing the final grades in this class with the final grades in a highly similar class that did not receive any study guides. For instance, he could compare the final exam grades for this class with the final exam grades from the same class when he taught it a year earlier. It just so happens that Dr. Pelton teaches exactly the same class every spring semester. Furthermore, because Pelton is so lazy, he uses *exactly* the same exams every year, withtou even correctgin the newmerous typso that drive students crazy. Thus, there is no obvious reason to expect final exam grades to be different in the two classes in the absence of the study guide manipulation. This new design is referred to as a **posttest-only design with nonequivalent groups** (Campbell & Stanley, 1966). When this comparison is carried out, Pelton sees that the class receiving the study guides averaged a 90 on the

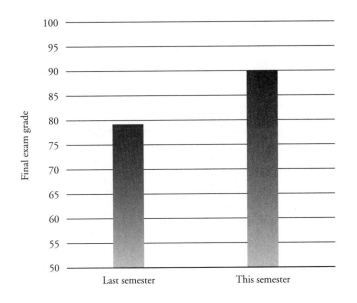

FIGURE 7.6 *Posttest-only design with nonequivalent groups*

final, whereas the previous class averaged a 79. The results of this further patched up design are shown in Figure 7.6. This is a large difference in grades, and it certainly suggests that the study guides may be beneficial. However, upon further reflection, Dr. Pelton realizes that last year's class was taught in the afternoon, whereas this year's class was taught early in the morning. This could be a *treatment confound* because students who are willing to sign up for a 6 a.m. class might be more serious than students who sign up for the same class offered at 3 p.m. To deal with this problem, Pelton should test to see if the two classes were roughly the same at the beginning of the two courses, prior to the time that he posted the study guides in the second course. This is an example of *matching*. We criticized matching before, but that was because we had the option of using random assignment. Now that random assignment is no longer possible, and now that nature has done the matching for us, matching doesn't look so bad after all. To see if these two groups are well matched, Pelton compares both the midterm and the final grades for the two classes. His prediction is that the two groups should get similar grades on the midterm (because this test was given before the treatment) but should get different grades on the final (because this exam was given after the treatment). This design is referred to as a **pretest-posttest design with nonequivalent groups** (Campbell & Stanley, 1966). When Pelton uses this design, he observes the findings depicted in Figure 7.7. The two classes only began to look different after the point at which Class 2 received the study guides.

At this point, Pelton would have pretty good reason to believe that the study guides are beneficial. However, his confidence in this assertion would hinge on (1) the assumption that experimenter bias was not very likely to

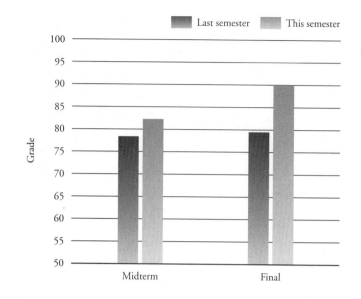

FIGURE 7.7   *Pretest-posttest design with nonequivalent groups*

have occurred in this situation and (2) that the small between-groups difference observed on the midterm is not meaningful. In short, Pelton has to convince himself (and his critics) that these minor differences halfway through the semester cannot somehow produce the major differences observed on the final exam. These small differences at pretest (or midterm) might show that the treatment group is slightly more prepared at the start than the control group. As a result, they might have been in a better position to improve after the midterm. In light of this, Pelton might want some harder evidence that the two groups were roughly equivalent before the treatment. *This is a common dilemma for researchers using quasi-experimental designs.* They often want to compare two groups, and they often want to state that the two groups would be equivalent, if not for the influence of some independent variable being studied. However, one or two comparisons will not usually be enough for someone who wishes to be extremely confident of the equivalence of two groups prior to a manipulation.

It is for this reason that researchers often use **time-series designs.** With time-series designs, researchers look at long runs of data to show equivalence prior to a quasi-manipulation. The professor might not have time-series data for the two classes for major exams because he gives only a midterm and a final. However, he could look at performance on weekly quizzes. By looking at quiz performance in the first six weeks of the semester, which happened before the posting, and in the second six weeks of the semester, which happened after the posting, he can get a strong sense of the comparability of the two groups. If the addition of the study guide is beneficial, the two classes should show very similar quiz performance in the first six weeks, but the experimental group should start to pull away from the control group at the

FIGURE 7.8   *Time series design*

point at which the study guides were first provided. A pattern of data like this is shown in Figure 7.8. With the increased information gained from having multiple pretest and posttest scores, Pelton now feels pretty confident that study guides are useful teaching tools. The two classes were doing about the same over an extended period, but then at the precise point when the study guides were introduced in the second class, this second class began to do better. It now seems very likely that the study guides had an effect. It is always *possible* that some confounding factor caused this shift, but many confounds that would have been serious cause for alarm using less sophisticated designs are no longer a problem.

Even if Pelton was pretty confident of his account for these findings, however, a critic might attack Pelton's interpretation. Remember, Pelton believes that study guides improve grades because they help students study more effectively than usual. Perhaps study guides do improve grades but do so for a different reason. The guides might cause better grades, but for reasons that have more to do with student spirits than with student study habits. More specifically, students might do better in classes when study guides are provided because they interpret the study guides as a sign that the professor cares about their well-being. By showing that he cared, Pelton may have encouraged students to ask more questions during lectures, to come to office hours more regularly, or to simply feel more optimistic about the course. These things might all lead students to perform better in the course, but they involve an entirely different psychological process than the one Pelton assumed. How might we resolve this issue?

When psychologists want to pinpoint the precise mechanism behind a finding, they often patch by making use of some kind of **internal analysis.**

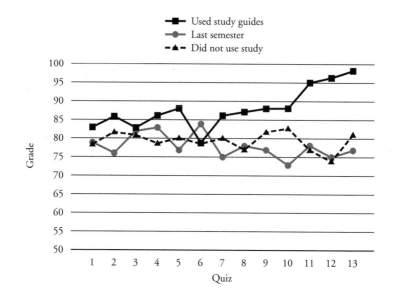

FIGURE 7.9   Time series with internal analysis

When conducting internal analyses, psychologists break one or more groups into additional subgroups to test for subgroup differences that are consistent with the focal theory or with competing theories. To illustrate, Pelton assumed that if study guides improve grades, they do so by helping students study more effectively. The alternative theory was that study guides have no actual influence on the way students organize and internalize the material. Instead, they just serve as a morale booster. If this latter account is true, it shouldn't really matter whether students actually view the guides on the Web or not. All that matters is that they know that Pelton cared enough to provide the study guides. These two theories lead to different predictions based on a specific kind of internal analysis. Unlike the alternative theory, the original theory suggests that students should improve their grades only to the degree that they actually *used* the study guides. This suggests an internal comparison between the students in the second class who did versus did not use the study guides. If these two groups were pulled out of the time-series design in the last figure, this might lead to the pattern of data shown in Figure 7.9. This pattern, if obtained, would strengthen the interpretation that study guides truly *guide studying* rather than merely boosting morale.

Can we be absolutely positive that this is the case? Unfortunately, the answer is still no. If we study Figure 7.9 carefully, we can still dream up some other reasonable explanations for this pattern of findings. For instance, students who report that they actually used the study guides could simply be more motivated and diligent than students who report that they did not. Pelton might counterargue that if this were the case, these highly diligent students should have done better on the *first* exam, too, which they did not. We might counter this counterargument by pointing out that we believe motivation ebbs and flows from week to week rather than operating as a permanent aspect of students' personalities. If this didn't prompt Pelton to call us nasty names, it might prompt him to come up with yet another patch based on a different kind of internal analysis. Although we might never settle the issue once and for all, we hope you can see that the more times a study survives a new patching process, the more confident you should become that a researcher's preferred explanation was at the root of his or her findings. A theory that survives a great deal of patching will gain a lot of scientific credibility. The canon of parsimony dictates that we should usually prefer a simple theory that can explain an entire patchwork quilt of research findings rather than relying on three or four alternative explanations.

Example 2: Would a Rose by Any Other Name Move to Rosemont?

The last example used fictitious data to illustrate the general concept of patching. In the world of real quasi-experiments, however, it is almost never possible to perform all the many forms of patching one might ideally like to perform. Sometimes pretest data simply do not exist. At other times, a researcher might be unable to identify a group of people who serve as an ideal control group for the people who were subjected to a natural manipulation. The real world does not sit around trying to dream up ways of making things easy for quasi-experimenters. Nonetheless, researchers who work hard at it can usually come up with patches that will address the most serious criticisms of their quasi-experimental findings. In the next section, we provide you with some examples of real research findings that address the question of whether human beings are truly in control of their major life decisions. In this case, the researchers in question used patching to try to make the point that people make important life decisions (where to live, what to do for a living) for unusual reasons that most people would probably find slightly embarrassing.

Before we discuss this research, however, please take a minute to list your six *favorite* and your six *least favorite* letters of the English alphabet. Work as quickly as possible, based on your gut impressions. When you are done, be sure to give each list of six letters a label such as "favorites" and "least favorites." Please do not continue until you have done this! When you are done, you should then circle all the letters (from each list) that happen to occur in either your first or your last name. Most people who do this activity find that the letters in their first and last names frequently make it to the list of strongly liked letters but rarely make it to the list of strongly disliked letters. This is usually true even for people whose names contain relatively rare and typically disliked letters of the alphabet such as J, K, or Z.[2] This is an example of a very well-documented laboratory finding called the **name-letter effect.** The name-letter effect refers to the finding that people like letters that occur in their own names quite a bit more than they like letters that do not. This effect occurs for all the letters in people's names, but it is particularly pronounced for people's first and last initials. This preference for one's own name letters was first documented by Josef Nuttin (1985; 1987), and it has subsequently been observed in at least 15 countries (e.g., Greece, Japan, Spain, the United States, and Singapore).

Presumably, the reason that most people prefer the letters in their own names is that most people feel very good about themselves. Ultimately people's good feelings about the self seem to rub off onto their feelings about anything that becomes *associated* with the self. Thus, in much the same way that people or animals come to like arbitrary things (e.g., musical tones, symbols) that are associated with food, praise, or other rewards, people seem to like anything that becomes associated with the self. Nuttin was so convinced that name-letter preferences reflect people's good feeling about the self that he referred to the name-letter effect as a form of unconscious narcissism. Like the mythical Narcissus, who fell in love with his own reflection, most people seem to fall in love with things (like names or possessions) that have come to symbolize who they are. OK, so people are a little stuck on themselves. Justin and Jordan probably think that J is totally phat, whereas Amber and Alyse probably think that A is completely sweet. But what do name-letter preferences have to do with major life decisions?

Pelham, Mirenberg, and Jones (2002) reasoned that if people really do have strong preferences for the letters in their names, then people's real-life decisions should reflect these preferences. As hypothetical examples, a person named Cruise might feel an inexplicable attraction to someone named Cruz, a TV cowboy named Roy Rogers might be especially interested in singing songs such as "Rudolph the Red-Nosed Reindeer," and a person named Judy might be more interested than the average person in becoming a judge. Pelham et al. referred to this general idea as *implicit egotism:* If people prefer things (e.g., the letters in their own names, their birthday numbers) that they associate with the self, then by extension people should prefer people, places, and occupations whose names or titles resemble their own first or last names (or their birthday numbers).

Pelham et al. first tested this idea by systematically generating a couple of European American male and female first names that closely resembled large American city names. They then narrowed down this list to the two male and two female first names that they were able to match most closely for age (e.g., Which would be a better match for Virginia? Dorothy or Jennifer?). The male name pairs they chose in this way were Jack and Philip, and if you know a little bit about Florida and Pennsylvania, we bet that you can guess which city names from these states most closely resemble these two male first names. Finally, these researchers consulted U.S. death records to see exactly how many men with each of these first names (regardless of their last names) had died while living in each of the two cities that resembled these two first names. The results of this study are shown in Table 7.1. As you can see, just as Jacksonville seems to have been disproportionately inhabited by Jacks, Philadelphia seems to have been disproportionately inhabited by Philips. This effect replicated, by the way, for the female first names Virginia (Virginia Beach) and Mildred (Milwaukee). So there you have it. If you think of people's first names as arbitrary variables, you have ironclad quasi-experimental evidence that people make major life decisions (where to live) on the basis of the associations they have to their own first names. Or do you? Can you think of any alternative explanations for these initial findings?

TABLE 7.1 Likelihood of living in a city as a function of one's first name (adapted from Pelham et al., 2002)

City	First Name Jack	First Name Philip	Row Totals
Jacksonville	436 (288)	111 (259)	547
Philadelphia	968 (1,116)	1,153 (1,005)	2,121
Column Totals:	1,404	1,264	2,668

Note. Numbers in parentheses indicate expected values, that is, the number of men with each name one would expect to live in each city if people's first names were unrelated to where they lived.

One very plausible alternative explanation is an interesting form of reverse causality. Do people's names cause them to live in certain cities, or does living in certain cities cause parents to give their children certain kinds of names? One way to patch up this design would be to perform an unusual variation on a pretest-posttest design by seeing how many of these men and women had *moved to* the cities where they died. For example, if Jack Florian's "pretest" score for place of birth was any place *other* than Jacksonville, and his "posttest" score for last known residence was Jacksonville, this would be much stronger evidence for the idea that name-letter preferences were actually at work. Unfortunately, it was usually impossible to tell exactly where people were born from the archival records used to generate the data from this study. Thus, most of the time this patch was simply unavailable.

However, in a series of follow-up studies, Pelham et al. performed a different kind of patch to address the same concern. Although it's possible that people living in Jacksonville are especially likely to name their children Jack, it's *not* very plausible that people ever change their *surnames* because they happen to live in a specific city. On the basis of this idea, Pelham et al. conducted a number of very large replication studies in which they tested to see if people were disproportionately likely to live in cities or states whose names began with the first few letters of their surnames. People were. For example, just as people whose surnames began with "Cal" were disproportionately likely to live in California, people whose surnames began with "Tex" were disproportionately likely to live in Texas. Furthermore, because these two states have very similar proportions of White and Latino residents, it's pretty unlikely that this finding reflects some kind of ethnic confound. In additional patches, Pelham et al. controlled for people's age and ethnicity in other ways (e.g., by focusing solely on people born in the same year), and they still observed strong support for their predictions. People still gravitated toward places that resembled their own first or last names. In one very large study, Pelham et al. were also able to identify a large subgroup of people who moved from one state to another during their adult lives. Just as women named Georgia were disproportionately likely to move to Georgia as adults, women named Virginia were disproportionately likely to move to Virginia. Women named Florence and Louise showed the same effect, as did men with names such as George, Kenneth, and Louis.

These results notwithstanding, we could still quibble about whether these studies truly constitute natural experiments. Exactly how arbitrary is a person's first or last name? Although our names clearly chose us rather than the reverse, we have already listed quite a few variables that are confounded with people's names. These include gender, age, and ethnicity, all three of which are pretty serious potential confounds. So try as we might to rule out all possible confounds, there is always a nagging concern that some unknown confound might be lurking beneath the surface. However, what about the case of people's birthdays rather than their names? The specific month and day on which a person is born comes pretty darn close to being truly random. Consider people who are born on February 2 (02-02), March 3 (03-03), or April 4 (04-04). It would be pretty shocking if the people born on these specific dates differed from one another on any meaningful demographic characteristics. If women were more likely than men to be born on February 2, for example, this would be pretty weird. Pelham et al. took advantage of this natural manipulation by assuming that people's preferences for their birthday numbers (especially for people whose day and month of birth were the very same number) operate very much like people's preferences for their names. If we could find a reasonable number of cities that began with words like "two," "three," or "four," we could see if the deceased residents of these cities were disproportionately likely to have had birthday numbers that strongly resembled these city names. As it turns out, in a country as large as the United States, there are quite a few cities whose names begin with numbers. Some examples include Two Harbors, Minnesota; Three Forks, Montana; and Five Points, Alabama. Pelham et al. analyzed exhaustive death records from every city in the United States whose name contained a usable number word (e.g., there are no cities whose names contain the word "eleven"). They found that people were, in fact, disproportionately likely to live in cities whose names strongly resembled their birthday numbers.

A close cousin of patching occurs when researchers move from one specific kind of dependent measure (one that is prone to a specific kind of confound) to a different kind of dependent measure, which is not prone to all the same confounds. In the case of research on implicit egotism, Pelham et al. showed that people's preferences for their name letters appear to predict people's choices of what to do for a living as well as people's choices of where to live. For example, they showed that people with names such as Dennis, Denis, Denny, Denver, Denise, Dena, Denice, and Denna are overrepresented among dentists. Studies of this sort rule out reverse causality because almost everyone is given a name well before the time that the person chooses an occupation. The likelihood of ethnic confounds can be minimized by adding direct comparisons with traditionally European American names whose objective frequency is identical to that of target names such as Dennis or Denise. By making repeated use of patching and studying more than one major life decision, Pelham et al. argued that their findings are pretty likely to reflect true name letter preferences (see also Jones, Pelham, Mirenberg, & Hetts, in press; Pelham, Jones, Mirenberg, & Carvallo, 2002).

Finally, several of Pelham et al.'s studies allowed them to make use of the specific form of patching that we referred to as *internal analysis*. For example, they found that behavioral name-letter preferences were larger than usual for people who had highly uncommon rather than common first or last names. If people's behavioral preferences really are based on their preferences for their names, it stands to reason that people might show stronger name-letter preferences (behavioral or otherwise) when their names do a good job of distinguishing them from other people. Whereas relatively rare names such as Hart, Brett, or Nebuchadnezzar do an excellent job of discriminating their owners from most other people, more common names such as Tom, Dick, or Harry probably do a lot less to discriminate people from every other Tom, Dick, or Harry in the world. This internal analysis involving name frequency thus lends some support for a name-letter interpretation of Pelham et al.'s findings.

As a second example of an internal analysis, laboratory research has also shown that relative to men, women usually show stronger preferences for the letters in their first names (because their first name is the only name that many women know they will keep forever; see Kitayama & Karasawa, 1997). Pelham et al.'s archival studies revealed a similar pattern. Preferences based on people's first names were usually stronger for women than for men. As was the case with our hypothetical example involving study guides, internal analyses are always open to criticism. However, they can go a long way toward increasing our confidence in a specific interpretation of an effect. So remember that if you really, really like this textbook and your name is Harbrett Pelton, the book may not be quite as good as it seems. Even more important, of course, remember that patching is one of the best ways to minimize the drawbacks of quasi-experiments.

When True Experiments and Quasi-Experiments Collide

Now that we have discussed most of the basic features of quasi-experiments, we are in a good position to address an important issue that was raised earlier—validity. It should be clear by now that true experiments, especially laboratory experiments, are superior to quasi-experiments when it comes to identifying causes. For this reason, good quasi-experimental researchers are often their own harshest critics. They are constantly looking at their own work and trying to think of potential confounds, so that they can address them as carefully as possible. On the other hand, perhaps good quasi-experimenters are their own biggest fans. If they truly believe in an effect, then they do not give up easily when critics launch attacks on their findings. By paying careful attention to potential confounds and identifying patches that help to address these confounds, quasi-experimental researchers can sometimes silence critics who are reluctant to believe in their findings. Of course, this will happen only if the results of a patched-up study actually turn out to support a researcher's favored theory.

Unfortunately, confounds actually do prove to be the true reasons behind some otherwise interesting research findings. For example, for many years, experimenters felt they had identified a simple and potent way of demonstrating gender bias in people's evaluations of other people's work. Specifically, in experiments in which judges were asked to evaluate an essay that had presumably been written by either "John" or "Joan," lots of studies showed that Joan's essay was rated more negatively than John's (Goldberg, 1968). This simple, potent experimental manipulation of gender appeared to reveal a large bias in the scales of social justice. As it turns, out however, there was a big problem with virtually all the studies that made use of this simple, clever manipulation. Most of these studies confounded the gender of names such as John or Joan with other important variables such as apparent age, likability, or apparent intelligence. Instead of showing a preference for men over women, these studies may have shown only that people strongly prefer certain specific names over others. If one selects equally youthful, equally smart sounding, and equally likable male and female names in studies of the John-Joan variety, the same essay that is purportedly written by either Christine or David usually gets identical marks (Kasof, 1993).

Incidentally, does this mean that there is no gender bias in work evaluation? No, not at all. It just means that there is no good evidence of gender bias using this particular method. We still know that real women in the real world are paid a lot less than real men for performing the same kind of real work. The challenge to researchers who wish to understand social injustices regarding gender and labor is to identify valid ways of studying social injustice in the laboratory. One solution to this problem, by the way, is to get women and men to work on some kind of engaging and meaningful task and then to ask people how much they should be paid for their own work. Studies making use of this self-pay paradigm are free of any concerns regarding name confounds. Interestingly, they also reveal a clear bias for women to pay themselves less than men pay themselves for exactly the same work (Jost, 1997; Major, 1994). On the basis of this research, we have learned that gender bias may be even more profound than it might have seemed from the John-Joan studies. That is, it is pretty clear that when it comes to gender discrimination, many women are so strongly socialized to believe in the fairness of the status quo that they may unknowingly play a hand in perpetuating biases in pay. An important social implication of this finding is that the members of underprivileged groups must sometimes resocialize themselves (as well as the rest of the world) if they wish to change the status quo.

To get back to our major theme, when concerns regarding internal validity can be carefully addressed, quasi-experiments have some methodological advantages over their true-experimental cousins. First and foremost, quasi-experiments can determine whether effects observed in the laboratory generalize to the real world. As we discussed before, researchers often want to know that the basic theories they test in the laboratory generalize to important applied problems. Quasi-experiments can do this because they often focus on real-world outcomes.

Quasi-experiments are also useful for testing basic theories. Moreover, quasi-experiments can test theoretically derived hypotheses that simply cannot be studied in the lab. We cannot conduct true experiments on the effects of tornados, or home-field advantages any more than we conduct true experiments on what factors influence longevitiy or major life decisions. Any theories related to these topics are based on the aspects of life that simply cannot be manipulated in the laboratory. To date, researchers have not developed tornado manipulations that they can use in the laboratory, and they have yet to get approval from human participant review boards to keep people in their laboratories long enough to study longevity. As these examples show, there are times when only quasi-experiments allow researchers to test the most important hypotheses that can be derived from their theories. In these instances, laboratory studies might be conducted to gain important information about some pieces of a theoretical puzzle (e.g., exactly what aspects of immune system functioning are compromised by stress), but they cannot close the circle completely and allow a full test of a large-scale theory. Theories of longevity cannot be fully tested in the short confines of the laboratory.

Having said this, of course, we hasten to add that true experiments and quasi-experiments are often carried out at roughtly the same level of analysis, with the intent of making roughly the same point, about roughly the same theory. In these instances, the benefits of quasi-experiments are that they provide us with the opportunity to see if laboratory findings that get right to the heart of a theory travel well outside the lab. When they do, we have usually learned something important. When they do not, things often get really interesting. It now becomes a challenge to understand why two different windows on the world reveal different pictures.

As an example of this kind of phenomenon, consider experimental versus quasi-experimental research on self-esteem. True experimenters have often tried to get a handle on self-esteem in the laboratory by using random assignment to temporarily *manipulate* people's self-esteem levels. A researcher who adopted this approach might attempt to create groups of participants who are high versus low in self-esteem by randomly assigning participants to receive either positive (esteem-enhancing) or negative (esteem-diminishing) feedback. The researcher could then study the judgments or behavior of the two groups to examine the consequences of experimentally engineered self-esteem levels. For instance, suppose that an experimenter manipulated self-esteem by telling people that they had scored really well or really poorly on a test of social perceptiveness. After this manipulation, all participants are asked to take a recently developed test of creativity, presumably to help the experimenter decide if the new test is valid or not. All participants learn that they performed poorly on the test. The dependent measure in this experiment might be the degree to which people make excuses for their poor performance (e.g., by reporting that they got very little sleep last night, by reporting that the test was probably biased) versus deciding that they simply aren't all that creative.

In such a study, we strongly suspect that the participants in the manipulated high self-esteem condition would make fewer excuses for their failure at the second task. The reason for this is that a great deal of research shows that people respond to positive feedback by becoming *less* defensive than they would otherwise be (Blanton, Cooper, Skurnik, & Aronson, 1997; Blanton, Pelham, DeHart, & Carvallo, 2001; Steele & Liu, 1987). Thus, true experiments on the judgmental consequences of self-esteem should lead us to the reasonable conclusion that being low in self-esteem causes people to be self-serving (e.g., by making self-protective excuses), whereas high self-esteem causes people to steer away from self-protective explanations. However, this reasonable conclusion would be erroneous. Quasi-experimental research that has *measured* trait self-esteem rather than manipulating it has consistently shown that people who are high rather than low in self-esteem make more self-serving and self-protective judgments (e.g., see Campbell, 1986; Taylor & Brown, 1988). In short, true experimental research using manipulations of self-esteem has consistently shown that high levels of self-esteem lead to *less* defensive judgments. In contrast, quasi-experimental research using measures of self-esteem has consistently shown that high levels of self-esteem lead to *more* defensive judgments. This would seem to be a problem.

Although we do not claim to have the definitive solution to this puzzle, we think a road trip to a Nazi concentration camp (i.e., a case study) could reveal some answers. In his classic case study of Jews who were imprisoned by Nazis in World War II, Bettleheim (1947) made a number of very interesting observations. Almost without exception, prisoners initially resisted the insults and psychologically abusive statements of their captors. That is, they worked very hard to maintain a sense of self-worth in the face of horrific feedback about who they were. After a while, however, many of the prisoners were worn down by all the physical and psychological abuse they received at the hands of the guards. Many of them eventually adopted patently anti-Semitic beliefs, siding with the guards. Bettleheim referred to this as "identification with the aggressor," and he believed that it was much more than a simple act designed to gain the approval of the guards. Sadly, many of the prisoners seemed to really internalize a profound sense of their own inferiority while simultaneously admiring and respecting their captors. Some prisoners even collected scraps of clothing and patches from the guards as souvenirs of the people they admired. Bettleheim's analysis suggests that the way people respond to an initial self-concept threat (e.g., laboratory feedback suggesting that one is socially unskilled) is very different from the way they respond to a long series of threats (e.g., growing up in poverty and being told by your teachers that you are a bad kid).

Research on self-esteem and social development are consistent with Bettleheim's analysis. That is, it seems likely that self-esteem manipulations do influence self-evaluation but they do not do so by creating a low level of self-esteem. Because most people have a clear, and positive, sense of who they are, and because people do not like to change their identities from moment to moment, most people seem to respond to recent self-relevant experiences by working to *restore* their self-esteem to its naturally existing level (see Swann, 1987, 1992). In the short run, that is, self-esteem regulation may operate much like a thermostat that is set at a specific level. For most people, this level is pretty high, and thus most people respond to suggestions that they aren't so wonderful by thinking up ways in which they actually *are* wonderful (just as they have always known).

In other words, a high-self-esteem person who has just been told by an experimenter that she is a loser is likely to behave very differently than a person who has received no experimental feedback but whose parents have been telling her that she is a loser ever since she was a child. Presumably, it is developing a true and stable sense that one is not worthwhile that causes people who are chronically low in self-esteem to make self-disserving judgments relative to their high self-esteem counterparts. To make this point a little more dramatic, imagine that researchers interested in gender concluded that we can understand gender differences only by ignoring participants' preexisting conceptions of their gender and randomly assigning people to be treated like men or women during an experiment ("OK, Candice, since your previously sealed medical records indicate that you are genetically male, I'm sure you won't mind if we all call you Buster during today's group activity . . ."). Although a highly creative researcher might be able to figure out a way to experimentally manipulate some specific aspects of gender, it is hard to imagine that an experimenter could reverse 20 or 30 years of sex-role socialization during a brief experimental manipulation. Assuming that our explanation holds up to more careful scrutiny, does this mean that quasi-experiments involving self-esteem yield more valid information than true experiments? In this specific case, yes, as long as we agree that self-esteem per se is difficult if not impossible to manipulate in the lab. However, the laboratory experiments we mentioned presumably *have* yielded valid information about how people respond to different kinds of feedback. To a great degree resolutions of debates such as this one boil down to questions about construct validity and conceptual validity. At any rate, we hope that you can see that it is possible to learn something from contradictory results.

On a more positive note, we should note that there are plenty of times when the results of true experiments and quasi-experiments prove to be very similar. As an example, one of the authors recently tested a theory about *image appeals* using both true experimental and quasi-experimental methods (Blanton, Stuart & VandenEijnden, 2001). An image appeal is a persuasion technique designed to change a person's attitudes or beliefs by capitalizing on people's desire to adopt positive and avoid negative images. If you grew up in a highly industrialized country, you have undoubtedly been the target of thousands of image appeals in your life. Marketers are constantly trying to get you to buy particular brand names by linking them to "cool" or desirable images. Tommy Hilfiger took this method to new heights when he worked hard to get people to associate his name with coolness and then got dozens of different clothing companies to sell him items of clothing to which he merely attached his name. (To our knowledge, Tommy Hilfiger has never designed or manufactured any of the popular items of clothing that bear his name.)[3] Of course, image appeals can be used for the public good as well as for the good of Tommy Hilfiger. For example, health psychologists often try to persuade people to live healthier lifestyles by linking safe sex practices with images of responsibility or by linking drunk driving with images of irresponsibility.

As it turns out, image appeals can be a complex as well as a profitable business. For instance, are image appeals that capitalize on negative images as effective as those that capitalize on positive images? Blanton et al. addressed this question by using image appeals to try to influence people's intentions to use condoms. They focused on whether one should try to promote condom use by using positively framed appeals (e.g., *"Be responsible. Use condoms every time you have sex."*) versus negatively framed appeals (e.g., *"Don't be irresponsible.* Use condoms every time you have sex."). Blanton et al. felt that effects of framing would depend heavily on the perceived social norms surrounding condom use. Specifically, they thought that a positive frame would be most effective when people thought that most other people were behaving badly (by practicing unsafe sex). This prediction was based on the assumption that image appeals are most effective when they tell people the social consequences of being *different.* When people think that others are *not* using condoms, a positive frame says it is different to be responsible. By the same logic, it should be more effective to use a negative frame when people think that most people behave well (by consistently using condoms). When people think that most people use condoms, a negative frame says it is different to be irresponsible, and people do *not* like to be different when it means being something bad.

These predictions were tested in two different studies. In one study, these researchers *manipulated* norm perceptions by randomly assigning participants to read one of two studies: one study suggested that most sexually active students use condoms, and the other study suggested that most sexually active students do *not.* In a quasi-experimental follow-up study, Blanton et al. *measured* norm perception by simply asking participants to rate the prevalence of condom use among sexually active students. Whether norm perception was measured or manipulated, the results were the same. Image appeals were most effective when they focused on what it took to feel different in a desirable way. Thus, positive frames worked best when people believed that most of their peers were *not* using condoms, and negative frames worked best when people believed that most of their peers *were* using condoms. The consistency of results across methods suggests that norm perception is an important determinant of message framing, across many social contexts.

Conclusions

In this chapter, we hope you have learned at least two important things. First, there are many different kinds of quasi-experiments, and each unique quasi-experimental design has its own unique strengths and weaknesses. Second, quasi-experiments solve a great number of practical and theoretical research problems. They do so by allowing researchers to study the otherwise unstudiable, by providing information about the external validity of laboratory experiments, and, occasionally, by revealing that the lessons that are revealed in laboratory experiments are in need of revision. The ideal research strategy involving quasi-experiments is often the same as the ideal research strategy involving any other research design: It is to make use of different designs that complement one another in an ideal way. In short, quasi-experimental designs are an important tool that can help psychologists better understand human nature. However, simply using quasi-experiments, alone or in conjunction with other techniques, is no guarantee of being a successful researcher. A successful researcher must certainly be aware of the different tools and methods that are available to psychologists. However, he or she must also have a keen appreciation of how to put different tools to use. This topic, effective tool use, is the focus of Chapters 8 and 9. These chapters focus, respectively, on how to choose and implement a specific research design and how to use specific research tools in the best way possible.

Notes

1. Cubic zirconium is an artificial stone that strongly resembles a real diamond but is not very valuable.

2. We used this simple measure of preferences only because it is much easier to score (and to explain) than more sensitive and methodologically rigorous measures. For instance, a more sophisticated measure of name-letter preferences requires people to report how much they like each of the 26 letters of the alphabet using 7- or 9-point rating scales. Using this measure, it is possible to calculate how much a person likes each individual letter in his or her name relative to how much other people like that same letter when their names do *not* include this same letter. Scoring this measure, however, is a bit of a pain in the butt. If you want to see exactly how it's done, see Koole, Smeets, Dijksterhuis, and van Knippenberg (1999).

3. We thank Shira Gabriel for this example.

8

Choosing the Right Research Design

One Obscure Movie

The independent film *El Norte* offers a sobering view of the difficult lives of two illegal immigrants to the United States, Enrique and his sister Rosa. After narrowly escaping death at the hands of guerillas in their rural village in Guatemala, Enrique and Rosa eventually make their way to the United States, where they take on any work they can find. Because Rosa speaks no English, she encounters some serious problems in her first day at work as a housekeeper. These problems are compounded by the fact that Rosa's only exposure to modern appliances in Guatemala came from her indirect exposure to the magazine *Buen Hogar* (*Good Housekeeping*). After struggling unsuccessfully for a long time with the modern washer and dryer she has been charged to use, Rosa eventually resorts to doing her first day's wash by hand in the kitchen sink, and laying it on the lawn to dry in the sun. Needless to say, Rosa did not win many points with her employer in her first day on the job.

The problem had nothing to do with Rosa's general knowledge of washers and dryers. She understood exactly what these appliances are designed to do. The problem was that Rosa didn't know how to *operate* a washer or dryer. Rosa fully appreciated the magic of these modern conveniences, but she didn't know the words to any good spells. That is, she simply didn't know which buttons to push. At this point, we suspect that you are in a position that is very similar to Rosa's. Of course, you have a lot more general information about research methods than Rosa had about washing machines, but your position is similar to hers in the sense that you have been given almost no instructions about how to put your general knowledge of research methods to work. This is the basic goal of the remainder of this book: to provide you with the missing details that you would need if you planned to conduct and interpret your own research. Learning these missing details will also put you in a much better position to evaluate research conducted by others. Thus, even if you are not planning a career as a researcher, the remaining chapters in this book should provide you with some specific knowledge that will make you a better consumer of research.

In keeping with this general goal, this chapter introduces you to two of the most important categories of information about research design. We begin by discussing two basic kinds of designs, those that have only a single independent variable (one-way designs) and those that have two or more independent variables (factorial designs). We follow this with a discussion of two basic approaches to design, designs that use between-subjects manipulations and those that use within-subjects manipulations. Although we will focus heavily on the design of experiments in this chapter, almost all the basic ideas we introduce apply to nonexperimental as well as experimental research. For example, when planning both experimental and nonexperimental research, researchers usually begin by deciding exactly how many independent variables they should include. Counting begins at one, and thus we begin with a discussion of designs that include only a single independent variable.

One-Way Designs

The simplest possible experimental design is a one-way design, a design in which there is one and only one independent variable. Furthermore, the simplest possible kind of one-way design is the aptly named **two-groups design.** In experiments employing a two-groups design, there is only one independent variable (i.e., only one experimental manipulation), and this variable has only *two levels*. A two-groups design often consists of an experimental group (a group that receives a treatment) and a control group (a group that does not). Strictly speaking, however, many two-groups studies do not really fit this scheme. For instance, a researcher interested in figuring out the ideal dosages for a new pain reliever might give people either 50 or 100 mg of the new drug, wait for the drug to kick in, and check to see whether the 50-mg group or the 100-mg group reported less discomfort while performing a cold-pressor task (i.e., while submerging one hand for an extended period in a bucket of ice water). In cases such as this, the important thing is whether the two groups differ from each other on the dependent variable. It is not always necessary that one group fail to receive a treatment at all.

Dooling and Lachman (1971) made use of a two-groups design to investigate some simple properties of memory. Put yourself in the place of the participants in their control group. These participants were asked to read the following cryptic passage:

> With hocked gems financing him, our hero bravely defied all scornful
> laughter that tried to prevent his scheme. Your eyes deceive, he had said. An
> egg, not a table, correctly typifies this unexplored planet. Now three sturdy

sisters sought proof. Forging along sometimes through calm vastness, yet more often over turbulent peaks and valleys, days became weeks. As many doubters spread fearful rumors about the edge, at last, from nowhere, welcome winged creatures appeared signifying momentous success.

When these participants were asked to remember this story after a delay, they had great difficulty doing so. Participants in Dooling and Lachman's experimental group read exactly the same story. However, prior to doing so, they were provided with a telling title for the story: "Christopher Columbus Discovering America." In comparison with the participants in the control group, those who got the title remembered the story quite well. If you read the story again with this title in mind, you'll see why this was so. The title allowed people to make sense of the story by using a well-learned knowledge structure (a schema). When people can make sense of things, they are much more likely to remember them. (Please try to remember that!)

Some intriguing examples of two-groups designs can be found in the literature on person perception and stereotyping. Figure 8.1 provides a crude picture of some potential stimuli that might be used in a very simple two-groups study of person perception. Take a look at the character on the left-hand side of Figure 8.1. How would you size him up intellectually? Now look at the character on the right. Does he look any smarter? How about any less sociable, or athletic? If we used the two characters depicted in Figure 8.1 as stimulus persons in a two-groups experiment, we would want to show each of our two groups of participants one and only one of these two drawings and ask them to rate the character on whatever traits we expected to be influenced by the manipulation involving eyeglasses. And we'd expect our simple manipulation to have a pretty dramatic effect. Most people usually judge characters wearing eyeglasses to be more intelligent than their eagle-eyed counterparts. Person perception studies in which participants have been presented with photos of real people instead of cartoon characters have yielded exactly this result. When you are going out on a first date, it may be safe to leave your

FIGURE 8.1 Potential stimuli for a simple two-groups study of person perception

glasses at home. However, when you are going out on your first job interview, you would be well advised to wear them.

In addition to two-groups designs, experimenters often make use of one other kind of one-way design, namely, the **one-way, multiple-groups design.** This is another design in which there is only a single independent variable. In this case, however, the independent variable takes on three or more levels. A one-way, multiple-groups design would be very appropriate for a more sophisticated version of the hypothetical drug-dosing study described above. To get a more precise estimate of the ideal dosage for the new drug, an experimenter might give one group of participants a *placebo* (a pill with no active ingredients) and give four other groups of participants increasingly large doses of the drug. For example, participants might receive 0, 25, 50, 75, or 100 mg of the new drug.

One-way, multiple-groups designs also come in handy in studies of person perception. For instance, a researcher interested in whether people "judge a book by its cover" might present three different groups of participants with identical written descriptions of a target person's personality while systematically varying the target person's level of physical attractiveness. Past research of this type has identified the existence of a *physical attractiveness stereotype*. Most people assume that physically attractive people possess a specific set of personality characteristics, most of which are favorable. Specifically, relative to their less attractive peers, physically attractive people are judged to be happier, better adjusted, and much more sociable (see Eagly, Ashmore, Makhijani, & Longo, 1991, for a review). By including multiple levels of an independent variable in this kind of experiment, researchers will sometimes discover things that would go undetected in a two-groups design. For example, if both physically attractive and physically unattractive people were judged to be less intelligent than *moderately* attractive people, researchers could only learn this by conducting studies that include at least three levels of physical attractiveness. Of course, the additional information that can be gained from multiple-groups designs comes at a cost. It almost always takes more time, more resources, and more research participants to conduct experiments that have more than two conditions.

As you may recall from our discussion of quasi-experiments, both experimenters and quasi-experimenters often begin a new research program by studying only high and low levels of an independent variable. Only after documenting an effect by looking at two groups (e.g., people very low versus very high in self-esteem, a very comfortable versus an uncomfortably hot room) do researchers typically begin to test hypotheses involving multiple levels of a variable (e.g., low, medium, or high levels of self-esteem). This initial bias toward simpler designs often saves time and energy. Moreover, in the absence of a theory suggesting that there is something interesting going on at the middle levels of an independent variable, this approach is often justified. As research accumulates, however, it often becomes useful to ask more precise questions about the dosing of an independent variable, and thus it often becomes worthwhile to invest some time and energy into examining multiple levels of an independent variable.

Factorial Designs

Although one-way designs have been the workhorses of psychological research for many years, there is only so much work that even a workhorse can do. The major limitation of one-way designs is the fact that they allow researchers to look at only one independent variable at a time. A great deal of human behavior is the product of multiple variables *acting together.* With this idea in mind, R. A. Fisher popularized the use of **factorial designs.** Factorial designs are designs that contain two or more independent variables that are completely crossed—meaning that every level of every independent variable appears in combination with every level of every other independent variable. That's a lot of everys, but it's not quite as complex as it sounds. It just means that you create every possible combination of all the levels of all your independent variables.

Ins and Outs of Factorial Designs

Factorial designs come in many shapes and sizes, and so researchers have developed precise conventions for describing specific factorial designs. The label a researcher gives a factorial design specifies both (1) how many independent variables exist in the design and (2) how many levels of each independent variable exist in the design. Thus, a 2×3 factorial design (stated "two by three") has two independent variables (because there are two numbers in the description), the first of which has two levels and the second of which has three. The two numbers in the design are separated by a multiplication sign (the "by" sign), which is a reminder that the two variables are completely crossed. Using this coding scheme, a 2×2 has two independent variables (because there are two numbers), both of which have two levels. The description of a factorial design also tells researchers exactly how many "cells" (i.e., how many unique conditions) there are in a study. You can easily figure this out in a factorial design by simply multiplying the numbers that identify the design. Thus, a 2×2 factorial design always has 4 cells. A 2×3 design always has 6 cells, and a $2 \times 2 \times 3$ (three different independent variables, two with two levels and one with three) has 12 cells.

This system also serves as a reminder of the kind of *statistical analysis* that should be conducted to analyze the data from a factorial experiment. If you conducted an experiment with a 2×2 factorial design, you would need to conduct a two-way analysis of variance (abbreviated ANOVA) to analyze your data. If your experiment had a more complex $2 \times 2 \times 2$ design, you would conduct a three-way ANOVA, and so forth. In this system, the word "way" simply indicates the number of independent variables there are in the experiment. If you were wacky, and hardworking, enough to conduct a $2 \times 2 \times 2 \times 2 \times 2 \times 2$ design, you would need to conduct a (count 'em) *six-way* ANOVA to analyze the data from the 64 unique conditions in your experiment. Incidentally, if you've been wondering why we referred to designs with only one independent variable as "one-way" designs, you now have your answer. Because they have only one independent variable, these simple designs are typically analyzed using a one-way ANOVA.

If little white stars are beginning to spin around your head as you ponder the potential complexity of factorial designs, we have some very good news. One of the most commonly used experimental designs in psychology is the 2×2 factorial, which is the simplest possible factorial design. Designs such as a 2×3 design are also pretty common, but many seasoned experimenters devote themselves almost exclusively to 2×2 designs. As a result, if you can understand a basic 2×2 factorial design, you will be well on your way to understanding most of the experimental designs you are likely to encounter in psychological research.

Because the basic idea behind factorial designs is to yield a more complete picture of the world than we can gain from one-way designs, you may be wondering why some researcher doesn't just conduct the study to end all studies by running something like a $2 \times 2 \times 3 \times 3 \times 4 \times 4 \times 5 \times 5$ factorial. That is, why doesn't someone just identify *all* the known causes of a phenomenon and examine all these independent variables at once, in a single, huge factorial study? There are many reasons, but the simplest answer is purely pragmatic: This huge study would simply be *too* huge. Remember that the more variables you have in a design, and the more levels you have of each variable, the more cells (i.e., unique conditions) you always have in your design. Conducting research is a resource-limited enterprise, and thus you have to think very carefully about whether you really *need* to know all about a particular variable before you incorporate it into your design. In the hypothetical eight-way factorial design we just mentioned, there are 14,400 unique conditions! At 20 participants per cell, this study would require 288,000 research participants! Assuming that most of the adult population of Wyoming was willing to serve as your participant pool for this study, and assuming it took about an hour to run each participant, it would take a small army of 10 full-time experimenters about 15 years to complete this study! By this time, your multibillion-dollar research grant would be exhausted, your list of likely causes would be 15 years out of date, and no one anywhere would be able to understand findings as complex as those you'd be likely to observe. Worse yet, we'd worry that if you had used a slightly different manipulation of a couple of your independent variables, you would have observed very different results. A simpler way to put this is that increasingly complex factorial designs do not become more enlightening at the same rate as they become more exhausting.

Even when studies are quick and easy to run, researchers still turn to the 2×2 design more often than any other factorial design. A second reason why researchers usually stick to simple rather than complex factorial designs was first mentioned in Chapter 2. Many researchers test and refine theories by engaging in *qualification.* When they do this, they attempt to show that a theory is true under some conditions but not under others. The easiest way to do this is to show that the effect of an independent variable on a dependent variable *depends* on the level of a second independent variable. When the effect of one independent variable differs depending on the level of a second independent variable, these two variables are said to *interact.* McGuire (1989) endorsed qualification as an approach to theory testing when he said that researchers pursue interactions to clarify the "circumstances under which a hypothesis is true and those under which it is false." (p. 7). We will discuss interactions in more detail in the next section. For now, we simply wish to emphasize that the concept of qualification in scientific hypothesis testing is tightly linked to the concept of interactions. Furthermore, it is possible to test for interactions only by making use of factorial designs. Finally, because it is usually hard for people to keep track of more than one qualification of an effect at a time, 2 × 2 factorial designs usually provide researchers with the most efficient way of specifying when an effect is and is not observed.

A slightly different way of understanding why researchers typically lean toward simple as opposed to complex factorial designs has to do with the fact that the goal of most research is usually to test predictions derived from one or two theories at a time. Most theories consist of one or two core principles, and thus they usually generate predictions that usually involve one or two variables. Even in the interesting case when two theories make opposing predictions about a phenomenon, this is true precisely because each theory suggests that the *same* manipulation will have different effects on some important outcome. Thus, it is often possible to conduct a simple factorial study whose findings will be relevant to more than one theory. Finally, most theories exist in some kind of logical "If A, then B" form. Cognitive dissonance theory states that if people realize that their behavior is inconsistent with their attitudes, they will try to resolve this inconsistency. Frustration aggression theory states that if frustrated, people will behave aggressively. These simple causal accounts of a phenomenon usually map onto only one independent variable. Thus, it usually takes only one manipulation (e.g., a high versus a low level of frustration) to provide initial support for a theory, and it usually takes only one more manipulation (e.g., whether the person who frustrated you did so on purpose or by accident) to *qualify* the first manipulation. Additional manipulations (e.g., whether the person who frustrated you can see you) often represent interesting but unnecessary detours into the domain of a totally different theory. If theories were typically more complex ("If A *and* B *and* C, then D) then higher-order factorial designs might be a lot more popular. Thankfully, most theories are simple, and thus most factorial designs are simple as well.

Main Effects

Given that factorial designs are so popular, it is important to know exactly what's so special about them. What can we learn from factorial designs that we cannot learn from one-way designs? To answer this question fully, let's begin at the beginning. First, because experiments with factorial designs always have at least two independent variables, such experiments can answer questions that cannot be addressed by studies that have only a single independent variable. One obvious sense in which this is true has to do with the fact that factorial designs allow researchers to answer questions about *more than one independent variable at the same time*. The simple, straightforward effects of independent variables in factorial studies are referred to as **main effects.** Main effects are the factorial equivalent of the only kind of effect you

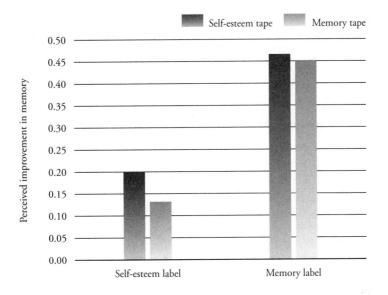

FIGURE 8.2 *Perceived memory improvement as a function of expectancies for memory improvement (from Greenwald et al., 1991)*

can detect in one-way designs. A main effect in a factorial design refers to the overall effect of an independent variable, averaging across all levels of the other independent variable(s). For instance, if you conducted a quasi-experiment involving the effects of gender and frustration on aggression, you might observe a main effect of *gender*. All else being equal (ignoring the frustration manipulation), men might engage in higher levels of aggression than women. In your study of gender, frustration, and aggression, you might also observe a main effect of *frustration*. Averaging across men and women, people who were experimentally frustrated might have generally been more aggressive. Main effects are simple. They only have to do with one variable. Thus, to determine whether your factorial study yielded a main effect of a specific variable, you collapse across all the levels of all other independent variables in a factorial design.

Another example of a main effect in a 2 × 2 factorial study is summarized in Figure 8.2. Greenwald, Spangenberg, Pratkanis, and Eskenazi (1991) conducted a clever 2 × 2 study to assess the effects of expectancies on memory. Participants in their study listened to one of two different subliminal self-help tapes for five weeks. Some of the tapes contained hidden messages designed to improve *self-esteem,* and some included hidden messages designed to improve *memory.* This was one of Greenwald et al.'s manipulations: the true subliminal content of the tapes. The other manipulation was how the tapes were labeled, regardless of what was actually on the tapes. This second variable was manipulated by simply switching the labels on half of the tapes. Thus, regardless of what subliminal messages participants were *actually* listening to, half of them *thought* they were listening to messages that would boost their memory, and the other half thought they were listening to messages that would boost their self-esteem. When Greenwald et al. looked at perceived memory improvement over the course of the study, they observed only one finding: a large *main effect* of the tape *labels*. There was no main effect of the actual tape content, meaning that the content of the tapes had no significant effect on whether people felt they had improved their memories. Consistent with other research on participant expectancies, people's *expectations* about the tapes had a dramatic effect on the degree of perceived improvement in people's memories.

In this study, one advantage to using a 2 × 2 design was that these researchers were able to demonstrate expectancy effects in exactly the same sample of participants and in exactly the same context in which they observed no evidence at all for the effectiveness of this popular form of subliminal message. This increases our confidence that this was a fair test of the effects of each of these two independent manipulations because any idiosyncrasies associated, for example, with this specific sample were common to both manipulations. If Greenwald et al. had run a one-way design in which they had *only* manipulated the true content of the messages, all they presumably would have found was a null effect (a noneffect) of tape content. This wouldn't be all that informative. We might worry, for instance, that this particular group of research participants just wasn't paying any attention at all to anything about the tapes. The 2 × 2 factorial design makes this worry unlikely. If these people simply weren't paying attention, then why did the tape labels have such a large effect? A second advantage of using a 2 × 2 design, by the way, is that Greenwald et al. were able to show that they observed an expectancy effect *regardless* of whether their participants were in a situation that might have justified this expectation. This suggests that expectancy effects truly are independent of message content effects (at least when it comes to this particular kind of subliminal content). It also suggests that expectancy effects occur in at least two different contexts (when people get one kind of subliminal message, and when they get another). We will return to this final point later in this chapter.

Interactions

In addition to yielding information about main effects, studies making use of factorial designs can yield a second, very important kind of information, a kind of information that can never be gained from studies making use of one-way designs. As we noted earlier, factorial designs allow researchers to detect the presence of **interactions.** Recall that interactions always mean "it depends." Interactions exist when the effect of one independent variable on a dependent variable depends on the level of a *second* independent variable. To explore the concept of interactions in more detail, let's take a close look at a couple of 2 × 2 factorial experiments in which researchers observed interactions. Let's begin with one of the first author's favorite examples of a 2 × 2 factorial design: a study of causal attribution conducted by Gilbert, Pelham, and Krull (1988, Study 1).

Most theories of causal attribution share the basic assumption that people come to understand other people's attitudes and personalities by considering the behavior of other people in its *social context*. Gilbert et al. were interested in the question of when people are most likely to take the social context into consideration when they are judging other people's personalities. To put this more concretely, imagine that you saw a woman who was behaving very anxiously (e.g., shifting around nervously in her seat, averting her eyes from her conversation partner). Furthermore, imagine that you couldn't hear anything the woman was saying but learned that she was involved in a getting-acquainted conversation with a stranger. Your first inclination might be to conclude that the woman is the kind of nervous person who is always uncomfortable in social situations. However, that's where the idea of the social context comes into play. Imagine that you learned that the woman had been asked to talk about anxiety-provoking *topics* such as whether she has ever been publicly humiliated, what her sexual fantasies are, and what she considers her most significant personal failures. Would this change your impression of her disposition? It should! If you were able to give the issue a little thought, you should realize that almost *anyone* would feel uncomfortable talking about these sensitive topics with a stranger. With this in mind, you should not necessarily conclude that the woman is a highly anxious person.

Now imagine that you observed the same woman engaging in exactly the same nervous behavior, but under very different conditions. In this case, suppose you learned that the woman had been asked to discuss pleasant topics such as foreign films, ideal vacations, and her favorite hobbies. Knowing this should also change your impression of the woman. People who give this second piece of contextual information a little thought might conclude that the woman is a real basket case (i.e., that she is an *extremely* anxious person). After all, if she gets this anxious when she is talking about relaxing topics like these, there is no telling how anxious she would be in a more stressful situation.

Notice that we could conduct a simple two-groups study to see if people engage in this kind of carefully reasoned logical analysis. In such a study, we could manipulate the social context under which the woman's behavior presumably took place by showing two groups of participants the same videotape of the same woman behaving anxiously while manipulating their beliefs about the discussion topics. Relative to participants who thought the woman was discussing relaxing topics, those who thought she was discussing anxiety-provoking topics should judge her to be a less anxious *person*. Gilbert et al. made use of exactly this manipulation of social context in their study of person perception. However, they also manipulated a second variable, making their study a 2×2 factorial. The second independent variable in this study was the level of *cognitive load* participants experienced as they tried to figure out the woman's personality. Half of the participants in this study simply tried to figure out the woman's personality. The other half tried to figure out her personality while they *also* performed a cognitively taxing secondary task (in this case, a memory task). A summary of the design of Gilbert et al.'s 2×2 factorial study appears in Figure 8.3. Notice that the two independent variables were completely crossed. The study included every combination of every level of the two independent variables.

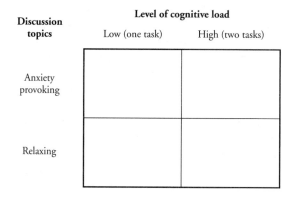

FIGURE 8.3 The design of Gilbert et al.'s study of automatic and controlled attributions: because this was a factorial design, every combination of every level of every variable was present in the design.

Note: Higher scores indicate higher levels of judged anxiety.

FIGURE 8.4 Judged trait anxiety of target as a function of cognitive load and situational constraint information (from Gilbert et al., 1988)

Gilbert et al. found that when people were not cognitively loaded, they did an excellent job of taking the situation into account when they judged the woman's personality. As you can see in Figure 8.4, participants who thought that the woman had been placed between a rock and a hard place decided that she was probably hardier than she appeared. Relative to people who thought she was talking about pleasant, innocuous topics, they concluded that she probably *wasn't* such an anxious person. However, Gilbert et al. found that when people had two things to do at once, they were unable to make any corrections in their judgments. The manipulation involving the anxiety-provoking versus pleasant discussion topics no longer had any effect on participants' judgments. Instead, they simply concluded that the woman was an anxious person, period. This pattern of findings means that Gilbert et al. observed an *interaction* between the information provided about the discussion topics and the cognitive load variable. Recall that interactions occur when the effects of one independent variable depend on the level of some other independent variable. In this case, the effect of the information about discussion topics on people's judgments of the woman's anxiety level *depended on* people's level of cognitive load.

On the basis of findings such as these, Gilbert (1989) concluded that person perception is a multistep process. During the early stages of this process, anyone who sees a person behaving a certain way (e.g., anxiously, aggressively, sadly) automatically jumps to the conclusion that the person is a certain *kind* of person (in this case, an anxious person). Whether people are able to correct their initial conclusions about a person in light of information about the situation depends on the degree to which people have full access to their higher-order cognitive resources at the time that they render their judgments. Many other studies of social judgment—including studies of attitude change, stereotyping, and judgment under uncertainty—have yielded results highly similar to these (see Petty & Cacioppo, 1986). When people's cognitive resources are taxed, they are much more likely to rely on simplistic judgments ("The people in that commercial look so happy; maybe *I'd* be that happy if I bought that car")—and much less likely to engage in more sophisticated forms of reasoning ("On second thought, that car has a very poor reputation for reliability. How fun would it be to get pulled around in that car by a tow truck?"). Studies such as these are almost always factorial studies because they make the point that judgment is a joint product of *more than one variable:* some aspects of the information people are given to make their judgments and some aspects of people's willingness or ability to use this information.

Notice that interactions are very different from main effects. For example, if there had simply been a main effect of cognitive load in the Gilbert et al. experiment, we might have seen that the cognitively loaded participants—as a group, independent of the manipulation about the discussion topics—judged the woman to be more anxious than did the cognitively unloaded participants. We *didn't* see this, of course, but we *could* have. Similarly, if we had only observed a main effect of discussion topic (no main effect of cognitive load and no interaction), we would have simply observed that, averaging across the two levels of cognitive load, the discussion topics influenced people's judgments. If we had *not* observed an interaction, the effects of the discussion topics would have been roughly equal in the load and no-load conditions. The effect of the discussion topics would *not* have depended on the cognitive load manipulation. Our findings would have resembled Greenwald et al.'s findings on the effects of subliminal tape labels.

To get a better feel for the difference between main effects and interactions in factorial studies, let's consider a hypothetical factorial study that might have been conducted by R. A. Fisher. Suppose we were interested in how the growth rate of bean plants is influenced by (1) the amount of sunlight to which the plants are exposed and (2) the amount of water the plants are given. If we wanted to conduct a 2×2 factorial study to address this question, we might take

Amount of water received

Amount of sunlight received

FIGURE 8.5   Design of a hypothetical study of plant growth

TABLE 8.1   Results of a hypothetical study of plant growth

Amount of Water Received	Amount of Sunlight Received		
	Low	High	Row Means
Low	22.4	25.6	24.0
High	10.8	37.2	24.0
Column means	16.6	31.4	

a group of 40 healthy bean sprouts and randomly assign the plants to the four treatment conditions summarized in Figure 8.5. Let's begin with the plants in the *low* sunlight condition. For the duration of the study (say 30 days), some of these plants would get only a little sunlight along with very little water, and some would get only a little sunlight along with a lot of water. Now consider the plants in the *high* sunlight condition. Like those in the low sunlight condition, some of these plants would get very little water and some would get a lot. In other words, the two independent variables would be completely crossed.

The results of this hypothetical study are summarized in Table 8.1. If we analyzed the data from this hypothetical study using a traditional two-way analysis of variance (ANOVA), we would probably observe three findings. As suggested by the means in Table 8.1, this study appears to have yielded (1) a main effect of sunlight, (2) no main effect of water, and (3) a Sunlight × Water interaction. The main effect of sunlight is indicated by the fact that the plants that received high levels of sunlight grew to be about twice as tall (31.4 versus 16.6 inches) as those that received low levels of sunlight. Similarly, the absence of a main effect for water reflects the fact that the plants that got a lot of water and the plants that got very little water grew to exactly the same average height. However, the presence of an interaction indicates that the main effects do not tell the whole story about sunlight, water, and plant growth. As it turns out, the effect of water on plant growth depended heavily on how much sun the plants received. Plants that got very little sun actually

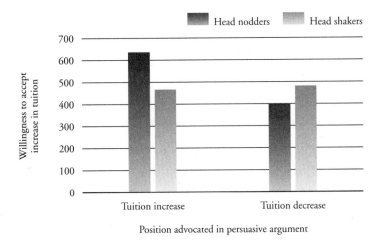

FIGURE 8.6 *Size of tuition increase participants were willing to accept as a function of head nodding and topic of persuasive argument (from Wells & Petty, 1980)*

did better when they got only a little water. Plants that got a lot of sun did much better when they got a lot of water.

Notice that if we had looked only at main effects in this study, we would have come away with a very misleading picture of the role of water and sunlight in plant growth. First of all, we would have concluded that water plays no role in plant growth! Second, we would have come away with an imprecise understanding of the role of sunlight. Whereas the main effect of sunlight (i.e., the average effect of sunlight, averaged across watering levels) was pretty large, the true size of this effect depended heavily on watering levels. When plants received very little water, high levels of sunlight made only a tiny contribution to growth. However, when plants received a lot of water, the effects of sunlight were enormous. This second point reveals another important characteristic of interactions. Interactions are *always* about two (or more) variables. In this case it is not only true that the effects of water depended on the levels of sunlight; it is also true that the effects of sunlight depended on the levels of water. In the case of two-way interactions, it is always possible, at least in principle, to look at the same interaction from two different vantage points.

Another important thing to know about interactions is that not all interactions are identical. Even in the case of two-way interactions, researchers often make a distinction between two distinct varieties of interactions. The most common form of two-way interaction occurs when an independent variable has an effect under some conditions but has less of an effect (or no effect at all) under other conditions. When an effect exists at one level of a second independent variable but is weaker or nonexistent at a different level of the second independent variable, the observed interaction is often referred to as an **ordinal** or **spreading interaction.** An example of a spreading interaction appears in Figure 8.6. This figure is based loosely on the results of an experiment on attitude change conducted by

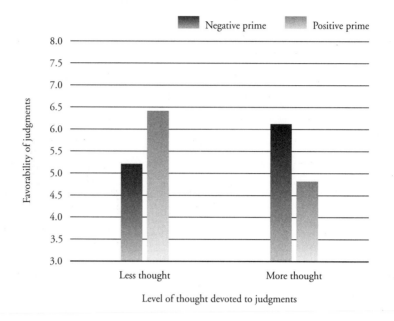

FIGURE 8.7   Favorability of judgments of a target as a function of priming and amount of thought devoted to judgment (data approximate overall findings of Martin, Seta, & Crelia, 1990)

Wells and Petty (1980). Wells and Petty believed that people sometimes infer their attitudes from their own physical responses to a persuasive argument. To test this idea, they asked participants to help them evaluate some stereo headphones that presumably had been designed for use during exercise. While listening to one of two different persuasive arguments about tuition over the headphones, some participants were asked to *shake* their heads from side to side, and others were asked to *nod* their heads up and down (presumably to simulate the head motions of different forms of exercise). As you can see in the left half of Figure 8.6, head nodding facilitated attitude change, but *only* when participants listened to a counterattitudinal argument (in favor of *increases* in tuition). Another way of looking at this same interaction is that the counterattitudinal argument (in favor of tuition increases as opposed to decreases) led to attitude change only when people were nodding their heads up and down.

A second kind of two-way interaction is depicted in Figure 8.7. This figure is based loosely on the results of a series of experiments on person perception conducted by Martin, Seta, and Crelia (1990). Martin et al. made use of some well-established priming manipulations to get people into the mind-set of thinking about either negative (e.g., "stubborn") or positive (e.g., "persistent") personality traits. They also examined the effects of variables (such as cognitive load or personal accountability) that they expected to influence how carefully people would think about a judgment. Thus, all their experiments were 2 × 2 factorials. Each of their factorial experiments yielded an interaction. The particular kind of interaction they observed was a **disordinal** or **crossover interaction.** A disordinal or crossover interaction occurs (1) when there are no main effects

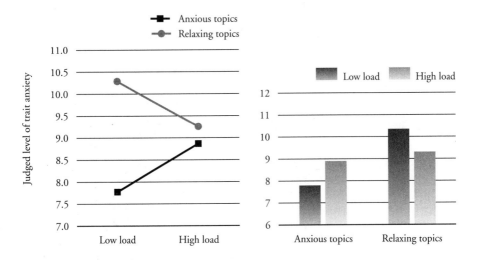

FIGURE 8.8 *Two different ways of graphing the results of Gilbert et al.'s (1988) anxious woman study*

of either independent variable and (2) when the effects of each independent variable are opposite at different levels of the other independent variable. In the case of Martin et al.'s studies, the effects of the primed concepts were opposite for people who gave a little versus a lot of thought to the person-perception task. Those who devoted very little thought to their judgments judged the target person *more favorably* when they had been primed to think about the favorable as opposed to unfavorable concepts. In contrast, those who devoted a great deal of thought to their judgments judged the target person *less favorably* when they had been primed to think about the favorable as opposed to unfavorable concepts. Another way to put this is that Martin et al. observed *assimilation* toward the primed categories when their participants weren't thinking hard about their judgments but observed *contrast* when their participants were.

When the results of a factorial study are represented in line graphs, an interaction will always show up in the form of *nonparallel lines*. (This lack of parallel lines is a direct reflection of the meaning of an interaction: the effects of one variable are *different* at different levels of some other variable.) In the case of a crossover interaction, these nonparallel lines actually cross over one another at or very near the middle of the two lines; hence the term "crossover" interaction. If you would like to see another approximation of a crossover interaction, take a look back at Figure 7.1. If you converted this bar graph to a line graph, you would see that the two lines are not only nonparallel but also cross over one another pretty near the middle. There were no main effects of Swann et al.'s persuasion techniques, and these techniques had roughly (though not perfectly) opposite effects for people who differed in terms of their level of self-certainty.

Whether an interaction in a 2 × 2 design is a spreading interaction or a crossover interaction can sometimes be a tricky issue. For example, take a look at the two graphs that appear in Figure 8.8. *Each* of these two graphs summarizes the results of the same experiment, namely the Gilbert et al. experiment. According to the way that some methods texts define spreading and crossover interactions, the graph on the left appears to depict a spreading or ordinal interaction. Specifically, the line graph shows that the discussion topics had no effect when people were cognitively loaded but had a substantial effect when people were not. However, according to the way that some texts define spreading and crossover interactions, the graph on the right appears to depict a crossover or disordinal interaction. This graph shows that the cognitive load manipulation had *opposite effects* for the two different kinds of discussion topics. When the topics were anxiety provoking, being cognitively loaded caused participants to judge the woman as *more* anxious. When the topics were relaxing, however, being cognitively loaded caused participants to judge the woman as *less* anxious (the bar graph, incidentally, is merely a rearrangement of Figure 8.4).

Which kind of interaction did Gilbert et al. observe? As we have defined the terms here, they observed a *spreading interaction*. The main reason that this is so is that they observed a main effect (a main effect of their discussion topics). This meant that even though their cognitive load manipulation did have opposite effects for different kinds of topics, the two lines that represent their findings do not cross at all (much less cross in the middle). When a researcher observes a true crossover interaction in a two-way factorial study, the effects of *both* independent variables are opposite (and roughly equal) at the different levels of the other independent variable. In the first of Martin et al.'s (1990) two studies of person perception, it was not merely the case that the effects of the priming manipulation were opposite at different levels of load. It was *also* the case that the effects of load were opposite at different levels of the priming manipulation. This symmetrical situation can be the case only when researchers observe an interaction *in the absence of any main effects*.

Because experimenters like to know exactly what kind of interactions they have observed in their research, and because a visual inspection of a set of means can sometimes be misleading, researchers usually conduct a set of very specific statistical tests after they have observed a statistically significant interaction in a two-way factorial design. In particular, they usually conduct **simple effects tests,** also known as **simple main effects tests,** to see which specific mean comparisons are significant in their factorial study. Simple effects tests are typically very simple statistical tests. In fact, most often they are simply *t*-tests. In the case of the first Martin et al. study, for example, one simple effects test would be conducted to determine whether the positive effect of the priming manipulation observed for cognitively loaded participants was significant. That is, did the loaded participants who received the positive prime judge the target person significantly more favorably than did the loaded participants who received the negative prime? The other simple effects test would be exactly the same specific comparison except that it would be conducted for the participants who were *not* cognitively loaded. This statistical test would tell us whether the nonloaded participants who received the positive prime judged the target significantly less favorably than did the nonloaded participants who received the negative prime. If we are dealing with a cut-and-dried case of a crossover interaction, each of these simple effects tests will be significant. If either one of these two simple effects tests is not quite significant, there will be some question as to whether we have observed a true crossover interaction.

Putting together everything that we've seen so far about factorial designs, let's consider what Fisher had to say about the advantages of factorial designs over simpler, one-way designs. Fisher noted that two of the major selling points of factorial designs are that they are both more *efficient* and more *comprehensive* than one-way designs. Factorial designs are efficient in the sense that they allow us to look for more than one main effect at a time in a single study. They are comprehensive in the sense that, unlike one-way designs, they tell us more of the whole story behind a specific phenomenon—by allowing us to see how different variables work together to influence the phenomenon. In addition to these two advantages of factorial designs, Fisher also noted that there is a third, less commonly appreciated, advantage of factorial designs. Although the term hadn't yet been coined in Fisher's day, modern methodologists would say that this third advantage has to do with external validity. As Fisher (1935) put it:

> There is a third advantage . . . which, while less obvious than the former two . . . has an important bearing on the utility of the experimental results in their practical application. This is that any conclusion, such as that it is advantageous to increase the quantity of a given ingredient, has a wider inductive basis when inferred from an experiment in which the quantities of other ingredients have been varied, than it would have from any amount of experimentation, in which these had been kept strictly constant. The exact standardisation of experimental conditions, which is often thoughtlessly advocated as a panacea, always carries with it the real disadvantage that a highly standardised experiment supplies direct information only in respect of the narrow range of conditions achieved by standardisation. Standardisation, therefore, weakens rather than strengthens our ground for inferring a like result, when, as is invariably the case in practice, these conditions are somewhat varied.

In other words, a researcher who observes main effects in a factorial study can be reasonably sure that any observed main effects will *generalize* across whatever levels of the other independent variables exist in the study. If these other variables were held at a single, constant value, as is necessarily the case in a one-way design, it would always be possible that the researcher had identified the one and only one set of conditions under which the observed effect usually occurs. Of course, main effects are often qualified by interactions, but as we have noted repeatedly, learning about the existence of interactions is also something that we can do only by using factorial designs. The topic of interactions is sufficiently important that we have created a special methodology exercise on interactions. This exercise is included at the end of this chapter to help you review and apply your knowledge of interactions. If you are still feeling a little unclear about the nature of main effects and interactions, this exercise should help you sharpen your knowledge of these important concepts.

Within-Subjects Designs

Earlier in this chapter, we said we were going to discuss two basic kinds of experimental designs and two basic approaches to experimental design. As you now know, the two basic kinds of experimental designs we were talking about are one-way designs and factorial designs. The two basic approaches to research design include between-subjects designs—the only approach to experimental design that we've discussed thus far—and within-subjects designs, which are the final topic of this chapter. **Between-subjects designs** are designs in which each participant serves in one and only one condition of an experiment. If you think back to all the studies we discussed in the first part of this chapter, it should be clear that participants in these studies experienced only one level of each manipulation they received. In contrast, **within-subjects** or **repeated measures designs** are those in which each participant serves in *more than one* (perhaps all) of the conditions of a study.

Most of the design issues that apply to between-subjects designs also apply to within-subjects designs. Most notably, within-subjects designs include both one-way designs (that have only a single independent variable) and factorial designs (that range from simple 2×2 factorials to designs with three or more independent variables). Like between-subjects designs, within-subjects designs are also analyzed using ANOVA. Of course, there are differences in the exact calculations that underlie between-subjects and within-subjects ANOVAs. In this regard, the main difference between a between-subjects and a within-subjects ANOVA is the fact that the within-subjects ANOVA takes it into account that the observations in the different cells of a within-subjects design are not statistically independent (because they are no longer coming from separate people). However, the precise calculations that reflect this fact are largely beyond the scope of this text (and they are typically handled by powerful computer software programs such as SAS or SPSS).

Advantages of Within-Subjects Designs

Within-subjects designs have some enormous advantages over between-subjects designs. The most straightforward is the fact that within-subjects designs require *fewer participants* than between-subjects designs—especially when it comes to complex factorial designs that have many different conditions. As an example, consider a study in which a researcher working for a national testing service wants to investigate the joint effects of three different variables on intellectual performance. Specifically, imagine that she has designed a factorial study in which she wants to examine the joint effects of task difficulty, time pressure, and type of task on the quality of people's performance. If she designed a 3 (task difficulty: low, medium, or high) × 3 (task type: verbal, mathematical, or analytical) × 2 (time pressure: low versus high) between-subjects factorial study to address her research question, her design would have 18 ($3 \times 3 \times 2$) unique conditions! If she needed to randomly assign 50 people to each condition to get a stable estimate of what's going on in each condition of the study, she would need to run 900 participants! On the other hand, if this researcher ran a completely within-subjects study, and exposed each participant to all 18 cells of her study, she would need to run only 50 participants to have 50 in each cell. That's a good deal! But wait, there's more! In all likelihood, if the researcher in this study used a within-subjects design, she would be able to get away with running far fewer than 50 participants (perhaps 25 or 30) to have the same ability to detect effects she would have needed 50 per cell to detect in a between-subjects design. This is because the factors in a within-subject design do not have to "fight" all the noise occurring between conditions due to *individual differences.* This leads to the second advantage of within-subject designs.

Another way to describe this second advantage is to say that within-subject designs eliminate *person confounds.* Recall that researchers usually eliminate person confounds by randomly assigning different participants to different conditions in between-subjects experiments. When researchers use within-subjects manipulations, however, they eliminate person confounds in a much more direct fashion. They ask the *very same people* to serve in the different experimental conditions in which they happen to be interested. In a sense, then, within-subjects designs take advantage of the only perfect form of matching. In so doing, they totally eliminate person confounds. If the very same people serve in both your experimental condition and your control condition, you don't have to worry very much about whether the people in these two conditions are different from one another. If Alfredo is a highly intelligent, extroverted lobbyist when he serves in your experimental condition, then we can rest assured that he is still a highly intelligent, extroverted lobbyist when he serves in your control condition. Needless to say, this is a very nice feature of within-subjects designs.

With this in mind, you may be wondering why anyone would ever bother to run more than a single person in a within-subjects experiment. After all, a single person could participate in all the conditions in a within-subjects study, and we wouldn't have to worry at all about person confounds. There are several reasons why within-subjects studies require multiple participants, but the most important reasons all have to do with the fact that we would like to be sure that the results we observe in an experiment apply to people in general, rather than to one particular person. In other words, running only one person in a within-subjects study would raise serious concerns about external validity. We'd have no way of knowing whether the findings of a single-participant study would apply to anyone else. This concern about external validity gets translated into a statistical concern as well. Recall that statistical analyses essentially tell us whether we can safely draw conclusions about the general population of people from whom our participants were drawn. When we have sampled only one participant, we cannot draw any safe statistical inferences about populations (This concept makes its way into statistical analyses in the sense that you can't even conduct most standard statistical tests unless you have a minimum of five to ten participants per condition in an experiment). On the other hand, within-subjects studies are generally more powerful than between-subjects studies. Thus, when researchers are fairly certain that their within-subjects studies are high in *psychological realism,* they can often make pretty safe inferences about people in general by sampling surprisingly small numbers of research participants. Within-subjects designs represent a very powerful research technique.

Disadvantages of Within-Subjects Designs

In light of how well within-subjects designs control for person confounds, and in light of how powerful and efficient they are, you may be wondering why anyone would ever waste his or her time running between-subjects studies! There are several very good reasons, but the simplest answer is that, despite all the advantages of within-subjects designs, they also have some disadvantages. Studies that use within-subject designs often introduce sources of bias that are unlikely to emerge in between-subjects designs. Although it is possible to reduce or eliminate *most* of these potential biases, some of them are potent enough that they sometimes force researchers to stick with between-subjects designs.

There are three primary, and closely related, biases that are applicable to within-subjects designs. The first bias has to do with the fact that people's psychological states change as they spend time working on one or more tasks. More specifically, **sequence effects** can pose serious problems for within-subjects designs. Sequence effects occur when the simple passage of time begins to take its toll on people's responses (e.g., when people get bored or tired). In the hypothetical within-subjects study of intellectual abilities described above, you can probably see how anyone would start to get a little tired by the time he or she reached the set of 10 problems that constituted the 18th unique condition of the study. Of course, researchers could compensate for this problem to some degree by giving people breaks or making their experimental tasks as brief as possible. However, this would not completely eliminate this serious problem. Most people are simply going to be in a different frame of mind when they are about to finish a task than they were when they first began it. In other words, within-subjects studies run the risk of confounding a specific condition or manipulation with a specific level of boredom, fatigue, or excitement that a task is almost over.

A second, closely related, drawback of within-subjects designs has to do with **carryover effects.** Carryover effects occur when people's responses to one stimulus in a study directly influence their responses to a second stimulus. As an example, consider a study by Stapel and Schwarz (1998). They had participants report their attitudes about the Republican Party after answering a simple question about either General Colin Powell or Senator Bob Dole. Both Colin Powell and Bob Dole are Republicans. However, at the time of Stapel and Schwarz's study, Powell was very popular, but Dole was not. As a result, participants who first reported their attitudes toward Powell rated the Republican Party more favorably than those who first reported their attitudes toward Dole. We can imagine that many of the participants in the Colin Powell condition thought something like "Colin Powell is a Republican, and I really like him. So I guess the Republican Party can't be all that bad." For similar reasons, participants in the Bob Dole condition may have allowed their negative feelings about Bob Dole to spill over into their feelings about the Republican Party.

Their thoughts might have even resembled the thoughts of the misinformed political activists who once boycotted Dole pineapples because of their distaste for Bob Dole (who has nothing to do with the Doles who sell pineapples).

This particular kind of carryover effect is known as an **order effect.** Order effects occur when a question takes on a different meaning when it follows one question than when it follows another. As a second example of order effects, Strack, Martin and Schwarz (1988) asked college students to report both their general life satisfaction and their dating frequency. When the general life satisfaction question came first, the two items had practically nothing to do with one another ($r = -.12$). However, when the dating frequency question came first, the two items were very strongly correlated ($r = .66$). The more people said they dated, the happier they said they were with their lives. Apparently, students who answer life satisfaction questions do not usually give much thought to their dating frequency, *unless they have just been asked to think about dating.* Thus, a single question that drew attention to dating frequency caused students to interpret life satisfaction from the idiosyncratic vantage point of dating frequency. Carryover effects such as question order effects can create serious problems for within-subjects studies.

Another kind of carryover effect can occur when participants knowingly or unknowingly learn something by performing an experimental task. When participants' experience with one task makes it easier for them to perform a different task that comes along later, they have benefited from **practice effects.** As you might guess, this is a problem because researchers cannot tell if people's superior performance on the second task happened because of an experimental manipulation or because of simple practice. Practice effects are closely related to *testing effects,* which we discussed in Chapter 4. Recall that testing effects occur when people perform better on a test the second time they take it. The primary difference between testing effects and practice effects is that practice effects occur even when the second test measures something very different than the first. (In the case of testing effects, the second test is designed to measure exactly the same thing as the first test, and the two tests are very similar if not often identical.) For instance, a person who benefits from practice effects might respond more accurately to multiple choice questions during the latter part of an experiment merely because he or she was becoming familiar with a multiple-choice question format. The specific topic of the questions wouldn't necessarily matter.

Of course, people's experience doing one thing does not *always* make it easier for them to do something else. In fact, the reverse is sometimes the case, especially when two tasks follow one another in close succession. When performing one task disrupts people's performance on a second task, this is referred to as an **interference effect.** Interference effects constitute a third kind of carryover effect. To see what we mean by an interference effect, please provide a brief, *one-word answer* to each of the following questions. It is important that you answer each question as quickly as possible!

What's a three-letter synonym for police officer?
What do you do with an ax?
What's the opposite of bottom?
What do you do at a green light?

If you were tempted to stop at the green light, you experienced a subtle form of interference effect. Interference effects are the opposite of practice effects, but they are equally problematic in within-subjects designs. If a person's performance in the second of two conditions in a within-subjects study deteriorates, we always have to worry that an interference effect, rather than an experimental manipulation, could have been at work.

Even if sequence or carryover effects are not a problem in within-subjects studies, a third drawback of within-subjects designs is that they increase the likelihood that participants will be able to figure out an experimenter's hypothesis. Consider, for instance, a study of gender stereotypes in which participants view a videotape of a man aggressing against a woman. After making some trait ratings of both the man and the woman, the same participants watch a very similar videotape. In fact, *everything* is the same except that the woman is now aggressing against the man. Most participants in a within-subjects study such as this one would quickly realize that the study has something to do with how we judge men and women who perform exactly the same behavior. Participants might not be able to spell out the experimenter's exact hypothesis, but they certainly wouldn't offer the kinds of natural responses to the second videotape that they might have offered to the first. We suspect that most participants would probably assume that the experimenter is *hoping* to see evidence that men are seen as more aggressive than women. If participants were sufficiently motivated to please the experimenter, they might fall prey to *demand characteristics* (see Chapter 4). If they did so, they might try to act in ways that were consistent with the experimenter's hypothesis. That is, they might try to be "good subjects" and thus might report what they felt the experimenter wanted to hear (Orne, 1962). Most likely, this would mean rating the man as more aggressive than the woman. Alternatively, it is possible that participants might succumb to *evaluation apprehension* (also reviewed in Chapter 4). If they did so, they'd report whatever they felt would portray them in the most favorable light possible (Tedeschi, Schlenker, & Bonoma, 1971). Given that stereotyping people on the basis of gender is generally frowned upon, participants might report that the man and the woman seemed equally aggressive, even if they secretly felt that the man seemed more aggressive than the woman.

Solutions

In light of all the problems that apply to within-subjects designs, you may be wondering why anyone would ever waste his or her time running within-subjects studies! The reason is that these problems can be reduced or eliminated using some specially designed control techniques. Let's review some of these useful techniques. We'll begin with the two general categories of problems that we reviewed first: sequence effects and carryover effects. A very useful control technique for reducing or eliminating both sequence and carryover effects is **counterbalancing.** This is a method of control whereby the researcher varies the order in which participants experience the different conditions of a within-subjects study. Because there are many different kinds of within-subjects studies, there are many different kinds of counterbalancing. The most comprehensive form of counterbalancing is appropriately referred to as **complete counterbalancing.** Researchers who use complete counter-balancing present *every possible order* of all their experimental treatment conditions. This means, of course, that different participants receive different orders (by virtue of their random assignment to these different orders). Complete counterbalancing works best when a within-subjects study has only two or three conditions. You can compute all the possible orders needed to perform complete counterbalancing by taking the *factorial* of the number of unique conditions that you have in your study. If you have only two within-subjects conditions, you have only 2! (two factorial = 2 × 1) or 2 possible orders. These orders are often written in a shorthand in which a different letter is used to represent each unique condition of the study. These letters are then written in the order in which they are presented to participants. In a simple one-way, within-subjects experiment with only two levels of the independent variable, the 2 orders would be summarized AB and BA. Some people get condition A followed by condition B. Others get condition B followed by condition A. It's that simple.

Once you graduate to within-subjects studies that have three or more unique conditions, you start to find that there are a lot of possible orders of presentation of your experimental conditions. When you have three different conditions in a one-way within-subjects study, there are 3! (3 × 2 × 1) or 6 possible orders of presentation, and when you have just four conditions, there are 4! or 24 possible orders. Jump up to a 2 × 3 factorial (with six unique conditions), and you have 720 possible orders (that's 6! = 6 × 5 × 4 × 3 × 2 × 1). In the 18-cell study of intellectual performance mentioned earlier, there would be a cumbersome 18! possible orders. That's $6.402373706 \times 10^{15}$ or about 6 quadrillion, 402 trillion, 373 billion, 706 million possible orders. Even if we only ran one participant in each order, we'd run out of people on earth before we had finished even a *millionth* of all these possible orders. From this perspective, the between-subjects study that requires 900 participants probably doesn't sound so bad after all!

When it is impractical to use complete counterbalancing, researchers typically make use of one of two kinds of *incomplete counterbalancing.* The simplest kind of incomplete counterbalancing is **reverse counterbalancing.** Researchers who use this technique simply generate a single order (either a meaningful order or a random order), and then they reverse it. This not only produces two different orders but also guarantees that the average serial position of any given condition in a study (e.g., whether this condition came first, second, third, and so forth) is exactly the same for all the unique conditions. Notice, for example, that if a researcher simply used the orders ABCDE and EDCBA, then each of the five unique conditions would occur, on the average, in the *third* of the five possible positions. Take condition B, for example. For half of the people this condition came second, and for half it came fourth. The average of second and fourth is third. It's that simple.

However, there is a fairly serious drawback of reverse counterbalancing. Although it does control for average serial position, it doesn't control for how frequently all possible conditions occur first or last. In the case of reverse counterbalancing just provided, condition C always occurs smack in the middle of the experiment. It's never first, and it's never last. Most forms of **partial counterbalancing** (a second general category of incomplete counterbalancing) take care of this problem. One commonly used form of partial counterbalancing involves choosing a limited number of orders (say 10 or 12) at *random* from the pool of all possible orders. In this way, the experimenter is using *random selection* and choosing a sample of orders from the entire population of possible orders. One conceivable problem with this is that it is always possible for the random selection process to turn out orders that share many similar features. For instance, it is always possible that condition A will always appear in the first half of the study. By choosing many different random orders, a researcher can minimize the likelihood of this problem. However, he or she will have to go to the trouble of choosing, creating, and keeping track of dozens of different orders.

As an alternative to choosing orders at random, a researcher who wants to control as completely as possible for order might also make use of a **Latin square** procedure to generate a fixed number of orders. In the case of four within-subjects experimental conditions, a Latin square could be used to generate four orders such that each of the four unique conditions appeared (1) exactly once in each possible serial position (first through fourth) and (2) exactly twice *before* and exactly twice *after* each of the other three unique conditions. Such an ideal Latin square for four orders is summarized in Table 8.2. Unfortunately, this ideal Latin square is impossible to achieve for many other designs. For example, when there are an odd number of unique orders, it will never be possible to achieve this second criterion. However, the one thing you can *always* do in any kind of Latin square is to arrange things so that each condition appears exactly once in each possible serial position. A Latin square for five conditions that fulfills this requirement also appears in Table 8.2. Finally, because there are some drawbacks to this specific approach to a Latin square (e.g., condition B usually occurs immediately after condition A), researchers sometimes choose several different Latin squares at random and make use of more than one Latin square in a single study. A detailed treatment of Latin squares is beyond the scope of this text. If you run into a particularly complex problem involving Latin squares, you can find advice in most advanced statistical texts. For most purposes, however, one of the basic

TABLE 8.2 An ideal Latin square for four within-subjects conditions and a regular Latin square for five within-subjects conditions

ABCD	ABCDE
BADC	BCDEA
CDAB	CDEAB
DCBA	DEABC
	EABCD

forms of counterbalancing we have reviewed here will suffice. The basic point we wish to emphasize is that counterbalancing goes a very long way toward resolving problems such as sequence and carryover effects. The specific form of counterbalancing you use to resolve these problems will depend on the complexity of your within-subject design.

Incidentally, we should make it clear that counterbalancing does *not* erase sequence or carryover effects. These effects exist sometimes, and there is usually little we can do to make them go away. Instead of erasing these effects, counterbalancing simply unconfounds them with particular treatment conditions. If all your treatment conditions occur with equal frequency in the early and late portions of an experimental session, then you have controlled for problems such as order and contamination effects. This doesn't mean that people don't get tired, or don't get better or worse at experimental tasks as they work their way through a study. These effects still exist, but they have been balanced (you might even say *counter*balanced) equally across all your treatment conditions. Moreover, if you went to the trouble to randomly assign your participants to the different orders of your within-subjects studies, you could check to see if order had any effects on your findings by treating order as an independent variable in an ANOVA and analyzing for it. When you do so, you will usually be hoping that you *don't* find any effects of order. However, in case there are any order effects, you will know that you have controlled for them. Moreover, you will also be able to take a close look at them to see if they tell you anything interesting about what you have been studying.

So counterbalancing can help solve two of the three big problems that sometimes affect within-subjects designs. But what about the problem that participants in within-subjects studies are especially likely to figure out a researcher's hypothesis? Counterbalancing can also make a small contribution to dealing with this problem. Recall that researchers randomly assign people to different orders in a within-subjects design. This means that researchers who are worried that their use of a within-subjects manipulation has clued participants in to what they are studying can simply look at people's judgments in the *first* condition to which participants were exposed (before they could have easily figured out what was being manipulated). This boils down to conducting a between-subjects analysis on a limited portion (the very first portion) of a within-subjects study. If the between-subjects analyses strongly resemble the within-subjects analyses, then this suggests that the within-subjects manipulation may not have created any problems by cluing participants in to what is being studied.

On the other hand, maybe things are even worse than the researcher had feared. Perhaps the manipulation is so transparent that many participants figured out what was being studied before they ever got to the second experimental condition! This is to say that an analysis of participants' responses on a dependent measure cannot completely reassure us that participants haven't figured out what was being manipulated in a study (regardless of whether the study involves a within-subjects or a between-subjects manipulation). When researchers really wish to know what people were thinking while they took part in a within-subjects study, they need to find good ways to ask them. With this idea in mind, researchers who use repeated measures designs often rely on some kind of **structured debriefing.** A structured debriefing is an interview conducted with participants immediately after they have completed a study to determine exactly what participants thought the researcher expected to find. Because it makes participants seem smart to have figured out what a researcher was studying, it is often possible to just come right out and ask people what they think the researcher's hypothesis was or what they think he or she expected to find. At other times, it might be necessary to provide participants with some options to see if they can guess the hypothesis at an above-chance level. If they can, this is usually a pretty serious problem. However, all may not be lost. For example, the researcher could reanalyze his or her data, focusing only on the participants who did not figure out (or guess) the hypothesis. This isn't as ideal as running a study in which no one realizes what you are expecting to find, but it's a step in the right direction. Because of the complexity of solving the "transparency problem" with within-subjects designs, researchers often avoid using within-subjects designs when doing so would make it clear what they are studying.

In some cases, that is, the only real solution to worries about transparency is to use a between-subjects design. Returning to the last example, a participant who sees *either* a film of a man aggressing against a woman *or* a film of a woman aggressing against a man will usually have no idea the experimenter has created multiple versions of the same video. As a result, participants in this between-subjects study will probably rate the aggressors just as they see them, without realizing that stereotypes may have influenced their judgments.

In short, one reason why experimenters sometimes rely on between-subjects designs is that some experiments are difficult to pull off using within-subjects designs. In addition to this problem, an even more serious problem is that some experiments are absolutely impossible to pull off using within-subjects designs. Within-subjects designs are feasible only to the degree that you can readily alter a state once you have created it. It's very easy to show participants a big circle and later show them a little circle to see if the size of the circle affects how much they like it. However, it would be much trickier to put participants in a good mood and expect to be able to put them in a bad mood a few seconds (or even a few minutes) later. And in some cases, what's done can never be undone at all, no matter how hard you try. For instance, behavioral neuroscientists or other biologically oriented psychologists who give their participants brain lesions or injections of hormones cannot usually return their participants to their original state to see how they would behave under a different set of experimental conditions. Similarly, natural manipulations such as gender, ethnicity, and a person's name are essentially irreversible. You can't study something on a within-subjects basis if you can't push it back and forth on a within-subjects basis.

Mixed-Model Designs

As we just noted, one solution to the problem of participant expectancies in within-subjects designs is to forget about using within-subjects designs anytime it could be easy for a participant to figure out your experimental hypoth-

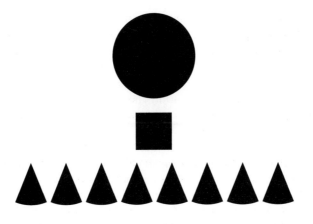

FIGURE 8.9   Stimuli from one of the between-subjects conditions of Pelham et al. (1994). Using the square as a 1.0 unit frame of reference, (1) estimate the area of the single circle above the square (e.g., 1.2 units, 3.8 units) and (2) estimate the total area of the eight triangles below the square.

esis. However, a better solution is probably to utilize the advantages of both within-subjects and between-subjects designs by conducting studies with **mixed** or **mixed-model designs.** Mixed-model designs are designs in which (1) at least one independent variable is manipulated on a between-subjects basis and (2) at least one other independent variable is manipulated on a within-subjects basis.

You probably won't be too surprised to learn that one of the first author's favorite examples of this kind of design is a study conducted by Pelham and colleagues. Pelham, Sumarta, and Myaskovsky (1994) were interested in a judgmental heuristic they referred to as the *numerosity heuristic:* the tendency to estimate quantity or magnitude by basing one's judgments disproportionately on the *number of units* into which a stimulus is divided—without fully adjusting for other important variables (like the size of the units). In one very simple study, Pelham et al. (1994; Study 1) presented people with two different stimuli: (1) an intact circle similar to the one at the top of Figure 8.9 and (2) a lot of little triangles similar to those at the bottom of Figure 8.9. Because people judged the total area of *each* of these two stimulus sets,* the study contained a within-subjects manipulation (whether a stimulus was divided into a lot of pieces or not). Pelham et al.'s participants judged the total area of the nine triangles to be quite a bit greater than the area of the single, intact circle.

However, if you look ahead to Figure 8.10 (at the very end of this chapter), you will see that participants paid too much attention to the numerosity information. When we made it easy for a second group of participants to see how the triangles could be pushed together to form a circle—by showing them a set of stimuli similar to those that appear in Figure 8.10—these participants

*Using the square in the middle as a standard, 1-unit comparison.

were much less likely to base their judgments on numerosity. This second manipulation, the difficulty of reassembling the little triangles into a single circle, was manipulated on a purely between-subjects basis. If we had tried to manipulate this variable on a within-subjects basis, a counterbalancing procedure would have been pretty useless. In particular, the participants who got the easy version of the problem first would almost certainly approach the difficult version of the problem differently than would naive participants. Just as quasi-experiments sometimes allow researchers to take advantage of the best aspects of experimental and nonexperimental research, mixed-models designs (whether they involve purely experimental manipulations or quasi-experimental manipulations) sometimes allow researchers to take advantage of the desirable qualities of between- and within-subjects designs.

HANDS-ON ACTIVITY 3

A Double-Blind Taste Test with Popular Colas

One good way to familiarize yourself with research methods is to ask yourself how you might go about answering a simple, everyday question the way a research psychologist would go about doing so. For example, suppose you wanted to know which of two nationally advertised soft drinks people really prefer. Specifically, what if you wanted to find out whether people prefer Coca-Cola or Pepsi-Cola? You might start by assuming that people have no preference. In fact, you might start by assuming that, if the two drinks weren't labeled, people couldn't even tell them apart. In this hands-on activity, you and your classmates will take part in a blind taste test designed to address two simple questions. First, can people correctly identify Coke and Pepsi in a blind taste test? Second, regardless of whether people can correctly identify the two colas, do people prefer one cola over the other? Because we think it will be useful for you to see what is taking place behind the scenes while you serve as a taster in this activity, we have summarized the procedures here from the experimenter's perspective. A set of instructions for tasters and a brief survey for indicating your responses to the test are included after these instructions to the experimenter.

Information for the Experimenter

For this activity, you will need (1) some chilled 2-liter bottles of Coca-Cola and Pepsi-Cola (2 to 2½ ounces of each cola for each of your participants), (2) two 3-ounce paper cups for each of your participants, (3) a box of saltine crackers (at least one cracker per participant), (4) some napkins, (5) some stickers or tape that you can use to number the paper cups, and (6) a large partition that permits you to pour the colas at the front of the room without allowing students to see which cola is being poured into which cup (a partition can be readily assembled from cardboard or foam board). Before beginning the taste test, you should set up your materials by numbering your cups consecutively (e.g., from 1–60 if you have 30 students). In addition, before beginning the tasting, participants will answer a few background questions about their cola-drinking behavior and their established preferences for the two colas (see the rating surveys). Once you have set up all your materials, you should recruit an assistant to serve the colas. To minimize the possibility of experimenter bias and participant expectancies, you will make use of a double-blind procedure in which neither the server nor the participants are informed of the content of the cups.

The basic procedure involves filling one of each pair of cups with Coke and the other one with Pepsi. For example, if you pour Coke into cup 17, you will pour Pepsi into cup 18. This will guarantee that each participant receives *one serving of each cola*. After you have filled each consecutively numbered set of cups using a chart that contains a list of random serving orders, your research assistant (the server) will give each participant two consecutively numbered cups of cola along with a napkin and a saltine cracker. As noted in the instructions below, participants will take a bite of the saltine cracker, drink the first cup of cola, take another bite of the saltine cracker, and then drink the second cup of cola. Tasting the cracker prior to tasting each cola should minimize contamination effects. After finishing both of the colas, participants will (1) try to identify each of the two colas and (2) report their degree of liking for each cola. To maintain the integrity of the counterbalancing procedure, it is important that participants taste the cups of cola in *numerical order* (e.g., the fifth participant should drink the cola in cup number 9 before drinking the cola in cup number 10). A table that you can use to determine the order in which the colas are served follows. Before beginning the taste test, you should flip a coin to determine which of the two charts you will use. Because the charts (order 1 and order 2) represent "opposite" orders, even a participant who had memorized the two charts would have no way of knowing which cola he or she was served first.

Instructions for Participants in the Cola Taste Test

Before beginning the blind taste test, you should fill out the top half of the Cola Rating Sheet. During the blind taste test itself, you will be asked to taste each of the two numbered colas (in numerical order). You will then try to identify the brand name of each cola and report how much you liked each cola.

1. Fill out the top half of your Cola Rating Sheet. Once you have received your cola samples, you should notice that you received two consecutively numbered cups of cola (e.g., cups numbered 31 and 32).

2. Eat a bite (about half) of the saltine cracker.

3. Drink all the cola in the cup with the *lower* number.

4. Eat the remaining half of the saltine cracker.

5. Drink all the cola in the cup with the *higher* number.

6. Fill out the remaining portion of your Cola Rating Sheet.

Two Possible Orders (Counterbalancing Schemes) for Serving the Colas

Order 1		Order 2	
001 = Coke	002 = Pepsi	001 = Pepsi	002 = Coke
003 = Pepsi	004 = Coke	003 = Coke	004 = Pepsi
005 = Pepsi	006 = Coke	005 = Coke	006 = Pepsi
007 = Pepsi	008 = Coke	007 = Coke	008 = Pepsi
009 = Coke	010 = Pepsi	009 = Pepsi	010 = Coke
011 = Coke	012 = Pepsi	011 = Pepsi	012 = Coke
013 = Coke	014 = Pepsi	013 = Pepsi	014 = Coke
015 = Pepsi	016 = Coke	015 = Coke	016 = Pepsi
017 = Pepsi	018 = Coke	017 = Coke	018 = Pepsi
019 = Pepsi	020 = Coke	019 = Coke	020 = Pepsi
021 = Pepsi	022 = Coke	021 = Coke	022 = Pepsi
023 = Coke	024 = Pepsi	023 = Pepsi	024 = Coke
025 = Coke	026 = Pepsi	025 = Pepsi	026 = Coke
027 = Coke	028 = Pepsi	027 = Pepsi	028 = Coke
029 = Coke	030 = Pepsi	029 = Pepsi	030 = Coke
031 = Coke	032 = Pepsi	031 = Pepsi	032 = Coke
033 = Coke	034 = Pepsi	033 = Pepsi	034 = Coke
035 = Coke	036 = Pepsi	035 = Pepsi	036 = Coke
037 = Pepsi	038 = Coke	037 = Coke	038 = Pepsi
039 = Coke	040 = Pepsi	039 = Pepsi	040 = Coke
041 = Pepsi	042 = Coke	041 = Coke	042 = Pepsi
043 = Coke	044 = Pepsi	043 = Pepsi	044 = Coke
045 = Coke	046 = Pepsi	045 = Pepsi	046 = Coke
047 = Pepsi	048 = Coke	047 = Coke	048 = Pepsi
049 = Pepsi	050 = Coke	049 = Coke	050 = Pepsi
051 = Coke	052 = Pepsi	051 = Pepsi	052 = Coke
053 = Pepsi	054 = Coke	053 = Coke	054 = Pepsi
055 = Pepsi	056 = Coke	055 = Coke	056 = Pepsi
057 = Coke	058 = Pepsi	057 = Pepsi	058 = Coke
059 = Pepsi	060 = Coke	059 = Coke	060 = Pepsi
061 = Pepsi	062 = Coke	061 = Coke	062 = Pepsi
063 = Pepsi	064 = Coke	063 = Coke	064 = Pepsi

Note. If you have more than 32 participants, you can simply start over (at the top of a chart) for your 33rd participant. To minimize errors, it is wise to cover the unused order while pouring the colas.

Questions for Students

1. You will notice that there are two versions of the Cola Rating Sheet—see pages 250–251. Why are there two versions? After you have taken part in the blind taste test, your instructor will probably summarize the primary results of the test for you. To get in the habit of thinking like a statistician, you should give some thought to what kind of comparisons you would make to answer the basic questions that are addressed in this study.

2. Specifically, how would you determine whether people are able to tell the two colas apart? For example, to see if people are able to label the colas correctly, you will probably want to make a statistical comparison of (a) your class's overall performance with (b) some kind of reasonable performance standard. What should that performance standard be?

3. What kind of comparison(s) should you make to see which of the two colas people prefer (before taking part in the study and in the actual taste test)?

1   **Cola Rating Sheet**   **Gender: M F**

1. About how many 12-oz. servings of cola do you currently drink on a typical day? (Enter a whole number): _____

2. What percentage of the cola you drink is regular cola (rather than diet cola)? (Enter a whole number): _____

3. In the last six months . . .

   ____ percent of the cola I've consumed has been Coca-Cola

   ____ percent of the cola I've consumed has been Pepsi-Cola

   ____ percent of the cola I've consumed has been other brands

(Please be sure these three values add up to 100%.)

4. How much do you like Coca-Cola? (Circle one number)

1	2	3	4	5	6	7	8	9
not at all							very much	

5. How much do you like Pepsi-Cola? (Circle one number)

1	2	3	4	5	6	7	8	9
not at all							very much	

6. Which of these two brands do you prefer? _____

STOP: PLEASE WAIT FOR INSTRUCTIONS ON THE TASTE TEST.

7a. The cola I tasted first was labeled with the # ____.

7b. I think this cola was: (Circle one) Coke Pepsi

7c. I liked this cola:

1	2	3	4	5	6	7	8	9
not at all							very much	

8a. The cola I tasted second was labeled with the # ____.

8b. I think this cola was: (Circle one) Coke Pepsi

8c. I liked this cola:

1	2	3	4	5	6	7	8	9
not at all							very much	

9. Of the two colas I tasted, the one I preferred was:

   (a) the first

   (b) the second

2   **Cola Rating Sheet**   **Gender: M F**

1. About how many 12-oz. servings of cola do you currently drink on a typical day? (Enter a whole number): _____

2. What percentage of the cola you drink is regular cola (rather than diet cola)? (Enter a whole number): _____

3. In the last six months . . .

   ____ percent of the cola I've consumed has been Pepsi-Cola

   ____ percent of the cola I've consumed has been Coca-Cola

   ____ percent of the cola I've consumed has been other brands

(Please be sure these three values add up to 100%)

4. How much do you like Pepsi-Cola? (Circle one number)

1	2	3	4	5	6	7	8	9
not at all							very much	

5. How much do you like Coca-Cola? (Circle one number)

1	2	3	4	5	6	7	8	9
not at all							very much	

6. Which of these two brands do you prefer? _____

STOP: PLEASE WAIT FOR INSTRUCTIONS ON THE TASTE TEST.

7a. The cola I tasted first was labeled with the # ____.

7b. I think this cola was: (Circle one) Pepsi Coke

7c. I liked this cola:

1	2	3	4	5	6	7	8	9
not at all							very much	

8a. The cola I tasted second was labeled with the # ____.

8b. I think this cola was: (Circle one) Pepsi Coke

8c. I liked this cola:

1	2	3	4	5	6	7	8	9
not at all							very much	

9. Of the two colas I tasted, the one I preferred was:

   (a) the first

   (b) the second

METHODOLOGY EXERCISE 3

Interactions

Does your dog bite? Will this pain reliever make me feel better? Are people attracted to those who say good things about them? When people ask important questions such as these, they usually want straightforward answers. That is why people typically become frustrated when they pose questions such as these to psychologists (especially social psychologists). That's because many psychologists give the same answer to every question: "It depends." "Spot usually bites men, but he almost never bites women." "Sodium salycarbanol is a great pain reliever, but it'll kill you if you take it with antihistamines." "Most people like to be flattered, but people who are very low in self-esteem prefer to be viewed negatively rather than positively."

Experimenters (especially experimental psychologists) are so intrigued with the "it depends" notion that they have developed a special statistical analysis to tell us when it depends. They have developed techniques, that is, for detecting interactions. Technically, an interaction means that a particular independent variable has different effects on a dependent variable at different levels of some other independent variable. It means, in short, that we cannot predict the effects of A on C without knowing something about variable B. The key is that the two independent variables work **together** to determine behavior. Information about one variable by itself tells you very little, but information about both variables tells you a lot.

To test for an interaction between two variables, you have to independently manipulate both of the variables in a **factorial** design. In its simplest form a factorial design is an experimental design that includes every possible combination of two independent variables. It is easiest to illustrate both an interaction and a factorial design with an example. Medical doctors often use the phrase "drug interaction precaution." Although they may not realize it, they are using the term "interaction" exactly the way a methodologist or statistician would. What they mean is that drug A by itself is good, and drug B by itself is good, but drug A and B together are bad. In the table below, you will find the results of a hypothetical study that illustrates this point. The study makes use of a 2 (drug A: placebo versus treatment) × 2 (drug B: placebo versus treatment) factorial design (remember, the "×" is pronounced "by"), and the dependent variable is the amount of pain that migraine sufferers reported 30 minutes after receiving their specific combination of treatments (higher numbers mean more self-reported pain on a 7-point scale).

	Level of Drug A	
Level of Drug B	Placebo	Treatment
Placebo	5.8 (ouch!)	1.2 (aaah . . .)
Treatment	1.5 (aaah . . .)	6.3 (ouch!)

Notice, first of all, that the design includes every possible treatment combination of the two drugs. According to their random assignment to one of four experimental conditions, (1) some patients got drug A only (along with a placebo that they thought was drug B), (2) some got drug B only (along with a placebo that they thought was drug A), (3) some got neither drug (they got two placebos), and (4) some got both drugs. (Notice, by the way, that all the patients *thought* that they got both drugs; the manipulation had to do with what the patients actually got.) If we had a large sample in this hypothetical study, a statistical test would definitely indicate that there was an interaction between the two treatments. When given alone, each drug was very effective, but when given together, the two drugs canceled each other out (in this case, however, they did not produce death).

Of course, interactions do not always take the form described above. For instance, some drugs probably work better in combination than they do alone. An interaction means that the effects of variable A are *different* at different levels of variable B. The effects of A could be strengthened, weakened, or totally reversed at a particular level of variable B, and you would still say that there was an interaction between the two variables. If all these different patterns qualify as interactions, does this mean that factorial designs always reveal some kind of interaction? Definitely not. Some drugs are absolutely unaffected by the presence of other drugs, just as some dogs are equally likely to bite people of either sex. According to self-enhancement theory, it should also be the case that everybody (whether high or low in self-esteem) prefers positive feedback rather than negative feedback. In statistical terms, straightforward ideas and theories such as the above would be reflected by *main effects* rather than interactions. The presence of a main effect in a factorial design (without an interaction) means that you don't need to know anything about B to describe the effect of A on your dependent variable. If the drug experiment just described had yielded only a main effect of drug A (no main effect of B and no interaction), the results might look something like those tabled below.

| | Level of Drug A | |
Level of Drug B	Placebo	Treatment
Placebo	6.2 (ouch!)	1.4 (aah . . .)
Treatment	6.3 (ouch!)	1.5 (aah . . .)

This would mean that the effects of drug A had nothing to do with drug B. People who got drug A felt better. Period.

To give you a better feel for how interactions work, we would like you to consider some data from a hypothetical study involving feedback and self-esteem. In this quasi-experiment, ten high-self-esteem participants and ten low-self-esteem participants were randomly assigned to receive either negative or positive feedback from a confederate (e.g., "You don't seem to be very good at this task; it seems like the kind of thing you're just not cut out for" versus "You did a really great job on this task; you really seem to have what it takes"). The dependent variable was participants' liking for the confederate measured on a 9-point scale (on which higher scores indicate greater liking). Thus the design was a 2 (self-esteem: low versus high) × 2 (feedback: negative versus positive) factorial. The raw data (not the means) are as follows:

	Self-Esteem	
Feedback	Low	High
Negative	7, 8, 7, 9, 9	3, 2, 3, 4, 3
Positive	2, 3, 4, 5, 1	6, 9, 9, 7, 9

After computing the mean liking score in each cell of this design and comparing these means, you should have a pretty clear idea of whether you observed (1) a main effect of self-esteem, (2) a main effect of feedback, and (3) an Esteem × Feedback interaction.

1. Which of these effects did you observe? Be sure to defend your answers by describing the findings with whatever mean comparisons are appropriate.

2. What do these results tell you about the nature of self-esteem? For example, is there evidence for self-enhancement theory (the theory that people always prefer positive feedback)?

3. In addition to checking for main effects and an interaction, are there any additional (follow-up) analyses you might want to conduct on these data?

4. Finally, if you had failed to include self-esteem as a factor in this study, and you had simply run a t-test to see if people preferred positive or negative feedback, what would you have found? Would these results have been misleading in any way?

FIGURE 8.10   Stimuli from the other between-subjects condition of Pelham et al. (1994)

Chapter 9

Being a Successful Researcher

If a man will begin with certainties, he shall end in doubts; but if he will be content to begin with doubts, he shall end in certainties.
  —Francis Bacon

In keeping with its title, this chapter is very pragmatic. We begin with a discussion of how to generate research ideas. After suggesting a few basic principles that can be used to generate good hypotheses for empirical investigation, we summarize some practical tips about how to translate good ideas and good methodology into good studies (e.g., writing clear instructions, running pilot studies). Finally, we discuss the most important sense in which anyone can be a successful researcher: being an ethical one.

How to Generate Research Ideas

During his distinguished scientific career, Charles Darwin published some extremely influential books on some very important topics. These include such famous books as *On the Origin of Species by Means of Natural Selection,* first published in 1859, and *The Expression of the Emotions in Man and Animals,* published in 1872. In 1881, the year before he died, Darwin capped off his career by publishing a book that, frankly speaking, didn't exactly bowl a lot of people over. The title of this book was *The Formation of Vegetable Mould, Through the Action of Worms: With Observations on Their Habits.* Although we have not read this book, our suspicion is that Darwin exercised the same care and attention to detail in this book that he had exercised in his earlier work. Although we do not want to make light of the scientific contribution of Darwin's final book,

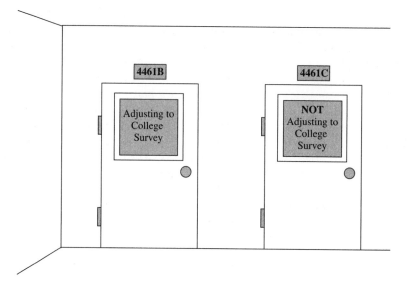

We typically fail to realize that the answers we get to research questions are determined largely by the questions we ask in the first place.

this book clearly did not have the same kind of scientific impact as his earlier work. Why not?

Of course, there are many answers to this rhetorical question (including regression toward the mean), but if we are willing to ignore a bit of folk wisdom and judge a book by its cover, the most obvious answer is that questions about the nature and formation of mold simply aren't as provocative as questions about the nature and origins of human beings. There was only so much that even Charles Darwin could do to pique people's curiosity about mold and worms. This point is related to one of the major themes of this chapter: the theme of how to generate research ideas. Being methodologically sophisticated is an important key to becoming a good scientist, but it is even more important to have an interesting topic to study in the first place.

McGuire (1973) made a similar point long ago. He wrote:

> It is my guess that at least 90% of the time in our current courses in methodology is devoted to presenting ways of testing hypotheses and that little time is spent on the prior and more important process of how one creates these hypotheses in the first place.

McGuire's estimate that 90% of all methodology courses are devoted to hypothesis testing (rather than hypothesis generation) is probably pretty generous. In fact, very few research methods texts make any mention of hypothesis generation at all. Fortunately, however, McGuire (1973, 1989) tackled this problem head-on by identifying some fruitful rules of thumb for generating specific research hypotheses (as well as general programs of research). In fact, McGuire has done such an excellent job of mapping out heuristics for hypothesis generation that we have found it difficult to add much to what he has already said. Thus, this section of this chapter is based almost exclusively on McGuire's previous analysis. Although we have organized McGuire's principles into two general categories and must take credit for a couple of omissions, most of what follows here is simply our attempt to recapitulate what McGuire (1973) had to say about this topic in the early 1970s.

Philosophers, logicians, and psychologists generally agree that there are two basic ways in which people reason (i.e., develop hypotheses) about the world. The first way of thinking, **induction,** refers to reasoning *from the specific to the general.* (Remember Hume's analysis of the inductive problem?) The second way, **deduction,** refers to reasoning *from the general to the specific.* To emphasize the fact that different kinds of reasoning are data driven or theory driven, respectively, cognitive psychologists use the terms "bottom-up" and "top-down" processing to make a very similar distinction. As it turns out, McGuire's rules for generating research hypotheses may be organized around these two basic themes.

Inductive Techniques

The inductive techniques McGuire identified are all based loosely on some kind of specific observation. As detailed in Chapter 5, one very useful source of observations that can be used either to test or to generate hypotheses is **case studies,** that is, carefully documented observations of a specific group or person. McGuire notes that great thinkers such as Freud and Piaget formulated many of their theories and hypotheses on the basis of formal or informal case studies. Freud carefully observed his patients' mental disorders, and Piaget carefully observed his children's cognitive development. As a social psychological example, Cialdini (1993) states that he became interested in the topic of social influence techniques early in his career precisely because he was always falling for the social influence techniques of real-world persuasion artists such as panhandlers and automobile salespersons. In fact, Cialdini reports that he discovered at least one social influence technique, the lowball technique, by simply observing automobile salespersons in action.[1] After discovering how effectively the technique worked on him, Cialdini used it, for example, to get people to do crazy things like sign up as participants in psychology experiments that begin at 7 A.M. (see Cialdini, Cacioppo, Bassett, & Miller, 1978). To some extent, we suspect that all researchers base at least some of their research hypotheses on life experiences that they themselves have found puzzling or intriguing. If you ask yourself what psychology courses you have found most intriguing, or what you would like to study if you could do research on any topic you wish, we suspect that you could identify some personal reasons why you are interested in certain issues and some important experiences you have had that might give you special insights into these issues.

A second inductive approach to generating research hypotheses is what McGuire refers to as trying to account for **paradoxical incidents** (i.e., puzzling or nonsensical observations). He cites a case in which the rumors that circulated after an earthquake were almost always disturbing rather than gratifying. This observation presumably played a role in Festinger's formulation of a revolutionary theory about how people try to make sense of their worlds by minimizing inconsistencies in their belief systems. Cognitive dissonance theory may have arisen, in part, from the rubble of an earthquake in Bihar, India. Asking why so many people gamble when doing so is clearly a long-term losing proposition, why some people remain in abusive romantic relationships, why John F. Kennedy's popularity increased after he publicly took the blame for the Bay of Pigs invasion, or why being the home team sometimes seems to be a disadvantage in the World Series are other examples of how unusual events can prompt researchers to develop theories and hypotheses to account for unusual or paradoxical events.

A third inductive technique is what McGuire calls **analyzing the practitioner's rule of thumb,** that is, analyzing things that experts in a particular area do to achieve certain outcomes. Cialdini's examples of techniques used by automobile salespersons could have also been placed in this category. Observing the favored strategies of athletes or chess champions, asking waiters and waitresses how they remember which dish to serve to each customer, or asking successful coaches how they motivate their players to perform well are additional examples of how we can identify psychological principles by observing people who have picked up special knowledge or skills in the real world. McGuire also reminds us that we can often learn as much from failure as we can from success. Asking novice chess players or losing coaches the same questions that we put to their more skillful counterparts may also yield useful information about what works, what doesn't work, and why.

Probably no thinker in the history of psychology was a bigger fan of the inductive method than B. F. Skinner. Although Skinner might quibble with McGuire's assumptions about the usefulness of people's self-reports about their behavior, he would probably approve of McGuire's inductive principles. In fact, he might insist on adding a fourth important inductive technique to McGuire's list. Skinner was fond of noting that **serendipity** (luck or good fortune) played an important role in most of his big discoveries. For example, one of Skinner's most important discoveries about learning was the *partial reinforcement effect*—the tendency for responses to be more resistant to extinction when they are reinforced inconsistently rather than uniformly. In addition to having enormous practical applications, this finding flew in the face of certain traditional conceptions of the nature of reinforcement. For example, it was inconsistent with the assumptions of early learning theorists that rewards "stamp in" responses. If they do, why does a little bit of sporadic stamping make a stronger impression than a lot of consistent stamping? Skinner reports that he discovered this principle completely by accident when he ran low on food pellets while running a simple conditioning experiment (see Schultz, 1981). Of course, to benefit from serendipity, a researcher has to be willing and able to put two and two together. But according to researchers like Skinner, the very nature of the experimental method (e.g., the isolation of variables) often sets the stage for fortuitous observations.

Deductive Techniques

McGuire also identifies a series of techniques for generating research hypotheses that we consider primarily deductive. One of the foremost of these is **reasoning by analogy.** McGuire himself has made excellent use of this technique in his own research on *attitude inoculation* and persuasion. Specifically, McGuire drew an analogy between biological resistance to disease and psychological resistance to persuasion. One of the basic forms of inoculation against disease consists of exposing people to a weakened version of a virus or antigen, a version that the person's immune system easily resists. In the process of dealing with the weakened version of the biological threat, the immune system becomes better able to defend itself against a full-blown version of the same virus or antigen. McGuire demonstrated a psychological analogue of this effect by giving people practice defending themselves against weakened versions of persuasive arguments. When people are later exposed to full-blown attacks on their belief systems, those who have been psychologically inoculated are much more resistant to persuasion (McGuire, 1961). This technique has proven to be an especially useful means of preventing adolescents from taking up smoking. Interestingly enough, biologists also explain the basic activity of the immune system by relying on analogies. Antigens (substances that attack the immune system) and antibodies (part of the body's defense system) are said to be analogous to locks and keys, respectively. Only antibodies with specific physical and chemical properties can attach themselves to specific antigens. And of course, if you noticed our use of words like "attack" and "defense" to describe the operation of the immune system, you can probably appreciate just how much we rely on analogy to understand—and test hypotheses about—all kinds of difficult concepts.

Carver and Scheier's (1990) reliance on the thermostat as a metaphor for understanding self-regulation, Dennett's (1991) reliance on the computer monitor as a metaphor for understanding consciousness, and Bowlby's (1977) reliance on observations of attachment behavior in primates as a metaphor for adult romantic attachment also represent profitable lines of research that have been enriched (and constrained) by the metaphors and analogies that have been used to derive many of the basic predictions and implications of these models.

A second deductive heuristic for generating research ideas is what McGuire calls **applying a functional or adaptive analysis** to a particular research question. Researchers who adopt this strategy ask themselves basic questions about what organisms have to do to successfully master their environments. For example, McGuire notes that Hull (1943) built up much of his theory of drive states and learning by asking questions about the minimum structural and procedural requirements of a behavioral system that can learn from experience (without abandoning old rules the first time they fail to work and without failing to detect changes in what does work). What, exactly, does any system have to do to be able to learn (and relearn) things about the environment? More recently, Gilbert (1991) developed a model of how mental systems represent incoming information whose truth or falsity is unknown. He appears to have done so, at least in part, by considering the functional or adaptive significance of different kinds of representational systems.

A third deductive technique for generating research ideas is the **hypo-thetico-deductive method.** This approach was popularized by Hull (1943), who believed that a good way to go about research is to begin with a set of a basic assumptions (or observations) and to derive one or more logical consequences from these basic principles. Swann's (1992) work on self-verification theory is an excellent example of this approach to research. A great deal of Swann's research builds on two intuitively appealing ideas. The first idea is that organisms prefer environments that are stable, predictable, and controllable. The second idea is that people's relationships and social interactions play an important role in regulating their beliefs about themselves. However, by building upon each of these intuitive assumptions, Swann has generated a wide range of counterintuitive hypotheses about how people take active steps to confirm their existing self-views (e.g., by seeking out information about one's weaknesses in areas in which one possesses negative self-views).

Tesser (1986) has adopted a very similar approach in his research on self-evaluation maintenance. He begins with three basic variables that presumably play a role in people's general self-evaluations: (1) people's feelings of closeness to a partner in a social interaction, (2) social comparison information about how people are performing relative to this partner, and (3) the personal relevance of a given self-concept dimension (or area of performance). By making a couple of simple assumptions about how these three variables work together to influence self-evaluation (e.g., if Eric is a math major, his best friend's perfect score on a calculus midterm will be more threatening to Eric's self-concept than it would be if Eric were an art major), Tesser has developed an entire research program to investigate the ways in which people orchestrate their performances, their relationships, and the relevance of their self-views in ways that maximize overall self-evaluation.

To provide a few more examples of the hypothetico-deductive approach, Petty and Cacioppo's (1986) elaboration likelihood model of persuasion; Chaiken, Liberman, and Eagly's (1989) heuristic-systematic model of social inference; Taylor and Brown's (1988) work on optimistic illusions; Wegner's (1994) research on ironic thought processes; and Higgins's (1989) research on self-discrepancies all build on this approach. These researchers all begin with a few guiding principles and derive specific hypotheses by combining the principles together in novel ways. The result of these derivations is typically a set of research hypotheses that researchers would have been unlikely to generate in the absence of a coherent theoretical framework.

A fourth deductive strategy for generating research hypotheses is trying to **account for conflicting results.** McGuire notes that primacy and recency in learning are principles that make opposite predictions about what people will learn best. Self-verification and self-enhancement theories also make opposite predictions about people's behavior under at least some conditions. When do people strive to maintain a positive overall self-evaluation (as predicted by Tesser's self-evaluation maintenance model), and when do people strive to confirm their negative self-views (as predicted by Swann's self-verification theory)? When do people engage in perceptual assimilation (overemphasizing the similarity between two stimuli), and when do they engage in perceptual contrast (exaggerating or enhancing the differences between two stimuli)? By struggling to fit contradictory theories together into a more comprehensive theory, researchers will often generate research ideas that would not have been generated by either theory alone.

A fifth deductive approach to hypothesis generation is **accounting for exceptions** to well-established psychological principles. Much of McGuire's approach to research is based on a contextualist theory of knowledge that assumes that almost everything is true under some circumstances. Social behavior is, in fact, a very complex can of worms, and thus many tried-and-true principles of behavior have their limitations and exceptions. From this perspective, the goal of psychological research should not be to determine what is true; instead it should be to determine when (or for whom) a given psychological principle is true (see also Schaller, Crandall, Stangor, & Neuberg, 1995). McGuire cites Hovland's classic research on the "sleeper effect" as an example of this principle. Persuasive messages are generally thought to have their greatest impact shortly after people have digested them, but in some cases the impact of a persuasive message actually increases over time (see Hovland & Weiss, 1951). Trying to figure out the situations under which a sleeper effect was most likely to occur apparently prompted Hovland to consider a number of important ideas about when and why delayed psychological responses to stimuli occur. Similarly, research on taste aversion and one-trial learning contradicted the accepted wisdom of the day that learning is a slow and gradual process. Usually it *is,* but researchers who dared to ask whether this rule is truly ironclad prompted a very interesting and influential area of research.

A more contemporary example of this approach can be found in Krull's (1993) research on the correspondence bias. In the wake of a large body of research suggesting that people tend to focus too much on dispositional explanations for people's behavior, Krull showed that when people's goals are to figure out *situations* rather than people, this otherwise robust inferential bias can be eliminated or even reversed (see also Fein, Hilton, & Miller, 1990; Krull & Erickson, 1995). Research on the "pratfall effect" (the tendency to like a talented person more when you discover that person has made a blunder; see Aronson, Willerman, & Floyd, 1966), research on the positive consequences of depressive symptoms (Pelham, 1991b), and research on overjustification (the tendency for rewards to diminish people's interest in an activity; see Lepper, Greene, & Nisbett, 1973) represent additional examples of the principle of finding exceptions to general rules.

The Five or Six R's of Being a Successful Researcher

By this point, you have a pretty large arsenal of research skills at your disposal. In addition, you should also have at last some sense of how to generate research hypotheses. However, there's knowing about feet and about water, and there's having gotten your feet wet. So far you have read a lot about the do's and don'ts of research methods, but you may need to know a little bit more if you want to survive the exciting but slippery ordeal of actually getting your feet wet as a researcher. In this section we provide some simple advice about maximizing one's chances of conducting successful research. Although this advice is couched primarily in terms of experimentation, almost all of it also applies to nonexperimental research.

Reading

One of the first things a person should do before beginning a new line of research is to check to be sure that the line of research is in fact new. At university and public libraries, personal computers with excellent literature-search programs are now almost as commonplace as card catalogs were in days gone by. And if you can't make it to the library, you can probably dial up some kind of search program (e.g., PsychINFO, PsychLit) from either your home psychology department or your home itself. These days there is little excuse for not knowing what's already out there. Once you locate what has already been done on your topic, you should read this work carefully to get a sense of (1) interesting and important things like whether researchers agree about what theories best account for the phenomenon in which you are interested, and (2) uninteresting but important things like how big the effect is that you're after (do people run studies with 20 participants or 200?) and what kind of equipment you will need (if the dependent measure in this line of research is response latencies, you will need access to a personal computer and some sophisticated software; if it's self-reports of anxiety, you may need only a ream of paper and a copy machine).

In addition to being gratifying in its own right, learning about what has already been done on your topic can save you the trouble of traveling down many of the same blind alleys that your predecessors traveled down years ahead of you. Starting an empirical research project without doing any background reading is a lot like starting a trek into the wilderness without carrying a map— except that there is usually no one to call the authorities when you get hopelessly lost. Of course, if you happen to be collaborating with an expert in your area of interest, this is a lot like taking a trip into the wilderness with an experienced guide. Even in cases such as this, however, it's nice to have a sense of where you're going—in case you get separated from your guide along the way.

Writing

In addition to reading, it's also important to work hard on your writing. At this point we are talking not about writing research papers but about more basic things like the written instructions you give your research participants or the questions that make up your dependent measures. Because many of the rules that apply to writing good items in a survey or a set of dependent measures also apply to writing good instructions, we will begin with a summary of ten rules for writing survey questions or dependent measures. We will then comment briefly about additional concerns that apply to writing experimental instructions.

Rule 1: Think carefully about the order of your questions.   The first piece of advice about writing survey questions has to do with doing things *gradually*. As a concrete example of the kind of thing we're talking about, consider the following story about a soldier who gets a brief letter from an old friend. The letter cuts right to the chase:

Dear Pete:
I'm sorry to say that your favorite cat Fluffy keeled over dead yesterday.

Sincerely,

Ben

The soldier is crushed not only by the sad news about his favorite cat but also by his friend's insensitivity in communicating the news so bluntly. He writes a letter back to his friend, trying to give some constructive advice about breaking bad news to people:

Dear Ben:
I can't believe your last letter. Here I am trying to cope with a war, and I get this letter from you just telling me that Fluffy keeled over dead. You just don't do that kind of thing to a guy, Ben. You need to break that kind of news to a guy more slowly. You might start off with a letter telling a guy that his cat is on the roof. In your *next* letter, you might add that the cat won't come down and that you're starting to get a little worried. In the *third or fourth* letter, you might let a guy know that you had to call the fire department to get the cat down, that they finally retrieved her, and that she is in intensive care at the veterinary hospital. In your *fifth* letter, you might let a guy know that his cat's chances of pulling through don't look very good. And in a *sixth* letter, you might finally tell the guy that they did everything they could for her but that Fluffy just didn't pull through. Finally, in the *seventh* letter, you tell the guy about the wonderful memorial service everyone had for Fluffy and remind him of what an inspiration she was to you. I hope you will be a little more careful in dealing with matters like this in the future.

Sincerely,

Pete

About a week later, Pete gets another very brief letter from Ben:

Dear Pete:
Your wife is on the roof.

Sincerely,

Ben

One of the premises that makes this story amusing is the idea that people deal better with tragedy if it is broken to them slowly. We're not really sure if this is true, but we do know that people deal better with sensitive survey questions if such questions are broken to them slowly. In light of this fact, one of the first things to consider when you are creating a survey or a set of dependent measures is *what* to ask people *when*. If you have to ask people sensitive questions, it's usually best to warm people up with easy or innocuous questions first and to ask the sensitive questions once people are feeling pretty comfortable. If questions about masturbation or sexual positions appear on the first page of a survey, the researcher has probably cut to the chase too quickly. A little methodological foreplay can go a long way toward enhancing the validity of sensitive survey research.

Rule 2: Use informal language.
A second, more technical, piece of advice about writing questions has to do with the kind of language you should use. Unless your audience is extremely sophisticated, it's usually best to use proper and grammatical but *relatively informal* language. It's equally important to avoid using any kind of psychological jargon or catchphrases. Even after you get people warmed up, don't ask people if they have ever suffered from auditory hallucinations. Instead, ask them if they have ever heard any voices or sounds that may not have been real. Instead of asking people if they are bulimic or anorexic, ask people simple and specific questions about eating, body image, and concerns about weight. Instead of asking people about their yearnings and aspirations in life, ask people about their wishes and dreams. If your 14-year-old cousin has difficulty understanding your survey questions, you should simplify them. And if you are studying 14-year-olds or people who are not highly educated, you should simplify them even further. A good rule of thumb is that your survey questions should make comfortable reading for people several grade levels lower than your intended audience.

Rule 3: Be clear and concise.
A third rule of writing is to be clear and concise. If your survey, or your specific question, is too long, participants may lose interest or simply get lost. Imagine that you wanted to measure global self-esteem without reference to the specific content of people's self-views. Consider the following two items:

1. My overall feelings and thoughts about myself are predominantly favorable most of the time, leading me to feel pretty satisfied about who I am.
2. On the whole, I am satisfied with myself.

The second item is taken from Rosenberg's (1965b) self-esteem scale. The first item addresses the same issue, but it is three times as long as the second. The law of parsimony applies to questions as well as to theories.

Rule 4: Avoid double-barreled questions.
This rule is closely related to rule 3. In an effort to be thorough or efficient, researchers sometimes try to ask people about two things at once. For example, to measure self-esteem, a researcher might be tempted to ask people to respond to the following item:

I am lovable and capable. (Circle one number.)

1	2	3	4
strongly disagree	disagree	agree	strongly agree

Similarly, to assess graduate students' feelings of being overworked, we might ask them the following true/false question:

I am in favor of cutting back to a six-day workweek and letting people take regular lunch and restroom breaks.

(Circle one option.)   true   false

If Mauricio feels lovable but not capable, or capable but not lovable, how is he supposed to respond to the first question? Similarly, if Tracy is opposed to cutting back to a six-day workweek, undecided about regular lunch breaks, and in favor of regular restroom breaks, how is she supposed to respond? The simple solution to double- (or triple-) barreled questions is to break them up into two (or three) separate questions. Changing the first item to "I am lovable" and adding the separate item "I am capable" would be a big improvement.

Rule 5: Ask sensitive questions sensitively.   If you need to ask people about sensitive topics such as stereotypes, sexual behavior, or illicit drug use, you should remember that people will not always be dying to tell you about all their deepest secrets. Unless you are willing and able to hook people up to a bogus pipeline, you will want to word your questions very carefully to diminish people's concerns about socially desirable responding. For example, if you wanted to know whether people have ever used marijuana, and you simply asked people "Have you ever used marijuana?" many people would be reluctant to admit having done so. However, if you listed a wide range of legal and illegal drugs (e.g., caffeine, alcohol, heroin, crack cocaine, marijuana), and you asked people to place a check mark next to all the drugs they had ever used, most people would probably feel less inhibited about checking off a drug like marijuana (especially if the list included more serious drugs such as heroin and crack cocaine). When you are asking people about sensitive topics, it is even more important than usual to be clear about what you mean, and to phrase your questions in ways that are not pejorative or judgmental. Giving people a clear idea of what you mean by "sexual partner" and then asking people how many sexual partners they have had would probably yield more useful and accurate information than asking people if they are "sexually promiscuous."

Rule 6: State things in the affirmative.   Research in cognitive psychology has shown that people process affirmations ("Brett is writing this chapter in the nude") more quickly and efficiently than negations ("Brett is writing this chapter while not wearing any clothing"). In fact, research has shown that when people process negative statements, they will sometimes interpret them in ways in which the statements may not have been intended. Reading the newspaper headline "Chris Federico Not Linked to Mafia" will be unlikely to give you the impression that Chris Federico is an especially upstanding citizen (Wegner, Wenzlaff, Kerker, & Beattie, 1981; see also Gilbert, 1991). When it comes to writing questions, the only thing worse than using negatively worded questions is using *double negatives*. Ignoring possible concerns about social desirability, an item such as "It's OK to run a stop sign every now and then" is better than "No one should be ticketed for not stopping at stop signs." Similarly, "Actually, Brett is writing this chapter while fully clothed" is better than "It's actually not the case that Brett is not fully clothed while writing this chapter."

Rule 7: Avoid questions that no one or everyone will endorse.   When you are conducting a study on a new topic, it is especially important to try to get a feel for what kinds of questions people will and will not endorse. If you are concerned that few people in your sample will say it's OK to run stop signs now and then, you might replace this item with something more like "I think we have too many traffic laws." If you are studying budding friendships, an item such as "My love for my friend is immeasurable" might not be very useful because very few people in your sample might endorse it (and if anyone does, you might be studying romantic relationships instead of friendships). Conversely, if you are studying close friendships, items such as "I like my friend" or "I feel close to my friend" might have the opposite problem. A more methodological way of putting this is that it is important to avoid both floor effects and ceiling effects when you are writing questions. **Floor effects** occur when almost everyone in a sample responds at the same *low* level on a question or dependent measure (e.g., when everyone circles a 1 on a 7-point Likert scale). **Ceiling effects** are just the opposite, but they are equally problematic. They occur when almost everyone in a sample responds at the same *high* level on a question or dependent measure. Floor and ceiling effects are both examples of the problem of **restriction of range.**

When there is little or no variation on a measure—that is, when there is restriction of range—it is difficult to impossible to find anything that will predict people's scores on the measure. Restriction of range on some measures is almost impossible to avoid (e.g., if you correlate people's GRE scores and their grade-point average in graduate school, you will usually see very little correlation—not because GRE scores don't predict performance but because only students with high GRE scores make it into graduate school in the first place). When you are writing survey questions, the main thing you can do to avoid restriction of range is to know your sample and to adjust your questions—and your Likert scales—accordingly. As an example, suppose you are studying dating relationships. Being the careful type, you conduct a pilot survey on 20 participants and ask them to respond to the following:

I am in love with my partner. (Circle one number.)

1	2	3	4	5
not at all true	slightly true	somewhat true	mostly true	very true

If your pilot study reveals that virtually everyone circles a 5 on this scale, there are several things you can do. First of all, you might check to see how long the people in your pilot sample have been dating. If they are all in established relationships, you might consider sampling people who haven't been dating so long. On the other hand, if it's important to you to study established relationships, you might try changing "in love" to "deeply in love." You might also consider expanding your 5-point Likert scale to a 9-point scale, or simply adding a sixth point ("extremely true") to your existing scale. Finally, in addition to the more-is-better rule of reliability, a good practical reason to measure any construct with more than one item is that multiple-item scales are less likely than single-item measures to yield a restriction of range.

The problem of restriction of range applies to all kinds of measures, not just survey questions or written dependent measures. If you are interested in upper-body strength, choose your weights carefully. If you are interested in how close someone sits to an experimental confederate, experiment with situations that produce reasonable amounts of variation in seating distance. If you are refining new measurements, a small pilot study that helps you adjust and refine your measures is often the difference between a complete success and a complete disappointment. In research, celebration is usually preceded by calibration.

Rule 8: Avoid vague numerical referents.   If you are asking people how frequently they have engaged in a specific behavior (e.g., How many times in the past week have you skipped a meal?), it is usually better to provide people with clear numerical answer options ("never," "once or twice," "three or four times," etc.) rather than phrases like "a couple of times" or "a few times." The reason for this is that there is a surprising amount of disagreement about exactly what is meant by phrases like "a couple" or "a few." To many people, a couple of things means exactly *two* of those things and a few means three or four. However, to many other people, three or four things can qualify as both a couple and a few. In fact, if we are talking about beers or packets of M&Ms, we have a close mutual friend for whom seven or eight can easily qualify as a couple.

Rule 9: Avoid leading questions and anchoring or framing effects. Although these closely related problems are more serious when it comes to survey research, they can mean trouble for experimenters as well. If you ask people if they are in favor of welfare, they will often give you a different answer than they would have if you had asked them if they are in favor of government assistance to the poor. And as you may recall from the section on scaling in Chapter 3, things as subtle as the endpoints that you choose to include in your Likert scales or whether you frame a question in terms of gains or losses can play a big role in the kinds of answers people give to your questions. Although these problems should not be taken lightly, we should note that they threaten the internal validity of experimental research only when they lead to a restriction of range. If you are trying to sample public opinion, and 60% of the people in your random sample engage in a behavior, but the wording of your survey question shifts this value to 40%, this is a serious problem. However, if you used the same biased wording in an experiment, this bias would be constant across your different experimental conditions. To the degree that you care only about relative differences between the experimental groups, biases such as this aren't all that serious unless they start to create floor or ceiling effects.

Rule 10: Make sure your questions are relevant to everyone in your study.   A final piece of advice about writing survey questions and creating dependent measures is to make sure that your questions make sense to everyone in your sample. For example, if you are studying close relationships, you should not take it for granted that everyone in your sample is heterosexual. If you are studying family dynamics, you should not take it for granted that everyone in your study has a meaningful relationship with both parents. Similarly, you should work hard to write questions that are gender-neutral and culturally unbiased. This is not simply a matter of political correctness; it is also about professional courtesy and construct validity. If the questions in your survey are written from a perspective that ignores the thoughts and feelings of a significant portion of your sample, this portion of your sample is unlikely to give you useful data.[2]

As we said earlier, almost all the rules and tips that apply to writing survey items or dependent measures also apply to writing experimental instructions and survey cover sheets. However, there are three important things that any good set of instructions should do that pertain to content rather than writing style. The first thing you should do in your instructions is to give your participants some idea (even if it is necessarily an incorrect one) of exactly why they are taking part in your study and exactly what they will be doing. People will do some pretty ridiculous things just because an experimenter has asked them to, but their behavior may not be meaningful if they are not in the mind-set you care about. The most important thing a set of instructions does is to orient people toward your task, that is, to get them in a certain frame of mind. This includes not only letting people know what the study is about but also letting them know exactly what sequence of activities and events will occur in the experiment.

If your research topic is at all sensitive, another extremely important thing that your instructions should do is to guarantee participants that their responses in the study are private and anonymous. This not only solves some important ethical dilemmas but also makes people more likely to report their true thoughts and feelings during the experiment. To emphasize anonymity in self-concept research, some researchers give research participants cover sheets to use while they respond to questionnaires. Researchers may also give people blank envelopes—instructing them to seal their responses in the envelope when they are done. Although we have never made a formal study of this, it is also our impression that giving people optically scanned answer sheets—and telling them that their answers will be scored by computer—increases the accuracy of people's self-reports.

A third useful tip about writing instructions is to include some redundancy in your instructions. By repeating your important points in slightly different ways, and including labeled summary statements that cover the bare bones of your instructions, you will increase the likelihood that even participants who only skim your instructions will know what is going on (or what is supposed to be going on) in your experiment. Finally, in most experiments, we not only give participants a complete set of written instructions but also supplement these written instructions with a verbal summary of what the experiment is about. By giving participants both written and spoken instructions, you make it difficult for even the most absentminded or unmotivated participants to remain in the dark about what they should be doing.

Running and Revising

In addition to taking great care about preparing your written materials, you may want to conduct a brief **pilot study** (a preliminary study or "practice experiment") before you conduct a full-blown version of your experiment. As suggested in the last section, one useful function of pilot studies is that they allow you to refine newly created questions. However, pilot studies can also help you in many other ways. They can allow you to identify potential holes in your cover story, to find out that people are falling asleep in the middle of your response-latency task, or to learn that your primary manipulation is or is not having the psychological consequences you intended. In short, pilot studies can help you identify almost anything that is wrong (or right) with your experiment. If Francis Bacon were around today, we suspect that he would be very much in favor of pilot studies. To pilot-test is to be content to begin with uncertainties.

One way to maximize the chances that you benefit from a pilot study is to include a **manipulation check** in your pilot study. A manipulation check is literally a check on your manipulation. It's a measure taken to see if participants in different experimental conditions were, in fact, experiencing different levels of the variable you were hoping to manipulate. For example, if you were conducting an experiment to see if anxiety facilitates certain kinds of problem solving, you might wait until your participants had completed your problem-solving task and then ask them how anxious they felt while they were performing the task. If your manipulation of anxiety was successful, you should find that, relative to the participants in the low-anxiety condition, those in the high-anxiety condition report having felt much more anxious. If they don't, you will need to look for either a more effective manipulation of anxiety or a more effective manipulation check.

Of course, even if you do not run any pilot studies, it is always a good idea to include a manipulation check in your actual experiment. Even a failed study is more informative when it includes a manipulation check. For example, if your manipulation check for anxiety suggested that your manipulation was extremely effective, but you observed no effects of your anxiety manipulation on problem solving, it would be safer than usual to conclude that anxiety has no effect on this particular form of problem solving. Despite their enormous advantages, one tricky aspect of manipulation checks is that they aren't always easy to perform. One of the biggest hurdles to conducting manipulation checks is the fact that participants may be either unwilling or unable to report on some of their experiences during an experiment (see Nisbett & Wilson, 1977). When this is the case, you might need to look for indirect ways of documenting that your manipulation created the psychological state that you intended (e.g., having blind judges decide how anxious participants appear to be, measuring anxiety by measuring people's galvanic skin response).

Alternately, if giving participants a manipulation check would get in the way of your experimental task itself, you might want to run a pilot study whose sole purpose is to document the effectiveness of your manipulation. For instance, if you want to document that participants who are rehearsing an 8-digit number are more cognitively taxed than those who are not, you might conduct a pilot study in which you enact this manipulation while people attempt to perform a cognitively demanding signal-detection task. If the cognitively taxed participants have longer reaction times or make more errors than the participants in the control group, you will have independent evidence of the effectiveness of your manipulation of cognitive load. If they do not, it is probably time to go back to the drawing board and develop a new and improved manipulation.

Regardless of whether you include any manipulation checks in any pilot studies you run, such preliminary studies can go a long way toward increasing the likelihood that your revised experiment will reveal something informative. Pilot studies are never as fun to conduct as the real thing. After all, they usually end up telling you more about what you were doing wrong than about what you were doing right. However, more than any other aspect of research preparation, pilot research can turn ordinary researchers into apparent geniuses. If you want to look like an experimental genius, remember the advice of Thomas Edison. Edison argued that "genius is 1% inspiration and 99% perspiration."

Rehearsing and Playing the Part

Once you have finished your literature review and your three informal pilot studies conducted on friends, family members, and anyone else you could cajole into helping you out, there is usually one more thing you will need to do before you start running participants in your actual experiment. The main thing is to rehearse all your instructions and directions until you can run participants through your study like a true expert. Practicing the entire experiment a few times on a friend, a graduate student collaborator, or your academic advisor will help you identify and correct any weaknesses in your delivery. Because one of us often forgets to tell his students—especially his best students—that experimentation is a complex skill that must be practiced and mastered, he recently devised a list of do's and don'ts that he shares with any beginning student who comes to work in his lab. Here, then, is our adaptation of these six commandments of being a good experimenter:

Commandment 1: Be suave.   Dress and behave professionally. The only cues that your participants have about your expertise are the ones that you give them during the course of your 5- to 50-minute interaction. Your participants do not know that you have a master's degree in engineering or that you were on the dean's list for 23 consecutive quarters, and so you must let them know that you are a professional by speaking and, most of all, *dressing,* professionally. As a graduate student, one of us dressed very informally. He wore sleeveless T-shirts and sweatpants to class, to colloquia, and to company picnics. But after experimenting with his dress as an experimenter, he quickly realized that, unlike his colleagues, his *participants* took him seriously only when he *looked serious* on the outside. Thus, after a few of his participants treated him like a kid, he began to dress like a grown-up. He quickly found that dressing more professionally made most participants take him much more seriously. When you dress the part, your data won't magically begin to confirm all your predictions, but your participants will definitely be more likely to take you seriously.[3]

Commandment 2: Be nice.   It is important to be professional, but it's also important to be polite and friendly. Even if a participant is rude, you should try to maintain a pleasant demeanor throughout the experiment (while keeping careful notes about the participant's rudeness). Does this mean you should let rude participants bully you into doing the experiment their way? Absolutely not. Be polite, but keep the experiment running the way it was designed to be run. If an obstinate participant absolutely refuses to comply, then you may either (1) continue the experiment and make a note of the fact that the participant failed to follow instructions or (2) stop the experiment and give the participant full credit for taking part in the study. Even if people aren't very likable, they have the right to refuse to participate in a study.

Commandment 3: Be educated.   Know your experiment well. It's hard to run a good experiment if you don't know what you are predicting or why you are predicting it. If you are going to pick up on the subtle things that may be going wrong in a study, you must know how things should look if the experiment is going right. If you don't know your experiment, do some homework or talk with someone who knows more about it (e.g., your advisor) to get a better understanding of what should be happening in the study.

Commandment 4: Be honest.   One of the dangers of knowing your study is that knowing exactly how your participant should be responding opens the door to the Pandora's box of experimenter bias. There is nothing worse than an experiment that works for the wrong reasons, and if you know your hypothesis well, it is possible that you may let your participant know in subtle ways how you would like him or her to respond. For example, if you give verbal instructions or clues about how the experiment works, it is always possible that you may give better instructions or clues to the experimental group than to the control group. You do not always have to be blind to the condition of your participants to avoid experimenter bias, but you should be aware of the subtle ways in which you can bias a participant's responses—so that you can work hard to treat all participants exactly the same way (except, of course, for the delivery of your manipulation). The easiest way to do this is to have a script that you stick to very closely during the experiment. After you have run 20 or 30 lab experiments, you may find that you no longer need a script to be suave, nice, smart, and honest, but during your first few years of experimentation, a script is a good idea.

Commandment 5: Be a good liar.   If you are running a deception study, remember that you can never blow your cover until the experiment is over. Use mechanical props to help aid you in your deception if necessary (in some studies, one of us has played tape-recorded conversations between himself and a fictitious participant in the next room to be sure that the real participant believed the fictitious person was actually present). In addition, if a participant expresses suspicion about your cover story, try to think on your feet and answer his or her concern without stepping out of the imaginary world that you have tried to create. For example, "Well, it is a little strange that your partner has exactly the same birthday as you, but it's probably not as unusual as it seems because we usually try to pair people up who are as close as possible in age. In this case, it looks like your ages happen to be identical." (You then proceed to the adjacent room and casually, in a very soft voice, ask the stack of journal articles there if she noticed that she has the same birthday as her partner in the next room. "Yeah, I wondered if you noticed. The other participant noticed it, too.")

Commandment 6: Be attentive.   If you really care about your experiment, you will watch your participants the way you watch a person you care about deeply. If your participant appears apathetic or confused, you will try to find out why, and you will make a written record of this. If your participant shows up drunk and smothered in mayonnaise—or stone sober and wearing a chicken suit—you may want to make a polite excuse to end the experiment early. This, too, is the kind of unusual thing you should carefully document. In short, you should pay close attention to your participant, and you should try to put yourself in his or her shoes so that if something is going seriously wrong with your experiment, you can fix it before your next participant arrives.

Replicating

Once you have gone to all the trouble to find just the right manipulation, just the right dependent measure, and just the right delivery in your experiment, there will always be a good chance that you have done just the wrong thing. Specifically, it is always possible that you have happened upon the one particular set of circumstances under which your hypothesis is true. In keeping with his contextual approach to research, McGuire (1973) expressed a very similar sentiment about experimental research in social psychology. After noting that almost all research hypotheses are both correct and incorrect (under different conditions), McGuire wrote:

> If the experiment does not come out "right," then the researcher does not say that the hypothesis is wrong but rather that something was wrong with the experiment, and he corrects and revises it, perhaps by using more appropriate subjects, by strengthening the independent variable manipulation, by blocking off extraneous response possibilities, or by setting up a more appropriate context, etc. Sometimes he may have such continuous bad luck that he finally gives up the demonstration because the phenomenon proves to be so elusive as to be beyond his ability to demonstrate. The more persistent of us typically manage at last to get control of the experimental situation so that we can reliably demonstrate the hypothesized relationship. But note that what the experiment tests is not whether the hypothesis is true but rather whether the experimenter is a sufficiently ingenious stage manager to produce in the laboratory conditions which demonstrate that an obviously true hypothesis is correct. In our graduate programs in social psychology, we try to train people who are good enough stage managers so that they can create in the laboratory simulations of realities in which the obvious correctness of our hypothesis can be demonstrated.

McGuire's point was not that research is a bankrupt enterprise or that experiments do not reveal any truths. Instead, he was mainly making the point that the simplistic and pristine image that we get of research in journal articles is often a far cry from what actually happens in the lab. In fairness to both McGuire and experimental social psychology, we think that to some extent researchers have finally begun to take his advice about research. Researchers still work hard to confirm their hypotheses, and they are still more likely to interpret failed experiments as failures of technique rather than failures of their hypotheses. However, social psychology (like many other areas of psychology) has become much more of a contextual enterprise over the past quarter century. Instead of simply predicting that two variables are related, contemporary psychologists are much more likely to try to identify the conditions under which an effect *does* and *does not* turn out to be true. In statistical terms, many of the hypotheses that psychologists test these days are hypotheses about *interactions*.

Another trend that appears to have taken place over the past couple of decades is that major journals in the more experimentally focused areas of psychology rarely publish empirical research papers unless these papers contain two or more experiments that demonstrate consistent support for a hypothesis. In other words, journal editors and reviewers who make recommendations about whether papers should be published in major journals have become more and more insistent on seeing novel research findings replicated (i.e., repeated) before they approve a paper for publication. A **replication** is sort of the opposite of a pilot study. It's a follow-up experiment that tests the idea behind an initial experiment again, usually in a different way. To the degree that a research finding replicates when different researchers use slightly different operational definitions of the constructs in question, it should increase our confidence in the validity of the original findings. If the findings were merely an artifact of the particular manipulations and measures that were chosen by the original researcher, they will be unlikely to replicate when the researcher (or someone else) tests the hypothesis in a novel way. What all this boils down to is that you should try to replicate your own research findings before you leave it up to someone else to do so. To the degree that you can specify the precise conditions under which your findings are and are not likely to be obtained, you will increase other people's confidence in the validity of your findings. In addition, you will protect yourself from at least a few attacks by people who may choose to test your hypothesis under conditions that are less ideal than those that you may have chosen yourself.

As an example of the value of replication, consider a pair of studies on the allure of secret relationships. If you have ever had the feeling that there is something exciting, almost erotic, about keeping a secret, you are not alone. Research on the paradoxical effects of thought suppression suggests that trying to suppress secret or forbidden thoughts can actually increase our obsession with these thoughts. The harder we try not to think about a scrumptious but forbidden bowl of chocolate ice cream, the more preoccupied we may become with it. Wegner, Lane, and Dimitri (1994) felt that this might be true of secret passions for other people as well as secret passions for things like ice cream. To test this idea, they first conducted a couple of survey studies in which they asked people about the degree to which various past romantic relationships had been secret. In addition, they asked people about the degree to which they were still obsessively preoccupied with these past relationships. The more their participants reported that a past relationship had been a secret one, the more these participants reported that they were still preoccupied with the relationship. Of course, nonexperimental findings such as this are consistent with the idea that secrecy intensifies preoccupation, but they are also consistent with the idea that preoccupation somehow intensifies people's memories of the secrecy of a past relationship—or that some third variable (e.g., whether one's parents disapproved of the relationship) is associated with both secrecy and preoccupation.

Wegner et al. were aware of such criticisms, and thus they replicated their correlational findings in a laboratory experiment. Specifically, they brought college students to their laboratory in groups of four people (two women and two men), and they paired each participant with an opposite-sex teammate in

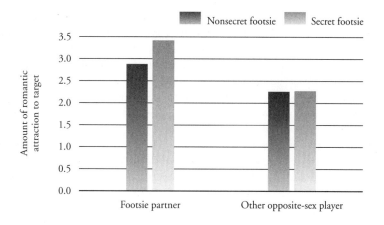

FIGURE 9.1 Reported attraction to a partner and to an opponent after playing secret or nonsecret footsie with partner (from Wegner, Lane, & Dimitri, 1994)

a card game. Before the game began, the members of one of the two mixed-sex teams were always instructed to play the game using a form of "natural nonverbal communication." More specifically, the members of one couple were always told to maintain foot-to-foot contact during the game in an effort to transmit useful information to each other. The members of the other couple were given no such instructions. (In fact, they were seated far enough apart—at a rectangular table—that they couldn't have maintained any foot-to-foot contact even if they had spontaneously decided to.)

Importantly, the couples who were randomly assigned to the footsie condition were further divided into (1) those who were instructed to keep their footplay a secret from the other team and (2) those who were told that it was fine if the other team knew what they were doing. After the couples had been allowed to play the game for about 10 minutes, the male and female participants were separated, and all the participants were asked to report, among other things, their level of romantic attraction (1) to their opposite-sex partner and (2) to their opposite-sex opponent. Figure 9.1 contains a summary of some of the major findings of the experiment. As you can see, those who secretly played footsie with their partner reported being more attracted to their partner than did those who openly played footsie with their partner. Moreover, this increase in attraction was directed specifically toward their footsie partner. Participants' reported level of attraction to their opposite-sex opponents was not influenced by the secrecy manipulation. Together with the findings from their two nonexperimental studies, this experimental replication suggests that Wegner et al. have probably latched onto an important truth underlying secret versus open romantic relationships.

Being an Ethical Experimenter

One particularly tricky thing about doing experimental research in psychology (especially social psychology) is the fact that it is often necessary to distract or deceive people to get them to behave naturally. In the specific case of social psychology, another tricky thing is the fact that social psychologists are interested in some of the most sensitive topics anyone could ever wish to study. To pick only a select few, delicate topics such as aggression, confession, depression, drug possession, and romantic obsession are all of great interest to social psychologists. In fact, some of the most famous and important studies in the history of social psychology have also proven to be some of the most ethically controversial. In the remainder of this chapter, we provide a couple of historical examples of studies that have raised important ethical questions among social psychologists, psychologists, and researchers in general. We then summarize how the American Psychological Association (APA) has responded to controversial or unethical studies such as these by summarizing the current ethical guidelines of the APA regarding research with human participants.

During the early days of research with human participants, there were no real guidelines concerning either the rights of human participants or the responsibilities of researchers to their participants. Most researchers simply put their faith in the good judgment of their fellow researchers and assumed that no one would ever allow anything bad to happen to his or her participants.

This faith in the good judgment (and good will) of all researchers turned out to be somewhat misguided. For example, in an infamous medical study begun in 1932, the researchers wanted to learn about the effects of untreated syphilis (untreated syphilis eventually leads to insanity and death). In the early days of the study, there was no known cure for syphilis, and thus the study didn't violate any ethical rules. However, in 1943, researchers discovered that penicillin cures syphilis. Instead of seeking out their patients and treating them, the researchers specifically ordered doctors *not* to treat their patients. When some of the men were drafted during World War II, the researchers even broke state and federal laws to prevent the men from receiving the treatment that otherwise would have been given to them after their medical examination for the draft. It is probably no coincidence that the patients in the study were about 600 rural Black men living in Alabama (whereas the researchers—though not all of those involved in the project—were White).

Although this study was conducted by medical researchers rather than psychologists, this study and others like it prompted enough attention to ethics in research with human participants that the APA eventually came up with a set of ethical standards for psychological research with human participants. The first set of standards was published in 1958, but psychologists didn't pay much attention to these standards until much later—in the wake of controversial studies that *were* conducted by psychologists. One of the controversial studies that rekindled people's interest in ethical issues was Milgram's famous study of obedience to authority. As you may recall, Milgram (1963) demonstrated that about 65% of a sample of normal, healthy men were willing to deliver what they thought were extremely painful and potentially life-threatening shocks to a learner.

Critics of Milgram's famous study (e.g., Baumrind, 1964) argued that his study was probably unethical. They pointed out, for example, that his research procedure was inherently coercive. Milgram responded that he was studying the important social problem of coercion. Critics noted that Milgram lied to his participants. He retorted that he conducted extensive debriefing sessions with his participants. During these sessions, his participants were given a great deal of information about the true purpose of the study, were told why it was necessary to use deception, and were told that the study was yielding information that could have widespread positive social consequences. Critics noted that the experiences Milgram put his participants through could cause them serious psychological harm. Milgram replied that most of his participants reported feeling that they had learned something extremely important about themselves by taking part in the study.

Although debates over the ethics of the Milgram study continue to this day, most contemporary researchers would probably consider the study unethical. Regardless of one's opinion on the ethicality of these studies, almost all researchers agree that one positive consequence of these studies is that they prompted serious action on the part of the APA. When the APA came out with a revision of its ethical principles in 1972, many more people took note of these principles. These principles were elaborated and revised again in December of 1992, and in the past couple of decades virtually all universities whose students and professors conduct research with human participants have created committees whose job it is to review this research. The point of these reviews is to make certain that the research is conducted in ways that are consistent with the principles of professional governing bodies such as the APA, the ASA (the American Sociological Association), and the AMA (the American Medical Association). The ethical guidelines of the APA are pretty extensive. They deal with a wide range of issues ranging from how practitioners should present themselves to the public to how collaborators should determine authorship on research papers. However, for the current purposes, the most important principles have to do with how we should conduct research with human participants. The five most important of the APA guidelines can be summarized as follows.

Rule 1: Informed Consent. Before participants agree to take part in research, they must be informed about any potential risks of the research (e.g., they must be told about any aspect of the research experience that may be embarrassing or harmful). This does not mean that researchers have to compromise the integrity of their investigations by telling their participants their hypotheses in advance. Instead, it means that if a study poses any foreseeable risk of anxiety, discomfort, or embarrassment, participants should be informed of this fact prior to agreeing to take part in the study, so that they can make an enlightened decision about whether to participate.

Rule 2: Freedom from Coercion. No undue pressure should be placed on participants to take part in a study. This means that researchers cannot place people under any kind of psychological pressure to take part in or remain involved in a study. Researchers are not only forbidden to order people, threaten people, or make them feel guilty in an effort to secure participation, but they are also forbidden to offer people exorbitant payments or rewards for taking risks that they might not otherwise take.

Rule 3: Protection from Physical and Psychological Harm. Researchers may not knowingly place participants in any kind of meaningfully risky or dangerous situation. All reasonable precautions and safeguards that minimize risks of physical or psychological harm should be followed during all phases of a study. In the case of a survey study, keeping people's responses anonymous (and telling people so) is a useful way to protect people while also increasing the likelihood that participants will respond honestly. In the case of a sensitive lab experiment in which people are asked to think about suicide, it might be necessary to screen potential participants for depression and to eliminate depressed people from the study.

Rule 4: The Risk-Benefit Rule. It's impossible to completely eliminate risk from research. If you ask people to fill out a seemingly harmless survey, there is always some risk that a participant could accidentally stab him- or herself with a pencil or get a nasty paper cut that leads to a serious infection. More realistically, if you have people pedal an exercise bike for five minutes before asking them to make some social judgments or if you mislead people slightly about the true purpose of your study, there is always a small chance that some participants will become physically injured or psychologically upset during the study. For this reason, the APA specifies that the kinds of risks to which people can be exposed during research should not be any greater than the risks to which they are routinely exposed during their day-to-day lives. Moreover, even if a study exposes participants to only very small risks, researchers must consider the benefits of the research to society against these potential risks. The benefits must always outweigh the risks.

Rule 5: Debriefing. If any deception takes place during a study, the researcher must inform the participant of the deception and the reason for it as soon as possible. In addition, whenever possible, researchers should share information about their research hypotheses with their participants. One of the benefits of taking part in any investigation should be learning something useful about the topic of the investigation. Finally, whenever possible, participants should leave the study in a psychological state that is at least as positive as the state in which they showed up for the study. For example, if some participants are put in a negative mood in a study of mood and memory, then something should probably be done to put them in a positive mood before they leave the experiment.

Following principles such as these requires some common sense and forethought, and it can also be expensive. For example, in the experiment on secret footsie conducted by Wegner et al. (1994), the researchers had experimentally generated higher than usual levels of attraction between about half of their opposite-sex dyads. To extricate themselves from the ethically questionable role of matchmaker, the researchers seated the men and women in separate rooms while the participants filled out their dependent measures. After separately debriefing the men and the women, Wegner et al. dismissed the women five minutes earlier than they dismissed the men (and politely asked them to leave the area). Similarly, after finishing their experiments on alcohol consumption and judgment, MacDonald et al. (1995) always checked people's blood alcohol levels before dismissing them. If participants showed any signs of intoxication after a reasonable waiting period, the experimenters got them a taxi and paid for their ride home. Sometimes researchers need to take preemptive rather than corrective action. To minimize the possibility that depressed participants would become even more depressed when trying to tell whether suicide notes were real or bogus, Bui (1997) prescreened all her participants and invited people to take part in her study only if they scored in the nondepressed range on a standard screening instrument for depression.

Although this review of the ethical principles of the APA should give you a good feel for the major issues that researchers need to consider when planning and conducting ethical research on human participants, you might wish to familiarize yourself with some of the details of these principles. The most recent version of the ethical principles of the APA can be found in the December 1992 issue of *American Psychologist*.

Over the past 20 or 30 years, the most important practical consequence of the development of the APA's ethical guidelines has been the formation of committees for the protection of research participants at all colleges and universities where psychological research is conducted. These committees are typically made up of (1) a group of instructors and researchers employed at the university, (2) one or more university staff members with special expertise in the area of research protocol, and (3) one or more laypeople from the local community (e.g., a minister or businessperson who is active in community service). If a researcher wants to conduct research on human participants, he or she must submit a formal proposal to the protection committee at the university with which she or he is affiliated. Such proposals typically include (1) a careful but nontechnical summary of the practical and theoretical goals of the research project, along with (2) a detailed description of the procedures to be followed in the research.

The description of the procedures is quite comprehensive. It includes information about how participants will be selected for inclusion in the study, a description of the setting in which the research will be conducted (e.g., a classroom, a laboratory), and copies of all the materials that participants will be given during the study (e.g., the informed consent form, copies of survey questions or experimental stimuli, debriefing sheets, etc.). It also includes a description of any procedures the researcher will use to minimize risks to his or her participants (e.g., a description of how participants' responses will be kept anonymous). When a study (1) does not make use of deception and (2) does not pose any meaningful risks to research participants, some universities provide a route through which the study may be "exempted" from a review by the full committee. When a researcher requests such an exemption from full review, one or two of the experienced members of the committee (usually the committee chair) will read the proposal and make a decision regarding its suitability for exemption. If it is very clear that the study poses no reasonable ethical risks, it may be exempted from a full review (and approved directly by the chair or acting committee members). On the other hand, if the reviewer disagrees with the researcher's conclusion that the study poses no ethical risks of any kind, the researcher may be asked to make changes to the study, or he or she may be asked to resubmit the study for review by the full committee. In either case, the researcher must await some kind of approval from the committee. Although the exact review procedures vary slightly from university to university, the days in which researchers could decide for themselves whether their research is ethically defensible are in the past.

METHODOLOGY EXERCISE 4

Repeated Measures Designs

In the first methodology exercise, we learned that matching is very bad. In fact, matching isn't *all* bad; it just has a few drawbacks (like being imperfect and impractical). However, if matching worked perfectly, and if it were practical, it would be pretty wonderful. Imagine, for example, that you could somehow create perfect clones of ten people and assign one member of each pair of clones to one of two conditions in an experiment. Notice, first of all, that you would no longer need random assignment. If the clones were truly *perfect* clones, there would be no need to worry about which member of a pair of clones went into which condition. Now suppose you ran your experiment and found that the clones in your experimental group behaved differently from those in your control group. How confident would you feel that the behavioral differences you observed were the result of your experimental manipulation? You should feel extremely confident, because a major source of behavioral variability (individual differences) has been completely eliminated from your study (remember that random assignment controls pretty well for individual differences but it never eliminates them entirely).

Given the recent media attention paid to cloning, it has probably occurred to you by now that cloning for experimental control has some pretty serious ethical and practical drawbacks. Even though we can't clone people to serve in research experiments, we can come pretty close. How? By allowing each person in an experiment to serve in more than one condition of the study and thus to serve as his or her own control. This is exactly what repeated measures or within-subjects designs do. They place each participant in more than one condition of an experiment to see if the same person's thoughts, feelings, or behavior will be different under different experimental conditions.

Besides giving you a great deal of control in your experiment, repeated measures designs can also increase the impact of certain manipulations. Suppose you wanted to vary either (1) the strength of two electric shocks people had to rate for painfulness or (2) the physical attractiveness of a woman whom participants had to rate for friendliness. Wouldn't your manipulations be more salient if each participant were exposed to both levels of shock or attractiveness? In addition to the advantages of control and impact, repeated measures designs have a final practical advantage. In comparison with traditional (between-subjects) designs, they typically require less of the two most valuable resources any experimenter has: time and research participants.

To give you a feel for how repeated measures designs work, this exercise will allow you to analyze a hypothetical data set from an experiment on the self-concept. One of the most widely accepted theories of the self is self-enhancement theory, which states that people have a strong need to think well of themselves and usually try to boost their own egos in any way that they can. Suppose two experimenters each ran a study in an effort to gain support for self-enhancement theory. In particular, suppose they both decided to see if people would be more likely to endorse positive rather than negative traits as self-descriptive. Suppose further that in an effort to gain evidence that self-enhancing self-ratings exist independent of potentially accurate self-knowledge, the researchers decided to study experimentally generated positive versus negative beliefs. That is, suppose they decided to examine people's tendencies to endorse *nonexistent* positive or negative traits as self-descriptive.

For example, suppose one researcher (Dr. A) gave half of her ten participants the following "personality measure" and asked them to place a "yes" or a "no" next to each trait to indicate whether they consider it self-descriptive:

_____ immature	_____ considerate
_____ humorless	_____ hardworking
_____ untruthful	_____ friendly
_____ boring	_____ open-minded
_____ gamant	_____ creative
_____ disagreeable	_____ talented

Suppose she gave the other (randomly assigned) half of her participants a different version of the same measure:

_____ immature	_____ considerate
_____ humorless	_____ hardworking
_____ untruthful	_____ friendly
_____ boring	_____ open-minded
_____ unreliable	_____ gamant
_____ disagreeable	_____ talented

If you examine the two personality scales carefully, you will see that people who receive the first scale will probably assume that being gamant isn't very good. People who receive the second scale, however, will be likely to assume that gamanticity is pretty wonderful.

Although we think that Dr. A has designed a pretty clever experiment, we don't think her experiment was quite as nice as a similar experiment run by Dr. B. Dr. B took a within-subjects approach and presented *each* of her ten participants with a measure that looked like this:

_____ immature	_____ considerate
_____ humorless	_____ hardworking
_____ untruthful	_____ friendly
_____ boring	_____ gamant
_____ casortic	_____ open-minded
_____ disagreeable	_____ talented

Notice that Dr. B's design is essentially the equivalent of giving ten people the first scale devised by Dr. A and then giving ten clones of the original participants the second scale devised by Dr. A. In fact, for the sake of this exercise, assume that Dr. B did just that by making use of ten perfect clones of the ten participants who took part in Dr. A's experiment. Like Dr. A, Dr. B was interested in the hypothesis that people would be more likely to endorse a bogus trait (i.e., to say that it was self-descriptive) if it happened to be positive rather than negative. The data from both studies appear below:

	Experiment A			Experiment B	
Participant	Valence of bogus trait	Endorsed?	Clone	Endorsed – trait?	Endorsed + trait?
01	–	**N**	01	**N**	Y
02	–	**Y**	02	**Y**	Y
03	–	**N**	03	**N**	Y
04	–	**Y**	04	**Y**	N
05	–	**N**	05	**N**	Y
06	+	**Y**	06	N	**Y**
07	+	**Y**	07	N	**Y**
08	+	**Y**	08	N	**Y**
09	+	**Y**	09	N	**Y**
10	+	**N**	10	N	**N**

Note: Valence of bogus trait refers to whether the bogus trait was negative (–) or positive (+).

Questions

1. Compare each clone with the original participant from whom he or she was cloned. How do the responses of clones 1–5 compare with the responses of the original participants from whom they were cloned? How about clones 6–10? How do their responses compare with those of original participants 6–10? Be specific by making it clear which responses can be compared and which ones can't.

2. Summarize the results of experiment A. What percentage of participants endorsed the bogus trait in the positive and negative trait conditions? Do the results provide any support at all for the hypothesis? Suppose you were to conduct a traditional ANOVA on the data from experiment A. Which of the following F ratios and p values do you think you would obtain? (Recall that only p values of less than .05 are significant.)

   (a) $F(1, 8) = 1.60, p = .2415$.
   (b) $F(1, 9) = 7.36, p = .0239$.

3. Summarize the results of experiment B. If you conducted a repeated measures ANOVA on both sets of scores in experiment B, which of the following F ratios and p values do you think you would obtain?

   (a) $F(1, 8) = 1.60, p = .2415$.
   (b) $F(1, 9) = 7.36, p = .0239$.

   Answer questions 2 and 3 by trying to decide which experiment (A or B) would yield significant results (only one would). Now explain why you think one study would yield more significant results than the other (there is more than one reason).

4. The results of this exercise might suggest that we should always use repeated measures designs, but despite all of their advantages, repeated measures designs also have some drawbacks. Can you think of any? First, can you think of a potential confound or problem that could "spoil" repeated measures designs? How do researchers typically deal with this problem? (You should be able to answer this from material provided in this text.) Second, can you think of any experiments or types of experiments that would be difficult or impossible to run using a repeated measures design?

HANDS-ON ACTIVITY 4

The Stroop Interference Effect

In 1935, J. Ridley Stroop conducted a clever and elegant experiment that had a powerful influence on a great deal of psychological research (Stroop, 1935, Experiment 2). Stroop was interested in the fact that many forms of knowledge come at a cost. Specifically, he noticed that in a wide range of situations, well-learned habits often interfere with the production of competing responses. For example, if you emigrated to a culture in which green traffic lights indicated that you should stop at an intersection, your established associations about traffic lights could get you into quite a bit of trouble. Similarly, if you tried to learn to speak Spanish as an adult, you could be guaranteed that the habits of pronunciation you had learned in English would interfere with the quality of your pronunciation of many Spanish words and phrases.

Effects such as these are typically referred to as *interference effects,* and Stroop developed a very elegant procedure for studying interference effects. Specifically, in the experimental condition of his study, Stroop presented participants with a long list of color words ("red," "blue," "green," "brown," and "purple") that were always printed in an ink color that differed from the color named by the word (e.g., the word "red" was printed in blue, green, brown, and purple ink at different places in the list; the word "blue" was printed in red, green, brown, and purple ink at different places in the list). Participants were instructed to work their way through the list as quickly as possible by *correctly naming the ink color* that printed each individual word. In the control condition of this same experiment, the ink color identification task was very similar except that the ink colors didn't print any words—they simply printed little squares. Stroop compared (1) the length of time it took people to name the ink colors in a list of 100 "mismatched" color words with (2) the length of time it took people to name the same 100 ink colors when the ink colors printed the squares. If you are having difficulty picturing this situation, take a peek at the inside front cover of your textbook, where you will find an abbreviated version of Stroop's stimuli. When Stroop compared people's performance in the two conditions, he found that it took the average person almost 75% longer to name all the ink colors in the mismatched condition. This finding—increased naming latencies for ink colors when the ink colors spell color words that are different from the color of the ink—has been appropriately dubbed the *Stroop interference effect.*

In this hands-on activity, you will serve as an experimenter in an abbreviated version of Stroop's classic experiment. Of course, this means that you will need a partner to serve as a participant. However, one of the interesting aspects of the Stroop interference effect is that even people who are fully aware of the effect cannot usually avoid falling prey to it. This means that after you have served as an experimenter in this demonstration, you can reverse places with your partner and serve as a participant as well. We are assuming that your instructor will want you to conduct this demonstration during a class session with a classmate or classmates. However, in case you have to conduct the experiment outside class, we have written the instructions for the task as if you were planning to conduct the experiment on a naive volunteer.

Advance Preparation

The materials you will need for this activity are (1) the inside front cover of your textbook, (2) a stopwatch (a wristwatch that indicates seconds will do in a pinch), (3) a slip of paper and a pencil, (4) a fair coin, and (5) two half-sheets of thick paper or cardboard (to hide the upper and lower halves of the Stroop page prior to the beginning of the activity). You should have all these materials in hand and be ready to begin the task *before* you recruit your participant. In addition, before recruiting your participant, you should make an answer key by numbering a slip of paper from 1 to 20 and writing down the correct ink colors for each of the 20 stimuli. This is very important because it will be difficult for you to check your participant's performance if you haven't recorded the correct answers.

Task Instructions

Once you and your participant are ready to begin, you should allow your participant to take a *quick peek* at the inside front cover of the book and explain that he or she will be trying to *name the colors of 20 inks as quickly as possible, without making any errors.* To be certain that your participant is familiar with the appropriate labels for the five colors, you should direct his or her attention to the five color words printed at the very top of the page. In fact, you should ask your participant to name these five ink colors as quickly as possible as a warm-up for performing the real experimental task. You should also explain that the experiment has two separate trials—one involving the list of squares and one involving the list of color words. When you are certain that your participant understands the task, you should place the Stroop page in front of your participant. However, before doing so you should *carefully* cover up the top and bottom halves of the page (except for the color labels at the very top) with your half-page cover sheets.

Before your participant begins the task, you should flip a fair coin to determine which list your participant will use first. If the coin comes up *heads,* announce that your participant will begin by naming all the colors in the *top* list. If it comes up *tails,* announce that your participant will begin by naming all of the colors in the *bottom* list. Of course, your participant will have little choice about following these instructions because you will uncover only *one* of the two lists when you give the signal to begin. On your signal (Stroop used "Ready! Go!"), you will uncover the appropriate list and start your stopwatch while your participant tries to name the 20 ink colors as quickly as possible. As soon as your participant announces the 20th color, stop your watch and record the time. After a brief pause, you will repeat the activity, but this time you will uncover the other list. This will allow you to compare your participant's performance in the two different conditions. You should record your participant's time for each task, and you should also make a note of which task your participant completed first. If your participant is like the large majority of Stroop's participants, he or she will take longer to name all the ink colors in the mismatched list. To familiarize you with the way these data would be analyzed in a formal research paper, your instructor may wish to collect and aggregate your data for analysis.

Methodological Notes

In this activity we presented an abbreviated version of Stroop's original interference task. Most contemporary psychologists who are interested in the Stroop effect present their stimuli one at a time on a computer monitor and assess participants' response latencies to each individual stimulus. In Stroop's day the technology wasn't available to do this, and thus part of Stroop's ingenuity was to make small differences in response latencies measurable by stringing a lot of them together. Refinements in our measurement techniques have led to some interesting developments that Stroop would have had difficulty uncovering. For example, by assessing interference effects on a stimulus-by-stimulus basis, Klopfer (1996) demonstrated that Stroop interference effects get larger as ink colors and color words get more similar. For example, larger interference effects are observed when green ink is used to print the word "blue" than they are when green ink is used to print the word "red." Another advantage of assessing Stroop effects using a computer is that computers do not have expectancies. Thus, in most computerized versions of the Stroop task, there is not much need to worry about problems such as experimenter bias. (Incidentally, if you were worried about experimenter bias, you could have recruited a third experimenter who held the answer key, gave the start command, and controlled the stopwatch—but wasn't informed of which list your participant was working on during the two experimental trials.)

Contemporary psychologists have put the Stroop task to a wide variety of uses. For example, clinical psychologists have made extensive use of the Stroop technique to investigate whether emotionally threatening words (e.g., "spider," "death") can produce interference in ink naming, especially among people with certain clinical disorders (e.g., spider phobics, people who are unduly anxious about death). They can (see Williams, Mathews, & MacLeod, 1996). Similarly, social and personality psychologists have adapted the Stroop interference effect to study phenomena such as thought suppression (see Wegner, 1994) and emotional regulation (see Rusting, 1998). Stroop would be happy to know that his simple color-naming task has contributed greatly to our understanding of how people process many different kinds of information.

Notes

1. When social influence agents use this tactic, they get people to agree to a "good deal" (or a prosocial request) that becomes less desirable (or more costly) once people have committed themselves. Once they become committed, people are reluctant to back out even if the deal is one they never would have agreed to up front. Salespeople often take advantage of this technique by offering potential customers a seemingly great deal on a product (such as a new car) and later informing the potential customer that they can't quite honor the original promise (e.g., "Oh Larry, I hate to tell you this, but my boss just told me that the free air conditioner only applies to last year's model. You know what, though? I think I can still get you a discount on it.").

2. For a more detailed treatment of survey construction (and administration), see Neuman (1991).

3. There is at least one interesting exception to the general rule that experimenters should dress professionally. In a study of terror management (a defensive process that people engage in after having been asked to think about their own mortality), Simon et al. (1997) directly manipulated whether their experimenter dressed (and acted) in a highly formal or informal fashion. Simon et al. found that participants who had been asked to contemplate their own mortality made defensive judgments (e.g., derogating a person who expressed negative opinions of the United States) only when the experimenter dressed informally. Apparently, highly formal experimenters induce a deliberative, rational form of information processing that short-circuits certain kinds of primitive defensive mechanisms.

10

A Brief Course in Statistics

Figures can't lie, but liars sure can figure.
  —*American folk saying*

Although few students are so disenchanted with statistics as to adopt this folk saying as a personal credo, most of the students who take methodology courses are thumbs-down on statistics. In fact, many students report that some of the most frustrating aspects of research methods are the parts that have to do with statistics. It's true that it's difficult to be a really good methodologist without having at least a working knowledge of statistics. However, it's also true that it's easy to be a really good methodologist *without* being a statistical genius. The statistical skills it takes to be a good methodologist are mainly conceptual rather than computational. If you can understand the logic of inferential statistics and familiarize yourself with a few relatively simple statistical tests, then you will have the kind of working knowledge of statistics that it takes to be a superb methodologist. The purpose of this chapter is to give you that working knowledge. Because inferential statistics are grounded partly in descriptive statistics, we begin this chapter with a discussion of descriptive statistics and then move on to a discussion of inferential statistics.

Descriptive Statistics

Statistics are a set of mathematical procedures for summarizing and interpreting observations. These observations are typically numerical or categorical facts about specific people or things, and they are usually referred to as **data.** The most fundamental branch of statistics is **descriptive statistics,** that is, statistics used to summarize or describe a set of observations.

The branch of statistics used to interpret or draw inferences about a set of observations is fittingly referred to as **inferential statistics.** Inferential statistics are discussed in the second half of this chapter. Another way of distinguishing descriptive and inferential statistics is that descriptive statistics are the *easy* ones. Almost all the members of modern, industrialized societies are familiar with at least some descriptive statistics. Descriptive statistics include things such as means, medians, modes, and percentages, and they are everywhere. You can scarcely pick up a newspaper or listen to a newscast without being exposed to heavy doses of descriptive statistics. You might hear that Priest Holmes is averaging 4.8 yards per carry this season, that Shaq is a 46% free-throw shooter, or that the Atlanta Braves have won 95% of their games this season when they were leading after the eighth inning (and 100% of their games when they outscored their opponents). Alternately, you might hear the results of a shocking new medical study showing that, as people age, women's brains shrink 67% less than men's brains do, or you might hear a meteorologist report that the average high temperature for the past seven days has been over 100°. The reason that descriptive statistics are so ubiquitous is that they are so useful. They take what could be an extremely large and cumbersome set of observations and boil them down to one or two highly representative numbers.

In fact, we're convinced that if we had to live in a world without descriptive statistics, much of our existence would be reduced to a hellish nightmare. Imagine a sportscaster trying to tell us exactly how well Priest Holmes has been rushing this season without using any descriptive statistics. Instead of simply telling us that Holmes has gained an average of 4.8 yards per carry this season, the sportscaster might begin by saying, "Well, on his first rushing attempt in the first game of the season, Smith gained an impressive 17 yards. However, on his second attempt in that same game, he only rushed for . . . and of course in that big breakaway play during game 7 . . . and on the 14th carry of his 9th game this season, Holmes actually lost about 5 yards." By the time the announcer had documented all of the rushes in Holmes's season (without even mentioning *last* season), the game would be over, and we would never have even heard the score. Worse yet, we probably wouldn't even have a very good idea of how well Holmes was rushing this season. A sea of specific numbers just doesn't tell people very much. A simple mean puts a sea of numbers in a nutshell.

Central Tendency and Dispersion

Although descriptive statistics are everywhere, the descriptive statistics used by laypeople are typically incomplete in an important respect. Laypeople make frequent use of descriptive statistics that summarize the **central tendency** (loosely speaking, the average) of a set of observations ("But my man Marshall Faulk has rushed for an average of 5.3 yards per carry"; "A follow-up study revealed that women also happen to be exactly 67% less likely to spend their weekends watching football and drinking beer than men are"). However, most laypeople are relatively unaware of an equally useful and important category of descriptive statistics. This second category of descriptive statistics consists of statistics that summarize the **dispersion, or variability,** of a set of scores. Measures of dispersion are not only important in their own (descriptive) right, but as you will see later, they are also important because they play a very important role in inferential statistics.

One common, and relatively familiar, measure of dispersion is the **range** of a set of scores. The range of a set of scores is simply the difference between the highest and the lowest value in the entire set of scores. ("The follow-up study also revealed that virtually *all* men showed the same amount of shrinkage. The smallest amount of shrinkage observed in all the male brains studied was 96 cc, and the largest amount observed was 103 cc. That's a range of only 7 cc. In contrast, many of the women in the study showed no shrinkage whatsoever, and the largest amount of shrinkage observed was 72 cc. That's a range of 72 cc.") Another very common, but less intuitive, descriptive measure of dispersion is the **standard deviation.** It's a special kind of average itself—namely, an average measure of how much each of the scores in the sample *differs* from the sample mean. More specifically, it's the square root of the average squared deviation of each score from the sample mean, or:

$$S = \sqrt{\frac{\Sigma(x - m)^2}{n}}$$

Σ (sigma) is a summation sign, a symbol that tells us to perform the functions that follow it for all the scores in a sample and then to add them all together. That is, this symbol tells us to take each individual score in our sample (represented by x), to subtract the mean (m) from it, and to square this difference. Once we have done this for all our scores, sigma tells us to add all these calculations together. We then divide these summed scores by the number of observations in our sample and take the square root of this final value.

For example, suppose we had a small sample of only 4 scores: 2, 2, 4, and 4. Using the formula above, the standard deviation turns out to be:

$$\sqrt{\frac{(2 - 3)^2 + (2 - 3)^2 + (4 - 3)^2 + (4 - 3)^2}{4}}$$

which is simply:

$$\sqrt{\frac{1 + 1 + 1 + 1}{4}}$$

which is exactly 1.

That's it. The standard deviation in this sample of scores is exactly 1. If you look back at the scores, you'll see that this is pretty intuitive. The mean of the set of scores is 3.0, and every single score deviates from this mean by exactly a point. There is a computational form of this formula that is much easier to deal with than the definitional form that we have shown here (especially if you have a lot of numbers in your sample). However, we included the definitional formula so that you could get a sense of what the standard deviation means. Loosely speaking, it's the average ("standard") amount by which all the scores in a distribution differ (deviate) from the mean of that same set of scores. Finally, we should add that the specific formula we presented here requires an adjustment if you hope to use a sample of scores to estimate the standard deviation in the population of scores from which these sample scores were drawn. It is this adjusted standard deviation that researchers are most likely to use in actual research. Conceptually, however, the adjusted formula (which requires you to divide by n – 1 rather than n) does *exactly* what the unadjusted formula does. It gives you an idea of how much a set of scores varies around a mean.

Why are measures of dispersion so useful? Like measures of central tendency, measures of dispersion summarize a very important property of a set of scores. For example, consider the two groups of four men whose heights are listed below:

	Group 1	Group 2
Person 1	6'2"	6'9"
Person 2	6'1"	6'5"
Person 3	5'11"	5'10"
Person 4	5'10"	5'0"

A couple of quick calculations will reveal that the mean height of the men in both groups is exactly 6 feet. Now suppose you were a heterosexual woman of average height, and you needed to choose a blind date by drawing names from one of two hats. One hat contains the names of the four men in group 1, and the other hat contains the names of the four men in group 2. From which hat would you prefer to choose your date? If you followed social conventions regarding dating and height, you would probably prefer to choose your date from group 1. Now suppose you were choosing four team-mates for an intramural basketball team, and you had to choose one of the two *groups* (in its entirety). In this case, we assume that you would choose group 2 (and try to get the ball to the big guy when he posts up under the basket). Your preferences reveal that dispersion is a very important statistical property because the only way in which the two groups of men differ is in the dispersion (i.e., the variability) of their heights. In group 1 the standard deviation is 1.58 inches. In group 2 it's 7.97 inches.[1]

Another way of thinking about dispersion is that measures of dispersion complement measures of central tendency by telling you something about how *well* a measure of central tendency represents all the scores in a distribution. When the dispersion or variability in a set of scores is low, the mean of a set of scores does a great job of describing most of the scores in the sample. When the dispersion or variability in a set of scores is high, however, the mean of a set of scores does not do such a great job of describing most of the scores in the sample (the mean is still the best available summary of the set of scores, but there will be a lot of people in the sample whose scores lie far away from the mean). When you are dealing with descriptions of people, measures of central tendency—such as the mean—tell you what the *typical* person is like. Measures of dispersion—such as the standard deviation—tell you how much you can expect specific people to differ from this typical person.

The Shape of Distributions

A third statistical property of a set of observations is a little more difficult to quantify than measures of central tendency or dispersion. This third statistical property is the *shape* of a distribution of scores. One useful way to get a feel for a set of scores is to arrange them in order from the lowest to the highest and to graph them pictorially so that taller parts of the graph represent more frequently occurring scores (or, in the case of a theoretical or ideal distribution, more probable scores). Figure 10.1 depicts three different kinds of distributions: a rectangular distribution, a bimodal distribution, and a normal distribution. The scores in a **rectangular distribution** are all about equally frequent or probable. An example of a rectangular distribution is the theoretical distribution representing the six possible scores that can be obtained by

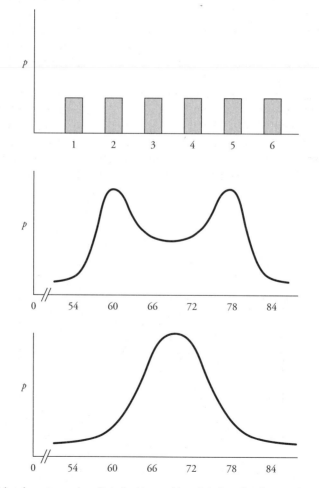

FIGURE 10.1   A rectangular distribution, a bimodal distribution, and a normal distribution

rolling a single six-sided die. In the case of a **bimodal distribution,** there are two distinct ranges of scores that are more common than any other. A likely example of a bimodal distribution would be the heights of the athletes attending the annual sports banquet for a very large high school that only has two sports teams: women's gymnastics and men's basketball. If this example seems a little contrived, it should. Bimodal distributions are relatively rare, and they usually reflect the fact that a sample is composed of two meaningful sub-samples. The third distribution depicted in Figure 10.1 is the most important. This is a **normal distribution:** a symmetrical, bell-shaped distribution in which most scores cluster near the mean and in which scores become increasingly rare as they become increasingly divergent from this mean. Many things that can be quantified are normally distributed. Distributions of height, weight, extroversion, self-esteem, and the age at which infants begin to walk are all examples of approximately normal distributions.

The nice thing about the normal distribution is that if you know that a set of observations is normally distributed, this further improves your ability to describe the entire set of scores in the sample. More specifically, you can make some very good guesses about the exact proportion of scores that fall within any given number of standard deviations (or fractions of a standard deviation) from the mean. As illustrated in Figure 10.2, about 68% of a set of normally distributed scores will fall within one standard deviation of the mean. About 95% of a set of normally distributed scores will fall within two standard deviations of the mean, and more than 99% of a set of normally distributed scores will fall within three standard deviations of the mean. For example, scores on modern intelligence tests (such as the Wechsler Adult Intelligence Scale) are normally distributed, have a mean of 100, and have a

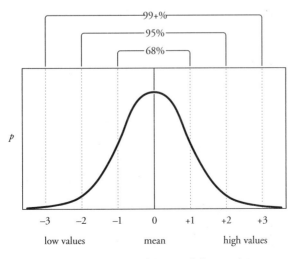

FIGURE 10.2 Approximate proportion of scores falling within one, two, and three standard deviations from the mean of a normal distribution

standard deviation of 15. This means that about 68% of all people have IQs that fall between 85 and 115. Similarly, more than 99% of all people have IQs that fall between 55 and 145.

This kind of analysis can also be used to put a particular score or observation into perspective (which is a first step toward making *inferences* from particular observations). For instance, if you know that a set of 400 scores on an astronomy midterm (a) approximates a normal distribution, (b) has a mean of 70, and (c) has a standard deviation of exactly 6, you should have a very good picture of what this entire set of scores is like. And you should know exactly how impressed to be when you learn that your friend Amanda earned an 84 on the exam. She scored 2.33 standard deviations above the mean, which means that she probably scored in the top 1% of the class. How could you tell this? By consulting a detailed table based on the normal distribution. Such a table would tell you that only about 2% of a set of scores are 2.33 standard deviations or more from the mean. And because the normal distribution is symmetrical, half of the scores that are 2.33 standard deviations or more from the mean will be 2.33 standard deviations or more *below* the mean. Amanda's score was in the half of that 2% that was well above the mean. Translation: Amanda kicked butt on the exam.

As you know if you have had any formal training in statistics, there is much, much more to descriptive statistics than what we have covered here. For instance, we skipped many of the specific measures of central tendency and dispersion, and we didn't describe all the possible kinds of distributions of scores. However, this overview should make it clear that descriptive statistics provide researchers with an enormously powerful tool for organizing and simplifying data. At the same time, descriptive statistics are only half of the picture. In addition to simplifying and organizing the data they collect, researchers also need to draw conclusions about populations from their sample data. That is, they need to move beyond the data themselves in the hopes of drawing general inferences about people. To do this, researchers rely on inferential statistics.

Inferential Statistics

As you may recall, we discussed the logic behind inferential statistics in Chapter 2. In that discussion, we used the metaphor of the courtroom to summarize the logic of statistical testing. Instead of repeating that discussion here, we will try to enrich your understanding of the nature of inferential statistics by using inferential statistics to solve a couple of simple problems. In an effort to keep formulas and calculations as simple as possible, we have chosen some very simple problems. Analyzing and interpreting the data from most real experiments will require much more extensive calculations than those you will see here, but these labor-intensive calculations are usually carried out by computers rather than by people. Regardless of how extensive the calculations are, however, the basic logic underlying inferential statistical tests is almost always the same—no matter which specific inferential test is being conducted.

Probability Theory

All inferential statistics are grounded firmly in the logic of probability theory. Probability theory deals with the mathematical rules and procedures used to predict and understand chance events. For example, the principle of regression toward the mean can easily be derived from probability theory. Similarly, the odds in casinos and predictions about the weather can be derived from straightforward considerations of probabilities. What is a probability? From the classical perspective, the **probability** of an event is a very simple thing: It is (a) the number of all specific outcomes that qualify as the event in question divided by (b) the total number of all possible outcomes. The probability of rolling a 3 on a single roll with a standard six-sided die is 1/6, or .167 because there is (a) one and only one roll that qualifies as a 3, and (b) exactly six (equally likely) possible outcomes. For the same reason, the probability of rolling an odd number on the same die is ½, or .50—because three of the six possible outcomes qualify as odd numbers. It is important to remember that the probability of *any* event (or complex set of events, such as the observed results of an experiment) is the number of ways to observe that event divided by the total number of possible events.

With this in mind, suppose the Great Hartini told you that he had telekinetic powers that allow him to influence the outcome of otherwise fair coin tosses. How could you test his claim? One way would be to ask him to predict some coin tosses and to check up on the accuracy of his predictions. Imagine that you pulled out a coin, tossed it in the air, and asked Hartini to call it before it landed. He calls heads. Heads it is! Do you believe in Hartini's self-proclaimed telekinetic abilities? Of course not. You realize that this event could easily have occurred by chance. How easily? Fully half the time we performed the test. With this concern in mind, suppose Hartini agreed to predict exactly 10 coin tosses. Let's stop and consider a number of possible outcomes of this hypothetical coin-tossing test. To simplify things, let's assume that Hartini always predicts heads on every toss.

One pretty unremarkable outcome is that he'd make 5 out of 10 correct predictions. Should you conclude that he does, indeed, have telekinetic abilities? Or that he is *half* telekinetic (perhaps on his mother's side)? Of course not. Making 5 of 10 correct predictions is no better than chance. To phrase this in terms of the results of the test, the number of heads we observed was no different than the *expected frequency* (the average, over the long run) of a random series of 10 coin tosses. In this case, the expected frequency is the probability of a head on a single toss (.50) multiplied by the total number of tosses (10). But what if Hartini made six or seven correct predictions instead of only five? Our guess is that you still wouldn't be very impressed and would still conclude that Hartini does not have telekinetic abilities (in statistical terms, you would fail to reject the null hypothesis). OK, so what if he made a slightly more impressive eight correct predictions? What about nine? You should bear in mind that Hartini never said his telekinetic powers were absolutely flawless. Hartini can't *always* carry a glass of water across a room without spilling it, but his friends usually allow him to carry glasses of water unassisted. Despite your firmly entrenched (and justifiable) skepticism concerning psychic phenomena, we hope you can see that as our observations (i.e., the results of our coin-tossing test) depart further and further from chance expectations, you would start to become more and more convinced that something unusual is going on. At a certain point, you'd practically be forced to agree that Hartini is doing something to influence the outcome of the coin tosses.

The problem is that it's hard to know exactly *where* that certain point is. Some people might be easygoing enough to say they'd accept eight or more heads as compelling evidence of Hartini's telekinetic abilities. Other people might ask to see a perfect score of 10 (and still insist that they're not convinced). After all, extraordinary claims require extraordinary evidence. That's where inferential statistics come in. By making use of (a) some basic concepts in probability theory, along with (b) our knowledge of what a distribution of scores should look like when nothing funny is going on (e.g., when we are merely flipping a coin 10 times at random, when we are simply randomly assigning 20 people to either an experimental or a control condition), we can use inferential statistics to figure out exactly how likely it is that a given set of usual or not-so-usual observations would have been observed by chance. Unless it is pretty darn *un*likely that a set of findings would have been observed by chance, the logic of statistical hypothesis testing requires us to conclude that the set of findings represents a chance outcome.

To return to our coin-tossing demonstration, just how likely *is* it that a person would toss 9 or more heads by chance alone? One way to figure this out is to use our definition of probability and to figure out (a) all the specific ways there are to observe 9 or more heads in a string of 10 coin tosses and (b) all the specific outcomes (of any kind) that are possible for a string of 10 coin tosses. If we divide (a) by (b), we should have our answer. Let's begin with the number of ways there are to toss 9 or more heads. At the risk of sounding like the announcer who was describing Priest Holmes's rushing history without using inferential statistics, notice that one way to do it would be to toss a tail on the first trial, followed by 9 straight heads. A second way to do it would be to toss a head on the first trial and a tail on the second trial, followed by 8 straight heads. If you follow this approach to its logical conclusion, you should see that there are exactly 10 specific ways to observe exactly 9 heads in a string of 10 coin tosses. And in case you actually want to see the 10 ways right in front of you, they appear in Table 10.1—along with all of the unique ways there are to observe exactly *10* heads. As you already knew, there is only one of them. However, it's important to include this one in our list because we were interested in all of the specific ways to observe 9 *or more* heads in a series of 10 coin tosses.[2] So there are 11 ways.

But how many total unique outcomes are there for a series of 10 coin tosses? To count all of these would be quite a headache. So we'll resort to a less painful headache and figure it out logically. How many possible ways are there for 1 toss to come out? Two: heads or tails—which turns out to be 2^1 (2 to the first power). How about 2 tosses? Now we can observe 2^2 (2×2) or 4 possible ways, namely:

HH, HT, TH, or TT

TABLE 10.1 All the possible ways to toss nine or more heads in ten tosses of a fair coin: a single tail can come on any of the ten trials, or it can never come at all.

1.	**T**	H	H	H	H	H	H	H	H	H
2.	H	**T**	H	H	H	H	H	H	H	H
3.	H	H	**T**	H	H	H	H	H	H	H
4.	H	H	H	**T**	H	H	H	H	H	H
5.	H	H	H	H	**T**	H	H	H	H	H
6.	H	H	H	H	H	**T**	H	H	H	H
7.	H	H	H	H	H	H	**T**	H	H	H
8.	H	H	H	H	H	H	H	**T**	H	H
9.	H	H	H	H	H	H	H	H	**T**	H
10.	H	H	H	H	H	H	H	H	H	**T**
11.	H	H	H	H	H	H	H	H	H	H

What about 3 tosses? Now we have 2^3 ($2 \times 2 \times 2$), or 8 possible ways.

HHH, HHT, HTH, THH, HTT, THT, TTH, or TTT.

Notice that our answers always turn out to be 2 (the number of unique outcomes for an individual toss) raised to some *power*. The power to which 2 is raised turns out to be the number of trials or specific observations we are making. So the answer is 2^{10} ($2 \times 2 \times 2 \times 2 \times 2 \times 2 \times 2 \times 2 \times 2 \times 2$) or 1,024 possible unique outcomes for a series of 10 coin tosses. This value of 1,024 includes every possible number of heads (from 0 to 10) and every possible order or position (first through tenth) for all of these possible numbers of heads. So now we have our probability. The probability of observing 9 or more heads in a series of 10 truly random coin tosses is thus 11/1024, or .011. So for every hundred times we conducted our coin-tossing study, you'd expect to see 9 or more heads only about once. That's only 1% of the time, and it's pretty impressive. (In fact, it's exactly as impressive as Amanda's score on the astronomy midterm, and we, for what it's worth, were very impressed with Amanda.) So if we had treated the study like a real experiment, if we had set alpha at .05, and if we had observed 9 heads, we would have had to conclude that Hartini does, in fact, possess the ability to influence the outcomes of otherwise fair coin tosses.

Now perhaps you're the literal type who is saying "But wait a minute. I still wouldn't believe Hartini has telekinetic abilities; and I certainly don't think most scientists would, either." You are correct, of course, because the theory that you have been asked to accept flies in the face of everything you know about psychology and physics. A much more reasonable explanation for the observed findings is that Hartini has engaged in some form of trickery, such as using a biased coin. However, this simply means that, like any scientific practice, the practice of conducting statistical tests must be carried out using a little common sense. If someone is making a truly extraordinary claim, we might want to set alpha at .001, or even .0001, instead of .05. Of course, setting alpha at a very low value might require us to design a test with a much greater number of coin tosses (after all, 10 out of 10 tosses—the *best* you can possibly do—has a probability higher than .0001; it's 1/1024, which is closer to .001), but the point is that we could easily do this. The exact design of our study is up to us (and, to some extent, to our critics). If people are sufficiently skeptical of a claim, they might also want to see a *replication* of a questionable or counterintuitive finding. If Hartini replicated his demonstration several times by correctly predicting 9 or more heads, and if we enacted some careful control procedures to prevent him from cheating (e.g., we let a group of skeptics choose and handle the coins), even the most ardent anti-telekinetician should eventually be persuaded. And if he or she weren't, we would argue that this person wasn't being very scientific.

The logic of the coin-tossing experiment is exactly the same as the logic underlying virtually all inferential statistical tests. First, a researcher makes a set of observations. Second, these observations are compared with what we would expect to observe if nothing unusual were happening in the experiment (i.e., if the researcher's hypothesis were incorrect). This comparison is ultimately converted into a *probability,* namely, the probability that the researcher would have observed a set of results at least this consistent with his or her hypothesis if the hypothesis were incorrect. Finally, if this probability is sufficiently low, we conclude that the researcher's hypothesis was probably correct. Because inferential statistics are a very important part of the research process, let's look at another highly contrived but informative question that could be answered only with the use of inferential statistics.

A Study of Cheating

Suppose we offered a group of exactly 50 students the chance to win a very attractive prize (say, a large amount of cash, or an autographed copy of this textbook) by randomly drawing a lucky orange Ping-Pong ball out of a large paper bag. Assume that each student gets to draw only one ball from the bag, that students return the drawn balls to the bag after each drawing, and that the bag contains exactly 10 balls, only 1 of which is orange. Because our university is trying to teach students the values of honesty and integrity, university regulations require us to administer the drawing on an honor system. Specifically, the bag of Ping-Pong balls is kept behind a black curtain, and students walk behind the curtain—one at a time, in complete privacy—to draw their balls at random from the bag. After drawing a ball, each student holds it up above the curtain for everyone else to see. Anyone who holds up an orange ball is a winner.

Suppose that we're the curious types who want to find out if there was a significant amount of cheating (peeking) during the drawing. At first blush, it would seem like there's nothing we could do. Unless we engage in a little cheating ourselves (e.g., by secretly videotaping the drawings), how can we figure out whether people were peeking as they selected their balls? We're at a complete loss to observe the unobservable—unless we rely on inferential statistics. By using inferential statistics, we could simply calculate the number of winners we'd expect to observe if *no one* was cheating. By making a comparison between this expected frequency and the number of winners we actually observed in our drawing, we could calculate the exact probability (based on chance alone) of obtaining a result as extreme as, or more extreme than, the result of our actual drawing. If the probability of having so many winners were sufficiently low, we might reluctantly reject the null hypothesis (our initial assumption that the students were all innocent until proven guilty) and conclude that a significant amount of cheating was happening during the drawing.

Let's find out. To begin with, we need to assume that our suspicions about cheating are completely unfounded and that no one peeked (as usual, we begin by assuming the null hypothesis). Assuming that no one was peeking, what's your best guess about how many students should have selected a winning ball? If you are a little fuzzy on your probability theory, remember that you can figure out the expected frequency of an event by multiplying (a) the probability of the event on a single trial by (b) the total number of trials in the series of events. This is how we knew that 5 was the expected number of observed heads in a series of 10 coin tosses. It was .50 × 10. The answer here is also 5 (it's .10 × 50). Now imagine that we had 6 winners. Or 9 winners, or 15—or 50. Hopefully, you can see, as you did in the coin-tossing study, that as our observed frequencies depart further and further from the frequency we'd expect through the normal operation of chance, we become more and more strongly convinced that our observed frequencies are *not* the product of normal chance processes.

For the purposes of actually seeing some inferential statistics in action, let's assume that we had exactly 10 winners in our drawing. Because our outcome was a categorical outcome ("success" or "failure" at the draw), and because we had a pretty large sample, we'd probably want to conduct a χ^2 (chi-square) test on these data. The formula for this test appears below:

$$\chi^2 = \Sigma \frac{(f_o - f_e)^2}{f_e}$$

Recall that Σ (sigma) is a *summation sign* that tells you to add together all the appropriate examples of the basic calculation.

f_o refers to the *observed frequencies* of each of the events you care about (successes and failures when it comes to sampling a lucky orange ball).

f_e refers to the *expected frequencies* for each of these same events.

You could think of a χ^2 statistic as a "surprise index." Notice that the most important thing the formula does is to *compare* expected and observed frequencies. Specifically, expected frequencies are compared with (i.e., subtracted from) observed frequencies, and then a couple of simple transformations are made on these difference scores. The more our observed frequencies depart from what you'd expect if chance alone were operating (that is, the more surprising our results are), the bigger our χ^2 statistic will become. And as our χ^2 statistic grows, it will be telling us that it's less and less likely that we're observing a chance process (and, in this case, more and more likely that we're observing cheating).

The χ^2 value for 10 winners (out of 50) when only 5 were expected is computed as follows:

$$\chi^2 = \frac{(10-5)^2}{5} + \frac{(40-45)^2}{45}$$

The 10 in the first half of the equation is the *observed* number of successes, and the two 5s both refer to the *expected* number of successes. The 40 in the second half of the equation is the *observed* number of failures, and the two 45s both refer to the *expected* number of failures (this has to be the sample size, which is 50, minus the expected number of successes). When we do the math, we get 25/5 + 25/45, which works out to 5.55. Notice that this *isn't* a probability. The way most inferential statistics work is that you generate both the statistic itself (e.g., a correlation coefficient, a *t*-value, an *F*-ratio), and then use the exact value of the statistic to determine a probability value (one that corresponds to the value of your statistic). If you are doing your calculations on a computer, the software program you are using will always do this for you. That is, it will give you the exact *p*-value (i.e., the exact probability) that corresponds to your results after they have been converted to the unambiguous language of your statistic. However, if you are doing your calculations by hand, as we have here, you will need to consult some kind of statistical table to see what the *critical values* are for your statistic. In the case of our study of cheating, the critical χ^2 value that corresponds to an alpha level of .05 is 3.841. Any χ^2 value that exceeds this score will have an associated *p*-value that is lower than .05, and will thus be significant when alpha is set at .05. If we were a little bit more stringent, we might set alpha at .02 or .01. Our χ^2 table happens to include critical values for each of these levels of alpha (i.e., for each of these probability values). In a study such as ours, the critical χ^2 value for an alpha of .02 is 5.412, and the critical χ^2 value for an alpha of .01 is 6.635. By these criteria, our result is still significant even if alpha is set at .02. However, if we move to the still more stringent alpha level of .01, the number of winners we observed would no longer be significant (because we're effectively saying that it'd take more than 10 winners to convince us).

Suppose we followed standard practice and set alpha at .05. We'd have to conclude that some people cheated. Notice, however, that we couldn't draw any safe inferences about exactly *who* cheated. Presumably about 5 of our 10 winners just got lucky, and about 5 cheated. Realizing that *only* about 5 people cheated provides a different sort of perspective on our findings. Specifically, it highlights the fact that there is often more than one way to look at a set of observations. Notice also that an alternate, and equally correct, perspective on our observation is that people are significantly honest! It appears to be the case that about 45 of our 50 students were completely honest—even in a situation that allowed rampant cheating. Why did we say 45? Because we just decided that only about 5 people are likely to have cheated. In light of how hard it is to win the game by playing fairly, this 5 or so cheaters led to a significant amount of cheating. However, if we had started out with the hypothesis that 49 out of 50, or 98%, of all people should be expected to cheat under these conditions, and if we had taken 49 (nearly absolute dishonesty)

as our standard of comparison rather than 5 (absolute honesty), we would
have obtained an *extremely* large χ^2 value. It would have been

$$\chi^2 = \frac{(10 - 49)^2}{49} + \frac{(40 - 1)^2}{1}$$

which is 1552.04, and which corresponds to an infinitesimally small *p*-value. Even
if we set alpha at a very, very, very low level (say one in a billion, or .000000001),
this would still be significant. In other words, it's important to keep in mind that
we appear to have observed a lot more honesty than cheating.[3]

A final aspect of this exercise about drawing Ping-Pong balls from a bag
is that it provides a useful metaphor for thinking about what researchers do
when they draw inferences about people in their research. Notice that in the
lottery involving Ping-Pong balls, we could not directly observe the phenomenon in which we were interested. The activities we cared about were
shrouded behind a black curtain—just as the activities that psychologists often
care about (e.g., dissonance reduction, feelings of passionate love, parallel
distributed representations of language) are hidden inside the black box of
people's minds. Inferential statistics work hand in hand with things like operational definitions to allow us to make scientific inferences. Operational definitions allow us to draw inferences about *processes* that we cannot observe
(those that occur inside the person), and inferential statistics allow us to draw
inferences about *people* we can't observe (those we didn't sample in our
study). When we conclude that a research finding is significant, we are concluding that it is real and thus that it applies to people who did not take part
in our study. This is one sense in which the Ping-Pong ball demonstration is
a little different from most significance tests. Although it would probably be
safe to generalize our findings about cheating to other college students, what
we really cared about most in this particular test was finding out what was
going on in our particular sample.

Virtually every inferential statistic that you will ever come across will be
based on the logic that was explicated here. Of course, the particular distributions of responses that researchers examine vary enormously from one
study to the next, and this, among other things, influences the particular statistics that researchers use to summarize and draw inferences about their data.
Moreover, once a researcher has chosen a particular statistic, the specific calculations that she or he will have to carry out (or get a computer to carry out)
will typically be a good bit more involved than those you have seen here. For
example, in a two-way analysis of variance (ANOVA), there are separate calculations (and separate *degrees of freedom*) for each of the two possible main
effects as well as for the two-way interaction. No matter what statistics they
are computing, however, researchers will always rely on the logic of probability theory to help them make their case that something significant is at the
root of their empirical observations.

Things That Go Bump in the Light: Factors That Influence the Results of Significance Tests
Alpha Levels and Type I and II Errors

Now that you have a better feel for what it means for a research finding to be statistically significant, we feel that it is our duty to warn you that when we look at significance testing in the cold, hard light of day, it has a couple of limitations. In other words, there are a few things that can go wrong when people are conducting statistical tests. First of all, it is important to remember that when a researcher conducts a statistical test and obtains a significant result, this does not *always* mean that his or her hypothesis is correct. Even if an experiment is perfectly executed with no systematic design flaws, it is always possible that the researcher's results *were* due to chance. In fact, the *p*-value we observe in an experiment tells us exactly how likely it is that we would have obtained results like ours even if nothing but dumb luck was operating in our study. Statisticians refer to this worrisome possibility—incorrectly rejecting the null hypothesis when it is in fact correct—as a **Type I error.** The likelihood of making a Type I error is a direct function of where we set our alpha level. As suggested earlier, if we think it would be a practical or scientific disaster to falsely reject the null hypothesis, we might want to set alpha at a very conservative level, such as .001. Then we would be taking only one chance in a thousand of falsely rejecting the null hypothesis.

So why not set alpha at .001 (or beyond) all the time? Because we have to strike a balance between being cautious and being so cautious that we become downright foolish. In statistical terms, if we always set alpha at an extraordinarily low level, we would decrease the likelihood of committing a Type I error at the expense of increasing the likelihood of committing a **Type II error.** A Type II error occurs when we fail to reject an incorrect null hypothesis—that is, when we fail to realize that our study has revealed something meaningful (usually that our hypothesis is correct). The reason it is useful to know about Type I and Type II errors is that there are things we can do to minimize our chances of making both of these troublesome mistakes. As suggested above, one of the easiest ways to minimize Type I errors is to set alpha at a pretty low level. Over the years, most researchers have pretty well agreed that .05 is a reasonable level for alpha (i.e., a reasonable risk for making a Type I error). And of course, if we want to be a little more cautious, but we don't want to ask anyone to adjust any alpha levels, we can always insist on seeing a replication. In the grand scheme of things, replications are what tell us whether an effect is real.

Effect Size and Significance Testing

Although no one wants to make a Type I error, no one really wants to make a Type II error either. There are several things that influence the likelihood that a researcher will make a Type II error (and fail to detect a real effect). Some of these are things over which researchers have little or no control, and some of them are things over which researchers have almost complete control. One thing that researchers can't do too much about is their "effect size," the magnitude of the effect in which they happen to be interested. If you collected a sample of 20 people and measured their heights and their foot sizes, you could probably expect to observe a statistically significant correlation between height and foot size, even though your sample was pretty small. This is because there is a pretty robust tendency for big people to have big feet. Of course there are exceptions, but they are relatively rare. We doubt that you will ever meet a gymnast who squeezes into a size 14 (or an NBA center who slips comfortably into a size 9). On the other hand, if you gave a sample of 20 people a measure of extroversion and a measure of self-esteem, you might not necessarily observe a significant correlation. Although self-esteem and extroversion do tend to go hand in hand, this correlation is much more modest than the substantial correlation between height and foot size. To return to our example about peeking and Ping-Pong balls, it would have been much easier to detect an effect of cheating if cheating had been much more rampant. In fact, notice that in this study it was quite easy to detect an effect of honesty—precisely because honesty was so rampant.

Measurement Error and Significance Testing

Although it's obviously impossible to change the true size of an effect, one thing that researchers can sometimes do to maximize their chances of detecting a small effect is to conduct a within-subjects or repeated measures study. As suggested in Chapter 6, within-subjects designs are usually more sensitive than between-subjects designs. One of the reasons this is the case is that within-subjects designs cut down on extraneous sources of variability that can mask an effect. A person in a cool room might deliver high levels of shock to a confederate just because this person happens to be an unusually aggressive person. However, if we could observe the behavior of the same person in both a hot and a cool room (and if we could make sure the person didn't know that she or he was being studied), we would presumably see that the person would deliver even higher levels of shock when the temperature was cranked up a bit. Of course, another reason why within-subjects designs are more powerful than between-subjects designs is that they simply increase the number of observations in a study. If we measure the aggressive behavior of each of our 20 participants in both a hot and a cool room, it is almost as if we had 40 participants in our study rather than 20 (see Pelham, 1993, for a further discussion of the advantages of within-subjects designs, but remember the disadvantages we discussed in Chapter 8).

Sample Size and Significance Testing

When researchers are unable to make use of within-subjects designs, there are still a couple of things they can do to maximize their chances of detecting a real effect. One simple, albeit potentially expensive, thing that researchers can do is to conduct studies with a lot of participants. Increasing your sample size in a study (whether it be an experiment, a quasi-experiment, or an archival

Conclusions based on small samples can be highly misleading.

study) can greatly increase the chances that you will detect a real effect. For example, suppose that the true correlation between extroversion and self-esteem among American adults is exactly .32. And suppose that you conducted a survey of 27 randomly sampled American adults and observed a correlation of exactly .32 in your study. Would this be statistically significant? Unfortunately not. In a sample of only 27 people, a correlation of .32 would have a p-value slightly greater than .10—at best a marginally significant value. On the other hand, if you had sampled 102 people rather than 27, and if you happened to hit the nail on the head again by observing another correlation of exactly .32, this result would be significant even if you had set alpha at .001. That's because when you have a sample as large as the second, it's quite unusual to observe a correlation as large as .32 when the two variables in question are actually unrelated. If this doesn't quite seem right to you, consider your own intuitive conclusions when we asked you earlier what you'd think if Hartini were able to correctly predict 6 heads in 10 coin tosses. If he produced exactly the same proportion of heads (600) in 1000 tosses, you should be much more impressed.

Restriction of Range and Significance Testing

As we suggested in Chapter 9, limits in the *range or variability* of the variables you are measuring or manipulating (i.e., restriction of range) can also limit your ability to detect a true effect. Wording your dependent measures carefully, choosing the right population, or making sure that your independent variable is as potent and meaningful as possible (which means not shooting yourself in the foot by artificially *diminishing* your real effect size) are all potential solutions to the problem of restriction of range, and thus they are all potential solutions to the problem of avoiding Type II errors. The particular statistical analysis that you conduct can also play an important role in whether your research findings are significant. When you have a choice between conducting a powerful test (one that can detect even relatively small effects) and a less powerful test, you should always perform the more powerful of the two. For example, performing a correlation between two continuous variables (e.g., self-esteem and the number of minutes people spent reading positive feedback about themselves) is usually more powerful than performing a median split (e.g., on self-esteem) and then conducting an ANOVA or t-test to see if the mean difference between the low group and the high group is significant. Similarly, making use of continuous ("how much did you like your partner?") rather than dichotomous ("did you like your partner?") dependent measures usually allows for more powerful statistical tests. As a second example, when you have a choice of conducting more than one separate between-subjects analysis (e.g., three different between-subjects ANOVAS, one on each of your three different dependent measures) versus a single within-subjects or mixed-model analysis on the same set of research findings (e.g., because you asked people to rate a target person on positive, neutral, and negative traits), you will usually be better served by the analysis that incorporates the within-subjects aspect of your design.

The issues discussed here can help you to conduct better research studies. Just as important, they can also help you to better interpret the findings of other people's studies. For example, if a team of researchers claims that they failed to replicate an important effect, you would do well to ask a few questions about the nature of their manipulation, the nature of their sample, the wording of their dependent measures, and the number of participants they included in their between- or within-subjects study before you abandon your own research on the same topic. If Dr. Snittle noted that he failed to replicate Phillips's archival research on suicide by noting that none of the 23 people in his small Nebraska farming community committed suicide after reading about a front-page suicide, this wouldn't be much cause for concern. However, if Dr. Snittle learned to speak fluent Mandarin, traveled to China, gained access to media and suicide records in several very large Chinese provinces, duplicated Phillips's analytical strategies perfectly, and failed to replicate some aspect of Phillips's findings, we'd want to figure out why. Perhaps some aspect of Chinese culture (or Chinese media coverage) is responsible for the difference. This way of thinking about how to interpret statistics is consistent not only with common sense but also with the logic of the scientific method. It is important to remember that statistics are simply a tool. When effectively applied to an appropriate problem, statistics can be incredibly powerful and effective. However, when misapplied or misinterpreted, statistics—like real tools—can be useless or even dangerous.

The Changing State of the Art: Alternate Perspectives on Statistical Hypothesis Testing

As you may recall from our discussion of the experimental paradigm in Chapter 2, statistical hypothesis testing has become a methodological touchstone for evaluating specific research findings. When a provocative research finding proves to be statistically significant, it is considered scientifically meaningful. When an equally provocative research finding proves to be nonsignificant, it is not taken seriously in scientific circles. As we have just seen, however, an absolute reliance on significance testing—when divorced from basic considerations involving things like effect size or sample size—can lead researchers to inappropriate conclusions. Another way of putting this is that there is more to hypothesis testing than simple significance testing. Critics of significance testing have pointed out, for example, that even when a study is well designed, basing a decision about whether an effect is real solely on the basis of statistical "significance" is not always advisable. In actual practice, for example, when a researcher conducts a study whose results are promising but not significant, the researcher will often run additional participants—or modify the design and run the study again—rather than concluding that the original hypothesis is incorrect. In fact, some researchers have argued that the traditional use of significance testing is an inherently misleading process that should be abandoned in favor of other approaches (Cohen, 1994).

Although it seems unlikely that significance testing will be abandoned anytime in the near future, most researchers would probably agree that it is often useful to complement significance testing with other indicators of the validity, meaningfulness, or repeatability of an effect. A complete review of the pros and cons of alternate approaches to significance testing is beyond the scope of this book. However, it is probably worth noting that researchers have recently begun to complement significance testing by making use of special statistics to assess the practical or theoretical meaningfulness of research findings. One way in which researchers have done this is to compute estimates of **effect sizes,** that is, indicators of the strength or magnitude of their effects. A second way is to compute estimates of (a) the overall amount of existing support for an effect or (b) the consistency or repeatability of the effect. The statistical approach most suited to this second category of questions is referred to as **meta-analysis**.

Estimates of Effect Size

When researchers want to assess the practical or theoretical rather than the statistical significance of a specific research finding—that is, when they want to know how big or meaningful an effect is—they typically calculate an **effect size.** Although there are many useful indicators of effect size, the two most commonly reported indicators of effect size are probably r and d. The statistic r is the familiar correlation coefficient, and thus you already have some practice at interpreting one frequently used indicator of effect size. Psychological effects that are considered small, medium, and large correspond respectively to correlations of about .10, .30, and .50. The less-familiar statistic d is more likely to be used to describe effect sizes from experiments or quasi-experiments because d is based on the difference between two treatment means. Specifically,

$$d = (\text{mean } 1 - \text{mean } 2)/\Delta$$

where Δ is simply the overall standard deviation of the dependent measure in the sample being studied (see Rosenthal & Rosnow, 1991, p. 302). Thus, d tells us *how different two means are in standard deviation units* (or fractions thereof). Because two means in a study can sometimes be more than one standard deviation apart, this means that d, unlike r, can sometimes be larger than 1. Otherwise, the interpretation of d is pretty similar to the interpretation of r. The respective values of d that correspond to small, medium, and large effects are about .20, .50, and .80 (see Rosenthal & Rosnow, 1991, p. 444).

Notice that we used the word "about" when we listed the specific values of r and d that correspond to different effect sizes. The reason we did so is that what makes an effect big or small is partly a judgment call. Moreover, how "big" an effect must be to qualify as meaningful varies quite a bit from one research area to another. If a cheap and easy-to-administer treatment (e.g., a daily vitamin C tablet) could reduce the risk of cancer and turned out to have a "small" effect size (e.g., $r = .10$ or less), this could easily translate into millions of saved dollars in medical expenses (and thousands of saved lives). Moreover, as you learned earlier, the size of an effect that researchers observe in a particular study is as much a function of how carefully the study is crafted as it is a function of the state of the world. Thus, considerations of effect size, like considerations of statistical significance, should reflect the theoretical or practical significance of a given finding—regardless of its absolute magnitude. If our easy-to-administer experimental treatment gets blood from only 10% of the turnips that we treat, we will have to consider the relative value of blood and turnips before deciding how meaningful the treatment is.

For many years, when researchers wanted to know how strongly two variables were related, they would compute a **coefficient of determination** by squaring the correlation associated with a particular effect. So if researchers learned, for example, that people's attitudes about a politician correlated .40 with whether people voted for that politician, the researchers might note that attitudes about candidates account for only 16% of the variance in voting behavior ($.40 \times .40 = .16$, or 16%). Although this is a technically accurate way of summarizing the association between two variables, some researchers have noted that it provides a misleading picture of the true strength of the relation between two variables. In particular, Rosenthal and Rubin (1982) developed the **binomial effect-size display** as a more intuitive way to illustrate the magnitude and practical importance of a correlation. The binomial effect-size display is referred to as binomial because it makes use of variables that can take on only two values (success or failure, survival or death, male or female) to illustrate effect sizes. As matters of convenience and simplicity, Rosenthal and Rubin demonstrate effect sizes using two dichotomous variables whose two values are equally likely. To simplify matters further, they express binomial effect sizes using samples in which exactly 100 people take on each of the two values of each of the two dichotomous variables.

Consider a hypothetical example involving attendance at a review session and performance on a difficult exam. Assume (a) that exactly 100 of 200 students attended the review session and (b) that exactly 100 of 200 students passed the exam. If we told you that the correlation between attending the review session and passing the exam was .20 (meaning that attendance at the review session accounts for only 4% of the variance in exam performance), you

TABLE 10.2 Performance on an exam as a function of attendance at a review session

Attendance at Review	Exam Performance		
	Passed	Failed	Total
Attended	60	40	100
Did not attend	40	60	100
Total	100	100	200

might not bother to attend the review session. However, if you examine the binomial effect-size display that appears in Table 10.2, you can see that a correlation of .20 corresponds to 20 more people passing than failing the exam in the group of attendees (and 20 more people failing than passing the exam in the group of nonattendees). *More generally, when summarized in a binomial effect-size display, a correlation coefficient corresponds to the difference in success rates that exists between two groups of interest on a dichotomous outcome.* If the correlation summarized in Table 10.2 had been .40, we would have seen that 70% of those attending the review (and only 30% of those failing to attend) passed the exam (70 – 30 = 40). Similarly, if we had observed a potential cookie thief for 200 days, if the person had been present in the kitchen for exactly 100 of the 200 days, and if cookies had disappeared on exactly 100 of the 200 days, then a correlation of .66 would mean that when the potential thief visited the kitchen, cookies disappeared on 83 out of 100 days (83 – 17 = 66). Even though the presence of this person accounts for only about 44% of the variance in cookie thefts ($.66^2 = .436$), notice that cookies are almost five times more likely to disappear when the person is present than when the person is absent ($.17 \times 5 = .85$). Notice also that the binomial effect-size display can be easily translated into the formula for r that was discussed in the exercise on partial correlation (r = matches – mismatches/n).

Regardless of what format researchers use to illustrate effect sizes, reporting effect sizes provides a very useful complement to traditional significance testing. For example, suppose we know that the effect size for a specific research finding corresponds to a d of .43. If a researcher claims that he failed to replicate this finding, it would be useful to consider the effect size the researcher observed (rather than focusing solely on his observed p-value) before concluding that his finding is different from the original (see Rosenthal & Rosnow, 1991, for a much more extensive discussion). In some cases, researchers have claimed that they failed to replicate findings when they observed effects that were just as large as those observed by previous researchers (e.g., when the second group of researchers had a much smaller sample than the first).

Meta-analysis

Estimates of effect size, such as r or d, provide a useful metric for describing and evaluating the magnitude of specific research findings. Regardless of how big a specific finding is, however, researchers are often interested in questions that have to do with the consistency or repeatability of the finding. Questions about the repeatability of a finding almost always have to do with a *group* of studies (and perhaps even an entire literature) rather than a single specific study. How many failed studies would have to exist to indicate that a set of findings is a statistical fluke rather than a bona fide phenomenon? If a phenomenon is bona fide, how consistently has it been observed from study to study? Even more important, what are the limiting conditions of the effect? That is, when is the effect most and least likely to be observed? Questions such as these can rarely be answered by any single study. Instead, researchers need systematic ways to summarize the findings of a *large number of studies*.

Fortunately, researchers have developed a special set of statistical techniques to summarize and evaluate entire sets of research findings. Not surprisingly, R. A. Fisher (1938) was one of the first researchers to address the question of how to combine the results of multiple studies. In the days since Fisher offered his preliminary suggestions, researchers have developed a wide array of techniques for summarizing and evaluating the results of multiple studies (see Rosenthal & Rosnow, 1991, for an excellent conceptual and computational review of such techniques). Statistical techniques that are designed for this purpose are typically referred to as *meta-analytic* techniques. The more commonly used term **meta-analysis** thus refers to the use of such techniques to analyze the results of studies rather than the responses of individual participants. From this perspective, meta-analyses are to groups of *studies* what traditional statistical analyses are to groups of specific *participants*. Literally, meta-analysis refers to the analysis of analyses.

Prior to the development of meta-analysis, the only way researchers could summarize the results of a large group of studies was to logically analyze and verbally summarize all the studies. Meta-analyses complement such potentially imprecise analyses by providing precise mathematical summaries of different aspects of a set of research findings. For example, a meta-analysis of effect sizes can provide a good estimate of the average effect size that has been observed in all the published studies on a specific topic. Other meta-analytic techniques can be used to indicate how much *variability* in effect sizes has been observed from study to study on a specific topic (see Hedges, 1987). Finally, meta-analysis can be used to determine the kinds of studies that tend to yield especially large or small effect sizes (e.g., studies that did or did not make use of a particular control technique, studies conducted during a particular historical era, studies conducted in a particular part of the country). This final kind of meta-analysis can provide very useful theoretical and methodological information about the nature of a specific research finding.

As an example of this third approach, consider a couple of meta-analyses conducted by Alice Eagly. Eagly (1978) analyzed findings from a large number of studies of the effects of gender on conformity and social influence. Many researchers had argued that women are more easily influenced than men are. When Eagly looked at studies published prior to 1970 (i.e., prior to the beginning of the women's movement), this is exactly what she found. However, when she focused on studies published during the heyday of the women's movement (during the early to mid-1970s) Eagly observed very little evidence that women were more easily influenced than men. Furthermore, in a second meta-analysis,

Eagly and Carli (1981) found that (a) the gender of the researcher conducting the study and (b) the specific influence topic under investigation were good predictors of whether women were more conforming than men. When studies were conducted by men or when the topic of influence was one with which women were likely to be unfamiliar, most studies showed that women were more conforming than men. However, when studies were conducted by women or when the topic of influence was one with which men were likely to be unfamiliar, men often proved to be more conforming than women.

Although meta-analysis may be used for many different purposes, the biggest contribution of meta-analysis to psychological research is probably an indirect one. The growing popularity of meta-analytic techniques has encouraged researchers to think about research findings in more sophisticated ways. Specifically, instead of treating alpha as an infallible litmus test for whether an effect is real, contemporary researchers are beginning to pay careful attention to the question of *when* a given effect is most (and least) likely to be observed. Ideally, when a meta-analysis suggests that an effect is magnified or diluted under certain conditions, researchers should conduct a study in which they directly manipulate these conditions. Doing so boils down to designing *factorial* studies in which at least two independent variables are completely crossed. As it turns out, then, researchers who have developed and promoted meta-analytic techniques have encouraged a perspective on research that is very similar to McGuire's contextualist perspective reviewed in Chapter 9. It is difficult to fault anyone for adopting this kind of sophisticated approach.

Notes

1. We adapted this example of men of varying heights from an illuminating statistics lecture by Daniel Gilbert.

2. Computing the probability of an event as extreme as *or more extreme than* an observed event (or set of events) is standard practice for most statistical tests. At first blush, paying attention to events even more extreme than an observed event may seem a little odd. However, if we care about events *as unusual as or more unusual than* our observed event—which we almost always do—it makes a lot of sense. If you think of the unusualness of a set of observations (e.g., a lot of heads tossed, a pair of means that are noticeably different) as a standard of experimental performance that a researcher hopes to meet or exceed, this may help make sense of this practice. If we set a high-jump bar at exactly 6 feet and Amanda clears it, the set of outcomes that Amanda, the judges, and the fans all care about is jumps of exactly 6 feet *or higher*. Furthermore, if we tried to calculate the probability of a specific observation or event, probabilities would almost always be pretty low—because the probability of any specific event is always quite low. For example, the probability of tossing a fair coin 20 times and observing *exactly* 10 heads is .176, even though this is the *most* likely of all the possible outcomes. Once we move to continuous rather than discrete events, this is even more true. The

probability that a particular high jump would be *exactly* 6 feet—even for a very good jumper who was trying to jump exactly 6 feet—is extremely low.

3. Speaking of cheating, we cheated. Unless we increased our sample size to about 250 people, we couldn't actually conduct this second χ^2 analysis. That's because we're allowed to use the χ^2 statistic only in situations in which all our expected frequencies have a value of at least 5.0. With values lower than five, the χ^2 values that are generated can be pretty unstable, and pretty inaccurate. In an extreme case such as this one, however, it's safe to say that people were significantly honest. If nothing else, we could always choose to make a very conservative comparison and set 90% (instead of 98%) dishonesty as our standard of comparison. This would yield 5 rather than 1 as the expected number of nonwinners. In case you want to practice your calculations, the value you should get if you do the analysis this more conservative (but legal) way is χ^2 (1, $N = 50$) = 272.22. The 1 in the parenthesis indicates the *degrees of freedom* you'd report in an actual research report in which you conducted this analysis. We'll come back to this in the section on reporting commonly used statistics.

Chapter 11

Telling the World About It

In this . . . chapter, there is nothing new to be said and it will not be possible to avoid repeating what has often been said before.
—Sigmund Freud
   (1962/1923)

One of the most gratifying aspects of the research process is publishing a research paper in a scholarly journal or giving a research talk to one's peers. Publishing papers and giving talks are public signs that the long weeks and months you have devoted to a research project were not spent in vain. Your work means something. In the case of a talk, someone invited you to tell other people about it. In the case of a publication, an editor and several expert reviewers voted to publish your work, and researchers in your area of investigation will presumably read about it. To focus on writing papers for the moment, we are also of the opinion that, even if you do not intend to publish a paper in a scholarly journal, the exercise of writing up a research report can be an inherently gratifying experience. Writing is a complex skill that most people can master only through great dedication and effort. We realize that this may sound a little like something your grandparents would tell you, but there is something inherently gratifying about mastering any complex skill.

The best metaphor we can offer for either writing research papers or giving academic talks is that these activities are a lot like juggling. First, there is almost no one who can honestly say that he or she wouldn't like to be able to do these things and do them well. Second, there are a few people who are so good at these activities that they can do them for a living. Third, for the most part, the people who do these things beautifully and make them look easy are those who have spent countless hours *practicing* these activities. Of course you can't entertain children at birthday parties by showing off your beautiful prose, but you can do equally important things like impressing the professors who provide your letters of reference for graduate school (or writing memos that your co-workers actually understand). From the perspective of this metaphor, the purpose of this chapter is to help beginning writers and speakers turn themselves into the literary equivalents of reasonably competent three-ball jugglers: people who don't make too many drops—and who don't hurt anyone along the way.

Like the introduction to Freud's *The Ego and the Id,* much of what we will say in this chapter has already been said before. Of course in Freud's case, he could at least take credit for having said it *himself* the first time. In contrast, many of the ideas that we will express in this chapter are borrowed from others. To be more specific, about two-thirds of this brief chapter deals with general points about writing empirical research papers and has been inspired heavily by Daryl Bem's (1987) excellent treatment of this topic. Most of what little we have added to Bem's analysis is simply a description of what we have observed among the best writers in social psychology and social cognition (including Bem). In keeping with the hands-on approach we have adopted in this text, we have supplemented this chapter on writing with an appendix that begins on page 361. This appendix contains the manuscript version of an entire APA-style research paper written by John Jost. The paper provides you with a complete model of what an APA-style paper looks like in draft form. More important, it also provides you with a complete model of clear, concise, scholarly, and provocative writing. We suspect that when you are composing your own research papers, you will find yourself referring to this manuscript much more often than you find yourself referring to this chapter. Incidentally, if you want to see what the manuscript would look like in published form, check out Jost (1997). The manuscript was published in 1997 in the *Psychology of Women Quarterly.* To complement both this sample paper and the first two-thirds of this chapter, we have also included a table in this chapter summarizing what goes into a good research paper.

The last third of this chapter consists of a discussion of how to give a good research talk in psychology. In the case of this discussion, we demoted ourselves from the role of inspired borrowers to the role of inspired typists. That is, instead of trying to give you advice about giving talks, we have simply provided you with a verbatim account of someone else's advice on giving talks. This advice comes in the form of an informal paper by Dan Gilbert, and the paper is included with his permission. As you will see, Gilbert has also contributed to this chapter in a second way: by providing an excellent example of someone who follows the rules of good writing. Finally, in Chapter 12, we address a very specific but important aspect of writing that is typically neglected in research methods texts—namely, how to report the results of some commonly used statistical tests. Because the material about reporting statistics is a little more technical, and challenging, than the material reported here, we have set this special discussion of writing aside as a brief chapter unto itself.

The Hourglass Approach to Empirical Research Papers

The most important thing you can know about writing an empirical research report is that the structure of the report should follow an *hourglass* form. In the Introduction to your paper, you should open broadly by asking a general question or making a general statement about people. You should work your way toward your specific research hypothesis by reviewing previous research and making a logical case for the study or set of studies that you will be reporting. In your Method and Results sections you should become still more specific. You should focus on the important details of your design and analysis, and you should stick very, very close to your data when interpreting your findings. Finally, in your General Discussion section, you should begin to broaden your scope by offering some theoretical and practical insights about what your findings mean (e.g., how they complement or invalidate the theories that you reviewed in your Introduction). Finally, you should end as broadly as you began, by summarizing the implications of your research in a very general way.

To see an hourglass approach at work, consider some excerpts from a paper by Gilbert, Krull, and Malone (1990). Gilbert et al. were interested in an idea that goes all the way back to the 17th century, when it was discussed by such luminaries as René Descartes (1644/1984) and Baruch Spinoza (1677/1982). The idea is a little slippery; it has to do with whether it is possible to *comprehend* something without briefly *believing* it (i.e., considering it to be true). Descartes considered it patently obvious that we can consider newly encountered ideas as abstract possibilities—that is, that we can represent ideas without reference to whether the ideas are true or false. Spinoza, on the other hand, believed that the act of *thinking about* something was tantamount to *thinking it so* (at least momentarily). Of course, Spinoza realized that we can identify what is true and what is false, but his position was that to consider an idea is *first* to accept it, and then to reject it if it proves to be unsupportable. Perhaps because their research problem began with Descartes, Gilbert et al. (1990) open their paper with a quotation from Descartes. Here is that quotation along with their first few sentences:

> That we have the power . . . to give or withhold our assent at will, is so evident that it must be counted among the first and most common notions that are innate in us.
>   —Descartes (1644/1984, p. 205)

> René Descartes was right about so many things that he surely deserved to be wrong about something: How people come to believe certain ideas and disbelieve others may be the something about which he was mistaken. Descartes insisted that ideas are initially represented in the mind without reference to their veracity. Thus, upon hearing the utterance "Armadillos may be lured from a thicket with soft cheese," Descartes suggested that the listener's mind simply held that proposition *in aequilibrio,* and only later submitted the proposition to a rational analysis by which it was determined to be true or false. . . .

After reviewing the basics of the Spinozan alternative to Descartes's hypothesis, Gilbert et al.'s report gradually becomes more specific. By the end of the introduction they report:

> The Spinozan hypothesis asserts that rejecting an idea requires the extra step of unaccepting or "tagging" a mental representation as false. If this is so, then people should initially accept both true and false ideas upon comprehension but, when the processing of the idea is interrupted, should not be able to go on and unaccept (or tag) false ideas. As such, interruption should cause Spinozan systems to mistake false ideas for true ones, but not vice versa.

After offering a competing description of mental representation suggested by Descartes's analysis, the authors become more specific still by reporting that:

> Study 1 was an initial attempt to test these competing predictions.

One paragraph later, the authors provide an overview of their first experiment:

> In the context of a language-learning experiment, subjects were presented with novel propositions on a computer screen. On most trials, subjects were subsequently informed that the preceding proposition was either true or false. On some of these trials, subjects' processing of the proposition was interrupted by having them quickly perform an unrelated task (namely, pushing a button in response to a tone). Finally, subjects were presented with the original propositions (in question form) and were asked to determine whether they were true or false.

The ensuing body of the Method section is even more detailed than this thumbnail sketch. It provides details about the research participants, the instructions, the procedure, and the dependent measures that would allow theoretical friends or foes to attempt an exact replication of their experiment. For example, because the authors presented their participants with some pretty unusual stimuli that had never been used in previous research (sentences like "A trica is a weasel," "A nasli is a snake," and "A suffa is a cloud"), they include all these stimuli in a table. The Results section is equally detailed, and equally concise. It provides a summary of the relevant findings in both verbal and graphical form, and briefly addresses some potential criticisms of the observed findings (which findings, by the way, supported the position of Spinoza rather than Descartes).

After providing equally precise descriptions of the methods and results of two additional experiments, the authors come to their General Discussion, where their language begins to take on the same broad form it took in the introduction. Instead of repeating the kind of specific statements they made in their Results sections ["Subjects responded much more rapidly on comprehension trials ($M = 1,336$ ms) than they did on assessment trials ($M = 1,899$ ms), $F(1, 28) = 65.9$, $p < .001$."], they quote Scottish philosophers, mention rhinoceroses, and discuss research in psycholinguistics—in much the same way that they had originally quoted Descartes, mentioned armadillos, and discussed research on automatic versus controlled information processing. After reiterating the basic theme of their report—that propositions are initially coded as true and must later be recoded as false when they prove to be logically untenable—they end their report as broadly as they began it:

> On occasion, of course, such attempts to recode false information will fail, and when this happens, a Spinozan system will find itself believing what it should not. This method of initially presenting ideas as true may be economical and it may be adaptive, but any system that uses it will err on the side of belief more often than doubt. That human beings are, in fact, more gullible than they are suspicious should probably "be counted among the first and most common notions that are innate in us."

In our usual style of taking back a little bit of what we have just told you, we should let you know that writers who have just been introduced to the hourglass approach often take this advice a bit *too* seriously. They open *too* broadly, they narrow too narrowly (especially in the Method section), and they close even more broadly than they opened. If your opening or closing paragraphs say anything about the origins of life on earth, the entire field of psychology, or even the entire field of interpersonal relationships, you may have overdone it. An intelligent reader who has read only your opening paragraph should be starting to get some idea of the exact research hypothesis you tested. An intelligent reader who has read only your closing paragraph should have about the same kind and amount of information. If these things are not the case, you need to become a little more focused. The litmus test for the right level of specificity in your Method section has already been provided above. A reader who wishes to replicate your study should be able to get all the information needed to do so by reading your Method section. However, the reader shouldn't be distracted by details that weren't an important part of your study. Unless you are studying the effects of paper color and survey length on people's survey responses, telling readers exactly how many pages were in your survey, or the color of paper on which it was printed, is likely to be distracting rather than enlightening. On the other hand, providing people with the exact phrases that anchored the endpoints of your dependent measure or telling them exactly what your confederate did to be annoying are both highly specific and highly relevant.

At the end of this chapter, we have provided a checklist of important things to include in a research paper. That checklist serves as a final reminder to organize research papers like an hourglass. If you do so, there is no guarantee that your paper will be as seamless as Gilbert et al.'s paper on Spinozan belief systems, but we can guarantee that it will be better than it otherwise would have been.

The Seven C's (and One G) of Good Research Papers

If you have crafted your paper in the design of an hourglass and you wish to polish your hourglass up a bit, there are still quite a few things you can do to improve the quality of your writing. In this section, we briefly summarize some of these things.

Rule 1: Be Correct

Reading an otherwise beautifully written paper that turns out to be filled with mistakes is like opening a beautiful silk purse and finding it stuffed full of sow's ears. Whether it is typographical, grammatical, or factual, any kind of error in a research paper is an embarrassing sign that the author hasn't done his or her homework (because part of an author's homework is double-checking his or her paper for errors). Misinterpreting or misquoting the work of another researcher is probably the most serious error a writer can make, because when writers do this they run the risk of embarrassing those they have miscited and those they have misled as well as themselves. Similarly, reporting a statistic incorrectly or getting a crucial result backward is an easy way either to lose credit with the instructor who is reading your assignment or to lose credibility with the colleagues who are reading your submission to a journal. After you have carefully proofread a draft of your paper once, the second-best way to avoid missing any further mistakes is to let the paper sit for a couple of days and to read it again. The *best* way is to show your carefully rewritten second or third draft to a friend or colleague who is willing to play the role of copy editor and identify the mistakes that you and your computer's spellcheck program never caught.

"Yes, Helen, get me the #@*!% employment agency again. And tell them I asked for ELVES, tiny little ELVES!"

Choose your words and check your spelling carefully. Seemingly small mistakes can sometimes lead to serious misunderstandings.

Rule 2: Be Clear

On the other hand, if you do prove to be wrong about something, the least you can do is to try to be clear about it. There is no greater virtue in writing than clarity. When an author's writing is not clear, most readers will take it as a sign that the writer's *thinking* isn't clear either. If your ideas are truly horrible, you may want to disguise them from others. Otherwise, you will want to write lucid prose that makes your ideas as compelling to others as they are to you. Although it is hard to give general advice about how to be clear, one thing that authors can try to do is to put themselves in the shoes of a person who is completely ignorant about everything that has to do with their research. This is difficult. Once you have thought long and hard about your research problem, it is hard to get back in touch with all the subtle but important things you didn't know before you started it. On the other hand, if you credit yourself with having a good imagination, try to imagine what an audience who has never seen your survey, your apparatus, or your laboratory will need to know to understand your study. And then tell them exactly what they need to know—as clearly as possible.

There are also things that you can do about your writing style to make it as clear as possible. One thing is to use *parallel constructions*. Just as parallel parking strategies are counterintuitive to most beginning drivers, parallel construction strategies are counterintuitive to most beginning writers. If you are wondering what parallel constructions are, you were just exposed to one in the last sentence. It was easy to write it, and it was easy to read it. There! You were just exposed to one again. We bet you're starting to notice them, and we bet you're starting to like them. Whenever you have to express two logically related ideas, the use of parallel constructions makes it easy for your reader to see whatever logical relation you are trying to point out. Opposites become clearly different. Similarities become clearly the same. As Bem (1987) noted:

> Inexperienced writers often substitute synonyms for recurring words and vary their sentence structure in the mistaken belief that this is more creative, stylish, and interesting. Instead of using repetition and parallel construction, as in "Men may be more expressive than women in the domain of negative emotion, but they are not more expressive in the domain of positive emotion," they attempt to be more creative: "Men may be more expressive than women in the domain of negative emotion, but it is not true that they are more willing and able to display the more cheerful affects." Such creativity is hardly more interesting but it is certainly more confusing.
>
> If you have developed the bad habit of avoiding parallel constructions in your writing and you don't know how to break it, consider writing the way you speak. Spoken language has to be produced and comprehended on the fly, and for this reason we often speak using parallel constructions. We say things like "I love him a lot, but I don't like him very much." Similarly, our friends and grandparents express their sympathy for our situation by reminding us that "You can't live with 'em, and you can't live without 'em." Anyone who says "I love him a lot, but my level of liking for him is definitely on the low side" runs the risk of slowing down the conversation. Anyone who responds with "You can't live with 'em, and yet it's pragmatically and emotionally untenable to go about your life in their absence" runs the risk of

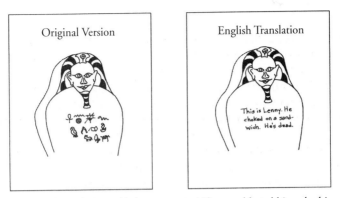

Maybe hieroglyphics wouldn't seem so cool if we could read hieroglyphics.

Some writers couch their meanings in obscure language, perhaps on the assumption that it's hard for readers to criticize what they can't understand. Avoid this temptation. If you're going to be wrong, at least be clear about it.

bringing the conversation to a screeching halt. If you want to be a good scientific writer, you can't live without parallel constructions.

A final thing most writers can do to improve the clarity of their research reports is to avoid the use of abbreviations, jargon, and grandiose ideophones (big words). Abbreviations save space, but they can lead to confusion. Because many readers consume papers in bits and pieces, they may have forgotten, by the time they get to the second half of your paper, whether your AA and AAA conditions had to do with battery sizes or alcoholism and motor vehicle clubs. Even when you use commonly understood (and thus acceptable) abbreviations, you should define them the first time you use them. In an empirical research paper, the first time readers learn that your participants are from UCLA or USC, they should learn it in parenthesis: "Participants were 20 undergraduates enrolled in an advanced juggling workshop at the University of California, Los Angeles (UCLA)." Similarly, the first time you reveal that you conducted an ANOVA, you should describe it as "an analysis of variance (ANOVA)." Once you have done this, you are free to use the abbreviation throughout the rest of your paper. For similar reasons, technical jargon should be used only when it clarifies rather than mystifies. Whenever technical but potentially unfamiliar terms do impart a more precise meaning than informal terms, you should use them but make sure to define them the first time they come up: "In this report, we focus on *implicit self-regard,* that is, on people's overlearned—and presumably unconscious—positive and negative evaluations of themselves."

Rule 3: Be Comprehensive

This rule is closely related to the rule about being correct, but it refers mainly to errors of omission rather than errors of commission. It's very important not to omit important results, to discuss your manipulation checks if you had any, and to include the references for all the work you cite. Including all your references is so important that when copy editors are proofreading an accepted paper to get it ready for publication, they go through the entire paper, marking and numbering every reference in the paper and cross-checking it against the reference list. Of course, you won't have that kind of assistance before you submit your paper for consideration in the first place, and so you should do the same kind of thing yourself. When we have read drafts of papers that were not yet published, we have occasionally become pretty upset at the authors for citing and describing a really interesting study and failing to include the citation in the reference list.

This rule also applies to theoretical comprehensiveness. Unless you are already a true expert in the area of your paper topic, you should probably perform a literature search (or update your old one) before you even begin to compose your paper. Although you do not need to cite everything that has ever been done on your topic, there will usually be a number of previously published papers that truly paved the way for your own thinking and research. You should make sure that you cite these—not only to help tell a coherent story but also to give credit where credit is due.

Rule 4: Be Coherent

Speaking of telling a coherent story, failing to do so is probably the most common shortcoming we have observed in the papers of inexperienced writers. Our smartest and hardest-working graduate students sometimes have the same problem. We have each struggled many times with this problem, and we suspect that even the most gifted and experienced writers often struggle with finding the best possible organizational scheme for their papers. If it is a struggle, it is one that is well worth the effort. Unfortunately, we can only give you a little bit of concrete advice about how to be coherent. Using the hourglass model is a good start. Using headings to identify and organize your major ideas is a good second step. However, writing coherently on a line-by-line, paragraph-by-paragraph, section-by-section basis is a skill that is best learned by observing other writers who do it well—and by practicing it yourself.

The only other additional piece of advice we can offer about coherence is to make sure that you engage in *telling* rather than *listing*. Papers that are otherwise competent but lacking in coherence often read like a list of previous findings instead of the story of an idea. Dr. Snittle's study is summarized beautifully in paragraph three, and Dr. Nettle's study is summarized beautifully in paragraph four, but the two studies are described as if they existed in isolation. They don't. If an author is citing both studies, he or she must have some reason for thinking the two studies are related. If the studies (or areas of research) that you review build upon one another by representing successive approximations to your hypothesis, arrange them in an order that brings you progressively closer to your hypothesis. In addition, describe the studies and ideas that you review from the unique vantage point that is provided by your own particular research hypothesis. If you tell a meaningful story that leads readers to your hypothesis, and if you put up headings along the way to your hypothesis (to let your readers know what is coming next), your readers will be able to navigate your paper well, and they may even enjoy the journey.

Rule 5: Be Concise

When the first author of this text was an undergraduate, he was selected for an award that meant he not only got his photo printed in the college year-book but was also allowed to include a statement regarding his philosophy of life, school, or anything else he wanted to write about. He wrote a *very long* essay. To make matters worse, it wasn't very coherent, and it certainly wasn't very concise. Beneath the essay, there was a photo of this person dressed in some bizarre clothing that presumably complemented his obtuse points about communicating with other people, marching to the beat of a different drum-mer, and walking the fine line between genius and mental illness. If he had followed the example of some of the people who had won the award before he did, he probably would have written a very different essay. A year or so before he graduated, his college yearbook included a photo of T. Mack Brown, wearing a suit and tie, and making a much subtler point about how to communicate with people. His essay was much shorter than the first author's. The essay was so inspiring that the first author committed it to mem-ory. The essay read as follows:

> Be concise. Don't bore people.

Being concise is another tricky aspect of good writing. It can be hard to be concise without sacrificing clarity, correctness, or comprehensiveness. Nonetheless, the solution to the problem is pretty straightforward. As Bem (1987) put it, "Omit needless words." This will often mean writing and rewrit-ing a passage until you have squeezed the maximum meaning out of every word. Consider what Bem had to say about the importance of being concise:

> Virtually all experienced writers agree that any written expression that deserves to be called *vigorous writing,* whether it is a short story, an article for a professional journal, or a complete book, *is* characterized by the attribute of being succinct, *concise,* and to the point. *A sentence*—no matter where in the writing it occurs—*should contain no unnecessary* or superfluous *words,* words that stand in the way of the writer's direct expression of his or her meaning and purpose. In a very similar fashion, *a paragraph*—the basic unit of organization in English prose—should contain *no unnecessary* or superfluous *sentences,* sentences that introduce peripheral content into the writing or stray from its basic narrative line. It is in this sense that a writer is like an artist executing a drawing, and it is in this sense that a writer is like an engineer designing a machine. Good writing should be economical *for the same reason that a drawing should have no unnecessary lines, and* good writing should be streamlined in the same way that *a machine* is designed to have *no unnecessary parts,* parts that contribute little or nothing to its intended function.
>
> *This* prescription to be succinct and concise is often misunderstood, and *requires* judicious application. It certainly does *not* imply *that the writer* must *make all* of *his* or her *sentences short* or choppy *or* leave out all adjectives,

adverbs, and qualifiers. Nor does it mean *that he* or she must *avoid* or eliminate *all detail* from the writing *and treat his* or her *subjects only in* the barest skeleton or *outline* form. *But* the requirement does imply *that every word* committed to paper should *tell* something new to the reader and contribute in a significant and non-redundant way to the message that the writer is trying to convey.

Bem then asks the reader to take the advice offered in this essay and to omit all the nonitalicized words. The result is an original remark by Strunk and White (1979), through which Bem intentionally wove his much longer statement:

> Vigorous writing is concise. A sentence should contain no unnecessary words, a paragraph no unnecessary sentences, for the same reason that a drawing should have no unnecessary lines and a machine no unnecessary parts. This requires not that the writer make all his sentences short, or that he avoid all detail and treat his subjects only in outline, but that every word tell.

If you would like to see an example of concise writing in *research* (as well as another example of the hourglass model), we will spare you the wordier version and take you directly to the opening and closing paragraphs of a paper by Swann, Stein-Seroussi, and Giesler (1992). The paper is succinctly entitled "Why People Self-Verify."

> Nearly half a century ago, Prescott Lecky (1945) proposed that people strive to confirm their self-conceptions, even if those self-conceptions are negative. Over the years, his proposal has provoked considerable controversy. Initially, critics questioned the assumption that self-confirmation strivings were powerful enough to override a desire for positive, self-enhancing information. Their skepticism grew stronger when the first widely cited study to support Lecky's claim (Aronson & Carlsmith, 1962) proved difficult to replicate (for reviews, see Dipboye, 1977; Shrauger, 1975). By the mid-1970s, even those who sympathized with Lecky reluctantly concluded that his hypothesis referred to a relatively circumscribed phenomenon (e.g., Shrauger, 1975).

In the next paragraph, Swann et al. discuss how the tables have begun to turn, and they review research suggesting that people *will* sometimes forgo positive feedback out of a concern for self-confirmation. They then discuss the results of two studies designed to figure out *why* people engage in self-confirmation. They end their paper with a paragraph even more concise (and just as broad) as their opening paragraph:

> Our findings therefore bring us closer to understanding the phenomenon that Prescott Lecky (1945) introduced so long ago: the tendency for people with negative self-views to embrace the very persons who think poorly of them. Apparently, people enact such paradoxical behaviors because negative evaluations bolster their perception that their social worlds are predictable and controllable. From this vantage point, people go to great lengths to maintain the perception that they are in touch with social reality, however harsh that reality might be.

Enough said. Be concise: Don't run on and on about being concise.

Rule 6: Be Cautious

Caution is not always a desirable quality in writing. A cautious romantic adventure is probably a bad romantic adventure. However, caution in scientific writing is a very desirable feature. This applies both to the kind of logical leaps you expect readers to make to get to your research hypothesis and to the kind of interpretations you expect readers to accept for your research findings. If there is little or no previous support for your hypothesis, say so in your introduction. If your findings provide only partial support for your hypothesis, say this as well—before your critics do. This doesn't mean selling yourself short or downplaying what is important about your research. Instead, it means expressing your excitement about your findings while sticking to the rules of careful interpretation. If you have demonstrated a significant amount of cheating in a context in which this has never been previously demonstrated, point out that you also observed significant levels of honesty—and if it is possible to do so, document this alternate perspective with a statistical analysis. In your General Discussion make sure to say something about the important practical and theoretical implications of your findings. But make sure to say something about their practical and theoretical limitations as well.

If it is appropriate to do so, offer some speculations about what your findings tell us about models of moral development, but make it clear that your speculations are just that (and await empirical scrutiny). Most important, do not conclude your paper with any grandiose statements about whether people are inherently good or evil. That is an appropriate debate to have over lunch with the other members of your lab group, but it strays too far from your data to make its way into your written research report. We know of some pretty good examples of a researcher who has occasionally violated this rule by drawing sweeping conclusions in his General Discussion section. Understandably, however, this researcher was unwilling to allow us to quote the offenses directly. If you want to find them yourself, you'll have to track down the actual papers (Pelham, 1991b, is a good place to start).

Rule 7: Be Creative

Like conciseness, humor and flair can add vigor to otherwise mundane writing. Thus it's good to allow yourself a little creative license in your writing. At the same time, being creative is merely the icing on the cake, and icing is a poor substitute for cake itself. Worry hard about the other important points we have summarized here before you worry at all about being creative. And once you do get around to worrying about creativity, remember that the amount of creative license you can give yourself will be determined in part by the kind of paper you are writing. Each of us, especially the first author, has a somewhat rambunctious writing style, and thus we often have to keep some of our wackier tendencies in check. In fact, one of the things that we have both enjoyed about writing this book is that doing so has allowed us to be a little more playful than we could risk being in an empirical research paper. Be creative, but know both yourself and your audience—so that your creative juices don't get the better of you.

Rule 8: Be Gender-Neutral

The final rule of good writing in research is more like an ironclad law than a rule. The American Psychological Association (APA) has clearly dictated that writers must avoid the use of sexist language. If you send an editor a paper in which you use the generic masculine "he" to mean people in general rather than one of your 43 male participants, the editor may very well send it back to you and ask you to correct your mistake before reviewing it. At the very least, you will be embarrassed when the three female and two male reviewers of your paper all comment on your use of sexist language. For reasons such as this, we have tried to use gender-neutral language throughout this book. In addition to resorting to an occasional use of "he or she" (e.g., "If an author is citing both studies, he or she must have some reason for thinking the two studies are related"), we have usually tried to solve this problem more elegantly by speaking of people in the plural whenever possible, as in "According to Aristotle, just as people with thick necks were strong in character and fierce tempered (like bulls), people with long, thin necks were backward and cowardly, like deer." Of course, if you are quoting someone verbatim or if you really are *just* talking about men, women, or a particular man or woman, it is perfectly appropriate to use gender-specific pronouns. Thus, instead of correcting Aristotle's gender-biased language, we quoted him verbatim (through his translators). Thus we wrote, "Similarly, it seemed self-evident to Aristotle that 'men with small *ears* have the disposition of monkeys' and that 'those with large ears [have] the disposition of asses.'"

Although it may not be an explicit part of the APA's publication guidelines, most researchers agree that the rule about not being sexist also extends to not being racist, classist, fascist, or *hetero*sexist. For example, when we were writing about how a person might choose a date from a pool of men who did or did not vary enormously in their heights, we asked you to "suppose you were a heterosexual woman of average height, and you needed to choose a blind date by drawing names from one of two hats." We needed our example of women choosing male dates to make a point about variability, but we didn't need to assume that *all* women always choose male dates. Of course, we could have been even more explicitly nonheterosexist by explicitly specifying that the men in the two groups all happened to be heterosexual, but we assumed that one reminder about sexual orientation was enough to make the point.

That's it. We don't have a lot more to say about how to write good empirical research papers. To summarize the basic structure of empirical research papers, and to remind you of some of the important things that should always be included in research papers, we have created a checklist of important things to include in empirical research papers. This checklist appears in Table 11.1. Although this checklist should cap off much of what we have said about writing, we should add that writing good papers is not the end of the story when it comes to communicating with your fellow researchers. Giving good talks is

TABLE 11.1   A checklist of concerns for empirical research papers

I. Introduction

    A. Abstract: Does it provide a clear and simple summary of the study?

    B. Justification of Hypotheses: Do readers know why the study is being done and what it will tell us?

    C. Explication of Hypotheses: Do readers know exactly what you expect to find (or find out) in the study?

II. Method

    A. Participants: Is the sample identified and described correctly?

    B. Materials and Procedure: Are the procedure and design of the study clear?

    C. Dependent Measures: Is it clear exactly what they were and how they were worded?

    D. Control Procedures: Are any special control procedures discussed appropriately? Examples: random assignment, experimenters/participants kept blind to hypothesis, anonymity of responses, counterbalancing in within-subjects designs.

III. Results

    A. Statistical Tests: Are the statistical tests (e.g., ANOVAS, correlations, etc.) described correctly?

    B. Results: Are the correct results reported (including results for any manipulation checks)?

    C. Interpretations: Are the findings interpreted correctly?

IV. Discussion

    A. Limitations, Clarifications, and/or Interpretations of Results: Are they discussed?

    B. Practical Implications of Results: If appropriate, are they discussed?

    C. Theoretical Implications of Results: Are they discussed?

V. Paper as a Whole

    A. Coherence: Are the arguments developed in a logical, orderly fashion?

    B. Clarity: Is the writing clear?

    C. Conciseness: Could you have said the same thing in fewer words?

also an extremely important skill that most researchers have to use on a pretty frequent basis. Finally, although there is obviously some overlap between writing and speaking, the two are more distinct than many people realize. With this in mind, savor the advice of someone who has learned to do both of these things extremely well.

How to Give a Good Talk in Psychology (by Daniel T. Gilbert)

Gilbert wrote this guide for people who were preparing to give a 45- to 50-minute job talk or invited colloquium. Obviously, you will need to adjust the time periods of different aspects of the talk to match the amount of time you have for *your* talk. For example, Gilbert indicates that you should be talking about your specific research hypotheses within the first 10 minutes of a 50-minute talk. In the case of a 15-minute talk, for example, this would roughly translate into talking about your specific hypotheses within the first 3 minutes.

Have a Plan

Nothing else is as important as having a cohesive organizational plan in which one point leads naturally to another. Usually this begins with (1) some background about the area of research, which leads into (2) background on the specific hypothesis, which leads into (3) the specific research question you want to address, which leads into (4) the procedures you followed, which leads into (5) your findings, which leads into (6) their interpretation, which leads into (7) the relevance of your findings for the problem you are addressing, which leads into (8) implications for "the big picture." In addition, each of these sections must be logically organized in and of itself. A logical argument is the basis for communicating with your audience. If you don't have one (a logical argument) you won't have one (an audience). Write your plan in (at least) outline form, and use these notes during your talk. If you must, you can write the talk out word for word. If you must have a canned talk, memorize it! Then use your notes as a prop. Ultimately, reading a talk is better than giving a terrible talk—but only a little better.

Tell the Plan

It is often useful to give listeners a road map for the terrain you wish to cover. Tell them the organizational plan in just a sentence or two. For example:

> I'd like to talk today about the effects of alcohol on reasoning; specifically, how alcohol enhances some cognitive performances and impairs others. I'll start with some general background information about research in this area, and then I'll present to you some research that professor Snorkwerth and I have conducted on alcohol use and motor performance. Finally, I'll try to show you how this research addresses the important question of whether motor systems can function independently.

On occasion, you may wish to use suspense, and thus this "tell the plan" heuristic will be inappropriate. Generally, however, you should forego suspense in favor of comprehension. Also, you should use speech markers as transitions to tell your audience where you currently are in the organizational plan (e.g., "Having briefly outlined the past research in this area, let me now turn to the experiment that we recently conducted . . .").

Start at the Beginning

Every study is part of a long story that begins with an idea by Aristotle. There are two things you can do wrong in choosing a point in the story at which to begin your talk.

First, you can start *too late*. You have started too late if you are not talking about your specific hypotheses within 10 minutes. You are starting too late if you mention Aristotle anytime after the first sentence. You must know the audience and try to figure out what they already know. You can refresh their memories *briefly*, but get to the point as quickly as your audience's knowledge will allow.

Second, you can start *too early*. You have started too early if your first sentence has anything to do with an experimental manipulation (or any other aspect of your method). An introduction sets the stage and explains *why* you did the study you did. Don't say "I did an experiment on alcohol and reasoning because alcohol abuse is a real problem in society," but say:

> For centuries, people have been using substances that affect their ability to think, feel, and act. Alcohol is one such substance. Yet we still don't know precisely how alcohol affects performance . . .

Don't relate the entire history of psychology, but don't act as though there were no history. Even if your study is completely novel and revolutionary, you must tie it into something your audience already knows and cares about. The introduction of a talk locates your work in the body of other work.

Before you can tell what you did, you must tell why. You must make the audience realize that your study is potentially an important one. You must intrigue them by showing the hole in the body of knowledge that your study serves to fill. It is wrong to assume that everyone shares your interests or that any study is worth doing. In the introduction, you must impress your audience with what needs to be done (and later you'll impress them even more by having done it). Thus, a rationale like "Emotions are important because everybody has them" does little to make the audience ready for your contribution. On the other hand, you might intrigue the audience with something like:

> Emotions lie at the heart of social behavior—from altruism to aggression, the emotions we feel compel us to act toward each other in a variety of ways. Yet very little is known about the physiological basis of emotion . . .

You must have had a reason for doing the research you want to talk about, so tell the audience what it was in the most interesting way possible.

Be Painfully Clear

Once you are talking about your study, you should strive for three things: clarity, clarity, and clarity. Nothing matters if the audience doesn't understand what you did and why. A few points to remember:

1. When you describe your study, explain first what *conceptual* variables you examined: "To test this hypothesis, we manipulated the anxiety level of our participants." Only then should you explain the *operational* variables:

> We did this by exposing half of our participants to an uncaged lion. These participants were in the "high anxiety" group. We exposed the other participants to an uncaged rabbit. These participants were in the "low anxiety" group.

2. Be redundant. Say the same thing several different times in different ways. Be repetitive. Remember that your audience cannot process your speech nearly as well as they can process your writing because they cannot go back and reread something you have said and because they cannot listen at their own pace. Any important point should be stated twice:

> We think alcohol impairs some cognitive processes but not others. More specifically, whereas some performances suffer after alcohol consumption, others actually benefit.

3. It is generally unprofessional to say "Is all of this clear so far?"—but it is better to do this than to lose the audience. If you think the audience is lost, you can ask. But ask someone whom you expect to tell you the truth. Most audience members will be too embarrassed to tell you that they are lost, but they will look around, exchange glances, and make you feel foolish.

4. Make use of visual aids (e.g., a drawing of your 2×2 design). A picture is worth 1,234 words. Supplement your speech with pictures. But remember that a complicated picture is worthless and causes the audience to stop listening to you while they figure out your picture. Thus, when you use a picture, use a *simple* one with *big* letters. Also, give the audience a moment to read all of the words on a slide before you start talking again; otherwise, they may miss what you're saying as they scrutinize the slide. Remember also to get rid of a slide when you're done with it. It can prove distracting when left up too long. Last, you should note that handouts are usually a bad idea, because you cannot determine where the audience will focus their attention at any given time. People always look ahead with handouts, and may miss your preliminary comments while they peruse the handout. Use slides or overhead transparencies instead.

5. Present data kindly. If you must present a lot of data, present each piece separately on a different slide. Nothing is worse than a slide full of numbers. Use figures instead of tables wherever possible. Present the most important data first! Don't present the manipulation checks first unless it is absolutely necessary to your argument. What the audience wants to know is "Did your study support your primary hypothesis?" So answer this question before they start asking "Can I go home yet?"

6. Take the audience's perspective. This is true in every facet of the talk. Try to see your ideas as a naive audience member would. Of course, *you* know that exposure to lions is a way of manipulating anxiety, but does the audience? If not, did you say it? Don't leave anything important unsaid. The best way to get the audience's perspective is to get a practice audience (intimate others and friends are traditional victims) and give your talk to them. Did they follow? You shouldn't have to be a psychologist to understand the talk; any reasonably bright person should follow it. Address your talk to a bright colleague in the art history department. And listen to the practice audience's advice! Think about this: When listeners tell you that something is confusing, they are always, by definition, correct.

Talk About One Interesting Thing

A good talk must have substance. You can't give a great talk on a dull, stupid, or boring idea. However, the converse is not necessarily true. A brilliant and exciting idea can easily be the topic of a very bad talk. Thus, the first rule for giving a good talk is "Have something interesting to say." In his *Rules for Writing,* M. Polya added an important second rule: "Have something to say. If by chance you have two things to say, control yourself." A talk must have a central theme—people can handle one major idea per talk. Ask yourself: "What is the major, take-home point here?" That is, what is the one-sentence summary that you hope a listener will give to his or her friends when they ask "What was the talk you heard today about?" Of course your study has complexities and nuances of great beauty. Go home and write a poem about them. But give your audience one and only one message, and give it clearly.

Talking clearly means not doing certain stylistic things that distract your audience. Do you pace? Chain yourself to a chair. Do you say "uh" between every sentence? Get therapy. Do you touch your nose or your chin all the time? Cut off your hand. All of these things can be very distracting, because when you are anxious you will do them very fast. As a result, you will not pace in a relaxed and professional manner; you will actually run from one end of the room to the other. (A note on pacing: If you pace you will often find that you need to look at your notes and that they are on a different side of the room than you are.) To find out what annoying stylistic nuances you have, videotape yourself.

Humor can be useful. A light remark puts the audience at ease and shows them that you are relaxed and confident. However, too much humor is probably worse than none at all. People will only consider your work to be as serious as you seem to think it is. If you think of it as a big joke, they will come to agree with you. In addition, nothing is worse than a joke that just doesn't cut it. Here's a good rule: If you don't know how much humor is too much, don't use humor. Not everyone can or should. And never, under any circumstances, tell a long joke that sidetracks you.

Take Charge of the Interaction

This is *your* talk. Don't let someone else take control of it by forcing you to deviate from your organizational plan. If someone requires clarification ("Were the anxious people ever eaten by the lion?"), then answer them briefly and continue. If someone wants to argue philosophy ("But don't you think psychology errs when it thinks of people as real?"), don't take the bait. Audience members may try to throw you off track, and you must not let them—but you must stop them with tact. Anyone can say "Shut up please, I'm trying to give a talk here." But the expert can say this *in other words* and still maintain an air of confidence and professionalism. A good standby is something like:

> That's an interesting question to which I've given much thought. I'll be addressing just that issue in a few minutes, but if I don't answer your question, please remind me at the end of the talk.

Of course, you better damn well be prepared to answer it at the end of the talk. If you can't even understand the question, you can always resort to something like:

> To be honest, I'm not quite sure I see the full implications of what you've said, but if I'm going to cover all the ground that I've set out to cover, I think I'd best delay a discussion of that until later.

You may be scared to interrupt a questioner who is persistent, but remember what Ann Landers would say: The interrupting questioner is acting impolitely. You have every right to get the exchange back on track by taking charge. In fact, you *owe* it to the rest of the audience who have come to hear *you,* not the questioner.

Novices often make the mistake of agreeing with criticisms they can't understand, because they think they will look foolish otherwise, and they think that the questioner will get off their backs if they just agree with him or her. By no means should you verbally agree with any critic unless you really understand her or his point and agree with it. If you do, you will find yourself backed into a corner later on ("But earlier you agreed when I said people weren't real, so how can you maintain that your data tell us anything about people?").

Novices often make the opposite mistake: They are sometimes too defensive. If a person attacks your study, she or he is not attacking you. If people have a valid criticism of a bad (or a good) study, your refusal to acknowledge their point will make you look both stupid and immature. If you acknowledge their point, you'll just look stupid. The best way to avoid damning criticisms is by letting others hear your talk first. Let a practice audience member (who loves and adores you) find the weaknesses in your argument, and then repair them before you speak in front of people who don't even love you a little. This is another benefit of writing an organizational plan (see "Have a Plan"). When you try to write your argument, you will see most of the flaws in your own logic. Better you than your audience.

End at the End

The same sins that pertain to starting also pertain to ending. You have ended too soon if, after presenting your results, you say "So that's what we found. Any questions?" You must summarize in two steps: First, summarize your findings (e.g., "So these data show that people who are made anxious tend to show substantially more interest in sex than do people who are not made anxious . . ."). Second, show the meaning of your findings for the "big picture" (e.g., "Theorists have always construed anxiety as a deficit, but our findings show that it can indeed have positive consequences . . ."). Finally, it is nice if you can point out what other provocative questions your findings suggest (e.g., "It would be interesting to know if the anxious person's increased *interest* in sex is accompanied by an increased ability to *perform.* We have several field studies in the works that attempt to show . . .").

You have ended your talk too late if (1) the clock tells you so, (2) the audience is yawning, or (3) you are spinning your wheels. Part of being a good teacher is knowing how to pace yourself, and at a job talk, people will be watching to see if you can end on time. If you have a one-hour talk, plan a 45-minute presentation. If you run over your limit by more than 10 minutes, look for another job. In any context, a verbose speaker may lose all the points he or she has won by going on and on and on and on. Don't leave the audience with a "bored taste in their mouths"—even if the talk was good, all good things must come to an end. So make your point, make it clearly, show why it's important, and shut the hell up. Like this.

Chapter 12

How to Describe the Results of Statistical Analyses

Although we hope that Chapter 11 provided you with some useful information about writing empirical research papers, it is missing a very important category of information. This is information about how to write the trickiest and most unfamiliar part of a research report—namely, reporting statistical analyses. If there is anything harder than understanding the ins and outs of statistics, it is knowing how to describe them in written research reports. We find that even students who understand a particular statistic perfectly well often have little idea how to describe the outcome of the statistical analysis in a research paper. When we have learned all about a new statistical test—because we have needed to use it in our research—we may still find ourselves at a loss when we have to write about it for the first time in a research paper. With this in mind, we have devoted this chapter to a discussion of how to report some commonly used statistics.

The particular statistics that a researcher uses to summarize and analyze his or her data are dictated partly by the designs the researcher has adopted (e.g., whether it's a within- or a between-subjects design), partly by the kind of measurement scale the researcher has used (e.g., whether it's a nominal or an interval scale), and partly by the particular question the researcher wants to answer about the data (e.g., whether a particular scale is internally consistent or whether two means are significantly different from one another). In an effort to facilitate direct comparisons between different statistical tests (and how they are reported), we will report the results of some fictional statistical tests that were all conducted to address some aspect of the *same* basic research question: a question about mysterious colorful spheres. Finally, although this is primarily a chapter about reporting statistics, a secondary goal here is to provide you with a fictional example of how different research techniques may be brought to bear on the same basic research question.

The Mysterious Spheres

Imagine that you are relaxing in front of the TV and have your favorite program interrupted by a special news bulletin. A newscaster reports that several dozen strange, colorful spheres have appeared here and there throughout the city. The spheres aren't very big; they range in diameter from about 4 to 10 inches (in fact, careful descriptive studies eventually reveal that the spheres are normally distributed in size, with an average diameter of exactly 7 inches and a standard deviation of exactly 1 inch—meaning that exactly 99.74% of them are between 4 and 10 inches in diameter). However, the spheres are getting a lot of attention. Early speculations about the origin of the spheres range from theories about government conspiracies or alien invasions to theories that the spheres are simply a large-scale practical joke. You eventually learn that the spheres have made sporadic appearances across the country and possibly across the globe.

The strange spheres are collected and analyzed by dozens of experts ranging from military experts and bomb-squad specialists to physicists, chemists, and electrical engineers. The spheres are a scientific mystery. It is impossible to determine their mass because they defy gravity, always hovering a few inches above the ground. Most interesting, and perhaps most disturbing, the spheres are completely indestructible. They defy all attempts to bend, break, crush, or otherwise reshape them, and they cannot be taken apart. They also cannot be x-rayed, sonographed, magnetically imaged, thermoscanned, or otherwise analyzed internally. In short, no one has a clue about what's up with the spheres. The spheres also happen to be completely immovable, which makes them a bit of a hazard when they settle down in places such as airport runways and major freeways. The only thing that is certain about the spheres is (1) that they come with equal frequency in two colors (green and yellow) and (2) that they appear to have a strange influence on human behavior.

Study 1: The Murder Rate Study

Although everyone agrees that the spheres have a strange influence on human behavior, no one can seem to agree on exactly what this influence is. One of the first clues comes from a team of applied social psychologists who conducted a large-scale *archival study* of the influence of the spheres. The study compared police reports of murders in two large American cities known to have had nearly identical murder rates prior to the arrival of the spheres. Importantly, the researchers noted that it happens to have been the case that a preponderance of spheres of a *particular color* landed in each of the two cities. In one city a disproportionate number of *green* spheres fell (86% to be precise), and in the second city a disproportionate number of *yellow* spheres fell (83% to be equally precise). The researchers examined murder rates in the two cities as a function of the color of the spheres that predominated in each particular city. Because murders are categorical events (either a murder occurs or it doesn't), the researchers simply counted up the murders in each city during a one-year period and checked this number against the official population of each city. This gave them an estimate of the number of people who had and had not committed a murder in each city in a given year. This got a little tricky, by the way, because it is possible that some people were responsible for more than one murder in a given year. (If 20 murders occurred, that doesn't guarantee that 20 different people committed murder. In principle, a single person could have committed them all.) However, the researchers addressed this critique very carefully in a footnote—a footnote that we will conveniently ignore.

Without getting too enmeshed in the researchers' exact methods, notice that their dependent measure is a *categorical* variable. That means their study is a good candidate for a χ^2 analysis (similar to, but a bit more complex than, the one we did with the Ping-Pong balls). With this in mind, let's take a look at some hypothetical results (depicted in Table 12.1) and see how the researchers might have described them in the Results section of their groundbreaking paper.[1]

> Our findings revealed a clear and significant association between city status and observed murder rates over the one-year period. As suggested by the pattern of observed and expected frequencies that appear in Table 12.1, murders were not equally distributed between the two cities, χ^2 (1, $N = 3,000,000$) = 21.34, $p < .001$, equivalent $\phi^2 = .00267$. In the absence of any differences associated with the spheres, we would have expected exactly twice the number of murders in the city in which most of the spheres were green. Instead, we observed that the number of murders committed in this city was more than eight times as high as the number of murders committed in the city in which most of the spheres were yellow. It is possible that green spheres act as a green light to murder.

There are several things to note about this description. First of all, notice that the statistics took a backseat to the verbal description of what was going on. The information about the χ^2 test is extremely important. Without it, we don't know whether to make much of the observed differences. As important

TABLE 12.1   Estimated number of people who did and did not commit murder in a 1-year period in 2 cities with previously comparable murder rates

	Predominant Color of Spheres Observed	
	Green	Yellow
Murderers	83	10
	(62)	(31)
Nonmurderers	1,999,917	999,990
	(1,999,938)	(999,969)

Note: Expected frequencies appear in parentheses below observed frequencies. Despite the assumption of identical murder rates, the expected numbers of murders differed for the two cities because the population of the "green" city was twice that of the "yellow" city.

as it is, however, it is not nearly as important as a simple description of what happened in the study. A second thing to notice is that, for the most part, the researchers avoided the use of causal language. Instead of saying that the spheres caused the observed differences, they said that they observed an association between the preponderance of the spheres and murder rates. The only suggestion of causality was the little flourish thrown in at the very end (and it was qualified by the word "possible"). Later in the paper, the authors may choose to make arguments about causes, but in the primary part of the Results section, it is best to be pretty cautious. Finally, notice that the researchers supplemented their χ^2 statistic with a ϕ (phi) value. This is the conceptual and mathematical equivalent of r (a correlation coefficient), and it is typically reported instead of r when the two variables being correlated are both dichotomous. You might also have noticed that the value of ϕ is *extremely* small. Whenever scores on a variable are highly skewed (e.g., when there are many, many more nonmurderers than murderers), this places some extreme limits on the size of a contingency coefficient. To steer readers away from the inappropriate assumption that the effect they observed in their study was extremely small, the authors expressed their findings in terms of observed versus expected murder rates.

Study 2: The Survey Study of Apathy and Energy

The first group of researchers made a breakthrough discovery. They were the first people to document the possibility that the *color* of the spheres might be a significant marker of what the spheres do. As is often the case with real research, however, this early breakthrough turned out to represent only an imperfect truth. A second group of researchers felt that the color of the spheres was very informative, but they had noticed that the spheres seemed to influence a lot more than just murder rates. For instance, they noticed that in the green city several unusually impressive sports records had also been set during the year of the archival study of murder. The researchers' casual observations also suggested that certain kinds of heroic behaviors (e.g., jumping into a freezing river to save a drowning child) had increased in the green city. Finally, during the summer of the first year of the spheres, ice cream sales tripled in the green city! The researchers had difficulty getting hold of ice cream sales records in the yellow city, but it seemed to be the case that ice cream sales had actually decreased there during the same period. In short, a mixture of formal and informal observations convinced the second team of researchers that the green spheres might act as some kind of *general* energizer, increasing the vigor with which people pursue any kind of activity (whether it be murdering one's enemies, competing with one's opponents, or rescuing someone else's enemies). They were less certain about the yellow spheres, but they suspected that they simply mellowed people out, making people's psychological responses to stimuli less intense.

To test their hypotheses, the second team of researchers conducted a large-scale survey study in which they asked a randomly sampled group of participants to recall the last time they had come into close contact with one of the spheres, to report whether the sphere had been green or yellow, and to answer a series of questions about their experience in the presence of the sphere. In particular, they created multiple-item measures of what they called *apathy* and *energy* (without labeling them as such), and they asked their participants to report the degree to which they had felt apathetic or energized the last time they had come into close contact with one of the spheres. The researchers expected to find that the color of the sphere people reported having most recently come into contact with would be strongly correlated with people's self-reported experiences of apathy and energy while in the sphere's presence. Because the researchers realized that numerically coding for nominal data is arbitrary, they simply coded reports of yellow-sphere experiences as –1 and reports of green-sphere experiences as +1 (they could have just as readily used values of –17 and +142.68; the only important thing would be to remember *which color* got the higher of the two arbitrary values). The researchers tested their hypotheses by simply computing point-biserial correlations between people's color codes and their reported experiences on the apathy and energy scales.

Because the researchers had developed their own measures of apathy and energy, they wanted to show that these measures were *reliable* before showing that they correlated as expected with people's self-reported exposure to a particular kind of sphere. As you may recall, in the case of multiple-item survey measures, the most relevant form of reliability is usually *internal consistency*. Before we take a look at how the researchers might have discussed the reliability of their measures, we should note that they probably *wouldn't* have presented information about reliability in their Results section. Because reliability is a property of survey measures, information about reliability is most likely to be found in a paper's Method section. Here is an example of what this paragraph of the authors' Method section might have looked like:

> *Measures of Apathy and Energy.* Because we were unable to find any existing measures of apathy and energy, we developed a new measure of each of these constructs. Based on pilot tests, we selected a set of 10 items for each scale. The *apathy* scale included items such as "When I was in the presence of the sphere, I didn't feel much like doing anything," and "When I was in the presence of the sphere, things that usually seemed important just didn't seem to matter." The *energy* scale included items such as "When I was in the presence of the sphere, I felt all revved up," and "When I was in the presence of the sphere, my feelings were more intense than usual." Participants answered the items in both scales using Likert scales that ranged from 1 *(not at all true)* to 9 *(extremely true)*. Coefficient alpha for the resulting measures of apathy and energy was high (.88 and .91, respectively).

Although there are many other ways to describe a set of measures, this description summarizes the important characteristics of the scales. If it were important for readers to see all the items in these scales (as it usually is for new scales), the authors would want to include all of the items in the scales, along with any important instructions, in an appendix. The final sentence in the paragraph provides the crucial information about the reliability of the scales. There are many other ways to state this (and you should develop your own). Another way to have said this is: "The items in both scales proved to be internally consistent (respective αs for the measures of apathy and energy were .88 and .91)." Incidentally, the Greek character alpha is short for Cronbach's alpha, and it is very different from an alpha level for statistical testing.

Measures of temporal consistency wouldn't make much sense for the kinds of items included in these two measures, but if they did, and if they were available, the researchers would probably want to present this information too. They might add: "In a separate sample of 100 participants, these scales also proved to be stable over time. The respective test-retest correlations for a 2-week period were r (98) = .77 and .84 for apathy and energy respectively." (Given both the magnitude of these correlations and the size of their sample, the researchers might not bother to report the obvious fact that these correlations are significant at $p < .001$.)

What about the results themselves? This part would be pretty straightforward. Given that there are only two correlations to report, reporting them in a table would be unnecessary. The researchers' description might look something like this:

> The correlations we observed provided strong support for our predictions. First, there was a moderately strong negative association between reports of sphere color and reported experiences of apathy, r (134) = −.46, $p < .001$. Because reports of having been in the presence of the green sphere were coded with higher values, this negative correlation means that participants who reported having been in the presence of the *yellow* sphere were substantially more likely to have reported overall feelings of apathy. Second, there was a very strong positive association between reports of sphere color and reported experiences of energy, r (132) = .71, $p < .001$. Participants who reported having been in the presence of the *green* sphere were especially likely to report having experienced high levels of energy and excitement. One participant who reported having been exposed to the green sphere spontaneously wrote on his survey: "Yellow spheres suck but green spheres our [*sic*] great! I wish I could can that stuff and sell it!" One wonders how long it had been since he had last been exposed to a green sphere.

There are a few things to note about this description. First, the value in parenthesis after each r indicates the *degrees of freedom* associated with that correlation. It's always $n - 2$, and so the researchers must have had 136 people in their sample. We intentionally made the degrees of freedom a little different for the second correlation. That kind of thing could easily happen if a couple of people completed the apathy measure but left part of the energy measure blank. If this did happen, the authors would probably want to point it out in a footnote so that readers didn't get the impression that the authors had made some kind of mistake. Second, notice that these authors, too, were pretty cautious about their language when they were describing the correlations (though they, too, may have been guilty of waxing a little causal in their final sentence). Finally, although we presented these data in the form of two correlations, it would have been equally reasonable to have divided participants up into two groups based on sphere color and to have conducted a simple one-way ANOVA (or a *t*-test) on the data. The statistics would have been a little different, but the probability values would have been *exactly* the same. So in this particular case, which statistic to conduct (and report) is largely a matter of taste. One possible advantage of running an ANOVA or *t*-test is that experimentally inclined researchers—who are more accustomed to seeing means—would probably get a better sense of the nature of your findings if each finding were presented in the form of two means rather than a single correlation.[2]

Study 3: The Newlywed Marriage Study

One limitation of the second study is that the participants' expectancies (or naive theories) about the spheres could have biased what they were report-ing. Of course, expectancies are grounded in folk wisdom, and folk wisdom often proves to be correct. On the other hand, it would be nice to have some evidence about the operation of the spheres that was less susceptible to this criticism. A third group of researchers was sympathetic to the view of the sec-ond group but wanted to address this criticism and to broaden the empirical basis for the other researchers' conclusions. They obtained records from mar-riage licenses in Los Angeles County over a one-year period. Except in the case of confidential licenses, marriage licenses always provide the mailing address of the newlywed couple. The researchers used these addresses to locate the single-family dwellings of a very large group of newlyweds, and then sent interviewers into the field to identify couples on whose lawns either a green or a yellow sphere had landed. Whenever the researchers identified such a home, they recorded the color of the sphere and attempted to secure an interview with one of the newlyweds. If no one was home, the interview-ers returned to the dwelling on as many as three different occasions before giving up on a particular couple.

When the interviewers did find someone home and were able to secure an interview, they queried interviewees on a number of mundane topics such as who was responsible for what chores and how much time participants spent watching television each week. However, these questions were mostly warm-up questions. When the interviewers had exhausted their short list of questions, they told the interviewees that they were asking a few questions that most people felt more comfortable answering in a confidential survey. They then gave participants a small survey card and an envelope and asked them if they would be willing to conclude the interview by privately answer-ing the questions on the card and sealing the card in the envelope. Everyone who agreed to the initial interview agreed to fill out the card. The card asked people to think about their relationship for the *last month* and to report: (1) how happy they were with their marriages, (2) how many times in an aver-age week the couple had gotten into an argument, and (3) how frequently (i.e., how many times per week) the couple had engaged in sexual inter-course. During the interview, the researchers made it a point *not* to mention anything about the spheres. In those few cases in which an interviewee spon-taneously mentioned the spheres, the researchers remarked that they hadn't really noticed them, and politely moved on with the interview. At the conclu-sion of the interview, however, the researchers always made a record of this comment on the participant's data-record sheet. This way, they could later check to see if the responses of these participants were different from those of the rest of the group.[3]

The three primary questions answered on the card constituted the researchers' dependent variables, but the researchers also measured a couple of other variables that they expected to be related to the dependent measures. The most important one was how many months the couple had been married. This measure served two purposes. First of all, it allowed the researchers to be sure that they had, in fact, sampled who they were after (because participants' reports could be compared with the date of the marriage given on the actual marriage license). Second, as long as this measure agreed with the researchers' records (which it almost always did), it could be used as an additional predictor of people's responses to the three questions on the card. To be more specific, because the researchers were unable to get an extremely large sample, they wanted to minimize "noise" or unpredictable fluctuations in their participants' responses. One pretty good predictor of how happy people report being with the quality of their marriages is how long people have been married. During the first year of a marriage (and beyond), you often see a gradually dwindling "honeymoon effect." People are extremely happy at first, but their level of happiness gradually tapers off over time. By measuring how long people had been married and controlling for this difference across the couples, the researchers hoped to gain a little extra control over their participants' responses.

Because the researchers measured more than one variable that they expected to influence their participants' responses and because at least one of these predictors (length of marriage in months) was a continuous (ratio) variable, the researchers decided to test their hypotheses by conducting a *multiple regression* analysis. Multiple regression is essentially a souped-up version of partial correlation, and thus if you took part in the methodology exercise on partial correlation (in Chapter 5) you should have at least a cursory idea of what multiple regression is about. For the time being, the most useful thing about multiple regression is that it allows researchers to control for one variable when they're examining the potential effects of a second variable. The controlled-for variable could be a suspected confound—like Bart when we really care about Lisa—or it could merely be a source of noise that the researchers wish to minimize, like how long people have been married in months when we really care about green and yellow spheres. There are many specific kinds of multiple regression analyses, and so researchers who use multiple regression have to be very clear about which particular kind of regression they conducted when they report their findings. Here is an example of what the researchers might have reported had they conducted a multiple regression analysis on their data. Before you check it out, however, here are a couple of important pieces of vocabulary. In multiple regression, the variables that researchers treat as independent variables are referred to as **predictors,** and the variable that researchers treat as the dependent variable is referred to as the **criterion.** Regression analyses also yield the logical equivalent of partial correlations. These measures of association are referred to as

regression coefficients, and they are conceptually identical to partial correlation coefficients.

As noted earlier, we tested our hypothesis by conducting three separate
simultaneous multiple regression analyses. Our criterion variable in each of
these analyses was always one of the three different measures of marital
quality (happiness, arguments, and sex). Our predictors were always (1) the
dummy coded sphere variable and (2) the number of months that
participants had been married. Table 12.2 summarizes the results of each of
these regression analyses. As suggested by the pattern of correlations and
standardized regression coefficients shown in Table 12.2, marital length was
related in the expected ways with each of the three criterion variables. The
longer participants had been married, the less happy they reported being, the
more they reported arguing, and the less frequently they reported engaging
in sexual intercourse (though the significant zero-order correlation observed
for happiness fell somewhat short of significance in the simultaneous
regression). More important, however, all three of the regression analyses
revealed strong and significant effects of the color of sphere. Moreover, unlike
the measure of length of marriage, the presence of the green as compared with
the yellow sphere was not simply associated with an across-the-board increase
or decrease in reported marital quality. Instead, the green sphere seemed to
magnify all three of these (self-reported) marital experiences—including both
the two positive experiences (happiness and sex) and the one negative
experience (arguments). In fact, the largest effects of the sphere appear to

TABLE 12.2   Marital happiness, frequency of arguments, and frequency
of sexual intercourse as a function of length of newlywed marriage in
months and proximity to green versus yellow spheres

Predictor	Results for Happiness			
	r	t	β	p
Length of Marriage	−.230	−1.82	−.186	.078
Sphere Type	.612	11.47	.587	< .001

Predictor	Results for Frequency of Arguments			
	r	t	β	p
Length of Marriage	.356	2.48	.256	.023
Sphere Type	.740	14.29	.853	< .001

Predictor	Results for Frequency of Sexual Intercourse			
	r	t	β	p
Length of Marriage	−.400	−6.49	−.393	< .001
Sphere Type	.553	9.02	.540	< .001

Note: Beta weights and t values have the same probability values. Respective r's with
absolute magnitudes greater than .217, .283, and .357 are significant at p <.05, .01,
and .001. The yellow and green spheres were dummy coded −1 and +1, respectively.

have occurred for arguments. Relative to the yellow spheres, the green spheres appear to have magnified couples' tendencies toward arguments even more than they magnified their tendencies toward happiness and sex.

One thing you may have noticed about this description is that it is chock-full of technical terms like "dummy coded" and "standardized regression coefficient." Multiple regression analyses yield a great number of statistics, including many (such as R^2 and adjusted R^2 values) that we chose not to include here. Researchers in training who want to become comfortable with multiple regression techniques usually take one or more courses in multiple regression, and regression techniques are continuously being refined and developed (see Edwards, 1976, for an excellent introduction, and see both Aiken & West, 1991, and Pedhazur, 1982, for excellent treatments of more advanced topics). Although a detailed treatment of regression is well beyond the scope of this text, there is one thing you can easily do to become a little more familiar with multiple regression. Later in this chapter, we will take a look at how the researchers who conducted this hypothetical study might have described exactly the same set of findings using the analysis of covariance (ANCOVA). By making a comparison of these two techniques, you can probably get a slightly better feel for how to think (and write) about regression.

A second thing you may have noticed about this description is that the authors avoided the use of causal language when it came to the association for marriage length, but sometimes indulged in causal descriptions when it came to the naturalistic manipulation of sphere type (e.g., by using words like "effect" and "magnify"). Because the study in question was a natural experiment rather than a true experiment, many researchers would have been a little more cautious about the use of causal language. Some researchers might also have been a little more cautious about making any relative statements about the *size* of the sphere effect for the different criterion variables (strong statements of this sort should really be supported by a special significance test). Finally, even though this write-up was a little on the bold side, notice that the researchers were generally pretty cautious when it came to making direct statements about behavior. Because the researchers didn't actually measure any behavior, they didn't speak directly about arguing and having sex. Instead, they wrote that people who had been married longer *reported* having had more arguments (and less sex).

Study 4: The Stereotyping Study

So far, the evidence is starting to suggest that the green and yellow spheres respectively magnify and water down normal human psychological responses. However, all the evidence we have seen so far is either correlational or quasi-experimental. It'd be nice to see what the spheres do to people in the carefully controlled confines of the laboratory. Another limitation of the existing studies is that they tell us the two kinds of spheres are different but don't necessarily guarantee that *both* of the spheres are having an effect on people. Are the yellow spheres really mellowing people out, or are they simply failing to rev people up the way the green spheres do? To answer this question, we'd need some kind of control group of people who are not exposed to the spheres at all. To address concerns such as these, and to extend studies of the effects of the spheres to yet another area of human experience, a fourth group of researchers decided to conduct a laboratory experiment on the influence of the spheres. In the early days of spherical research, no one considered trying to conduct any experiments on spherical issues because of the simple fact that the spheres were immovable. It's pretty hard to bring an immovable object to the lab. A few enterprising psychologists solved this problem by bringing their laboratories to the spheres! In particular, they simply identified spheres that had fallen in open (though usually inconspicuous) areas on college campuses, and built small laboratories around them. It was well established that the range of influence of the spheres was about 40 feet, and thus it was easy for researchers to disguise the fact that their new labs had been built next to or around the spheres. Of course, participants in different conditions of the experiments had to be herded off to different parts of campus, but this was easy to arrange.

One particularly fortunate, and well-funded, pair of researchers was even able to set up a 2 × 2 factorial experiment on their campus. In particular, the researchers independently manipulated whether people were exposed to each of the two spheres. The design of their study was a 2 (yellow sphere: absent or present) × 2 (green sphere: absent or present) completely between-subjects factorial. This meant, by the way, that there happened to be an accessible spot on these researchers' campus where a green and a yellow sphere had landed in close proximity to each other (which allowed them to create the present/present cell in all their 2 × 2 experiments). By simply setting up the same psychological situation in the four laboratories they had set up across campus, the researchers could investigate any topic in which they were interested to see how the spheres influenced different kinds of behaviors.

In their first study, the researchers decided to study ethnic stereotyping. Normally, they might have studied stereotyping by *manipulating* the apparent ethnicity of a target person (e.g., by describing a protagonist as "Robert Gardner" or "Roberto Garcia") and examining stereotype-relevant judgments of this person (for a real example of how this might work, see Bodenhausen, 1990). However, in the case of their study of the spheres, the researchers merely described a case in which an eyewitness who wasn't wearing his eyeglasses claimed to identify the defendant, Roberto Garcia, as the person who had stolen his new sports car. (Notice that including a "Robert Gardner" condition would have required a more complex 2 × 2 × 2 design.) The researchers' dependent measure was simply the length of the prison sentence that participants recommended for the defendant. From their informal observations of people's behavior when they were exposed to both spheres at once, the researchers predicted that the presence of the two spheres together would lead to a different pattern of judgment than what would be expected based on observations of how each sphere influenced people in isolation. In other words, the researchers predicted an *interaction* between the presence of the yellow sphere and the presence of the green sphere. Here is how the researchers described their results:

> The sentencing measure was submitted to a 2 (yellow sphere: absent or present) × 2 (green sphere: absent or present) completely between-subjects

analysis of variance (ANOVA). This analysis revealed both a main effect of the presence of the yellow sphere, $F (1, 40) = 12.84$, $p < .001$, $d = 1.113$, and a main effect of the presence of the green sphere, $F (1, 40) = 7.32$, $p = .010$, $d = 0.856$. The first main effect reflected the fact that those exposed to the yellow sphere recommended *shorter*-than-average prison sentences. The second main effect reflected the fact that those exposed to the green sphere recommended *longer*-than-average prison sentences. Each of these main effects was consistent with the effects of the spheres observed in previous studies. However, the analysis also revealed that these main effects were qualified by a significant Yellow Sphere x Green Sphere interaction, $F (1, 40) = 8.31$, $p = .005$, $d = 0.911$. As suggested by the means appearing in Table 12.3, the nature of this interaction was consistent with predictions. Specifically, when the yellow sphere was absent, the presence of the green sphere had a large effect on sentencing. Those exposed to the green sphere recommended sentences almost three times as long as usual, $t(20) = 5.03$, $p < .001$, $d = 2.250$. However, when the yellow sphere was present, the presence of the green sphere had no effect whatsoever on participants' judgments. Participants recommended equal (and equally lenient) sentences for the defendant regardless of their level of exposure to the green sphere, $|t| < 1$, n.s., $d = -0.081$. Apparently, the yellow spheres not only minimize people's normal psychological responses to a situation but also neutralize any effects of the green spheres. At any rate, it is clear that the spheres do not simply cancel each other out. If they did, participants' responses in the present/present cell would have looked more like their responses in the absent/absent cell.

Interestingly, extensive discussions with participants in the yellow-sphere condition (during debriefing) revealed that they typically reported feeling little sympathy for Roberto. Instead, most of them reported that they just didn't see why it was such a big deal to steal a car or two every now and then. Two separate participants in the yellow-sphere condition also insisted on referring to the defendant as "Rob," and when queried about this habit reported that they simply hadn't bothered to read the rest of his name. Finally, the few participants in these conditions who did report that they felt it was wrong to steal cars all reported that it just wasn't worth the trouble to incarcerate hardened criminals. In the yellow-sphere-absent condition, however, not a single participant reported any of these apathetic responses. In fact, a few participants who were exposed to the green sphere and nothing else spontaneously reported that in the case of

TABLE 12.3 Length of recommended prison sentence for Roberto Garcia as a function of exposure to green and yellow spheres

	Yellow Sphere	
Green Sphere	Absent	Present
Absent	2.21	0.45
Present	6.58	0.32

Note: Means are recommended sentences in years (theoretical range = 0–10). There were 11 participants in each condition.

particularly heinous crimes such as Roberto's, they were strongly in favor of capital punishment (preferably by pressing, breaking on the wheel, burning, hanging in chains, bludgeoning, or gibbeting; see Sidanius & Pratto, 2000).

The first paragraph is a standard discussion of main effects, interactions, and the ensuing simple effects tests that are conducted to clarify the nature of an observed interaction (along with some supplemental reports of effect sizes). The second paragraph is a slightly exaggerated version of the kind of thing researchers might add to their Results section (or possibly their General Discussion) to give readers some added insights into the experiences of their participants. In a real experiment, of course, participants' responses wouldn't normally be quite this colorful, but they might be just as telling.

Study 5: A Brief Return to Roberto and to the Newlywed Study

Imagine that the researchers who conducted the last study had pretested all of their participants a few weeks before their experiment to determine the strength of their participants' stereotypes about Latinos. If the spheres hadn't proven to have such a potent effect on people's behavior, these pretest scores might have come in very handy in such a study because we might expect these scores to be correlated with people's tendencies to recommend harsher sentences for Roberto Garcia. If this were true, the researchers in question could conduct a more sensitive experimental test of their hypotheses by conducting an analysis of covariance (ANCOVA)—rather than a regular ANOVA—on their participants' recommended sentences. ANCOVA is very similar to ANOVA except that the scores that are analyzed are first statistically adjusted for any effects of the covariate (the measured variable that is expected to *covary* with the researcher's dependent measure). Thus, ANCOVA is a hybrid analysis that incorporates desirable features of both multiple regression and the analysis of variance. Like regression techniques, ANCOVA can statistically adjust for variables that may be *confounded* with a researcher's independent variables. In addition, it can reduce what would otherwise be random noise or error in a set of scores—to make it easier to detect the effects of the variables in which researchers are most interested. In this second case, ANCOVA is the loose experimental equivalent of a noise-reduction system (such as a Dolby noise-reduction system in a stereo system). It allows researchers to bypass a good deal of noise to get a better idea of whether a set of data has anything beautiful to tell us.

The main difference between reporting the results of an ANCOVA and reporting those of an ANOVA is that researchers typically report the effects of any covariates *first* (much like main effects—because both conceptually and mathematically they *are* main effects) and then report all the usual things that are reported in a typical ANOVA. The only other notable difference in how the results are discussed is that the resulting means are referred to (quite appropriately) as *covariate-adjusted means,* both in the body of the results and in any tables that might refer to them. If the researchers who conducted the interview study of newlyweds had decided to analyze their data by using ANCOVA, their first set of results (for happiness) might have been reported like this:

Our primary analyses consisted of three separate one-way (sphere type: yellow or green) analyses of covariance (ANCOVAS) in which length of marriage was treated as the covariate (and thus statistically controlled). Each ANCOVA focused on one of our three separate dependent measures (happiness, arguments, and sexual intercourse). The analysis of participants' reported happiness with their marriage revealed that the covariate (length of marriage) was only marginally associated with participants' reports of being happily married, $F(1, 102) = 3.20$, $p = .078$. Nonetheless, because of its *a priori* importance (and because it was significant in the other two ANCOVAS) the covariate was retained in the analysis. More important, the analysis also revealed a very large effect of sphere type, $F(1, 102) = 131.56$, $p < .001$. As suggested by the covariate-adjusted means for marital happiness, newlyweds whose lawns contained green spheres ($M = 8.53$) rather than yellow spheres ($M = 4.88$) reported much higher levels of marital satisfaction. In fact, the modal response in this condition was 9, which was the upper endpoint of our scale. Whereas green spheres appear to intensify feelings of marital happiness, yellow spheres appear to minimize these same feelings.

Similar descriptions should be provided for the other two dependent measures, and the psychological interpretation of the observed findings should obviously be the same as they were in the case of the discussion of the regression analyses. In fact, if you were minding your p-values carefully, you may have noticed that the two p-values reported here were identical to the two p-values reported in the upper section of Table 12.2. Although the results for both the regressions and the ANCOVA are fictional, this aspect of the results is not an accident. If we had provided the results of an ANCOVA for a variation on the stereotyping study and we had run a regression to analyze the same data, the results of both the ANCOVA and the regression would be more complex than those reported here (because there would be two main effects and an interaction to report, not to mention simple effects tests). However, the p-values from the regression and the ANCOVA that corresponded to the same effects (e.g., the p-value for the main effect of the green sphere) would be identical in the two analyses.

Study 6: The Duck in the Drugstore Study

So far we have seen that the mysterious spheres appear to influence a wide range of responses, including aggression, stereotyping, general feelings of apathy and energy, and specific feelings and behaviors related to interpersonal relationships. However, figuring all this out has been a laborious and time-consuming enterprise. To answer questions about the spheres, the researchers you've read about thus far were looking at reams of police records, sending teams of people out into the field to conduct interviews, and when they had to, even building new laboratories. In addition, the researchers generally had access to pretty large samples of participants. What would the researchers have done if they hadn't had so much time or money, or so many

Q: What's the difference between a duck? A: Eliphino.

research participants? Presumably, they might have been forced to design more economical studies. It's pretty likely that such studies might have made use of *within-subjects* manipulations. It's also pretty likely that you, too, will someday have to design a pretty economical study. With this in mind, let's take a look at a final study that investigated the effects of the spheres (one of them at least) on a shoestring budget.

Suppose a group of students wanted to conduct an experiment on the effects of the spheres without having to build their own laboratory or run dozens and dozens of research participants. The students had located a relatively inconspicuous green sphere near a commonly used campus thoroughfare, and they decided to focus solely on the effects of the green sphere in their study. Knowing that they would have to take their study to the sphere, they decided to conduct an experiment in which they could present people with their stimuli using nothing more than a portable stereo (with headphones) and a clipboard. One of the students had long been interested in the psychology of humor, and she convinced the others to conduct a study of how the green sphere influences people's perceptions of the humorousness of jokes.[4]

To minimize the number of participants they would need to run, the students designed a study with a mixed-model design. They had one between-subjects variable (whether participants responded to some audiotaped jokes in close proximity to the green sphere—which the students covered with a backpack and a jacket—or whether they responded to the same jokes in an area devoid of any spheres). They also had one within-subject variable—whether the jokes their participants heard did or did not contain canned laughter (i.e., a dubbed-in laugh track). Because the students obviously couldn't expect people to respond to the same joke twice (with and without a laugh track), they pilot-tested a large group of jokes (on 14 of their friends) to identify two equally, and only moderately, funny jokes. The first joke was about a duck in a drugstore: A duck walks into a drugstore and asks for some Chapstick. When the cashier asks him if he'll be paying in cash, the duck says, "No, I was hoping you could just put it on my bill." The second joke is also an animal joke—Question: What do you get when you cross an elephant with a rhinoceros? Answer: Elephino. (It's pronounced "Ell-if-I-know.")

Because the students had been well trained in research methods, they prepared four different versions of their joke tapes. These four versions are summarized below:

Tape A: (1) duck joke without laugh track followed by (2) elephino joke with laugh track

Tape B: (1) duck joke with laugh track followed by (2) elephino joke without laugh track

Tape C: (1) elephino joke without laugh track followed by (2) duck joke with laugh track

Tape D: (1) elephino joke with laugh track followed by (2) duck joke without laugh track

In other words, the students *counterbalanced* both (1) the particular joke that came first, and (2) whether the laugh track was paired with the first or the second joke. In so doing, they unconfounded their within-subjects laugh track manipulation with (1) any potential differences in the humorousness of the two jokes, and (2) any effects of whether a joke came first or second. For reasons that should become clear below, the students predicted an interaction between the sphere manipulation and the laugh track manipulation. Here is how the students summarized their findings:

> Because our experiment had both a between-subjects and a within-subjects manipulation, we submitted the data to a 2 (green sphere: absent vs. present) × 2 (laugh track: absent vs. present) mixed-model analysis of variance (ANOVA). The ANOVA revealed main effects of both the sphere manipulation, $F(1, 23) = 18.97$, $p < .001$, and the laugh track manipulation, $F(1, 23) = 7.86$, $p = .011$. Both the presence of the sphere and the presence of the laugh track increased people's ratings of the humorousness of the jokes. The ANOVA also revealed the predicted Sphere x Laugh Track interaction, $F(1, 23) = 11.41$, $p < .001$. As suggested by the means in the left half of Table 12.4, when there was no laugh track, the sphere still intensified people's responses to the jokes, $F(1, 23) = 4.35$, $p = .048$. However, as suggested by the means in the right half of the table, the effect of the sphere was noticeably greater when the jokes were accompanied by a laugh track, $F(1, 23) = 27.67$, $p < .001$. It appears that the green sphere not only

TABLE 12.4 Judged humorousness of jokes as a function of the presence of green spheres and laugh tracks

Green Sphere	Laugh Track	
	Absent	Present
Absent	5.25	5.84
Present	6.80	8.92

Note: Means reflect the rated humorousness of the jokes (theoretical range = 1–10). There were 12 participants in each of the two sphere conditions.

magnified people's responses to the jokes themselves but also magnified people's responses to the laugh track manipulation.

Notice that there is very little that is special about how to discuss the results of a mixed-model ANOVA. The students duly mentioned that they had conducted a mixed-model ANOVA to analyze their data, but except for this fact the students could just as easily have been describing the results of a completely between-subjects factorial. The same thing would be true if the students had somehow been able to conduct a 2 × 2 completely within-subjects design (in which every participant served in every condition of the study). The only exception to this rule is that when you are reporting the results of studies that have within-subjects manipulations, you will sometimes want to report any effects of your counterbalancing procedures (i.e., you may want to report whether you observed any order effects). Of course, if there were any order effects, you took care of them by balancing them out across your within-subjects conditions. Thus, most readers don't really care that much about seeing this kind of discussion. On the other hand, if order effects would be interesting in their own right, or if you observe an interaction between order and an experimental manipulation, you should always report such effects.

Because the hypothetical studies discussed here span the range from archival to experimental studies, you may be wondering if we have spanned the entire range of statistical tests that researchers might need to report. We haven't. Although the tests reviewed here are some of the most commonly conducted statistical tests, there are literally hundreds of statistical tests. However, a good portion of these other tests will bear at least a passing resemblance to the tests reported here. For example, if you had measured a lot of separate dependent measures that weren't organized along any kind of continuum (i.e., that didn't really represent levels of a within-subjects manipulation), you might want to conduct a MANOVA (a multivariate analysis of variance) on your data. However, the basic approach you adopted to describe the results of your MANOVA would be very similar to the approach adopted here. Of course, your writing style is probably very different from either of ours, and thus even if your analysis was exactly like one of those we have reported here, you would never say things *exactly* the way we have said them (in fact, if you did, we would be forced to report you for plagiarism). Regardless of your writing style, however, if you were writing about your results *well,* you would do three important things: you would focus primarily on the meaning of your findings, you would organize these findings in a coherent way, and you would document all of your findings by mentioning the statistical tests that made them scientifically meaningful. That, in a nutshell, is how to write about results.

Notes

1. As a compromise between simplicity and the kind of real differences you'd be likely to see in the sizes of different real cities, notice that we computed the statistics you see in the description based on populations of 2 mil-

lion and 1 million, respectively, for the green and yellow cities. Given that we started out with 93 total murders to split between the two cities, and given that the green city was twice as big as the yellow city, this meant that our expected frequency for murders in the green city had to be twice the expected frequency of murders in the yellow city. This works out to exactly 62 and 31 murders, respectively. Though it now requires more calculations, the χ^2 formula used to compute this statistic was exactly the same one you saw in Chapter 10.

2. Because participants in this study responded to two different kinds of questions that were measured on the same scale, the researchers could also have conducted a 2×2 mixed-model ANOVA in which the between-subjects variable was the color of the sphere and the within-subjects variable was the measure of apathy versus the measure of energy.

3. Except for the part about the spheres, this fictional study is loosely inspired by a project on newlywed marriage conducted by Bradbury and his colleagues (see Davila, Bradbury, Cohan, & Tochluk, 1997; Karney & Bradbury, 1997).

4. The student also happened to be familiar with the research of James Olson. The study described here is partly inspired by Olson's (1992) experiment on the effects of laugh tracks on people's perceptions of humor.

13

Putting Your Knowledge to Work: 20 Methodology Problems

This chapter contains 20 methodology problems designed to allow you to exercise the methodological skills you have developed by reading this text. Most of these problems provide a specific interpretation of some kind of empirical observation (e.g., the claims made in a commercial, the findings of a laboratory experiment). Your job is usually to provide an *alternate interpretation* for the same empirical observation. Many of these problems also ask you for advice about improving the way in which the observation was made (e.g., correcting potential design flaws in an experiment). Finally, a couple of the problems ask you to design your own study to test a particular research hypothesis. The common thread that unites all the problems is the fact that they all provide you with a chance to demonstrate your methodological expertise. We have found that students usually enjoy working on these problems with other students. In fact, we usually ask students to work on the problems in groups of five to eight people (during class—so that it is possible to monitor students' progress and make suggestions as they work). Regardless of how you approach the problems, however, we hope you will find it as gratifying to solve them as we did to pose them.

Except where otherwise indicated, the problems in this chapter are all based on real studies or real claims made by advertisers, laypeople, or trained researchers. In some cases, however, we have consolidated several closely related studies into a single study or changed unimportant details of a study (often to protect the identity of the party who made the original claim). Although our inspiration for each individual problem was always a specific empirical claim or research finding, our main inspiration for creating this set of methodology problems was a scholarly and engaging text by Huck and Sandler (1979). If you would like some additional practice flexing your methodological muscle, we heartily recommend their text.

1. In Search of a Delicious, Low-Fat TV Show

In late July of 1992, a Los Angeles TV station reported the results of a surprising and alarming medical study. The reporter covering the story stated that watching too much TV may be bad for children's hearts as well as their heads. In particular, he said that a study of television viewing and blood cholesterol revealed that, relative to kids who watched very little TV, kids who watched a lot of TV had especially high cholesterol levels. The reporter implied that TV watching actually increases blood cholesterol levels, but we are skeptical of this interpretation. Can you come up with a more reasonable explanation for the results of the study?

2. Let's Get Supernatural

Despite the efforts of many to debunk astrology and parapsychology, many people believe that you can predict a person's personality or future from the motion of stars and planets to which the person has never even traveled. Others believe that although the stars cannot predict your future, other people can do so using their psychic powers. If you wanted to conduct a study to test the validity of either (1) astrology and horoscopes or (2) a specific person's claim that he or she could predict future events, how would you do so? In answering this question, try to think of a test that is both simple and fair (i.e., scientific). In doing so, you should pay special attention to the closely related issues of (1) coming up with a good operational definition of a correct prediction and (2) choosing a good dependent variable or variables.

3. Fly Away Home

We believe that notices on milk cartons can help authorities to recover missing children. We also believe that the television show *America's Most Wanted* has helped law enforcement agencies put away some very dangerous criminals. Similarly, we think it's likely that flyers such as the ones the first author used to receive in the mail on a regular basis can help people recover missing children. The problem is that we'd like to know exactly *how* effective these approaches are. After all, if we could find out which approaches are most effective, we could rescue more children and capture more criminals for the same amount of effort. A flyer that the first author often received in the mail (from an organization called ADVO) seems to answer this question in clear and simple terms. In this flyer, ADVO claimed, "Over 55 children featured have been recovered." The implication of ADVO's claim is that their treatment (the flyers) caused the recovery of over 55 missing children. What are some potential problems with this claim? If ADVO hired you to perform a large-scale study to evaluate the effectiveness of their flyer, how would you go about doing so? In other words, if you had sufficient resources at your disposal, how would you correct any potential threats to the validity of ADVO's implicit claim about the flyers?

FIGURE 13.1 Is the vacuum cleaner the first author is using to pick up this 16-lb. bowling ball the best vacuum that money can buy?

4. Impressive Pickup Lines

Vacuum cleaner companies often distribute advertisements that promote the amazing cleaning powers of their particular model of vacuum cleaner. For example, some ads show vacuum cleaners picking up heavy objects such as nails, bolts, or ball bearings. However, an advertisement that each of us has received in the mail many times seems to top them all by showing that the compact version of a particular canister vacuum can pick up a 16-lb. bowling ball! (See Figure 13.1) One of us happens to know a couple of excellent homemakers who insist that this particular vacuum cleaner really does do an excellent job, and thus we are not necessarily disputing this manufacturer's claim. However, as skeptical consumers (and even more skeptical scientists), we would like to know more before we decide that this vacuum is one of the best on the market. For the purposes of this exercise, we would like you to assume that the compact canister vacuums produced by this particular company *really can* pick up a 16-lb. bowling ball (as we believe they can). However, even if you make this assumption, it is still possible to criticize this specific demonstration of the superior performance of this vacuum. What are your criticisms? As a clue, we think that a consideration of the first three basic forms of *validity* discussed in Chapter 3 suggests a different methodological critique of this claim (and a different way of improving the demonstration).

5. Clever Who?

As statistics instructors who have frequently seen math anxiety at work among extremely bright and motivated college students, we can easily relate to high school math teachers who become frustrated trying to get kids interested in math. About 100 years ago, a German math teacher named Mr. von Osten appears to have gotten so frustrated that he gave up on his regular students and turned his teaching attention to his horse! Interestingly, Mr. von Osten seems to have had better luck with his horse than he had with many of his human students. In fact, he taught his horse to perform such a wide array of intellectual feats that the horse eventually became known as Clever Hans. Not only could Clever Hans perform routine mathematical tasks such as addition, subtraction, and multiplication, but he could also perform more complex tasks such as finding the square root of a number, raising a number to a power, or telling the day of the week that corresponded to a particular date. As if this wasn't enough, Hans could also identify musical tones and answer general-knowledge questions about history, geography, or the arts.

Of course, even Clever Hans had his limits. For example, he couldn't write or speak. However, his owner prepared a special tablet containing all the letters of the alphabet, and Clever Hans could tap out his answers to most questions by using this tablet. Similarly, to give his answers to mathematical questions, Hans would tap his hoof a certain number of times to indicate a certain number. Hans was studied by a wide variety of experts who initially concluded that his amazing abilities were genuine. However, further investigation eventually revealed that Hans wasn't quite as clever as people had originally thought. How do you suppose people eventually discovered the secret behind Hans's performances? What was this secret?

6. Life Sucks and So You Die

A large body of research in health psychology suggests that negative life events (such as the death of a loved one or the loss of one's job) can have negative consequences for people's physical well-being. One common way of studying the relation between negative life events and illness involves making use of retrospective survey designs. In studies making use of such designs, people who are physically ill and people who are physically healthy are asked to report the number of negative life events they have experienced in the recent past (e.g., the past month). Such studies typically reveal that people who are ill report having experienced a greater number of negative life events. Although such findings are consistent with the possibility that negative life events contribute to physical illness, these findings are open to alternate interpretations. What kinds of alternate interpretations can you suggest? If you wanted to gather more rigorous support for the idea that life events can contribute to illness, how might you improve upon this kind of retrospective design?

7. On the Drawbacks of Liking Yourself

Researchers who study the self-concept have identified numerous advantages of high self-esteem. Relative to people low in self-esteem, for instance, people high in self-esteem appear to be happier, better adjusted emotionally, more successful, less lonely, and more likely to succeed at work. Although we believe that all these things are true, the first author once conducted a preliminary study in which he examined the potential *disadvantages* of high self-esteem. After giving people an established, well-validated measure of self-esteem at the beginning of the quarter, he asked them a few questions about their driving behavior two months later. His most important findings were that, in comparison with people low in self-esteem, those high in self-esteem (1) were more likely to report owning a motorcycle or scooter, (2) reported having received more speeding tickets during the last year, and (3) reported a greater frequency of driving while under the influence of alcohol. All these findings were statistically significant, and we hope you will agree that they can all have very serious negative consequences. At least one of us would like to conclude that self-esteem has negative consequences (at least in the area of driving behavior). However, we each have to admit that there are some problems with this claim. How many can you think of? How might you try to fix them?

8. The Early Bird Gets the Win?

When the first author was a freshman in high school, his wrestling coach claimed that his careful analysis of high school wrestlers indicated that you could usually predict who would win a wrestling match by noticing who got the takedown at the beginning of the match (loosely speaking, by noticing which wrestler was the first to score points for controlling the other wrestler during the opening seconds of a match). The coach claimed that wrestlers who got the "takedown" won more than 80% of the more than 100 matches that formed the basis of his informal study. On the basis of this observation, this coach concluded that if he could teach all his wrestlers to master the basic moves involved in a takedown, his team could greatly improve its win-loss record from the previous year. Thus, the coach had his wrestlers spend a disproportionate amount of training time learning about takedowns. Because the first author was a mediocre wrestler, he really wanted to believe that he could greatly improve his winning percentage by simply improving his skills at the takedown. Of course, the coach was wrong. The first author did improve his takedown skills (perhaps due to sheer regression toward the mean), but doing so didn't do very much for his win-loss record. Moreover, the overall team record that year was far from stellar. What was wrong with this coach's conclusion about takedowns?

9. Testosterone Makes Better Dive Bombers

A researcher recently argued that, because of our culture's emphasis on competition among boys and men, men should perform better than women under the pressure of competition. To test his hypothesis, he gave 20 women and 20 men the task of assembling a model airplane as quickly as possible. To create a competitive atmosphere, the researcher promised that the person assembling his or her plane most quickly would win four tickets to the Super Bowl (and you can assume that his participants believed him). As a group, the men assembled their planes in about half the time required by the women, and a statistical test showed that this difference was highly significant. The researcher concluded that men do indeed work better than women under competitive conditions. We can think of at least three problems with the researcher's study that might render this conclusion suspect. How many can you think of? How would you correct them?

10. Working Your Fingers to the Dean's List

As an undergraduate, one of us worked part-time jobs 20–30 hours per week, and he sometimes wished that he had more time to devote to his studies. However, an ad that used to appear frequently in UCLA's student newspaper (the *Daily Bruin*) suggests that we should all take on as many part-time jobs as possible. The ad depicts an attractive young woman who claims, "Last quarter, I earned $3,000 and a 3.5." The ad implies that being employed by UPS can actually improve one's GPA. "Think of it—great pay, flexible hours, and maybe even better grades." Although UPS may run the tightest ship in the shipping business, it appears to run one of the loosest ships in the methodology business. What are some of the problems with its claim?

11. To Thine Own Selves Be True

One of the most fascinating phenomena in psychology is *dissociative identity disorder* (what is more commonly known by laypeople as "multiple personality disorder"). According to some psychologists, some people possess several distinct personalities, each of which is as rich and elaborate as the single personality that you yourself possess. As an example, at different times, a person with dissociative identity disorder might possess (1) a friendly, easygoing, and confident personality, (2) a shy, self-critical, and withdrawn personality, and (3) a grandiose, self-absorbed, manipulative personality. According to some psychologists, the different personalities of people with dissociative identity disorder may differ dramatically in their skill at particular tasks, their intelligence, or even their biological reactions to different allergens! To provide some empirical evidence for the existence of dissociative identity disorder, one psychologist repeatedly gave a standard intelligence test to a patient believed to be suffering from this problem. In particular, the psychologist asked a colleague who was blind to his hypothesis to administer the revised version of the Wechsler Adult Intelligence Scale (the WAIS-R) to one of his clients on four different occasions. This particular client, whom we will call Cari, appeared to have 11 distinct personalities, and each time she took the test she identified herself as a different person.

The first personality to take the test was "Wanda," who received a score of 114 (somewhat above average) on the WAIS-R. A week later, "Melanie" took the same test and received a score of 123 (a score that is clearly above average). The third week, "Jasmine" received a score of 140 (a score that approaches the genius range). Finally, on the fourth week, "Bassandra" received a high but not amazing score of 131. The psychologist who had been treating Cari concluded that each of Cari's personalities has a different IQ and that this finding supports the validity of dissociative identity disorder. Although there now appears to be some pretty solid evidence for the existence of dissociative identity disorder, we would not place the evidence about Cari in that category. Critique this researcher's conclusion. Can you suggest some things the researcher could do to improve upon the design of his study?

12. A Rosy Mood by Any Other Name?

Some people claim that whenever we are in a bad mood, we tend to see ourselves through mud-colored lenses. In particular, it appears to be the case that being in a negative mood causes people to evaluate themselves more negatively than usual. For example, being in a negative mood apparently causes people to focus selectively on negative self-relevant memories—due to a "spreading activation" process in memory. The crucial point is that *affect* (people's feelings) influences *cognition* (people's thoughts about themselves). To demonstrate this point, a researcher recently used a mood-induction procedure to put participants into happy versus sad moods. In particular, participants were asked to "relive" (i.e., to focus on and write about) a significant positive or negative experience from their past. After participants experienced the positive or negative mood induction to which they had been randomly assigned, they were given a well-validated measure of their self-perceived abilities in many different areas. The results were clear. Participants in the negative mood condition reported much more negative mood than did those in the positive mood condition, and they also reported significantly more negative self-evaluations (e.g., less self-perceived competence) than those in the positive mood condition. In fact, the effects of the mood manipulation on self-perceived competence were even more dramatic than the effects on mood itself! The researcher concluded that mood causes people to change their beliefs about themselves. Can you think of any problems with this conclusion? A clue: manipulation check versus dependent measure. Another clue: manipulation.

13. Old Geniuses Never Die Young?

A recent study appeared to provide good news for geniuses. Compared with people in "regular" occupations that do not require any special form of genius, people like Nobel prize–winning scientists and orchestra conductors appear to live especially long lives. One recent study revealed that Nobel Prize–winning scientists appear to live noticeably longer than either cooks or plumbers and that orchestra conductors lived even longer than Nobel Prize winners. There are many possible explanations for these findings. For example, one could conceivably argue that geniuses can afford superior health care. However, if we assume that there is nothing about being a genius per se that predisposes a person to living a long life, can you think of any additional confounds that could explain why maestros and Nobel Prize winners live longer than cooks, plumbers, and other blue-collar workers? In addition to any confounds involving the life experiences of these two different groups, can you think of a more sweeping methodological critique that might completely invalidate this claim about genius and longevity? A clue: great-grandmothers.

WIN $50! Fill out the survey below and return to the Daily Bruin by TODAY at 4pm. Positive and negative feedback are equally welcomed. Look in the April 1 Issue of the Daily Bruin for the Names of the 3 lucky $50 winners! **WIN $50!**

- -

TELL US ABOUT YOURSELF

1. Name:_____ 2. Phone #:_____

3. Personal Information: (to better understand who is giving us feedback) **sex:** M☐ F☐ **age:** _____

   UCLA status: Student Faculty Staff How many Football games did you attend this year? _____

   How many Basketball games?_____ How many Daily Bruin Sports Supplements did you read this year? ____

GIVE US SOME FEEDBACK!

Rate the following on a scale of 1-5 (1=poor/never, 5=GREAT!/ALWAYS!)

Feel free to give us extra info under your rating.   WHY? (give us some details...)

1. Did you enjoy the Sports Supplement? 1 2 3 4 5 NA _____
2. Was game day coverage thorough?   1 2 3 4 5 NA _____
3. Was coverage as informative as
   other game day media?   1 2 3 4 5 NA _____
4. How was the design & use of color? 1 2 3 4 5 NA _____
5. Were you aware of them in advance? 1 2 3 4 5 NA _____
6. Did you look forward to reading them? 1 2 3 4 5 NA _____
7. Were they easily accessible at games? 1 2 3 4 5 NA _____
8. Did you like having them at games? 1 2 3 4 5 NA _____
9. Did you respond to any of the ads? 1 2 3 4 5 NA _____

10. How can the Sports Supplement be improved? _____
_____

11. Would you like to see the Sports Supplement again next year? YES☐ NO☐ I don't care☐
    Why or Why not? _____
_____
_____

14. Sampling Student Opinion

The survey above appeared in the Basketball Supplement (NCAA Tournament Issue) of the *Daily Bruin* on March 14, 1991. As you can see from reading the survey, it was designed to give the editors of the *Bruin* some objective feedback about student attitudes toward the special Basketball Supplement appearing in that particular issue of the *Bruin*. Although we commend their efforts to be sensitive to student needs, we do not think the approach used by these researchers gave them an accurate feel for students' feelings. Why should we be skeptical about the validity of the survey?

15. I'm Speechless

One of the most controversial debates in psychology has to do with the language capabilities of higher primates such as gorillas and chimpanzees. Although a number of researchers claim that they have taught gorillas and chimps to use symbolic language systems such as American Sign Language, many researchers would argue that the case for higher language capacities in nonhuman primates has yet to be made. Imagine that an extremely well-funded researcher decided to take a novel approach to this problem by randomly sampling ten normal, healthy American adults and ten normal, healthy adult chimpanzees. The researcher decided to expose the people and the chimps to *the same training program* in an effort to teach them an artificial language—a language that required "speakers" to communicate by placing arbitrary plastic shapes on a magnetic communication board. The basic idea behind the study was to provide the people and the chimps with an equal amount of exposure to the artificial language and to compare the performance of the two groups.

In an effort to make the training identical for the people and the chimps, the research assistants who attempted to teach participants (i.e., the people and the chimps) the artificial language were forbidden from ever speaking to the human participants (as this would have given the human participants an obvious advantage over the chimps). Moreover, in an effort to minimize experimenter bias, the research assistants were carefully trained to present their language lessons in a highly standardized fashion. Both groups of participants were given three hours of daily training in the artificial language, and this training lasted for 30 days. Every five days, the participants were tested extensively in several aspects of language comprehension and production. For example, there were separate tests for vocabulary and for understanding of grammar or syntax. Importantly, these tests were scored by blind raters who were shown only the responses the participants had made on their magnetic boards (i.e., the raters did not know whether a given set of responses had been produced by a person or a chimp). When asked to summarize the primary findings of the study, the principal investigator reported three important findings. First, at each of the six testing sessions, the human participants performed significantly better than the chimps. Second, the advantages displayed by the humans were larger for the tests involving grammatical rules than they were for the tests involving simple vocabulary. And third, the advantages displayed by the human participants generally grew larger over the course of the six testing sessions. On the basis of these findings, the researcher concluded that, unlike people, chimpanzees do not have the ability to learn and use language.

Critique this interpretation of the study and formulate a more "pro-chimp" interpretation. First, in light of the primary findings, is the researcher's conclusion justified? What else might you want to know about the details of these findings before you decide whether you agree with the researcher's interpretation? Second, are there any additional control procedures you would like to see included in the study before you conclude that the overall learning situation was really equal for the people and the chimps? Third, even if you included every imaginable control procedure during the administration of the study itself, can you think of any preexisting differences between the ten people and the ten adult chimps (i.e., any confounds) that would be virtually impossible to control in a study such as this?

16. He May Be Small but He's Slow

The similarity hypothesis in interpersonal attraction suggests that "birds of a feather flock together"—that is, people are attracted to similar others. Both correlational and experimental studies suggest that this is true. For example, married couples tend to be similar at a much greater than chance level on dimensions as diverse as age, religion, eating habits, and shoe size. Thus, we know that similar people tend to pair off together. But once people are together, does similarity predict happiness? That is, if some couples are *more* similar than others, will those same couples be more satisfied than others? To address this question, a researcher classified married couples as high versus low in similarity by using established methods. He then assessed various aspects of each couple's level of relationship satisfaction by asking them 50 different questions in a confidential survey. He found that on two of the 50 items ("in love" and "committed") the high-similarity couples scored significantly higher than the low-similarity couples (both p's < .05). In addition, on one of the remaining questions ("sexually attracted") the low-similarity couples actually scored higher (p < .05). He concluded that "among married couples, a high degree of attitudinal similarity appears to lead to love and commitment but may simultaneously reduce sexual attraction." Besides pointing out that correlation does not guarantee causation, how would you criticize his findings? How might you remedy the problem(s) you see?

17. Everyone's a Winner

If you are familiar with grocery stores in southern California, and you've heard the results of Lucky's price surveys, you have heard that Lucky is the "low-price leader" among southern California grocery stores. Of course, if you've heard the results of surveys conducted by Ralphs' or Von's grocery stores you have also heard that *these* grocery stores have the best prices in southern California. We haven't bothered to conduct our own price survey, but we feel certain that when several stores all claim to be the least expensive store around, they can't *all* be correct. To add to the confusion, however, we feel pretty sure that the researchers who conducted many of these price surveys had some training in statistics and methodology. For example, most of the price surveys we've heard about involve randomly sampling a large number of items at different grocery stores and simply comparing the price totals of these same items (brand for brand) at two or more stores. At first blush it seems that nothing could possibly be more fair or scientific. After all, no known sampling technique is better than simple random sampling. We may never get to the bottom of who is correct, but we can think of an important change these researchers should make in their sampling procedures if they really wish to get things right. If the stores really wanted to know who's the cheapest, what advice would you give them about improving their sampling procedure?

18. Can a Couple of Beers Really Go Straight to Your Belly?

The results of a recent study of 12,000 people conducted by a group of researchers in North Carolina (reported in the *News of the Weird*—we're not making this up) showed that people who drink a lot of beer tend to put on a lot of weight in their bellies. In contrast, people who drink a lot of wine do not. Thus, there appears to be empirical support for the existence of "beer bellies."

We know that alcohol has a lot of useless calories, but we are skeptical of the claim that different alcoholic beverages turn into fat that goes to different parts of our bodies. Can you think of any factors that should be controlled before we conclude that beer bellies are truly a direct consequence of beer consumption?

19. What's in a Name?

In a classic experiment published in 1968, Goldberg devised a simple and elegant way to study gender discrimination. Goldberg simply asked people to evaluate an essay. However, he gave some people the impression that the essay had been written by a man while giving others the impression that the essay had been written by a woman. He did this by merely providing bogus, sex-typed author names on otherwise identical versions of the essay. For example, people asked to evaluate an essay could learn that the essay had been written by John or Joan McKay, Stephen or Stella Hamilton, or Paul or Pauline Conger. Goldberg found that people evaluated the essay more favorably when they thought it had been written by a man. Following the publication of Golberg's findings, the use of sex-typed names became a very popular way to study topics such as gender discrimination and stereotyping.

Although there is ample evidence that gender discrimination is alive and well in our culture, it now seems pretty clear that there was a problem with Goldberg's original study—and with many of the studies that followed in its footsteps. Although you may wonder how an experiment as simple and elegant as Goldberg's could possibly involve a serious confound, consider the ratings of essay quality provided by participants in the hypothetical study summarized below. These ratings should provide you with a clue about the confound that appears to have existed in Goldberg's study. In case this clue isn't very helpful, you might want to take a peek at Kasof's (1993) insightful review of research using sex-typed names. In fact, as an additional clue, we should confess that we used Tables 4 and 5 of Kasof's paper to generate the means that appear below. Finally, as a really big clue, you might recall that we reviewed this specific research topic in your text. Can you remember what we had to say?

TABLE 13.1 Judged quality of essay and gender of essay writer

Brian	Gary	David	Harry	Male Average
4.93	4.24	5.43	3.11	4.43
Louise	Ruth	Lisa	Dorothy	Female Average
3.97	3.68	4.62	2.79	3.77

Note: Each pair of names (i.e., each of the first four columns) reflects the findings of a different experiment. Higher values correspond to higher ratings of essay quality, and you may assume that differences of a quarter of a point or greater are statistically significant.

20. Are You Threatening Me?

In case you may have drawn the inappropriate conclusion that our culture is relatively free of gender bias, we should remind you that regardless of how people evaluate hypothetical male and female essay writers, there is plenty of solid evidence that people are predisposed to see women (and men) in ways that are consistent with culturally shared sex-role stereotypes. In fact, as you may recall from the discussion of meta-analysis in Chapter 10, gender stereotypes are so pervasive that even scientists who study gender sometimes allow their assumptions about gender to get the better of them. Specifically, recall that early studies of conformity and persuasion appeared to show that women are more easily persuaded than men. However, subsequent research demonstrated that when the topic of influence is one with which men happen to be less familiar than women, men are more easily persuaded than women. Early research on gender and persuasion was misleading.

A great deal of contemporary research on gender, ethnicity, and intellectual potential may also be misleading. Specifically, researchers interested in intelligence and academic performance have sometimes tried to develop "SES-free," "culture free," or "gender neutral" tests of general intelligence, mathematical ability, etc. For example, in the case of tests aimed at identifying ethnic differences in intelligence, researchers might present people with problems to which neither highly educated nor highly uneducated people are likely to have ever been exposed. Similarly, researchers interested in gender and mathematical ability might present sixth- or seventh-grade kids with math tests that focus on questions that even well-educated sixth and seventh graders have yet to learn about (e.g., by giving seventh graders math questions from the SAT or GRE). Many such studies have revealed that boys (or men) outperform girls (or women). Other studies have revealed that whereas boys and girls perform at about the same average level, there are many more boys who manage to earn extremely high scores on such inappropriately difficult tests. In addition to problems such as experimenter bias or participant expectancies, we can think of at least two very serious confounds that appear to plague studies such as these. Because these confounds are both rather subtle, we will tell you that one confound has to do with the question of whether these difficult tests are, in fact, equally unfamiliar to boys and girls who come from the same schools. The other confound is sort of a cousin of participant expectancies, and it has to do with the inherently social nature of achievement tests. For a further clue about this second confound, you might want to take a look at the research of Steele and Aronson (1995) on "stereotype threat."

Coda

We began this book by saying that it was our goal to depart from traditional treatments of research methods by making them both interesting and easy to understand. Although it is hard for us to know how close we have come to achieving this difficult goal, we hope that we have achieved the more modest goal of emphasizing what is logical and intuitive about research methods—and thus minimizing some of the discomfort that is part of any learning process. We also hope that we have communicated some degree of enthusiasm for research. In short, we hope that you have learned something valuable, and that you have had at least a little fun in so doing.

Finally, we would like to add that in the process of writing this book we have learned a few things ourselves. Although this may sound heretical, the most important thing we learned about research methods was that, prior to writing this text, we had probably overestimated the importance of the laboratory experiment in scientific advancement. This does not in any way mean that we do not value experimentation. The experiment is a symbol of what distinguishes science from music and literary criticism—and as far as we know, neither of us could ever make a living at either of these other disciplines. However, as we worked on this book, we realized that, without a little help from logic, intuition, and nonexperimental research methods, the lab experiment simply is not enough to get the whole job done. From this perspective, if our goal is to move from vague guesses about psychological truths to closer and closer approximations of the real thing, we think that we will probably get closer more quickly by paying attention both to "experience carefully planned" and to experiences that can be carefully looked for (or stumbled across) only in the field. This does not mean becoming armchair philosophers. Instead, it means complementing our laboratory experiments with observations made in the real world—or supplementing our statistical analyses with logical analyses derived from creative thought experiments. In short, it is the *logic* of experimentation more than the mere practice of conducting experiments that lies at the heart of the scientific method. Although the experimental paradigm is an incredibly powerful tool, complete researchers will want to remember the purpose of this tool, and they may often want to supplement it by using other useful research tools. Because we are in the business of trying to understand things as ephemeral and elusive as the weight of smoke, we must learn to make careful use of every tool at our disposal.

Appendix

An Experimental Replication of the Depressed Entitlement Effect Among Women

John T. Jost
Stanford University

Running Head: DEPRESSED ENTITLEMENT AMONG WOMEN

An Experimental Replication of the Depressed Entitlement Effect among Women

John T. Jost

Graduate School of Business

Stanford University

Author's Note: The author wishes to thank William J. McGuire for providing personal and financial support for the research described herein and Mahzarin Banaji for her encouragement and influence on this and related work. Gratitude is expressed also to Jay Bartletti and Jennifer Roberts for acting as independent judges. Helpful comments for revision were offered by Brenda Major, Jim Shah, Eddy van Avermaet, and two anonymous reviewers. The study was conducted while the author held a Robert M. Leylan Graduate Fellowship in Social Science at Yale University. Other funding for the project was provided by a grant from the Faculty Research Assistant Program at the University of California at Santa Barbara.

Abstract

Previous research has suggested that women pay themselves significantly less than

men pay themselves for the same amount of work (Callahan-Levy & Messé, 1979;

Major, McFarlin, & Gagnon, 1984). In an experimental study involving 132

participants (68 men and 64 women), this "depressed entitlement effect" was

replicated in a current sample of university students. Independent judges unaware of

participant gender perceived no differences in quality between products of men and

women, indicating that the two groups' efforts did not differ in objective terms.

Results are interpreted in terms of a general "system justification" framework (Jost

& Banaji, 1994), according to which members of disadvantaged groups internalize

ideological justifications for their own disadvantage.

An Experimental Replication of the Depressed Entitlement Effect among Women

It has been suggested often that members of oppressed groups internalize aspects of their oppression, coming to believe in the legitimacy of their own inferiority (e.g., Allport, 1954; Kidder & Stewart, 1975; Lewin, 1941). Marxian social theorists have invoked the concept of "false consciousness" to describe these and other social and cognitive effects of material domination (see Jost, 1995; Jost & Banaji, 1994). Insofar as dominant groups in society wish to preserve their "hegemonic rule", they will use their control over educational and cultural resources to win the "spontaneous consent" of subordinate groups (Gramsci, 1971). According to the theory of "system justification" (Jost, 1996; Jost & Banaji, 1994; Stangor & Jost, 1996), there is a learned tendency to accept and justify existing systems of social arrangements in such a way that these arrangements are perceived as rational, just, natural, and perhaps even inevitable. Stereotypes and other social judgments, according to this view, function to preserve a sense that inequalities between groups are justified, despite potential costs to individuals' self-esteem and groups' social identity (Jost & Banaji, 1994).

One oppressed group that has been studied with increasing frequency in this context is women. It has been argued that women in general are relatively unaware of their status as an oppressed group and that they hold many beliefs that are consonant with their own oppression (Gurin, 1985; Major, 1994). Gender socialization practices are so thorough in their justification of inequality that girls and women may develop system justifying attitudes with little or no conscious awareness (Bem & Bem, 1970).

One example of the internalization of gender inequality is the "depressed sense of entitlement" observed among female, as compared with male, research

Depressed Entitlement Among Women   4

participants (Callahan-Levy & Messé, 1979; Major, McFarlin, & Gagnon, 1984). These studies suggest that in the absence of clear-cut standards of comparison, women pay themselves significantly less money than do men for the same amount of work. This phenomenon has been related to the "paradoxical contentment effect" whereby women are just as satisfied with their employment situations as men, despite massive gender differences in earned wages (Major, 1994). It would appear that in the context of gender relations at least, "the disadvantaged often come to believe that they are personally entitled to less than do members of more advantaged groups" (Major, 1994, p. 307).

Historical factors are decisive when it comes to the acceptance or rejection of particular forms of inequality (e.g., Gramsci, 1971). It has been found, for instance, that Maori children in New Zealand expressed preferences for white over brown dolls before but not after the advent of the "Brown Power" Movement there (Vaughan, 1978). There is some reason to think that women as a group are more collectively aware of their disadvantaged state than in previous decades and that they are less likely to hold beliefs supporting this disadvantage. According to research by Lottes and Kuriloff (1994), "Ivy League" students in the late 1980's and early 1990's have tended to hold fairly favorable attitudes toward feminism. These researchers reported that mean scores on the Attitudes Toward Feminism Scale were between 1.21 and 1.42 standard deviation units above the scale's neutral point during the years 1987-1991. During this same time period, mean scores on an attitudinal measure of "male dominance" were found to be between 1.52 and 2.01 standard deviation units below the neutral point (see Lottes & Kuriloff, 1994). The goal of the present study was to seek replication of the "depressed entitlement" effect in a sample of current male and female students at an elite American university, where consciousness of gender issues was expected to be relatively high.

Method

One hundred and thirty-two undergraduate students (68 men and 64 women) of Yale College completed measures of self-evaluation and self-payment in the context of another experiment on intergroup relations (see Jost, 1996). The students received either course credit or $6 for their participation. Ages of participants ranged from 17-22 years, with a mean of 18.8 years (SD=1.16).

Early in the experiment, participants were asked to list up to five thoughts in response to the following prompt, which was borrowed from McGuire and McGuire (1991, p. 19): "Do you think that it would be better or worse if most *shopping* were done from home computer terminals rather than in stores?" Approximately 20-30 minutes later, after rating the quality of several other thought-lists on different topics (see Jost, 1996), both men and women were asked to turn back to the thought-lists they had generated and to evaluate them on the following seven dimensions: meaningfulness, logicality, sophistication, vividness, persuasiveness, originality, and insightfulness. All judgments were made on 15-point scales ranging from "Not at all" to "Extremely". Finally, participants were asked: "If you were an employer in charge of paying authors for their thought-listing contribution based on their quality, how much (from $1 to $15) would you pay the author of the thoughts you listed?" Thus, research participants first generated open-ended thought-lists and then later in the same experimental session evaluated the quality and deservingness of their own efforts.

Depressed Entitlement Among Women   6

The original thought-lists were subjected to ratings by two external, independent judges (one woman and one man), both of whom were blind to the hypotheses of the study and to the gender of each of the original research participants. (Two thought-lists were found to be unusable, one of which was left blank and one of which was found to be illegible, reducing the number of thought-lists rated from 132 to 130). Judges were instructed to evaluate each thought-list on the same seven dimensions (meaningfulness, logicality, sophistication, vividness, persuasiveness, originality, and insightfulness) that the original participants had used and to render the same decision as to payment deservingness (again based on a scale ranging from $1 to $15). The purpose of this rating procedure was to ensure that there were no differences in the objective quality of thought-lists generated by men and women.

Results

First, neither of the independent judges perceived any differences between the thought-lists of women and men. Multivariate analyses of variance were conducted in order to assess the impact of participant gender on the eight ratings taken as a whole, and univariate analyses were conducted in order to assess the impact of participant gender on each of the eight ratings separately. Whether multivariate effects are assessed by combining the ratings of the two judges or by examining each judge's ratings individually, there were no general effects of participant gender on ratings of quality ($F < 2$ in all three cases). Furthermore, not one of the univariate tests reached statistical significance ($p < .05$) for either of the judges, so the conclusion is clear: independent judges were unable to perceive any differences in quality between thought-lists written by men and thought-lists written by women on any of the eight dimensions.[1]

Although independent judges perceived no differences between the thought-lists of men and women, self-ratings indicated that women and men evaluated and paid themselves differently for their thought-list contributions. Multivariate analysis of variance yielded a significant main effect of participant sex on combined evaluation and payment ratings (F (8, 123) = 2.41, p < .02). Univariate analyses indicated that women's self-ratings were significantly lower than men's self-ratings on only two of the dimensions, self-payment (F (1, 130) = 6.05, p < .02) and insight (F (1, 130) = 7.87, p < .01). Differences attained marginal significance (p < .10) for two other self-ratings, sophistication and originality, again in the same direction of women rating themselves lower than men. No gender differences were observed for ratings of how meaningful, logical, vivid, or persuasive the thought-lists were (see Table 1).

The strongest piece of evidence in support of the depressed entitlement hypothesis was that women judged their own thought-lists to be worth significantly less than men judged their thought-lists to be. Whereas men estimated the value of their contributions at $9.73 (SD = 3.21), women estimated the value of theirs at $8.22 (SD = 3.37). Thus, men "paid" themselves $1.51 or 18% more than did women for the same amount of work and, according to independent judges, the same quality of work.

A composite measure of evaluation was created by averaging across the seven dimensions of evaluation, and this composite measure was used as a covariate in order to determine whether or not the depressed entitlement effect on payment would persist even after controlling for gender differences on evaluation in general. Results of the analysis of covariance were that women paid themselves significantly less than men did (F (1, 129) = 4.04, p < .05), even when mean evaluation scores were covaried out. Thus, the effects of gender on self-payment cannot be attributed solely to differences in evaluation.

Discussion

It has been argued that girls and women internalize their group's relative economic disadvantage and consequently experience a depressed sense of entitlement (e.g., Major, 1994). We replicated the findings of Callahan-Levy and Messé (1979) and Major *et al.* (1984) in the context of an experimental study involving male and female students at an elite North American university, where gender consciousness was expected to be relatively high (Lottes & Kuriloff, 1994). For measures of self-payment, women's ratings were significantly lower than men's, indicating that women believed their contributions to be less valuable than did men. Results such as these are supportive of a system justification perspective, which stresses the power of dominant ideologies to affect the attitudes and behaviors of disadvantaged group members (Jost, 1995, 1996; Jost & Banaji, 1994; Stangor & Jost, 1996).

Several explanations for the depressed entitlement effect among women have been offered (see Major *et al.*, 1984, p. 1400). First, by drawing intrapersonal comparisons, women may be using a standard of payment that is consonant with their own past situations of disadvantage and which is lower than the standard that men hold based on their personal experiences. Secondly, by drawing intragroup (rather than intergroup comparisons), women may compare their wages to those of other women, resulting in a lower standard than that used by men. Thirdly, it has been suggested that women and men may possess different value systems, and that women may value material rewards less than men. Fourthly, women may devalue their work inputs, assuming that their efforts are not as great as those of men. A fifth and final explanation is that women may perceive less of a direct connection between work and pay, so that their self-rewards may be more susceptible than those of men to contextual influences. Of course, these proposed mechanisms are not mutually exclusive (Major, 1994); all of them may operate in concert to produce depressed entitlement effects.

Still, each of these "explanations" requires an explanation in itself. One may reasonably ask why women in general do not compare their wages to those of men, why they devalue material rewards in general, why they underestimate the value of their own efforts, and why they perceive less of a connection between work and reward. These phenomena are best understood in terms of a general framework for understanding the social and cognitive effects of material inequality (e.g., Jost, 1995). It would appear that people tend to explain and justify differences in status, power, prestige, or success in such a way that the legitimacy of the overall system is seldom, if ever, called into question (Jost & Banaji, 1994; Major, 1994; Stangor & Jost, 1996). As the present findings demonstrate, it may take years, even decades, for members of oppressed groups to develop oppositional ideologies which reject the justifications promulgated by members of dominant groups (e.g., Gramsci, 1971; Gurin, 1985; Vaughan, 1978).

References

Allport, G. W. (1954). *The nature of prejudice.* Cambridge, MA: Addison Wesley.

Bem, S. L., & Bem, D. J. (1970). Case study of a nonconscious ideology: Training the woman to know her place. In D.J. Bem (Ed.) *Beliefs, attitudes, and human affairs* (pp. 89-99). Belmont, CA: Brooks/Cole Publishing Co.

Callahan-Levy, C. M., & Messé, L. A. (1979). Sex differences in the allocation of pay. *Journal of Personality and Social Psychology, 37,* 433-446.

Gramsci, A. (1971). Selections from the prison notebooks. New York: International Publishers.

Gurin, P. (1985). Women's gender consciousness. *Public Opinion Quarterly,* 49, 143-163.

Jost, J. T. (1995). Negative illusions: Conceptual clarification and psychological evidence concerning false consciousness. *Political Psychology, 16,* 397-424.

Jost, J. T. (1996). *Ingroup and outgroup favoritism among groups differing in socio-economic success: Effects of perceived legitimacy and justification processes.* Unpublished doctoral thesis, Yale University.

Jost, J. T., & Banaji, M. R. (1994). The role of stereotyping in system-justification and the production of false consciousness. *British Journal of Social Psychology, 33,* 1-27.

Kidder, L. H., & Stewart, V. M. (1975). *The psychology of intergroup relations: Conflict and consciousness.* New York: McGraw-Hill.

Lewin, K. (1941). Self-hatred among Jews. In *Resolving social conflicts: Selected papers on group dynamics* (pp. 186-200). New York: Harper & Brothers.

Lottes, H. L., & Kuriloff, P. (1994). The impact of college experience on political and social attitudes. *Sex Roles, 31,* 31-55.

Major, B. (1994). From social inequality to personal entitlement: The role of social comparisons, legitimacy appraisals, and group memberships. *Advances in Experimental Social Psychology, 26,* 293-355.

Major, B., McFarlin, D., & Gagnon, D. (1984). Overworked and underpaid. *Journal of Personality and Social Psychology, 47,* 1399-1412.

McGuire, W. J., & McGuire, C. V. (1991). The content, structure, and operation of thought systems. In R. S. Wyer and T. K. Srull (Eds.) *Advances in social cognition, Volume IV* (pp. 1-78). Hillsdale, NJ: Erlbaum.

Stangor, C., & Jost, J. T. (1996). Individual, group and system levels of analysis and their relevance for stereotyping and intergroup relations. In R. Spears, P. J. Oakes, N. Ellemers, & S. A. Haslam (Eds.) *The social psychology of stereotyping and group life* (pp. 336-358). Oxford: Blackwell.

Vaughan, G. M. (1978). Social change and intergroup preferences in New Zealand. *European Journal of Social Psychology, 8,* 297-314.

TABLE 1
Means (and Standard Deviations) on Dimensions of Self-Evaluation and Self-Payment by Sex of the Participant

Dimension	Women (n = 64)	Men (n = 68)	Univariate F-test (df = 1,130)
Meaningful	8.56	8.94	0.75
	(2.11)	(2.41)	
Logical	9.30	9.74	1.03
	(2.50)	(2.30)	
Sophisticated	7.73	8.68	3.52*
	(2.49)	(2.55)	
Vivid	8.00	7.88	1.00
	(2.75)	(2.60)	
Persuasive	8.78	9.19	0.63
	(2.75)	(2.74)	
Original	8.17	9.09	3.08*
	(2.56)	(2.54)	
Insightful	8.23	9.66	7.87***
	(2.80)	(2.37)	
Self-Payment	$8.22	$9.73	6.05**
	(3.37)	(3.21)	

*$p < .10$; **$p < .05$; ***$p < .001$.

Footnote

[1] Given that the evaluation task involved judjments of a highly subjective nature, it is not surprising that inter-rater agreement was modest, with inter-rater correlations for the eight judgments ranging in magnitude from +.32 to +.56.). The mean inter-rater correlation for the eight judgments was +.48 ($p. < .001$). All eight correlations did attain statistical significance at the level of $p < .001$ (n=130), so there is some evidence at least that the two judges were in fact differentiating among the thought-lists in terms of quality but that gender of the author was irrelevant to determinations of quality.

Glossary

accounting for conflicting results: Attempting to come up with theoretical reasons why different studies on the same topic have yielded different findings. McGuire noted that this is a good way to generate research hypotheses.

accounting for exceptions: Attempting to generate exceptions or limiting conditions to well-established psychological principles or empirical findings. McGuire noted that this is a good way to generate research hypotheses.

alpha level: The probability value that serves as the standard for rejecting the null hypothesis in a statistical test. Alpha is most commonly set at .05, meaning that researchers typically conclude that their findings are "real" only if findings as extreme as or more extreme than theirs would have occurred fewer than 5 times in 100 based on chance.

alternative hypothesis: The statistical assumption that there is a relation between the independent and dependent variables of interest in an investigation (i.e., the assumption that the researcher's prediction is true).

analyzing the practitioner's rule of thumb: Analyzing things that experts in a specific area do to achieve certain outcomes. McGuire noted that such an analysis can serve as a means of generating research hypotheses.

animism: The belief that natural phenomena are alive and influence behavior. This is the earliest category of metaphysical explanations for human behavior. See also **astrology** and **mythology and religion.**

applying a functional or adaptive analysis: Analyzing what an organism has to do to successfully master an environment or achieve a desired end state. McGuire noted that this is a good way to generate research hypotheses.

archival research: Research in which investigators examine naturally existing public records to test a theory or hypothesis.

astrology: The belief that human behavior and personality are influenced by the positions of celestial bodies such as planets and stars. This is one of the three categories of metaphysical explanations for human behavior. See also **animism** and **mythology and religion.**

attrition: See **experimental mortality.**

authority: Expertise or status in a specific area. People often rely on the opinions of authorities or experts as a way of answering questions. Relying on authority is one of four ways of knowing emphasized in this text.

behavioral confirmation: The tendency for social perceivers to elicit behaviors from a person that are consistent with the perceivers' initial expectations about the person (e.g., expecting a person to be aggressive and being more aggressive than usual with the person, which leads the person to behave in a very aggressive fashion toward you).

between-subjects design: An experimental design in which each participant serves in one and only one condition of the experiment. See also **within-subjects design.**

bidirectionality problem (reverse causality): An interpretive problem that occurs in most forms of passive observational research (e.g., in cross-sectional survey research). When an investigator documents that two variables are related, it is not usually possible to tell which variable is the cause of the other.

bimodal distribution: A distribution of scores in which there are two distinct ranges of scores that are more common than any other scores.

binomial effect size display: A simple, intuitive way to illustrate the strength of the relation between two dichotomous variables. It involves categorizing participants in terms of their scores on each of the two dichotomous variables and entering the frequencies of these categorizations in a contingency table whose rows and columns sum to 100. See Table 10.2 (page 306).

canon: A fundamental assumption that is accepted on faith. The four canons of science are **determinism, empiricism, parsimony,** and **testability.**

carryover effects: A methodological problem that occurs in within-subjects designs. This occurs when participants' responses in one condition of a study influence their responses in a subsequent condition. See also **order effects, counterbalancing.**

case study: A systematic analysis of the experiences of a particular person or group of people. In addition to serving as studies in their own right, case studies often serve as sources of inspiration for more traditional scientific investigations such as experiments.

categorical scale: See **nominal scale.**

ceiling effect: A methodological problem that occurs when everyone or almost everyone in a sample responds at the same high level on a survey question or dependent measure. A specific example of the problem of **restriction of range.**

census: An exhaustive survey of an entire population of people. Censuses are typically conducted to gather basic demographic information about people and to provide a total head count in a population. The U.S. government conducts a national census every ten years.

central tendency: A statistical term for the average or most representative score in a set of observations.

cluster sampling: A variation on true random sampling in survey research. Researchers who use this technique identify large, usually natural, groups of people (e.g., specific schools, specific cities, people living in specific zip codes) and first randomly sample a limited number of groups (e.g., 30 zip codes from the entire United States) before sampling individual people randomly from each of these groups.

coefficient of determination: The percentage of variance in one variable that is accounted for by a person's score on another variable. This is r^2, the square of the correlation coefficient describing the relation between the two variables.

complete counterbalancing: A comprehensive form of counterbalancing in which the researcher presents every possible order of the different experimental conditions in a within-subjects experiment.

conceptual validity: One of the four basic forms of validity emphasized in this text. Conceptual validity refers to the degree to which the procedures followed in a study (i.e., the specific variables that are measured and/or manipulated) map onto the specific hypothesis being tested.

conciseness (in writing):   Brevity, efficiency.

confederate: A trained research assistant who pretends to be a research participant by acting out a specific part during an experiment. This is usually done to create a psychological state that would otherwise be difficult to achieve in the real participant(s).

confound: A design problem in which some additional variable (a nuisance variable) varies systematically along with the independent variable(s) in which the researcher is interested.

construct validity: The degree to which the independent and dependent variables in a study truly represent the abstract, hypothetical variables (i.e., the constructs) in which the researcher is interested.

contamination effects: A methodological problem that occurs in experiments utilizing within-subjects designs. This occurs when participants' experiences in an earlier condition of the experiment influence their responses in a later condition of the experiment (e.g., because of learning, interference, or insight). This problem can sometimes, but not always, be corrected by the use of counterbalancing.

convenience sample: A sample of research participants who are selected into a study because they are readily available to a researcher rather than because they are highly representative of a population.

correlational methods: An approach to research in which researchers gather a set of observations about a group of people and test for associations (i.e., correlations) between different variables. Questionnaires, interviews, and archival studies are good examples of correlational studies.

counterbalancing: A method of control in within-subjects studies whereby the researcher varies the order in which participants experience the different experimental conditions (by presenting the conditions in different orders to different participants).

covariation: The principle of correlation, that is, the co-occurrence of or association between two events (e.g., when it is cloudy, it usually rains). According to John Stuart Mill, covariation is the first of three requirements that must be met to establish that one thing (such as clouds) causes something else (such as rain). See also **temporal sequence** and **elimination of confounds.**

cover story: A false story about the nature and purpose of a study. Researchers make use of a cover story to divert participants' attention from the true purpose of the study whenever they are concerned about participant reaction bias (i.e., when they believe that participants would not behave naturally if they knew the true purpose of the study). Most forms of deception in research are part of a cover story.

criterion: The outcome variable in a multiple regression analysis (the regression equivalent of the dependent variable in an experimental design).

cross-over interaction (disordinal interaction):   A specific kind of statistical interaction. This describes the situation in which (1) there are no main effects of either independent variable and (2) the effects of each independent variable are opposite at different levels of the other independent variable.

data: Numerical or categorical facts about specific people or things, especially when such people or things are the objects of systematic investigation.

debriefing: The ethical principle of educating participants about the nature and design of an investigation and making sure that they leave the study in a frame of mind at least as favorable as the one they brought to the study. When deception was used in a study, this includes informing participants about the nature of and reasons for the deception at the conclusion of the study.

deduction: Reasoning from the general to the specific (e.g., drawing a conclusion about human memory by logically deriving it from a set of higher-order principles about human cognition). See also **induction.**

demand characteristics: Aspects of an experiment that subtly suggest how participants are expected to behave. Demand characteristics often contribute to the problem of **participant expectancies.**

dependent variable: The variable in an experiment that is measured by an experimenter. The experimenter expects the dependent variable to be influenced by the independent variable.

descriptive statistics: Statistics used to summarize or describe a set of observations.

determinism: The idea that the universe is orderly—that all events have meaningful, systematic causes. It is one of the four canons of science emphasized in this text.

disordinal interaction: See **cross-over interaction.**

dispersion (variability):   A statistical term for the degree to which the typical score in a set of scores deviates from the mean or most representative score. As measures of dispersion increase, the mean becomes progressively less representative of the entire set of scores. The range and standard deviation are common measures of dispersion.

double-barreled question: A question, especially a survey question or dependent measure, that contains two different assertions (e.g., "I like going to movies and eating popcorn."). Such questions are problematic because participants who agree with one assertion and disagree with the other do not know how to respond.

double-blind procedure: A method of controlling for both participant expectancies and experimenter bias by keeping both research participants and experimenters unaware of participants' treatment conditions during an experiment.

effect size: An indicator of the strength of the relation between two or more variables. Two common indicators of effect size are r and d.

elimination of confounds: Ruling out other plausible causes of an event before concluding that one thing (e.g., touching poison ivy) is the cause of another (e.g., developing a rash). This is the third of John Stuart Mill's requirements for establishing causality. See also **covariation** and **temporal sequence.**

empiricism: An approach to understanding the world that involves collecting data or making observations. It is one of the four canons of science emphasized in this text.

environmental confound: A confound that occurs in nonexperimental research when a measured variable (e.g., depression) seems to cause something because people who are high or low on this variable also happen to be high or low on some contextual or situational variable (e.g., the recent loss of a loved one) that is associated with the outcome variable of interest (e.g., physical illness).

epidemiology (general definition):   The scientific study of the causes of disease.

epidemiological research (in clinical psychology):   Descriptive studies that focus primarily on the prevalence of different psychological disorders within different populations.

equifinality: The notion that the same behavior is often produced by many different causes.

evaluation apprehension: The form of participant reaction bias that occurs when participants attempt to behave in whatever way they think will portray them most favorably. Evaluation apprehension is a threat to internal validity.

expected value(s):   The most likely outcome (or the entire distribution of all possible outcomes) in a probabilistic situation that is repeated a great number of times under ideal conditions. For example, the expected value of an 80% chance of winning $100 is $80 because if you take this gamble a great number of times, the average amount of money you will gain will be $80 per trial of the gamble.

experiment: A research design in which the investigator manipulates one or more variables and then assesses the impact of this manipulation. An experiment isolates the effect of a variable by holding all other variables constant while this variable is manipulated.

experimental mortality (attrition):   The failure of some research participants to complete an investigation. In an experiment or quasi-experiment this may include *homogeneous attrition* (when attrition rates are equal across experimental conditions) and *heterogeneous attrition* (when attrition rates are different across experimental conditions). Heterogeneous attrition is primarily a threat to internal validity, and homogenous attrition is primarily a threat to external validity.

experimental paradigm: The approach to research (popularized by R. A. Fisher) in which the researcher randomly assigns participants to different treatment conditions, measures some outcome of interest, and makes use of inferential statistical tests to draw conclusions about the effects of the manipulation(s).

experimental psychology: A branch of psychology that emphasizes the systematic manipulation of variables as a means of learning about human experience and behavior. See **experimental paradigm.**

experimental realism: The degree to which the subjective experiences of research participants are realistic or psychologically meaningful. Well-designed experiments can be high in experimental realism even when they bear little physical resemblance to the real world (e.g., participants can be made fearful or anxious by being convinced that they are about to receive electric shocks to their big toes). See also **mundane realism.**

experimental simulation: An experiment in which participants are randomly assigned to treatment conditions but are asked to play a specific role or act out a part rather than engaging in wholly natural behavior.

experimenter bias: The bias that occurs in research when the investigator's expectations about participants lead to false support for these expectations. One form of experimenter bias occurs when experimenters interpret ambiguous behaviors in ways that are consistent with their expectations. A second form occurs when experimenters actually treat participants differently in different experimental conditions and thus influence participants' real behavior in hypothesis-consistent ways.

external validity: The degree to which a research finding provides an accurate description of what typically happens in the real world. The degree to which the observed relation between an independent and a dependent variable in a specific study applies to people, times, and settings not examined in the study of interest.

extreme groups approach: An approach to selecting people for inclusion in a laboratory study. In the case of this approach, experimenters recruit people to take part in a study only if such people receive extreme (i.e., very high or very low) scores on an individual difference measure of interest. See **prescreening** and **median split.**

factorial design: A research design containing two or more independent variables that are completely crossed, meaning that every level of every independent variable appears in combination with every level of every other independent variable.

false consensus effect: The tendency to overestimate the proportion of other people whose attitudes and behaviors are similar to one's own.

falsifiability: Openness to disconfirmation. This is closely related to the scientific canon of **testability** and may refer either to a philosophy of science or to a property of a specific theory or hypothesis.

falsification: An approach to scientific hypothesis testing in which a researcher attempts to gather evidence that would invalidate or disprove a specific hypothesis. This is one of the three common approaches to scientific hypothesis testing emphasized in this text.

floor effect: A methodological problem that occurs when everyone or almost everyone in a sample responds at the same low level on a survey question or dependent measure. A specific example of the problem of **restriction of range.**

freedom from coercion: The ethical principle of respecting participants' rights to drop out of a study if they choose to do so. This mainly consists of making it clear to participants that they have the right to stop participating without any fear of negative consequences.

Hawthorne effect: The increases in productivity that may occur when workers believe that their behavior is being studied or believe that they are receiving special treatment. Because participants who are receiving an experimental treatment are more likely to believe these things than are participants in a control condition, Hawthorne effects may be mistaken for treatment effects and thus are a threat to internal validity.

heterogeneous attrition: See **experimental mortality.**

history: Changes that occur over time in a very large group of people such as those living in a city, state, nation, or culture. When an investigator conducts a pretest-posttest study in which all participants receive a treatment, changes due to history may masquerade as treatment effects. Thus, history represents a threat to internal validity. See also **maturation.**

homogeneous attrition: See **experimental mortality.**

hourglass approach: A symmetrical approach to writing an empirical research paper in which the writer opens the Introduction broadly, becomes increasingly more focused throughout the Introduction, remains highly focused and detailed in the Method and Results sections, and then becomes increasingly broader in the Discussion or General Discussion section.

hypothesis: A prediction about a specific event or events. Hypotheses are usually derived from one or more theories.

hypothetico-deductive method: Beginning with a working set of assumptions and deriving one or more logical conclusions from these basic assumptions. McGuire noted that this is a good way to generate research hypotheses.

illusory correlation: The false association that people often form between membership in a statistical minority group and rare (and typically negative) behaviors.

incomplete counterbalancing: Any form of counterbalancing other than complete counterbalancing. A counterbalancing scheme in which the researcher *does not* present every possible order of the different experimental conditions in a within-subjects experiment.

independent variable: The variable in an experiment that is manipulated by an experimenter. The experimenter expects the independent variable or variables to influence the dependent variable.

induction: Reasoning from the specific to the general (e.g., drawing a conclusion about human memory by noticing that a certain pattern of findings shows up in many different studies of memory). See also **deduction, problem of induction.**

inferential statistics: Statistics used to make inferences, that is, to interpret or draw general conclusions about a set of observations.

informed consent: The ethical principle of advising participants about any foreseeable risks that are posed by a specific study and getting participants' permission to take part in the research prior to the beginning of the study.

interaction: A statistical term indicating that the effect of an independent variable on the dependent variable is different at different levels of another independent variable. The presence of an interaction means that one cannot make a simple, blanket statement about the independent and dependent variables in a factorial study. See also **main effect.**

interference effect: A problem that occurs in within-subjects designs when people's experience in one within-subject condition disrupts or diminishes their performance in a later within-subject condition. Interference effects are roughly the opposite of **practice effects.**

internal analysis: A specific form of patching in quasi-experiments in which a researcher breaks a group of participants into one or more subgroups to test for subgroup differences that are consistent with the focal theory or with competing theories. As an example, a researcher interested in whether the trauma of being exposed to a tornado leads to anxiety disorders might identify participants who were and who were not physically injured during a tornado to see if those who were injured showed a greater subsequent increase in their level of anxiety disorders.

internal consistency: The degree to which the total set of items or observations in a multiple-item measure behave in the same way. For example, the degree to which individual participants respond in relatively consistent ways to each of the specific items in a ten-item self-esteem survey. This is one of the three kinds of reliability emphasized in this text.

internal validity: The degree to which a research finding provides accurate or compelling information about causality. The degree to which changes in the independent variable in a particular study really do influence the dependent variable in the way suggested by the results of the study.

interobserver agreement (interrater reliability):   The degree to which different judges independently agree upon a measurement, judgment, or observation. This is one of the three kinds of reliability emphasized in this text.

interrater reliability: See **interobserver agreement.**

interval scale: A measurement scale that uses real numbers designating amounts to reflect relative differences in magnitude. Interval values can be negative, and adjacent scores on different parts of interval scales (e.g., 10 versus 11 and 25 versus 26) are typically, but not always, separated by equal amounts. Temperature, SAT scores, self-esteem scores, and most psychological scales are examples of interval scales. See also **nominal, ordinal,** and **ratio scales.**

intuition: An implicit understanding of a phenomenon that a person develops in the absence of any formal training on the topic. Loosely speaking, common sense or folk wisdom. It is one of four ways of knowing emphasized in this text.

judgment and decision making: A kind of scientifically rigorous single-variable research in which participants' judgments or decisions on a specific topic are compared with the judgments or decisions that would be made by a purely rational decision-maker.

Latin square: A form of partial counterbalancing in a within-subjects experiment in which each condition appears with equal frequency in every possible ordinal position (e.g., 1st, 2nd, 3rd, etc.). For example, an ideal Latin square for a within-subjects experiment with four conditions can be represented (1) A B C D, (2) B A D C, (3) C D A B, and (4) D C B A.

law: A precise, coherent, well-developed account of the relation between two or more variables. A universal statement that allows reliable predictions of future events.

leading questions: Questions that are worded in ways that suggest that some kinds of answers are more appropriate than others (e.g., "What do you like most about this wonderful textbook?").

logic: The formal rules of correct and incorrect reasoning. The use of logic is one of four ways of knowing emphasized in this text.

logical positivism: The idea that science and philosophy should be based solely on things that can be observed with absolute certainty. Many logical positivists (e.g., Karl Popper) also emphasize falsification as an approach to scientific discovery. See **falsification.**

longitudinal design: A nonexperimental research design (often involving questionnaire, interview, and/or observational techniques) in which researchers track participants' response over time (e.g., to track changes in children's social development or adults' personalities).

main effect: A statistical term indicating that, on the average (i.e., collapsing across all levels of all other independent variables), an independent variable in a factorial design had a significant effect on the dependent variable. Main effects can be taken at face value only when there are no interactions between the independent variables in a factorial study. See also **interaction.**

manipulation: Systematically varying the level of an independent variable in an experiment, with the goal of seeing whether doing so has any effect on the measured level of a dependent variable. Manipulation and **random assignment** are the two defining ingredients of the experimental method.

manipulation check: A measure taken to see if participants in different experimental conditions were truly experiencing different levels of the independent variable the researcher was hoping to manipulate.

marketing research: Research designed to assess consumers' attitudes about and preferences for different kinds of products and services. This kind of scientifically rigorous, single-variable research is very similar to public opinion polls.

maturation: Changes that occur over time in a specific person or group of people due to normal development or experience (e.g., growth, learning). When an investigator conducts a pretest-posttest study in which all participants receive a treatment, changes due to maturation may masquerade as treatment effects. Thus, maturation represents a threat to internal validity. See also **history.**

median split: An approach to selecting people for inclusion in a laboratory study. In the case of this approach, experimenters recruit people who score in either the top half or the bottom half (i.e., people above or below the median) on an individual difference measure of interest. This approach is usually inferior to the extreme groups approach. See **prescreening** and **extreme groups approach.**

meta-analysis: A set of statistical techniques for summarizing findings from a large set of studies to (1) determine the total amount of existing support for an effect, (2) assess the consistency or repeatability of the effect, and (3) identify determinants of the strength or magnitude of the effect across different studies.

metaphysical systems: An early set of explanations for human behavior and the operation of the physical world. Metaphysical explanations attribute behavior or experience to the operation of nonphysical forces such as deities. Metaphysical explanations include (1) **animism,** (2) **mythology and religion,** and (3) **astrology.**

method of deduction: A method of theory testing in which a specific hypothesis is derived from a broader theory and then tested empirically. This is contrasted with the method of induction because researchers first begin with a theory and then make observations. Logically, this method can be used only to falsify or qualify a theory because support for a theory in one instance never proves that the theory is true in all other instances (see the **problem of induction**).

method of induction: A method of scientific reasoning popularized by Francis Bacon. It refers to making many specific observations in an effort to draw general conclusions (to formulate theories or laws) about the nature of things. This is contrasted with the method of deduction because researchers first begin with observations and then try to formulate theories on the basis of these observations (but see the **problem of induction**).

mixed design: See **mixed-model design.**

mixed-model design: An experimental design in which at least one independent variable is manipulated on a between-subjects basis and at least one independent variable is manipulated on a within-subjects basis.

"more is better" rule of reliability: The idea that, all else being equal, measurements based on a large number of items, events, or observations are usually higher in reliability than measurements based on a small number of items, events, or observations.

multiple-groups design: A one-way experimental design in which there is a single independent variable that takes on three or more levels (e.g., a drug dosage study in which participants receive 0, 50, 100 or 150 mg of an experimental drug). See also **two-groups design.**

mundane realism: The degree to which the physical setting in an experiment is similar to the real world setting(s) in which the experimenter's independent and dependent variables are most likely to operate. See also **experimental realism.**

mythology and religion: The belief that human behavior and experience are influenced by the operation of spiritual forces such as the wishes of a deity. This is one of the three categories of metaphysical explanations for human behavior. See also **animism** and **astrology.**

name-letter effect: The finding that people like the letters in their own names (1) more than they like other letters of the alphabet and (2) more than other people like these same letters (when these letters do not occur in their names).

natural experiment: A kind of quasi-experiment in which the researcher makes use of archival data documenting the consequences of a natural manipulation such as a natural disaster or a change in traffic laws in a particular state. The best natural experiments typically involve arbitrary or near-chance events that affect a large group of people.

noise: An extraneous variable in an experiment that influences the dependent variable but is evenly distributed across experimental conditions. Contrast with **confound.**

nominal (categorical) scale: A measurement scale that uses meaningful but typically arbitrary, and nonnumerical, names or categories. Gender, HIV-status, license plate number, favorite color, and pet ownership are examples of nominal variables. See also **interval, ordinal,** and **ratio scales.**

nonresponse bias: The bias that occurs in research when a substantial proportion of those invited to take part in a study refuse to do so. If those who agree to take part are different from those who refuse, the resulting bias is similar to selection bias and represents a threat to external validity. See also **selection bias.**

normal distribution: A symmetrical, bell-shaped distribution of scores in which there is one distinct score that is more common than any other score. Most continuous physical and psychological measures (e.g., height, SAT scores) approximate a normal distribution.

null hypothesis: The statistical assumption that there is no relation between the independent and dependent variables of interest in an investigation (i.e., the assumption that the researcher's hypothesis is false).

observation: The practice of taking measurements of an object or phenomenon to figure out its nature (e.g., looking at something, measuring its weight). This is one of four ways of knowing emphasized in this text. See also **empiricism.**

observational research: Research in which investigators record the behavior of people in their natural environments without influencing people's behavior. Such observations are usually made secretly or unobtrusively.

one-group design: A very simple research design in which all the participants are in a single group that received a natural or experimental manipulation. This is the rough equivalent of a pseudo-experiment. It is usually very difficult to draw any clear conclusions from a study making use of a one-group design.

one-group, pretest-posttest design: A quasi-experimental research design in which measures are taken from a single group of research participants both prior to and after the participants receive a natural manipulation. Because this design does not include a control group, it usually yields findings that are open to many alternative explanations.

one-way, multiple-groups design: A research design in which there is only one independent variable but in which there are at least three levels of this variable (e.g., a drug effectiveness study in which participants receive 0, 50, 100, or 150 mg of a drug). See also **redundancy** and **multiple-groups design.**

operational confound: A confound that occurs when a measure designed to assess a specific construct such as self-esteem, time pressure, or happiness inadvertently measures something else as well. Operational confounds are applicable to both experimental and nonexperimental research designs and are closely tied to the notion of **operational definitions.**

operational definition: A definition of a theoretical construct that is stated in terms of concrete, observable procedures (e.g., defining helping as the number of minutes a child spends assisting a friend with a problem). See also **testability.**

order effects (sequence effects):   A methodological problem that occurs in experiments utilizing within-subjects designs. This occurs when participants' responses change over the course of the experiment due to fatigue, boredom, or the simple passage of time. This problem can almost always be corrected by the use of counterbalancing.

ordinal interaction: See **spreading interaction.**

ordinal scale: A measurement scale that uses order or ranking. Birth order, ranking in a foot race, or liking rankings for four different kinds of breakfast cereal are examples of ordinal variables. See also **interval, nominal,** and **ratio scales.**

paradigm: A widely shared set of guiding assumptions and research methods that make up a scientific research tradition.

paradoxical incidents: Puzzling, counterintuitive, or nonsensical observations. McGuire noted that such observations are a rich source of research hypotheses.

parsimony: The idea that, all else being equal, one should prefer simple theories or explanations over complex ones. It is one of the four canons of science emphasized in this text.

partial correlation: A statistical technique for determining the unique (i.e., non-redundant) relation between two variables when the relation between an additional variable (i.e., a potential confound) and each of the first two variables is taken into account. This also refers to the result of such an analysis.

partial counterbalancing: A category of incomplete counterbalancing in which several different orders are presented and in which each condition appears with equal or roughly equal frequency in every possible ordinal position in the experiment (e.g., 1st, 2nd, 3rd, etc.). The two most common forms of partial counterbalancing include (1) choosing several orders at random from the pool of all possible orders and (2) making use of a **Latin square** procedure.

participant expectancies: The form of **participant reaction bias** that occurs when participants consciously or unconsciously try to behave in ways they believe to be consistent with the experimenter's hypothesis. Participant expectancies are a threat to internal validity. See also **demand characteristics.**

participant reactance: The form of **participant reaction bias** that occurs when participants attempt to assert their sense of personal freedom by choosing to behave in ways they believe to be in opposition to the experimenter's expectations. Participant reactance is a threat to internal validity.

participant reaction bias: The bias that occurs when research participants realize they are being studied and behave in ways in which they normally would not. The three forms of participant reaction bias emphasized in this text are (1) **participant expectancies,** (2) **participant reactance,** and (3) **evaluation apprehension.** Most forms of participant reaction bias threaten the internal validity of an investigation.

patched-up designs: The term Campbell and Stanley (1966) used to refer to a set of quasi-experimental findings in which a researcher has made repeated use of patching (the addition of control groups) to refine and strengthen the design. See **patching.**

patching: A research method in which a researcher adds new conditions to a quasi-experiment to help establish the size of an effect, to test for the influence of conceivable confounds, or both.

person-by-treatment quasi-experiment: A research design in which the researcher *measures* at least one independent variable and *manipulates* at least one other independent variable. Person-by-treatment designs are always **factorial designs.**

person confound: A confound that occurs in nonexperimental research when a variable (e.g., income level) seems to cause something because people who are high or low on this variable also happen to be high or low on some *individual difference* variable (e.g., education level) that is associated with the outcome variable of interest (e.g., scores on an IQ test). True experiments eliminate person confounds by virtue of their use of **random assignment.**

philosophy: The systematic study of human behavior and experience by means of logic, intuition, and empirical observation. Philosophers are interested in the nature of knowledge, ethics, aesthetics, logic, etc. Along with physiology, philosophy was one of the two most important precursors of psychology.

physiology: A branch of biology focusing on the functions, operations, and interrelations between different parts of the brain and body. Along with philosophy, physiology was one of the two most important precursors of psychology.

pilot study: A preliminary study or "practice study" conducted by researchers before they conduct the full-blown version of the study in which they are interested. Pilot studies often allow researchers to refine their experiments and/or hypotheses by revealing errors or problems in the design of the study.

population survey: A survey designed to provide a description of the members of a population by sampling a representative portion of the population. If researchers make use of random sampling, they can typically provide accurate estimates of the characteristics of a very large population based on a relatively small number of people.

positive test bias: The tendency for hypothesis testers to attempt to confirm rather than disconfirm a hypothesis. This bias in hypothesis testing is similar to (1) behavioral confirmation in social interaction and (2) validation as an approach to scientific hypothesis testing.

posttest-only design with nonequivalent group: A quasi-experimental design in which a researcher compares two similar but nonidentical groups after one and only one of the groups experiences a treatment condition.

practice effect: A problem that occurs in within-subjects designs when people's experience in one within-subject condition facilitates their performance in a later within-subject condition. Practice effects are thus very similar to **testing effects** and are roughly the opposite of **interference effects.**

predictor(s): The variable(s) used to predict an outcome of interest in a multiple regression analysis (the regression equivalent of the independent variables in an experimental design).

prescreening: A procedure for identifying the participants who will take part in a laboratory study (usually a person-by-treatment quasi-experiment). Researchers who use this technique give an individual difference measure to a large group of people prior to the time that they run their laboratory studies. People who receive specific scores (usually extreme scores) on the individual difference measure are then recruited to take part in the laboratory study.

pretest-posttest design with nonequivalent groups: A quasi-experimental research design in which data are collected from two presumably comparable groups of research participants both prior to and after one of the groups receives a natural manipulation. To the degree that one can safely assume that the two groups truly were similar prior to the time that they experienced different levels of the manipulation, this is a relatively strong quasi-experimental design.

probability: The number of specific outcomes that qualify as an event divided by the total number of all possible outcomes (e.g., the probability of drawing an ace from a fair deck of cards is 4/52 or 1/13). Probabilities can never be lower than 0 or higher than 1.0.

problem of induction: A shortcoming of the method of induction. The problem, pointed out by David Hume, is that one can never safely infer anything with absolute certainty on the basis of induction (reasoning from specific observations to general principles). The problem exists because a single disconfirming instance can invalidate a principle that has received consistent support in hundreds of previous observations.

procedural confound: A confound that occurs in a laboratory experiment or quasi-experiment when a researcher mistakenly allows a second variable to vary along with a manipulated variable. See also **environmental confound.**

protection from physical and psychological harm: The ethical principle of taking steps to eliminate or minimize any physical or psychological risks to the participants taking part in an investigation.

pseudo-experiment: A "false" experiment. A research design in which the investigator exposes one or more people to a variable of interest and notes that the people exposed to this treatment felt, thought, or behaved as expected.

psychology: The scientific study of human behavior.

public opinion poll: A survey study designed to determine the attitudes, opinions, or preferences of large groups of people such as voters or consumers. This is one kind of scientifically rigorous single-variable research. See also **marketing research.**

qualification: An approach to scientific hypothesis testing in which a researcher attempts to identify the conditions under which a hypothesis is and is not true. This is one of the three common approaches to scientific hypothesis testing emphasized in this text.

quasi-experiment: A research design in which the researcher has only partial control over his or her independent variables. Quasi-experiments include both natural experiments that are typically based on archival data and person-by-treatment quasi-experiments that are typically conducted in the laboratory.

questionnaire research: Research in which an investigator asks participants to respond to a standard set of written questions about their attitudes, moods, experiences, and/or background characteristics.

random assignment: A technique for assigning participants to different conditions in an experiment. The use of random assignment means that every person in the study has an equal chance of being assigned to any of the conditions of the study. The use of random assignment makes it highly likely that the groups of participants in different experimental conditions are highly similar to one another.

random sampling (random selection):   A technique for deciding which participants in a population are selected for inclusion in a study. When true random sampling is used, every person in a population (e.g., American adults) has an equal chance of being selected into the study. The use of random sampling makes it highly likely that the participants who take part in an investigation are highly similar to the entire population of people from whom they were sampled.

random selection: See **random sampling.**

randomization: Random sampling and random assignment. See also **experimental paradigm.**

range: A statistical term for the difference between the highest and the lowest score in a set of scores. The range is a measure of dispersion.

ratio scales: Measurement scales that use real numbers designating equal amounts to reflect relative differences in magnitude. Ratio scales have all the properties of interval scales except that ratio scales always have a true zero point (at which none of the quantity under consideration is present). Thus, ratio scales literally allow researchers to designate ratios (e.g., David is 6.1 times as heavy as Alisa; Faith solved 3.4 times as many anagrams as David did), and ratio scores cannot be negative. See also **nominal, ordinal,** and **interval scales.**

reasoning by analogy: Analyzing similarities or concordances between different phenomena to shed light on the less-well-understood of the two phenomena. McGuire noted that this is a good way to generate research hypotheses.

rectangular distribution: A distribution of scores in which all of the scores occur with equal frequency or likelihood (e.g., the distribution of the probabilities of drawing cards of different values from a fair deck).

redundancy (in writing):   A stumbling block, problem, flaw, error, mistake, quandary, hitch, mess, snag, or fault in writing (i.e., composition, inscription, written communication, prose production) that often or frequently, if not typically, involves unnecessarily, without useful purpose and for no good reason, repeating, restating, duplicating, saying over again, replicating, or reiterating oneself to the point of causing, producing, or creating suffering, distress, pain, and unhappiness (not to mention boredom or monotony) on the part of the reader or consumer of written prose rather than enlightening, edifying, educating, or informing said same reader or consumer of written prose. Contrast with **conciseness.**

regression coefficients: The statistical measures of association between variables that are generated when one conducts a multiple regression. They are conceptually identical to partial correlations.

regression toward the mean: The tendency for people who receive extreme scores on a specific test or measure to score closer to the mean when given the test or measure at some point in the future. Regression toward the mean occurs because performance is influenced by error or luck as well as by a person's true score. When an investigator conducts a pretest-posttest study in which all participants receive a treatment, regression toward the mean may masquerade as a treatment effect. Thus, it is a threat to internal validity.

reliability: The consistency, coherence, or repeatability of a measure or observation. The three kinds of reliability emphasized in this text include (1) interobserver agreement or interrater reliability, (2) internal consistency, and (3) temporal consistency or test-retest reliability.

repeated measures design: See **within-subjects design.**

replication: A follow-up experiment that tests the idea behind the original experiment again—often by making use of different operational definitions of the independent and dependent measures and sometimes by testing the idea on a different kind of research participant (e.g., adults versus children).

restriction of range: The methodological problem of a lack of variability in participants' response to a survey question or dependent measure. This includes both floor effects and ceiling effects.

reverse causality: See **bidirectionality problem.**

reverse counterbalancing: A form of counterbalancing the order of presentation of the experimental conditions in a within-subjects experiment. Some participants are presented with one specific order, and other participants are presented with the opposite order.

risk-benefit rule: The ethical principle of weighing (1) any potential risks to research participants taking part in an investigation against (2) the benefits to participants or to society as a whole that are likely to accrue from the research. The benefits must outweigh the risks.

sample: A subgroup drawn from a population that is being studied.

sampling error: The likely discrepancy between the results one obtains in a specific survey sample and the results one would have been likely to have obtained from the entire population. This estimate of a survey's potential inaccuracy is also known as the *margin of error.* All else being equal, surveys taken from larger samples usually suffer from less sampling error.

selection bias: Choosing research participants from a nonrepresentative sample by using imperfect (i.e., biased) sampling techniques rather than true random sampling. This typically represents a threat to external validity.

semantic priming: The finding that people recognize most words more quickly than usual when they have just been exposed to words that have a similar meaning. For instance, people are usually able to identify the word "smile" more quickly than usual if they have just been exposed to the word "happy." Semantic priming also refers to the experimental procedures used to demonstrate this effect.

sequence effects: See **order effects.**

serendipity: Luck or good fortune. B. F. Skinner noted that many important scientific discoveries are partly the result of serendipity.

simple effects tests (simple main effects tests): A set of follow-up tests that are conducted when the statistical analysis in a factorial design yields a significant interaction. Simple effects tests clarify the precise nature of an interaction.

simple main effects tests: See **simple effects tests.**

spreading interaction (ordinal interaction): A specific kind of statistical interaction. This describes the situation in which an independent variable has an effect at one level of a second independent variable but has a weaker effect, or no effect at a different level of the second dependent variable.

standard deviation: A statistical term for the average amount that each of the scores in a sample differs from the sample mean. The standard deviation is a very commonly used measure of dispersion.

statistical testing: A technique, popularized by R. A. Fisher, for drawing conclusions about the results of empirical studies. It involves considering the likelihood that the observed findings would have occurred by chance. If the results are unlikely to have occurred by chance, researchers conclude that the results support the hypothesis being investigated.

statistics: A set of mathematical procedures for summarizing and interpreting observations. See also **descriptive statistics** and **inferential statistics.**

structured debriefing: An interview conducted with participants immediately after they have completed a study to determine exactly what participants thought the researcher expected to find. This always occurs prior to the point at which the experimenter conducts a full debriefing in which he or she explains the true purpose of the study. Conducting a structured debriefing is more important than usual when researchers make use of **within-subjects designs.**

superstitious conditioning: The "false" conditioning that often occurs when an organism is provided with reinforcements at random intervals. It occurs because the organism comes to associate an arbitrary response with the delivery of the reinforcement and repeats the response until a reinforcement is eventually delivered.

survey research: Research in which investigators ask people to respond to written or verbal questions about their thoughts, feelings, and behavior. This includes pencil and paper questionnaires, face-to-face or telephone interviews, and—increasingly—electronic surveys filled out by e-mail or on the Internet.

temporal consistency (test-retest reliability): The degree to which participants' scores on an item or set of items remain stable over time. This is usually assessed by correlating participants' responses on a measure with their scores on the same measure assessed at some later date. This is one of the three kinds of reliability emphasized in this text.

temporal sequence: Establishing that a potential cause of an outcome occurs *prior to* the outcome in question. This is the second of John Stuart Mill's requirements for establishing causality. See also **covariation** and **elimination of confounds.**

test-retest reliability: See **temporal consistency.**

testability: The idea that scientific theories should be confirmable or disconfirmable using currently available research techniques. It is one of the four canons of science emphasized in this text.

testing effects: The tendency for most people to perform better on a test or personality measure the second time they take the test or measure. When an investigator conducts a pretest-posttest study in which all participants receive a treatment, testing effects may masquerade as treatment effects. Thus, testing effects represent a threat to internal validity.

theory: A general statement about the relation between two or more variables. A good theory should be testable or falsifiable. See also **hypothesis** and **law.**

third variable problem: The problem of confounds, especially as it applies to passive observational research.

time-series design: A quasi-experimental research design in which researchers collect multiple waves of data from two presumably comparable groups of research participants. If the two groups of participants receive highly similar scores on a dependent measure prior to a natural manipulation but begin to receive different scores immediately after the natural manipulation, this strongly suggests that the manipulation may be responsible for the observed post-manipulation differences.

two-groups design: An experimental design in which there is only one independent variable and only two levels of this variable. This is the simplest possible kind of experimental design.

Type I error: Rejecting the null hypothesis when the null hypothesis is actually correct. That is, concluding that a researcher's hypothesis is true when it is false.

Type II error: Failing to reject the null hypothesis when the null hypothesis is actually incorrect. That is, failing to conclude that a researcher's hypothesis is true when it is in fact true.

unobtrusive observations: Observations or measurements that are made secretly or surreptitiously (i.e., without asking participants any direct questions and without letting participants know that their behavior is being measured). An example of an unobtrusive measurement is assessing how far a participant sits from a confederate to determine how much the participant likes the confederate.

validation: An approach to scientific hypothesis testing in which a researcher attempts to gather evidence that supports or confirms the hypothesis. This is one of the three common approaches to scientific hypothesis testing emphasized in this text.

validity: The relative accuracy or correctness of a psychological statement or finding. The three kinds of validity emphasized in this text are internal validity, external validity, and construct validity.

within-subjects design (repeated measures design):   An experimental design in which each participant serves in more than one condition (typically all of the conditions) of the experiment. See also **between-subjects design**

References

ABRAMSON, P. R. (1984). *Sarah: A sexual biography.* Albany, NY: SUNY Press.

ABRAMSON, P. R. (1992). *A case for case studies: An immigrant's journal.* Newbury Park, CA: Sage Publications.

AIKEN, L. S., & WEST, S. G. (1991). *Multiple regression: Testing and interpreting interactions.* Newbury Park, CA: Sage Publications.

AJZEN, I. (1977). Intuitive theories of events and the effects of base-rate information on prediction. *Journal of Personality and Social Psychology, 35,* 303–314.

ALLOY, L. B., & ABRAMSON, L. Y. (1979). Judgment of contingency in depressed and nondepressed students: Sadder but wiser? *Journal of Experimental Psychology: General, 108,* 441–485.

ALLPORT, G. W. (1954). *The nature of prejudice.* Cambridge, MA: Addison-Wesley.

ALLPORT, G. W. (1961). *Pattern and growth in personality.* New York: Holt, Reinhart & Winston.

ANDERSON, C. A. (1987). Temperature and aggression: Effects on quarterly, yearly, and city rates of violent and nonviolent crime. *Journal of Personality and Social Psychology, 52,* 1161–1173.

ANDERSON, C. A. (1989). Temperature and aggression: Ubiquitous effects of heat on occurrence of human violence. *Psychological Bulletin, 106,* 74–96.

ARONSON, E., & CARLSMITH, J. M. (1968). Experimentation in social psychology. In G. Lindzey & E. Aronson (Eds.), *The handbook of social psychology* (pp. 1–78). Reading, MA: Addison-Wesley.

ARONSON, E., & METTEE, D. R. (1968). Dishonest behavior as a function of differential levels of induced self-esteem. *Journal of Personality and Social Psychology, 9,* 121–127.

ARONSON, E., WILLERMAN, B., & FLOYD, J. (1966). The effect of a pratfall on increasing interpersonal attractiveness. *Psychonomic Science, 4,* 227–228.

ASCH, S. E. (1955). Opinions and social pressure. *Scientific American, 193,* 31–35.

ASCH, S. E. (1956). Studies of independence and conformity: I. A minority of one against a unanimous majority. *Psychological Monographs, 70,* 1–70.

ASIMOV, I. (1964). *Asimov's biographical encyclopedia of science and technology.* Garden City, NY: Doubleday.

BAILLARGEON, R. (1994). How do infants learn about the physical world? *Current Directions in Psychological Science, 3,* 133–140.

BANAJI, M. R., & CROWDER, R. G. (1989). The bankruptcy of everyday memory. *American Psychologist, 44,* 1185–1193.

BANAJI, M. R., & HARDIN, C. D. (1996). Automatic stereotyping. *Psychological Science, 7,* 136–141.

BANDURA, A. (1977). *Social learning theory.* Englewood Cliffs, NJ: Prentice-Hall.

BARGH, J. A., CHEN, M., & BURROWS, L. (1996). Automaticity of social behavior: Direct effects of trait construct and stereotype activation on action. *Journal of Personality and Social Psychology, 71,* 230–244.

BARGH, J. A., & TOTA, M. E. (1988). Context-dependent automatic processing in depression: Accessibility of negative constructs with regard to self but not others. *Journal of Personality and Social Psychology, 54,* 925–939.

BARNES, J. (Ed.). (1984). *The complete works of Aristotle: The revised Oxford translation.* Princeton, NJ: Princeton University Press.

BARON, R. A., & BELL, P. A. (1976). Aggression and heat: The influence of ambient temperature, negative affect, and a cooling drink on physical aggression. *Journal of Personality and Social Psychology, 33,* 245–255.

BAUMEISTER, R. F. & STEINHILBER, A. (1984). Paradoxical effects of supportive audiences on performance under pressure: The home field disadvantage in sports championships. *Journal of Personality and Social Psychology, 47,* 85–93.

BAUMRIND, D. (1964). Some thoughts on ethics of research: After reading Milgram's "Behavioral Study of Obedience." *American Psychologist, 19,* 421–423.

BEAMAN, A. L., KLENTZ, B., DIENER, E., & SVANUM, S. (1979). Self-awareness and transgression in children: Two field studies. *Journal of Personality and Social Psychology, 37,* 1835–1846.

BEM, D. J. (1967). Self-perception: An alternative explanation of cognitive dissonance phenomena. *Psychological Review, 74,* 183–200.

BEM, D. J. (1972). Self-perception theory. In L. Berkowitz (Ed.), *Advances in experimental social psychology* (Vol. 6). New York: Academic Press.

BEM, D. J. (1987). Writing the empirical journal article. In M. P. Zanna & J. M. Darley (Eds.), *The compleat academic* (pp. 171–201). Hillsdale, NJ: Erlbaum.

BERKOWITZ, L., & LEPAGE, A. (1967). Weapons as aggression-eliciting stimuli. *Journal of Personality and Social Psychology, 7,* 202–207.

BETTLEHEIM, B. (1943). Individual and mass behavior in extreme situations. *Journal of Abnormal and Social Psychology, 38,* 417–52.

BIAGIOLI, M. (1993). *Galileo, Courtier: The practice of science in the culture of absolutism.* Chicago: University of Chicago Press.

BLANTON, H., COOPER, J., SKURNIK, I., & ARONSON, J. (1997). When bad things happen to good feedback: Exacerbating the need for self-justification through self-affirmation. *Personality and Social Psychology Bulletin, 23,* 684–692.

BLANTON, H., PELHAM, B. W., DEHART, T., & CARVALLO, M. (2001). Overconfidence as dissonance reduction. *Journal of Experimental Social Psychology, 37,* 373–385.

BLANTON, H., STUART, A .E., & VANDENEIJNDEN, R .J. J. M. (2001). An introduction to deviance-regulation theory: The effect of behavioral norms on message framing. *Personality and Social Psychology Bulletin, 27,* 848–858.

BODENHAUSEN, G. V. (1990). Stereotypes as judgmental heuristics: Evidence of circadian variations in discrimination. *Psychological Science, 1,* 319–322.

BOWLBY, J. (1977). The making and breaking of affectional bonds: I. Aetiology and psychopathology in the light of attachment theory. *British Journal of Psychiatry, 130,* 201–210.

BREHM, J. W. (1966). *A theory of psychological reactance.* New York: Academic Press.

BUI, K. V. T. (1997). A model of contrast and assimilation in social comparison. Unpublished doctoral dissertation, University of California, Los Angeles.

BUSS, A. (1988). Personal communication, October 1988.

CAMPBELL, D. T., & FISKE, D. W. (1959). Convergent and discriminant validation by the multi-trait multi-method matrix. *Psychological Bulletin, 56,* 81–105.

CAMPBELL, D. T., & STANLEY, J. C. (1966). *Experimental and quasi-experimental designs for research.* Chicago: Rand McNally.

REFERENCES   393

CAMPBELL, J. D. (1986). Similarity and uniqueness: The effects of attribute type, relevance, and individual differences in self-esteem and depression. *Journal of Personality and Social Psychology, 50,* 281–294.

CANDLISH, A. (1990). *The revised Waite's compendium of natal astrology.* London: Penguin Books.

CARVER, C. S., & SCHEIER, M. F. (1990). Origins and functions of positive and negative affect: A control-process view. *Psychological Review, 97,* 19–35.

CHAIKEN, S., LIBERMAN, A., & EAGLY, A. H. (1989). Heuristic and systematic information processing within and beyond the persuasion context. In J. S. Uleman & J. A. Bargh (Eds.), *Unintended thought* (pp. 212–252). New York: Guilford Press.

CIALDINI, R. B. (1993). *Influence: Science and practice* (3rd ed.). New York: HarperCollins.

CIALDINI, R. B., & ASCANI, K. (1976). Test of a concession procedure for inducing verbal, behavioral, and further compliance with a request to give blood. *Journal of Applied Psychology, 61,* 295–300.

CIALDINI, R. B., CACIOPPO, J. T., BASSETT, R., & MILLER, J. A. (1978). Low-ball procedure for producing compliance: Commitment then cost. *Journal of Personality and Social Psychology, 36,* 463–476.

COHEN, J. (1994). The earth is round ($p < .05$). *American Psychologist, 49,* 997–1003.

COLLINS, B. E., & HOYT, M. F. (1972). Personal responsibility-for-consequences: An integration and extension of the "forced compliance" literature. *Journal of Experimental Social Psychology, 8,* 558–593.

COOK, T. D., & CAMPBELL, D. T. (1979). *Quasi-experimentation: Design and analysis issues for field settings.* Boston: Houghton Mifflin.

COPI, I. M. (1978). *Introduction to logic* (5th ed.). New York: Macmillan.

COX, J. R., & GRIGGS, R. A. (1982). The effects of experience on performance in Wason's selection task. *Memory and Cognition, 10,* 496–502.

DAMASIO, A. R. (1994). *Descartes' error.* New York: Avon Books.

DAMASIO, H., GRABOWSKI, T., FRANK, R., GALABURDA, A. M., & DAMASIO, A. R. (1994). The return of Phineas Gage: The skull of a famous patient yields clues about the brain. *Science, 264,* 1102–1105.

DARLEY, J. M., & GROSS, P. H. (1983). A hypothesis-confirming bias in labeling effects. *Journal of Personality and Social Psychology, 44,* 20–33.

DARWIN, C. (1859). *On the origin of species by means of natural selection.* London: J. Murray.

DARWIN, C. (1872). *The expression of the emotions in man and animals.* London: J. Murray.

DARWIN, C. (1881). *The formation of vegetable mould, through the action of worms: With observations on their habits.* London: J. Murray.

DAVILA, J., BRADBURY, T. N., COHAN, C. L., & TOCHLUK, S. (1997). Marital functioning and depressive symptoms: Evidence for a stress generation model. *Journal of Personality and Social Psychology, 73,* 849–861.

DENNETT, D. C. (1991). *Consciousness explained.* Boston: Little, Brown.

DESCARTES, R. (1984). Principles of philosophy. In J. Cottingham, R. Stoothoff, & D. Murdock (Eds. & Trans.), *The philosophical writings of Descartes* (Vol. 1, pp. 193–291). Cambridge, England: Cambridge University Press. (Original work published 1644)

DEVINE, P. G. (1989). Stereotypes and prejudice: Their automatic and controlled components. *Journal of Personality and Social Psychology, 56,* 5–18.

DEWAAL, F. (1996). *Good natured: The origins of right and wrong in humans and other animals* (pp. 1–131) Cambridge, MA: Harvard University Press.

DIAMOND, J. (1992). *The third chimpanzee: The evolution and future of the human animal* (pp. 1–136). New York: Harper Collins.

DIENER, E., & WALLBOM, M. (1976). Effects of self-awareness on antinormative behavior. *Journal of Research in Personality, 10,* 107–111.

DOBSON, K .S. (1985). The relationship between anxiety and depression. *Clinical Psychology Review, 5,* 307–324.

DOOLEY, D. (1995). *Social research methods* (3rd ed.). Englewood Cliffs, NJ: Prentice-Hall.

DOOLING, D. J., & LACHMAN, R. (1971). Effects of comprehension on retention of prose. *Journal of Experimental Psychology, 88,* 216–222.

DUFFY, M. (1993). *Occam's razor.* London: Sinclair-Stevenson.

DUNNING, D., & STORY, A. L. (1991). Depression, realism, and the overconfidence effect: Are the sadder wiser when predicting future actions and events? *Journal of Personality and Social Psychology, 61,* 521–532.

EAGLY, A. H. (1978). Sex differences in influenceability. *Psychological Bulletin, 85,* 86–116.

EAGLY, A. H., & CARLI, L. (1981). Sex of researchers and sex-typed communications as determinants of sex differences in influenceability: A meta-analysis of social influence studies. *Psychological Bulletin, 90,* 1–20.

EAGLY, A. H., ASHMORE, R. D., MAKHIJANI, M. G., & LONGO, L. C. (1991). What is beautiful is good, but: A meta-analytic review of research on the physical attractiveness stereotype. *Psychological Bulletin, 110,* 109–128.

EDNEY, J. J. (1979). The nuts game: A concise commons dilemma analog. *Environmental Psychology and Nonverbal Behavior, 3,* 252–254.

EDWARDS, A. L. (1976). *An introduction to linear regression and correlation.* San Francisco, CA: W. H. Freeman.

EDWARDS, A. L., & THURSTONE, L. L. (1952). An internal consistency check for scale values determined by the method of successive intervals. *Psychometrika, 17,* 169–180.

ELLSWORTH, P .C. (1977). From abstract ideas to concrete instances: Some guidelines for choosing natural research settings. *American Psychologist, 32(8),* 604–615.

ETHICAL PRINCIPLES OF PSYCHOLOGISTS AND CODE OF CONDUCT. (1992). *American Psychologist, 47,* 597–1611.

FAZIO, R. H., JACKSON, J. R., DUNTON, B. C., & WILLIAMS, C. J. (1995). Variability in automatic activation as an unobtrusive measure of racial attitudes: A bona fide pipeline? *Journal of Personality and Social Psychology, 69,* 1013–1027.

FAZIO, R. H., SANBONMATSU, D. M., POWELL, M. C., & KARDES, F. R. (1986). On the automatic activation of attitudes. *Journal of Personality and Social Psychology, 50,* 229–238.

FAZIO, R. H., ZANNA, M. P., & COOPER, J. (1977). Dissonance and self-perception: An integrative view of each theory's proper domain of application. *Journal of Experimental Social Psychology, 13,* 464–479.

FEIN, S., HILTON, J. L., & MILLER, D. T. (1990). Suspicion of ulterior motivation and the correspondence bias. *Journal of Personality and Social Psychology, 58,* 753–764.

FESTINGER, L. (1957). *A theory of cognitive dissonance.* Stanford, CA: Stanford University Press.

FESTINGER, L., & CARLSMITH, J. M. (1959). Cognitive consequences of forced compliance. *Journal of Abnormal and Social Psychology, 58,* 203–210.

FISCHHOFF, B. (1982). Debiasing. In D. Kahneman, P. Slovic, & A. Tversky (Eds.), *Judgment under uncertainty: Heuristics and biases* (pp. 422–444). Cambridge: Cambridge University Press.

FISHER, R. A. (1925). *Statistical methods for research workers.* Edinburgh: Oliver & Boyd.

FISHER, R. A. (1935). *The design of experiments.* Edinburgh: Oliver & Boyd.

FISHER, R. A. (1938). *Statistical methods for research workers* (7th ed.). London: Oliver & Boyd.

FORER, B. R. (1949). The fallacy of personal validation: A classroom demonstration of gullibility. *Journal of Abnormal and Social Psychology, 44,* 118–123.

FREEDMAN, D., PISANI, R., PURVES, R., & ADHIKARI, A. (1991). *Statistics* (2nd ed.). New York: Norton & Company.

FREUD, S. (1962/1923). *The ego and the id* (translated by J. Riviere, revised and edited by J. Strachey). New York: Norton & Company.

GAO (1990). *Death penalty sentencing: Research indicates patterns of racial disparities. Report to Senate and House Committees on the Judiciary.* GAO/GGD-90-57.

GERGEN, K. J. (1973). Social psychology as history. *Journal of Personality and Social Psychology, 26,* 309–320.

GILBERT, D. T. (1989). Thinking lightly about others: Automatic components of the social inference process. In J. S. Uleman & J. A. Bargh (Eds.), *Unintended thought* (pp. 189–211). New York: Guilford Press.

GILBERT, D. T. (1991). How mental systems believe. *American Psychologist, 46,* 107–119.

GILBERT, D. T., KRULL, D. S., & MALONE, P. S. (1990). Unbelieving the unbelievable: Some problems in the rejection of false information. *Journal of Personality and Social Psychology, 59,* 601–613.

GILBERT, D. T., PELHAM, B. W., & KRULL, D. S. (1988). On cognitive busyness: When person perceivers meet persons perceived. *Journal of Personality and Social Psychology, 54,* 733–740.

GLENN, J. (1996). *Scientific Genius: The twenty greatest minds.* New York: Crescent Books.

GOLDBERG, P. (1968). Are women prejudiced against women? *Trans-Action, 5,* 28.

GREENWALD, A. G., & BANAJI, M. R. (1995). Implicit social cognition: Attitudes, self-esteem, and stereotypes. *Psychological Review, 102,* 4–27.

GREENWALD, A. G., MCGHEE, D. E., & SCHWARTZ, J. L. K. (1998). Measuring individual differences in implicit cognition: The implicit association test. *Journal of Personality and Social Psychology, 74,* 1464–1480.

GREENWALD, A. G., PRATKANIS, A .R., LEIPPE, M. R., & BAUMGARDNER, M .H. (1986). Under what conditions does theory obstruct research progress? *Psychological Review, 93,* 216–229.

GREENWALD, A. G., SPANGENBERG, E. R., PRATKANIS, A. R., & ESKENAZI, J. (1991). Double-blind tests of subliminal self-help audiotapes. *Psychological Science, 2,* 119–122.

GRICE, H. P. (1975). Logic and conversation. In D. Davidson & G. Harman (Eds.), *The logic of grammar.* Encino, CA: Dickenson.

HAMILTON, D. L., & GIFFORD, R. K. (1976). Illusory correlation in interpersonal perception: A cognitive basis of stereotypic judgments. *Journal of Experimental Social Psychology, 12,* 392–407.

HAMILTON, D. L., & ROSE, T. L. (1980). Illusory correlation and the maintenance of stereotypic beliefs. *Journal of Personality and Social Psychology, 39,* 832–845.

HAMILTON, D. L., & SHERMAN, J. W. (1994). Stereotypes. In R. S. Wyer, Jr. & T. K. Srull (Eds.), *Handbook of social cognition* (2nd ed., pp. 1–68). Hillsdale, NJ: Erlbaum.

HANEY, C., BANKS, C., & ZIMBARDO, P. (1973). Interpersonal dynamics in a simulated prison. *International Journal of Criminology and Penology, 1,* 69–97.

HARRÉ, R. (1981). *Great scientific experiments.* Oxford: Phaidon Press.

HEATHERTON, T. F., & POLIVY, J. (1991). Development and validation of a scale for measuring state self-esteem. *Journal of Personality and Social Psychology, 60,* 859–910.

HEDGES, L. V. (1987). How hard is hard science, how soft is soft science? The empirical cumulativeness of research. *American Psychologist, 42,* 443–455.

HEIDER, F. (1958). *The psychology of interpersonal relations.* Hillsdale, NJ: Erlbaum.

HEIMAN, G. A. (1995). *Research methods in psychology.* Boston: Houghton Mifflin.

HEISENBERG, W. (1955/1958). *The physicist's conception of nature* (translated by Arnold J. Pomerans). New York: Harcourt, Brace & World.

HETTS, J. J., & PELHAM, B. W. (2001). A case for the nonconscious self-concept. In G. B. Moskowitz (Ed.), *Cognitive social psychology: The Princeton symposium on the legacy and future of social cognition* (pp. 105–123). Mahwah, N. J.: Erlbaum.

HETTS, J. J., SAKUMA, M., & PELHAM, B. W. (2001). Two roads to positive regard: Implicit and explicit self-evaluation and culture. *Journal of Experimental Social Psychology.*

HIGGINS, E. T. (1989). Self-discrepancy theory: What patterns of self-beliefs cause people to suffer? In L. Berkowitz (Ed.), *Advances in experimental social psychology* (Vol. 22, pp. 93–136). San Diego: Academic Press.

HOOKE, R. (1665). *Micrographia or some physiological descriptions of minute bodies made by magnifying glasses with observations and inquiries thereupon.* London: The Royal Society.

HOVLAND. C. I., & WEISS, W. (1951). The influence of source-credibility on communication effectiveness. *Public Opinion Quarterly, 15,* 635–650.

HUCK, S. W., & SANDLER, H. M. (1979). *Rival hypotheses: Alternative interpretations of data-based conclusions.* New York: Harper & Row.

HULL, C. L. (1943). *Principles of behavior.* New York: Appleton–Century–Crofts.

HUSTON, T. L., & LEVINGER, G. (1978). Interpersonal attraction and relationships. *Annual Review of Psychology, 29,* 115–156.

ISEN, A. M. (1987). Positive affect, cognitive processes, and social behavior. In L. Berkowitz (Ed.), *Advances in experimental social psychology* (Vol. 20, pp. 203–253). San Diego: Academic Press.

ISEN, A. M., & LEVIN, P. F. (1972). Effect of feeling good on helping: Cookies and kindness. *Journal of Personality and Social Psychology, 21,* 384–388.

JONES, E. E., & SIGALL, H. (1971). The bogus pipeline: A new paradigm for measuring affect and attitude. *Psychological Bulletin, 76,* 349–364.

JONES, J. T., PELHAM, B. W., MIRENBERG, M. C., & HETTS, J. J. (2002). Name letter preferences are not merely mere exposure: Implicit egotism as self-regulation. *Journal of Experimental Social Psychology, 38,* 170–77.

JOST, J. T. (1997). An experimental replication of the depressed-entitlement effect among women. *Psychology of Women Quarterly, 21,* 387–393.

KAHNEMAN, D., & TVERSKY, A. (1973). On the psychology of prediction. *Psychological Review, 80,* 237–251.

KARNEY, B., & BRADBURY, T. N. (1997). Neuroticism, marital interaction, and the trajectory of marital satisfaction. *Journal of Personality and Social Psychology, 72,* 1075–1092.

KASOF, J. (1993). Sex bias in the naming of stimulus persons. *Psychological Bulletin, 113,* 140–163.

KENRICK, D. T., & MACFARLANE, S. W. (1986). Ambient temperature and horn honking: A field study of the heat/aggression relationship. *Environment and Behavior, 18,* 179–191.

KITAYAMA, S., & KARASAWA, M. (1997). Implicit self-esteem in Japan: Name letters and birthday numbers. *Personality & Social Psychology Bulletin, 23,* 736-742.

KLEIN, S. B., SHERMAN, J. W., & LOFTUS, J. (1996). The role of episodic and semantic memory in the development of trait self-knowledge. *Social Cognition, 14,* 277–291.

KLOPFER, D. S. (1996). Stroop interference and color-word similarity. *Psychological Science, 7,* 150–157.

KOOLE, S. L., SMEETS, K., VAN KNIPPENBERG, A., & DIJKSTERHUIS, A. (1999). The cessation of rumination through self-affirmation. *Journal of Personality and Social Psychology, 77,* 111–125.

KRULL, D. S. (1993). Does the grist change the mill? The effect of the perceiver's inferential goal on the process of social inference. *Personality and Social Psychology Bulletin, 19,* 340–348.

KRULL, D. S., & ERICKSON, D. J. (1995). Judging situations: On the effortful process of taking dispositional information into account. *Social Cognition, 13,* 417–438.

KUHN, T. S. (1970). *The structure of scientific revolutions* (2nd ed.). Chicago: University of Chicago Press.

LEAHEY, T. H. (1991). *A history of modern psychology.* Englewood Cliffs, NJ: Prentice-Hall.

LEPPER, M. R., GREENE, D., & NISBETT, R. E. (1973). Undermining children's intrinsic interest with extrinsic reward: A test of the "overjustification" hypothesis. *Journal of Personality and Social Psychology, 28,* 129–137.

LIEBERMAN, M. D., OCHSNER, K. N., GILBERT, D. T., & SCHACTER, D. L. (2001). Do amnesics exhibit cognitive dissonance reduction? The role of explicit memory and attention in attitude change. *Psychological Science, 12,* 135–139.

LOBEL, M., DUNKEL-SCHETTER, C., & SCRIMSHAW, S. C. (1992). Prenatal maternal stress and prematurity: A prospective study of socioeconomically disadvantaged women. *Health Psychology, 11,* 32–40.

MACDONALD, T. K., ZANNA, M. P., & FONG, G. T. (1995). Decision making in altered states: Effects of alcohol on attitudes toward drinking and driving. *Journal of Personality and Social Psychology, 68,* 973–985.

MAJOR, B. (1994). From social inequality to personal entitlement: The role of social comparisons, legitimacy appraisals, and group memberships. *Advances in Experimental Social Psychology, 26,* 293–355.

MARKUS, H. R., & KITAYAMA, S. (1991). Culture and the self: Implications for cognition, emotion, and motivation. *Psychological Review, 98,* 224–253.

MARSH, H. W. (1993). Relations between global and specific domains of self: The importance of individual importance, certainty, and ideals. *Journal of Personality and Social Psychology, 65,* 975–992.

MARTIN, L. L., SETA, J. J., & CRELIA, R. A. (1990). Assimilation and contrast as a function of people's willingness and ability to expend effort in forming an impression. *Journal of Personality and Social Psychology, 59,* 27–37.

MCGUIRE, W. J. (1961). Resistance to persuasion conferred by active and passive prior refutation of the same and alternative counterarguments. *Journal of Abnormal and Social Psychology, 63,* 326–332.

MCGUIRE, W. J. (1973). The yin and yang of progress in social psychology: Seven koan. *Journal of Personality and Social Psychology, 26,* 446–456.

MCGUIRE, W. J. (1989). A perspectivist approach to the strategic planning of programmatic scientific research. In B. Gholson, W. R. Shadish, Jr., R. A. Neimeyer, & A. C. Houts (Eds.), *Psychology of science: Contributions to metascience* (pp. 214–245). Cambridge, England: Cambridge University Press.

MCKEARNEY, J. W. (1987–1988). Asking questions about behavior. *Perspectives in Biology and Medicine, 21,* 109–119.

MCKELVIE, S. J. (1990). Student acceptance of a generalized personality description: Forer's graphologist revisited. *Journal of Social Behavior and Personality, 5,* 91–95.

MCKELVIE, S. J., & SCHAMER, L. A. (1988). Effects of night, passengers, and sex on driver behavior at stop signs. *Journal of Social Psychology, 128,* 685–690.

MICHAELS, J. W., BLOMMEL, J. M, BROCATO, R. M., LINKOUS, R. A., & ROWE, J. S. (1982). Social facilitation and inhibition in a natural setting. *Replications in Social Psychology, 2,* 21–24.

MILGRAM, S. (1963). Behavioral study of obedience. *Journal of Abnormal and Social Psychology, 67,* 371–378.

MILLER, A. G., COLLINS, B. E., & BRIEF, D. E. (1995). Perspectives on obedience to authority: The legacy of the Milgram experiments. *Journal of Social Issues, 51,* 1–19.

MILLER, J. (1984). Culture and the development of everyday social explanation. *Journal of Personality and Social Psychology, 46,* 961–978.

MOOK, D. G. (1983). In defense of external invalidity. *American Psychologist, 38,* 379–387.

MURRAY, S. L., HOLMES, J. G., & GRIFFIN, D. W. (1996). The benefits of positive illusions: Idealization and the construction of satisfaction in close relationships. *Journal of Personality and Social Psychology, 70,* 79–98.

NEELY, J .H. (1977). Semantic priming and retrieval from lexical memory: Roles of inhibitionless spreading activation and limited-capacity attention. *Journal of Experimental Psychology: General, 106,* 226–254.

NEUMAN, W. L. (1991). *Social research methods: Qualitative and quantitative approaches.* Boston: Allyn & Bacon.

NISBETT, R. E., & WILSON, T. D. (1977). Telling more than we can know: Verbal reports on mental processes. *Psychological Review, 84,* 231–259.

NUNNALLY, J. C., JR. (1970). *Introduction to psychological measurement.* New York: McGraw-Hill.

NUTTIN, J. M. (1985). Narcissism beyond Gestalt and awareness: The name letter effect. *European Journal of Social Psychology, 15,* 353–361.

NUTTIN, J. M. (1987). Affective consequences of mere ownership: The name letter effect in twelve European languages. *European Journal of Social Psychology, 17,* 381–402.

OLSON, J. M. (1992). Self-perception of humor: Evidence for discounting and augmentation effects. *Journal of Personality and Social Psychology, 62,* 369–377.

ORNE, M. T. (1962). On the social psychology of the psychological experiment: With particular reference to demand characteristics and their implications. *American Psychologist, 17,* 776–783.

PATERNOSTER, R. (1983). Race of victim and location of crime: The decision to seek the death penalty in South Carolina. *Journal of Criminal Law and Criminology, 74,* 754–785.

PEDHAZUR, E. J. (1982). *Multiple regression in behavioral research: Explanation and prediction* (2nd ed.). New York: Holt, Rinehart & Winston.

PELHAM, B. W., JONES, J. K., MIRENBERG, M. C., & CARVALLO, M. C. (2002). *The man who took a wife because of an H: Implicit egotism and marriage.* Under review.

PELHAM, B. W., MIRENBERG, M. C., & JONES, J. T. (2002). Why Susie sells seashells by the seashore: Implicit egotism and major life decisions. *Journal of Personality and Social Psychology, 82,* 469–87.

PELHAM, B. W. (1991a). On confidence and consequence: The certainty and importance of self-knowledge. *Journal of Personality and Social Psychology, 60,* 518–530.

PELHAM, B. W. (1991b). On the benefits of misery: Self-serving biases in the depressive self-concept. *Journal of Personality and Social Psychology, 61,* 670–681.

PELHAM, B. W. (1993). The idiographic nature of human personality: Examples of the idiographic self-concept. *Journal of Personality and Social Psychology, 64,* 665–677.

PELHAM, B. W. (1998). Unpublished raw data, University of California, Los Angeles.

PELHAM, B. W., & HETTS, J. J. (2001). Implicit and explicit personal and social identity: Toward a more complete understanding of the social self. In T. Tyler & R. Kramer (Eds.), *The psychology of the social self.* New York: Erlbaum.

PELHAM, B. W., & NETER, E. (1995). The effect of motivation on judgment depends on the difficulty of the judgment. *Journal of Personality and Social Psychology, 68,* 581–594.

PELHAM, B. W., & SWANN, W. B., JR. (1989). From self-conceptions to self-worth: On the sources and structure of global self-esteem. *Journal of Personality and Social Psychology, 57,* 672–680.

PELHAM, B. W., SUMARTA, T. T., & MYASKOVSKY, L. (1994). The easy path from many to much: The numerosity heuristic. *Cognitive Psychology, 26,* 103–133.

PETERSON, C., & SELIGMAN, M. E. P. (1987). Explanatory style and illness. *Journal of Personality, 55,* 237–265.

PETTY, R. E., & CACIOPPO, J. T. (1986). *Communication and persuasion: Central and peripheral routes to attitude change.* New York: Springer-Verlag.

PHILLIPS, D. P., & CARSTENSEN, L. L. (1986). Clustering of teenage suicides after television news stories about suicide. *New England Journal of Medicine, 315,* 685–689.

PLOUS, S. (1993). *The psychology of judgment and decision making.* New York: McGraw-Hill.

POPPER, K. (1974/1990). *Unended quest: An intellectual autobiography.* LaSalle, IL: Open Court.

PYSZCZYNSKI, T., GREENBERG, J., & SOLOMON, S. (1997). Why do we need what we need? A terror management perspective on the roots of human social motivation. *Psychology Inquiry, 8,* 1–20.

REBER, P., & KOTOVSKY, K. (1997). Implicit learning in problem solving: The role of working memory capacity. *Journal of Experimental Psychology: General, 126,* 178–203.

REGIER, D. A., & BURKE, J. D. (1987). Psychiatric disorders in the community: The epidemiologic catchment area study. In R. E. Hales & A. J. Frances (Eds.), *American Psychiatric Association Annual Review* (Vol. 6, pp. 610–624). Washington, DC: American Psychiatric Press.

REIFMAN, A. S., LARRICK, R. P., & FEIN, S. (1991). Temper and temperature on the diamond: The heat-aggression relationship in major league baseball. *Personality and Social Psychology Bulletin, 17,* 580–585.

RENSBERGER, R. (1986). *How the world works: A guide to science's greatest discoveries.* New York: William Morrow.

ROESE, N., & JAMIESON, D. W. (1993). Twenty years of bogus pipeline research: A critical review and meta-analysis. *Psychological Bulletin, 114,* 363–375.

ROMANES, G. J. (1882). *Animal intelligence.* London: Routledge & Kegan Paul.

ROSENBERG, M. J. (1965a). When dissonance fails: On eliminating evaluation apprehension from attitude measurement. *Journal of Personality and Social Psychology, 1,* 28–42.

ROSENBERG, M. J. (1965b). *Society and the adolescent self-image.* Princeton, NJ: Princeton University Press.

ROSENTHAL, R., & FODE, K. L. (1963). The effect of experimenter bias on the performance of the albino rat. *Behavioral Science, 8,* 183–189.

ROSENTHAL, R., & JACOBSON, L. (1966). Teachers' expectancies: Determinants of pupils' IQ gains. *Psychological Reports, 19,* 115–118.

ROSENTHAL, R., & ROSNOW, R. L. (1991). *Essentials of behavioral research: Methods and data analysis* (2nd ed.). New York: McGraw-Hill.

ROSENTHAL, R., & RUBIN, D. B. (1982). A simple general purpose display of magnitude of experimental effect. *Journal of Educational Psychology, 74,* 166–169.

ROSS, L. (1977). The intuitive psychologist and his shortcomings. In L. Berkowitz (Ed.), *Advances in experimental social psychology* (vol. 10, pp. 173-220). San Diego: Academic Press.

ROSS, L., GREENE, D., & HOUSE, P. (1977). The false consensus effect: An egocentric bias in social perception and attribution processes. *Journal of Experimental Social Psychology, 13,* 279–301.

ROSS, L., LEPPER, M. R., & HUBBARD, M. (1975). Perseverance in self-perception and social perception: Biased attributional processes in the debriefing paradigm. *Journal of Personality and Social Psychology, 32,* 880–892.

RULE, B. G., TAYLOR, B. R., & DOBBS, A. R. (1987). Priming effects of heat on aggressive thoughts. *Social Cognition, 5,* 131–143.

RUSTING, C. L. (1998). Personality, mood, and cognitive processing of emotional information: Three alternative models. Under review.

SACKS, O. W. (1985). *The man who mistook his wife for a hat and other clinical tales.* New York: Summit Books.

SCHACTER, D. L. (1996). *Searching for memory: The brain, the mind, and the past.* New York: Basic Books.

SCHALLER, M., CRANDALL, C. S., STANGOR, C., & NEUBERG, S. L. (1995). "What kinds of social psychology experiments are of value to perform?" A reply to Wallach and Wallach. *Journal of Personality and Social Psychology, 69,* 611–618.

SCHULTZ, D. (1981). *A history of modern psychology* (3rd ed.). San Diego: Academic Press.

SCHUMAN, H., & SCOTT, J. (1987). Problems in the use of survey questions to measure public opinion. *Science, 236,* 957–959.

SCHWARZ, N., & CLORE, G. L. (1983). Mood, misattribution, and judgments of well-being: Informative and directive functions of affective states. *Journal of Personality and Social Psychology, 45(3),* 513–523.

SCHWARZ, N., HIPPLER, H. J., DEUTSCH, B., & STRACK, F. (1985). Response scales: Effects of category range on reported behavior and comparative judgment. *Public Opinion Quarterly, 49,* 388–395.

SEARS, D. O. (1986). College sophomores in the laboratory: Influences of a narrow data base on social psychology's view of human nature. *Journal of Personality and Social Psychology, 51,* 515–530.

SHADISH, W. R., COOK, T. D., & CAMPBELL, D. T. (2002). *Experimental and quasi-experimental designs for generalized causal inference.* Boston: Houghton-Mifflin.

SIDANIUS, J., & PRATTO, F. (2000). *Social dominance: An intergroup theory of social hierarchy and oppression.* Cambridge: Cambridge University Press.

SIMON, L., GREENBERG, J., HARMON-JONES, E., SOLOMON, S., PYSZCZYNSKI, T., ARNDT, J., & ABEND, T. (1997). Terror management and cognitive-experiential self-theory: Evidence that terror management occurs in the experiential system. *Journal of Personality and Social Psychology 72,* 1132–1146.

SKINNER, B. F. (1948). "Superstition" in the pigeon. *Journal of Experimental Psychology, 38,* 168–172.

SKINNER, B. F. (1971). *Beyond freedom and dignity.* New York: Bantam Books.

SMITH, E. R., & MACKIE, D. M. (1995). *Social psychology.* New York: Worth.

SNYDER, M., & SWANN, W. B. (1978). Hypothesis-testing processes in social interaction. *Journal of Personality and Social Psychology, 36,* 1202–1212.

SNYDER, M., TANKE, E. D., & BERSCHEID, E. (1977). Social perception and interpersonal behavior: On the self-fulfilling nature of social stereotypes. *Journal of Personality and Social Psychology, 35,* 656–666.

SPELKE, E. S. (1991). Physical knowledge in infancy: Reflections on Piaget's theory. In S. Carey & R. Gelman (Eds.), *The epigenesis of mind: Essays on biology and cognition* (pp. 133–169). Hillsdale, NJ: Erlbaum.

SPINOZA, B. (1982). *The ethics and selected letters*. (S. Feldman, Ed., and S. Shirley, Trans.). Indianapolis, IN: Hackett. (Original work published 1677)

STAATS, A. W., & STAATS, C. K. (1958). Attitudes established by classical conditioning. *Journal of Abnormal Psychology, 57,* 37–40.

STAPEL, D. A. & SCHWARZ, N. (1998). The Republican who did not want to become president: Colin Powell's impact on evaluations of the Republican party and Bob Dole. *Personality and Social Psychology Bulletin, 24,* 690–698.

STEELE, C. M., & ARONSON, J. (1995). Stereotype threat and the intellectual test performance of African-Americans. *Journal of Personality and Social Psychology, 69,* 797–811.

STEELE, C. M., CRITCHLOW, B., & LIU, T .J. (1985). Alcohol and social behavior: II. The helpful drunkard. *Journal of Personality and Social Psychology, 48(1),* 35–46.

STEELE, C. M., & LIU, T. J. (1983). Dissonance processes as self-affirmation. *Journal of Personality and Social Psychology, 45,* 5–19.

STERNBERG, R. J. (1996). *Successful intelligence: How practical and creative intelligence determine success in life.* New York: Simon & Schuster.

STEWART, I. (1989). *Does God play dice? The mathematics of chaos.* Cambridge, MA: Blackwell.

STRACK, F., MARTIN, L .L., & SCHWARZ, N. (1988). Priming and communication: The social determinants of information use in judgments of life-satisfaction. *European Journal of Social Psychology, 18,* 429–442.

STROOP, J. R. (1935). Studies of interference in serial verbal reactions. *Journal of Experimental Psychology, 18,* 643–662.

STRUNK, W., JR., & WHITE, E. B. (1979). *The elements of style* (3rd ed.). New York: Macmillan.

SUTER, W. N., & LINDGREN, H. C. (1989). *Experimentation in psychology: A guided tour.* Boston: Allyn & Bacon.

SWANN, W. B., JR. (1987). Identity negotiation: Where two roads meet. *Journal of Personality and Social Psychology, 53,* 1038–1051.

SWANN, W. B., JR. (1992). Seeking "truth," finding despair: Some unhappy consequences of a negative self-concept. *Current Directions in Psychological Science, 1,* 15–18.

SWANN, W. B., JR., PELHAM, B. W., & CHIDESTER, T. R. (1988). Change through paradox: Using self-verification to alter beliefs. *Journal of Personality and Social Psychology, 54,* 268–273.

SWANN, W. B., JR., PELHAM, B. W., & KRULL, D. S. (1989). Agreeable fancy or disagreeable truth? Reconciling self-enhancement and self-verification. *Journal of Personality and Social Psychology, 57,* 782–791.

SWANN, W. B., STEIN-SEROUSSI, A., & GIESLER, R. B. (1992). Why people self-verify. *Journal of Personality and Social Psychology, 62,* 392–401.

TAFARODI, R. W., & SWANN, W. B., JR. (1995). Self-liking and self-competence as dimensions of global self-esteem: Initial validation of a measure. *Journal of Personality Assessment, 65,* 322-342.

TASSINARY, L. G., & CACIOPPO, J. T. (1992). Unobservable facial actions and emotion. *Psychological Science, 3,* 28–33.

TAYLOR, S. E., & BROWN, J. D. (1988). Illusion and well-being: A social psychological perspective on mental health. *Psychological Bulletin, 103,* 193–210.

TAYLOR, S .P. & GAMMON, C .B. (1975). Effects of type and dose of alcohol on human physical aggression. *Journal of Personality and Social Psychology, 32(1),* 169–175.

TAYLOR, S. E., REPETTI, R. L., & SEEMAN, T. (1994). Health psychology: What is an unhealthy environment and how does it get under the skin? *Annual Review of Psychology, 48,* 411–447.

TEDESCHI, J .T. SCHLENKER, B. R., & BONOMA, T .V. (1971). Cognitive dissonance: Private ratiocination or public spectacle? *American Psychologist, 26(8),* 685–695.

TESSER, A. (1986). Some effects of self-evaluation maintenance on cognition and action. In R. M. Sorrentino & E. T. Higgins (Eds.), *Handbook of motivation and cognition: Foundations of social behavior* (pp. 435–464). New York: Guilford Press.

TESSER, A., & VALENTI, A. C. (1981). On the mechanism of thought-induced attitude change. *Social Behavior and Personality, 9,* 17–22.

TETLOCK, P. E. (1985). Accountability: A social check on the fundamental attribution error. *Social Psychology Quarterly, 48,* 227–236.

TRIANDIS, H. C. (1989). The self and social behavior in differing cultural contexts. *Psychological Review, 96,* 506–520.

TRIPLETT, N. (1898). The dynamogenic factors in pacemaking and competition. *American Journal of Psychology, 9,* 507–533.

TULVING, E. (1993). Self-knowledge of an amnesic individual is represented abstractly. In T. K. Srull & R. S. Wyer, Jr. (Eds.), *The mental representation of trait and autobiographical knowledge about the self: Advances in social cognition* (Vol. 5, pp. 147–156). Hillsdale, NJ: Erlbaum.

TURNER, C. W., SIMONS, L. S., BERKOWITZ, L., & FRODI, A. (1977). The stimulating and inhibiting effects of weapons on aggressive behavior. *Aggressive Behavior, 3,* 355–378.

TVERSKY, A., & KAHNEMAN, D. (1981). The framing of decisions and the psychology of choice. *Science, 211,* 453–458.

TVERSKY, A., & KAHNEMAN, D. (1982). Evidential impact of base rates. In D. Kahneman, P. Slovic, & A. Tversky (Eds.), *Judgment under uncertainty: Heuristics and biases* (pp. 153–160). Cambridge: Cambridge University Press.

TVERSKY, A., & KAHNEMAN, D. (1983). Extensional versus intuitive reasoning: The conjunction fallacy in probability judgment. *Psychological Review, 90,* 293–315.

VARGAS, P. T., VON HIPPEL, W., & PETTY, R. E. (1998). It's not just what you think, it's also how you think: Using measures of biased processing to predict behavior. Under review.

WASON, P. C. (1971). Problem solving and reasoning. *British Medical Bulletin, 27,* 206–210.

WEBB, E. J., CAMPBELL, D. T., SCHWARTZ, R. D., & SECHREST, L. (1966). *Unobtrusive measures.* Chicago: Rand-McNally.

WEGNER, D. M. (1994). Ironic processes of mental control. *Psychological Review, 101,* 34–52.

WEGNER, D. M., LANE, J. D., & DIMITRI, S. (1994). The allure of secret relationships. *Journal of Personality and Social Psychology, 66,* 287–300.

WEGNER, D., WENZLAFF, R., KERKER, R. M., & BEATTIE, A. E. (1981). Incrimination through innuendo: Can media questions become public answers? *Journal of Personality and Social Psychology, 40,* 822–832.

WELLS, G. L., & PETTY, R. E. (1980). The effects of overt head movements on persuasion: Compatibility and incompatibility of responses. *Basic and Applied Social Psychology, 1,* 219–230.

WILLIAMS, J. M. G., MATHEWS, A., & MACLEOD, C. (1996). The emotional Stroop task and psychopathology. *Psychological Bulletin, 120,* 3–24.

WILSON, T. D., LINDSEY, S., & SCHOOLER, T. Y. (2000). A model of dual attitudes. *Psychological Review, 107,* 101–126.

WILSON, T. D., & SCHOOLER, J. W. (1991). Thinking too much: Introspection can reduce the quality of preferences and decisions. *Journal of Personality & Social Psychology, 60,* 181–192.

WUNDT, W. (1900–1920). *Folk psychology.* Leipzig, Germany: Engelmann.

ZAJONC, R. B. (1965, July 16). Social facilitation. *Science, 149,* 269–274.

Name Index

Subject Index

TO THE OWNER OF THIS BOOK:

We hope that you have found *Conducting Research in Psychology: Measuring the Weight of Smoke, Second Edition,* useful. So that this book can be improved in a future edition, would you take the time to complete this sheet and return it? Thank you.

School and address: ——————————————————————————

Department: —————————————————————————————

Instructor's name: ————————————————————————————

1. What I like most about this book is: ————————————————

——————————————————————————————————

——————————————————————————————————

2. What I like least about this book is: ——————————————

——————————————————————————————————

——————————————————————————————————

3. My general reaction to this book is: ——————————————

——————————————————————————————————

4. The name of the course in which I used this book is: ——————

——————————————————————————————————

5. Were all of the chapters of the book assigned for you to read? ————

    If not, which ones weren't? ——————————————————

6. In the space below, or on a separate sheet of paper, please write specific suggestions for improving this book and anything else you'd care to share about your experience in using the book.

——————————————————————————————————

——————————————————————————————————

——————————————————————————————————

——————————————————————————————————

Optional:

Your name: _____ Date: _____

May Wadsworth quote you, either in promotion for *Conducting Research in Psychology: Measuring the Weight of Smoke* or in future publishing ventures?

Yes: _____ No: _____

Sincerely,

Brett W. Pelham and Hart Blanton

FOLD HERE

BUSINESS REPLY MAIL

FIRST CLASS   PERMIT NO. 358   PACIFIC GROVE, CA

POSTAGE WILL BE PAID BY ADDRESSEE

ATT: *Brett W. Pelham and Hart Blanton*

**Wadsworth/Thomson Learning
511 Forest Lodge Road
Pacific Grove, CA 93950-5098**

NO POSTAGE
NECESSARY
IF MAILED
IN THE
UNITED STATES

FOLD HERE